Race and Ethnicity

BLACKWELL READERS IN SOCIOLOGY

Each volume in this authoritative series aims to provide students and scholars with comprehensive collections of classic and contemporary readings for all the major subfields of sociology. They are designed to complement single-authored works, or to be used as stand-alone textbooks for courses. The selected readings sample the most important works that students should read and are framed by informed editorial introductions. The series aims to reflect the state of the discipline by providing collections not only on standard topics but also on cutting-edge subjects in sociology to provide future directions in teaching and research.

Race and Ethnicity

Comparative and Theoretical Approaches

Edited by

John Stone and Rutledge Dennis

Blackwell
Publishing

Editorial material and organization © 2003 by John Stone and Rutledge Dennis

350 Main Street, Malden, MA 02148–5018, USA
108 Cowley Road, Oxford OX4 1JF, UK
550 Swanston Street, Carlton South, Melbourne, Victoria 3053, Australia
Kurfürstendamm 57, 10707 Berlin, Germany

First published 2003 by Blackwell Publishers Ltd, a Blackwell Publishing company

Library of Congress Cataloging-in-Publication Data

Race and ethnicity : comparative and theoretical approaches / edited by John Stone and Rutledge Dennis.
    p. cm. – (Blackwell readers in sociology ; 11)
  Includes bibliographical references and index.
    ISBN 0-631-18633-6 (alk. paper) – ISBN 0-631-18634-4 (pbk. : alk. paper)
    1. Ethnicity. 2. Ethnic attitudes. 3. Race discrimination. 4. Ethnic conflict. 5. Transnationalism. I. Stone, John, D. Phil. II. Dennis, Rutledge M. III. Series.

  GN495.6 .R32 2002
  305.8–dc21

2002071223

A catalogue record for this title is available from the British Library.

Set in 10 on 12pt Sabon
by Kolam Information Services Pvt. Ltd., Pondicherry, India

For further information on
Blackwell Publishing, visit our website:
http://www.blackwellpublishing.com

Contents

Contributors

John Stone is Professor and Chairman of the Department of Sociology at Boston University. He is the Founding Editor of the journal *Ethnic and Racial Studies* and author of *Ethnic Conflict in the Post-Cold War Era: Problems in Advanced Industrial Societies* (1995).

Rutledge Dennis is Professor of Sociology at George Mason University and the editor of the JAI/Elsevier series on *Research in Race and Ethnic Relations*. Among his recent publications is *The Black Intellectuals* (1997).

Heribert Adam is Professor of Sociology at Simon Fraser University. His most recent book (co-authored with Kogila Moodley and F. Van Zyl Slabbert) is *Comrades in Business: Post-Liberation Politics in South Africa* (1997).

Kevin Avruch is Professor of Anthropology and Conflict Resolution at George Mason University. His publications include *Culture and Conflict Resolution* (1998).

Michael Banton was Professor of Sociology at the University of Bristol 1965–92 and a member of the UN Committee on the Elimination of Racial Discrimination 1986–2001 (Chairman, 1996–8). His most recent book is *The International Politics of Race* (Polity Press, 2002).

Derek Bok is Professor of Law and President Emeritus at Harvard University. His most recent book is *The Trouble with Government* (2001).

William G. Bowen is President of the Andrew W. Mellon Foundation and a former President of Princeton University. He is co-author (with James L. Shulman) of *The Game of Life: Sports and Educational Values* (2001).

Walker Connor is a Distinguished Visiting Professor of Political Science at Middlebury College. His publications include *Ethnonationalism: The Quest for Understanding* (1994).

Frank Dikötter is Senior Lecturer in History and Director of the Contemporary China Institute at the School of Oriental and African Studies, University of London. His publications include *The Construction of Racial Identities in China and Japan* (1997).

Richard Jenkins is Professor of Sociology at the University of Sheffield. His latest book is *Foundations of Sociology: Towards a Better Understanding of the Human World* (2002).

Christian Joppke is Professor of Sociology at the European University Institute. His most recent book (co-edited with Virginie Guiraudon) is *Controlling a New Migration World* (2001).

Barbara Ballis Lal is Associate Professor of Sociology at the University of California, Los Angeles and the author of *The Romance of Culture in an Urban Civilization: Robert E. Park on Race and Ethnic Relations in Cities* (1990).

Roger N. Lancaster is Associate Professor of Anthropology and Director of the Cultural Studies program at George Mason University. His latest book is *The Trouble with Nature: Sex in Science and Popular Culture* (2002).

René Lemarchand is Emeritus Professor of Political Science and former Director of the African Studies Center at the University of Florida. His publications include *Burundi: Ethnic Conflict and Genocide* (1997).

Peggy Levitt is Associate Professor of Sociology at Wellesley College. Her most recent book is *The Transnational Villagers* (2001).

Roel W. Meertens is Professor of Social Psychology at the University of Amsterdam. Among his publications (co-authored with H. Wilke) is *Group Performance* (1994).

John McGarry is Associate Professor of Political Science at King's College, University of Western Ontario. He is the editor of *Northern Ireland and the Divided World* (2001).

Daniel J. Monti is Associate Professor of Sociology at Boston University. He is the author of *The American City: A Social and Cultural History* (Blackwell Publishing, 1999).

Kogila Moodley holds the David Lam Chair in Educational Studies at the University of British Columbia. She is the co-author (with Heribert Adam) of *The Opening of the Apartheid Mind: Options for a New South Africa* (1993).

Brendan O'Leary is Professor of Political Science at the University of Pennsylvania. His most recent book is *Rightsizing the State: The Politics of Moving Borders* (2001).

Ellen Oxfeld is Associate Professor of Sociology and Anthropology at Middlebury College. Among her publications is *Blood, Sweat, and Mahjong: Family and Enterprise in an Overseas Chinese Community* (1993), which was awarded the Thomas and Znaniecki Prize of the American Sociological Association.

Thomas F. Pettigrew is Professor of Psychology at the University of California, Santa Cruz and a former President of the Society for the Psychological Study of Social Issues. He is the author of *How to Think Like a Social Scientist* (1996).

Alejandro Portes is Professor of Sociology at Princeton University and a former President of the American Sociological Association. His latest book (co-authored with Ruben Rumbaut) is *Legacies: The Story of the Immigrant Second Generation* (2001).

Anthony H. Richmond is Professor Emeritus in the Department of Sociology at York University. Among his publications is *Global Apartheid: Refugees, Racism and the New World Order* (1995).

Beth Roy is a sociologist and mediator at the University of California, Berkeley. Her most recent book is *Bitters in the Honey* (1999).

Rubén G. Rumbaut is Professor of Sociology and Director of the Center for Research on Immigration, Population and Public Policy at the University of California, Irvine. He is the co-author (with Alejandro Portes) of *Ethnicities: Children of Immigrants in America* (2001).

Dusko Sekulic is Professor and Chairman of the Department of Sociology at The Flinders University of South Australia. He is the author of *Market, Planning and Self-management, Contradictions, Conflicts and Development* (1987), *Structures in Decline, Classes, Conflicts and Social Mobility* (1991), and co-author (with I. Zivkovic and Z. Sporer) of *Assimilation and Identity: Study of Croatian Immigrants in the USA and Canada* (1995).

Anthony D. Smith is Professor of Political Science and Sociology at the London School of Economics. His latest publications include *Nationalism: Theory, Ideology and History* (Polity Press, 2001).

Yasemin Nuhoğlu Soysal is Senior Lecturer in Sociology at the University of Essex and President of the European Sociological Association. Her publications include *Limits of Citizenship: Migrants and Postnational Membership in Europe* (1994).

Alex Stepick is Professor of Sociology at Florida International University. He is the author of *Pride Against Prejudice: Haitians in the United States* (1998).

Charles Taylor is Professor of Philosophy and Political Science at McGill University. His latest book is *Varieties of Religion Today: William James Revisited* (2002).

Igor Zevelev is Professor of Russian Studies at the George Marshall European Center for Security Studies in Garmisch-Partenkirchen, Germany. His most recent publication is *Russia and its New Diasporas* (2001).

Preface

Given the plethora of anthologies on race and ethnic relations, there are several reasons why we have put together the present collection. First, we believe that the core problems posed by race and ethnicity can be best interpreted when theoretical guideposts are in place to help us assess prevailing attitudes and behavior. The three theorists we have selected to start this work provide us with important reference points from which such issues as power, domination, exclusion, and inequality may be understood. Second, we wanted to include essays by contemporary scholars of race and ethnicity so as to trace the manner in which the basic ideas of Du Bois, Weber, and Park have been re-shaped and re-formulated. Of special interest in the writings of recent theorists has been changing identities and the creation of new ethnicities, ideas central in the formulations of all three theorists. Third, we planned to explore issues pertaining to the changing definitions of color, ethnicity, nationalism and citizenship, and how massive immigration from Third and Fourth World states into the industrial and post-industrial regions of Europe and North America have prompted a reassessment of the meaning of labor, citizenship, and basic human rights.

We also intended that the authors included in this volume would represent a wide diversity of perspectives. This point is clearly seen in the chapters focusing on affirmative action and conflicting ethnonational claims. Finally, we decided to include papers which reveal important insight into the existing world: a Janus-faced entity reflecting both high levels of tension and conflict as well as a significant measure of cooperation and mutual trust. Our aim is to get readers to understand and, to a degree, "experience", in the works included here, some of the reality of racial and ethnic violence, warfare, and genocide. Along with this we intended that readers should use the essays included in this volume to appreciate that an understanding of race and ethnicity in contemporary societies entails a probing of social structure and its affiliated political, economic, religious, and cultural networks. Only within this broad framework can we hope to comprehend the complexity of race and ethnicity as we move into a new millennium.

The gestation of this book has been somewhat longer than usual. During the process we have been helped by numerous people including the patient editors at Blackwell Publishing – most notably Simon Prosser, who initiated the project, and Ken Provencher, who saw it to its conclusion. We are grateful to our many contributors; to our colleagues and students in the Department of Sociology and Anthropology at George Mason University and the Department of Sociology at Boston University; to the Woodrow Wilson Center for Scholars in Washington, D.C., and the Rockefeller Foundation's Bellagio Conference and Study Center, for support in hosting conferences relevant to the central themes of this work; and to Dusko Sekulic and Heribert Adam for their early attempts to place orders for the book, confirming the truth of W. I. Thomas's famous maxim, "If men define situations as real, they are real in their consequences."

Acknowledgments

The editors and publishers gratefully acknowledge the following for permission to reproduce copyright material, which is here listed in alphabetical order of author:

Heribert Adam and Kogila Moodley, "Reconciliation without Justice." From *Race and Ethnicity*, edited by John Stone. Copyright © 2001 Heribert Adam and Kogila Moodley. Published by Blackwell Publishing. Printed by permission of the authors.

Kevin Avruch, "Culture and Ethnic Conflict in the New World Disorder." From *Race and Ethnicity*, edited by John Stone. Copyright © 2001 Kevin Avruch. Published by Blackwell Publishing. Printed by permission of the author.

Barbara Ballis Lal, "R. E. Park's Approach to Race and Ethnic Relations." From *The Romance of Culture in an Urban Civilization*. Copyright © 1990 Barbara Ballis Lal. Published by Routledge, pp. 49–64. Reprinted by permission of the publisher.

Michael Banton (1990), "The International Defence of Racial Equality." From *Ethnic and Race Studies*, Vol. 13 (4), pp. 568–83. Reprinted by permission of Taylor and Francis Ltd. http://www.tandf.co.uk/journals

William G. Bowen and Derek Bok, *The Shape of the River*. Copyright © 1998 Princeton University Press. Reprinted by permission of Princeton University Press.

Walker Connor, "Beyond Reason: The Nature of the Ethnonational Bond." From *Race and Ethnicity*, edited by John Stone. Copyright © 2001 Walker Connor. Published by Blackwell Publishing. Printed by permission of the author.

Rutledge Dennis, "W. E. B. Du Bois and Double Consciousness." From *Research in Race and Ethnic Relations*, Vol. 9, pp. 69–90. Copyright © 1996 JAI Press Inc. Reprinted by permission of the publisher and the author.

Frank Dikötter, "The Discourse of Race in Modern China." From *The Construction of Racial Identities in China and Japan: Historical and Contemporary Perspectives*, edited by Frank Dikötter. Copyright © 1997 Frank Dikötter. Published by University of Hawaii Press, pp. 12–33.

Richard Jenkins (1994), "Rethinking Ethnicity: Identity, Categorization and Power." *Ethnic and Race Studies*, Vol. 17 (2), pp. 197–223. Reprinted by permission of Taylor and Francis Ltd. http://www.tandf.co.uk/journals

Christian Joppke, "Multicultural Citizenship in Germany." From *Race and Ethnicity*, edited by John Stone. Copyright © 2001 Christian Joppke. Published by Blackwell Publishing. Printed by permission of the author.

René Lemarchand, *Burundi: Ethnic Conflict and Genocide*. Copyright © 1994, 1995 the Woodrow Wilson International Center for Scholars. Published by The Woodrow Wilson Center Press and The Press Syndicate of The University of Cambridge, pp. 1–16. Reprinted with the permission of Cambridge University Press.

Peggy Levitt, "Transnational Communities." From *The Transnational Villagers* by Peggy Levitt, pp. 199–216. Copyright © 2001 The Regents of the University of California. By permission of the Regents of the University of California and the University of California Press.

John McGarry and Brendan O'Leary (1995), "Five Fallacies: Northern Ireland and the Liabilities of Liberalism." From *Ethnic and Racial Studies*, Vol. 18 (4), pp. 837–61. Reprinted by permission of Taylor and Francis Ltd. http://www.tandf.co.uk/journals

Roger N. Lancaster, "Skin Color, Race and Racism in Nicaragua." From *Life is Hard: Machismo, Danger, and the Intimacy of Power in Nicaragua* by Roger Lancaster. Copyright © 1992 The Regents of the University of California. By permission of the Regents of the University of California and the University of California Press.

Ellen Oxfeld, *Blood, Sweat and Mahjong: Family and Enterprise in an Overseas Chinese Community*. Copyright © 1993 by Cornell University Press. Reprinted by permission of the publisher.

Daniel J. Monti, "Ethnic Economies and Affirmative Action." From *The American Sociologist*, Vol. 28 (4) (Winter 1997), pp. 101–12. Copyright © 1997 by Transaction Publishers. Reprinted by permission of Transaction Publishers.

Thomas F. Pettigrew and Roel W. Meertens, "The *Verzuiling* Puzzle: Understanding Dutch Intergroup Relations." From *Current Psychology*, Vol. 15 (1), pp. 3–13. Copyright © 1996 by Transaction Publishers. Reprinted by permission of Transaction Publishers.

Alejandro Portes and Alex Stepick, "The Transformation of Miami": From *City of the Edge: The Transformation of Miami* by Alejandro Portes and Alex Stepick, pp. 203–21. Copyright © 1993 The Regents of the University of California. By permission of the Regents of the University of California and the University of California Press.

Anthony H. Richmond, "Postindustrialism, Postmodernism and Ethnic Conflict." From chapter two of *Global Apartheid: Refugees, Racism and the New World*

Order. Published by Oxford University Press, 1994. Reprinted by permission of the author.

Beth Roy, "Rioting Across Continental Divides." Copyright © Beth Roy 2000. An earlier version of this paper was published by the Japan Center for Area Studies, National Museum of Ethnology, Osaka in JCAS Symposium Series No. 11, edited by K. Hiroyuki, F. Takeshi, and O. Fumiko, "State, Nation and Ethnic Relations" (2000) pp. 147–64. Printed by permission of the author.

Rubén G. Rumbaut, "Assimilation and its Discontents: Ironies and Paradoxes." From *The Handbook of International Migration: The American Experience*, edited by Charles Hirshman, Philip Kasinitz, and Josh DeWind. Copyright © 1999 Russell Sage Foundation, 112 East 64th Street, New York, NY 10021. Reprinted with permission.

Dusko Sekulic, "The Creation and Dissolution of the Multinational State: The Case of Yugoslavia." From *Nations and Nationalism*, Vol. 3 (2), 1997, pp. 165–79. Permission granted by the editors of *Nations and Nationalism*, Journal of the Association for the Study of Ethnicity and Nationalism (London School of Economics).

Anthony D. Smith, *Nationalism and Modernity.* Copyright © 1998 Anthony D. Smith. Published by Routledge, pp. 199–220. Reprinted by permission of the publisher and the author.

Yasemin Nuhoğlu Soysal, "Toward a Postnational Model of Membership." From *Limits of Citizenship: Migrants and Postnational Membership in Europe* by Yasemin Nuhoğlu Soysal. Published by University of Chicago Press, 1994, pp. 137–55 (abridged). Reprinted by permission of the publisher and author.

John Stone, "Max Weber on Race, Ethnicity and Nationalism." From *American Behavioral Scientist*, Vol. 38 (3) (January 1995), pp. 391–406. Special Issue edited by John Stanfield © Sage Publications Inc. Published by permission of the author and publisher.

Charles Taylor, *Multiculturalism: The Politics of Recognition.* Copyright © 1992, expanded paperback edition © 1994 Princeton University Press. Reprinted by permission of Princeton University Press.

Igor Zevelev, "Russia and the Russian Diasporas." From *Post-Soviet Affairs*, Vol. 12(3), pp. 265–84. © V. H. Winston & Son, Inc., 360 South Ocean Boulevard, Palm Beach, FL 33480. Reprinted by permission. All rights reserved.

The publishers apologize for any errors or omissions in the above list and would be grateful to be notified of any corrections that should be incorporated in the next edition or reprint of this book.

Introduction: Race Against Time – The Ethnic Divide in the Twentieth Century

At the end of the nineteenth century, during a period when academic sociology was still in its formative stages, three major social thinkers were engaged in the task of developing a systematic study of society. Two of them, W. E. B Du Bois and Robert Ezra Park, were Americans and the third, Max Weber, was German. Each was concerned with a central feature of all complex societies, their division into diverse racial and ethnic groups. This diversity often formed the dividing lines shaping both conflict and hierarchy, and was believed by many to provide a justification for racial inequality, colonialism and the widespread practice of racial and ethnic segregation.

In the course of the twentieth century, the central importance of race relations, ethnic attachments and national loyalties was a recurrent theme in an era marked by global warfare, mass migrations and the continual rise and fall of states and nations. Against this turbulent background, a famous prediction of Du Bois, was to be proved correct time and again. In 1903, he had stated that the problem of the twentieth century would be "the problem of the color-line – the relation of the darker to the lighter races of men in Asia and Africa, in America and the islands of the sea." By the end of the century, the truth of Du Bois's prophecy had withstood the test of time. Racial struggles had marked every decade of the century, and ethnonational conflicts were as much a matter of concern and anguish in the 1990s as they were in the period leading up to the First World War. While social science had provided increasing insight into the nature of these conflicts, the practical means to prevent their recurrence seemed to be as elusive as ever.

The purpose of this book is to provide the reader with a broad overview of the major issues confronting the student of race and ethnic relations at the beginning of a new century. While the problems posed by racial and ethnic diversity date back to the dawn of mankind, their expression in contemporary global society does raise fresh questions and demand new solutions. This stated, it is also true that many of the current conflicts can only be fully understood against a background of the historical roots of present day relationships and identities. In some cases, attitudes and behavior may remain relatively stable despite momentous political and social upheavals – as, for example, in China (chapter 9) – but in other settings group definitions and relationships may be transformed in a short space of time. In Burundi and Bosnia formerly friendly and peaceable ethnic neighbours have become hostile enemies in the wake of "ethnic cleansing" and genocide. However, this does not prevent us from seeking general patterns and causal explanations, that is the only long-term method to find practical solutions to these critical problems. This was indeed the agenda of Du Bois, Weber and Park (chapters 1–3), and it is a measure of the difficulty of the challenges involved that we are still groping towards bitterly contested strategies of the best way to move forward.

A hundred years ago the world was a very different place. The United States, although experiencing rapid industrialization in the second half of the nineteenth century, had yet to achieve its dominating position during what has been called "America's century." Russia was still under the rule of the Czars and remained a largely feudal society awaiting its revolutionary destiny. Germany and Great Britain vied with one another for economic supremacy, while France and Germany were rivals for political domination in Europe. Japan's industrial development, growing out of the reforms of the Meiji restoration, would soon be recognized after its unexpected military defeat of Russia in the war of 1904–5. Most of Africa and Asia remained firmly under the domination of European colonial powers whose technological and military superiority had crushed the indigenous political rulers and allowed the imperial states to divide up whole continents on the basis of conquest and cartographic convenience. Many future problems, especially the critical mismatch between nations and states (chapter 10) would be created by these unthinking acts of imperial arrogance.

Most of the racial and ethnic problems considered by our three sociologists fit into this world of decaying empires and emergent new nationalisms. In the United States, the destruction of slavery and the move towards greater racial democracy, following the defeat of the Confederacy during the Civil War, had been slowly but relentlessly overturned after the period of Reconstruction. So by the turn of the century, the slave system had been replaced by a new form of racial oppression, Jim Crow segregation, that effectively relegated African Americans to second class citizenship. It would take much of the century to reverse this regression and redirect the United States towards fulfilling its Constitutional promise that all of its citizens are created equal and that no one should be denied the right to vote, or the enjoyment of civil rights, on the basis of racial or ethnic background.

The outbreak of the First World War (1914–18) marked an important turning point and, for many, represents a critical divide between a world securely in the grip of European imperial powers to one that was about to witness their decline and fall from hegemonic domination. The war saw the collapse of the Austro-Hungarian and Ottoman empires, the transfer of power from Czarist Russia to Lenin's Bolshevik republic, and the emergence of both the United States and Japan as military and industrial powers of global significance. All these events sowed the seeds for many subsequent racial and ethnic conflicts that were to be exposed in the coming decades. Ethnic Russians started a diaspora into the furthest reaches of the Soviet empire and new states like Yugoslavia were created in an attempt to stabilize the ethnic fragmentation in the Balkans (chapters 21 and 15).

The Turkish genocide against the Armenians signalled the beginning of a series of murderous events that were to rival the military carnage of the two world wars. It was Adolf Hitler, a dictator emerging from the wreckage of the defeated German state, who made the cynical, but largely accurate remark: "who remembers the Armenians?" By the 1940s, Hitler's henchmen were busy repeating this generally forgotten genocide of the early years of the century – some would claim that the massacres in the Belgium Congo under King Leopold were the first genocide of the twentieth century – in the even larger and more systematic slaughter of European Jews in the Holocaust. And in the decades that followed the end of the Second World War, the killing did not stop, erupting in very diverse settings such as Cambodia, Rwanda and Burundi, and Bosnia.

The interwar years were marked by the economic problems culminating in the Great Depression. This was a genuinely global development that affected all the major industrial economies and had a powerful impact on the rest of the world. Economic decline generated massive unemployment, international migration was reduced to a trickle, and as economic opportunities evaporated most industrial societies did not need the harsh new immigration controls to stem the flow of economic migrants. The political and social disruption prepared the ground for authoritarian regimes of fascists and communists, who promised their followers stability, in exchange for a loss of liberty and unquestioned obedience. In the 1930s, Mussolini attacked Abyssinia and the rest of the world looked on as Haile Selassie pleaded in vain for the League of Nations to intervene. Such appeasement of fascism was to prove equally ineffective in Europe as Spain, Czechoslovakia, and Poland were successively attacked and overrun by the Nazi military machine. The Second World War may have been the inevitable outcome of the short-sighted and punitive terms of the Versailles Peace Treaty, but the unintended results of this second global conflict were to fundamentally reshape the direction of global race and ethnic relations.

The impact of this war cannot be exaggerated. Europe and Japan lay in ruins. The United States and the Soviet Union emerged as the two superpowers whose rivalry would shape the framework of world politics until the fall of the Berlin Wall in 1989. The Third World was poised to shake off the shackles of colonial domination and start the long struggle to gain political independence and economic development. After the failure of the League of Nations, a fledgling United Nations was established, but rendered largely impotent by the post-war political stalemate. A bi-polar rivalry spawned by the Cold War ensured that strategic politics, rather than human rights and racial and ethnic justice, would dominate the international agenda.

One of the unanticipated consequences of the war against fascism was the exposure of the shortcomings of the Allies in their own record of racial equality. The United States army was segregated throughout the conflict, the premise of inequality and injustice inherent under colonialism was revealed to both colonized and colonizer, and the terrible consequences of racist ideologies were seen in the extermination camps and occupying brutality of the Axis forces. While the Nuremberg and Tokyo trials provided evidence of the extent of these crimes against humanity, the need to change patterns of segregation and racial hierarchy became part of the unfinished business of the champions of democracy. In India, Gandhi's campaign of *satyagraha*, non-violent resistance, brought about independence in 1947, but not without terrible loss of life in the intercommunal violence perpetrated by Hindus and Muslims who did not share the Mahatma's peaceful philosophy (chapter 13).

In Africa, decolonization began a decade later with Kwame Nkrumah's campaign in Ghana leading the way and starting a process that would be largely complete within the next three decades. (It was an elderly and rather disillusioned W. E. B. Du Bois who moved to Ghana in 1961 and died there on the very day Martin Luther King gave his historic, "I have a Dream" speech, during the March on Washington in 1963.) Some of the most violent and protracted struggles on the continent took place in those societies under the control of European settlers, rather than those ruled from the colonial metropole; Algeria in the north and Rhodesia/Zimbabwe and South Africa in the south. These conflicts produced inspiring liberation leaders and advocates of racial equality as diverse as Frantz Fanon and Nelson Mandela. However, most of these newly independent states faced crippling legacies of ethnic inequality and competition from the colonial era so that the post-colonial period of state building was marked by protracted ethnic violence, particularly in Nigeria, Sudan, Rwanda, Burundi, and Angola.

The experience of South Africa, in the years following India's independence, was different from the trends elsewhere. With the triumph of a virulently racist strain of Afrikaner nationalism, in the elections of 1948, the society embarked on a course that was to become progressively out of step with the movements towards de-racialization in much of the rest of the world. In fact the doctrine of *apartheid*, the legislative enforcement of racial separation, began to be imposed with increasingly draconian measures just at the time when the United States' Supreme Court was ruling that "separate but equal is inherently unequal" in the famous *Brown* decision. Until its final defeat in the early 1990s, *apartheid* was one of the few doctrines that met with virtually unanimous disapproval at the United Nations, even though member states disagreed profoundly on the best strategies to end it. Race relations had become a prisoner of the ideological preoccupations of the Cold War and it is no coincidence that the final transition to non-racial democracy in South Africa took place following the sudden collapse of the Communist bloc.

Another major post-war development was the Civil Rights struggle in the United States which profoundly changed the one superpower leading a global crusade for capitalist free markets and liberal democracy. The persistence of what Gunnar Myrdal termed "the American Dilemma" – the clash between the universalistic ideals of the US Constitution and the discriminatory practices of American society – posed a difficult problem. In the ideological battle to win the hearts and minds of the non-aligned states, making up an increasing number of the new members of the United Nations, the failure of American society to rectify this glaring injustice remained an embarrassing issue. However, it was the internal mobilization and struggle of America's diverse minorities, led particularly by African Americans, that gradually challenged and brought about major changes in the system. Following the 1954 *Brown* decision that started the desegregation of public schools – like the one in Little Rock, Arkansas (chapter 13) – the Civil Rights Acts of 1957, 1960 and 1964, and the Voting Rights Act of 1965, finally established a legal framework for equality for all American citizens. The legislation of this period also ended the flagrant national origins bias in immigration policy established in 1924 and opened the country up to a new wave of migrants from Asia and South America (chapters 16 and 17).

The battle for racial justice in America has been a long and difficult struggle. While racial minorities have made remarkable progress in so many areas of public life, securing political office at all but the highest level, the economic record is much more uneven. It is the divergent pattern of material success that has been a focal area of debate during the final quarter of the century. Some sociologists have pointed to the persistence of residential segregation and the collapse of the employment base in the inner cities as critical remaining problems facing the African American community and the wider society in the 1990s. But why have some succeeded in escaping the urban ghettoes and others have not? Here interpretations tend to divide along the political spectrum with conservatives, from all ethnic backgrounds, stressing the need for cultural capital and strong community values, while radicals place a greater emphasis on the persistence of prejudice and the structural discrimination built into the fabric of society. Such views mirror the differences between Park and Du Bois in the early part of the century and can be seen in the variety of assessments of affirmative action by contemporary social scientists and educators (chapters 22 to 24).

Despite the enormous influence of the United States and its impact on race and ethnic relations throughout the world, the American experience is in many respects exceptional. Not only is the United States an immigrant society in a rather unique form, but its categorization of race – the so-called "one drop rule," whereby anyone with any observable black ancestry is defined as a member of the subordinate group – is by no means a universal mechanism of racial hierarchy. The diverse and continuous systems of color consciousness in Brazil, Morocco or Nicaragua generate a complex and multifaceted process that, in the long run, may actually be more difficult to challenge and eradicate than the crude racial dichotomy of the United States (chapter 7).

The post-war world witnessed many other variants on race and ethnic relations. Unlike South Africa, the Netherlands had a completely different reputation for intergroup tolerance but it was, ironically, based on a type of communal separation that formed the justification behind *apartheid*. The crucial difference, however, was that the Dutch, unlike their Afrikaner cousins, developed a system of elite cooperation that promoted genuine consensus and a fair distribution of resources. So the *verzuiling puzzle* (chapter 8) explains the divergent outcomes of two systems based on the structural separation of ethnic and racial groups.

Another type of separation resulted in the partition of Ireland in the 1920s. Seen as a solution to the conflicting nationalist loyalties of those who considered themselves Irish, and those whose identity was linked to Britain, the division of Ireland did not end the conflicts between Catholics and Protestants. Tensions in Northern Ireland remained dormant until the outbreak of "the troubles" in the 1960s. These were partly triggered by the Civil Rights movement in the United States, but once set in motion the polarizing impact of sectarian violence quickly set off a long and bloody civil war (chapter 12). It was only at the end of the century that forces came together to raise the prospects of a settlement with determined American mediation, a transformed Irish Republic prospering as a result of the economic opportunities generated by its membership of the European Union, a Britain prepared at last to support the devolution of power to its constituent nations, and a new generation of Northern Ireland leaders more pragmatic in their search for a solution. None the less, the outcome still remains uncertain and the basic ethnonational roots of this seemingly self-destructive conflict explain its remarkable tenacity.

While the conflict in Northern Ireland had authentic historical roots, stretching back to the early conquests that established Britain's first overseas colony, many of the other ethnonational conflicts were of more recent vintage. In Burundi, just as in Bosnia and the rest of Yugoslavia, much of the actual carnage was explained by the superficial inventions of contemporary nationalist leaders (chapter 14). The psychological bond evoked by national feelings generated a sense of loyalty and a destructive power that belied its often "artificial" or even fictitious origins. And while nationalism so often claims its legitimacy by reference to a history of heroic struggle or a lost golden age, it remains a fascinating paradox that nationalism and modernity are far from incompatible (chapter 11).

This dynamic quality of modern nationalism can also be seen in the consequences of renewed migrations in the latter part of the century. Waves of new migrants not only provided further diversity to the "nation of immigrants," but they also started a debate about the meaning and scope of modern citizenship. In the United States, Cuban refugees radically changed the politics and economy of Miami, suggesting that the transformative powers of the American city, analysed by Park and Weber in relation to Chicago (chapter 20), might need to be re-examined. An evaluation of the impact of assimilation has suggested that it may no longer be the unmixed blessing it was once considered to be for the migrants themselves. Furthermore, the generation of transnational communities, a product of the transportation and communications revolutions of the postmodern era, raises yet further questions about the long-run direction and outcome of assimilatory pressures. And these developments are truly global as overseas diaspora communities follow complex migratory patterns, like the Hakka Chinese of Calcutta and Toronto (chapter 18) or the Ugandan Asians that moved between India, Britain, and America.

Such diversity posed difficult policy dilemmas about multiculturalism and post-national citizenship (chapter 19). Europe, the United States, Australia, and Canada debated different models to apply to their particular circumstances. Germany's shift from a strict adherence to ethnic nationalism to a greater degree of civic inclusiveness could be traced to the evolutionary developments in the European Union after German unification, the demands of a new generation of Germans born in the country whose anomalous status as "guestworkers" became increasingly anachronistic, and the need to exorcise the ghosts of the Nazi past (chapter 24). Canada's circumstances opened up other issues. Not only was there the delicate balance between the demands of English Canada and Quebec, but there are also the claims of the indigenous peoples – the "First Nation" – and significant groups of immigrants who came from many parts of the world. The often conflicting demands of multiculturalism and the recognition sought by Quebec separatists, intent on preserving the Francophone culture of the province, remain outstanding issues that still await a long-term political resolution (chapters 5 and 25).

The overall picture of race and ethnic relations at the turn of the millennium is a complex blend of contradictory trends. Despite the continuing levels of strife and oppression, and the deep-seated tenacity of ethnonational bonds, the story is not always depressing. Much inter-ethnic change takes place in an incremental manner receiving little attention as it fails to catch the headlines. Some societies, like the

Netherlands and South Africa, defy all the predictions of conventional social science models and demonstrate how even the most divided societies can still resolve profound conflicts and move beyond discrimination and intolerance. Understanding "Mandela's Miracle" is clearly an important step in finding constructive resolutions of other seemingly intractable conflicts.

Another way in which the emerging theoretical perspectives developed by social scientists can contribute to this endeavor is by refining its theoretical models. A dominant paradigm in contemporary writing across the social sciences is the emphasis on the social construction of racial and ethnic groups (chapters 4 and 5). Although not a new idea by any means, and explicit in the work of Park's Chicago colleague, W. I. Thomas, this approach has gained increasing ascendancy by the end of the century. But racial and ethnic groups are not created solely by the internal structures and cultures of peoples, they are equally affected by the categorizations of outsiders. The constant dialectic between culture and power is a critical force shaping the developments of minorities and majorities in an ever-changing external environment. The outcome of these exchanges and interactions remain contingent on a range of circumstances, particularly in the highly fluid postindustrial and postmodern reality of global society (chapter 6).

For all the search for intellectual understanding, how to achieve progress towards the goals of tolerance and justice remains the burning practical issue on the ethnic agenda. Many of the societies torn apart by racial violence and genocidal massacres have explored the possibility of innovative institutions like South Africa's Truth and Reconciliation Commission that have attempted to find a balance between accountability and social reconstruction (chapter 26). Whether this is the right path to pursue or whether a more robust stance, involving War Crimes Tribunals, is a better long-term strategy remains a contentious issue. The international defence of racial equality and justice is a work in progress, but some limited success has been achieved in the second half of the twentieth century to set up the institutional framework under the umbrella of the United Nations, despite all the undeniable setbacks and tragic failures (chapter 27).

Taken as a whole, the twentieth century provides a dire warning for those trying to ignore the consequences of racial inequality and ethnic injustice. There is a profound need for social scientists to provide as much insight and concrete proposals to assess and guide the dynamics of these complex, but often deadly, social relationships. Our global society is more closely interdependent than ever before and failure to recognize the common humanity of all the peoples of the planet will be a costly mistake.

Part I

Setting the Agenda: Du Bois, Weber, and Park

At the beginning of the twentieth century W. E. B. Du Bois prophetically announced that the color line would be the major problem of the century. One of the
great ironies of our era is the reality that the color line remains one of the major
problems confronting us as we move into the twenty-first century. The pervasive-
ness of the color line and its correlation with status, power, inequality and domination, provides us with an opportunity for a reappraisal of the theoretical
contributions of Du Bois, and other sociologists of race, and of the practical uses
of these theories of race and ethnic relations. In Part I, papers are presented on the
racial and ethnic theories of W. E. B. Du Bois, Max Weber, and Robert E. Park, of
whom it would not be an overstatement to call "founding fathers" of the sociology
of race and ethnicity.

Rutledge Dennis's examination of Du Bois's concept of double consciousness
raises questions regarding the alleged unreconciled nature of the term in its most
popularized version which he labels Theme One. Dennis also probes the early
sociological writings of Du Bois to note the degree to which he continued to view
double consciousness as a central problem for oppressed groups. As Dennis
asserts, the concept of double consciousness remains one of the most popular
terms by Du Bois which continues to have relevance in contemporary sociology.
The question must be asked: Why did Du Bois elevate the idea of double consciousness as one of the first major themes in his *Souls of Black Folk* and then,
without an apparent second thought, simply abandon the concept? Additionally,
we might ask whether Du Bois's foray into the psychological realm of consciousness was simply a sociological aberration in as much as his approach to prejudice
and racial inequality had, heretofore, been structural rather than individual.
Finally, to answer the degree to which contemporary scholars have wrestled with
and sought to re-shape the concept of double consciousness, Dennis explores a few
of the more prominent re-statements of the concept. Dennis questions the sociological merits of Heinze's overly idealistic and psychological use of the term which,
in his view, takes us back to an almost nineteenth-century formulation. Gilroy's
use of the term is questioned from many angles. First, his approach in largely
idealistic connotations is challenged as being in opposition to the gist of Du Bois's
sociological writings. Secondly, Dennis raises questions relative to Gilroy's assertion of double consciousness as the genesis for the emergence and evolution of
ideas crucial to transcending nationalism, culture, and race.

John Stone's paper on Weber analyzes the theoretical contributions Weber made
to racial and ethnic issues. As Stone asserts, Weber did not produce a systematic
study of a racial or ethnic group per se. Despite this fact, however, he was to link
his contemporary observations of racial and religious groups, for example, Jews,
African Americans and Native Americans, to some existing ideas in his theoretical
arsenal, especially ideas of social closure and its relationship to domination,
power, and authority. As outlined by Stone, sociology is indebted to Weber for the

keen insights he proferred to issues such as group formation, group mobilization, caste relations, color and caste, and especially, his use of the term "pariah" to describe an excluded and oppressed group. Since the bulk of Weber's works remained untranslated until the 1930s, Americans probably first saw the word "pariah" in Du Bois's *Souls of Black Folk*. It is almost certain that Du Bois came across the concept while studying in Berlin where he met Weber. One of Weber's great contributions to sociology, according to Stone, was his ability to tackle the materialist–idealist issue by focusing on the subjective elements in human behavior and interaction as well as those in the realm of the structural and material. By doing so he was able to analyze the values, attitudes, and other individual features of ethnic relations as these are played out against the structural background of exclusion, domination, conflict, and power.

The final paper, by Barbara Ballis Lal, focuses on the ideas of another pioneer in the sociology of race and ethnicity. Lal highlights many of the contributions by Park in the area of racial and ethnic theory and relations: his critique of status groups and conflict, his views on the instruments of social control, his models for social change, and his use of subjective factors such as attitudes, motives and meanings to assess the core of inter-group and intra-group relations. Park, like Weber, highlighted the role of the subjective in group relations. Of the three sociologists Du Bois was least inclined to draw heavily upon the subjective elements. Lal outlines some of the merits in Park's use of subjective factors, though she criticizes Park's inability or unwillingness to include structural explanations as key factors of his analysis. Lal sees this as a major deficit in Park's sociology and this deficiency is revealed most clearly in Park's discussion of race and ethnic relations. For not only does he ignore important issues related to racial and ethnic conflict and domination which are central to the sociologies of Du Bois and Weber, but also, unlike these two, he appeared to neglect crucial elements of the world around him as he developed his sociology of race and ethnicity.

1 W. E. B. Du Bois's Concept of Double Consciousness

Rutledge Dennis

During his long life, W. E. B. Du Bois (1868–1963) almost single-handedly created and shaped a revolutionary discourse on race and ethnic relations in the United States. His insights and pronouncements on race and racial matters, and his poignant and prophetic remark that "the problem of the Twentieth Century is the problem of the color line" (Du Bois 1903 [1961], p. 10) helped forge a radical paradigm shift in the area of race and race relations. He viewed such a shift as vital in the transformation of the racial discourse from the subjective to the objective domain; from racial explanations rooted in theology and "folk knowledge" to those based on reason, logic, and the use of scientific methodology. History and sociology were to be anchor disciplines providing a framework within which racial theories and problems were to be explicated and understood.

In his book *The Souls of Black Folks* (1903 [1961]), Du Bois introduces the concept of "double consciousness." The concept, along with his theory of "the Talented Tenth" ("leaders of thought and missionaries of culture among their people") became one of the pillars of his sociology of race, for it represented a very personal attempt to rechart the history and sociology of a people: to use the past in order to both structure and explain the present.

The recent spate of books applying the idea of double consciousness (Early 1993; Gilroy 1993; Heinze 1993) to a variety of contemporary issues, invites us to take yet another look, perhaps an even sharper and more critical look, at the concept itself. This paper focuses on Du Bois's use of double consciousness to describe the racial identity dilemma and to assess racial, status, and power relations between blacks and whites. First, the paper examines the idea of double consciousness as it emerges out of the psychological theories and literary traditions of the nineteenth century. Second, we analyze Du Bois's definition(s) of double consciousness and some possible consequences for marginal groups. Finally, recent studies by Heinze and Gilroy, which focus on double consciousness from diverse perspectives, are examined. Here, we are interested in whether these authors adhere to Du Bois's earlier definition(s) of the term or whether they modify the term to make it more consistent with their disciplines or their theoretical positions.

Historical Perspectives on Double Consciousness

It is important to place the origins of double consciousness in historical context. When the term was first used by Du Bois, Southerners and Northerners (particularly the former) had already experienced and were continuing to live through a series of events, some of which occurred in rapid succession or simultaneously. The Civil War had been fought; reconstruction was attempted and had failed; the Ku Klux Klan and other terrorist groups had emerged; millions of African Americans had been freed from slavery without provisions for land or money and the political economy of the recently defeated Southern states moved quickly into neo-slavery and Jim Crowism.

Hundreds of thousands of Southerners began to migrate to the North and Midwest and encountered treatment not very different from the social relations they had experienced in the South; millions of European immigrants flocked to the large urban centers of the North and Midwest and quickly became "very" American by adopting the prevailing racial attitudes of their new country. Turner, Singleton, and Musick (1984) have provided an excellent socio-historical evaluation of these issues and events.

Du Bois analyzed these events and issues and framed his intra-group and inter-group analysis around the idea of what it meant to be a minority group within a majority culture with these unique socio-historical experiences and, secondarily, what might be the long-lasting consequences of this experience. It is this latter feature that concerns us in this paper, for, according to Du Bois, one of the most obvious predicaments of this particular situation is the condition he called double consciousness. The vividness and sharpness of the metaphors used in conceptualizing the term make it imperative for those seeking clarification of the idea to do several things: to present a critique of the double conscious; to understand the concept in conjunction with the ideas and situations of that era; to analyze Du Bois's empirical works in order to ascertain whether he presents and discusses concrete sociological situations that suggest the existence of a double consciousness, and, finally, to review some recent works by scholars who have used the concept in order to ascertain whether these scholars have moved beyond Du Bois's initial definition of the term.

It is appropriate to begin the analysis by presenting the passage on double consciousness in its entirety (Du Bois 1903 [1961], pp. 16–17):

> the Negro is a sort of seventh son born with a veil, and gifted with second sight in this American world – a world which yields him no true self-consciousness, but only lets him see himself through the revelation of the other world. It is a peculiar sensation, this double consciousness, this sense of always looking at one's self through the eyes of others, of measuring one's soul by the tape of a world that looks on in amused contempt and pity. One ever feels his two-ness – an American, a Negro; two souls, two thoughts, two unreconciled strivings; two warring ideals in one dark body, whose dogged strength alone keeps it from being torn asunder.

The famous passage, which I shall refer to as Theme One, is often cited to represent Du Bois's position on the double conscious. But there is a second theme in the very next paragraph that is less cited and less dramatic and which appears, on the surface, to contradict key aspects of the first (Du Bois 1903 [1961], p. 17):

> The history of the American Negro is the history of this strife – this longing to attain self-conscious manhood, to merge his double self into a better and truer self. In this

merging he wishes neither of the older selves to be lost. He would not Africanize America, for America has too much to teach the world and Africa. He would not bleach his Negro soul in a flood of white Americanism, for he knows that Negro blood has a message for the world. He simply wishes to make it possible for a man to be both a Negro and an American, without having the doors of opportunity closed roughly in his face.

Arnold Rampersad (1976, p. 74) informs us that the idea of double consciousness was undoubtedly developed by Du Bois from the works of the two leading psychologists of the nineteenth century, William James and Oswald Kulpe. James refers to the binary structure of the brain in which "one system give[s] rise to one consciousness, and those of another system to another *simultaneously* existing consciousness." Kulpe is more specific regarding the process of recognizing double consciousness itself, depicting it as "the phenomenon of double consciousness or the divided self [is] characterized by the existence of a more or less complete separation of two aggregates of conscious process... oftentimes of entirely opposite character." But there is yet another source of Du Bois's doubleness theme: that of literature.

Claire Rosenfield (1967) traces the emergence of the double theme in nineteenth-century Western literature, especially as represented in the works of Melville, Goethe, Dostoevsky, Poe, and Conrad. According to her, the idea of the double in literature relates to those conscious and unconscious features that influence and control individual behavior; moreover, it assumes the existence of a relatively high level of cohesiveness and uniformity in the original and "natural" personality of the individual; it alleges finally, that the idea of the double is intricately linked to "the loss of a sense of identity and continuity in time." This idea of a loss of identity, is crucial to Du Bois's explanation of double consciousness as developed in his second theme.

Du Bois transforms the idea of double consciousness from its nineteenth-century psychological and literary contexts and applies it to what he perceives to be the persistent duality of African-American life in the United States. The remaining sections of this paper will analyze the degree to which Du Bois was successful in this venture. We can note precisely two double consciousness themes presented by Du Bois: one, emphasizing the irreconcilable nature of the two opposing forces (one African, the other European) locked in an eternal battle the outcome of which cannot yet be known; the other theme offers the possibility of a synthesis of the two opposing forces suggesting that unity may yet emerge from great disunity, that a largely fragmented reality may give rise to a heretofore unthinkable coherence.

I will argue that Theme One represents a strand of Du Bois's thought that remained nationalistic and race-specific; the other represented a Du Bois who was universalistic and a race-generalist.

Both themes center on the then young Du Bois's adherence to a racial group theory which was quite popular during the latter part of the nineteenth century: the germ theory of races. This theory holds that in the grand scheme of things, races, not individuals, are the significant carriers of values. Moreover, the theory proffers the view that social values are primarily racial, hence, biological, and can be traced from the earliest origins of a group. S. P. Fullinwider (1969), Elliot

Rudwick (1982), and David Lewis (1993) have extensively examined the impact of this racial theory on the thoughts and ideas of the young Du Bois.

Even as he supports a theory of race that gives credence to certain psychic and psychological attributes, Du Bois's early empirical studies and essays present a picture of the dual social life and reality of blacks and whites – that American society consists of tightly controlled and separate racial worlds within which exists power differentials between groups in economics, politics, education, and social status. A close reading of Du Bois's critique of the American social structure leads to the conclusion that contrary to all of his discussions of the germ theory of races, there is a linear relationship between a group's position in the social structure and the nature and degree of its consciousness. In other words, blacks and whites represent and manifest different types of psychological consciousness because they inhabit different social worlds; it is, therefore, the group's social existence, ultimately, which is more significant in determining consciousness. This Du Boisian logic is one of the underlying themes in both *The Souls of Black Folk* and *The Philadelphia Negro*.

This perspective explains why he viewed the white position as representative of a system of exploitation, privilege, and domination. Such a position, according to Du Bois, results in a consciousness of the oppressor. This may be contrasted to a consciousness of the oppressed. Moreover, Du Bois's logic tells us, a consciousness of the oppressor results in a consciousness that is motivated around that group's self-interest.

The psychological and literary perspectives on double consciousness center on the psychic split within the individual. Du Bois's Theme One view of the concept does entail an interpretation suggestive of a psychic split framework. Beginning with Du Bois's brief introduction of the concept, the idea of a psychic split within the black population would not resurface again until the 1950s and 1960s with the publication of four very controversial psychological studies: *The Mark of Oppression* (Kardiner and Ovesey 1951); *Black Rage* (Grier and Cobbs 1968); *The Colonizer and the Colonized* (Memmi 1965), and *Black Skin, White Masks* (Fanon 1967).

What is striking in Du Bois's use of the term conscious and consciousness is that his conceptualization appears to reflect a static and generally surface understanding of the concept. His view also represents an antiquated psychological approach that was rapidly receding under the onslaughter of a new and revolutionary Freudian perspective on consciousness and the unconscious.

Du Bois's Empirical Studies

In this section we analyze whether the double conscious, and any of its behavioral manifestations, are clearly demarcated and delineated in Du Bois's major works. To guide us in this analysis we have extracted what we view to be the major assertions of the double conscious:

a.   that the American world "yields" to blacks no true self-consciousness;
b.   that blacks always see themselves through the eyes of others;

c. that there exists an eternal and unreconciled two-ness (two thoughts, two souls, two warring ideals) within the collective black population.

A probe in this direction is crucial: either we view the concept as theoretically fruitful with the potential to explain some variant of the empirical world or we see it merely as a provocative theme useful only as an ideological weapon in inter-racial and intra-racial struggles. If the double conscious idea is indeed important because it negatively predisposes a population to experience, under Du Bois's first theme, severe identity crises in which there are seemingly irreconcilable emotional, psychological, philosophical, and ideological splits within individuals and groups, it, therefore, describes a society fragmented beyond repair, hence a disintegrating society. However, if we look at Theme Two we approach a dialectical stretch in which those excluded, Weber's pariahs (Bendix 1960), have had to create as well as maintain their own special sociocultural world while simultaneously assaulting as well as participating in the larger society to the extent made possible by the political, economic, and legal restrictions of the majority culture. In such a scheme, the identity question is not a mutually exclusive issue, per se, and there is no inherent contradiction between being both American and black.

As we analyze Du Bois's empirical works it might be important to distinguish two types of "anguish." In one type of anguish we must delineate the anguish of a group due to Theme One of the double conscious – that of the "two warring souls" in one body and to questions of identity vis-à-vis another group; this an-guish must be distinguished from the second type of anguish which is linked to the unequal power, domination, deprivations, and exclusionary policies inflicted upon one group by a more powerful group.

Du Bois's initial empirical studies, "The Negroes of Farmville, Virginia: A Social Study" (1898), and his magnum opus *The Philadelphia Negro* (1899 [1967]) were conceived as a research unit: the study of social life in a Southern community and in a Northern city and the intra-racial and interracial dynamics in each locale. Since the Philadelphia study is grander in scope and encompasses a more compre-hensive world of blacks, if themes related to double consciousness were to emerge, they might do so in such a study. Unfortunately, there in not even a hint of this dilemma in the book. Hence, Theme One is not validated.

Theme Two appears to be validated only in the sense that Du Bois paints a picture of a highly regulated and relatively unified racial community that has created, under great obstacles, its specific institutions and organizations. It is the world of a people anchored in their churches, secret, beneficial, and insurance societies, labor unions, various political clubs, and many cooperative associations. There were many who rebelled against this special world and sought to penetrate the larger world of the more dominant group; their rebellion did not necessarily relate to their dislike of their self-created world as much as it represented a dislike of being excluded as a pariah group from the larger social body.

The only expression of anguish occurs when Du Bois writes of the impact of "color prejudice": "In the Negro's mind, color prejudice in Philadelphia is that widespread feeling of dislike for his blood, which keeps him and his children out of decent employment, from certain public conveniences and amusements, from hiring houses in many sections, and in general, from being recognized as a man.

Negroes regard this prejudice as the chief cause of their present unfortunate condition" (1967, p. 322).

When Du Bois discusses the behavior of the black middle class in Philadelphia, one gets the impression that he might indeed link this behavior to some idea of double consciousness, however, he does not, at least in the formal sense in which we define the term. He writes of the frustrations of this class (pp. 177–8): its inability to live where its income would permit; the problems of status inconsistency and cognitive dissonance *vis-à-vis* members of the white middle class and the vast majority of the black poor; the criticisms directed toward it by the lower classes, and its unwillingness to organize and spearhead race-specific organization, fearing that doing so would harden these institutions into permanent segregation units, thus delaying the possibility of their own entry into the larger society. (But one must seriously question Du Bois's assertion on that latter point, especially after his analysis of the many race-based institutions and organizations in Philadelphia. Without a doubt, the bulk of these institutions and organizations were created and sustained by members of the middle class.) The central point here is that the frustration of the middle class as described by Du Bois was not one necessarily of identity, whether to be an American or a Negro, or two warring souls. Rather it was the frustration from an inability to live like middle-class citizens.

The Farmville study utilized methodological approaches similar to the Philadelphia project; Du Bois concluded that beyond the great differences in size between the two communities, they have many things in common: the intricate organizational and institutional network and the dynamics of intra-racial and interracial relations. One major difference, of course, is that Farmville is located in Virginia about fifty miles from Richmond, the former capital of the Southern Confederacy. Like the assertions made in the Philadelphia study, Du Bois concludes that blacks and whites were separated in all their relations save that of economics. The surprising feature of Du Bois's analysis of Farmville, quite unlike the Philadelphia study, is his claim that rather than "the complete dependence of blacks upon whites," there is an "adjusted economic interdependence of the two races, which promises much in the way of mutual forbearance and understanding" (p. 34). However, again there is no discussion that in any way suggests the existence of double consciousness. In fact, Du Bois discusses Farmville in such an idyllic manner, very much unlike the specific examples outlined in his Philadelphia study, that we are hard pressed to find clear examples of racial conflict and strife in this Southern community.

Next, we present Du Bois's study *The Black North in 1901* (1901 [1969]), a brief analysis of the black communities in Boston, New York, and Philadelphia. Again, there is ample discussion of the inner world of blacks and the degree to which "the veil" has been drawn around that world by whites. In a very insightful analysis Du Bois draws out what he views to be an ongoing conflict between free blacks born in the North and the immigrant blacks who moved north from the South. His discussion *is* germane to the issue of identity when he states that "From the earliest times the attitude of the free negroes has been opposed to any organization or segregation of negroes as such. *Men like Fortune, McCune, Smith, and Remond insisted that they were American citizens, not negroes, and should act accordingly*" (p. 41, emphasis added).

That these men choose to view themselves as Americans rather than Negroes is the point to be observed here. However, Du Bois does not state this contradiction in a manner suggesting the anguish which is crucial to Theme One. He makes it clear that these men did indeed have reservations and ambivalences regarding what might have have described as the American/Negro dilemma. The paradox here is these same men were in the forefront of race-based organizations and institutions within their communities! Hence, there may have been theoretical or philosophical resistance to "being a negro," yet in their practical relations to others in their community, these men were just as much a part of what Du Bois called the "inner world" of blacks as others. Even if they did not want to belong to that black world, white resentment and segregation tied them tightly to that world.

Last, we look again at the book from whence the concept of double consciousness emergences, *The Souls of Black Folk* (1903 [1961]). Beyond the quotations and inferences from Chapter One of *Souls* (pp. 1–9), there is no other reference to the concept in any of the subsequent chapters. Du Bois does write of the legal, political, and economic restrictions blacks encounter, but the entire book is a masterful account of how blacks have been able to build and create an inner world for themselves in spite of efforts by many whites to curtail, intimidate, and destroy.

As our brief survey of Du Bois's works has shown, Du Bois apparently made no effort to validate or support his assumptions of double consciousness. It is imperative, therefore, that we move beyond his generalizations in order to arrive at some specifics: when, how, and in what circumstances did Du Bois believe these generalizations to be true? Without the benefit of history, context, or examples, these generalizations now stand as mere empty conjectures, assertions generations of scholars (Dennis and Henderson 1980; Dennis 1981, 1991) have accepted at face value simply because they had been enunciated by Du Bois. They appear, given Du Bois's descriptions of the concept at the time, to be reasonable and logical assumptions of what might be expected of a people, in Du Bois's terms "living behind the veil." But is it an accurate description of *actual behavior* or is it merely a supposition of *expected behavior*? In lieu of evidence supporting actual behavior, we must opt for the latter.

When we analyze *actual behavior* in the community studies cited by Du Bois, we note an elaborate degree of institution-building and intensive and extensive organizational networks. Thus, we note that racial structural constraints and barriers, as rigid as they were, did not prohibit all forms of institution-building. Or to state it in other terms, the structural constraints and barriers prohibited certain types of institutions but encouraged certain other types. This is Ralph Ellison's point: that the constraints, though powerful, did not, and could not prevent those elementary cultural features, based on the collective and historical experiences of a people from emerging. Du Bois's socio-historical account of race in America is an account of the importance of structure in determining a group's position in the society. However, the structural wall is never impenetrable; it is never sieveless.

One of the consequences of the interface of racial structural barriers and the unique collective experiences of blacks in America is, according to Du Bois (1903 [1961], p. 56), the emergence of racial social consciousness. He thus presents us with a paradox within a paradox: Just how accurate is his account of the double consciousness of Theme One if, in fact, blacks have been able to develop their own sense of racial and group consciousness, as he is now suggesting, to challenge, refute, and rebuff a prevailing white supremacist racial consciousness?

Recent Works Utilizing Double Consciousness

Two recent studies have applied the theme of double consciouness to an array of ideas and situations. Denise Heinze (1993) offers a critique of the double conscious via a study of the fictional communities of Toni Morrison; Paul Gilroy (1993) focuses on the idea of double consciousness as a substructural entity that lays the foundation for the idea of a transnational, transcultural, and transracial concept called *The Black Atlantic*.

Denise Heinze

Heinze's study lacks some of the most important nuances of Du Bois's approach to double consciousness as depicted in Du Bois's statement presented earlier in this paper. For example, her entire approach (Heinze 1993, p. 5), to double consciousness is simply a "state of affairs in which an individual is both representative of and immersed in two distinct ways of life." For Heinze, Du Bois's double consciousness becomes merely a "social dialectic" in which there are various competing ideas and "competing literary selves" presented in Morrison's novels. For example, Heinze's idea of "proving" the existence of double consciousness is merely to present a list of binary opposites presented in Morrison's works: materialism versus spiritualism; Afro-Centrism versus Euro-Centrism; white beauty versus black beauty; past versus present; good versus bad; nuclear family versus female-headed family; conformity versus rebellion, and community solidarity versus individual ambitions.

When Morrison presents an extended situation with which to demonstrate double consciousness, it turns out to be one-dimensional; it also turns Du Bois's logic on its head. Illustrative of this point is her discussion of Jadine and Son in *Tar Baby* (1981). She describes Jadine as one who chose to accept and live within the confines of the white side of the double conscious: she represented the best of white culture; she was constantly struggling to gain acceptance among whites, and she was addicted to the white world. Conversely, she describes Son as follows: he represented the best of black culture; he struggled to keep aspects of black culture alive, and that he could never become black middle class in as much as becoming that entails accepting Western values and meaning. Finally, Heinze depicts the relationship between Jadine and Son as a "manifestation of the psychic fragmentation of the culture as a whole." Heinze, of course, has a right to extend Du Bois's definition, and frankly, her conceptualization of the dualism so described does attest to the high level of social structural fragmentation.

In one sense Heinze de-psychologizes the double conscious by disallowing its dualistic black and white features from being present in one individual simultaneously. This simultaneous coexistence is, to be sure, the crux of the Du Boisian perspective: two warring souls in one body. Heinze has discretely removed the Du Boisian vision and has made the double conscious a representation of two separate individuals each residing in two separate and discrete worlds. By structuring her interpretation in this manner Heinze does make Morrison's character more internally consistent and more psychically whole; the price she pays for making this possible, however, is to make the characters more one-dimensional, less complex, and relatively static. Thus, Jadine and Son become, in Heinze's interpretation, "ideal types": representatives of their respective single-sided (white for Jadine and black for Son) consciousness in a society which, according to Heinze, is actually fragmented, and thus manifests a collective double conscious. One misses in this interpretation the anguish, challenge, and protestations that are so much a part of what we have called Theme One of Du Bois's definition, even though we have challenged this interpretation. The Heinze interpretation is no improvement on the Du Boisian version since it does not reflect, as does Du Bois's, the struggles of individuals who are in the process of challenging and calling into question, then refashioning, remolding, and reshaping their identities. Rather than representing individuals in the midst of an ongoing struggle for individual/group definition, her analysis reflects individuals who have concluded such a struggle.

Unlike Du Bois, Morrison, according to Heinze, does not seek a final resolution to the dilemma of duality. Du Bois suggests a synthesis of the opposing collective selves, voicing the hope that a "better self" might emerge out of the conflicting doubleness. Heinze (1993, p. 5) sees in Morrison the maintenance of a value that maintains that any final reconciliation of the opposing ideas and values are premature and next to impossible. In other words, the issues cannot be resolved; the true depiction of society and culture in the United States is the permanancy of a state of accommodation and the degree of connectedness between cultures (p. 10). Hence, the issues and ideas cannot be resolved or merged, but must remain as discrete units. So strangely enough, in the world of Morrison, as described by Heinze, there will not be a final synthesis; nor will there be a total victory for one side or the other in this struggle. No total victory is envisioned because, according to Heinze (p. 150), Morrision is not really interested in a clear victory of one side over the other. Morrision's great feat, according to Heinze, is to utilize issues dealing with double consciousness; but it was not to deal with double consciousness as a resoluable theme but rather as ideas with which to "enrich and expand the limits of human consciousness beyond the either-or mentality that sets people against each other in mutually destructive ways."

Paul Gilroy

Paul Gilroy's book, *The Black Atlantic* (1993), presents the thesis that many of the ideological and philosophical ideals and values of African-American cultural elites have become indelibly interwined with similar ideals and values enunciated by European cultural elites. As a result of this fusion, there has emerged, according to Gilroy, values, ideas, and positions that are transnational, transcultural, and transracial. This racial mutation and hybridity has only been possible, says Gilroy, because of the merger of ideas centered around modernity (ideas related to citizenship, freedom, and individuality) with that of double consciousness (dual perspectives of African-Americans and Afro-Europeans due to their less powerful position within more powerful American and European societies). Modernity and the double conscious have joined to produce something revolutionary in Western ideological, political, and philosophical thought: the formation of racial mutation and hybridity.

Gilroy does not ground the double conscious in the status and power inequities, contradictions, and ambiguities of the African-American experience in the United States. Instead, he views the European travel experience of African-Americans as a key link in the emergence of the black Atlantic which is the antecedent to double consciousness. Or as he states it: "the black Atlantic politics of location frames the doorway of double consciousness." A fuller explanation of the relationship between Du Bois, black Atlantic politics, and double consciousness is explored by Gilroy (p. 19):

> Du Bois's travel experiences raise in the sharpest possible form a question common to the lives of almost all these figures who begin as African-American or Caribbean people and are then changed into something else which evades those specific labels and with them all fixed notions of nationality and national identity. Whether their experience of exile is enforced or chosen temporary or permanent, these intellectuals and activists, writers, speakers, poets, and artists repeatedly articulate a desire to escape the restrictive bonds of ethnicity, national identification, and sometimes even 'race' itself.... The specificity of the modern political and cultural formation I want to call the black Atlantic can be defined, on one level, through this desire to transcend both the structures of the nation state and the constraints of ethnicity and national particularity.

Gilroy (p. 126) locates the double conscious as an instance in the "special difficulties arising from black internalisation of an American identity." Later in the chapter on Richard Wright, Gilroy (p. 147) highlights Wright's apparent movements "between the claims of racial particularity on one side and the appeal of those modern universals that appear to transcend race on the other arises in the sharpest possible form. Wright's sense of this opposition and the conflicting forms of identity to which it gives rise adds another notch of complexity and bitterness to formulations of double consciousness." It is perhaps in this immediate quote that we see the major difference between Du Bois's and Gilroy's interpretation of the origins of double consciousness.

There are two main problems with Gilroy's assessment of Du Bois's concept: the first is that he frames the logic for a double conscious around the idea that the African-American had to travel to Europe to discover and recognize its existence; the second is that unlike Du Bois, he does not emphasize the emergence of double consciousness from its social structural foundation.

Throughout his many books Du Bois carefully documented the issues and situations that had given rise to polarization and contradictions in American life. That these had been built into the very fabric of American life was evident in the manner Du Bois had described the American society and the role and position of blacks within that society beginning with his study of the African Slave Trade (Du Bois 1896 [1969]). He poses the question of what it means to be a free man in contrast to what it means to be a slave or a second-class citizen. Furthermore, Du Bois outlines a concise history of the making of black America: the construction of a dual society and all that it entails (the creation of institutions and organizations and the melding together of these into workable networks that were intercommunal in nature).

This need to construct a dual society and the constraints that forced blacks to live, in Du Bois's term, "behind the veil" was indeed conducive to "interpreting" one's realities in doubles, since one was "living" a double or dual existence. Thus, the assertion that Du Bois had to retreat to Europe to discover dualities or doubleness is not logical or reasonable because the very structure and organization of the American society itself represented these attributes. Frederick Douglass, Du Bois, David Walker, and others did not have to go to Europe to discover European political thinkers who, according to Gilroy, would then induce in them a double conscious, because they were already inspired by the American Constitution, the Bill of Rights, and the antislavery movement in its religious and political contexts. Each contributed initially toward an emancipation of the mind, later the body. Each also provided an opportunity for blacks to open the doors to political, social, and economic inclusion, in theory though not in reality.

The claim is not being made here that Du Bois, Douglass, and others did not learn from European thinkers or did not utilize some of their ideas. Nor is the claim being made that Du Bois and others did not include other cultures, nations, and struggles in their pronouncements on freedom. Rather, the assertion here is that the American society itself had, and did manifest, all of the elements which would have given African-American thinkers the impetus for double consciousness. Gilroy (p. 159) also appears to believe this when he favorably cites Richard Wright's conversation with C. L. R. James about volumes of Kierkegaard on a shelf:

'Look here Nello, you see those books there? Everything that he writes in those books I knew before I had them.' James suggests that Wright's apparently inituitive foreknowledge of the issues raised by Kierkegaard was not intuitive at all. It was an elementary product of his historical experiences as a black growing up in the United States between the wars: 'What [Dick] was telling me was that he was a black man in the United States and that gave him an insight into what today is the universal opinion and attitude of the *modern* personality' (emphasis added).

In another paper (Dennis 1979) Du Bois's nationalism and internationalism were briefly analyzed. Though one cannot explain the politics of Du Bois without examining his slow movement, first into socialism, then into formal communism, it can be argued, as this writer has, that Du Bois's understanding of and involvement in both movements were largely situational, very limited in scope, and beyond a few articles, very circumscribed in any semblance of theoretical richness and clarity. Du Bois clearly understood the importance of transcultural, transracial, and transnational values, however, the great impetus for his critiques and analyses always revolve around the particularities of the African-American experience, and the specialness of that experience analyzed in conjunction with the particularities of the experiences of the dominant white society. In the world that he knew existed, he could not and did not discuss one without the other.

The second issue raised against Gilroy is that his analysis of double consciousness is largely a search for identity among African-Americans, but he does not ground the identity search in the specifics of social structure. Rather, he presents the identity issue and double consciousness as givens, as preformed elements and as independent qualities, rather than what they actually are: the result of institutional, organizational, and value contradictions and polarizations. Gilroy proffers the view that the double conscious is a precondition for the sociopolitics of black Atlantic, but he does not adequately analyze the features which become the precondition for the double conscious itself. To be sure, it is in the manner in which he positions the issue of identity within the social structure, in contrast to Gilroy, that we perceive Du Bois's greater sociological depth. Without becoming entangled in any of the side issues of the materialist/idealist debate, we can observe certain tendencies in Du Bois and Gilroy that are germane to the debate: Du Bois believed that the preconditions for identity questions are always tied to the political, economic, class, and racial structure and one's location in that structure.

Du Bois's position on this issues lies clearly in the materialist camp. Gilroy's demonstration of the transition from double consciousness to the black Atlantic, with minimum attention to social structural matters, places him much more squarely in the idealist camp. That is the problem. When Du Bois wrote of double consciousness he related the concept to a condition affecting the entire black population. When Gilroy describes the concept, there is a degree of ambiguity. Ostensibly, he is primarily concerned with writers and scholars, their European experience, how double consciousness erupts from this interaction, and how and why the black Atlantic is a natural outcome of these co-joining forces. At other times, however, Gilroy (pp. 1–2) writes as if he, like Du Bois, is referring to all blacks, not just the cultural elite:

> Striving to be both European and black requires some specific forms of double consciousness. . . . The contemporary black English, like the Anglo-Africans of earlier generations and perhaps, like all blacks in the West, stand between (at least) two great cultural assemblages, both of which have mutated through the course of the modern world that formed them and assumed new configurations. At present, they remain locked symbiotically in an antagonistic relationship marked out by the symbolism of colours which adds to the conspicuous cultural power of their central Manichean dynamic – black and white.

Gilroy assures us that the black Atlantic is authentic and valid, but the very person who is at the centerpiece of the black Atlantic, Du Bois, may be the individual who most undermines the idea. As is so often the case when analyzing Du Bois, it is a matter of time and location. Gilroy is correct in moving Du Bois from the nationalist to the internationalist, from ethnic specificity to generalized ethnicity, but Du Bois (1968) simply refuses to stay in one corner. Du Bois understands why it is important to live in a world where transcultural and transnational values exist. But this acknowledgment does not mean that he abandoned his focus on black American. A reading of his books reveals the extent to which he, like Richard Wright, another central figure in the Gilroy book, was always a mixture of the divergent possibilities in black life: integrationist–separatist; capitalist–socialist/

communist; the common man–the cultural elite; nationalist–internationalist; the Europeanist–the Pan-Africanist. If Du Bois does represent the black Atlantic he does so by emphasizing the *black* and placing small caps on Atlantic.

There is an idealist strain in Gilroy's development of double consciousness almost similar to the Marxian development of dialectical materialism. To many Marxists, the success of the Proletarian Revolution will signal the end of class conflict and strife. In like manner, Gilroy proposes that the anguish of the double conscious will be assuaged by the emergence of the black Atlantic which will end the double conscious dilemma. A case can be made that Gilroy tries too hard to prove the reality of black Atlantic. He attempts to prove his case for European universalism prior to exhausting historical resources and situations that would have demonstrated an already existing level of universalism in a non-European setting. For example, he is so eager to prove the European origin of so much of Du Bois's thought that he virtually ignored a number of Harvard professors who shaped Du Bois's intellectual landscape before Du Bois travelled to Europe (see Du Bois 1968, p. 148).

While Gilroy takes the double conscious theme into a radically new area, he does not really improve upon Du Bois's sketchy pronouncements, and because his treatment of the concept is largely theoretical and drafted to define a condition of specific individuals (Du Bois, Wright, Douglass, etc.), we do not get an analysis that focuses on the behavior of groups in a particular society. Rather, Gilroy has provided us with acute insights into the psychology of Du Bois and especially Richard Wright and how each related to certain European philosophical themes. The individual psychological dimensions of double consciousness was noted by Ralph Ellison in an interview with William Penn Warren (1966). When asked by Warren to respond to Du Bois's assertion of the existence of double conscious or a psyche split among black Americans, Ellison rejected the claim. He stated that "the idea that the Negro psyche is split is not as viable as it seems – although it might have been true of Dr. Du Bois personally."

The problem with accounts of double consciousness by Heinze and Gilroy is that neither account is sociological though Gilroy's account purports to be. What appears to be true in the world of literary and philosophical thought may not in fact hold true in reality, though the results may be extremely interesting and in-formative as is true of the books cited here. The test of Du Bois's thesis might provide more tangible results if the basis for the inquiry were sociological and if such inquiry occurred in a research setting. This statement is based on the premise that Du Bois's original logic for double consciousness was indeed sociologically grounded.

Conclusion

In a sense Du Bois created the muddle now accompanying the idea of double consciousness. By situating the question as a psychic problem and by suggesting that the problem may be irresolvable, as expressed in Theme One, he ultimately imprisoned the logic and rationale of many thinkers who took his pronouncements of the issue as final rather than as a starting point. We would have been more advanced in approaching the issue of the duality of black life had Du Bois used a term he later used to describe the same phenomenon: double environment. That term has more of the tenor of, and is more suggestive of, the sociological. The issue here is that Du Bois had a mimimal understanding of psychology beyond his superficial introduction to Jamesian psychology. This limitation does not, however, minimize Du Bois's great psychological insights into the interracial and intra-racial worlds.

References

Bendix, R. 1960. *Max Weber: An Intellectual Portrait*. Garden City, NY: Doubleday and Company.

Dennis, R. M. 1979. "Race, Structured Inequality and the Consequences of Racial Domination: The Political Sociology of W. E. B. Du Bois." In *Lectures: Black Scholars on Black Issues*, edited by V. Gordon. Washington, DC: University Press of America.

——. 1981. "Socialization and Racism: The White Experience." In *Impacts of Racism on White Americans*, edited by B. Bowser and R. Hunt. Newbury Park: Sage Publications.

——. 1991. "Dual Marginality and Discontent among Black Middletown Youth." In *Research in Race and Ethnic Relations*, edited by R. M. Dennis. Greenwich, CT: JAI Press.

Dennis, R. M., and C. Henderson. 1980. "Intellectuals and Double Consciousness." In *Afro-American Perspectives in the Humanities*, edited by C. Hedgepeth, Jr. San Diego: Collegiate.

Du Bois, W. E. B. 1896. *The Suppression of the African Slave-Trade to the United States of America. 1638–1870*. New York: Longmans, Green and Company (Reprinted by Schocken Books, New York, 1969).

——. 1898. "The Negroes of Farmville: A Social Study." *Bulletin of the United States Department of Labor* 3: 1–38.

——. 1899. *The Philadelphia Negro*. Philadelphia: University Publishers (Reprinted by Schocken Books, New York, 1967).

——. 1901. *The Black North in 1901*. Articles originally published in the *New York Times* (Reprinted by Arno Press and *The New York Times*, New York, 1969).

——. 1903. *The Souls of Black Folk*. Chicago: A. C. McClurg and Co. (Edition cited is the Fawcett Publications, Greenwich, CT, 1961).

——. 1940. *Dusk of Dawn*. New York: Harcourt and Brace (Reprinted by Schocken Books, New York, 1968).

——. 1968. *The Autobiography of W. E. B. Du Bois*. New York: International Publishers.

Early, G. 1993. *Lure and Loathing*. New York: Penguin Books.

Fanon, F. 1967. *Black Skin, White Masks*. New York: Grove Press.

Fullinwider, S. P. 1969. *The Mind and Mood of Black America*. Homewood, IL: The Dorsey Press.

Garvey, M. 1967. *Philosophy and Opinions of Marcus Garvey*. London: Frank Cass and Company.

Gilroy, P. 1993. *The Black Atlantic*. Cambridge, MA: Harvard University Press.

Grier, W., and P. Cobbs. 1968. *Black Rage*. New York: Bantam Books.

Heinze, D. 1993. *The Dilemma of "Double-Consciousness": Toni Morrison's Novels*. Athens, GA: University of Georgia Press.

Kardiner, A., and L. Ovesey. 1951. *The Mark of Oppression*. Cleveland: Meridian Books.

Lewis, D. L. 1993. *W. E. B. Du Bois: Biography of a Race*. New York: Henry Holt and Company.

Memmi, A. 1965. *The Colonizer and the Colonized*. New York: Orion.

Morrison, T. 1981. *Tar Baby*. New York: New American Library.

Rosenfield, C. 1967. "The Conscious and Unconscious Use of the Double." In *Stories of the Double*, edited by A. J. Guerard. Philadelphia: J. B. Lippincott Company.

Rampersad, A. 1976. *The Art and Imagination of W. E. B. Du Bois*. Cambridge: Harvard University Press.

Rudwick, E. 1982. *W. E. B. Du Bois – Voice of the Black Protest Movement*. Urbana: University of Illinois Press.

Turner, J., R. Singleton, and D. Musick 1984. *Oppression: A Socio-History of Black–White Relations in America*. Chicago: Nelson Hall.

Warren, R. P. 1966, *Who Needs the Negro?* New York: Vintage Books.

2 Max Weber on Race, Ethnicity, and Nationalism

John Stone

Few writers in the sociological tradition can be compared to Max Weber as a prophet of the most fundamental social and political trends of the 20th century. His remarkable ability to focus on the central issues of the modern era, not to mention his increasing recognition as a precursor of some of the major themes that constitute the "postmodern" debate, are acknowledged by admirers and critics alike.[1] Weber's analysis of the cultural foundations and contradictions of capitalism, his skeptical vision of the future of socialism, his concern about the pervasive intrusion of bureaucracy in everyday life, and his seminal discussion of the complex interplay among economic, social, and political power are contributions that are generally recognized and are documented extensively (Gerth and Mills, 1948; Parkin, 1982; Runciman, 1978; Wrong, 1970). It might even be argued that much of the most valuable controversy in social theory during the past four decades has been, to rephrase Zeitlin, a "debate with the ghost of Weber."[2]

Nevertheless, Weber may be criticized, along with almost every other social thinker from the time of the French Revolution until the outbreak of World War I, for failing to give sufficient weight to racial, ethnic, and national conflicts.[3] He cannot, however, be accused of having ignored these issues, and much of his sociological analysis, even when it was not focused specifically on racial and ethnic groups, can be adapted to the study of race and ethnic relations without significant modification. In this essay, I outline Weber's own attempts to incorporate race and ethnicity into his sociological writings. Then I consider some of the principal ways in which aspects of the Weberian legacy have been adopted by a broad range of sociologists and other scholars concerned with race and ethnic relations.[4] Finally, I argue that a Weberian perspective still offers some of the most important insights into the enduring problems of racial and ethnic conflict.

Following in the footsteps of other prominent European social thinkers such as Tocqueville and Beaumont, Harriet Martineau, and James Bryce,[5] Weber found that contact with the United States greatly heightened his interest and sensitivity toward race and ethnic relations. In 1904, during a crucial visit to the Congress of Arts and Sciences of the Universal Exposition in St. Louis, Missouri, Weber not only derived inspiration for the completion of his most celebrated work, *The Protestant Ethic and the Spirit of Capitalism*, he was also brought face to face with what he began to realize was America's most serious problem. At this time, the specter haunting Europe appeared to be that of the class struggle, the dress rehearsal for the Bolshevik Revolution was only a year away, and the latent national rivalries, about to break out in global warfare during the next decade, were still masked by the waning years of Pax Britannica.

The situation in America was starkly different. Northern cities teamed with the ethnic diversity generated by the trans-Atlantic migrations combined with the movement of African Americans from the southern states. It was impossible for any perceptive observer to overlook the central significance of racial and ethnic diversity for American society. Weber was fascinated by the situation he observed in New York and Chicago:

> The Greek shining the Yankee's shoes for five cents, the German acting as his waiter, the Irishman managing his politics, and the Italian digging his dirty ditches...the whole gigantic city...is like a man whose skin has been peeled off and whose entrails one sees at work. (Gerth and Mills, 1948, p. 15)

Like Tocqueville, who visited America some 70 years earlier, Weber was particularly struck by the contrasting status of African Americans and Native Americans (cf. Manasse, 1947, p. 198).[6] Why was it that the former were treated with so much more hostility and contempt than the latter? He noted that this could not be attributed to physical differences, because both groups were clearly and visibly distinct from the majority White population. Nor could it be argued seriously that there was a natural repulsion between Blacks and Whites, as many southern Whites claimed, because of the large number of mixed-race offspring from interracial unions and sexual relationships. And yet it could be seen that the smallest trace of observable African ancestry would relegate an individual to a subordinate social status whereas significant amounts of "Indian blood" did not. Weber's explanation for this strange differential rested with the institution of slavery, which was, of course, unique to the Black experience in America. Paradoxically, the strength that Blacks had demonstrated by surviving the physical and psychological trauma of slavery (unlike the Indians, who generally could not adapt to these terrible conditions) led to their association with despised manual labor. This, according to Weber's interpretation, reflected the almost feudal contempt for such work found in southern White society.

Weber's views on American race relations were influenced by the contacts he made during his brief stay. He spent several days in the company of Cherokee Indians in Oklahoma and also visited Tuskegee, Alabama. Whether he actually met Booker T. Washington is unclear, but what is certain is that he spoke to W. E. B. Du Bois, Washington's great rival, and that from this encounter came an article titled "Die Negerfrage in den Vereinigten Staaten," which Du Bois published in the 1906 volume of the *Archiv für Sozialwissenschaft und Politik*, a journal that Weber jointly edited. It was Du Bois who made the claim, which in retrospect was not particularly exaggerated, that "the problem of the twentieth century would be that of the colour line," a prediction that Weber, no mean prophet himself, readily adopted, stating that the unresolved racial conflicts would hover over American society "like a big black cloud" (see Gerth and Mills, 1948, pp. 15–16).[7]

If Weber's American travels were to focus his attention on some of the most sharply defined issues of racial conflict and stratification, this was not his first attempt to grasp the significance of ethnic group differences. During the 1890s, he published a number of articles (including his inaugural lecture at Freiburg titled "The National State and Economic Policy"[8]) on agrarian life in eastern Germany, which involved comparisons between ethnic Germans and ethnic Poles, both as farmers and as farm laborers. In these early studies, Weber displayed a thorough-going German nationalism in which he castigated the Junkers, the landed aristoc-racy, for using cheap Polish labor that undercut and systematically displaced German farm workers from the great estates of the eastern parts of the country. At this time, Weber had not totally rejected the currently influential notions of inher-ent racial differences, as his references to "Slavic adaptability" implied (see Mana-sse, 1947, p. 194), but he was much too careful a scholar to pursue this line of reasoning without substantial evidence to support it. Time and again, he found concrete historical and social causes to explain observable differences in the eco-nomic behavior and social status of the Polish and German populations, which made the idea of inherent group characteristics redundant. His growing rejection of racial theorizing was not based on a conviction that no such differences could exist, and even in his later writings he always regarded the question, at least in principle, as an open one. What was crucial for Weber was the weight of evidence that the work habits of Germans and Poles were a product of historical circum-stances and environmental conditions rather than permanent biological or cultural attributes. As a result, references to such factors increasingly faded from Weber's subsequent writings on these issues.

There are two other major themes of Weber's work that illustrate this consistent rejection of racial "explanations" of historical change and national character. In contemporary historical debates surrounding the factors purporting to explain the decline of the Roman Empire, Weber attacked the notion that "barbarian" blood among the leadership groups could in any way account for the collapse of this great civilization. Such a hypothesis simply did not fit the facts: At the height of its power and prestige, the Roman Empire acquired many of its most brilliant leaders from the ethnic periphery of its vast territories, and there was no evidence that it was external rather than Roman cultural influences that accompanied the social and political disintegration of the regime. Explanations had to be found in other, less simplistic causes. In writing about another of the great historical civil-izations, that of the Chinese, Weber addressed the same basic issue from a differ-ent angle. He considered the question of outsiders' stereotypes of the Chinese "character" and showed how these were often mutually contradictory or that certain types of behavior could be interpreted as typical of most groups under similar circumstances. Once again, Weber's commitment to value-neutral methods to explore and test hypotheses, considered to be eminently plausible by many contemporary scholars, led him to reject racial explanations of social and political events.

Weber's mature position on ethnicity and ethnic stratification thus represented a significant and vital shift from the emphasis of his turn-of-the-century writings on agrarian life in Eastern Prussia. This is illustrated further by his analysis of the Indian caste system and the situation of post-diaspora Jews in Western societies. Manasse provides a characteristically balanced assessment, pointing to the crucial change in the type of question that Weber considered to be important in these later studies. The confusion between race and culture was resolved and "instead of asking which innate qualities distinguish one Indian caste from another, he raised the question why the solution of the racial problem in India differed so greatly from the solution in analogous situations, such as that in England after the Norman conquest" (Manasse, 1947, p. 207). A similar change of focus could be detected in his attempt to understand the factors inhibiting the assimilation of the Jews in the diaspora by their host societies. Turning attention away from any allegedly hereditary characteristics of the Jews as a minority group, he asked, "What historical and sociological experiences shaped those attitudes that caused the segregation of the Jews from their neighbours?" (p. 207).[9]

In both cases, Weber's interest in the historical development of the caste system or in the remarkable persistence of the Jews as a distinct minority – or "pariah group," to use his more controversial terminology – caused him to focus on the interaction between economics, religion, and ethnicity. Economic monopolization provided much of the rationale for the creation of these particular social structures, religion acted as a potent source of legitimation, and racial and ethnic characteristics acted as convenient types of group markers. He saw caste as originating in racial conflicts with the dominant, light-skinned conquerors forcing the darker-skinned, indigenous populations out of all those occupations that carried social prestige. Understanding the religious doctrine of karma and the taboos on intermarriage and commensality provided, as in his argument about the unique contribution of ascetic Protestantism to the birth of modern capitalism, vital clues to the resilience of the caste system in India. A similar appreciation of the special characteristics of traditional Judaism, such as the emphasis on strict dietary laws, also played an important part in explaining why the Jews had preserved their distinct communities in a largely gentile world.[10]

Weber's influence on the field of race and ethnic relations is by no means confined to his somewhat limited treatment of the subject itself. For two and a half decades after his death in 1920, Germany was submerged in the "polar night of icy darkness" that he anticipated so clearly in his final lectures. However, Weber's sociological legacy was passed on to the English-speaking world mainly through the translations and writings of Talcott Parsons. With the defeat of Nazism, much of the initial concern of race relations research, particularly among the refugee scholars from Central Europe, revealed a preoccupation with the psychodynamics of prejudice, as exemplified by the monumental study of the *The Authoritarian Personality* written by Adorno, Frenkel-Brunswick, Levinson, and Sanford (1950).[11] This represented an attempt to understand the fundamental roots of fascism that lay behind the horrors of the Holocaust. The limitations of this approach gradually became apparent, and emphasis shifted toward investigations of patterns and structures of racial discrimination. With this reorientation of research, Weber's central themes of power, domination, authority, and legitimation became increasingly relevant for the analysis of racial and ethnic conflicts.

There are few contemporary perspectives on race and ethnic relations that cannot be linked, in one way or another, to some theme of Weber's seminal writings. When the emphasis is on the microdynamics of racial interaction found among the symbolic interactionists, phenomenologists, and ethnomethodologists, Weber's methodological focus on action, and the importance he attached to the interpretative understanding of such action (*verstehen*), is clearly relevant. W. I. Thomas's famous dictum, "If men define situations as real, they are real in their consequences," echoes much of Weber's preoccupation with entering into the minds of social actors. "One does not have to be Hitler to understand Hitler" might be an interesting adaptation of his famous statement concerning Caesar.

This concern with ideas leads logically to the study of racism and other ethno-centric belief systems that have played an important part in the perpetuation, and possibly the genesis, of systems of racial stratification. Weber's ongoing debate with Marxist scholars, and his attempts to refine materialism to take seriously the importance of ideal interests, provided a solution to many of the self-inflicted problems of subsequent Marxist sociology. If these scholars had seen Weber's work as an attempt to extend and develop Marx's legacy in a more sophisticated and realistic direction rather than as a frontal assault on their cherished dogmas, they would have avoided an enormous amount of spurious controversy.[12] Finally, Weber's focus on power and domination is of critical relevance to a wide spectrum of approaches that emphasize a variety of different factors, from resource mobilization and competition to the role of world systems and the conflict between centers and peripheries. It is interesting to note that despite the importance placed on rationalization as a key concept and unifying theme in so much of Weber's work (cf. Brubaker, 1984, p. 2), his understanding of the term was rather different from the way in which it has been incorporated into modern rational choice theory. In fact, he anticipated some of the limitations of this particular perspective on race relations (cf. Stone, 1992, pp. 91–2).

Whereas the scope of Weber's vision is impressive, it is possible to isolate certain key contributions that, in my judgment, are especially valuable to the field. These I consider under the following broad headings: (1) the insight of his basic definitions, (2) the process of group closure and boundary maintenance, (3) the role of racist ideas and the importance of legitimacy, and (4) the centrality of power and domination.

I   Definitions

Weber's evident frustration with the elusive quality of ethnicity is well captured by his statements in *Economy and Society*. Nevertheless, he did not abandon the concept and proceeded with great care to try to isolate its essential character. As a result, he produced a formulation that has been adopted, in most of its basic elements, by many subsequent scholars of the subject. Weber defined ethnic groups as "human groups (other than kinship groups) which cherish a belief in their common origins of such a kind that it provides a basis for the creation of a community" (Runciman, 1978, p. 364; see also Jackson, 1982/1983). In this definition, he isolates the fundamental characteristics of the phenomenon that center on a set of beliefs and not on any objective features of group membership such as shared language, religion, and especially biological traits associated with the everyday understanding of race. It is this sense of common ancestry that is vital, but the identification with shared origins is largely, if not wholly, fictitious. The elusive quality of ethnicity stems from the minimal core on which ethnic groups are based and accounts for the kaleidoscope of other elements that are found among the myriad examples of individual ethnic groups. Weber is adamant that the difference between ethnic groups and kinship groups lies precisely on the question of "presumed identity" (Roth and Wittich, 1968, p. 389). Ethnic membership per se does not necessarily result in ethnic group formation but only provides the resources that may, under the right circumstances, be mobilized into a group by appropriate political action.

The individual and social construction of ethnicity is a theme that has recurred in many subsequent analyses of the phenomenon. Attention is focused less on the content of ethnicity than on the processes and mechanisms that convert the potential ethnic attributes into fully fledged ethnic communities and organizations. Such a perspective applies across the spectrum of groups whether they are defined as racial or as ethnic, and it reinforces the critical truth that whether we are unmasking "the figment of pigment" (Horowitz, 1971, p. 244) or the "invention of tradition" (Hobsbawm and Ranger, 1983), it is vital to concentrate attention on the sociological process of group formation that is the central task of the social scientist. What causes the increased salience of ethnicity at a particular historical period? What determines which ethnic markers are selected as the basis of group membership? How are group boundaries demarcated and perpetuated? How are boundaries broken down and, in some cases, eradicated by assimilation into new and different social groupings? These are some of the basic question that Weber's deceptively simple definition of ethnicity provokes.

The third definition refers to nationalism, which Weber considered to be a political extension of the ethnic community because its members and leadership searched for a unique political structure by establishing an independent state (Smith, 1992b, pp. 62–3). Whereas, as Anthony Smith has noted, he did not provide a historical account of the rise of nationalism, he did nevertheless seek to discuss the important relationship between ethnicity and nationalism, which has been a key feature of much subsequent scholarship.

2 Group Closure and Boundary Maintenance

Apart from providing these basic definitions of race, ethnicity, and nationalism, Weber's discussion of what he termed "social closure" is another particularly helpful contribution to our understanding of the origin and dynamics of ethnic and racial groups. Weber noted the general tendency of social groups to attempt to form monopolies or, at least, to try to restrict the full force of open competition in a manner that was analogous to the behavior found in economic markets. By extending the tradition – long established in the literature of economics – of analyzing the reasons underlying the formation of monopolies and oligopolies to encompass the rationale behind a much wider range of social groups, Weber opened up an interesting new perspective on ethnic group formation. Whereas this approach could also be applied to classes and professional groups as much as to racial or ethnic groups, it did provide a convincing explanation for the persistence of these groups once they had been established, if not for their initial creation.

That question was largely a matter of historical or social circumstances: factors such as conquest or migration putting visibly or culturally identifiable groups together and unleashing the tendencies for the more powerful to entrench their privileges by monopolizing economic, social, and political advantages. This became particularly acute when competition for scarce resources increased so that

> one group of competitors takes some externally identifiable characteristic of another group of (actual or potential) competitors – race, language, religion, local or social origins, descent, residence, etc. – as a pretext for attempting their exclusion. It does not matter which characteristic is chosen in the individual case: whatever suggests itself most easily is seized upon. . . . [The purpose of] this monopolization . . . is always the closure of social and economic opportunities to outsiders. (Weber, 1922/1968, pp. 341–2)

Such an agnostic attitude to the importance of particular group markers has not commended itself to all subsequent scholars working on the question of social closure, with writers such as Murphy (1988) proposing a hierarchy of closure mechanisms rather than the almost random process of group demarcation suggested by Weber.

The theme of social closure has become an important element in the neo-Weberian literature; whereas it has been developed with particular focus on social stratification, it is of equal if not greater relevance to ethnic and racial stratification. Frank Parkin's (1979) trenchant critique of Marxism, along with the more recent studies by Murphy and Brubaker, has demonstrated how "the mechanisms of closure provide a key to understanding the formation of status groups and social classes engaged in the struggle over the distribution of rewards and opportunities" (Manza, 1992, p. 276). Although much of this debate has been concerned with aspects of class analysis, many of the examples have in fact been drawn from situations of deep racial and ethnic conflict. This has exposed the limitations of a sociology of stratification that has often ignored or downplayed these critical ethnic and racial divisions and is true of gender divisions as well.[13] As a result, modern stratification theory has steadily regained a wider vision that typifies the approach found in Weber's writings on these issues rather than being preoccupied by the more restricted view of the processes associated with economic classes found in industrial societies.

Concepts of closure, and the related question of group boundaries, can be seen as a central preoccupation of many scholars studying ethnicity in modern society. Michael Hechter's work, for example, has ranged across a spectrum of issues, from concern with the phenomenon of internal colonialism as an explanation for regionalist movements in the Celtic Fringe of Great Britain (Hechter, 1975; Stone and Hechter, 1979) to rational choice analyses of ethnic conflict (Hechter, 1986, 1987). Both approaches have some connection to questions of social closure, but his theoretical discussion of the principles of group solidarity clearly lies explicitly within the debates over types and forms of social closure. In social anthropology, the seminal writings of Fredrik Barth on boundaries, and the subsequent focus of scholars such as Wallman and Okamura, represent variations on a similar theme (Barth, 1969; Okamura, 1981; Wallman, 1986). Brubaker's (1992) study on *Citizenship and Nationhood in France and Germany* reveals yet another illustration of the manner in which Weber's emphasis on the centrality of social closure continues to appear in important new studies of societal diversity. As Brubaker (1992) notes,

> In global perspective, citizenship is a powerful instrument of social closure, shielding prosperous states from the migrant poor. Citizenship is also an instrument of closure within states. Every state establishes a conceptual, legal and ideological boundary between citizens and foreigners. (p. x)

Although it is not generally attributed to the Weberian legacy to the sociology of race and ethnic relations, as it is characteristically associated more with Simmel's essay on "the stranger" and Park's writings on "the marginal man," the body of literature devoted to "merchant minorities" can also be linked to Weber's interest in what he called pariah groups (Leresche, 1989; Stone, 1985). It is true that, as a recent critic such as Gary Abraham has stressed, Weber's concern with such minority groups was only peripheral to his major research interests; however, his analysis should not be dismissed, as Abraham (1992) implies, as simply a repetition of "contemporary stereotypes" (p. 293). His interpretation of the position of such groups in society contains much insight that is derived from seeing the phenomenon in a broad comparative context. Thus the ideal type may be based on the situation of European Jewry, but the characteristic features of a merchant minority can be found in groups residing in many different societies during various historical epochs. Among such groups, tendencies toward monopolization, albeit forced on the group by outside discriminatory pressures, can be developed with the assistance of ethnic markers or religious sanctions that are then used to limit access to group membership. Such status differentiation develops into caste-like structures, according to Weber, only when rooted in ethnic divisions. Thus

> The "caste" is actually the normal "societal" form in which ethnic communities which believe in blood relationship and forbid intermarriage and social intercourse with outsiders live alongside one another. This is true of the "pariah" peoples which have emerged from time to time in all parts of the world – communities which have acquired special occupational traditions of an artisan or other kind, which cultivate a belief in their common ethnic origin, and which now live in a "diaspora," rigorously avoiding all personal intercourse other than that which is unavoidable, in a legally precarious position, but tolerated on the grounds of their economic indispensability and often even privileged, and interspersed among political communities....The Jews are the most striking historical example. (Runciman, 1978, p. 50)

Later scholars have argued about the balance of characteristics that constitute the core features of such groups and particularly about the factors in the wider societies, and among the groups themselves, that account for the origin and persistence of the phenomenon. Others have criticized Weber for the apparently pejorative connotations of the term pariah group, but substitution of the politically more correct terms such as middleman or merchant minorities should not disguise the fact that these particularly vulnerable ethnic groups display many of the sociological characteristics found in Weber's original analysis of the subject.

3   Racism and Legitimacy

Two of the most distinctive features of Weber's sociological perspective were his concern for understanding the meaning that individual actors attributed to their behavior and the related importance that they invariably attached to the search for legitimacy in relation to such action. In *The Protestant Ethic*, Weber isolated a special set of ideas that he argued were particularly crucial in explaining why modern rational capitalism took off in one particular social setting during a specific historical period. Several sociologists and historians of race and ethnic relations have also speculated on the parallel role of ideologies and belief systems – in this case, those associated with racism – in contributing toward an explanation of the dynamics and persistence of particular forms of racial and ethnic stratification. John Rex, for example, who is one contemporary sociologist to explicitly identify with a Weberian perspective, has incorporated the presence and special character of "deterministic belief systems" in his attempt to define a "race relations situation" (Rex, 1970, 1980). Whereas other scholars, particularly those inclined toward a Marxist or materialist orientation, have tended to dismiss racial ideas as epiphenomena that are largely insignificant reflections of a particular mode of production, much of this is based on confusion concerning the social impact of false ideas.

It is certainly true that ideas of biological race have been discredited on scientific grounds – notions of pure races are wholly fictitious – but it is not the case that such beliefs are sociologically irrelevant. For Weber, it did not matter whether Calvinist notions of predestination had any validity; what counted was that people believed this to be the case and that this had real, if unanticipated, consequences for human action. Whereas there is certainly no absolute link between prejudiced beliefs and discriminatory action, to dismiss such ideas as irrelevant is unjustified. Thus Rex focuses on the debates over slavery and points to the importance that Weber attached to "the question of the role of religious and other ideological factors in shaping socio-economic systems" (Rex, 1980, p. 125). Although Weber's stress on the affinity between Calvinism and rational capitalism might imply an incompatibility between slavery and capitalism, the situation was in reality much more complex than this. Rex uses Weber's basic approach to develop a broad sociological portrait of colonialism and post-colonial societies that revealed that "slavery is one means of achieving ends which may also be achieved through a variety of alternative forms of unfree labor" (p. 130). Where, then, does racism enter the picture? On this question, Rex makes the interesting claim, following both Tocqueville and Weber, that racist ideas are particularly salient in circumstances where legal sanctions no longer support racial inequality. Under these conditions, the social order has to "depend upon the inculcation in the minds of both exploiters and exploited of a belief in the superiority of the exploiter and the inferiority of the exploited" (p. 131). In this way, as Rex continues to argue, "the doctrine of equality of economic opportunity and that of racial superiority and inferiority are complements of one another. Racism serves to bridge the gap between theory and practice" (p. 131).

Such a position not only suggests that racial ideas are far from irrelevant, it highlights the circumstances where they may be critically important. It also raises the second major preoccupation of Weber's sociology of domination: the question of legitimacy. For, as Weber noted,

> [There is] the generally observable need of any power, or even of any advantage of life, to justify itself. . . . He who is more favored feels the never ceasing need to look upon his position as in some way "legitimate," upon his advantage as "deserved," and other's disadvantage as being brought about by the latter's "fault." (Weber, 1922/1968, p. 953; also quoted in Wrong, 1979, p. 104)

Slavery, apartheid, and other forms of racial oppression are generally associated with elaborate ideological justifications, but it may well be the case that racist ideas are particularly important when such rigid status systems are being questioned and are under attack by egalitarian social philosophies. Those following in the Weberian tradition would have little doubt that such ideas should be taken seriously and analyzed as part of the causal chain that brings about systems of racial hierarchy, helps them to endure, and also leads to their eventual demise.

4 Power and Domination

Many, although by no means all, interpreters of Weber's political sociology have noted the element of naked power that lies ominously below the surface of his discussion of legitimacy and authority. As Parkin (1982) comments, "inside the velvet glove is always an iron fist. . . . The terminology of violence, coercion and force is as natural to Weber's sociology as the terminology of moral integration is to Durkheim's" (p. 71). Weber himself is quite explicit about the matter and in *Economy and Society* declares

> Domination in the most general sense is one of the most important elements of social action. Of course, not every form of social action reveals a structure of dominance. But in most of the varieties of social action domination plays a considerable role, even where it is not obvious at first sight. . . . Without exception every sphere of social action is profoundly influenced by structures of dominance. (Weber, 1922/1968, p. 941)

This is particularly relevant for the study of race and ethnic relations, and it is no accident that an important survey of the state of global race relations written by Philip Mason during the late 1960s, and based on research monographs from all five continents, should have been given the simple title of *Patterns of Dominance* (Mason, 1970). Philip Mason was neither a sociologist nor someone particularly influenced by Weber's writings, but the choice was characteristically Weberian in its stress on structures of power. Weber's preoccupation with power has a special resonance for the study of race and ethnic relations. By breaking down the components of power and by stressing the analytically distinct concept of "status group," Weber opened up a means of understanding the special sociological character of ethnic group formation that had for so long troubled those trying to impose a largely materialist perspective on ethnic loyalty, racial identity, and national affiliation. The example of the poor Whites in the southern states of America is frequently cited by Weber as a dynamic illustration of the interplay between low economic class and high ethnic status, which has important repercussions for race relations. While explaining the lack of class conflict between the planters and the non-slave-owning Whites, he noted that "the 'poor white trash' were much more hostile to the Negroes than the planters, who, because of their situation, were often swayed by patriarchal feelings" (Runciman, 1978, p. 58). In this way, he draws a distinction between what Pierre van den Berghe (1965, 1978) was to characterize as the "competitive" and "paternalistic" ideal types of race relations.

The famous discussion of "class, status and party" in *Economy and Society* also points to the special spheres in which market conditions prevail and those areas in which they do not, anticipating some of the limitations of rational choice-based theories of race relations. Thus he notes that "when the fate of a group of men is not determined by their chances of using goods or labor in the market (as in the case of slaves), that group is not in the technical sense a 'class' but a 'status group'" (Runciman, 1978, p. 45).[14] This does not mean that status groups are unrelated to the economic structure of society, but it does imply that their special dynamics are not wholly driven by the mode of production, by the distribution of wealth in society, or by a set of preferences originating, in any meaningful way, at the individual level. Race and ethnic relations have been defined by one social theorist, Herbert Blumer, as a "sense of group position" (as quoted in Lal, 1990), which is very close to the preoccupation with social worth, prestige, and styles of life that are the hallmarks of status groups in general and ethnic groups in particular, as found in the Weberian conceptualization. Whereas it would be wrong to deny the direct economic costs and benefits associated with ethnic and racial group membership (and exclusion), a purely materialist reductionism totally fails to capture the complex reality of some of the most fundamental bases of individual identity and social life.

Despite the theoretical primacy of power in Weberian sociology and its practical relevance for studies of race and ethnic relations, these two aspects of social relationships are not always closely associated. Of the major sociological perspectives on race and ethnic relations, the writings found within the plural society tradition are perhaps the most implicitly Weberian in their emphasis. These start from Furnivall's (1948, pp. 304–11) classic formulation of a "plural society," one consisting of separate ethnic and racial groups living in distinct social spheres and cultural universes, where group interaction is confined to the impersonal relationships of the marketplace and where the whole society is held together by the political power of the dominant (colonial) rulers. Such a model has many of the ingredients of Weber's approach, including a recognition of the social reality of discrete ethnic and racial boundaries, and the fundamental significance of power in underpinning group relationships. Its subsequent development by M. G. Smith and Leo Kuper reveals even more parallels. Thus Smith's focus on what he calls the differential incorporation of minority groups is not unlike the mechanisms of closure that I discussed earlier. What is noteworthy is that much of this literature refers to the societies of the Caribbean and sub-Saharan Africa reflecting the degree to which these concepts have broad cross-cultural relevance (Kuper and Smith, 1969).

Not all contemporary power analyses of race relations emerged out of this tradition; some, such as Rex's, clearly do, whereas those of Lieberson and Blalock have come to emphasize similar variables by somewhat different routes. Thus

Lieberson has pointed to the importance of the initial contact situation between different ethnic groups and which of them possesses the dominant power at that crucial time. Blalock has stressed the many components that make up the balance of power between contending ethnic and racial groups, thus providing insight into the enormous complexity of the struggles that underlie so many contemporary ethnic conflicts. All three approaches, however, share the core Weberian premise that power must remain at the center of any serious attempt to understand the nature and dynamics of ethnic and race relations (Blalock, 1989; Lieberson, 1961; Stone, 1992).

Notes

1   Most classical sociologists touched on the questions of race, ethnicity, and nationalism but tended to mention them as aspects of other problems (Stone, 1977). Alexis de Tocqueville's writings provide us with quite an extensive analysis (Stone and Mennell, 1980) and a possible exception to Isaiah Berlin's claim that the subject was largely ignored by 19th-century social thinkers. A full recognition of the central significance of racism and nationalism by sociologists dates from the early decades of the present century and can be found in the writings of Park and the Chicago School, together with the seminal work of W. E. B. Du Bois (cf. Lal, 1986, 1990).

2   This is an allusion to Zeitlin's (1968) earlier claim concerning Marx in *Ideology and the Development of Sociological Theory.*

3   In this article, I subsume the questions of nationalism under the general term ethnicity. Weber's own definitions of nationalism viewed it as a form of politicized ethnicity aimed at establishing a separate and independent state. For an equally insistent distinction between the terms nation and state, see the influential writings of Walker Connor (1972, 1993), in which this issue has been stressed in the context of global studies of ethnonationalism.

4   Weber, like Marx, never saw himself as a professional sociologist. His interests and training were too broad for such a narrow categorization, and he lacked Durkheim's zeal for establishing an exclusive sociological discipline (cf. Lukes, 1973; Parkin, 1982).

5   Bryce's contributions are explored and compared to Weber's in Stone (1972) and Tocqueville's in Stone and Mennell (1980). I thank Jacqui Callaghan for bringing Martineau's much undervalued work to my attention. One can extend this argument to Marx, whose writings for the *New York Daily Tribune* produced at least some serious attention to the issues of race relations and slavery by the founder of dialectical materialism. Thus the impact of America, albeit indirectly, did have some impact in moderating the ethnocentric preoccupations of the Marxist tradition. For a more recent review of the Marxist legacy on nationalism, see E. Nimni's (1991) *Marxism and Nationalism: Theoretical Origins of a Political Crisis.*

6   It is interesting to compare Tocqueville's robust rejection of Gobineau's racial thesis with Weber's much more tentative approach. In both cases, however, the use of historical evidence to refute such theories provides a comprehensive demolition of their plausibility. Whereas Tocqueville noted how the Romans would have dismissed the Britons as savages, belonging to a different race and destined to vegetate in ignorance, Weber showed how "barbarian blood" was an integral part of the glory that was Rome.

7   Weber's respect for Du Bois is clear and, at a meeting of the German Sociological Society in Frankfurt in 1910, he declared, "I wish to state that the most important sociological scholar anywhere in the Southern States in America, with whom no white scholar can compare, is a Negro – Burckhardt Du Bois" (Weber, 1910/1973, p. 312).

8   Compare Abraham's (1992) comment, "The way in which Weber brought his concern (for the social and cultural unification of Germany) to bear on the Polish problem reveals a central and perhaps irresolvable conflict between the liberal and nationalist aspects of his social outlook" (p. 73).

9   For a sharply divergent and highly critical interpretation of Weber on this issue, compare Abraham (1992, pp. 9, 287).

10   See Smith's (1992a, pp. 436–56) discussion of the survival of ethnic groups.

11   Contrast this search for the "fascist" personality with the subsequent arguments concerning the "banality of evil." For an excellent recent study in this tradition, see Fred Katz (1993).

12   See Hechter's (1976, p. 1168) related comments.

13   Compare the parallel arguments in Mirza (1992) and the comments of Komarovsky (1991).

14   The most comprehensive development of rational choice theory in sociology is found in Coleman (1990).

References

Abraham, G. (1992). *Max Weber and the Jewish question.* Urbana: University of Illinois Press.

Adorno, T. W., Frenkel-Brunswick, E., Levinson, D. J., and Sanford, R. N. (1950). *The authoritarian personality.* New York: Harper & Row.

Barth, F. (ed.). (1969). *Ethnic groups and boundaries.* Boston: Little, Brown.

Berlin, I. (1992). *The crooked timber of humanity.* New York: Vintage.

Blalock, H. (1989). *Power and conflict: Toward a general theory.* Newbury Park, CA: Sage.

Brubaker, W. R. (1984). *The limits of rationality: An essay on the social and moral thought of Max Weber.* London: Allen & Unwin.

Brubaker, W. R. (1992). *Citizenship and nationhood in France and Germany.* Cambridge, MA: Harvard University Press.

Coleman, J. (1990). *The foundations of social theory.* Cambridge, MA: Harvard University Press.

Connor, W. (1972). Nation-building or nation-destroying? *World Politics,* 24, 319–55.

Connor, W. (1993). *Ethnonationalism: The quest for understanding.* Princeton, NJ: Princeton University Press.

Furnivall, J. S. (1948). *Colonial policy and practice.* Cambridge: Cambridge University Press.

Gerth, H., and Mills, C. W. (eds.). (1948). *From Max Weber.* London: Routledge.

Hechter, M. (1975). *Internal colonialism: The Celtic Fringe in British national development.* London: Routledge.

Hechter, M. (1976). Response to Cohen: Max Weber on ethnicity and ethnic change. *American Journal of Sociology,* 81, 1162–8.

Hechter, M. (1986). Rational choice theory and the study of race and ethnic relations. In J. Rex and D. Mason, *Theories of race and ethnic relations* (pp. 264–79). Cambridge: Cambridge University Press.

Hechter, M. (1987). *Principles of group solidarity.* Berkeley: University of California Press.

Hobsbawm, E., and Ranger, T. (eds.). (1983). *The invention of tradition.* Cambridge: Cambridge University Press.

Horowitz, D. (1971). Three dimensions of ethnic politics. *World Politics,* 23, 232–44.

Horowitz, D. (1985). *Ethnic groups in conflict.* Berkeley: University of California Press.

Jackson, M. (1982/1983). An analysis of Max Weber's theory of ethnicity. *Humboldt Journal of Social Relations*, 10, 4–18.

Katz, F. (1993). *Ordinary people and extraordinary evil*. Albany: State University of New York Press.

Komarovsky, M. (1991). Some reflections on the feminist scholarship in sociology. *Annual Review of Sociology*, 17, 1–25.

Kuper, L., and Smith, M. G. (eds.). (1969). *Pluralism in Africa*. Berkeley: University of California Press.

Lal, B. (1986). The "Chicago School" of American sociology. In J. Rex and D. Mason (eds.), *Theories of race and ethnic relations* (pp. 280–98). Cambridge: Cambridge University Press.

Lal, B. (1990). *The romance of culture in an urban civilization*. London: Routledge.

Leresche, D. (1989). *Middleman minority theory reconsidered*. Unpublished manuscript, George Mason University, Institute for Conflict Analysis and Resolution.

Lieberson, S. (1961). A societal theory of race and ethnic relations. *American Sociological Review*, 26, 902–10.

Lukes, S. (1973). *Emile Durkheim: His life and work*. Harmondsworth, Middlesex, England: Penguin.

Manasse, E. (1947). Max Weber on race. *Social Research*, 14, 191–221.

Manza, J. (1992). Classes, status groups and social closure: A critique of neo-Weberian social theory. *Current Perspectives in Social Theory*, 12, 275–302.

Mason, P. (1970). *Patterns of dominance*. London: Oxford University Press.

Mirza, H. (1992). *Young, female and Black*. London: Routledge.

Murphy, R. (1988). *Social closure*. New York: Oxford University Press.

Nimni, E. (1991). *Marxism and nationalism: Theoretical origins of a political crisis*. London: Pluto.

Okamura, J. (1981). Situational ethnicity. *Ethnic & Racial Studies*, 4, 452–65.

Parkin, F. (1979). *Marxism and class theory: A bourgeois critique*. New York: Columbia University Press.

Parkin, F. (1982). *Max Weber*. London: Tavistock.

Rex, J. (1970). *Race relations in sociological theory*. London: Weidenfeld & Nicolson.

Rex, J. (1980). The theory of race relations: A Weberian approach. In M. O'Callaghan (ed.), *Sociological theories: Race and colonialism* (pp. 117–42). Paris: UNESCO.

Roth, G., and Wittich, C. (eds.). (1968). *Max Weber: Economy and Society*. New York: Bedminster.

Runciman, W. G. (ed.). (1978). *Weber: Selections in translation*. Cambridge: Cambridge University Press.

Smith, A. D. (1992a). Chosen peoples: Why ethnic groups survive. *Ethnic & Racial Studies*, 15, 436–56.

Smith, A. D. (1992b). Nationalism and the historians. *International Journal of Comparative Sociology*, 33, 58–80.

Stone, J. (1972). James Bryce and the comparative sociology of race relations. *Race*, 13, 315–28.

Stone, J. (ed.). (1977). *Race, ethnicity and social change*. Belmont, CA: Wadsworth.

Stone, J. (1985). *Racial conflict in contemporary society*. Cambridge, MA: Harvard University Press.

Stone, J. (1992). Power, ethnicity and conflict resolution. In S. Silbey and A. Sarat (eds.), *Law, politics and social change* (pp. 89–105). Greenwich, CT: JAI.

Stone, J., and Hechter, M. (eds.). (1979). Internal colonialism in comparative perspective (special issue). *Ethnic & Racial Studies*, 2(3).

Stone, J., and Mennell, S. (eds.). (1980). *Alexis de Toqueville on democracy, revolution and society*. Chicago: Chicago University Press.

Van den Berghe, P. (1965). *South Africa: A study in conflict.* Middletown, CT: Wesleyan University Press.

Van den Berghe, P. (1978). *Race and racism: A comparative perspective.* New York: Wiley.

Wallman, S. (1986). Ethnicity and the boundary process in context. In J. Rex and D. Mason (eds.), *Theories of race and ethnic relations* (pp. 226–45). Cambridge: Cambridge University Press.

Weber, M. (1968). *Economy and Society* (Trans. G. Roth and C. Wittich, Eds.). New York: Bedminster. (Original work published 1922.)

Weber, M. (1971). Max Weber on race and society (Trans.). *Social Research*, 38, 30–41. (Original work published 1910.)

Weber, M. (1973). Max Weber, Dr. Alfred Ploetz and W. E. B. Du Bois (Trans.). *Sociological Analysis*, 34, 308–12. (Original work published 1910)

Wrong, D. (ed.). (1970). *Max Weber.* Englewood Cliffs, NJ: Prentice-Hall.

Wrong, D. (1979). *Power: Its forms, bases and uses.* Oxford, England: Blackwell.

Zeitlin, I. (1968). *Ideology and the development of sociological theory.* Englewood Cliffs, NJ: Prentice-Hall.

3 Robert Ezra Park's Approach to Race and Ethnic Relations

Barbara Ballis Lal

The Subjective Aspects of Collective Action

Park, along with W. I. Thomas, was an early advocate of the view that the subjective dimension of human behaviour must be included in sociological investigation. Subjective factors such as attitudes, motives, and meanings are derived from individual experience but also reflect the culture and the history of social groups. The acquisition of culture, which plays the crucial role of orienting the individual in his activities by transmitting to him 'a pattern of symbolic meanings through which the members of a collectivity grasp their world', is available only through communication within society and 'social' forms of association (Higham 1984: xi).

The importance placed upon the subjective aspects of action and the symbolic dimension of group life urges scrutiny of the mass media, art, and literature. It also requires the examination of the statements of politicians and civic leaders on behalf of dominant and subordinate groups and of the 'process of collective definition' that makes public opinion, scientific belief, ideologies, and mythologies available to members of a society.

Park's and Thomas's second significant contribution was to require that the sociologist know the culture and the history of social groups in order to interpret the experience and the world view of its members accurately. The sociologist was responsible for recognizing the coherence (or dissonance) between ideas, activities, and institutions.

Thus, for example, Park's field-work in the South while working at Tuskegee in Alabama and his knowledge of both southern culture and history led him to discount popular racial theories of his contemporaries, which viewed race prejudice as a reflection of an instinctual dislike between different races. Instead, Park noted that contemporary southern culture and southern history were replete with situations of intimacy between blacks and whites belying theories of race prejudice based on instinct. Racial etiquette, he thought, was intended to *enforce* social distances rather than reflecting a natural, instinctual dislike between races (Park (1928b) 1950: 230–4; Park (1937a,b) 1950).

Third, Park's concern with culture, history, and the subjective world of meaning led him to conclude that men are not always motivated by 'interest' – whether self-interest or class interest. Under certain conditions, ideas and passions, rather than either material interests, such as that of social class, or even ideal interests having to do with status and privilege, become the most important factors in the explanation of action. Human beings, he believed, 'live in the world of imagination' and are able to entertain ideas and feel emotions which may lead them to act over against what *appears to the sociologist* to be in their self-interest. Empathy, which Park considered a concomitant of communication and collective action, may result in altruistic behavior. According to Park, both empathy and altruism are normal features of social life.

The sociology of race and ethnicity abounds with examples of the substitution of interest-oriented explanations framed by the investigator for explanations that take the *prima facie* ideas and explanations of the actor seriously. For example, the writer Harold Cruse, in his study *The Crisis of the Negro Intellectual*, suggests that an adequate explanation of the 'relationship between groups in America, and on the international plane' is that they 'are actuated by power principles and not by morality and compassion for the underdog classes' (Cruse 1967: 494). This leads him to expunge ideas of morality and compassion from his explanations of race and ethnic relations.

Similarly, in her otherwise excellent study, *In the Almost Promised Land: American Jews and Blacks, 1915–1935*, the historian Hasia Diner argues that 'for many Jewish leaders, black issues provided a forum in which to work out certain tensions of acculturation' and to pursue 'Jewish ends'. However, the material in her book lends itself equally well to alternative interpretations which take the motives acknowledged by Jewish leaders at the time at their face value. Her decision to pit alleged Jewish self-interest against 'genuine' but none the less 'overstated and unrealistic' sentiments, such as empathy with blacks and the pursuit of elementary justice, is an example of the logic of procedure that follows from an interest-oriented approach to race and ethnic relations (Diner 1977).

An interest in 'hidden interests' may also result in looking behind the avowed motives of analysts of race and ethnicity. Ralph Ellison's denunciation of Park is the classic example of the substitution of the observer's agenda of hidden interest-oriented motives for the *prima facie* ideas of the sociologist. Ellison condemns the work of the sociologists at the University of Chicago during the 1920s and 1930s on the grounds that it was financed by guilt-ridden, white, northern philanthropists of a liberal political bent who had an interest in the continued subordination of black American labourers. Nowhere does Ellison address himself to the question of either the analytical usefulness of the approach developed by the Chicago scholars or the adequacy of their description of race relations in the United States (Ellison (1994) 1972: 303–17). In a similar vein, Cruse asks, 'Just what is *behind* Nathan Glazer's fervent insistence that Negroes be integrated as fast as possible, and by any means?' (Cruse 1967: 494–7).

Park assumed that there is a range of experience available to members of the same social class, both within and between racial and ethnic groups. The sources of experience and subjective meaning – including beliefs about what the world 'is really like' – include communication within associations as disparate as the immediate family, kin, the church, trade unions, professional societies, and neighbours. The school and the mass media are also purveyors of cultural imagery and sources of belief. Why should a unitary class interest emerge and become of greatest importance in influencing behaviour given such variety?

(Park's concept of the 'marginal man' is based on the idea of a social world in which there are multiple sources of imagery and meaning, and underscores the diversity – and in some sense idiosyncratic range – of experience available to individuals and groups in modern urban societies (Park (1928a) 1950; (1931) 1950; (1937c) 1950: 372–6; Stonequist (1937) 1961).)

Park's preference, was to link interest to status groups. However, his vision of the multiplicity of sources of experience and meaning in urban life led him to advocate that the attribution of motive be an outcome of empirical investigation. This last point directs attention to the advantages of research strategies that take the actor seriously as a source of knowledge about his own activities.

Status Groups and Social Conflict

Park's conclusion that social conflict is most often the outcome of the efforts of status groups to enhance or preserve their position relative to others is another important component of his approach to race and ethnicity that follows from his general perspective on group life. In American society, race, and, to a lesser extent, ethnicity are among the major bases of status group formation. According to Park, conflicts between native-born white Americans, African-Americans, and immigrants had to do with relative group position, style of life, and corresponding beliefs about deference, obligation, identity, and self-worth.

Here it is crucial to remember that Park stretched the concepts of culture and society, communication and collective action to include a corresponding social psychological theory that related these concepts both to individual needs, such as the need for recognition, esteem, and identity, and to the needs of social groups for cohesion and morale.

Park's conviction of the importance of status groups in the explanation of social conflict opposes the view that attributes such as colour, national origin, language, religion, and gender mask the fundamental cleavages around which 'genuine' groups, motivated by 'real' shared concerns, should cohere (Castles and Kosack 1973; Phizacklea and Miles 1980; Stone 1985: 62–82). The latter influential strand of thought assumes that social conflict between racial and ethnic groups, as opposed to social classes, is a manifestation of false consciousness arising from the cynical manipulation of the proletariat or the have-nots at the hands of a ruling class and their representatives in government, the media, and the schools. In the United States, it is argued, racism itself 'is built into the structure of modern capitalism' (Sherman and Wood 1979: 96).

Yet, studies of slavery, immigration, nationalism, and contemporary race relations contain examples of groups that have acted to preserve a set of social relationships from which they do not appear to have gained much. Thus, for example, in the debate about the causes of the American Civil War the historian Kenneth Stampp points out that only one-quarter of free whites in the antebellum South owned slaves and, among this number, only a small percentage owned more than fifty slaves (Stampp 1956). Moreover, even among slave owners, plantations were not always profitable. How then to explain the persistence of slavery and a civil war which was supported by non-slaveholding white Southerners?

This question is posed and answered by Eugene Genovese, himself a Marxist social historian, who points out in a discussion of materialistic and idealistic interpretations of slavery, that members of a dominant racial group may become committed to a style of life, or a set of beliefs and a mythology, which motivates them to act in ways that are not economically rational, politically expedient, nor likely to result in their own prosperity (Genovese (1966) 1972: 23–52).

Park placed status groups and the study of conflict at the centre of his approach to the sociology of race and ethnicity because he took the view that racial and ethnic studies had to do with the interactions between cultural groups. In addition, his appraisal of the importance of status groups and, in particular, of their role in influencing individual stability suggests that he was fundamentally convinced that human beings survive and succeed when they are incorporated into 'sentimental groups'. Sentimental groups, as conceived here, are based upon a shared culture, social solidarity, and affective relationships between members.

Sentimental groups share some of the properties of primary groups. However, they do not necessarily have an ecological basis such that members participate in 'intimate, face-to-face association' over a long period of time and in many different role relationships (Cooley (1909) 1962: 23–31). Along with other types of associations, they are the purveyors of values and ideals.

Sentimental groups may limit membership on the basis of characteristics, such as race, nationality, and gender. On the other hand, the concept of 'ethnicity by consent' suggests that sentimental groups may consist of volunteers who share a mystical or mythical connection and participate in a newly created culture.

Sentimental groups may or may not further interests and perform 'functions'. For example, ethnically based fraternal lodges fostered solidarity and identity while at the same time performing useful services such as the provision of social insurance. Events such as dinners, dances, and picnics, while not of instrumental value, provided individuals with psychological and social support. The 'storefront' church established by African-American migrants from the South represented their attempt 'to re-establish a type of church in the urban environment... in which they were known as people' (Frazier (1963) 1974: 58).

Recent events and current social analysis impart credibility to what twenty years ago might have been evaluated as Park's naive vision of the needs of human beings and the basis of an orderly society. Thus, for example, the growth of fundamentalist, born-again Christian sects, as well as a renaissance in Jewish orthodoxy, has not escaped the notice of contemporary social scientists. Why, it is asked (although not necessarily answered), do people seek to give up the liberty and freedom from authoritarian social institutions so recently won? Of equal significance in this respect is the growth of organizations such as Weight Watchers Anonymous and Debtors Anonymous which foster the belief that the group and its teaching will enable individuals to attain values which are impervious to unaided individual effort. Each of these instances affirms the necessity for sentimental bonds whether of ancient or relatively recent origin.

Social Control

Park also supported efforts to integrate individuals into groups which provided them with a coherent vision of the world, a notion of desirable behaviour, and affective ties to others. Such groups, whether parochial minority groups, sentimental groups, or sects, were a source of social control.

Traditionally, a shared culture and, in particular, informal mechanisms of social control lodged within language, as well as primary groups and local institutions such as the church and school, worked to restrain individual impulse and unbridled egoism. More recently, Park thought, urbanization, the predominance of secondary associations, and an ethic of individualism eroded these mechanisms of social control and sanctioned in their place unbridled self-expression and gratification, both of which contributed to demoralization.

Park and Thomas believed that in twentieth-century urban America the social sciences could also promote socially controlled behaviour by increasing an awareness of the interdependence and reciprocal obligations between individuals and groups. As Thomas pointed out,

> if we recognize that social control is to be reached through the study of behaviour, and that its technique is to consist in the creation of attitudes appropriate to desired values, then I suggest that the most essential attitude at the present moment is a public attitude of hospitality toward all forms of research in the social world, such as it has gained toward all forms of research in the physical world. (Thomas (1917) 1981: 38)

Park and Thomas hoped to use sociological findings to resurrect a citizenry of 'character'. Character, according to the political scientist James Wilson, is based on 'virtue', that is, 'habits of moderate action; more specifically, acting with due restraint on one's impulses, due regard for the rights of others, and reasonable concern for distant consequences' (Wilson 1985: 15).

The concept of social control is no longer fashionable among sociologists. Nor has the idea of character gained much of a hearing. However, social disruption stemming from drug misuse, child abuse and neglect, broken families, crime and violence, all press for a response from sociologists. Solutions to these problems may involve greater reliance upon formal mechanisms of social control initiated by the state, such as more effective policing, greater numbers of social workers, and subsidies to community-care facilities. Park and Thomas, however, pinned their hope upon education, including greater knowledge about the social world, and increased communication, as the ways to encourage the growth of informal mechanisms of social control which relied upon self-restraint rather than externally imposed regulation for its effectiveness. They endorsed movement towards a society based upon 'voluntary cooperation' in which 'consent' rather than 'force' predominated (Fisher and Strauss 1979: 465).

Park's positive attitude towards informal mechanisms of social control based upon self-restraint and consensus complemented his belief that African-Americans and immigrants should be integrated into urban America mostly as a result of their own voluntary efforts. In particular, effective mechanisms of social control among blacks and foreigners were those based upon the internal discipline imposed by the minority group and internalized by the individual rather than a result of efforts by a dominant group to force acquiescence to a particular style of life deemed to be beneficial. Park's liberal vision of social control, which was to be achieved through education and self-help within the community, contradicted the programmes of racists and Americanizers who argued that both the black community and the immigrants required externally imposed programmes to enforce conformity to a prescribed way of life.

Three Models of Social Change

Park presented three models of social change, each of which has implications for his analysis of race and ethnic relations and his prognosis of the future of minorities. The first model emphasizes the process of social conflict and is characterized by the rational adjustment of activities among a plurality of groups on the basis of negotiation and the reconciliation of conflicting interests. Communication between contentious groups, either through the mass media, art, and literature or within the framework of political institutions such as elections, is the activity that typifies this mode of social change. The public, consisting of a variety of self-interested groups, is the form of association exemplifying this model.

Park's hope for the future rested with the efforts of a 'democratic public' to alter its own destiny on the basis of public opinion, education, and socially controlled conflict. He held this view despite his acknowledgement that politics, social reform, and planning often resulted in unanticipated and undesired outcomes because they are as subject to the limitations imposed by human nature as they are to the resistance of aggrieved groups.

Fisher and Strauss draw attention to the connection between Park's vision of 'a democratic public' and the incorporation of minorities into the mainstream of American life. 'This public', they note,

> required the supportive social conditions and a level of general education that enabled communication over what provincial peoples might see as insuperable barriers... The problem of democracy was: under what conditions would who be able to speak to whom? The difficulties of the American attempt to build a variable nation-state were linked to the reality that so many barriers to communication existed. Racial and ethnic groupings constituted the foremost barriers. (Fisher and Strauss 1979: 466)

Park's second model of social change is based upon collective behaviour and, more specifically, the transformation of social unrest into crowds or into social movements which generate leadership and culminate in new social institutions. This second model is based upon the initially irrational response of isolated, socially disconnected individuals to a collective unease brought about by a dimly perceived deficiency in the environment. The religious sect, for example, represents the efforts of people to adapt their religious beliefs and their church to a new environment.

The Montgomery bus boycott organized by Martin Luther King and the emergent Southern Christian Leadership Conference is one example of how relatively unorganized protest may be transformed into a coherent social movement capable of mobilizing the energy of an oppressed group, of jogging the sensibilities of a minority of liberal whites, and eventually bringing about significant changes in racial stratification in the American South.

Other examples of the collective behaviour model of social change are the 'ghetto revolts' in major American cities during the 1960s and the related rise of the Black Muslims under the leadership of Elijab Muhammed and Malcolm X at about this same time. In both of these instances, angry groups of African-Americans were able to call attention to what they perceived to be the inequities of racial stratification in America through popular appeals made without benefit of great financial resources or access to the usual avenues of political change.

Park departed from the conventional wisdom of many European social theorists and took an optimistic view of the creative potential of crowds rather than emphasizing their mindless, destructive capabilities. Although he does not himself suggest it, this second model of social change based upon collective behaviour is the poor man's alternative to social change based upon politics and access to resources such as the mass media, influence, and political organization. Park did not advocate ghetto revolt as a way of bringing about social equality. None the less, his second model of change remains a useful way of understanding how aggrieved groups that are relatively impoverished may use numbers and disruption as weapons to protest and change existing social arrangements.

Park's third model of social change is based upon cyclical processes, such as a race relations cycle or a 'natural history', in which a series of transformations occur as a result of the properties inherent in phenomena or events or on the basis of 'social forces'. Since social forces are treated as analytically separable from conscious human volition, the outcome of this type of social change is not directly effected by the values or desires of individuals and groups.

The 'social forces' model is the most metaphysical and least persuasive model of change. It contradicts Park's own account of cognizant individuals directing their activities in a cultural order. Instead, this model of unpremeditated change is most suitable when used to describe ecological processes such as that of succession and dominance. It is of less interest as a model of specifically *social* processes.

The numerous criticisms of the race relations cycle highlight the deficiencies of this model of social change (Cox (1948) 1970; Lyman 1973; Persons 1987; Smith 1988).

In order to set out the basic features of a viable approach to the study of race and ethnicity which builds upon the strengths of Park's contributions, it is now necessary to consider the problematic features of his approach. By and large, objections revolve around Park's undue emphasis upon the volitional elements in group life and his unwillingness to acknowledge the constraints inherent in the environment in which individuals and groups construct their activities and in which cultures flourish, are transformed, and disappear.

Status Groups without Social Classes

Park considered status groups, such as racial and ethnic minorities and occupational groupings, to be more important than social classes in the analysis of collective action. But relegating social class to the periphery of sociological investigation leads Park to overlook the fragmentation of status groups along the dimension of social class. The consequence of such neglect was to overestimate social cohesion and social consciousness among minority group members.

Thus, for example, Park predicted that an embryonic, aspiring black middle class would provide leadership among African-Americans. Moreover, he assumed that the 'bi-racial organization' of businessmen and professionals would eventually predispose members of different racial groups to act together on the basis of a shared world-view stemming from similarities in education, occupation, and life-styles.

In his monograph *Black Bourgeoisie* published in 1957, Park's student E. Franklin Frazier studied the black middle class identified earlier by Drake and Cayton in their study of Chicago. Frazier established that the black middle class was fundamentally different from the white middle class because it had no foundation in the larger American economy and therefore exercised power and influence only on the basis of holding strategic positions in segregated institutions within the African-American community. This resulted in the emergence of an opportunistic middle class which claimed to speak for the black community as a whole but whose retention of power was dependent upon residential segregation and real and symbolic separation rather than integration into mainstream American life.

Frazier's study suggested differentiating members of the black community along the line of social classes rather than assuming that race obliterated differences within this population. Moreover, he challenged Park's assumption that the black middle class would be more or less equivalent to its white counterpart in a bi-racially organized society. Finally, Frazier's study noted the ways in which the different constituencies of white and black leaders effected the reconciliation of an interest in retaining power with the adequate representation of the objectives of their supporters.

It is also clear that Park overlooked the extent to which class influenced both the kinds of situations in which different class strata within each racial group experience each other, and the variety of meanings within each racial group brought into play in their resolution. Thus, for example, in their comparison of upper-class blacks who comprise 5 percent of Bronzeville's population and lower-class blacks making up 65 percent of this group, Drake and Cayton pointed out that the former, in 'carrying the responsibilities of the major Negro institutions', are likely to find themselves 'cooperating with sympathetic and liberal whites who give them financial and moral support' such that 'this Negro upper class becomes symbolic of racial potentialities'. However, the lower social classes, '[n]ot alone by choice but tossed by the deep economic tides of the modern world', are 'pressed and moulded by an unusually indifferent and occasionally unkind white world' (Drake and Cayton (1945) 1962: 522–3).

The puzzle of where the balance between status interests and class interests lies, both from the point of view of the sociologist and from the point of view of those being studied, underlies the often vitriolic debate about the significance of class strata among both African-Americans in the United States and Afro-Caribbeans in Great Britain today. It also lies behind the quarrel about the relative importance of cultural differences based upon country of origin among 'non-whites' or 'blacks' in the USA and Britain (Modood 1988).

Thus, for example, the American sociologist William Julius Wilson suggests that in general the influence of race on minority class stratification has decreased and 'class takes on greater importance in determining the life chances of minority individuals'. Wilson points out that

> whether one focuses on the way race relations was structured by the system of production or the polity or both, racial oppression (ranging from the exploitation of black labour by the business class to the elimination of black competition for economic, social and political resources by the white masses) was a characteristic and important phenomenon in both the pre-industrial and industrial periods of American race relations. (Wilson 1978: 149)

He goes on to assert that in the 'modern industrial period', beginning after the Second World War, the significance of race has yielded its pre-eminence to social class. 'As race declined in importance in the economic sector,' observes Wilson, 'the Negro class structure became more differentiated and black life chances became increasingly a consequence of class affiliation' (Wilson ibid.: 153).

Wilson's argument is not that race is insignificant in influencing the life chances of African-Americans but that the effect of race upon education, job placement, and occupational mobility has declined. He is careful to note the possibility of white resistance in eroding such hard-won gains in the future.

The problem, in Park's day as now, is to differentiate between those aspects of living in which being black limits choice, diminishes life chances and constitutes a disability shared by all blacks, from situations in which the differential distribution of resources, such as wealth, education, and market position, means that at least for some members of the group, race is no longer the predominant constraint upon choice and range of available options. For example, the *de jure* abolition of restrictive covenants in northern cities in the USA as a result of the 1968 Civil Rights Act resulted in middle-class blacks being able to exercise the option of living in suburbs even in the face of the resistance of their white residents.

Park had little more to say about the effects of the formation of social classes among African-Americans than his observations concerning the impact of the new middle class in cities. Surprisingly, in an era punctuated by conflict between labour and big business, the communist revolution in Russia, discussion of the ideals of socialism and of the welfare state, Park was relatively silent about the importance of social class divisions among and between native-born American whites and immigrants, as well as African-Americans.

Clearly for Park the barriers of race and, to a lesser extent, of ethnicity were the crucial factors dividing Americans from one another, inhibiting communication, and threatening the durability of democracy in urban America. His use of the concepts of class and class conflict is incidental to his analyses in which cultural conflict between status groups predominates.

Social Conflict without Tears and Social Control without Force

According to Park, in most cases, the resolution of social conflict involves negotiation and adjustment through the process of communication. He suggested that there are few conflicts between groups that cannot be solved through greater efforts by members to scrutinize their own position and to better understand their opponent's point of view. Thus, for example, when Park dealt with industrial disputes he, like Durkheim, found the source of conflict in a lack of understanding between workers and management. He concluded that 'The ills from which civilisation is suffering are not fundamentally political; they are cultural ills that can be cured not by legislation but by concert, collective action and leadership.' He endorsed the industrial psychologist Elton Mayo's suggestion that what was needed was an 'administrative élite' trained to improve 'worker morale' (Park 1934) 1955: 299).

Park's vision of the peaceful, rational nature of social conflict was also sustained in his belief in the efficacy of communication and personal friendship in undermining racial antagonism (Park (1939) 1950).

Park's interpretation of social conflict and his relative lack of interest in the concepts of power and of force are inherent in his view of social control and in his overall perspective on group life. He believed that understanding and self-restraint are the bonds that hold groups and society together. He also argued that a shared heritage and language – both of which are aspects of culture – rather than force and coercion lead people to identify with the interest of the group or the society as a whole, rather than to pursue unrestrained self-interest or self-expression.

In short, Park's imagery of the co-operative nature of individuals and the consensual basis of society recognized no necessity for coercion, force, and the predominance of formal mechanisms of social control in the analysis of social life. This view underlies his analysis of social conflict.

In addition, Park's interest in the symbolic nature of group life led him to examine the point of view of individuals and social groups and to pay less attention than warranted to the constraints within which subjective orientations are expressed and social processes unfold. Park did not wish to reduce historical events to a social psychology of inter-subjective orientations. However, he sometimes seemed to forget that slavery, discrimination, and segregation stand for relationships which consist of more than just the subjective orientations of groups towards one another.

This bias in the direction of social-psychological reductionism – which Park hoped to avoid – also led him to overestimate the role of communication and empathy in mitigating racial injustice. It is a major element in his romantic vision of what Vidich and Lyman identify as a 'moral brotherhood' (Vidich and Lyman 1985: 195–208).

Finally, Park's interpretation of social control as essentially self-control emphasized the volitional aspects of action and deflected interest away from the limitations arising from the differential distribution of resources, and in particular economic and political power. For example, Park emphasized social ritual and etiquette rather than legislation – such as the Black Codes and physical abuse, including torture and death – in ensuring compliance with the requirements of chattel slavery. In a similar way, a natural history approach to the dispersion and concentration of minorities neglected the role of restricted covenants and unlawful methods of harassment in ensuring residential segregation in cities (Park (1929) 1952).

Park's relative lack of interest in social class and social structure, and in the role of power in influencing race and ethnic relations, stemmed from his emphasis upon the volitional aspects of human group life. It resulted in his unwillingness to consider the constraints which frustrate the realization of individual wants and which influence the ways in which social processes unfold. The problem intrinsic to the analysis of race relations is to find the balance between imposed constraints, on the one hand, and self-generated possibilities, on the other.

References

Castles, S. and Kosack, G. (1973) *Immigrant Workers and Class Structure in Western Europe*, London: Oxford University Press.

Cooley, C. H. ((1909) 1962) *Social Organization: A Study of the Larger Mind*, New York: Schocken Books.

Cox, O. C. ((1948) 1970) *Caste, Class and Race*, London: Modern Reader Paperbacks.

Cruse, H. (1967) *The Crisis of the Negro Intellectual*, New York: Morrow.

Diner, H. (1977) *In the Almost Promised Land: American Jews and Blacks, 1915–1935*, Westport, Conn.: Greenwood Press.

Drake, St Clair and Cayton, H. R. ((1945) 1962) *Black Metropolis: A Study of Negro Life In A Northern City*, 2 vols, New York: Harcourt, Brace.

Ellison, R. ((1944) 1972) 'An American dilemma: a review', in R. Ellison *Shadow and Act*, unpublished, written in 1944 for *The Antioch Review*, New York: Random House, pp. 303–17.

Fisher, B. M. and Strauss, A. (1979) 'Interactionism', in T. Bottomore and R. Nisbet (eds) *A History of Sociological Analysis*, London: Heinemann, pp. 457–98.

Frazier, E. F. ((1963) 1974) 'The Negro Church in America', in E. F. Frazier and C. E. Lincoln *The Negro Church in America, The Black Church Since Frazier*, New York: Schocken Books, pp. 9–98.

Genovese, E. D. ((1966) 1972) 'Rebelliousness and docility in the Negro slave: a critique of the Elkins thesis', originally published in *Civil War History*, 13 December 1966: 293–314; reprinted in E. D. Genovese (ed.) in *Red and Black: Marxian Explorations in Southern and Afro-American History*, New York: Random House, (1972), pp. 73–101.

Higham, J. (1984) *Send These to Me: Jews and Other Immigrants in Urban America*, Baltimore, MA: The Johns Hopkins University Press.

Lyman, S. (1973) *The Black American in Sociological Thought: A Failure of Perspective*, New York: Capricorn Books.

Modood, T. (1988) '"Black", racial equality and Asian identity', *New Community* XIV (Spring): 397–404.

Park, R. E. ((1928a) 1950) 'Human migration and the marginal man', *American Journal of Sociology* XXXIII (6) (May 1928): 881–93; reprinted in *Race and Culture* (1950), pp. 345–56.

——((1928b) 1950) 'The bases of race prejudice', *Annals of the American Academy of Political and Social Science* CXL (November 1928): 11–20; reprinted in *Race and Culture* (1950), pp. 230–43.

——((1929) 1952) 'Sociology, community and society', in W. Gee (ed.) *Research in the Social Sciences*, New York: Macmillan Co. (1929), pp. 3–49; reprinted in *Human Communities* (1952), pp. 178–209.

——((1931) 1950) 'Personality and cultural conflict', *Publications of the American Sociological Society* XXV (May 1931): 95–110; reprinted in *Race and Culture* (1950), pp. 357–71.

—— ((1934) 1955) 'Industrial fatigue and group morale', *American Journal of Sociology* 40 (November 1934): 349–56; reprinted in *Society* (1955), pp. 293–300.

—— ((1937a) 1950) 'Introduction', in B. W. Doyle *The Etiquette of Race Relations in the South*, Chicago: University of Chicago Press (1937), pp. xi–xxiv; reprinted in *Race and Culture* (1950), pp. 177–88.

—— ((1937b) 1950) 'Cultural conflict and the marginal man', 'Introduction', in E. V. Stonequist *The Marginal Man*, New York: Charles Scribner (1937), pp. xiii–xviii; reprinted in *Race and Culture* (1950), pp. 372–6.

—— ((1939) 1950) 'The nature of race relations' in E. Thompson (ed.) *Race Relations and the Race Problem*, Durham, NC: Duke University Press (1939), pp. 3–45; reprinted in *Race and Culture* (1950), pp. 81–116.

Persons, S. (1987) *Ethnic Studies at Chicago 1905–45*, Urbana and Chicago, Ill.: University of Illinois Press.

Phizacklea, A. and Miles, R. (1980) *Labour and Racism*, London: Routledge & Kegan Paul.

Sherman, H. J. and Wood, J. L. (1979) *Sociology, Traditional and Radical Perspectives*, New York and London: Harper & Row.

Smith, D. (1988) *The Chicago School: A Liberal Critique of Capitalism*, London: Macmillan Education.

Stampp, K. (1956) *The Peculiar Institutions: Slavery in the Antebellum South*, New York: Vintage Books.

Stone, J. (1985) *Racial Conflict in Contemporary Society*, London: Fontana Press/Collins.

Stonequist, E. V. ((1937) 1961) *The Marginal Man: A Study in Personality and Culture Conflict*, New York: Russell & Russell.

Thomas, W. I. ((1917) 1981) *Social Behavior*, ed. E. Volkart, Greenwood, Conn.: Greenwood Press.

Vidich, A. J. and Lyman, S. M. (1985) *American Sociology, Worldly Rejections of Religion and their Directions*, New Haven and London: Yale University Press.

Wilson, J. Q. (1985) 'The rediscovery of character: private virtue and public policy', *The Public Interest* (Fall): 3–16.

Wilson, W. J. (1978) *The Declining Significance of Race: Blacks and Changing American Institutions*, Chicago: University of Chicago Press.

Part II

Emerging Theoretical Perspectives

INTRODUCTION TO PART II

The sociologists of the early twentieth century set out many of the fundamental questions of racial and ethnic relations that would provide valuable insight for students of the field. By the end of the century, a radically new world had generated a further set of questions that demanded answers from the academic community. In response several central themes emerged in the scholarly literature on race and ethnic relations and some of the most critical of these were concerned with the construction of ethnic identity, the origin and dynamics of group boundaries and the impact of postindustrial and postmodern forces on ethnic relations. Both anthropologists and sociologists were particularly influenced by Fredrik Barth's seminal writings on ethnic groups and boundaries that exemplified the fluid nature of ethnogenesis and the permeable reality of ethnic boundaries. Starting with Barth's transactional emphasis, Richard Jenkins makes the case for giving as much weight to the external as to the internal processes of group formation. The development of ethnic groups is not always the result of their members' self-definition, that they share common traits and experiences, but it is often also a product of the categorization of outsiders. Taken together, social identity – of which ethnic identity is one particular form – can be seen as the interaction of internal and external forces operating at both the individual and group level. Jenkins explores the way in which this model can throw light on ethnic relations in a wide range of settings, from the conflicts between Catholics and Protestants in Northern Ireland and the interactions between the Mapuche indigenous peoples and the dominant society in southern Chile. The power of categorization, and the contexts in which it takes place, requires a careful rethinking of ethnic dynamics.

In his learned essay, Kevin Avruch provides further insight into the social construction of ethnicity which has probably become the dominant mode of academic interpretation of race and ethnic relations at the beginning of the twenty-first century. He notes how variable the definitions of race, color and community have become, whether in Morocco, the United States, Quebec or Nigeria. Both the postmodern concern with discourse, and the Barthian emphasis on resource competition, seem to share a common focus on power. In concluding his analysis, Avruch considers the role of the international refugee camps, and the impact of the United Nations and the NGOs, as incubators of ethnic identity. The experience of the Palestinians, and the Hutus in Tanzania being prominent examples of this increasingly relevant form of the political construction of ethnicity.

Anthony Richmond sets out to explore the impact of post-industrialism on ethnic relations as mediated through the particular characteristics of postmodern society. Sorting out the diverse consequences of the economic, political and social changes brought about by globalization is no easy task. Richmond summarizes the debates surrounding the revolutions in information technology, travel and migratory patterns, global capital and production markets, and their multidimensional impact on ethnic and race relations. Richmond shows that these complex and diverse trends in modern societies have a variety of different impacts on ethnic and race relations whose net consequences are difficult to assess. While some factors challenge the structures of racial hierarchy and ethnic domination, others create situations of competition and insecurity that can lead to the resurgence of ethnic nationalism and the global movements of ethnic mobilization. The challenge of "global apartheid" remains the ongoing agenda for those seeking to defuse the explosive potential of racial and ethnic loyalties.

4 Rethinking Ethnicity: Identity, Categorization, and Power

Richard Jenkins

One of the most influential models of ethnicity and inter-ethnic social relations is that which was outlined by social anthropologist Fredrik Barth and his colleages in *Ethnic Groups and Boundaries* (Barth 1969a). The perspective put forward in that collection drew, on the one hand, upon the meta-theoretical model of social forms as generated by interpersonal transactions outlined in Barth's earlier *Models of Social Organisation* (Barth 1966) and, on the other, upon a structural-functionalist tradition concerned with the study of 'plural societies' (R. Cohen 1978; Jenkins 1986a). However, the Barthian approach departed in a significant fashion from the then-dominant structural functionalism of social anthropology inasmuch as it emphasized the perceptions and purposive decision-making of social actors, rather than viewing individuals as more-or-less determined, general 'bearers' of the norms and values of their culture.

Barth's original view of ethnicity consists of a number of elements. Pride of place must be given to the insight that ethnicity is not an immutable bundle of cultural traits which it is sufficient to enumerate in order to identify a person as an 'X' or a 'Y' or locate the boundary between ethnic collectivities. Rather, ethnicity is situationally defined, produced in the course of social transactions that occur at or across (and in the process help to constitute) the ethnic boundary in question. Ethnic boundaries are permeable, existing despite the flow of personnel or interaction across them; criteria of ethnic ascription and subscription are variable in their nature and salience.

While remaining firmly grounded in his original 1966 *Models* project, Barth has subsequently modified his vision of ethnicity somewhat. His recent discussions of cultural pluralism in complex societies emphasize the importance of history, in addition to the transactional ebb-and-flow of the here-and-now (Barth 1984; 1989). Barth invokes history in two distinct senses: as the ongoing progress of events which constitutes the context and content of the here-and-now, and as 'streams' of 'tradition' – the reference here to Redfield is explicit – within which people are to differing degrees located and of which they differentially partake. Emphasizing history produces a shift of emphasis away from the individualistic voluntarism of his earlier writings (which has always been one of the standard criticisms of Barth's work: Paine 1976; Evens 1977) towards a Weberian acknowledgement of the unintended consequences of action. Further, recognizing the centrality of history entails a search for pattern, influence and effect within a wide social and geographic arena; attention must be given to factors both within and without the social setting, local community or region which is the object of analytical interest.

In most respects, however, Barth has remained true to his original point of view in *Ethnic Groups and Boundaries*, particularly with respect to the primacy accorded to the perceptions and definitions of actors. It is on this aspect of his work that I shall concentrate in this article, hoping to develop our understanding of ethnicity while capitalizing at the same time upon the strengths and insights of the Barthian paradigm and the tradition of work that it has inspired.

Groups and Categories

Barth emphasizes the transactional nature of ethnicity; these transactions are of two basic kinds. First, there are processes of *internal definition*: actors signal to in- or out-group members a self-definition of their nature or identity. This can be an ego-centred, individual process or a collective, group process, although it only makes sense to talk of ethnicity in an individual sense when the identity being defined and its expression refer to a recognizable socially-constructed identity and draw upon a repertoire of culturally-specified practices. Although conceptualized in the first instance as internal, these processes are necessarily transactional and social (even in the individual case) because they presuppose both an audience, without whom they make no sense, and an externally derived framework of meaning.

Second, there are processes of *external definition*. These are other-directed processes during which one person or set of persons defines the other(s) as 'X', 'Y' or whatever. This may, at its most consensual, be the validation of the others' internal definition(s) of themselves. At the conflictual end of the spectrum of possibilities, however, there is the imposition, by one set of actors upon another, of a putative name and characterization which affects in significant ways the social experience(s) of the categorized.

This process of external definition may, in theory, be an individual act: person A defines person or persons B as, say, 'X' or 'Y'. For two reasons, however, it is difficult to imagine external definition as a primarily individual process. In the first place, more than an audience is involved: the others here are the object(s) of the process of definition, and implied within the situation is a meaningful intervention in their lives, an acting upon them. Thus, external definition is necessarily embedded within social relationships. Secondly, the capacity to act successfully upon other people's lives implies either the power or the authority to do so. The exercise of power implies competitive access to and control over resources, while authority is, by definition, only effective when it is legitimate. Power and authority are thus necessarily embedded within social relationships.

The distinction between internal and external definition is primarily analytical. In the complexity of day-to-day social life, each is chronically implicated in the other. The categorization of 'them' is too useful a foil in the identification of "us" for this not to be the case, and the definition of 'us' too much the product of a history of relationships with a range of significant others (Hagendoorn 1993). Which is, of course, one of Barth's original claims: ethnicity, the production, reproduction and transformation of the social boundaries of ethnic groups, is a two-way process that takes place across the boundary between 'us' and 'them'. At the individual level, in the creation of personal identities, much the same can be said: identity is located within a two-way social process, an interaction between 'ego' and 'other', inside and outside. It is in the meeting of internal and external definition that identity, whether social or personal, is created.

It may be objected that the suggested equivalence of collective/social identity and individual/personal identity is misleading: the boundaries of the self are secure and unproblematic in a way that is not, for example, true of social groups, particularly inasmuch as the notion of the self is bounded by and within the body. There are a number of reasons for rejecting this argument. First, and regardless of whether one chooses to follow Freud or Piaget, it seems clear that a relatively secure sense of the boundary of self is acquired as the infant separates itself psychologically from the significant other(s) in its life through an early interactive process of defining and being defined (Stern 1985). Secondly, there is a well-established understanding of adult personal or self-identity which sees its content(s), boundaries and, most critically, security as variable over time in interaction with changing circumstances (e.g., Giddens 1991). Finally, even if the boundaries of the self are, most of the time, stable and taken for granted, this is only true as long as it *is* true. When it is not, when the boundary between the self and others weakens or dissolves, the result is a range of more-or-less severe, and not uncommon, disruptions of self that in Western culture are conceptualized as psychiatric disorder (for one understanding of which, within a model that is analogous to the distinction between external and internal definition, see Laing 1971). To extend the logic of this last point, the boundaries of collective identity are also taken for granted until they are threatened.

The contrasting processes of identity-production, internal and external, can be illuminated further by drawing upon concepts derived from the methodology of the social sciences. Basic to the sociological and anthropological enterprises is the classification of human collectivities. One of the most enduringly useful distinctions which we employ for this purpose is that which we draw between *groups and categories*:

> category. A class whose nature and composition is decided by the person who defines the category; for example, persons earning wages in a certain range may be counted as a category for income tax purposes. A category is therefore to be contrasted with a group, defined by the nature of the relations between the members. (Mann 1983, p. 34)

A group, therefore, is rooted in processes of internal definition, while a category is externally defined. This distinction is concerned, in the first instance, with the procedures that we employ to constitute the social world as a proper object for empirical inquiry and theoretical analysis. As such, it is relevant beyond the study of ethnicity and ethnic relations. Debates about social class, for example, are often characterized by disagreement about which principle of definition is most appropriate for the adequate constitution of classes as objects of/for analysis. The distinction here may be vividly exemplified in this context by Marx's famous contrast between 'a class in itself' (a category) and 'a class for itself' (a group). This reference to Marx reminds us that the distinction is, of course, something more than methodological. Social groups and social categories are different kinds of collectivities existing in the social world. Marx's understanding of the development of class consciousness involves a social category, defined with reference to alienation from the means of production, becoming a social group, the members of which identify with one another in their collective misfortune and have the potential for collective action on the basis of that identification.

So, whereas social groups define themselves, their name(s), their nature(s) and their boundary(s), social categories are identified, defined and delineated by others. Most social collectivities can be characterized as, to some extent, defined in both ways. Each side of the dichotomy is implicated in the other and social identity is the outcome of the conjunction of processes of internal *and* external definition. Whether, in any specific instance, one chooses to talk about a group or a category will depend on the balance struck between internal and external processes in that situation. It is a question of degree.

Although it is undoubtedly true that historically social anthropology has, inasmuch as it has considered *individual* indentity at all, privileged social or external knowledge over self- or internal knowledge (A. P. Cohen 1992, p. 222), the emphasis of the post-Barthian anthropology of ethnicity and *communal* identity (e.g., Wallman 1978, 1986; A. P. Cohen 1982, 1985, 1986; Eriksen 1991) has tended to fall on the other side of the internal–external dialectic: upon processes of group identification rather than social categorization (Jenkins 1986a). There are at least three reasons why this should be so. First, anthropology, in its enthusiasm for 'otherness' and its (still) essentially non-conflictual model of the social world – regardless of internal theoretical debates between transactionalism or structuralism, for example, or the impact of various threads of post-modernism – tends to celebrate ethnicity as a social resource. This is at the expense of paying sufficient attention to ethnicity as a social liability or stigma. Secondly, this is reinforced by the fact that enthusiasm for a transactional model of social life – ethnicity as process – has typically been accompanied by a view of social relationships as rooted in reciprocation, exchange and relatively equitable negotiation. Thirdly, anthropology's continued emphasis upon participant observation as the discipline's methodological *sine qua non* has led its practitioners to concentrate upon the collection of data during face-to-face encounters or through direct observation. Processes of collective internal definition may be easier to study using such an approach than their external counterparts.

This anthropological bias is not, however, *entailed* by the Barthian model, as is well illustrated by Eidheim's essay, 'When ethnic identity is a social stigma', in *Ethnic Groups and Boundaries* (Eidheim 1969). Ideally, the exploration of processes of ethnic and other forms of categorization should represent the extension, refinement and development of the Barthian perspective.

Before proceeding, however, it is necessary to clarify one further point, which has so far only been implied. In talking about the names, natures and boundaries of groups and categories, I am suggesting that identity is 'made up' of a number of distinct strands, even if they may only be analytically distinguishable. Two of these strands, in particular, are significant here. Social identity, whether it be ethnic or whatever, is both nominal, i.e., a name, and virtual, a meaning or an experience, a contrast that is implicit in the distinction between boundaries and their contents, and approximately analogous to the well-worn distinction between 'status' and 'role'. This distinction is important because one can change without the other doing so; similarly one can be the product of internal processes of identification, the other of categorization. For example, although categorization may not necessarily change the name or boundary of an identity, it may have considerable potential to define what it means to bear it, the experience of 'being an X'. The implications of this are explored later in the article.

Social Categorization

Distinguishing between internal and external definitions, and between groups and categories, allows us to think about ethnic identity at a number of different levels within a unified analytical framework. One basis for doing so is presented schematically in figure 4.1. Perhaps the first thing to explain about figure 4.1, however, is that, as suggested in its caption, it is not specifically about ethnicity. If it has any application at all, it applies to all forms of social identity. Second, the vertical lines $\updownarrow$ indicate a continuum of graded differentiation, the horizontal ones ———— a dialectical synthetic unity. In this sense, the internal:external distinction should not be read as implying an acceptance of intellectual dualisms such as thinking: doing or subjective:objective (and one could doubtless add a further long list). These are difficult to maintain and do not seem to contribute anything useful to the attempt to understand the social world (Jenkins 1981; see also Bourdieu 1990, pp. 23–141).

So what does figure 4.1 mean? The representation of the internal:external dichotomy by a line, rather than a sharp break, indicates a number of interrelationships. First, there is the influence of external definition (by others) on internal definition(s). Next, it is important to recognize the role in internal definition of the categorization, or external definition, of others: the process of defining 'us' demands that 'they' should be split off from or contrasted with 'us'. Finally, there is the defence which pre-existing internal definitions may provide against the imposition of external definitions. The experience of categorization may strengthen existing group identity through a process of resistance and reaction. Thus, the experience of being categorized may contribute to the formation of group identity (although the ways in which it will do so are a matter for empirical research rather than theoretical prediction). Similarly, group identification is likely to proceed, at least in part, through categorizing others (whether positively or negatively). Arguments analogous to all the above could also be offered at the individual/psychological level.

The next step is to unpack further some of the social processes that are summarized in figure 4.1. At the most individually-focused level, the distinction between 'I' and 'me', while it is inspired ultimately by Cooley (1902; 1965 ed., pp. 168–263), is derived in this formulation from Mead (1934, pp. 173–226), a theorist who has been 'curiously unacknowledged' by social anthropology (A. P. Cohen 1992, p. 226). To paraphrase Mead, the 'I' is that aspect of the self which responds to others, whereas the 'me' comprises the attitudes and responses of others as they are incorporated into the self. In this sense, it might be more appropriate to rename the latter the 'What, me?'

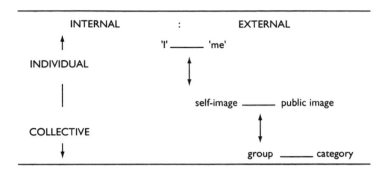

Figure 4.1 Forms and processes of social identity

This is a distinction that can also, of course, be interpreted as drawing upon the basic Freudian distinction between 'ego' and 'superego'. In the course of earliest socialization each human being develops a unique personality, a sense of self which, although it may not always be available to us consciously, is one of the bedrocks of our 'ontological security' (Giddens 1991, pp. 36–46). Much of this 'sense of self' is located in that hinterland of unreflexive habit – neither conscious nor unconscious – that is the generative site of practices which Bourdieu calls the 'habitus' (Bourdieu 1990, pp. 53–97). This 'sense of self' is not simply a 'mental' phenomenon but is intimately bound up with the physical integrity of the individual. Selves are located within bodies....

It is easy to imagine how primary socialization is likely to include an ethnic component: the child will learn not only that he/she is an 'X', but also what this means, in terms of self-esteem and worth or appropriate and inappropriate behaviour, and what it means not to be an 'X', a 'Y' or a 'Z' perhaps (Epstein 1978). This is emphatically the case, for example, in societies where 'racial' categorization is a powerful principle of social organization and stratification (Goodman 1964; Milner 1975; Troyna and Hatcher 1992).

Moving on to *self-image* and *public image*, the distinction has something in common with Mauss's conceptualization (1938; 1985 ed., p. 12) of the difference between, on the one hand, 'role' (*personnage*) and, on the other, the combination of 'person' (*personne*) and 'self' (*moi*). Self-image, in my definition, is the way we see ourselves and perhaps even more important, the way we would like to be seen by others.

The essential starting point for any attempt to understand how this works in social interaction is, of course, Goffman (1969). In the context of this discussion, Goffman's most important arguments about the 'presentation of self' are: (1) that it is a matter of performance; (2) that there is no single, consistent self, but rather a range of aspects or revelations of self, depending on the social situation; (3) that management of the awkward relationship between the desired presentation of self and other, countervailing aspects of one's biography and present situation is of great importance; and (4) that validation of the performance by others, if not their complicit collaboration, is central to successful impression management. The homology between Goffman's view of social selfhood as performative and processual and Barth's model of ethnicity as transactional is obvious.

The third and fourth points above direct our attention to the other side of the coin, public image, the vexed question of how others see us. It goes without saying that there is no necessary equivalence between self-image and public image. What is more, it is not always easy to know how other see us anyway. Apart from the obvious epistemological issue – the old philosophical problem of 'other minds' – there are a number of reasons why this should be so. First, the audience may attempt to conceal its opinion of both actor and performance. Second, the actor may, for various strategic or tactical reasons, attempt to present something other than their 'true' self-image. Third, there may be poor communication between the two sides, for various interactional, institutional or other external reasons. Fourth, the personal psychology that is integral to selfhood may, in the event of major disagreement between self-image and public image, block acknowledgement of the threatening public image. However, allowing for these qualifications, there will usually be at least some interaction between self-image(s) and public image(s), some process of conscious or unconscious adjustment in the ongoing process of the making and re-making of social identity. . . .

The implication of [this] for ethnicity is apparent if we look at discrimination in the labour market and the depression or encouragement of aspiration, either effect being possible, among those ethnic minorities who find themselves on its receiving end. The cumulative outcome of this kind of situation, if left unchallenged by currents of resistance within the ethnic community or communities concerned, may at best be the development of ethnic occupational niches and a communally accepted ceiling on occupational mobility. At worst the self-image of a stigmatized and discriminated-against minority will interact with discrimination and exclusion in a vicious circle of disadvantage, as in many North American urban neighbour-hoods (Liebow 1967; Hannerz 1969; Anderson 1978). 'Realism' becomes, at least in part, constitutive of 'reality'.

Ethnic disadvantage in the labour market may seem far removed from the micro-interactional concerns of Goffman. A better example for our purposes might be perhaps the subtlety with which people in Northern Ireland purport to 'tell' the difference between Catholic and Protestant in social interaction (Burton 1978, pp. 37–67; Jenkins 1982, pp. 30–1). However, the principles involved are essentially the same. The 'labour-market' is, after all, nothing more than an ab-straction from a myriad of encounters in which the choices of job-seekers are subject to categorizing decisions about who should get which jobs (Jenkins 1986b). Although for the moment there is a question begged here – that of who is authorized to make the decisions and to make those decisions count – the example serves to connect the micro-interaction of self-image and personal image with the larger social register of groups and categories.

Most discussions of ethnicity are pitched at the level of the *social group*, the emphasis being upon collective internal definitions of distinctiveness: 'ethnic groups are categories of ascription and identification by the actors themselves' (Barth 1969b, p. 10). While it is clear from Barth's discussion that the 'actors themselves' can signify actors on both sides of the ethnic boundary, it is equally, if only implicitly, clear that explanatory or analytical priority is accorded to identification within the ethnic boundary. There is a sense in which this is as it should be. A claim to ethnic identity must be validated by an audience of 'outsiders' or 'others', because without such an audience the issue would not arise, but it seems to make little sense to talk about an ethnicity which does not at some point recognize itself as such.

When the issue is expressed thus, the anthropological emphasis upon internal group identification becomes apparent. Leaving aside the massive body of work on caste and hierarchy in India and elsewhere, because it is not concerned with ethnicity as such (which is not only a major exception but also, for many readers perhaps, an indefensible one), there are few examples in the anthropological ethnicity literature of an explicit concern with *social categorization*. Those examples which can be found, however, are ample illustration of the value of such an approach. For our purposes, one such will do (Stuchlik 1979).

Looking at the history of European colonial expansion into Chile, the Spaniards came into contact relatively early – in the sixteenth century – with an indigenous people known today as the Mapuche. Stuchlik, using docmentary sources, identifies five distinct ways in which the Spanish, and subsequently the Chileans, categorized the Mapuche in the course of the centuries that followed: as 'brave and fearless warriors', 'bloodthirsty bandits', 'lazy drunken Injuns', 'the white man's burden' and 'gentle savages who lack education', in historical sequence. The main thrust of this analysis – which, while it does not tell us about the impact of categorization on Mapuche group identity, does suggest some of its effects upon Mapuche life – is that these categorical models of the Mapuche are not a reflection of 'factual' knowledge about the Mapuche. Rather, they tell us about native policies, the goals of the Spanish and the Chileans with respect to the Mapuche. Hence they tell us about the catego*rizers* – how they see themselves and their objectives – not the catego*rized*. It is Chilean ethnicity that is under construction as much as anything else.

A more general point can perhaps be made about the anthropological enterprise itself, particularly with respect to notions of 'primitiveness' as a means of categorizing other cultures (Boon 1982; Kuper 1988). Fortunately, unlike Spanish colonizers or Chilean administrators and politicians, the capacity of anthropologists to make their definitions count for those who they categorize has generally been modest, although their indirect influence should not be underestimated.

Broaching the issue of 'primitiveness' brings me to the relationship between ethnicity and 'race', and in looking at 'race' and racism, we are dealing with some of the most powerful processes of social categorization. The relationship between 'race' and ethnicity is far from clear in the literature. Wallman, for example, argues that the two concepts are essentially of the same order: phenotype, which is generally what we mean by 'race', is no more than 'one element in the repertoire of boundary markers' (Wallman 1986, p. 229). Elsewhere, she has dismissed the debate about the relationship between 'race' and ethnicity as a 'quibble' (Wallman 1978, p. 205). This is not, however, convincing. Ethnicity is historically and culturally more ubiquitous than those situations which we describe as 'race relations'. Ethnic relations are not necessarily hierarchical, exploitative and conflictual, as is arguably true for 'race relations' (Rex 1973, p. 184). Nor does ethnicity tend to appeal to a systematic body of justificatory, theoretical knowledge as the charter for its operation, as is frequently the case with 'racial' categorization and racism.

The group:category distinction may clarify the situation. Banton, for example, has suggested that, 'Membership in an ethnic group is usually voluntary; membership in a racial group is not' (Banton 1983, p. 10). Ethnicity, in this view, is about inclusion ('us'), while 'race' and racism are a matter of 'exclusion' ('them'); group identification versus categorization. At first sight this seems to be a plausible and useful approach to the matter. There are, however, a number of important *caveats* to be acknowledged.

In the first place, there is the routine implication, each in the other, of processes of group identification and categorization. The definition of 'them' in terms of 'race' is likely to be an important aspect of our definition of 'us' (which must, correspondingly, have a 'racial' dimension). Similarly, there are many processes of ethnic categorization which do not appear to involve the imputation of 'racial' difference (although one is entitled to ask whether it is not more a case of 'racial' rhetoric having been in the quarantine of disreputability in the decades following World War II). Thirdly, groups may actively seek to identify themselves in positively evaluated 'racial' terms. The best-known example here, perhaps, is the ideology of the *Herrenvolk*, as in Nazi Germany and Nationalist South Africa. Something similar, however, can also be discerned in the formation of modern Israeli Jewish identity and in various forms of 'black nationalism' in the United States and elsewhere. These latter cases, in particular, represent the 'turning round' of a powerful process of negative 'racial' categorization into a positive group identity. Finally, we should remember that the criteria of 'racial' classification are no less socially-constructed and culturally-selected than those upon which ethnic identification depends. It is emphatically not the case that the difference between ethnicity and 'race' is a simple difference between the physical and the cultural, although it may be a difference between purported physical and cultural, characteristics.

Viewed from this perspective, 'racial' differentiation and racism should perhaps best be viewed as historically-specific forms of the general – perhaps even universal – social phenomenon of ethnicity. As such, they characterize situations in which one ethnic group dominates, or attempts to dominate, another and in the process categorizes them with reference to their supposed inherent and immutable difference and inferiority. The role of 'racial' ideologies in the legitimation of conquest and domination should not be overlooked in this respect. However one might choose to recognize the distinction between them, the question of the relationship between 'race' and ethnicity remains something more than a 'quibble' (cf. Miles 1982, pp. 44–71).

The other kind of ethnic legitimation which deserves a mention here is nationalism. Understood strictly as a political philosophy relating to the exclusive right of occupation of territory, on the one hand, and freedom from alien rule, on the other, this is an historical development with its roots in the bourgeois revolutions of nineteenth-century Europe (Anderson 1983; Gellner 1983; Hobsbawm 1990). However, Smith is surely correct to insist (1986) that nationalism also has another set of roots, in the ethnic communality of the pre-modern world. The important point to recognize here is that nationalism involves once again processes of both group identification and social categorization, inclusion and exclusion. Whatever else it may be, it is perhaps most usefully regarded, like 'race' and racism, as another historically specific facet of ethnicity.

Categorization and Power

Categorization contributes to group identity in various ways. There is, for example, something that might be referred to as 'internalization': the categorized group is exposed to the terms in which another group defines it and assimilates that categorization, in whole or in part, into its own identity. Put this baldly, however, the suggestion seems to beg more questions than it answers: *why* should the external definition be internalized, for example, and *how* does it happen? There are at least five possible scenarios.

First, the external categorization might be more or less the same as an aspect of existing group identity, in which case they will simply reinforce each other. One might suggest that, in fact, some degree of external reinforcement or validation is crucial for the successful maintenance of internal (group) definitions. Similarly, categorization may be less likely to 'stick' where it is markedly at odds with existing boundaries.

Second, there is the incremental cultural change that is likely to be a product of any long-standing but relatively harmonious inter-ethnic contact. The ethnic boundary is osmotic, and not just in terms of personnel: languages and cultures may interact also, and in the process identities are likely to be affected.

Third, the external category might be produced by people who, in the eyes of the original group, have the legitimate authority to categorize them, by virtue of their superior ritual status, knowledge, or whatever. Such a situation implies greater social than cultural differentiation (if a distinction posed in terms as crude as this is admissible), inasmuch as legitimate authority necessarily requires at least a minimal degree of shared participation in values or cosmology.

Fourth, this might be a simpler case: external categorization is imposed by the use of physical force or its threat, i.e., the exercise of power. The categorized, without the capacity to resist the carrying of identity cards, the wearing of arm-bands, or whatever more subtle devices of identification and stigmatization might be deployed, may, in time, come to think of themselves in the language or categories of the oppressor.

Finally, there are the oppressed who do resist, who reject imposed boundaries and/or their content(s). However, the very act of defying categorization, of striving for an autonomy of self-identification, is, of course, an effect of being categorized in the first place. The rejected external definition *is* internalized, but paradoxically, as the focus of denial.

In these five possibilities, the distinction between power and legitimate authority can be seen in operation. However, the contribution of categorization to group identity depends upon more than 'internalization'. In particular, we should not underestimate the capacity of one group of people to define effectively or to constitute the conditions of existence experienced by another. This is the distinction that I have proposed between the *virtual* and *nominal* dimensions of ethnicity.

To return to an example mentioned earlier, the categorization in particular ways of the Mapuche by white Chileans must be expected to have influenced both groups. Specifically, it will have influenced the behaviour of the Chileans towards the Mapuche: 'native policy' as Stuchlik puts it. The Chileans, like the Spanish before them, because of their effective monopolization of violence within the local context and their consequent control of resources, were (and, indeed, still are) in a position to make their categorization of the Mapuche count disproportionately in the social construction of Mapuche life.

The effective categorization of a group of people by a more powerful 'other' is not therefore 'just' a matter of classification (if, indeed, there is any such thing). It is necessarily an intervention in that group's social world which will, to an extent and in ways that are a function of the specifics of the situation, alter that world and the experience of living in it. Just as the Chileans have the capacity to constitute, in part, the experience of 'being a Mapuche', so do, for example, employment recruiters in Britain, who are typically white, contribute to the social constitution of the collective experience of growing up as a member of a black ethnic minority.

To return to Barth (and Weber), here one sees the unintended consequences of action at work, and it is partly in the cumulative mutual reinforcement of these unintended consequences that the pattern of history, both in the present and as a framework of constraint and possiblity for future generations, is produced. If we accept that 'culture' is not independent of practical day-to-day life and its exigencies, then the power of others to constitute the experience of daily living is a further important contribution of categorization to group identity. It is also powerful support for the view of ethnicity and identity as day-to-day practice and historical process that is central to Barth's model.

Finally, a concern with external definition and categorization demands that we pay attention to *power* and *authority*, and the manner in which different modes of domination are implicated in the social construction of ethnic and other identities. This is not an original observation. It is, perhaps, worth suggesting further that if we do not do so the result will be a model of ethnicity which is as trivial as it is one-sided. Unless we can construct an understanding of ethnicity that can address *all* of ethnicity's facets and manifestations, from the celebratory communality of belonging to the final awful moment of genocide, we will have failed both ourselves and the people among whom we undertake our research.

References

Anderson, B. 1983 *Imagined Communities: Reflections on the Origin and Spread of Nationalism*, London: Verso.

Anderson, E. 1978 *A Place on the Corner*, Chicago, IL: University of Chicago Press.

Banton, M. 1983 *Racial and ethnic competition*, Cambridge: Cambridge University Press.

Barth, F. 1966 'Models of social organisation', *Occasional Paper No. 23*, London: Royal Anthropological Institute.

—— (ed.) 1969a *Ethnic Groups and Boundaries: The Social Organisation of Culture Difference*, Oslo: Universitetsforlaget.

—— 1969b 'Introduction', in Barth 1969a.

—— 1984 'Problems in conceptualizing cultural pluralism, with illustrations from Somar, Oman', in D. Maybury-Lewis (ed.), *The Prospects for Plural Societies*, Proceedings, American Ethnological Society.

—— 1989 'The analysis of culture in complex societies', *Ethnos*, vol. 54, pp. 120–42.

Boon, J. A. 1982 *Other Tribes, Other Scribes: Symbolic Anthropology in the Comparative Study of Cultures, Histories, Religions and Texts*, Cambridge: Cambridge University Press.

Bourdieu, P. 1990 *The Logic of Practice*, Cambridge: Polity.

Burton, F. 1978 *The Politics of Legitimacy: Struggles in a Belfast Community*, London: Routledge and Kegan Paul.

Cohen, A. P. (ed.) 1982 *Belonging: Identity and Social Organisation in British Rural Cultures*, Manchester: Manchester University Press.

—— (ed.) 1985 *Symbolising Boundaries: Identity and Diversity in British Cultures*, Manchester: Manchester University Press.

—— 1986 *The Symbolic Construction of Community*, London: Ellis Horwood/Tavistock.

—— 1992 'Self-conscious anthropology' in J. Okely and H. Callaway (eds), *Anthropology and Autobiography*, London: Routledge.

Cohen, R. (1978), 'Ethnicity: problem and focus in anthropology', *Annual Review of Anthropology*, vol. 7, pp. 379–403.

Cooley, C. H. 1965 *Human Nature and the Social Order*, New York: Schocken.

Eidheim, H. 1969 'When ethnic identity is a social stigma', in F. Barth (ed.), *Ethnic Groups and Boundaries*, Oslo: Universitetsforlaget.

Epstein, A. L. 1978 *Ethos and Identity: Three Studies in Ethnicity*, London: Tavistock.

Eriksen, T. H. 1991 'The cultural contexts of ethnic differences', *Man*, vol. 26, pp. 12–44.

Evens, T. M. S. 1977 'The predication of the individual in anthropological interactionism', *American Ethnologist*, vol. 79, pp. 579–97.

Gellner, E. 1983 *Nations and Nationalism*, Oxford: Basil Blackwell.

Giddens, A. 1991 *Modernity and Self-Identity: Self and Society in the Late Modern Age*, Cambridge: Polity.

Goffman, E. 1969 *The Presentation of Self in Everyday Life*, London: Allen Lane.

Goodman, M. E. 1964 *Race Awareness in Young Children*, rev. ed., New York: Collier.

Hagendoorn, L. 1993 'Ethnic categorization and outgroup exclusion: cultural values and social stereotypes in the construction of ethnic hierarchies', *Ethnic and Racial Studies*, vol. 16, no. 1, pp. 27–51.

Hannerz, U. 1969 *Soulside: Inquiries into Ghetto Life and Culture*, New York: Columbia University Press.

Hobsbawm, E. J. 1990 *Nations and Nationalism since 1780: Programme, Myth, Reality*, Cambridge: Cambridge University Press.

Jenkins, R. 1981 'Thinking and doing: towards a model of cognitive practice', in L. Holy and M. Stuchlik (eds), *The Structure of Folk Models*, London: Academic Press.

—— 1982 *Hightown Rules: Growing up in a Belfast Housing Estate*, Leicester: National Youth Bureau.

—— 1986a 'Social anthropological models of inter-ethnic relations', in J. Rex and D. Mason (eds), *Theories of Race and Ethnic Relations*, Cambridge: Cambridge University Press.

—— 1986b *Racism and Recruitment: Managers, Organisations and Equal Opportunity in the Labour Market*, Cambridge: Cambridge University Press.

Kuper, A. 1988 *The Invention of Primitive Society: Transformations of an Illusion*, London: Routledge.

Laing, R. D. 1971 *Self and Others*, Harmondsworth: Pelican.

Liebow, E. 1967 *Tally's Corner: A Study of Negro Streetcorner Men*, Boston: Little, Brown.

Mann, M. (ed.) 1983 *The Macmillan Student Encyclopaedia of Sociology*, London: Macmillan.

Mauss, M. 1985 'A category of the human mind: the notion of person; the notion of self', in M. Carrithers, S. Collins and S. Lukes (eds), *The Category of the Person: Anthropology, Philosophy, History*, Cambridge: Cambridge University Press.

Mead, G. H. 1934 *Mind, Self and Society from the Standpoint of a Social Behaviorist*, Chicago, IL: University of Chicago Press.

Miles, R. 1982 *Racism and Migrant Labour*, London: Routledge and Kegan Paul.

Milner, D. 1975 *Children and Race*, Harmondsworth: Penguin.

Paine, R. 1976 'Two modes of exchange and mediation', in B. Kapferer (ed.), *Transaction and Meaning*, Philadelphia, PA: ISHI.

Rex, J. 1973 *Race, Colonialism and the City*, London: Oxford University Press.

Smith, Anthony D. 1986 *The Ethnic Origins of Nations*, Oxford: Basil Blackwell.

Stern, D. N. 1985 *The Interpersonal World of the Infant: A View from Psychoanalysis and Developmental Psychology*, New York: Basic Books.

Stuchlik, M. 1979 'Chilean native policies and the image of the Mapuche Indians', in D. Riches (ed.), *The Conceptualisation and Explanation of Processes of Social Change*, Queen's University Papers in Social Anthropology, vol. 3, Belfast.

Troyna, B. and Hatcher, R. 1992 *Racism in Children's Lives: A Study of Mainly White Primary Schools*, London: Routledge.

Wallman, S. 1978 'The boundaries of race: processes of ethnicity in England', *Man*, vol. 13. pp. 200–17.

—— 1986 'Ethnicity and the boundary process in context' in J. Rex and D. Mason (eds), *Theories of Race and Ethnic Relations*, Cambridge: Cambridge University Press.

5 Culture and Ethnic Conflict in the New World Disorder

Kevin Avruch

I

For scholars of the postmodernist persuasion the great insight into ethnicity – ethnic identity, nationalism, culture, history, or most anything else that is social, for that matter – is that ethnicity is socially constructed: It is not a given but rather a thing which is made and thus potentially unstable, inconstant, and negotiable. Taken to an epistemological extreme, most elegantly by Richard Rorty perhaps, this position exercises different sorts of foundationalists, truth-correspondence theorists, and conservatives, and has generated tremendous turmoil in the teapot of the academy. But what makes this insight worth pursuing (and it is, at least in the long run, essentially correct), is that it so sharply flies in the face of what most ethnic "actors," the players themselves, believe. For they are convinced beyond doubt that their group – its "culture" (more on this troublesome term later), its customs, traditions, language, its religious beliefs and practices – stretches back in an unbroken chain to some primordial antiquity. This tension between the observers of ethnicity and the players, so to speak, has been remarked on by many: "Traditions," wrote Hobsbawm (1983:1), "which appear or claim to be old are often quite recent in origin and sometimes invented." Referring to nationalism (a special genre or manifestation of ethnicity broadly conceived), Anderson (1983:5) noted the "objective modernity of nations to the historian's eye versus their subjective antiquity in the eyes of the nationalists." But the notion of "invention" only takes us part way in understanding how ethnicity is constructed. Eller (1999) points out that the prime raw material for constructing ethnicity is usually the past – "history" as transparently conceived by the ethnics themselves (even if such "history" is legend, myth, or worse, to outsiders – "objective" analysts or opposing ethnics). And consideration of collective construals of the past means that supplementing mechanical invention demands the many arts of memory: of remembering *and* forgetting, and above all, of interpretation.

Let me give an example close to home. Many Americans (and perhaps especially African Americans) even today view the December festival called *Kwanzaa* as an ancient (if generic) African celebration as old as Christianity and Christmas. In a generation or two, after exposure to multicultural K-12 education, almost all Americans will believe this. In fact, *Kwanzaa* is "really" quite new. It was invented (out of African cultural materials, certainly) in 1966 by Maulana Ron Karenga, an African American academic and black nationalist who was quite explicitly politically motivated to create in America an *African* cultural counterweight to Christian Christmas and Jewish Hanukkah. But Hanukkah in fact is an earlier variation on the same theme. It is a traditionally minor Jewish festival that over time was blown up in importance in the US to serve American Jews as a cultural counterweight – to shield their culturally vulnerable children from an unstoppable combination of mythos, spirituality, and consumerism: from the powerful allure of Christmas.

Taking the long, or longitudinal, view to the insight of the constructed nature of ethnicity is properly the province of the historian. But the historical, or diachronic, view is not the only way to get a look at ethnicity's constructedness. My own insight came – appropriately for a cultural anthropologist – synchronically, in the course of ethnographic fieldwork, interacting with that epitome of postmodern encounters, The Other.

II

I was twenty-five years old, sitting anxiously in a room at the Hotel *Splendid* in Rabat, waiting for permission to come through from the Ministry of Interior that would allow me to reside for a year or so in a Moroccan village and "do" my doctoral fieldwork. It was a bad time to seek this permission, worse than usual, according to old Moroccanist hands. In Spain, Generalissimo Franco was sick and dying, and Moroccan newspapers were already reflecting the government's line that a new era was dawning in the struggle against colonialism, that the future of Spanish Sahara lay in its "reintegration" to Morocco. The noises from Spain were that after Franco this old remaining bit of the Empire would, indeed, be jettisoned. But the noises from the colony itself, from its indigenous *saharouis*, were quite different. Talk there was of independence from both Spain and Morocco. The *saharouis* claimed that they were never part of Morocco's Maghrebian empire. This was the beginning of a movement, soon to be called the Polisario, that would engage Morocco in a draining insurgency war for decades. But in fact in those days – commencing in September of 1975 – Morocco's main worry was not the Polisario guerrillas, but rather Algeria's (and to a lesser extent, Mauritania's) potential interest in the Spanish Sahara. It was war with Algeria that frightened Morocco the most and put the country, its ministries and armed forces, in a state of high alert. In November, King Hassan II sent hundreds of thousands of Moroccans down south in what was called *la marche verte*, "a green march of peace," to claim the territory for the Kingdom by virtue of their physical presence in it, well before Spanish troops even left. All transportation in the country was mobilized to move the marchers southward; all other work in the ministries stopped.

So I sat in Rabat, waiting out my three-month tourist visa, and hoping daily for word from the Ministry. From down the hall every afternoon came the pungent smell of a *tajine* being cooked (illicitly) in a room, and one day Mohammed, the cook, invited me in to share some. Mohammed was, to my American eyes, a young black man about my age. He was excited to hear I was an American, and told me he was in Rabat trying to get a passport so that he could leave Morocco and go to France or, better yet America. (Couldn't I help him, didn't I have a job for him? Perhaps my father did?) Increasingly worried about my own prospects for a job and career should doctoral field work collapse completely, I reflected on this: He was a Moroccan national in the capital trying to wring the bureaucracy in order to get out and I was a foreigner trying to wring it in order to be allowed in. One day I asked him why he wanted to leave. "Ah," he said, "I come from the south, and things there are bad and they are going to get worse. The worst thing is the Africans," he added. "The *who?*" I said, taken aback. "The Africans," he said, "*les noirs.* They are lazy and deceitful and not to be trusted. God help us if they ever get any power." I looked at him, confused. *Les noirs?* What did he think he was? I said: "I'm sorry, I'm confused, aren't you too African?" His eyes flashed angrily. "*Non! Je suis Arabe!* My father is a sheikh, I am a prince and a sherif, a descendant of the Prophet. I am no more African than you are."

At twenty-five this was my first direct contact with ethnicity's essentially post-modern sensibility. True, I had come from multiethnic and polyglot Brooklyn, and bethought myself a big-city sophisticate in racial matters and what we today call "diversity." But despite this and my advanced training in the social sciences and all-but-doctoral status as an anthropologist, I was in fact culture-bound and cogni-tively trapped in my own ethnic and racial categories and calculus, and had never been confronted by that of another. I was also a little angry, given something Mohammed had said with great self-righteousness the day before. So I said to him, not aiming to enhance the ethnographer's rapport, "But you know, Moham-med, in America, you would be thought of as a black man." It was as if I slapped him. He reared and said, "No! You are lying. I am as white as you are." And then, forsaking the *tajine* and further contact (I knew) I rudely put my arm next to his and said with mock mildness: "We are the same color?" Mohammed looked down at our arms and spat. "Yes, we are. But do you know why mine looks darker?" And before I could say a word he said, "Because unlike you, you rich and spoiled American bastard, I have had to work outdoors in the sun all of my life, and not in an office. If I had your life and your money in America, and you had mine in the south, you would be black and I would be white."

"Well," I said as I had gathered my wits, a thoroughly ungrateful guest as well as a hopeless fieldworker. "That may be. But if ever you make it to America, Mohammed, to Los Angeles or Chicago or Houston, and you are stopped by the police one night in your car, you would do best to remember, for your own safety that, like it or not, you are a black man." (Twenty years later, watching the awful video of Rodney King's beating for the *n*th time, Mohammed's face and that entire afternoon at the Hotel *Splendid* came back to me with a frightening clarity. Today, I realize also that I was then instinctively a good enough native informant of American culture to have recognized the mordant contingencies of what some call "driving while black.") That day in Rabat, looking at me aghast, gathering his wits, Mohammed repeated what he had said the day before, that which had gotten me angry in the first place. "Yes," he'd said, "America is a great country except for one great problem." "What is that?" I'd asked. "But of course," he said, "but of course you know, everybody does: it is *le racisme.*"

III

This encounter was revelatory for me in 1975 (which, indeed, is why one does fieldwork in foreign places – or teaches undergraduates about them), but by 2001 it must seem passé. Now there are many accounts that ring familiarly of this, of the chagrin – to reverse figure and ground – that some African Americans feel when they are classified, by their African brothers and sisters, as "Europeans" in many parts of Mother Africa (e.g., in Lee 1984); or the unhappiness of American Jewish immigrants to Israel (who often traded an American materially good-life for a less good one, but one which "maximized" their Jewishness) on being called "Anglo-Saxons" by other Israelis (Avruch 1981); or how the "subjective" perception of skin color seems to vary by "objective" social class in parts of Brazil (the higher you go, the lighter you are [Skidmore 1974]). The next time I ran into the Moroccan paradigm was on the other side of the African/Arab/Muslim world, in the Sudan. There "black" (to the eye of our paradigmatic Los Angeles patrol-man – or university/corporate equity officer, for that matter) northern (Muslim, Arabophone) Sudanese know themselves to be Arabs, and thus utterly different from the African (i.e., "black") southern (Christian, non-Arabophone) Sudanese, with whom they have struggled in a bloody civil war for more than two decades now.

One of the effects of looking at ethnicity as a social construct was that it changed our orientation: We initially regarded it as a thing completed (Narroll 1964) – a unit-vessel filled with cultural content (which is how the ethnic actors themselves continue to view it) – but soon began to regard it as a work-in-progress. (The completist impulse never disappears altogether; nevertheless I give short shrift here to the position, expressed by van den Berghe [1987], that roots ethnicity in ethology or evolutionary theory; here ethnicity is a vessel stuffed with DNA.) We focus less on the assumed "primordiality" of the cultural content of ethnicity and more on the processes of the production of this cultural content (Fox 1990). This revision has largely replaced an older concern in the ethnicity literature, a concern expressed by the Parsonian distinction between expressive and instrumental modalities. Both mo-dalities sought after the uses of ethnicity, but use-values were differently construed. The expressivists saw the actors' concerns with ethnicity as self-evident ends in themselves or, if not quite self-evident, perhaps as means towards identity integra-tion or "authenticity." This naturally led them to focus on the cultural content of ethnicity, especially as it dovetailed with religion. The instrumentalists in contrast saw actors' use of ethnicity as a strategy for the mobilization of resources and personnel. Like Barth (1969), these scholars were mostly not interested in ethnicity at all, but in ethnic groups. Ethnic groups organized actors to compete for scarce resources against other groups. What mattered most were the boundary-maintain-ing mechanisms that separated one group from another, not the rubbery cultural content – tradition, custom, cult, kinship: ethnicity – inside the boundaries. In a consummate elucidation of this view, Abner Cohen (1969) demonstrated how changeable this cultural content really was. He traced how, in post-colonial Nigeria, the Hausa of Sabo, in order to protect their monopoly of the north–south cattle and cola nut trade from other groups, transformed the basis of their group solidarity from "tribal" Hausa (the colonial locution) to "religious" Tijaniyya-Muslim (acceptable in a post-colonial political environment that proscribed open appeals to tribalism). Today, of course, in the midst of worsening Muslim–Christian violence exacerbating regional conflicts, many Nigerians rue this turn in the post-independence era to confessional identity.

Now fast-forward to a modern classic of the constructivist view of ethnicity, Richard Handler's *Nationalism and the Politics of Culture in Quebec* (1988). Handler demonstrates how, over the course of several decades, Quebecois nationalists sought self-consciously to construct a satisfying version of Quebecois culture. Some of the cultural "raw material" available to them, that which "naturally" set them off from the Anglophone majority – the French language, the Roman Catholic church, and indigenous rural village Quebec mores and folkways – were all, in one way or another, ultimately unsatisfactory to the intellectuals and elites who were the self-appointed culture-producers. As to language (with French language here standing metonymically for French culture, as well), a perception of France as the "neglectful mother," combined with a sense of inferiority to metropolitan (i.e., Parisian) French – abetted by the typical ungraciousness of the metropolis's speech community to all other variants (Marseilles or Nancy, much less Montreal or Quebec City) – rendered this suboptimal. And the Church, the bulwark of Francophone Canadian identity and solidarity through the nineteenth century, struck many liberal or leftist intellectuals by the late-middle twentieth century as theocratic, rigid, and reactionary. As to authentic, indigenous village culture, demographically Quebec was increasingly urban by the 1970s; the village as prototypically Quebecois was already a thing of the past. And besides, rural Quebecois – the genuine Quebecois "folk" – romanticism aside, were in the end villagers with wooden shoes and fiddle dances – folkish – *rustre* after all. So the intellectuals were caught in a bind: How could they construct a satisfying culture while rejecting the "real" culture that surrounded them? In the radical 1960s one solution was to follow Fanon (1986) and declare Quebecois culture a "culture born of oppression," a culture thus shared with other victims of colonial oppression, like that of the Algerians. (The colonial oppressors were Anglophone Canadians. However, comparing themselves to Algerians, just out of a very bloody war, had limited widespread political appeal.) But if the intellectuals bickered and faltered, the politicians knew exactly what to do. First gaining provincial power under the Parti Quebecois in the 1976 elections, one of the things they did was to empower a Ministry of Culture, charged with bureaucratically *creating* a culture for the ministry's *fonctionnaires* to administer. Gaining further power, as the 1980s and 1990s went on, the party spearheaded a move to separate from Canada. Ultimately they (re)turned to the French language to make their points. Within Quebec, they and the revivified culture-makers enacted a series of anti-English language and educational laws that have seemed unacceptably repressive to liberal champions of individual rights, as well as very frightening to the so-called *allophones* – the non-native French or English speakers, the new immigrants in increasing numbers, and aboriginal, First Nation, peoples. Separatists later charged that it was these people (especially new immigrants in Montreal) that provided the very thin margin of votes that defeated the last sovereignty referendum in 1995.

Works such as Handler's show some of the complications in connecting "culture" to "ethnicity." They are not isomorphic concepts, either conceptually (deployed by the analyst), or practically, as used by ethnic actors, politicians, and entrepreneurs. Objectively speaking, it can take a very little bit of cultural content – cultural *difference* – to mark off one ethnic group from another. As Cohen's

Nigerian work demonstrated decades ago, the "choice" of that content (from fictive kinship to religion; from language to dress) can be labile in the extreme. Ethnicity utilizes bits of culture that have been "objectified" by political actors, projected publicly, and then resourcefully deployed by actors for political purposes (Avruch 1998:29–31). "People who live their culture unproblematically tend not to be ethnic in the proper sense of the word," Eller remarks (1999:11), and he goes on to argue that ethnic groups in conflict are not fighting *about* culture but *with* culture. Indeed, this is one reason (among several) why one must treat the "clash of civilizations" approach to new world order ethnic or national conflict with some skepticism (e.g., Huntington, 1996).

Works such as Handler's can also be refracted through the lens that the older perspective for understanding ethnicity provides. One thing that comes into focus is power. Holding Barth and Cohen, on the one hand, and Handler, on the other, in the same frame, it would appear that the instrumentalists' view of ethnicity in effect presaged that of the postmodern constructivists, at least with respect to the transformable nature of ethnicity's cultural content. This is so because both regard ethnicity, whether viewed as resource or discourse, as a way that parties organize in order to contest with one another for power. Both see ethnicity as necessarily implying social conflict. The Barthian instrumentalist is likely to see all this as groups occupying some socio-ecological "niche" and in conflict for the resources of the niche. The postmodernist is likely to see groups as social congeries in more-or-less frangible states, competing for the fruits of hegemony, control over the dominant discourse of the society. The constructivist dismisses Barth's instrumentality for its ethnocentric "market model" of ethnic conflict. Seeking rather to reintegrate expressivist concerns with identity with instrumentalist ones of profit, the constructivist argues for the "constituting effect on individuals" of ethnic conflict (Fox 1990:6). From the contest flows identity. But does not the concern with power remain central to both views? Does it matter if the vocabulary is hegemony or market-share? Curriculum or cola nuts? Why fight to control the discourse if not to control the resources? (Gramsci *was* a Marxist.)

Looked at from the perspective of power, there is perhaps little – or less than one thought – to differentiate the postmodern from the instrumentalist view of ethnicity – or, indeed, the parameters of ethnic conflict in the "post-industrial" and "pre-post-industrial" (!) eras. Power seems to remain the obdurate social primitive in all manner of ethnic calculi. But there is another variable – hinted at in Handler's analysis – that perhaps serves better to distinguish ethnicity and ethnic conflict in the new world disorder, and that is the intervention of state (or, as we shall see, suprastate) bureaucracy in the matter of ethnic identity construction. There is, I shall argue in the last part of this paper, a new super-ethnic category in the making, one which transcends the traditional particularist confines of blood, cult, and shared history, but yet is crucial for their articulation. I refer to the category of international refugee, created on the one hand as a fall-out of the contests of states – this being an old process – and on the other, and rather more recently, by the new world order of UN and nongovernmental organizations (NGOs), in developing concert with the militaries of yet other states, and all in the context of new, twenty-first century political-cum-bureaucratic briefs like "conflict resolution," "peacekeeping," and "humanitarian assistance."

IV

In his prescient analysis of ethnicity first published in 1975, which was just about the time the term itself was making its way into the social scientist's lexicon, Harold Isaacs (who himself preferred the term "basic group identity," which never quite caught on) points to the forces which, since 1945, made ethnic conflict an inevitably increasing part of the world's political order. The main impetus came from the collapse of power systems which had hitherto held together disparate clusters of people, the collapse acting as a sort of political centrifuge that broke the clusters apart and sent them flying off in different directions. One result is what is today called "transnational" or "globalized" institutions or personnel. Isaacs mentions four sorts of power systems that seemed to be disintegrating in the post-1945 world: post-colonial, post-imperial, post-revolutionary, and post-illusionary.

Postcolonial. In Africa, for example, most of the national boundaries were drawn by Europeans in Berlin in 1884. The retreating Europeans (some of whom, the final backwash, I ran into in Morocco in 1975) left behind them African nationalist movements that cross-cut older tribal/ethnic identities, just as the boundaries of the new African states sundered some ethnic groups and bound others together. Biafra, the Ogaden War, the Polisario, etc., all come out as unfinished business in the wake of European colonialism.

Postimperial. Some time after the last European troops left, and the Colonial Office disbanded, the "periphery" returned the favor of colonialism, in some measure, and came as immigrants to the old colonial centers: North Africans to France, Moluccans to Holland, Indians and Pakistanis to the UK. This movement was connected to broader labor-flows, for example, the phenomenon of the guest laborer that also brought Turks to Germany, and Sicilians to Scandinavia, a not quite postimperial manifestation. As their numbers grew and certain aspects of their institutions and practices, especially those connected to Islam, became more visible, these migrants engendered ethnic and racial conflict in Northern and Western European democratic states, the very sort of conflict that in the past, *pace* Myrdal, could be ascribed to the United States alone.

Postrevolutionary. Here, in 1975, Isaacs seems most dismissible, as he predicted the collapse of the USSR and even China, the "revolutionary" states of modern times, the spinning off of their holdings (eastern Europe and the Soviet republics) and conflict among their minority "nationalities." From our perspective in 2001 (post-Ukraine and post-Chechnya, with Tiananman Square as unfinished business), Isaacs seems most prescient.

Postillusionary. Here, finally, Isaacs turns his eye on the United States, the "illusion" he refers to being that of white supremacy, and the progressive weakening of American apartheid since Truman integrated the Army, Eisenhower sent troops to Little Rock, and Johnson pushed forward the Civil Rights legislation of 1964. Following this came black power, black nationalism, and the ethnic revivals of the late 1960s and 1970s, which changed American society and would make of ethnicity and ethnic conflict, for the two decades since the publication of Isaacs's book, the hottest areas of social scientific inquiry.

For all his prescience, however, Isaacs did not see a fifth (post-1945 and specific-ally, post-1989, end-of-the-Cold War) dynamic: that ethnic conflict (in the post-colonial world, especially) would never stay isolated in the periphery. Partly as a precipitate of postimperial forces, which physically brought the lately decolonized to the centers, ethnic clashes in the unstable periphery threatened increasingly to involve the old colonial/imperial centers in their violent conflict. For example, disturbances in Algeria send yet more Algerians fleeing to France, which exacer-bates inter-ethnic tensions there. Chechnya, once regarded as the "tombstone of Russian power" (Lieven 1998), retains a destabilizing potential for subsequent governments. Indonesian repressions sends Ambionese to Holland. The reabsorp-tion of Hong Kong into the PRC precipitates a potential immigration crisis for the UK and reconfigures the true worth of a Commonwealth passport overnight. Often enough, the disturbances in the periphery are played out with acts of terror-ism in the cities of the old center. Yet even if they wanted to, the old imperial centers find it difficult to disengage entirely from their peripheries, for the formerly colonized now reappear not just as labor migrants but as political refugees, as ethnic problems waiting to happen. One response to this has been to declare immigration crises and tighten increasingly restrictive immigration laws: keep the refugees out. Linked to this is the rising electoral success of ultra-nationalist (and some argue, racist or proto-fascist) parties throughout western and central Europe.

When things get really bad – when the warlords and the civil war disrupt the harvest and famine comes; when the ethnic cleansing produces mass graves and the new world order of concentration camps – they also appear, thanks to CNN and satellite communications, on the television screens of citizens throughout Europe and North America. Especially the children appear. Now the visibility of refugees presents a different sort of problem for the governments of the center. Keeping them out is only a partial solution. (And neither the Europeans nor the North Americans have been overly successful in keeping them out.) For now, one's own citizens clamor that they be helped. And one's own security analysts argue that the best way to keep them out is to address the problems "out there," in the first place. Thus is born, along with new bureaucracies, the new international organizations (IO and NGO) and large-scale humanitarian assistance, as well as a new role for the formerly disengaged center: "peacekeeping operations," under the UN or some regional (NATO, OAU, ECOWAS, etc.) consortium. Here military operations get blended with an emerging rhetoric of conflict resolution (e.g., Durch 1993, Charters 1994). When that circle cannot be squared – and it is not easily squarable on the face of it, as Somalia demonstrated (Clarke and Herbst 1997) – its critics call the re-engagement neocolonialism. But that is hardly the whole story, if only because many of the so-called neocolonialists seem on the whole more Conrad than Kipling; they seem deeply conflicted and unenthusiastic about the task.

V

In some sense, of course, the refugee is as old as a neolithic clash between any two groups, in which one group vanquishes the other, destroys or occupies its habitation, and thus compels the other to flee to some new place. These refugees melded themselves into existing settlements, or started new ones, or perished somewhere between the two. This sort of refugee is as old as history. But the modern sense of refugee entails the state system, and refers to the human precipitate of the conflict dynamics of states – inter-state warfare, intra-state terrorism and repression, state collapse. There are no longer any land bridges to cross over to empty continents. The territories to which these refugees flee are no longer the virgin forests of the neolithic; they are usually territories that are in the domain of some other state, and more often than not already occupied by citizens of that state. Refugees may come as individuals or as family units to their place of refuge, and some are even admitted under special provisions of the refuge-state's immigration law (the so-called political refugee). But the dynamics of state conflict or state collapse mean that refugees often flee en masse, and must be dealt with en masse. The emergent socioecological setting (the niche, in Barthian terms) for this flight is the refugee camp, administered by a congeries of new bureaucracies – governmental and nongovernmental, public and private, but most often and paradigmatically by the United Nations High Commissioner for Refugees (UNHCR). Increasingly, too, the refugee camps are part of larger third-party operations organized under the rubric of peacekeeping, humanitarian assistance, and conflict resolution.

What are some of the implications for ethnic conflict of these new sociopolitcal forms?

First, these forms are the hitherto neglected manifestations of ethnic conflict in the post-industrial world, the newest, post-Cold War extensions of what Isaacs called postcolonial and postimperial disturbances. Although played out most often in the former periphery, these forms represent ways in which the centers get – willy-nilly and not always with great enthusiasm – re-engaged in their collapsing affairs. The newest form of engagement with ethnic conflicts outside the centers is in the form of "peace-keeping" operations, in which militaries are invited to reinvent themselves. The newest areas of the military crafts are "Operations Other Than War" (OOTW).

Second, the refugee camps themselves are veritable hothouses for the forced-growth and nurturance of ethnic (or national) identities. Probably the paradigmatic case is that of the Palestinians, who were also one of the first refugee groups to have been administered by the UN, under the United Nations Relief Works Agency for Palestinians Refugees (UNRWA), established in 1948 as part of the first Arab–Israeli armistice. Palestinian camps scattered in Gaza, the West Bank, and Lebanon provided the fighters for the most militant PLO factions such as Fatah, as well its ideological elite. (Financial resources came from elsewhere.) Schools – crucial elements in ethnogenesis – turned out the fiercest anti-Zionists and the most committed Palestinian nationalists. Increasingly, schools are combining with other social service-providing institutions under Islamist influences, like Hamas, thus marrying Palestinian nationalism to Islamism. The Palestinian state may well be the first state in history whose underlying governance structures were partially built on the formative framework of the refugee camp.

Although paradigmatic, Palestinians are hardly the only example of this. Work by Liisa Malkki (1990, 1995) on Hutu refugees from Burundi in Tanzania in the

1980s contrasts those living in organized camps with those who chose to live among Tanzanians in the nearby city. She points that the "camp Hutus," by creating and fostering a compelling "mythico-history" (as Malkki calls it) of their relations with the Tutsi and their victimization, maintained a strong sense of "pure" Hutu identity, while the city-dwellers sought to assimilate, even to inter-marry with Tanzanians. The camp Hutus strongly stressed their eventual return to Burundi (and, alas, their planned revenge on the Tutsis), while the city Hutus did not. Moreover, the camp Hutus directed some of their greatest hostility against their city-dwelling co-ethnics, whom they regarded as traitors and cowards.

If, as I said at the beginning of this essay, ethnicity is a constructed affair, then one of the prime sites of its construction is the refugee camp. Moreover, considering the range of political goals that ethnic groups can aspire to, the camp is especially important for constructing the sort of ethnicity that feeds overtly nationalistic movements, those claiming the existence of a unique *nation* entitled to sovereign control over a territory: a *state* (see Smith 1991, Connor 1994).

But more than this – and the third implication for ethnic conflict – *refugee* itself is a newly constructed category and, as my comparison of Palestinian and Hutu indicates, it can be construed as a sort of super-ethnicity. For it may be used to constitute a social group that is closely bounded, ecologically situated, with a shared history (oppression, persecution, ethnic/religious identity), a shared present (famine, isolation, uncertainty, the "wards" of UN and NGOs and reluctant host refuge-states) and shared visions of the future (a state of their own, a return to a homeland, revenge taken on their oppressors). What is also shared, increasingly, is their formative exposure to the "culture" of the "international community" – the militaries, IOs and NGOs – which certifies refugee status and creates, supports, and administers the camps.

Finally, to return at last to the issue of culture, one might ask what the "cultural content" of the category refugee is. Surely the Palestinian and the Hutu and the Bosnian Muslim do not share the same "culture," do they? Of course not, or at least not in the way "culture" was traditionally bestowed. But in another way, they do. To a great extent, it is the culture shared by all those unfortunate enough to be the human precipitate of the struggle or collapse of states. And it is a cultural "content" shared by dint of the shared cultures of the post-industrial institutions and bureaucracies (UN, NGO, PVO, ICRC, USAID, OXFAM, etc. etc.) – as well as the various "aid industries" (see Hancock 1989, Maren 1997) – that conjoin to create and sustain them, and each other.

References

Anderson, Benedict. *Imagined Communities*. London: Verso, 1983.
Avruch, Kevin. *American Immigrants in Israel: Social Identities & Change*. Chicago: University of Chicago Press, 1981.
Avruch, Kevin. *Culture and Conflict Resolution*. Washington D.C.: United States Institute of Peace Press, 1998.

Barth, Fredrik, ed. *Ethnic Groups and Boundaries*. Boston: Little, Brown, 1969.

Charters, David, ed. *Peacekeeping and the Challenge of Civil Conflict Resolution*. Halifax: Centre for Conflict Studies, University of New Brunswick, 1994.

Clarke, Walter and J. Herbst. *Learning from Somalia: The Lessons of Armed Humanitarian Intervention*. Boulder: Westview Press, 1997.

Cohen Abner. *Custom and Politics in Urban Africa*. Berkeley: University of California Press, 1969.

Connor, Walker. *Ethnonationalism: The Quest for Understanding*. Princeton: Princeton University Press, 1994.

Durch, William, ed. *The Evolution of UN Peacekeeping*. New York: St. Martin's, 1993.

Eller, Jack David. *From Culture to Ethnicity to Conflict*. Ann Arbor: University of Michigan Press, 1999.

Fanon, Frantz. *The Wretched of the Earth*. New York: Grove Press, 1986.

Fox, Richard, ed. *Nationalist Ideologies and the Production of National Culture*. Washington, D.C.: American Anthropological Association, 1990.

Hancock, Graham. *Lords of Poverty: The Power, Prestige & Corruption of the International Aid Business*. New York: Atlantic Monthly Press, 1989.

Handler, Richard. *Nationalism and the Politics of Culture in Quebec*. Madison: University of Wisconsin Press, 1988.

Hobsbawm, Eric. "Introduction: Inventing Traditions." In, *The Invention of Tradition*. (E. Hobsbawm & T. Ranger, eds.). Cambridge: Cambridge University Press, 1983.

Huntington, Samuel. *The Clash of Civilizations and the Remaking of World Order*. New York: Simon and Schuster, 1996.

Isaacs, Harold. *Idols of the Tribe: Group Identity & Political Change*. Cambridge: Harvard University Press, 1975.

Lee, Richard B. *The Dobe! !Kung*. New York: Holt, Rinehart & Winston, 1984.

Lieven, Anatol. *Chechnya: Tombstone of Russian Power*. New Haven: Yale University Press, 1998.

Malkki, Liisa. "Context and Consciousness: Local Conditions for the Production of Historical and National Thought among Hutu Refugees in Tanzania." In, *Nationalist Ideologies and the Production of National Culture*. (R. Fox, ed.). Washington, D.C.: American Anthropological Association, 1990.

——. *Purity and Exile: Violence, Memory, and National Cosmology among Hutu Refugees in Tanzania*. Chicago: University of Chicago Press, 1995.

Maren, Michael. *The Road to Hell: The Ravaging Effects of Foreign Aid and International Charity*. New York: The Free Press, 1997.

Narroll, Raoul. "Ethnic Unit Classification." *Current Anthropology* 5:283–312, 1964.

Skidmore, Thomas E. *Black Into White: Race and Nationality in Brazilian Thought*. New York: Oxford University Press, 1974.

Smith, Anthony. *National Identity*. Reno: University of Nevada Press, 1991.

Van den Berghe, Pierre. *The Ethnic Phenomenon*. New York: Praeger, 1987.

6 Postindustrialism, Postmodernism, and Ethnic Conflict

Anthony H. Richmond

The terms 'postindustrial' and 'postmodern' are sometimes used synonymously, but it is more appropriate to confine the former to the technological and economic developments that have occurred in the second half of the twentieth century, and the latter to the social and cultural changes that have taken place. It is debatable whether the postindustrial revolution (consequent upon the use of advanced technologies such as nuclear energy, jet propulsion, computers, automation, and telecommunication) is a radical departure from the changes initiated by the earlier Industrial Revolution or simply a logical continuation of trends that were already evident in the nineteenth century (Kumar 1978). In either case, it is clear that there has been a tremendous acceleration in the rate of change, consequent upon these technological advances. By the same token, it is arguable that contemporary societies that are part of the global capitalist system, as well as those in the less developed world, are in a transitional phase. Whether moving from traditional to modern or from modern to late modern, there is a potential for conflict arising from competing interests and values.

Edward Tiryakian, discussing the global crisis in the mid-1980s, showed that there has been a geographic shift in the centre of modernization from North America to East Asia. He noted that the deindustrialization of large zones within advanced Western societies was matched by the relocation of manufacturing investment in Third World countries and that the information processing revolution led to new modes of production: 'the global crisis is one not only of decline and destructuration but also one of underlying currents of restructuration' (Tiryakian 1984:125). The last decade (1981–90) has been one of those critical epochs that has profound implications for international migration, now and in the future.

Although interdependent, the global *ecological* system is analytically distinct from the global *state* system, the *military* order, the *information* system and world *capitalism* (Giddens 1985; Robertson 1990). There has always been a global system of commerce extending from the Mediterranean to the far north and from Ireland to the far east. What is new is the emergence of a global system of *production*, as well as commerce and communications. This is now truly universal. In its present form, this world system originated with the Eurocentred mercantile adventurers of the sixteenth and seventeenth centuries. Their exploits linked the New World with the Old, and led to the agrarian and industrial revolutions in western Europe. This paved the way for imperialist expansion and the beginnings of modern capitalism (Wallerstein 1974). Today, however, the global economy is multicentred and dominated by what has been called the ILE (i.e., the interlinked economies of the United States, Europe, and Japan, together with rapidly expanding economies such as those of Taiwan, Hong Kong, and Singapore). The interdependence of these economies is such that, as in chaos theory, a small movement anywhere can trigger a recession, a stockmarket crash, or a massive movement of capital and foreign exchange from one country to another. One of the major contradictions inherent in the current process of global change is that, notwithstanding residual protectionism (particularly in the agricultural sphere), money, goods, and information flow relatively freely across borders, but *people do not*. While economists examine the consequences of lowering barriers to trade, removing protectionism, and seeking ways of promoting prosperity through greater sensitivity to consumer preferences, sociologists and political scientists draw attention to the closing of doors to immigrants and refugees, and what Alan Dowty calls 'the contemporary assault on freedom of movement' between one country or continent and another (Dowty 1987).

Industrialism and Postindustrialism

Pre-industrial societies were typically small, closely-knit, and territorially-bounded communities based upon kinship. Tonnies ([1887] 1957) used the term *Gemeinschaft* to describe such a system of social relations. Relatively undifferentiated in terms of social position, such communities exhibited only an elementary division of labour based on age and gender. Status and political power were ascribed by birth and descent. There was little geographic or social mobility. Governed by orally transmitted traditions, such societies were slow to change. Beginning gradually with the iron and bronze ages and accelerating with the application of steam-generated power to transportation and manufacturing, the impact of industrialization transformed such communities into more complex social systems based upon association or *Gesellschaft*.

These new forms of social organization were superimposed on the old, transforming them without always eliminating them altogether. Family, kinship, neighbourhood, and a sense of community based on shared language, religion, and loyalty to traditional customs persisted, even when the effects of urbanization and industrialization introduced different ways and created new demands. Formal organizations, bureaucratic systems of government, and economic associations with complex systems of production and distribution created new classes with both cooperative and antagonistic interests. Simple barter and economic exchange gave way to complex markets facilitated by the development of money as a currency and a measure of the price, not only of goods and services but of labour itself. Through saving and investment, money became a source of power. When contracts were enforceable by law, the state became the agency through which property was protected. Inherited title to land and property survived the feudal system in which it originated, but a new bourgeois class of business persons, merchants, and entrepreneurs grew in size and importance. In the nineteenth century, the creation of the limited liability company with multiple investors brought industrial capitalism as we know it today. It became the dominant form of economic organization.

Again, earlier forms persisted, particularly in the less developed regions of the world still dependent on subsistence agriculture. Meanwhile, the political and economic expansion of industrial capitalist societies seeking abundant supplies of energy, raw materials, and cheap labour led to the imperial domination and colonization of whole continents.

Although the concept was used by earlier writers, the term 'postindustrial' entered the sociological lexicon in the 1960s and was popularized in the writings of David Riesman (1958), Daniel Bell (1973), Amitai Etzioni (1968), Alan Touraine ([1969], 1971) and Alvin Toffler (1970). As well as recognizing the impact of advanced technologies, these writers anticipated significant social changes, not all of which have been realized in the form that they expected. For example, Riesman expected that the increased industrial productivity resulting from new inventions would give rise to a leisure-oriented society, liberating people from the more arduous tasks associated with earlier phases of industrialism. Similar utopian visions were projected by others who were inclined to attribute benign consequences to technological innovation (Frankel 1987). In reality, the second half of the twentieth century has been characterized by higher labour force participation rates (particularly by women), cyclical economic fluctuations, and chronically high unemployment rates in most late capitalist societies. In other words, the 'leisure' anticipated by Riesman has been unevenly distributed and largely involuntary.

Daniel Bell (1973) forecast a shift from employment in primary and secondary industries into the tertiary and quaternary sectors of the economy. In this respect, a distinction between service occupations and service industries is important. As Kumar (1978) pointed out, service occupations were widely held in the nineteenth century, particularly by women in domestic service. Many of the occupations currently filled by women are simply the same jobs transferred to a new site, as in mass food processing and distribution, office cleaning, and hotel services. However, there has also been a growth in industries that are more closely linked to the technological innovations of postindustrialism. They include financial and management services, information processing, telecommunications and media, together with the education and health industries. All of these industries have a range of occupations requiring different levels of skill. As well as a professional and technocratic élite, there are also more routinized jobs (such as data entry and keypunching), although these may still require a level of education that traditional service occupations did not. Altogether service sector jobs in advanced industrial societies have doubled in the period 1960–90, while the share of manufacturing jobs has fallen to only one in five of all occupations. Agricultural employment is now only 4 percent of all jobs (Akyeampong and Winters 1993). Contemporary labour markets have become global in extent. They are also highly stratified and segmented. Not only is there a hierarchy in terms of status and rewards, but skills have become less transferable. Prolonged periods of education and training are a prerequisite for employment in specialized fields. Furthermore, labour unions and professional organizations are protective of their privileged access to employment. Credentialism governs hiring and there are barriers to the employment of those who lack the appropriate qualification or local experience.

A theme common to a number of writers concerning postindustrialism is the importance of applied science and technology and the emergence of a knowledge-based system. This, in turn, creates a class of information managers, technocrats, and decision makers with exceptional power to influence opinion and determine policies, leading to a 'technology of knowledge' and a 'programmed society' (Etzioni 1968; Touraine [1969] 1971). Peter Drucker (1993:19–47) described 'post-capitalist' society as one that has become a 'knowledge society'. While it is probably premature to speak of the end of capitalism, it is true that applied science and the 'application of knowledge to knowledge' has generated profound economic, political, and social changes. Among them are transformations in the characteristic forms of social organization.

The impact of structural change is most evident in transportation, communication, and the transmission of information and images. Beginning with the invention of printing and the spread of mass literacy, on the one hand, and the building of railways, steamships, and, in due course, the airplane, on the other, transportation and communications have been revolutionized. Marshall McLuhan was one of the first to recognize the importance of these developments, pointing out that 'when information moves at the speed of signals in the central nervous system, man is confronted with the obsolescence of all earlier forms of acceleration, such as road and rail. What emerges is a total field of inclusive awareness. The patterns of psychic and social adjustment become irrelevant' (McLuhan 1964:103).

I have argued elsewhere (Richmond 1969, 1988) that these postindustrial developments have important consequences for education, migration, and ethnic relations. Automation makes paid learning, experimentation, and programming the principal sources of increased productivity. All aspects of production, consumption, and recreation are rendered incidental to communication and the electronic feedback of information. Higher education and technical training, once the privilege of a minority, became prerequisites for all but the most menial forms of employment. International (and internal) migration becomes a multiway process of exchange based upon ease of access to information and transportation, in which net gains and losses of population in particular localities are a small proportion of the gross movements involved in labour migration, business, and tourism. The concept of transilient migration, originally limited to the highly qualified professional and managerial strata, is now applicable to a much wider range of movers whose permanence in any one locality is neither necessary nor expected, given the ease with which return and remigration can occur. The predominant mode of coaptation of migrants in postindustrial societies is active mobilization, i.e., a 'dynamic interaction between motile individuals and collectivities giving rise to information flow and feed-back effecting greater control over material and human resources' (Richmond 1969:281).

The instantaneous communication made possible through telephones, fax machines, satellite links, videotapes, etc., means that the maintenance of ethnic identity is no longer dependent on a territorial community (*Gemeinschaft*) or on formal organizations (*Gesellschaft*) but on networks (*Verbindungsnetzschaft*). Ethnic links are maintained with others of similar language and cultural background throughout the world (Richmond 1988:167–82). The political, economic, and social consequences of globalization are central features of both the postindustrial and postmodern revolution.

Globalization

The geography of labour migration is related to globalization and structural changes that are changing the international division of labour:

> The globalization of international labor migration is manifest in two ways. Firstly, all countries now engage in migration systems growing in size and complexity and producing an increasing diversity of flows. Second, many of the processes that create and drive these systems operate on a worldwide basis, the consequence of economic globalization, capital mobility, the activities of international business corporations, and the widespread realization by governments that human resources can be traded for profit like any other resource. (Salt 1992:1080)

Remittance from overseas workers are an important source of foreign currency for many developing countries. These transfers contribute to material development of the countries concerned, contributing to education, welfare, improving the status of women, and contributing to infrastructure building. They also facilitate debt repayment (Stahl 1988).

In terms of trade and commerce, transnational exchanges of goods have always occurred. Beginning in the Mediterranean and Asia Minor, the world system gradually spread to the rest of the globe with the incorporation of the New World into a system of exploitation and colonization (Wallerstein 1974). Money as a medium of exchange was universalized, first through the adoption of a gold standard, later through international banking and money markets, and, by 1986, through the electronic linkage of capital, stock exchanges, and commodity markets into a single system operating twenty-four hours a day. The so-called 'big bang' symbolized the economic integration of a world system (Dezalay 1990). There remained internal conflicts and contradictions between the proponents of free trade and those who continue to seek protection for agricultural and manufacturing industries in particular countries and regions. An international division of labour, with substantial inequalities in the distribution of wealth and in the level of technological and economic development, persists despite the relative integration of the world economic system. In turn, this gives rise to mass migrations of labour from the less to the more developed regions (Appleyard 1988).

The movement of people is also as old as history itself. From nomadic hunters and pastoralists to the inhabitants of space stations, human migration is a universal experience. Early traders, military invaders, explorers, religious evangelists (of many different faiths), pilgrims, travelling entertainers, pirates, and highway robbers have carried languages and cultures around the globe. In more recent times, immigrants, refugees, guest workers, tourists, drug peddlers, journalists, students, and scientists have been added to the growing body of motile individuals and groups. The revolution in transportation and communication that began with the railway and the steamship, accelerated with the automobile, the airplane, and the telegraph, became a dominant factor in the contemporary world system with the spread of radio, TV, telecommunications, satellites, and spacecraft. These new technologies not only convey people and information, they are also the vehicles through which political ideologies, alternative lifestyles, oppositional values, and social movements are spread. Appadurai (1990:295–310) calls these various dimensions of the globalization process ethnoscapes, technoscapes, finanscapes, mediascapes, and ideoscapes. He emphasizes that these are social constructs 'inflected very much by the historical, linguistic and political situatedness of different sorts of actors: nation-states, multinationals, diasporic communities, as well as subnational groupings and movements...' (1990:296). One could add to this list mediscapes as the universal consequences of the AIDS epidemic unfold. 'Thus the global health system is only the promissory side of a world disease system. Each generates the other. Here, once again, there is a potential for a rebarbarization of the global order through quarantine orders, immunization control and racism – witness the construction of Afro-AIDS' (O'Neill 1990:338).

Metaphorically, the global system can be understood as an immense spider's web of interlinked networks, without a spider in the middle! It would be tempting to consider the position of secretary-general of the United Nations as the spider at the centre of the web, but this is clearly not the case. In the absence of a system of world government, there is no central direction. States operate with a significant degree of autonomy, even though there is clearly a structure of dominance resulting from unequal economic, political, and military power. Nevertheless, there are many cross-cutting ties and the influence of the UN has increased considerably in recent years. The web of interlinked networks has many sectors (see figure 6.1). They include the interlinked economies of various countries, their political systems and diplomatic corps, as well as a variety of other networks, together with those of non-governmental and non-economic organizations representing various interests, ranging from religious faiths and humanitarian agencies to subversive political groups and terrorist organizations. Superimposed on all of these are the interpersonal networks based on kinship, friendship, ethnoreligious affiliation, and shared interests. The ability to maintain these links across long distances has been greatly assisted by modern communications technology....

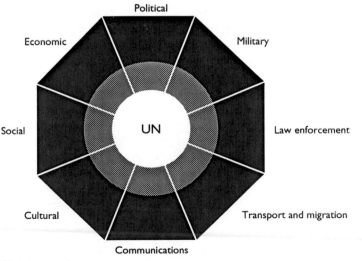

Figure 6.1   Global networks

In 'mapping the global condition', Robertson (1990:27) suggests that the period since 1960 has been a 'phase of uncertainty'. This phase of globalization has brought inherent contradictions arising from the inclusion of Third World countries in the global system, the increase in global institutions and media influence, problems of multiculturalism and polyethnicity, concern with human-kind as a 'species community', and interest in world civil society and world citizenship. The resolution of these contradictions and their consequent conflicts will determine whether an integrated global economy, polity, and society can become a reality. Postindustrialism, globalization, the communications revolution, and a resurgence of nationalism are related phenomena. In turn, they are connected to the political, social, and cultural movement that has been labelled 'postmodern'.

Postmodernism

The terms 'industrial' and 'postindustrial' refer to technological and economic developments. 'Traditional', 'modern', 'late modern', and 'postmodern' describe the social and cultural changes that are concomitant with the economic and tech-nological ones, although they are not necessarily predetermined by them in any absolute way. There is scope for considerable selectivity and variation in the ways in which particular individuals and groups respond to the challenges presented by globalization. Postmodernism is a philosophical and cultural movement. It is a reaction against previous forms of expression in art, architecture, literature, music, and theatre. It emphasizes the uniqueness of particular cultures and the relativity of aesthetic and value judgements. Its ideas have also been influential in the social sciences, giving rise to considerable controversy concerning the validity of theories and methods that claim 'scientific' or universal applicability. Some writers con-tinue to defend the positivist view that there can be a 'natural science of society', but even they agree that contemporary sociology does not claim such a status (Turner 1992:156–76)....

Postmodernism rejects the view that postindustrialism and globalization must lead to cultural homogenization through the spread of capitalism and mass markets. Although the instrumental forms of advanced technology may become universal, their expressive and symbolic meanings are used selectively, transformed, and adapted to the needs and interests of local communities. 'Indigenous cultural values shape the transformations that external forces engender and the ironies and resistances they generate' (Coombe 1991:198). If this is true of non-Western soci-eties, it may also apply to the cultural minorities within Western societies whose voices are being heard and responded to as never before. Frederic Jameson (1991:17) makes this point when he states that 'if the ideas of a ruling class were once the dominant (or hegemonic) ideology of bourgeois society, the advanced capitalist countries today are now a field of stylistic and discursive heterogeneity without a norm'. The micropolitics of gender, ethnicity, race and religion – that is, the politics of difference – ensure that new social and linguistic codes are more freely expressed. In turn, this raises the question whether 'anything goes'.

Taken to extremes, postmodernism leans towards nihilism and the rejection of all claims to knowledge as 'truth'. Objective truths are replaced by hermeneutic truths, which are entirely subjective and relative to the point of view of the interpreter. This argument fails to distinguish between instrumental and expressive knowledge. As Gellner suggests, scientific knowledge 'has proved so overwhelmingly powerful, economically, militarily, administratively, that all societies have to make their peace with it and adopt it' (Gellner 1992:61). However, this still leaves fundamental questions concerning human rights and political organization in dispute. Issues such as private property ownership, territorial claims, torture and the death penalty, the status of women, the rights of minorities, the preservation of lifestyles, the survival of languages, the practice of religion, and freedom of expression are caught in the paradox of universalism versus particularism. Whose values are to prevail? What if the values in question are themselves contradictory? How does one respond to the claims of fundamentalists (of whatever religious or political persuasion) who insist upon imposing their particular ideas and practices on others, by force if necessary, or of eliminating, through expulsion or genocide, those who are different? Such ideological fanaticism is one of the contributory factors in the spread of ethnic conflict today.

Ethnic Conflict

Ethnolinguistic and ethnoreligious heterogeneity by themselves are not a sufficient cause of conflict. In fact, I have argued that 'the complex communication networks of postindustrial societies will create the possibility of a new type of society, free of both religious and ethnic intolerance, by permitting great diversity within the structure of a supra-national state' (Richmond 1988:181–2). However, I went on to say that such a transition would not come about without conflict, and that there would be reactionary movements reasserting national sovereignty and seeking to impose ethnic and cultural uniformity. Fishman (1989:18) makes the same point when he states that 'a characteristic of postmodern ethnicity is the stance of simultaneously transcending ethnicity as a complete, self-contained system, but of retaining it as a selectively preferred, evolving, participatory system.' Fishman then identifies some of the factors that hinder the emergence of such benign forms of ethnic identification. They include the communication barriers induced by language and the persistence of nationalism and its manipulation by power élites. Also important are the contributions that economic deprivation, political authoritarianism, and the rapid changes induced by modernization make towards the generation of civil strife. He concludes that 'linguistic homogeneity/heterogeneity cannot be considered an important independent predictor of civil strife when an extensive panoply of deprivational, modernizational and non-ideological authoritarianism predictors are also considered' (Fishman 1989:623). In other words, a multivariate model of ethnic conflict is required in which the role of underlying conditions, intervening variables, precipitating events, and interacting feedback effects of policy responses by local and international agencies are taken into account (Richmond 1988:3–10).

Ethnic conflict takes several different forms and sometimes combines different elements. Firstly, there are the state-supported systems of domination and exploitation of minorities that may lead eventually to the extermination of a people or their relegation to the geographic and social margins of the society. This was the typical fate of indigenous populations in the colonial era and continues in varying degrees today. Neocolonialism is often more economic than political in form, but does not preclude the state's connivance in the activities of national and transnational corporations exploiting natural and human resources. Secondly, there are the conflicts that result from the emancipatory efforts of such minorities endeavouring to reclaim territory and reassert human rights, with or without the support of outside agencies such as the UN, churches, and other minorities joining in the common cause. Thirdly, there are interstate conflicts in which questions of language, religion, and irredentist aspirations are involved. Fourthly, intrastate conflict (sometimes leading to civil war) may occur when interethnic antagonisms, competition for scarce resources, political power struggles, and ideological disputes fail to be resolved by other means, such as negotiation, conciliation, and the peace keeping efforts of outside bodies. Fifthly, various manifestations of ethnic nationalism give rise to overt conflict when other constraining factors are removed. The lifting of imperialist rule or the end of a totalitarian system of government may precipitate latent conflicts that have been held in check by the superior military power and ruthlessly suppressive measures used by the previously governing parties. Sectarian violence, communal conflict, civil wars, and independence movements may assert themselves under these conditions. Finally, there are the conflicts that arise as a consequence of past and present migrations, particularly the movements from less developed to more economically developed countries. Beginning with the movements of slaves and indentured labourers, and continuing to the present day with migrant workers and asylum applicants, such migrations have left substantial ethnocultural minorities in Europe, North America, and elsewhere. Originally sought after for their contribution to the labour force or welcomed as political refugees, such minorities may face severe opposition and demands for their repatriation during times of economic recession....

The idea of society as a whole is precisely what postmodernist critics are sceptical of. Who determines what constitutes the whole society and whose voices will be heard in a system that is structured in dominance and that is hierarchical, patriarchal, competitive, and motivated by profit? Drawing on Derrida, Foucault, and poststructuralist writers, Radhakrishnan (1990) relates questions of ethnic identity to questions of difference and the politics of heterogeneity. He uses the example of Jesse Jackson's candidacy for the leadership of the Democratic party in the United States, the so-called 'rainbow coalition' that tried to bring together a wide spectrum of minority groups. Jackson was seen as representing special interests whereas, Radhakrishnan claimed, 'Corporate, military, business, male, "White," "non-ethnic interests" were regarded as "natural," "general," "representative," ideologically neutral and value-free' (1990:66).

In Canada there are similar tensions and conflicts between particular minorities competing for power, status, and recognition, as well as between these minorities and the dominant or founding anglophone and francophone majorities. The failure of several decades of effort to achieve constitutional reform in Canada (as in Australia) is evidence of the difficulty of reconciling competing interests. It is also evidence of globalization as both countries restrict immigration, adopt concepts such as 'multiculturalism', endeavour to accommodate Aboriginal concerns, and come to terms with the realities of a global economy (Russell 1993:41–61). There are inherent contradictions between the emphasis on individual rights, including those relating to property, which stem from the Western liberal philosophy and the recognition of collective rights. Quebec Premier Robert Bourassa defended his use of the 'Notwithstanding' clause in the Canadian Charter of Rights on the grounds that he had a special responsibility to defend French language and culture in North America. Similar arguments have been used by Aboriginal representatives, who consider that the cultural traditions of some Aboriginal communities place more emphasis upon the communal sharing of land than upon individualistic ideas about property rights (Hiebert 1993; Turpel 1990).

The combined effects of postindustrialism, postmodernism, and globalization have generated a crisis of integration in contemporary societies (McLellan and Richmond 1994). There are systemic contradictions between homogeneity and universalism, on the one hand, and heterogeneity and particularism, on the other. In extreme circumstances, other countries could follow the example of Yugoslavia and disintegrate into warring factions, acting out historic animosities and seeking revenge for past and present atrocities. All forms of collectivism (ethnicism, nationalism, statism, regionalism, and globalism) are in dialectical contradiction to the thesis of individualism. It remains to be seen whether a new synthesis will take the form of humanism. Ernest Gellner rejects both postmodern and fundamentalist positions when he makes a case for 'enlightened rationalism' (Gellner 1992). He rightly points out that societies are systems of real constraints and not just systems of 'meanings', as hermeneutics would suggest. Unfortunately, however enlightened it may be, rationalism does not carry with it the emotional appeal – the gut reaction – that ethnic nationalism provides.

Anthony Giddens (1990:151–73) prefers the idea of 'utopian realism' as expressed in emancipatory social movements, such as those concerned with economic equality, participatory democracy, human rights, demilitarization, and the protection of the environment. In the face of high-consequence risks, we (i.e., humanity as a whole) must 'harness the juggernaut' in order to minimize the dangers of a 'runaway world'. Among those dangers are the growth of racism, the revival of Nazi movements in Europe and elsewhere, the perceived threat of mass migration and refugee flows, and the consequent imposition of forms of global apartheid.

References

Akyeampong, E. B., and J. Winters. 1993. 'International Employment Trends by Industry – a Note'. *Perspectives* (Summer):33–45.

Appadurai, A. 1990. 'Disjuncture and Difference in the Global Cultural Economy', in *Global Culture: Nationalism, Globalization and Modernity*, edited by M. Featherstone. London: Sage Publications.

Appleyard, R., ed. 1988. *International Migration Today, Vol. 1: Trends and Prospects*. Paris: UNESCO.

Bell, D. 1973. *The Coming of Post-industrial Society. A Venture in Social Forecasting*. London: Heinemann.

Coombe, R. J. 1991. 'Encountering the Postmodern: New Directions in Cultural Anthropology'. *Canadian Review of Anthropology and Sociology* 28, no. 2:188–205.

Dezalay, Y. 1990. 'The Big Bang and the Law: The Internationalization and Restructuration of the Legal Field'. In *Global Culture: Nationalism, Globalization and Modernity*, edited by M. Featherstone. London: Sage Publications.

Dowty, A. 1987. *Closed Borders: The Contemporary Assault on Freedom of Movement*. New Haven: Yale University Press.

Drucker, P. F. 1993. *Post-Capitalist Society*. New York: Harper Business.

Etzioni, A. 1968. *The Active Society: A Theory of Societal and Political Processes*. New York: Free Press.

Fishman, J. A. 1989. *Language and Ethnicity in Minority Socio-Linguistic Perspective*. Philadelphia: Multilingual Matters Ltd.

Frankel, B. 1987. *The Postindustrial Utopians*. Cambridge: Polity Press.

Gellner, E. 1992. *Postmodernism, Reason and Religion*. London: Routledge.

Giddens, A. 1985. *The Nation–State and Violence*, Vol. 2 of *A Contemporary Historical Materialism*. Cambridge: Polity Press.

—— 1990. *The Consequences of Modernity*. Cambridge: Polity Press.

Hiebert, J. 1993. 'Rights and Public Debate: The Limitations of the "Rights Must Be Paramount" Perspective'. *International Journal of Canadian Studies* 7–8: 117–36.

Jameson, F. 1991. *Postmodernism, or the Cultural Logic of Late Capitalism*. Durham: Duke University Press.

Kumar, K. 1978. *Prophecy & Progress: The Sociology of Industrial and Post-Industrial Society*. Harmondsworth: Penguin Books.

McLellan, J. and A. H. Richmond. 1994. 'Multiculturalism in Crisis: A Postmodern Perspective on Canada'. *Ethnic and Racial Studies* 17, no. 2 (October): 662–83.

McLuhan, M. 1964. *Understanding Media: The Extension of Man*. New York: McGraw Hill.

O'Neill, J. 1990. 'AIDS as a Globalizing Panic'. In *Global Culture: Nationalism, Globalization and Modernity*, edited by M. Featherstone. London: Sage Publications.

Radhakrishnan, R. 1990. 'Ethnic Identity and Post-Structuralist Difference'. In *The Nature and Context of Minority Discourse*, edited by A. R. JanMohamed and D. Lloyd. New York: Oxford University Press.

Richmond. A. H. 1969. 'Sociology of Migration in Industrial and Postindustrial Societies'. In *Sociological Studies 2: Migration*, edited by J. Jackson. Cambridge: Cambridge University Press.

——.1988. *Immigration and Ethnic Conflict*. London: Macmillan.

Riesman, D. 1958. *The Lonely Crowd: A Study of the Changing American Character*. New York: Doubleday.

Robertson, R. 1990. 'Mapping the Global Condition: Globalization as the Central Concept'. In *Global Culture: Nationalism, Globalization and Modernity*, edited by M. Featherstone. London: Sage Publications.

Russell, P. H. 1993. 'Attempting Macro Constitutional Change in Australia and Canada'. *International Journal of Canadian Studies* 7, no. 8:41–62.

Salt, J. 1992. 'The Future of International Labour Migration'. *International Migration Review* 26, no. 4: 1077–111.

Stahl, C., ed. 1988. *International Migration Today, Vol. 2: Emerging Issues*. Paris: UNESCO.

Tiryakian, E. A. 1984. 'The Global Crisis as an Interregnum of Modernity'. *International Journal of Comparative Sociology* 25, 1–2:123–30.

Toffler, A. 1970. *Future Shock*. New York: Random House.

Tonnies, F. [1887] 1957. *Community and Society*. Translated and edited by L. P. Loomis. East Lansing: Michigan State University Press.

Touraine, A. [1969] 1971. *The Post-Industrial Society*. New York: Random House.

Turner, J. H. 1992. 'The Promise of Positivism'. In *Postmodernism and Social Theory*, edited by S. Seidman and D. G. Wagner. Oxford: Basil Blackwell.

Turpel, M. E. 1990. 'Aboriginal Peoples and the Canadian Charter: Interpretive Monopolies, Cultural Differences'. In *Canadian Human Rights Year Book 1989–90*, edited by M. Boivin et al. Ottawa: Human Rights Research and Education Centre, University of Ottawa.

Wallerstein, I. 1974. *The Modern World System: Capitalist Agriculture and the Emergence of the European World Economy in the Sixteenth Century*. New York: Academic Press.

Part III

The Diversity of Ethnic Patterns

INTRODUCTION TO PART III

Significant contrasts in the dynamics of racial inequality between the United States and Brazil are only the beginning of the true complexity of racial and ethnic systems. Even within major continental regions the variety of ways in which individuals and groups perceive one another and interact is astoundingly diverse. Roger Lancaster demonstrates, in his ethnographic research in Nicaragua, how the small minority of individuals of African descent, concentrated in the Atlantic Coast area, reveals a complex pattern of colour consciousness and hierarchy that permeates the whole society. The preference for lighter skinned children can be found in everyday discourse and the association of whiteness with wealth and blackness with poverty is widespread. Lancaster explains that this is yet another example of the impact of colonialism, playing out in subtle variations long after the end of the colonial era. The symbolism of colour reflects the inequalities of power set off by the historical legacy of conquest, and generates a self-perpetuating system of prejudice and domination that is extremely difficult to change. If Nicaragua illustrates the insight of Foucault's conceptualization of power, it also demonstrates the difficulties of transforming such a deeply entrenched system of thought and behavior.

Another variation is provided by Dutch society that has generally been regarded as one of the more tolerant and stable systems of intergroup relations in Europe, if not the world. The historical record is mixed and while over the centuries the Dutch have displayed significant religious tolerance at home, their colonial practices were far from ideal. Pettigrew and Meertens set out to explain what appears to be a contradictory feature of the Dutch experience, what they call the *verzuiling puzzle*. Over a period of centuries, the Dutch developed a system in which separate communities, initially Protestants and Catholics, retained a high level of autonomy and separation, but compromised and cooperated through their ethnic elites. Such a "separate but equal" arrangement, according to most social science theories, should be a recipe for social disaster. However, the Dutch seemed to have made it work and have maintained a level of tolerance that is the envy of many of their neighbors. Pettigrew and Meertens provide a number of historical reasons why this pattern should have had such an unexpected development in Holland and then explore whether the absence of blatant forms of discrimination and prejudice may not mask more subtle and latent types of intolerance. While their research does indeed confirm that the Dutch are by no means free from prejudice, nevertheless the strong norms against the public expression of intolerance and open discrimination seem to be a lasting legacy of this system. Understanding the forces that brought this about, and how similar principles might be applied more generally, is the practical benefit of solving the *verzuiling puzzle*.

A common explanation for the widespread notion of racial hierarchy throughout the world is to attribute it to the power of European expansionism and the legacy of colonialism. Frank Dikötter argues that this interpretation does not adequately explain the persistence of racial thinking in China over the past few

centuries. While it is true that Chinese intellectuals and political leaders did selectively adopt some of the ideas prominent in the West, such as eugenics, social
Darwinism and various types of racial theorizing, for the most part Chinese views
concerning the distinct and superior nature of the "yellow race" can be seen as a
social construction developed within the society itself. Some of it stems from the
traditional concern with lineage in Chinese thought and society, the powerful role
of family ties and respect for ancestral obligations that could easily be adapted to
the development of nationalist theories by the revolutionaries of the early twentieth century. What is interesting is the continuity of much of this racist thought in
both Republican and Communist China throughout the twentieth century. Notions
of Han superiority, stereotypes about the racial "Other," physical assaults on African students, and attempts to find fossil evidence to prove scientifically that Homo
sapiens developed independently in China – as a counterweight to the strongly
supported theory of the African genesis of all mankind – suggest that ideas of
biological racism are still quite prevalent in contemporary Chinese society. However, as Dikötter strongly emphasizes, the development of a racist discourse cannot
be attributed to "hegemonic" Western influences and must be explained in terms
of indigenous Chinese cultural and social factors.

7 Skin Color, Race, and Racism in Nicaragua

Roger N. Lancaster

It is sometimes stated that Nicaraguan society has historically been relatively free of racism (see T. Walker 1982, 10). And from certain points of view that claim is true. The common forms of racism prevalent in North American history – discrimination, segregation – strike most Nicaraguans with whom I have spoken as both irrational and immoral. Relative to certain other Latin American countries – where racial stratification approaches the form of a caste system – Nicaragua is by no means racially polarized. But I would begin any discussion of skin color, race, and racism by saying that Nicaragua does indeed have a "race problem" or, perhaps more to the point, a "color problem," and this problem manifests itself in insidious and destructive ways. Little that has transpired since the revolution deals directly with this topic, and, indeed, dealing with it will prove difficult because of deep-seated cultural conditioning.

The Atlantic Coast Question

Prejudice against natives of the Atlantic coast – the Costeños – is perhaps the most striking phenomenon (T. Walker 1986, 82–3). In the majority, mestizo (racially mixed), western sector of Nicaragua, Miskitos and African Caribbeans are felt to be "backward" and inferior in various ways. Such prejudicial sentiments, which generally treat the minority sector's "level of culture" or "level of economic development," occasionally take on "racial" forms, as well.

A typical pattern evinced itself in my discussions with ordinary people about the Atlantic coast problem: at an analytical level, almost everyone admits that indigenous Miskitos and African Caribbeans have been the victims of prejudice and misunderstandings by the Spanish-speaking mestizo majority; yet almost no one admits to harboring any personal ill will toward the minority sector. The peculiarity of the ethnic question in Nicaragua is its duplex structure in discourse. Revolutionary ideology recognized the problem of ethnic prejudice; as part of its negotiating position in bringing regional autonomy and peace to the Atlantic coast, the government put dealing with ethnic crisis near the top of its list of concerns. Government representatives spoke openly and frequently about their own "past errors" and the need to overcome chauvinism; in the process, ordinary people took their cues from this governmental discourse. A common refrain went something like this: "We have had our problems with the Atlantic coast, and we have our differences, but we have to learn to live together." True enough. But when individually questioned about racial and ethnic issues, most people have a stereotyped construction: racism exists; mistakes have been made; and no, I am not a racist myself. The density of real, everyday discourse betrays the good intentions of a thin, official discourse.

Elvis was cool and analytical on virtually any topic. A member of the Sandinista Youth, well aware of the status of the ethnic question, and a Marxist trained in materialism, Elvis took it as a matter of personal pride that he was not superstitious. One day I was asking him about his various tours of duty through the mountainous provinces of Nicaragua. He spoke of hunger, isolation, boredom, and danger. "We were in the rain a lot. There were almost no provisions, and I was starving for salt. It was especially bad, having to eat monkeys, because when you skin them, they look like men. But the worst was when they sent me to the Atlantic coast." "Why?" I asked. "Because there are a lot of *gente mala* [evil people] on the coast." "How so?" I wondered. Did he mean counterrevolutionaries? No, *gente mala* was not a political designation at all. "Look, I was never sick in the mountains. But on the Atlantic coast I got a fungus, a skin disease, that covered my whole arm. I still have scars from it." He showed me the patchwork of little scars. "But what's that got to do with bad people?" "Ah," Elvis clarified, "because they all practice witchcraft. A *negra* [black woman] from Bluefields was looking at me, very strange, for a long time, and a couple of days later, I got sick." "And you think she caused it?" "I know she caused it."

"It's doubtful – " I began. "You didn't see her eyes," he retorted. I pressed Elvis a bit further. "I didn't think you believed in witches, the evil eye, black magic and such." "Of course not!" he replied. "Not here. But the Atlantic coast, that's a different thing." Thus, for Elvis the Atlantic coast embodied pure otherness. It was a mysterious zone where all the normal rules of reason were suspended, inverted; a dark land untouched by science, populated by natives known by their rejection of rightness – *gente mala:* bad folks, evil people. As I questioned him further on his characterizations, Elvis grew increasingly uncomfortable and embarrassed; eventually we changed the subject.

Elvis's was a hushed, fearful, and somewhat ashamed discourse on Atlanticity. Sometimes the racism takes a harder, more overt edge. In practice, the basketball courts in Luis Alfonso Park are segregated: mestizos play separately from African Caribbeans, and I have never seen an integrated game. Jaime tells me that once he and some friends were playing a friendly game on one side of the court. A young man from the coast approached and began shooting baskets at the other end of the court. Instead of asking him to join their play, or even going about their game at the other end of the court, Jaime reports, the young men of his group all just walked away. I was surprised, because Jaime is not – or does not seem to be – a racist. Yet rather than try to convince his friends to stay and play ball, he walked away with them. And whenever African Caribbeans enter a bus in Managua, people tend to move away from them – in a country where there is generally little aversion to close physical contact, and on a public transportation system that is heavily overloaded.

The Atlantic coast minorities – African Caribbeans, who speak English, and indigenous peoples, who speak Miskito or English and occasionally Sumo, Rama, or Garífona – are not part of national Nicaraguan culture. Historically colonized by Britain and geographically isolated from the Spanish traditions of the majority sector, they remain both remote and distinct from the mestizo Pacific. No highway links the east coast to the west. Various causes exacerbate the ethnic tensions that already existed in Nicaraguan society. The FSLN was too aggressive in its early attempts to "bring the revolution" to the coast and to its distinctly nonrevolutionary peoples, who tended to see the revolution as a "Spanish thing" – and therefore not good. On the coast, the Sandinistas stimulated the formation of a multiethnic, indigenous mass organization, but Miskito demands soon outstripped the framework of that vehicle, and the organization splintered into increasingly militant and separatist organizations (see Bourgois 1982; Diskin 1987). Various Miskito factions joined the contras and organized their own armed groups. The Atlantic coast came to be seen as separatist, hostile, counterrevolutionary territory. Many Nicaraguan families from the western majority region lost sons in the fighting. Ultimately, working piece by piece with various armed groups, the Sandinistas negotiated a gradual peace on the Atlantic coast that entailed a large measure of economic, political, and cultural autonomy for that region – indeed, a separate constitution, with separate laws, education in the native tongue, and guarantees that youths drafted on the Atlantic coast would be stationed on the Atlantic coast (see Diskin et al. 1986). In perhaps its boldest move, the FSLN integrated their former enemies into the Sandinista Army, making what were formerly armed contra units into the guarantors of peace in the region. The war is now over, but the wounds remain.

Under such circumstances, even minor events can inflame passionate hatreds. Virgilio once asked me if I were a racist. I said no; to my surprise, he asserted that he was. He spoke openly of his hatred of the African Caribbeans in his high school. "I hate blacks," he told me. "They are immoral. And black is ugly. Better to just exterminate them all – cut their throats." Astonished by the vehemence of his remarks, I pressed Virgilio on his feeling until finally he yielded a "reason": he had made friends with an African-Caribbean boy at school, and his friend stole his girlfriend. "*Me traicionó* [he betrayed me], so that's why I hate blacks. Wouldn't you?" Virgilio concluded, "Whenever black people touch me, I feel dirty: I want to go wash it off. Black *is* dirty, isn't it?"

I do not want to give a misleading or one-sided picture here. Such extreme sentiments are rare. (Virgilio's girlfriend, for example, was clearly not averse to dating an African Caribbean, nor was Virgilio himself at first reluctant to befriend the youth.) It seems to me that racism toward the Atlantic coast minorities is generally less vicious and all-encompassing than racism as I know it in the United States. For instance, I have never heard anyone assert that these minorities are by nature intellectually inferior to mestizos. No Nicaraguan ever struck up a casual conversation with me around the topic of his contempt for or hatred of Costeños (nor were any such conversations conducted within my hearing). In many parts of the States – south and north – white people do just that, employing casual racism and white solidarity as a way of ingratiating themselves with white strangers. But this sort of casual racism is not the basis for an easy racial solidarity in Nicaragua. In fact, none of my informants ever revealed their racism to me – either directly, as did Virgilio, or indirectly, as did Elvis – until they were confident that we had already established a solid friendship. Moreover, those African Caribbeans and Miskitos who have migrated from the Atlantic coast to live and work in Managua do not inhabit segregated barrios, and they generally live on good terms with their mestizo neighbors.

After getting to know me, most politically conscious Nicaraguans would eventually ask me if I were a racist, and then (unlike Virgilio) deliver a quick comparative lesson by way of analogy with their own country. "You North Americans have a history of racism starting with slavery," Aida told me, "and even today there is a lot of racism in the States. Your country should treat all its people equally, with respect and dignity. You should learn how to live with your black neighbors. We've had problems with racism in Nicaragua, too. There's a lot of animosity between the Pacific and the Atlantic. But we are learning how to live in peace with our black neighbors on the Atlantic coast." And while it is true that Atlantic coast culture is generally thought to be "inferior" to mestizo culture, this perception did not prevent Dimensión Costeña from becoming Nicaragua's most popular native musical group, nor the Atlantic "Maypole dance" from becoming Managua's biggest dance craze since breakdancing. Finally, people were always telling me that, of the candidates for president in the United States, their favorite was *El Morenito* – Jesse Jackson. He was seen as a Third World candidate, good for minorities in the United States and all nonwhite nations in the world.

Thus, the racial situation in Nicaragua can be summed up as follows: first, racism really does exist in Nicaragua, and it can be detected, its logic diagrammed, in various ways; second, this is not as absolute or all-encompassing a racism as that which one encounters in the United States; and finally, it is nonetheless a significant social problem, posing a range of cultural and political issues that will continue to affect the course of Nicaraguan history.

Color Signs

But significant though this regionally defined racism may be, prejudice against the Atlantic coast minorities is scarcely the most pervasive form of "racism" in Nicaragua. Indeed, apart from the cultural and political tensions that clearly exist between the western majority and the eastern minority, it seems to me that whatever racism exists toward the Atlantic coast minorities is but an extension of a much deeper-seated pattern *internal* to mestizo culture, not external to it. A more apposite term for this pattern might be *colorism* rather than *racism*.

People put color into discourse in a variety of ways. The ambiguity of Nicaraguan speech about color is perhaps its crucial feature. *Negro* refers to Atlantic coast natives of African heritage, but it may also refer to dark-skinned indigenous peoples such as the Miskitos. It can also refer to dark-skinned mestizos – the majority of Nicaragua's population. For instance, it is common for parents to nickname their darkest-skinned child "Negro" or "Negra." I don't think I've ever been in a house where this was not the practice. When I mentioned this to Virgilio, his first reaction was to deny it – a remarkable thing, because his mother had summoned him to dinner that very afternoon by yelling out "Ne-gro!" at the top of her lungs, as she often does. Virgilio is the *negro* in his house, as is Jaime. In this sense, *negro* is a relative term, marking differences in coloration among the mestizo majority. It is sometimes used to mark very narrow differences indeed. One family in Barrio Sergio Altamirano had a set of twin boys: one had darker brown hair, the other's hair was lighter brown. I had to look closely, at the parents' insistence, to see the difference. One was nicknamed Negro, the other Chele.

Thus, in everyday usage and for most purposes, color terms are *relational* terms. The relativity of this sort of usage turns on the intention of the speaker, comparative assessments, and shifting contexts. Not one but three different, perpetually sliding systems are in use.

It was through an extended series of conversations with Virgilio and Jaime about race, racism, and skin color that this complex system became clear to me. I had seen a variety of perplexing things. On one day, someone would be described to me as negro, on another as moreno, and on yet another as blanco. How to reconcile these apparently contradictory descriptions? After Virgilio proclaimed that he was a racist, he, Jaime, and I discussed the meanings of various terms and usages in some detail. I was, after all, quite confused. Virgilio's skin was darker than that of many African Americans in the United States, although here his indigenous appearance would undoubtedly classify him as either Native American or Hispanic. But for Nicaraguan purposes, what was he? White, brown, or black? And Jaime's dark skin, full lips, and frizzy hair would probably classify him as "black" in the United States. So what was he? The answer is, it all depends on the context.

First, there is the phenotypic system, which is recognized by everyone in at least certain contexts:

Blanco (white)
Moreno (brown)
Negro (black)

This relatively "objective" system of classification is employed to describe the range of possible skin tones. *Blancos* are persons of primarily European ancestry. This is a small minority – by far the smallest of the three categories marked in this system. *Moreno* designates the brown hair and brown skin of the mestizo majority – and here *mestizo* is primarily a cultural, not phenotypic, term. Within fifty years of the Spanish conquest, Nicaragua's indigenous population declined from roughly one million to a few tens of thousands (T. Walker 1986, 10). There were at the same time a few hundred Spanish settlers in the country. Thus, without adequate support for indigenous continuity, Nicaragua's culture developed as a Spanish-speaking mestizo culture; but it is also clear that the vast majority of material in the gene pool was and remains indigenous, not Spanish. Nicaraguan national culture is mestizo; people's physical characteristics are primarily indigenous; and in the terms of this phenotypic system, most people are moreno. In this system, *negro* can denote either persons of African ancestry or sometimes persons of purely indigenous appearance, whether they are culturally classified as Indio or mestizo.

Second, there is the more common polite usage:

Polite terms	Corresponding phenotypic terms
Chele (sometimes *rubio*)	*Blanco* (light hair, blue eyes)
Blanco	*Moreno* (brown hair, brown skin)
Moreno	*Negro* (black or dark brown skin)

In this system, all the color terms are inflated. Europeans are denoted by a special term, *chele* (a Mayan word that literally means "blue," for the eyes of Europeans and Euro-Americans [T. Stephens 1989, 64]), but morenos become blanco and negros become moreno. This is the system normally used in the presence of the person about whom one is speaking. Even persons of African heritage are referred to as moreno in their presence. It is considered a grave and violent offense to refer to a black-skinned person as *negro*. "Never, ever, call a negro *negro*," Jaime warned me, "at least not to his face." "Why not?" I wondered. Virgilio laughed. "Do you want to die?" Indeed, this inflationary rule extends to a range of circumstances: in the countryside, Indians are called *mestizos* rather than *Indios*.

Finally, there is the pejorative and/or affectionate usage:

| *Chele* | (fairer skin, lighter hair) |
| *Negro* | (darker skin, darker hair) |

To posit a hostile difference between the speaker and the person spoken about or spoken to, Nicaraguans resort to a simplified dichotomy between white and black. On rare occasions the term *chele* may be thrown out as invective; this usage can occur when someone assumes more familiarity with the target than is socially appropriate. More commonly, *negro* is employed to disparage the victim of one's aggression. "Black as carbon," for instance, asserts the absolute negritude of one's target. Color can also be used to augment the standard invectives. For instance, *hijo de puta* becomes *negro hijo de puta* (black son of a whore). At the same time, these terms are common in affectionate discourse. *Chele* and *Negro* are common family nicknames, and *negrito mio* is a diminutive form commonly exchanged between *novios* (sweethearts). This is not to say that such affectionate nicknames carry with them a directly stigmatizing force. But *negro* or *negrito mio* are affectionate and intimate terms precisely because they are "informal"; and such terms are informal because they violate the rules of polite discourse. Even when motivated by affection rather than anger, such terms can never be innocent of the social relations in which they are embedded. Such terms of intimacy maintain at close range the system of contrasts that is, for other purposes and in other contexts, stigmatizing – and that might, in an argument or in a different tone, carry the force of strong invective.

Both Jaime and Virgilio confidently asserted, on first questioning, that they were blanco, white. After more questioning, they downgraded themselves to moreno. After yet more questioning, they finally admitted, "Well, we're all black from the point of view of rich white people." On the basis of this questioning, drawing out examples and scenarios, Jaime and Virgilio described to me all these various rules of interaction. The three of us sat out on the sidewalk late one night, sometimes talking in low voices, at Jaime's suggestion, lest our neighbors overhear us classifying and reclassifying them. I then drew up the rules of discourse into the three situational systems described above, until I understood the material, and it met with my informants' approval.

Jaime proved very perceptive on the subject and put the entire matter into perspective with one clever sentence. Citing the old aphorism, "In the land of the blind, the one-eyed man shall be king," he observed: "In the land of the negros, the moreno shall be blanco." As Jaime's maxim suggests, something of this very issue – power, status, wealth – clings irrevocably to color distribution and color descriptions. Of poor barrios, it is sometimes said, "They're very black" – and it seems to me that there really is a loose correlation between darkness and poverty. Of wealthier neighborhoods, it is also said, "They're whiter." And in this case there is a very clear connection between affluence, status, power, and whiteness.

Whiteness, then, is a desired quality, and polite discourse inflates its descriptions of people. Well, then, I wondered, how should I respond to Doña Jazmina, when she greets me as "Chele"? Should I respond, "*Buenas trades, morenita*"? No, not at all, I was informed. A proper and polite greeting would be "*Chela, por cariño*" (more or less, "You, too, are white, in my affection"). When I tried this formula out the following day, the results were exactly as the two had predicted. Doña Jazmina appeared flattered and even remarked on my mastery of polite conversation. Tellingly, she observed that I was speaking good *Castellano* (Castilian Spanish).

Jaime and Virgilio understood perfectly well how color was put into discourse and could describe all the rules for competent performance within the system of color discriminations. Nonetheless, their sociological knowledge of the phenomenon was not enough to permit them to "escape" the system. The competition for a claim to whiteness produces quirky self-deceptions, even among the most astute. At one point, my two best informants on the matter developed for me a Lamarckian, climatic theory of color. Jaime reasoned, and Virgilio agreed, "We would be much whiter than we are, but the sun is very direct, and the climate is very hot. Why, look at the Matagalpeños. They live up in the mountains, where the air is fresh, and they come out much whiter than we do."

As such remarks indicate, a desire to "whiten" oneself pervades the system of color discrimination. Many dark-haired women use manzanilla tea to lighten their hair. *Rubio* (fair) is virtually synonymous with *guapo* (sexy or attractive); indeed, fair-skinned people are considered good catches in a marriage because their children, too, will be lighter-skinned. When one man in the neighborhood learned that I was staying with the Ocampos, he first made various salacious innuendoes about my relationship with Yolanda, the oldest daughter in the household, and then reasoned, "She's a *buena hembra* [a good-looking woman], and a white woman, too." When Doña Flora's sister-in-law had her fourth son, she related the news to me and sympathized with her comadre's plight: "He came out *varón* [a boy]." The mother had been hoping for a girl. Then she shook her head and added, sympathetically, "And he came out negro, too. All her children came out negros."

One day I watched Doña Flora studying her son Charlie's face. He had been away from home for a couple of months in military training. He had spent much of the time outdoors in training exercises, and his brown skin was a shade darker than it had been before he left home. His first visit home was a festive occasion. Thoughtful and industrious, as usual, he had filled his duffel bag with mangos from a gigantic tree on base. Doña Flora made a pot of pinol, I joked with Charlie about his experiences in boot camp, and we all sat out in the backyard, eating and drinking and catching up on events. After the joy of reunion had passed a bit, Doña Flora examined her son's face, shook her head, and matter-of-factly stated, "*Puro Niquinohomo*." The boy's father was from Niquinohomo, a small farming community near Masaya. Its residents are considered country bumpkins in Managua; they have very dark skin and strongly indigenous features, and the town is still sometimes considered "indigenous." The point seemed lost on Flora that her son had in fact come out a very handsome young man, with fine bone structure, an appealing face, and a strong, well-proportioned physique. When I asked her what she meant, she responded, as though it were perfectly obvious, "He's very black."

Doña Jazmina once asked me which of her two grandsons was better looking. Josué-Luis was four, and Augusto César was two. For me, the choice was obvious. Josué-Luis had a perfectly proportioned, symmetrical face with even features and large, endearing black eyes. His half-brother had a poorly proportioned, asymmetrical face, uneven features, and small, undistinguished brown eyes; moreover, his bouts with parasites had left him looking sickly. Naturally, I first responded, "Well, they're both such fine-looking young boys." But Doña Jazmina insisted, "Yes, but one of them is much more handsome than the other. Which one?" "Well, Josué-Luis." Doña Jazmina's face showed surprise and disbelief. "No, Roger. Augusto César is much better looking." Now it was I who was incredulous. The difference was so extreme, and my own judgement was so strong in the other direction, that I queried: "How so?" "Well, just look at them!" she responded. "Augusto César is *muy fino* [very fine], rubio. He's clearly the more handsome of the two." She then solicited opinions from her sons and daughters in the house, including the boys' mother, who confirmed her judgment over mine.

Nicaragua's mestizos make a range of assertions about blackness vis-à-vis whiteness. Black is primitive and irrational; it is dirty; it is also less attractive than white. And blackness is clearly associated with evil. The devil is envisioned as black, not red, in Nicaraguan lore, and "black as sin" is a phrase whose meaning would not be lost in the translation from English to Spanish. One young man from a neighboring barrio was referred to by his friends with the nickname *El Diablo* (The Devil). When I asked why he should have such a name, his friends explained, "Why, because he's so black, of course!" In popular discourse, blackness becomes a sort of semiotic sponge, absorbing the entire range of possible negative connotations.

Power, Color, Discourse, and History

To return, then, to the question of racism toward the Atlantic coast populations: Nicaraguans apply to Costeños no rules that they do not apply more intimately to themselves. The categories with which they divide up the mestizo world are for them universal framers of experience. The color terms are the same, and the shifting rules of discourse are the same. Moreover, it is not only that many Nicaraguans see their Atlantic coast as a culturally backward region; they apply even that same logic to themselves, relative to other countries. One night at Doña Flora's house, we were watching a series of music videos on Sandinista television. The Mexican group Flans was coming to Nicaragua on a concert tour, and so their videos were getting constant airplay. One video after another depicted very fair-skinned young female singers in a variety of romantic situations, surrounded by opulence and luxury. Then the programming included a video from Nicaragua's own Atlantic coast group, Dimensión Costeña. Produced in Central America, it had simple production values; it was Nicaraguan and Caribbean in flavor. I casually opined that Dimensión Costeña was far superior to Flans. No one in the room agreed with me. Guto interjected, "How? How could *anything* produced here in poor little Nicaragua compare with things produced in Mexico? Or the United States? What good could come out of this poor country?" It was not simply that the band in question reflected the culture of the Atlantic coast; what was really in question was the status of Nicaragua itself. As the Atlantic coast stands to Nicaragua, so Nicaragua stands to the world. Backwardness, poverty, and blackness merge to define the deficient end of a scale.

If whiteness, like wealth, is a "limited good," in George M. Foster's (1965) sense of the term, then blackness, like poverty, is an abundant state of the *absence* of that good. The simultaneously envious and invidious nature of the social setting is clarified if we remember that envy is a state of hostile desire (Foster 1972). Things white are envied, desired; things black are denigrated, shunned. The envy manifests its workings in both centripetal and centrifugal motions. One discursive cycle builds up one's self and one's friends by employing an inflated conception of whiteness. But the countercycle to this is the sometimes teasing, sometimes overtly hostile use of *negro*, in which almost everyone comes out black, and all are drawn back into the color equivalent of shared poverty, shared blackness. People caught in this swirl of envy are thus propelled in two directions: to maximize their own goodness/color/status, and to minimize other people's. "Shared poverty" on the one hand, and the notion of an egalitarian "improvement for all" on the other.

These machinations represent not merely an ideology in the classical sense of the term – for an ideology proper would be easy to contest – but rather a real political economy of the body and its engagement with other bodies in society and history. Such transactions are political and economic in every sense.

Politically, color relations inside Nicaragua reproduce Nicaragua's own history of repression at the hands of other states. Where power and privilege are at stake, *white* implies might and right, as it were. When people employ the ambiguity of color terms to their own advantage, when they shift from one descriptive scale to another, and when they negotiate their own location within a system of contrasts, they are struggling over honor, to be sure, but they are no less struggling over privilege and power.

The transactions I have sketched are no less economic: value is assigned on the basis of exchange, but the values are assigned not to commodities but to human beings. In these daily exchanges, the many words associated with fair skin, with their arbitrary positive connotations, make up an inflated symbolic currency. Whiteness thus serves as a kind of symbolic capital, empowering its claimant to make advantageous exchanges in a host of other symbolic and material realms. Thus, Augusto César enjoys a social advantage over Josué-Luis, an advantage which will carry across family, neighborhood, and school; a fair-skinned woman will generally be judged more attractive than a dark-skinned woman, and she might parlay her complexion's perceived value into an economically advantageous marriage; a chele in the world of business could readily translate his whiteness into contacts, contracts, and an economic advantage over moreno competitors; Elvis and Virgilio feel intrinsically superior to African Caribbeans; and so on. Such exchanges locate human beings within a system of production that is simultaneously symbolic and material. Color terms constitute, symbolically, a series of representational strata; the people to whom they are applied experience, materially, differential life chances. Although not absolute, the correspondence of economic classes to the representational color scheme is by no means random. From a semiotic point of view, these color relations are ultimately *power* relations, and they constitute, in Marxist terms, a substratum as much as a superstructure.

To speak of a political economy of the body, or to conceive of the body as a field of productive relations, is not to draw rigorous, one-to-one analogies with material production but to reiterate that what is produced in any case is not a good but a "value." What "economy" means in all cases is a system where value is assigned based not on any "intrinsic" worth of an object but rather on that object's position in the system of production and exchange. Thus, the value of a commodity is calculated in relation to other commodities and by the comparative social labor that produced it. Classes, too, are defined relationally: by their relations to each other in the production process. In the political economy of machismo, one's standing as a man is gauged by the execution of certain transactions (drinking, gambling, womanizing) in relation to other men. And in the political economy of colorism, one's value as a person is determined within a system of exchanges and in terms of relations between the lexical clusters around *black* and *white*.

What is always at issue in these daily power plays is the ascent of whiteness over blackness that began with the Spanish conquest. Africanos, Indios, and lower-class mestizos have been lumped together under a single term – *negro* – that signifies defeat. This defeat, however, is not just a "legacy" in the passive sense of the term. It is not a trauma held at a distance on the historical and social horizon. This defeat reproduces itself daily in myriad interactions.

Spanish language and Spanish culture have long been ensconced in the commanding heights of Nicaraguan society. Things Spanish or white are superordinate; things Indian or black are subordinate. This Spanish imposition was one of the bloodiest conquests in history. From extermination, enslavement, forced marches, overwork, and European epidemics, the territory of what is now Nicaragua lost more than 90 percent of its population within fifty years. A more total destruction would be hard to imagine, and the conflicts it engendered remain as more than mere wisps. For most of Nicaragua's population, little remains of pre-Columbian culture. But the conquest has been problematic, uneasy. Traces of indigenous words still remain in the Nicaraguan vocabulary. Historically, in most parts of the country lower-class mestizos assumed the structural positions and cultural characteristics usually reserved for indigenous populations in other Latin American countries: their economic position was defined by patron–client relations with whiter, wealthy landowners; and classical popular culture was defined by participation in religious festivities involving symbolic inversion, economic leveling, and a cargo system (Lancaster 1988, 27–54) – the very hallmarks of indigenous communities in other parts of Latin America. The politics of this sort of "implicit Indianness" is not lost in real discourse. Upper-class Nicaraguans sometimes refer to lower-class mestizos, especially campesinos, as Indios (as well as negros) and attribute to them all the characteristics that Ladinos in other countries attribute to their own subordinate indigenous populations (laziness, ignorance, poor hygiene). On the other side of the divide, in heated and political moments ordinary people speak of their *sangre india, sangre rebelde* (Indian blood, rebel blood). And every Nicaraguan, save those few ruling class whites of primarily European ancestry, remains at war with himself: Spanish culture, indigenous skin.

Within this simultaneously symbolic and material system, there are moments of reprieve, flashes of rebellion, whose site, too, is the human body. During Carnaval and carnivalesque festivities such as the Coming of Santo Domingo, negritude is symbolically elevated over whiteness, and things indigenous take precedence over things Spanish. Celebrants appear drenched in grease and wearing indigenous costumes. Youths blacken their own and their elders' faces. As though in revenge against white envy and color climbing, blackness thus assaults the entire community, triumphantly asserting itself as a reversal of the people's baptism into a Spanish Catholic Church. But to date, this spirit of rebellion has not much escaped the confines of Carnaval.

Comparisons and contrasts might prove useful. Colonialism's long history, in Nicaragua as in the United States, puts race and color into discourse in subtle and invidious ways. Thus, colonialism can write and rewrite its text anew: in ways of perceiving and treating the human body; in all the ways we talk about ourselves and other people. But the history of colonialism is different in Nicaragua and in the United States. So history is embodied differently, spoken differently, structured differently, in the two countries.

In the United States' race system, at least from the point of view of the white majority, degree of coloration is not an issue: one falls on one side or the other of a boundary whose existence is scarcely subject to negotiation. "Race" is a very definite thing and gives every appearance of a structure. "Race" is no less a structure in those Latin American contexts where phenotypic traits count for nothing, and language, birthplace, and dress count for everything. In Nicaragua, though, "race" is a very different sort of thing. Color discriminations there constitute themselves not so much as solid, permanent structures but as a series of discursive gestures that are contingent and contextual and whose motives are eminently logical and self-interested. The site of these distinctions knows no bounds; they operate equally within the self, the family, the neighborhood, and society at large. Indeed, this system exists always as a practice, never as a structure: there is no race boundary, no line, no stopping point where negotiation and discourse cease. One can play the game with equal amounts of risk and self-interest in any given context. In mestizo company, Costeños, too, play the game, entering the same discourse by the same rules. Not an absolute boundary at all, these color distinctions are best seen as a series of concentric circles, which are in fact power plays, emanating from a highly problematic ego who may win or lose depending on contingent factors. Unlike our own tradition, in Nicaragua race hatred can scarcely be separated from self-hatred. Chauvinism toward the Atlantic coast minorities merely constitutes the furthest reaches of a discourse that ultimately afflicts the majority as severely as it castigates the minority....

Politics?

What is the prospectus for changing Nicaragua's political economy of the body? How to translate dignity and sovereignty into body and discourse? Writ into the body and carried out in myriad daily transactions, such practices cannot be suppressed by decree. Making them taboo might well drive them underground and render them all the more powerful. A massive consciousness-raising effort might at least bring these practices to the level of self-consciousness, but even the most sociologically minded of my informants were still fully subject to the logic of this system. The always negotiable nature of the system; the fact that any given person may always defer a final judgment on his or her location within the system of contrasts; the presence of racial thinking combined with the absence of corporate races: these factors distribute the weight of color in Nicaragua in a subtle and pernicious manner and militate against efforts to address – or even perceive – the issue as a problem, as an issue of power.

When I attempted to discuss the politics of color with my informants, I was often charged with racism. Why? First, because I pointed out the political implications of everyday discourses deemed apolitical and thus was accused of having an unhealthy interest in the subject. And, more often than not, because people felt that I was relegating them to an inferior color status. "I see, chele," I was told on more than one occasion: "You want to be the only blanco in the room!" Granted, the interpersonal dynamics of such discussions were less than ideal (and it is not my business to meddle, only to report), but they do point up the special constraints of the system. Nicaraguans are personally invested in the values of a system that rarely pays off, except in the little daily exchanges that validate the system.

Nicaraguans do develop a different way of appreciating racism when they come to visit or work in or live in the United States, for they then inhabit a solid "structure" of race (where to be Hispanic is to be brown), and not the sliding practices of their own color discourse. On the Nicaraguan terrain, a "negro" or "moreno" pride movement might be helpful, but the sliding of signifiers and signifieds would prove slippery soil indeed. Most people would have the option of resisting such a revolution in connotators, and they could take tactical refuge in their own "whiteness", unless it could be proven that they would come out ahead by changing the game. Worse yet, systematic consciousness raising might well resort to the "objectivity" of phenotypic variation and tactically freeze the sliding signs, but still fail to erase the stigma that clings to color's history. In so doing, the best of efforts might transform the color code into a truly totalitarian scheme of race classification.

The form, scope, and play of power analyzed here obviously recall Foucault's descriptions of power as decentered and nonbinary. Other than language itself, there is no "center" to this system of power. In most cases it would be hard to say who is dominated and who is dominating. It is not so much that white people dominate black and brown people; rather, *whiteness* dominates *blackness*. And someone is always whiter than any given speaker, just as someone is always blacker. Although color clearly participates in each generation's construction of economic hierarchy, the cleavage into white elites and dark subjects is by no means sharp. The original colonialism that sorted people into rulers and ruled is gone; the discourse of power – and the power of discourse – remains. This discourse feeds less on the energy of domination than on the despair of defeat. One could hypothesize that, although the original colonialism that invented the color terms and invested them in the human body is gone, its power/discourse has remained, supported by subsequent US colonialism.

Attractive as this thesis is, it shares the weakness of the classically Marxist analysis of base and superstructure: it cannot specify in any detail the links whereby US colonialism produces discourse. The thesis rests, ultimately, on its attractiveness alone, and it mystifies more than it illuminates. The Spanish origin is not mysterious. Spain imposed a language, a religion, and a culture on the territory of what is now Nicaragua; its colonists lived among, dominated, and intermarried with the indigenous natives and thereby created a mestizo culture. Its values established hegemony: white over black and brown, Christian over non-Christian, Spanish over Indian, and so on. Today's North American conquerors might occasionally refer to the land as "Niggeragua," but their colonialism has no power to compel Nicaraguans to call each other "nigger." And were that power/discourse supported only by the interests of the local, affluent, white elites, it could not compel the active participation of people in every household. Its overthrow would be a relatively simple matter.

Consequently, I have pursued a "how," not a "who," of power. This power "is not something that is acquired, seized, or shared, something that one holds on to or allows to slip away; power is exercised from innumerable points, in the interplay of nonegalitarian and mobile relations" (Foucault 1980, 94). Surely, its play is "strategic," "intentional," and "nonsubjective"; and just as surely, the system already accounts for "resistances" and diversionary tactics by its targets (ibid., 94–6), which by no means constitute a threat to the power that is ultimately held by no one, owned by no one, but firmly implanted in both discourse and body.

Even though the prospects for change seem remote, I do not want to construct a "winner loses" argument (Hoy 1986, 11) of the sort critiqued by Fredric Jameson in his analysis of postmodernism:

> What happens is that the more powerful the vision of some increasingly total system or logic – the Foucault of the prisons book is the obvious example – the more powerless the reader comes to feel. Insofar as the theorist wins, therefore, by constructing an increasingly closed and terrifying machine, to that very degree he loses, since the critical capacity of his work is thereby paralyzed, and the impulses of negation and revolt, not to speak of those of social transformation, are increasingly perceived as vain and trivial. (Jameson 1984, 57)

There is more pathos than terror in the machineries at hand, and while their operation exacts a very real human cost, the results for any particular individual are more often mundane than tragic. Perhaps this power resists politicization because it is so diffuse. Almost everyone suffers somewhat; almost everyone inflicts some pain on others; few suffer very greatly, and those who do are apt to redouble their efforts to exact vengeance on others *within* the system of values. The tragedy, of course, is cumulative: that this ceaseless whirligig should go on, ranking and sorting ad nauseam; that this monster of colonialism should endure as an internal and psychological colonialism.

Nor do I want to suggest that the situation is as bleak as that described by Vincent Crapanzano in South Africa, where "the tyranny of language," no matter how narrowly we inscribe it, "offers no escape" (1986, 29). Freedom is always, in Sartre's sense, the freedom to affirm or negate, the freedom to say yes or no – collectively, individually, and at every level of the question. Carnaval, the Coming and Going of Santo Domingo, and other carnivalesque festivities provide symbolic revolt against the system of values entailed by and reproduced within this system of power; they support the form of color discourse (black/white, Indio/Latino) but scramble and invert the values of the discourse. That is one way of negating. Some people refuse to participate in the ranking or use only the color terms of "polite" discourse; that is another, partial way of negating. Leftist political discourse often draws on "Indianness" and "Indian blood" to contest colonialism in all its dimensions. That is yet another way of negating. What was made by history can also be unmade by history; what is affirmed by language may also be negated by language.

One of Foucault's aphorisms states, "People know what they do; they frequently know why they do what they do; but what they don't know is what what they do does" (in Dreyfus and Rabinow 1982, 187). Therein lies the problem, and therein lie the seeds for a more systematic and explicit way of negating. To get a handle on any given system of power, one must first stop negotiating one's way through its series of mazes and options and realize it in its totality of consequences. Consciousness raising, change, social transformation: these are difficult, but possible.

A thoughtful *fotonovela* (photographic comic book) published by the Centro Valdivieso (the coordinating center for liberation theology in Nicaragua) follows the plight of a young working-class girl, teased by her peers and finally tormented to tears by the term *negra* and its associated abuses. When her mother finds her, weeping and distraught, she draws the story out of her and consoles her: black is the color of the soil; black is the color of your mother; black is beautiful. It is nothing to be ashamed of. Simple and direct, a child's tears suggest the bitter legacy of a colorized history and the lived realities of a present-day system of power. The words of consolation spoken by a loving mother offer a humane politicization of language and suggest a different way of living.

References

Bourgois, Philippe I. 1982. "The Problematic of Nicaragua's Indigenous Minorities." In T. Walker, *Nicaragua in Revolution*, 303–18.

Crapanzano, Vincent. 1986. *Waiting: The Whites of South Africa*. New York: Random House, Vintage Books.

Diskin, Martin. 1987. "The Manipulation of Indigenous Struggles." In T. Walker, *Reagan Versus the Sandinistas*, 80–96.

Diskin, Martin, Thomas Bossert, Salomón Nahmad S., and Stéfano Varese. 1986. *Peace and Autonomy on the Atlantic Coast of Nicaragua: A Report of the LASA Task Force on Human Rights and Academic Freedom*. Pittsburgh: Latin American Studies Association Secretariat.

Dreyfus, Hubert, and Paul Rabinow 1982. *Michel Foucault: Beyond Structuralism and Hermeneutics*. Chicago: University of Chicago Press.

Foster, George M. 1965. "Peasant Society and the Image of Limited Good." *American Anthropologist* 67:293–315.

——. 1972. "The Anatomy of Envy: A Study in Symbolic Behavior." *Current Anthropology* 13, no. 2:164–202.

Foucault, Michel. [1976] 1980. *The History of Sexuality*. Vol. 1, *An Introduction*. Translated by R. Hurley. New York: Random House, Vintage Books.

Hoy, David Couzens. 1986. *Foucault: A Critical Reader*. Oxford: Basil Blackwell.

Jameson, Fredric. 1984. "Postmodernism, Or, The Cultural Logic of Late Capitalism." *New Left Review* 146 (July–August):53–92.

Lancaster, Roger N. 1988. *Thanks to God and the Revolution: Popular Religion and Class Consciousness in the New Nicaragua*. New York: Columbia University Press.

Stephens, Thomas. 1989. *Dictionary of Latin American Racial and Ethnic Terminology*. Gainesville: University of Florida Press.

Walker, Thomas W. 1982. "Introduction." In T. Walker, *Nicaragua in Revolution*, 1–22.

——. 1986. *Nicaragua: The Land of Sandino*. 2nd ed. Boulder: Westview.

8 The *Verzuiling* Puzzle: Understanding Dutch Intergroup Relations

Thomas F. Pettigrew and Roel W. Meertens

The Puzzle

Dutch intergroup relations present a challenge to social science theory. Intergroup policy in the Netherlands has until recently revolved around a *verzuiling* system. This system divided the society into separate religious and social *zuilen*, and distributed resources with a form of "separate but equal" structure.

Experience in many parts of the world, most notably in South Africa and the US, leads one to expect such a political system would result in increasingly greater intergroup conflict. Indeed, other nations have fashioned intergroup systems closely comparable to that of the Netherlands – Austria (1945–66), Belgium (since World War I), Cyprus (until 1960), Lebanon (1943–75), and Malaysia (since 1955). None of these comparisons boasts the political stability of the Dutch, and none could serve as a model of intergroup harmony.

Yet the Netherlands is regarded as one of the most tolerant societies in the Western world. To appreciate the theoretical challenge this situation presents, we must discuss both the reputed tolerance of Dutch society and the *verzuiling* system itself.

Dutch tolerance

It is all too easy to romanticize Dutch intergroup relations. Historical evidence demonstrates the need to differentiate the tolerant tradition of the Dutch in terms of time, group and type of tolerance (Gijswijt-Hofstra, 1989). With respect to freedom of conscience and religion, the tradition of tolerance was relatively strong throughout most of the sixteenth and seventeenth centuries. In the eighteenth century, however, there was persecution of Gypsies as well as outbursts against Catholics and "sodomites." In the nineteenth century, the Dutch renounced slavery late, and colonial concerns dominated. The tradition of tolerance gained particular strength following World War II, though the military attempt to thwart Indonesian independence marked another exception.

There are also current intergroup problems in the Netherlands, most obviously in the employment area. The unemployment rates of Dutch minority groups rank among the highest for minority groups in western Europe. To be sure, the general unemployment rate in the Netherlands is extremely high, hovering around 13 percent in recent years. Yet table 8.1 shows that the figures for minorities living in the country attain rates two to three times greater.

These differential unemployment rates of Dutch majority and minority groups are, of course, influenced by sharp demographic differences. Veenman and Roelandt (1990) constructed a model that estimates how much of this discrepancy in unemployment rates can be explained by differences on five key demographic variables: education, age, sex, region and employment level. These factors accounted for only 2 to 6% of the higher unemployment of minority workers. This finding suggests that discrimination plays a significant role in the labor market in the Netherlands. Indeed, research shows that Dutch employers often prefer majority to minority job applicants (e.g., Brasse and Sikking, 1986). Moreover, field experiments at employment bureaus demonstrate that majority and minority applicants with equivalent qualifications often receive differential treatment (Den Uyl, Choenni, and Bovenkerk, 1986).

Yet there are many other indicators that strongly support the country's reputation as a tolerant society. The nation boasts a Christian Democratic Party that, unlike religious parties elsewhere, is the product of former Protestant and Catholic parties that merged to gain political strength. And interracial marriage is far more common than it is in the English-speaking world. For example, Eurasians are no longer considered a minority group, either officially or unofficially. Following Indonesian independence, they migrated to the Netherlands to escape discrimination. During the early 1950s, the Dutch government harbored doubts about how well they would manage in Dutch society (Surie, 1973; Schuster, 1991), and the Eurasians did encounter initial problems. But they had many advantages for rapid assimilation – prior fluency in the Dutch language, familiarity with the culture and widespread marriage into native Dutch families.

The inclusion of Eurasians continued a long Dutch tradition. In earlier times, French Huguenots, Sephardic Jews, Gypsies, and even accused witches came for a safe haven. Jews, escaping from the Nazis in the 1930s, also found the Netherlands to be one of few available havens. Anne Frank and her family fled from Germany only a few years before World War II.

From these data, two divergent positions have arisen among Dutch scholars concerning current intergroup relations in the Netherlands. *The special case theory*

Table 8.1 Dutch population and unemployment by ethnicity, January 1, 1990

Group[*]	Population in Thousands	Population Percentage	Unemployment Rate
Dutch	14,899	95.5%	13%
Surinamese	244	1.6	27
Antillians / Arubans	84	0.5	23
Moroccans	169	1.1	42
Turks	207	1.3	44

[*]Only foreign-born are included. Moluccans are included with the Indonesians under "Dutch" in these data and thus cannot be separated out.

Sources: *Reportage Arbeidsmarket 1989*, Ministrie van Sociale Zaken en Werkgelegenheid. Cited in Hooghiemstra (1991), *Maandstatistiek van de Bevolking*, Centraal Buro voor de Statistiek, March 1991.

emphasizes the country's long tradition as a haven for the dispossessed. It notes the comparatively high rates of racial intermarriage. And the theory points to the impressive foreign language skills of the Dutch as evidence for their openness to the world. In its more apologetic form, this perspective is sometimes used to deny current Dutch intergroup problems. In its more sophisticated version, this theory readily admits to current problems but insists that intergroup models drawn from other nations are likely to err by ignoring the nation's special history and traditions (e.g., Bovenkerk, Bruin, Brunt and Wouters, 1985).

The regular racism theory emphasizes the nation's past as a major colonizer. From Indonesia to Surinam, the Dutch empire stretched across the globe. Since modern racism has its nineteenth century origins as an ideological legitimation for western colonization, how could the Netherlands have escaped its effects? Racist phenomena noted in other countries are, therefore, likely to exist in the Netherlands. Witness the high minority unemployment rates and the evidence for discrimination in the labor market. Proponents of this racism perspective, such as Essed (1984), also distinguish between *tolerance* and *acceptance* of other peoples. The Dutch inclusion of various refugees, they concede, signifies a certain "patronizing" type of tolerance. But, argue these theorists, this tradition has not entailed a genuine acceptance of other peoples and cultures.

We shall present evidence that suggests each of these theories is partly right and partly wrong. For grasping the *verzuiling* puzzle, however, it is sufficient to note that the tolerance of Dutch society should not be romanticized. By absolute standards, there are limits to Dutch tolerance. Nonetheless, Dutch society is notable for its tolerance compared with other western societies.

The Dutch verzuiling *system of intergroup relations*

The *verzuiling* system is unique in several ways. Though the system has declined since the late 1960s, it took root centuries ago to ease religious conflict (Bax, 1990; Lijphart, 1968; Van Schendelen, 1984). *Zuilen* are separate "pillars" for each major religious or political group through which government funnels support to separate institutions – from religious schools to sports clubs and radio stations. Thus, in what would be a violation of the First Amendment of the US Constitution, the Dutch government has traditionally financed separate schools for its various religious groups. This tradition includes recent support for separate Islamic schools for its Turkish and Moroccan populations.

This system would seem to be a recipe for disaster. Social theory holds that the *verzuiling* principle should have led to increased separation of the various groups, correspondingly greater intergroup differences, and heightened intergroup conflict. The theory receives support from the horrendous case of *Apartheid* in South Africa, a system modeled directly after *verzuiling* by Dutch settlers in the seventeenth century. Thus, the relative tolerance of the present-day Netherlands seems to be a direct denial of theoretical predictions. Why?

Partial Solutions to the Problem

Five explanations are structural in nature; they stress historical and political pecu-
liarities of the Netherlands from the Middle Ages to the present. These explanations have been advanced by a wide variety of historians (e.g., Gijswijt-Hofstra,
1989; Schama, 1987), political scientists (e.g., Bax, 1990; Lijphart, 1968) and
sociologists (e.g., Van Schendelen, 1984).

1   *The lack of a Dutch feudal system.* Unlike much of Europe, the northwes-
tern corner of the continent that is the present-day Netherlands never had an
established feudal system. This has many positive advantages, two of which could
contribute to Dutch tolerance. An entrenched social class system, such as those of
France and the United Kingdom, did not arise. Moreover, Dutch society has not
had to overcome any form of "a fief mentality."

2   *Refugees have enhanced the Dutch economy.* Another partial answer to the
riddle stresses the economic benefits that seventeenth century Holland reaped from
allowing Huguenots and Sephardic Jews to enter. French Protestants brought international trading skills valued by an expansive Holland. Jews brought an entirely
new industry – diamond cutting. So it is argued that Hollanders learned early that
tolerance toward newcomers paid off. Without denying this factor, one can question its generality. Thus, admitting Gypsies and accused witches had no direct
economic benefits. Like other explanations, the economic argument is not fully
adequate.

3   *Small minorities amidst a homogeneous population.* As table 8.1 reveals, the
percentage of foreign-born minorities in the Netherlands is relatively small. Some
claim Dutch tolerance is made possible by this modest minority proportion (about
5% foreign born) in the midst of a homogeneous population. This factor may be
important; but it cannot be determining. This proportion is similar to that of other
western European nations. And the homogeneity of the Dutch population is often
exaggerated. Frisians in the North, maintaining their distinctive language with a
zeal that rivals that of the Welsh, provide convincing evidence against the point.

4   *The similar proportions of Catholics and Protestants.* The original *verzuiling*
system was devised to avoid the religious conflicts between Catholics and Protestants that plagued much of Europe. But unlike Northern Ireland, for example,
the population proportions of the two major religious groups have long been
about equal. This near-equality has been especially true since 1830, when southern
and heavily Catholic areas of the Netherlands left to form the northern tier of
Belgium. A "separate-but-equal" political system may well operate better when
both major groups have something to gain by taking the "equal" part of the
formula seriously.

5   *A tradition of elite cooperation.* While the groups were encased within
their *zuilen* and largely separated from each other, their leaders were not nearly
so separated. A long tradition of cooperation among the elite developed in
the seventeenth century, and its effects are still obvious. Indeed, the unique

Catholic–Protestant political party of Christian Democrats is perfectly natural and "rational" within this Dutch tradition of elite cooperation.

In agreement with Bax (1990) and Lijphart (1968), we place special emphasis on elite cooperation. The Dutch metaphor is that each *zuil* is a separate pillar that, together with other *zuilen*, support the roof that is the Netherlands. We extend the metaphor by emphasizing that, while the groups' members were largely separated in their various pillars, their leaders were in close communication in the attic under the roof. In fact, the elites made a common national roof possible. They were able to keep the *zuilen* upright and the whole construction standing because the masses followed them obediently.

To be sure, other structural conditions, such as the absence of a feudal system and similar proportions of Catholics and Protestants, contributed to this "attic contact" and leadership power of the elites. Yet the remarkable degree of elite cooperation was critical for the success of group separation in the Netherlands.

Further explanations concern modal Dutch attitudes and values.

6 *The dominance of the humanitarian values of Erasmus.* Many think of the Netherlands as sternly Calvinistic in the past. To be sure, fundamentalistic branches of the Dutch Reformed Church still strongly reflect Calvinistic values. And these sectors were overrepresented among Dutch settlers to South Africa and Michigan. But, generally the humanitarian philosophy of Erasmus was more influential than were Calvinistic tenets in shaping Dutch values. Schama (1987), in *The Embarrassment of Riches*, argues that this was true even for the Amsterdam elite in the early seventeenth century. To the extent that this has been the case for much of the nation, Dutch tolerance is a consistent result of a much wider Erasmus tradition.

7 *Conflict avoidance as a general Dutch characteristic.* Consistent with the Erasmus theory, Dutch tolerance may simply be part of a broader, more embedded characteristic of conflict avoidance. In a small land, with centuries of adapting to flood dangers and high population density, there have been good reasons to maximize cooperation and minimize conflict. Many Dutch cultural devices serve this function – from conversational forms and emotional control to low rates of violence. Lijphart (1968) sees it as a crucial component of the Dutch political system of accommodation.

Dutch tolerance can thus be another, highly adaptive, mechanism for maintaining order in an endangered, crowded society. Superordinate goals of survival, apparent to all, facilitated cross-*zuilen* cooperation. In short, conflict avoidance in a society faced with constant external and internal threats shifted the situation from a zero-sum to a mixed motive game for both the elites and the masses.

8 *As a trading nation, the Netherlands valued other cultures.* The most popular explanation for the *verzuiling* puzzle is to cite the Dutch tradition of international trade. Hollanders have been seafaring traders for four centuries. This experience, goes the argument, led to an early appreciation of other cultures and languages. They became skilled at international trade, thanks to an astute understanding of their foreign trading partners.

This factor undoubtedly plays a role. Yet it, too, cannot serve as a full account. There are many nations that are successful international traders, but none have developed a similar domestic tradition of tolerance. Indeed, modern Japan shows that it is possible to be highly effective world traders while maintaining a domestic xenophobia of peoples of other cultures and races.

A Social Psychological Contribution

Our understanding of the *verzuiling* puzzle and Dutch intergroup relations can be furthered by a more precise conceptualization of Dutch attitudes toward their minorities.

We begin by asking how current intergroup attitudes in the Netherlands differ from those of its European neighbors. For an answer, we draw on data from the fall 1988 Eurobarometer surveys of probability samples from Great Britain and West Germany as well as the Netherlands. Our two Dutch surveys, one asking for opinions about Turks and the other about Surinamers, use the same questions as surveys that ask about West Indians in Great Britain and Turks in Germany. These rich data allow cross-national tests for any distinctiveness of Dutch intergroup attitudes.

Based on earlier work in the US, we devised two reliable scales of 10 items each to measure contrasting types of prejudice (Pettigrew and Meertens, 1995). Blatant prejudice is the direct and traditional form of prejudice. The Blatant Scale sought agreement or disagreement to such statements as: "Turks have jobs that the Dutch should have;" and "Surinamers come from less able races and this explains why they are not as well off as most Dutch people."

The subtle variety is a more distant, modern form of prejudice. The subtle scale asked for agreement or disagreement with such statements as: "Surinamers living here should not push themselves where they are not wanted;" and "Turks living here teach their children values and skills different from those required to be successful in the Netherlands." Other questions asked about how culturally different the minority is and whether the respondent had ever felt admiration or sympathy for members of the minority.

For controls, we compare Dutch attitudes toward Turks on these two scales with those of Germans toward Turks, and Dutch attitudes toward Surinamers with those of the British toward West Indians. Figure 8.1 provides the results. When we compare the scale means for blatant prejudice, Dutch attitudes toward both the Turks and Surinamers are indeed distinctive. As the special case theory predicts, Dutch respondents express significantly less blatant prejudice toward these minority groups than do the Germans toward Turks or the British toward West Indians.

The picture changes sharply when we check the data on subtle prejudice. The Dutch means for subtle prejudice against Turks are significantly *higher* than those of Germans, and the Dutch means for subtle prejudice against Surinamers are the same as those of the British toward West Indians. These results are consistent with the regular racism theory of Dutch intergroup relations.

But is subtle prejudice really prejudice? Since the questions about cultural differences and positive feelings in the Subtle Scale are not traditional means of measuring prejudice, we must check on the criterion validity of the new scale. In all the probability samples, the subtle prejudice scale correlated highly with the more traditional blatant prejudice scale (+.48 to +.69). Moreover, the subtle scale scores in each sample predicted more restrictive attitudes toward immigration policy and the rights of minorities in the country (Pettigrew and Meertens, 1995).

In short, Dutch tolerance rejects crude, blatant expressions of intergroup prejudice and discrimination. Nonetheless, the Dutch express indirect, subtle forms of prejudice that predict outgroup rejection in ways similar to that of blatant prejudice. Making a clear distinction between the two forms of prejudice, blatant and subtle, allows a more precise restatement of the *verzuiling* puzzle.

A Normative Restatement of the Puzzle

These survey data on prejudice suggest a normative approach to the problem. We posit the existence of a four-centuries-old Dutch norm that proscribes blatant prejudice and discrimination against outsiders. This would account for the fact that Dutch means on blatant prejudice (see figure 8.1) are so below those of comparable countries. Yet subtle prejudice means in figure 8.1 suggest that these less direct forms often "slip in under" the antiblatant prejudice norm.

In proposing a normative explanation, we must be aware of its weaknesses. Too often social scientists invoke norms in an *ad hoc*, circular manner: they posit a norm to explain a particular social phenomenon, then they use the phenomenon itself to "prove" the existence of the norm. Independent evidence for the norm is obviously

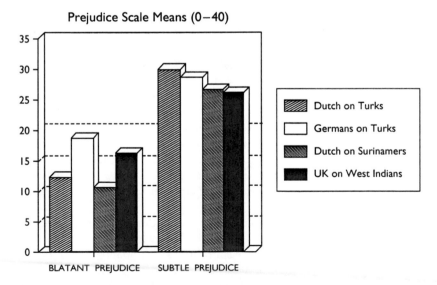

Figure 8.1   Blatant and subtle prejudice in three nations
Source: Pettigrew and Meertens, 1995.

needed. More precisely, the historical origins of the norm must be explored and cross-societal comparative data employed to specify the norm more carefully.

Recast in this context, the structural and value arguments cited to explain Dutch tolerance are potential causal factors in the creation of a distinctive Dutch norm. In particular, we believe that the elites established a generalized norm against blatant expressions of prejudice toward persons outside of one's own *zuil*, with an eye toward the best interests of both the nation and their *zuil*. The superordinate goals of survival against threatening seas and external enemies made the confluence of interests between nation and *zuilen* possible. Indeed, superordinate goals are a key element in generating intergroup harmony (Sherif, 1966).

We have seen that Dutch tolerance – defined here as a distinctive norm against blatant prejudice and discrimination – waxed and waned in particular situations and over past centuries. For the current operation of the norm in the Netherlands, we offer three types of additional evidence – from judges' ratings, independent survey data, and actual discriminatory behavior in the field.

We had psychology students from the University of Amsterdam rate the most prejudiced response to each of our 20 blatant and subtle prejudice scale items. For their ratings, the students used 10-point bipolar scales ranging from "socially not acceptable" (score = 1) to "socially acceptable" (score = 10). A sample of 22 students rated the items with Turks as the targets; and another sample of 26 rated the items with Surinamers as the targets. We assume that those prejudice answers thought by the judges to be the least socially acceptable violate a Dutch cultural norm. The judges did not know that the items were from prejudice scales, and they were requested to make their ratings according to what they believed "the Dutch in general would find socially acceptable." There was strong consensus among the judges in their ratings (mean intercorrelation = +.956).

As expected, the prejudiced answers to the 10 items from the blatant measure of prejudice were judged far less "socially acceptable" than were the prejudiced answers from the 10 items of the subtle measure of prejudice. These differences are highly significant (on Turks, mean blatant items = 26.64, mean subtle items = 50.09, t (21) = 8.16, p < .0001, or Wilcoxon signed-ranks test, Z = 4.01, p < .0001; on Surinamers, mean blatant items = 28.19, mean subtle items = 46.19, t (25) = 10.60, p < .0001, or Wilcoxon signed-rank test, Z = 4.46, p < .0001).

More importantly, these ratings of the social acceptability of the 20 prejudice responses correlate significantly and negatively with the item differences between the Dutch, German and British samples. That is, those items whose prejudiced responses were rated by our judges as the least socially acceptable with respect to Surinamers in Dutch society are the same items that most strongly differentiated the Dutch sample about the Surinamers from the British sample about West Indians (rho = −.76, p <.001).

Similarly, those items whose prejudiced responses were rated by our judges as the least socially acceptable with respect to Turks in Dutch society are the same items that most strongly differentiated the Dutch and German samples about the Turks (rho = −.52, p <.02). For example, our judges indicated that strong agreement with the overtly racist item "Turks come from less able races..." is highly unacceptable in the Netherlands. And it is this item that yielded the largest differences between the Dutch and German samples and one of the largest differences between the Dutch and British samples.

Another test is whether norm-violating behavior provokes negative reactions. In 1983, a survey asked Dutch respondents how they would react if confronted by friends or colleagues with the statement "All foreigners should be sent away from the country." Fifty-one percent answered they would contradict the statement, 26% would be annoyed or remain passive, only 16% would be indifferent and 7% would agree (Castenmiller and Brants, 1984).

The most direct test involves data on discrimination. Den Uyl (1986) conducted a field experiment to determine if there were discrimination by Dutch temporary job placement companies. Minority or majority testers sought jobs 75 times each at temporary job agencies. Only twice was the minority applicant rejected when the majority applicant with the same credentials was offered a job – a blatant form of discrimination. But in 28 of 75 comparisons (37%), the minority tester received less help from the agencies than did the majority tester – a subtle expression of discrimination.

Important for our thesis, the publication of these results in the press gained wide attention. Once made public, any form of minority rejection was seen as a norm violation. Under governmental pressure, the temporary job agencies drew up a new code of ethical behavior that proscribed even subtle expressions of discrimination. Later tests of the agencies revealed that there had in fact been effective changes made in the treatment of minority job applicants.

Such public indications of the antiblatant prejudice norm are common in Dutch society. For example, research on affirmative action employment programs in the Dutch urban police uncovers some overt but mostly subtle forms of majority resistance – though not nearly as intense as that usually found in the US (De Vries and Pettigrew, 1994). A national labor union presented the Amsterdam Police Force with a special award for its effective affirmative action program.

The *Verzuiling* Puzzle in Perspective

We have tried to unravel the *verzuiling* puzzle by recasting it. To summarize our contentions, we have advanced the following:

1   The intergroup tolerance of the Netherlands is a genuine phenomenon, though it needs to be carefully delimited and specified. It has not been a universal characteristic across the last four centuries, across all groups or all realms. Even today Dutch minorities suffer far higher unemployment rates than do others. Yet a tolerance influenced by Erasmus and rooted in the sixteenth and seventeenth centuries represents a distinctive Dutch cultural theme of special interest.
2   Recent survey data help to specify Dutch tolerance by distinguishing between blatant and subtle prejudice. The norm of intergroup tolerance in the Netherlands repudiates blatant forms, but often not subtle forms, of intergroup prejudice.
3   The *verzuiling* system of intergroup relations characterized Dutch intergroup relations over the past four centuries. This system required a systematic separ-

ation of the population into *zuilen*, or pillars, upon which were imposed some degree of segregation and "separate but equal" distribution of resources. An apparent contradiction to intergroup theory is raised by the coexistence of the distinctive pattern of intergroup tolerance with this system – which should have resulted in increased group differences and conflict. We labeled this "the *verzuiling* puzzle."

4   An array of possible solutions to the puzzle can be advanced. We described eight of them – ranging from special aspects of Dutch history and politics (no feudal system, refugee contributions to the Dutch economy, the modest size of Dutch minorities, similar proportions of Catholics and Protestants, and a strong tradition of elite cooperation) to modal values (the humanitarian values of Erasmus, a broad tradition of conflict avoidance, and the valuing of other cultures by a trading nation). In particular, we stress the importance of elite cooperation.

5   We posit a strong Dutch norm that proscribes blatant, but not subtle, prejudice and discrimination. This norm has a long history, and a variety of evidence reveals its operation.

Once one accepts the existence of a powerful Dutch norm against blatant forms of anti-minority prejudice and discrimination, the *verzuiling* puzzle is recast. We contend that Dutch tolerance has been achieved over the centuries largely in spite of, rather than because of, the *verzuiling* system. Dutch society managed this feat because of a unique normative structure. And this antiblatant norm has retained its force until the present, bolstered by the processes of secularization and individualization since the 1960s that have eroded the *verzuiling* system.

Thus, the puzzle is more apparent than real. It does not represent as serious a challenge to theory as it first appears. However, the puzzle does contribute a corollary to basic theory: namely, negative effects of intergroup separation and salience can, under particular circumstances, be overcome by a strong normative structure against blatant forms of prejudice and discrimination.

The problem, then, is not to solve the *verzuiling* puzzle, but to determine how this unique, pro-tolerance normative structure became established, how it has persisted, and how it operates to shape current Dutch intergroup relations. We suggest an important part of the answer lies in the strong Dutch tradition of cooperation in pursuit of superordinate goals that benefit both the individual groups and the nation.

References

Allport, G. W. (1954.) *The Nature of Prejudice*. Reading, MA: Addison-Wesley.

Bax, E. H. (1990.) *Modernization and Cleavage in Dutch Society*. Aldershot: Avebury.

Bovenkerk, F., Bruin, K., Brunt, L., and Wouters, H. (1985.) *Vreemd Volk, Gemengde Gevoelens* [Strange people, mixed feelings]. Meppel, The Netherlands: Boom.

Brasse, P., and Sikking, E. (1986.) *Positie en Kansen van Etnische Minderheden in Nederlandse Ondernemingen* [The position and chances of ethnic minorities in Dutch companies]. Den Haag, The Netherlands: Ministerie van Sociale Zaken en Werk-gelegenheid.

Castenmiller, P., and Brants, K. (1984.) (In)tolerantie ten opzichte van etniche minderheden [(In)tolerance of ethnic minorities]. Unpublished report, Department of Collective Political Behavior, University of Amsterdam. Amsterdam, The Netherlands.

Den Uyl, R., Choenni, C. E. S., and Bovenkerk, F. (1986.) *Mag het Ook eeh Buitenlander Wezen?: Discriminatie bij Uitzendburo's* [Is a foreigner allowed? Discrimination by temporary employment agencies]. Utrecht, The Netherlands: National Bureau Against Racism.

De Vries, S., and Pettigrew, T. F. (1994.) A comparative perspective on affirmative action: *Positieve actie* in the Netherlands. *Basic and Applied Social Psychology,* vol. 15 (1 & 2), pp. 179–99.

Essed, P. (1984.) *Alledaags Racisme* [Everyday racism]. Amsterdam, The Netherlands: Sara.

Gijswijt-Hofstra, M., Ed. (1989.) *Een Schijn van Verdraagzaamheid: Afwijking en Tolerantie in Nederland van de Zestiende Eeuw tot Heden.* [A semblance of tolerance: Deviance and tolerance in the Netherlands from the 16th century to the present]. Hilversum, The Netherlands: Verloren.

Lijphart, A. (1968.) *The Politics of Accommodation: Pluralism and Democracy in the Netherlands.* Berkeley: University of California Press.

Pettigrew, T. F., and Meertens, R. W. (1995.) Subtle and blatant prejudice in Western Europe. *European Journal of Social Psychology, 25,* 57–75.

Schama, S. (1987.) *The Embarrassment of Riches: An Interpretation of Dutch Culture in the Golden Age.* New York: Knopf.

Schuster, J. (1991.) The Dutch state and post-war immigration: The racialisation and assimilation of Eurasian immigrants from 1949 to 1968. Unpublished paper, Department of Cultural Anthropology. Utrecht University, Utrecht, The Netherlands.

Sherif, M. (1966.) *In Common Predicament.* Boston: Houghton Mifflin.

Surie, H. G. (1973.) De Gerepatrieerden [The Repatriates]. In J. Verwey-Jonker (Ed.) *De Allochtonen in Nederland* [Minorities in the Netherlands]. Den Haag, the Netherlands: Staatsuitgeverij.

Van Schendelen, M. P. C. M., Ed. (1984.) *Consociationalism, Pillarization and Conflict-Management in the Low Countries.* Meppel, the Netherlands: Boom.

Veenman, J., and Roelandt, T. (1990.) Allochtonen: Achterstand en achterstelling [Minorities: Disadvantage and subordination]. In J. J. Schippers (Ed.) *Arbeidsmarkt en Maatschappelijke Ongelickheid* [The labor market and societal inequality]. Groningen, the Netherlands: Wolters-Noordhoff.

9 The Discourse of Race in Modern China

Frank Dikötter

Was the notion of a 'yellow race' imposed on China by Europeans in the late nineteenth century? The term only appeared in Europe at the end of the seventeenth century, probably in response to Jesuit reports on the symbolic significance of the colour yellow in China. It did not exist in the ancient world, and was not used by travellers of the Middle Ages such as Marco Polo, Pian del Carpini, Bento de Goes or any of the Arab traders. In 1655 the first European mission to the Qing described the Chinese as having a white complexion, 'equal to the Europeans', except for some southerners whose skin was 'slightly brown'.[1] When a young inhabitant of the Celestial Kingdom was presented at the court of Louis XIV in 1684, he was described as a 'young Indian'. The first scientific work in which the notion of a 'yellow race' appeared was François Bernier's 'Étrennes adressées à Madame de la Sablière pour l'année 1688'.[2] In China, however, the symbolic meanings ascribed to the colour yellow placed it in a privileged position in the construction of social identities. Yellow, one of the five 'pure' colours in China, had long been symbolic of grandeur and of the emperor. In both popular and literate culture, yellow was the colour of the Emperor of the Middle Kingdom, ancestral home of the 'descendants of the Yellow Emperor' who, it was claimed, had originated in the valley of the Yellow River. Wang Fuzhi (1619–92), a seventeenth-century scholar who wrote after the fall of the Ming and the invasion of China by the Manchus, entitled one of his more important works the *Yellow Book* (*Huangshu*) (1656): the last chapter contrasted the imperial colour yellow to 'mixed' colours, and named China the 'Yellow Centre' (*huangzhong*).[3] On more popular discursive registers, legends circulated about the origins of mankind in which noble people were said to be made out of yellow mud and ignoble people of vulgar rope.[4] These folk accounts were appropriated and rearticulated into a racial identity by scholars in the late nineteenth century. Huang Zunxian (1848–1905), for instance, recorded in his diary when aged twenty that 'all men are fashioned out of yellow mud'. At the age of fifty-four, as one of the most outstanding reformers and an important architect in the racialisation of identity, he publicly wondered 'Why is the yellow race not the only race in the world?'[5] Far from being a negative label imposed on Chinese scholars by the 'cultural hegemony' of 'imperialism', the notion of a 'yellow race' was a positive symbol of imperial nobility which was actively mobilised by reformers who transformed it into a powerful and effective means of identification. The only sector of the social field which denounced the reformers' use of terms like 'yellow race' (*huangzhong*) and 'white race' (*baizhong*) were conservative scholars, mainly because it undermined imperial cosmologies on which their power and knowledge was predicated.[6]

Chinese reformers in the 1890s were active agents who participated in the invention of their identities. They were not the passive recipients of a 'derivative discourse', but creative individuals who selectively appropriated elements of foreign thought systems in a process of cultural interaction. More important, the reform movement which contributed so much to the invention of racial identities in China was largely the product of complex interactions and fusions of different indigenous schools of thought, such as New Text Confucianism, statecraft scholarship (*jingshi*), classical non-canonical philosophies (*zhuzixue*) and Mahayana Buddhism, all of which had virtually nothing to do with Western learning. In other words, racial identities during the late imperial period were created through cultural interaction with a variety of schools of thought by a group of reformers who actively responded to the decline of imperial cosmology. Far from being a 'derivative discourse' of a more 'authentic' form of 'white racism', narratives of blood and descent in China had an internal cohesion which was based on the active reconfiguration of indigenous modes of representation. Lineage discourse was perhaps one of the most prominent elements in the construction of symbolic boundaries between racially defined groups of people.

The Reconfiguration of Lineage Discourse and the Emergence of Racial Taxonomies

The racial categories of analysis which first emerged in China with the rise of nationalism were largely constructed on the basis of indigenous modes of representation, in particular lineage discourse. The Qing era was marked by a consolidation of the cult of patrilineal descent, centre of a broad movement of social reform that had emphasised the family and the lineage (*zu*) since the collapse of the Ming. Considerable friction arose between lineages throughout the nineteenth century in response to heightened competition over natural resources, the need to control market towns, the gradual erosion of social order and organisational disorders caused by demography pressures. Lineage feuds as well as interethnic conflicts (*fenlei xiedou*) prevailed throughout the empire, but were more common in the south-east, where the institution of the lineage had grown more powerful than in the north. The militarisation of powerful lineages reinforced folk models of kinship solidarity, forcing in turn more loosely organised associations to form a unified descent group under the leadership of the gentry. At court level, too, ideologies of descent became increasingly important, in particular with the erosion of a sense of cultural identity among Manchu aristocrats. Racial identity through patrilineal descent became important in the Qianlong period (1736–95), when the court progressively turned towards a rigid taxonomy of distinct descent lines (*zu*) to distinguish between Han, Manchu, Mongol or Tibetan.[10] Within three distinct social levels – popular culture, gentry society and court politics – the deployment of more stable folk notions of patrilineal descent became widespread in the creation and maintenance of group boundaries.

The racialisation of lineage discourse during the last decade of the nineteenth century was largely the work of the 1898 reformers, who championed a radical transformation of imperial institutions and orthodox ideology. In contrast to their precursors, they promoted an alternative body of knowledge which derived its legitimacy independently from the official examination system. It was the product of a fusion between different indigenous strains of knowledge and foreign discursive repertoires, with the principal object of political attention being the species. The scientific category of 'race' and the administrative category of 'population' were heralded as objects worthy of systematic investigation. Folk models of shared kinship and élite culture stressed patrilineal descent in the creation and maintenance of group boundaries. Cultural intermediaries like Liang Qichao and Kang Youwei selectively appropriated scientific knowledge from foreign discursive repertoires, actively manipulated evolutionary theories to bolster theories of pure origins; they reconfigured folk notions of patrilineal descent into a racial discourse which represented all inhabitants of China as the descendants of the Yellow Emperor. The semantic similarity between *zu* as lineage and *zu* as race was rearticulated in a new racialised identity called *huangzhong*, meaning both 'lineage of the Yellow Emperor' and 'yellow race'. Extrapolating from an indigenous vision of lineage feuds, which permeated the social landscape of late imperial China, the reformers ordered mankind into a racial hierarchy of biological groups where 'yellows' competed with 'whites' over degenerate breeds of 'browns', 'blacks' and 'reds'. Thriving on its affinity with lineage discourse, 'race' thus gradually emerged as the most common symbol of national cohesion, permanently replacing more conventional emblems of cultural identity. The threat of racial extinction (*miezhong*), a powerful message of fear based on more popular anxieties about lineage extinction (*miezu*), was often raised to bolster the reformers' message of change: 'They will enslave us and hinder the development of our spirit and body.... The brown and black races constantly waver between life and death, why not the 400 million of yellows?'[7] In the reformers' symbolic network of racialised Others, the dominating 'white' and 'yellow races' were opposed to the 'darker races', doomed by hereditary inadequacy to racial extinction. Liang Qichao rearticulated traditional social hierarchies into a new racial taxonomy of 'noble' (*guizhong*) and 'low' (*jianzhong*), 'superior' (*youzhong*) and 'inferior' (*liezhong*), 'historical' and 'ahistorical races' (*youlishi de zhongzu*). The widespread distinction between 'common people' (*liangmin*) and 'mean people' (*jianmin*) that had officially characterised late imperial China up till the early eighteenth century also found an echo in Tang Caichang (1867–1900), who opposed 'fine races' (*liangzhong*) to 'mean races' (*jianzhong*). He phrased it in evenly balanced clauses reminiscent of the classical language: 'Yellow and white are wise, red and black are stupid; yellow and white are rulers, red and black are slaves; yellow and white are united, red and black are scattered.'[8]

The myth of blood was further sealed by the turn of the century when the revolutionaries created a national symbol out of the Yellow Emperor. Liu Shipei (1884–1919), to take but one example, advocated the introduction of a calendar in which the foundation year corresponded to the birth of the Yellow Emperor. 'They [the reformers] see the preservation of religion as a handle, so they use the birth of Confucius as the starting date of the calendar; the purpose of our generation is preservation of the race, so we use the birth of the Yellow Emperor as a founding date.'[9] Early twentieth-century revolutionaries like Chen Tianhua (1875–1905) infused kin terms, previously deployed in lineage discourse, into racial frames of reference to foster the much needed bonds of national loyalty: 'The racial feeling comes from birth onwards. For the members of one's own race, there is surely mutual intimacy and love; for the members of a foreign race, there is surely mutual savagery and killing.'[10] The first issue of the *Tides of Zhejiang*, a nationalist journal published in Japan by Chinese students, stated that 'those who are able to group their own tribe into an organised body able to resist other groups will survive.' In an era dominated by 'racial competition', the key to survival lay in the cohesive force of the group (*qunli*). Nationalism fostered unity, as it 'erects borders against the outside and unites the group inside'.[11] A contributor to the journal *Yunnan* attributed the decline of the 'barbarian red and the savage black races' to their ignorance of the racial principles of nationalism: a nation needed a 'group strategy and group strength'.[12] World politics were expounded in terms of racial cohesion. India, for instance, had been conquered by the 'white race' because its class system inhibited racial homogeneity.[13] Russians were a 'crossbreed between Europeans and Asians and nothing else', another polemicist claimed. A cranial analysis and a detailed racial investigation revealed that the Russians had Asian blood running in their veins. This racial mix was responsible for Russia's inability to group.[14] The naval superiority of the United States, on the other hand, was ascribed to its racial quality: were not the Americans an inch taller than the English?[15] Culture, nation and race had become coterminous in the symbolic universe of China's revolutionaries.

Racial Discourse in Republican China

The imperial reformers failed to secure the power necessary to implement their vision of change. However, the promotion of racial definitions of identity would become widespread after the fall of the Qing empire in 1911, a momentous political event which was marked by a number of important developments. First came the rapid transformation of the traditional gentry into powerful new élites, such as factory managers, bankers, lawyers, doctors, scientists, educators and journalists – the result of new economic opportunities created through contacts with foreign traders and the closer integration of the country into a global economy. The gradual emergence of new social formations was particularly pronounced in the large metropolises of the coast. Based on a common ground of social values, a sophisticated network of relations webbed intellectuals, urban notables and financial élites together into a modernising avant-garde. Secondly, with the collapse of the imperial system, neo-Confucian knowledge rapidly lost its credibility and authority. Previously imagined as a purposeful whole, a benevolent structure which could not exist independently from ethical forces, 'nature' was now conceptualised as a set of impersonal forces that could be objectively investigated. No longer were physical bodies thought to be linked to the cosmological foundations of the universe: bodies were produced by biological laws inherent in 'nature'. With the decline of conformity to the moral imperatives enshrined in a canon of Confucian texts, a growing number of people believed 'truth' to be encoded in a nature which only science could decipher: identity, ancestry and meaning were buried deep inside the body. Embryology or genetics could establish differences between population groups, not philology or palaeography. Human biology replaced imperial cosmology as the epistemological foundation for social order. Thirdly, private printing houses, run by private associations of merchants, greatly profited from increased demand for new books and the general growth in literacy after the fall of the empire, and rapidly grew into huge publishing companies. The printed pages which poured forth from the vernacular press greatly facilitated the accessibility of new cultural modes to a larger public of consumers.

Shared consumption of cultural products which heralded the demise of 'primitive races' and the regeneration of the 'yellow race' contributed to the construction of imagined boundaries based on blood. The epistemic shift from cosmology to biology was particularly evident in studies in anthropometry, craniology and raciology. Racial categories of analysis were consolidated by endless references to science. Folk notions of biological discontinuity, of course, had long existed in popular culture. To this day, for instance, the Cantonese describe the Tanka, a population group of boat-dwellers in South China, as people with six toes on each foot: they are claimed to be of non-Han descent. The small toenails of the Mongols are said by the Han to be cloven, while minorities in Hainan have long been alleged to have a tail. A variety of cultural intermediaries – social reformers, professional writers, medical researchers, university professors – scientised these folk notions of common stock and legitimised racial discourse through appeals to the authority of science. Chen Yucang (1889–1947), director of the Medical College of Tongji University and a secretary to the Legislative Yuan, boldly postulated that cranial weight was the only indicator of the degree of civilisation: 'If we compare the cranial weights of different people, the civilised are somewhat heavier than the savages, and the Chinese brain is slightly heavier than the European brain.' Liang Boqiang, in an oft-quoted study on the 'Chinese race' published in 1926, took the blood's 'index of agglutination' as an indicator of purity,[16] while the absence of body hair came to symbolise a biological boundary of the 'Chinese race' for a popular writer like Lin Yutang (1895–1976), who even proclaimed that 'On good authority from medical doctors, and from references in writing, one knows that a perfectly bare *mons veneris* is not uncommon in Chinese women.'[17] Archaeologists, too, sought evidence of human beginnings in China. Like many of his contemporaries, Lin Yan cited the discovery of Peking Man at Zhoukoudian as evidence that the 'Chinese race' had existed on the soil of the Middle Kingdom since the earliest stage of civilisation. Excavations supported his hypotheses by demonstrating that migrations had taken place only within the empire. It was concluded that China was inhabited by 'the earth's most ancient original inhabitants'.[18]

If 'Chineseness' was thought to be rooted in every part of the body, cultural differences between groups of people were also claimed to be solidly grounded in nature, in particular in the case of Africans. The *Great Dictionary of Zoology* (1923), the first reference work of its kind, contended that the 'black race' had 'a rather long head, many protruding teeth and a quite low forehead, so that their face is inclined towards the back. This type of people have a shameful and inferior way of thinking, and have no capacity to shine in history.'[19] In a popular introduction to the 'human races of the world', professor Gu Shoubai wrote that black people could be recognised by their smell. They had a 'protruding jaw, very thick lips, a narrow forehead' and emitted an offensive stench.[20] Professor Gong Tingz-hang claimed that even the slightest physical contact with a black person was enough for the olfactory organs to be repelled by an 'amazing stench'.[21] The presumed inferiority of African people was made to appear permanent and immut-able through a discourse of race which firmly located social differences inside the body: the use of the term 'black slave race', common in China until the 1920s, most clearly expressed the conflation of social and racial differences. Chen Jian-shan, the popular evolutionist, classified the 'black slave' with the chimpanzees, gorillas and Australians as a branch of the propithecantropus.[22] A popular zoology textbook first published in 1916 included a paragraph on the differences between man and ape. The 'inferior races' (*liedeng zhongzu*) had a facial index similar to that of the orang-utan. The 'black slave' was classified in the gorilla branch, and Malays were represented as descendants of the orang-utan.[23]

Racialised senses of identity also permeated lower levels of education after the foundation of the Republic in 1911. The opening sentence of a chapter on 'human races' in a 1920 textbook for middle schools declared that 'among the world's races, there are strong and weak constitutions, there are black and white skins, there is hard and soft hair, there are superior and inferior cultures. A rapid overview shows that they are not of the same level.'[24] Even in primary schools, readings on racial politics became part of the curriculum: 'Mankind is divided into five races. The yellow and white races are relatively strong and intelligent. Because the other races are feeble and stupid, they are being exterminated by the white race. Only the yellow race competes with the white race. This is so-called evolution... Among the contemporary races that could be called superior, there are only the yellow and the white races. China is the yellow race.'[25] Although it is clear that individual writers, political groups and academic institutions had differ-ent ideas about the meanings of physical features, many people in China had come to identify themselves and others in terms of 'race' by the end of the Republican period. The success of racial discourse in China, in short, was the result of a significant degree of convergence between popular culture and officially sponsored discourses of race, of the scientisation of folk models of identity and of the recon-figuration of more stable notions of descent, lineage and genealogy.

Some isolated voices in China openly contested the existence of a racial tax-onomy in mankind: Zhang Junmai, for instance, wisely excluded 'common blood' from his definition of the nation.[26] Qi Sihe also criticised the use of racial categor-ies of analysis in China, and pointed out how 'race' was a declining notion in the West.[27] Generally, however, racial discourse was a dominant practice which cut across most political positions, from the fascist core of the Guomindang to the communist theories of Li Dazhao. Its fundamental role in the construction of racialised boundaries between Self and Other, its powerful appeal to a cultural sense of belonging based on presumed immutable links of blood, its authoritative worldview in which social differences could be explained in terms of stable bio-logical laws, all these aspects provided racial discourse with a singular resilience: it shaped the identity of millions of people in Republican China, as it had done for people in Europe and the United States.

Conflicting feelings of superiority and inferiority were part of the racialisation of social encounters. As Hong Yuan observed in 1930, 'Most of the [Chinese] people, however, continue to think of our race as inherently superior to that of our neighbours of lighter or darker skin. Indeed there is very often a set of superiority and inferiority complexes stirring within those who have constant or occasional contacts with foreigners. He constantly persuades himself of his unexplainable superiority over the foreigner, but frequently has to rationalize in order to disperse the inferiority complex'.[28] Racial classifications between different population groups were so important that they often preceded and shaped real social encounters. The poet Wen Yiduo, for instance, sailed for the United States in 1922, but even on board his courage ebbed away as he felt increasingly apprehensive of racial discrimination in the West. In America he felt lonely and homesick: he described himself as the 'Exiled Prisoner'. Wen Yiduo wrote home: 'For a thoughtful young Chinese, the taste of life here in America is beyond description. When I return home for New Year, the year after next, I shall talk with you around the fire, I shall weep bitterly and shed tears to give vent to all the accumulated indignation. I have a nation, I have a history and a culture of five thousand years: how can this be inferior to the Americans?'[29]

It is undeniable that some Chinese students genuinely suffered from racial discrimination abroad, although undoubtedly an element of self-victimisation and self-humiliation entered into the composition of such feelings. More important, however, they often interpreted their social encounters abroad from a cultural repertoire which reinforced the racialisation of Others. Even social experiences that had the potential to destabilise their sense of identity were appropriated and integrated into a racial frame of reference. Pan Guangdan, the most outspoken proponent of eugenics in China, expressed his disappointment with the unwillingness of a book entitled *The American Negro*, edited by Donald Young in 1928, to speak in terms of racial inequality:

> But to be true to observable facts, in any given period of time sufficiently long for selection to take effect, races *as groups are* different, unequal, and there is no reason except one based upon sentiment why we cannot refer to them in terms of inferiority and superiority, when facts warrant us. It is to be suspected that the Jewish scholars, themselves belonging to a racial group which has long been unjustly discriminated against, have unwittingly developed among themselves a defensive mechanism which is influencing their judgements on racial questions. The reviewer recalls with regret that during his students days [in the United States] he had estranged some of his best Jewish friends for his candid views on the point of racial inequality.[30]

Eugenic ideas, indeed, were also dominant among modernising élites in Republican China. Heredity, descent, sexual hygiene and race became the core themes of medical and eugenic discourses, which thrived on folk ideas of patrilineal descent. In their racialisation of the nation, the discourse of eugenics most clearly endowed the state with a responsibility in the production of a healthy population. Although eugenics in China never achieved legislative expression, in contrast to other countries like the USA and Germany, ideas of race improvement were eagerly appropriated and spread by the new medical professions. As a *Textbook of Civic Biology* (1924) for middle schools put it, 'the choice of a partner who is unfit harms society and the future of the race. To establish a strong country, it is necessary to have strong citizens. To have strong and healthy citizens, one cannot but implement eugenics. Eugenics eliminate inferior elements and foster people who are strong and healthy in body and mind.'[31] Proponents of eugenics claimed that breeding principles such as assortative mating and artificial selection could prevent further degeneration. Although modernising élites were instrumental in putting forward eugenic views, theories of race improvement circulated among a much wider audience in China. Cheap textbooks on heredity and genetics explained to the public the dangers of racial degeneration. Primers, self-study manuals, pamphlets and 'ABC' introductions to mainline eugenics were published throughout the 1920s. Hereditary principles, granting sex a biological responsibility for future generations, were thought to highlight further the need for social discipline. Mendelian laws were circulated by popular journalists and commercial writers to underline how genetic factors determined the endowment of an individual. Student magazines urged university students to undertake eugenic research for the sake of advancing the 'race', the state, and the individual.[32] In the 1930s, eugenic arguments became increasingly common in medical circles, 'degeneration' and 'racial hygiene' being the catchwords of the day. Official marriage guides encouraged 'superior' people to marry for the regeneration of the 'race',[33] since 'inferior' and 'weak' characteristics were transmitted through sexual congress; a popular guide for women published by the Commercial Press described hereditary diseases as the 'germs' which threatened the nation with degeneration and final extinction (*zhongzu zimie*).[34] Professor Yi Jiayue, a highly respected member of the academic community, made the forceful statement that 'if we want to strengthen the race, there is no time to waste. We should first implement a eugenic program. Strictly speaking, we should not just forbid the sexually diseased, the morons and the insane to marry. For those who abuse the sexual instinct and create a menace to future generations, there can be only one appropriate law of restraint: castration!'[35]

Racialised Identities in Contemporary China

Racial frames of reference never disappeared from the People's Republic of China, and have generally increased within popular culture, scientific circles and government publications in the Deng Xiaoping era. University students have been the social group most prominently involved in one of the more recent attempts to promote skin colour as a marker of social status. Physical attacks and demonstrations against African students on the university campuses of the People's Republic throughout the 1980s have been the most widely publicised feature of these racialised practices. Far from being a manifestation of a vestigial form of xenophobia, these events are an intrinsic part of racialised trends of thought which have been diversely deployed in China since the end of the nineteenth century. Articulated in a distinct cultural site (university campuses) by a specific social group (university students) in the political context of the reforms initiated by Deng Xiaoping since 1978, campus racism demonstrates how contradictory discourses of 'race' and 'human rights' can be harnessed together in politicised oppositions to the state: six months after their mass demonstrations against Africans in Nanjing, students were occupying Tiananmen square in the name of 'democracy'.

Images of foreign sexuality have been important in the racialisation of encounters between African and Chinese students, and have played an even greater role in the spread of collective anxieties about sexually transmitted diseases (STDs). On popular levels, the myth of 'international syphilis' (*guoji meidu*) has contrasted the pure blood of Chinese people to the polluted blood of outsiders, said to have become immune to syphilis after centuries of sexual promiscuity. Official discourse and popular culture have also explained AIDS as an evil from abroad, and prostitutes who offered their service to foreigners were singled out for severe punishment in the late 1980s. . . .

In contrast to recent efforts made by some other governments, there is no indication that the hierarchies of power maintained through racial discourse are being contested in any significant way by the cultural centres of authority in China. Critical intellectuals in Hong Kong and Taiwan have also failed to address the issue. Bo Yang's indignant exclamation that 'Chinese racism is far more serious than American racism' remains no more than a gratuitous statement which is never followed by any effort at critical inquiry.[36] In Singapore too, racialised identities have been promoted by the government in the official conflation of notions of culture, ethnicity and race. The desire to consolidate and expand a biologised notion of Chinese identity in mainland China and elsewhere may further be reinforced by the resurgence of overseas networks. Greater China, or the invention of a community that transcends the political boundaries of the People's Republic, can very well be based on the racialisation of 'Chineseness'.

Three conclusions might be drawn from this [analysis]. First, racialised identities are central, and not peripheral, to notions of identity in China: precisely because of the extreme diversity of religious practices, family structures, spoken languages and regional cultures of population groups that all define themselves as 'Chinese', ideologies of biological descent have emerged as powerful and cohesive forms of identity. Chineseness – in Taiwan, Singapore or mainland China – is primarily defined as a matter of blood and descent: one does not become Chinese like one becomes Swiss or Dutch, since cultural integration (language) or political adoption (passport) are both excluded. Racial discourse, of course, has undergone numerous permutations, reorientations and rearticulations since the end of the nineteenth century. Its flexibility and variability is part of its enduring appeal, as it constantly adapts to different political and social contexts, from the racial ideology of an economically successful city-state like Singapore to the eugenic policies of the communist party in mainland China. It is not suggested here that racialised senses of belonging were the only significant forms of identity available in China. However, it should be underlined that notions of culture, ethnicity and race have consistently been conflated throughout the twentieth century in efforts to portray cultural features as secondary to an imagined biological specificity. Secondly, this [analysis] has contended that racial discourse thrived largely thanks to, and not in spite of, folk models of identity, based on patrilineal descent and common stock. Instead of crude generalisations about the role of 'the state' in the deployment of racial categories which would have been disseminated from top to bottom, or the popular 'cloud to dust' theory of cultural change, a degree of circularity, or reciprocal interaction, between popular culture and officially sponsored discourses of race has been proposed. More stable folk notions of patrilineal descent, which were widespread in late imperial China, were reconfigured from the late nineteenth century onwards. Scientised by cultural intermediaries, indigenous notions of identity were reinforced and enriched by the use of new vocabularies. Moreover, the suggestion that racial narratives inevitably entail a rupture with traditional cultural categories, as is all too common in dominant theories of nationalism, has also been questioned. Thirdly, this [analysis] has been highly critical of attempts to reduce the complexities of racial discourse in China to so-called 'Western influence'. In contrast to current theories of 'derivation' and 'cultural hegemony', it emphasises how racialised identities have been actively reconstructed and endowed with indigenous meanings that can hardly be explained as 'Westernisation'. Cultural intermediaries in China drew inspiration from foreign cultural repertoires, appropriated the language of science, indigenised notions of 'race', invested new ideas with native meanings, and finally invented their own versions of identity.

Notes

1   Jan Nieuhof, *Het gezantschap der Neerlandtsche Oost-Indische Compagnie aan den Grooten Tartarischen Cham den tegenwoordigen Keizer van China*, Amsterdam: Jacob van Meurs, 1665, p. 173.

2   Pierre Huard, 'Depuis quand avons-nous la notion d'une race jaune?', *Institut Indochinois pour l'Etude de l'Homme*, 4 (1942), pp. 40–1.

3   E. Vierheller, *Nation und Elite im Denken von Wang Fu-chih (1619–1692)*, Hamburg: Gesellschaft fur Natur-und Völkerkunde Ostasiens, 1968, pp. 30 and 124.

4   *Taiping yulan* (Song encyclopaedia), quoting the Later Han work 'Fengsutong', Taipei: Xinxing shuju, 1959, p. 1693 (360: 5a). See also Zhou Jianren, 'Renzhong qiyuan shuo' (Legends about the origins of human races), *Dongfang zazhi*, 16, no. 11 (June 1919), pp. 93–100.

5   Noriko Kamachi, *Reform in China: Huang Tsun-hsien and the Japanese model*, Cambridge, MA: Harvard University Press, 1981, pp. 15, 141.

6   Charles M. Lewis, *Prologue to the Chinese revolution: The transformation of ideas and institutions in Human Province, 1891–1907*, Cambridge, MA: Harvard University East Asian Research Centre, 1976, pp. 64–5.

7   Yan Fu, *Yan Fu shiwen xuan* (Selected poems and writings of Yan Fu), Beijing: Renmin wenxue chubanshe, 1959, p. 22.

8   Tang Caichang, *Juedianmingzhai neiyan* (Essays on political and historical matters), Taibei: Wenhai chubanshe, 1968, p. 468.

9   Liu Shipei, 'Huangdi jinian shuo' (About a calendar based on the Yellow Emperor), *Huangdi hun* (The soul of the Yellow Emperor), 1904, p. 1; reprinted, Taibei: zhonghua minguo shiliao congbian, 1968.

10 Chen Tianhua, *Chen Tianhua ji* (Collected works of Chen Tianhua), Changsha: Hunan renmin chubanshe, 1982, p. 81.

11 Yuyi, 'Minzuzhuyi lun' (On nationalism), *Zhejiangchao*, 1 (Feb. 1903), p. 3.

12 *Yunnan*, 1 (Aug. 1906), pp. 7–12.

13 'Yindu miewang zhi yuanyin' (The reasons for the extinction of India), *Zhejiangchao*, 1 (Feb. 1903), pp. 4–6.

14 Feisheng, 'Eren zhi xingzhi' (The Russians' nature), *Zhejiangchao*, 1 (Feb. 1903), pp. 4–5, 2 (March 1903), pp. 77–9.

15 Taosheng, 'Haishang de Meiren' (The Americans on the sea), *Zhejiangchao*, 6 (Aug. 1903), p. 2.

16 Liang Boqiang, 'Yixueshang Zhongguo minzu zhi yanjiu' (Medical research on the Chinese race), *Dongfang zazhi* (Eastern miscellany), no. 13 (July 1926), pp. 87–100.

17 Lin Yutang, *My country and my people*, New York: John Ray, 1935, p. 26.

18 Lin Yan, *Zhongguo minzu de youlai* (Origins of the Chinese race), Shanghai: Yongxiang yinshuguan, 1947, p. 27.

19 Du Yaquan et al. (eds), *Dongwuxue da cidian* (Great dictionary of zoology), Shanghai: Shangwu yinshuguan, 1927 (1st edn 1923), p. 15.

20 Gu Shoubai, *Renleixue dayi* (Main points of anthropology), Shanghai: Shangwu yinshuguan, 1924, p. 51.

21 Gong Tingzhang, *Renlei yu wenhua jinbu shi* (History of the progress of mankind and culture), Shanghai: Shangwu yinshuguan, 1926, pp. 1 and 55.

22 Chen Jianshan, 'Shi renlei' (Explaining mankind), *Minduo zazhi*, 5, no. 1 (March 1924, p. 7.

23 Chen Darong, *Dongwu yu rensheng* (Animals and life), Shanghai: Shangwu yinshuguan, 1928 (1st edn 1916), pp. 8–13.

24 Fu Yunsen, *Renwen dili* (Human geography), Shanghai: Shangwu yinshuguan, 1914, pp. 9–15.

25 Léon Wieger, *Moralisme officiel des écoles, en 1920*, Hien-hien, 1921, p. 180, original Chinese text.

26 Zhang Junmai, *Minzu fuxing zhi xueshu jinchu* (The scientific foundations for national revival), Beijing: Zaishengshe, 1935, pp. 10, 22.

27 Qi Sihe, 'Zhongzu yu minzu' (Race and nationality), *Yugong*, 7, nos 1–2–3 (April 1937), pp. 25–34.

28 Frederick Hung (Hong Yuan), 'Racial superiority and inferiority complex', *The China Critic*, 9 Jan. 1930, p. 29.

29 Wen Yiduo, *Wen Yiduo quanji* (Complete works of Wen Yiduo), Hong Kong: Yuandong tushu gongsi, 1968, vol. 1, p. 40.

30 Pan Guangdan, review of Donald Young (ed.), *The American Negro* (1928) in *The China Critic*, 28 Aug. 1930, p. 838.

31 Wang Shoucheng, *Gongmin shengwuxue* (A textbook of civic biology), Shanghai: Shangwu yinshuguan, 1928 (1st edn 1924), p. 52.

32 Wu Zhenzi, 'Women wei shenme yao yanjiu youshengxue' (Why we should study eugenics), *Xuesheng zazhi*, 15, no. 9 (Sept. 1928), pp. 31–6.

33 For instance Ma Chonggan, *Jiehun zhidao* (Marriage guide), Shanghai: Qinfen shuju, 1931, pp. 11–12.

34 Zhang Jixiu, *Funü zhuance* (Special handbook for women), Shanghai: Shangwu yinshuguan, 1937, pp. 52–61.

35 Yi Jiayue, 'Zhongguo de xingyu jiaoyu wenti' (The problem of sex education in China), *Jiaoyu zazhi*, 15, no. 8. (Aug. 1923), p. 22160.

36 Bo Yang, 'Zhongzu qishi' (Racial discrimination), *Choulou de Zhongguoren* (The ugly Chinese), Taibei: Linbai chubanshe, 1985, pp. 212–14.

Part IV

Conflicting Ethnonational Claims

INTRODUCTION TO PART IV

Social scientists, as we demonstrated in the first two sections of this book, have a broad range of theories to explain how different ethnic and racial groups often strive towards the creation of autonomous political units or states. Two major problems immediately confront such models: firstly, that nations and states are not the same, despite the loose terminology employed by activists and scholars involved in trying to understand or construct nationalist movements; secondly, that the very nature of the identification created by national sentiment is deeply psychological, often unconscious, and extraordinarily difficult to translate into simple rational categories. Walker Connor seeks to illustrate these claims by looking at the speeches made by prominent political leaders, some strident advocates of nationalist ideologies, like Hitler and Mussolini, and others, such as Mao and Ho Chi Minh, who one would expect to have a much more limited interest in appeals to nationalism. The extent to which so many political leaders, no matter how different their political ideologies, have used national imagery and idioms to support their rhetoric, suggests the power of this particular form of identity.

Connor, however, is not arguing that national sentiments are an unchanging and immutable reality, still less that they are based on some sociobiological logic linked to shared genetic inheritance. Applying the insight of W. I. Thomas, that individuals are motivated by what they *believe* to be the case, no matter how false this may be in reality, Connor points to the appeals to common ancestry, shared blood, and to family ties that intersperse the language of nationalist leaders. Those social scientists who have been writing the obituary of ethnonational loyalties for the past thirty years should think again and recognize the deep-seated appeal of these ubiquitous movements.

Taking a long historical perspective on world history, McNeill has suggested that nationalism, and the dominance of nation states, represents an unusual interlude that characterizes European history from the French Revolution until the end of the Second World War. In his essay, Anthony Smith evaluates McNeill's interpretation and his prediction that "polyethnic hierarchy" will be restored in the postmodern period in which we are living. Smith considers the impact of migration, gender, liberal democracy and globalization, and whether these contemporary forces are likely to produce a return to polyethnicity. The fragmentation of contemporary societies and the ensuing sets of hybrid identities, the diverse implications of the feminist critiques of nationalism, the competing models of civic and ethnic nationalism, and the complex ramifications of globalization are all explored for their insight into this question. Smith concludes that postmodern interpretations, far from abolishing "grand narratives" to explain the current dynamics of nationalism, largely side-step the critical questions or simply leave their assumptions implicit while they embark on their deconstructionist analyses. Whether a new metatheory capable of explaining the direction of contemporary nationalism can be developed remains to be seen.

The third article in this section looks critically at what John McGarry and Brendan O'Leary call the liberal interpretation of the conflict in Northern Ireland. Following Walker Connor's assumption that the basis of the dispute is a deeply engrained ethnonational struggle, they set out to consider five basic propositions that they suggest typify liberal explanations of the situation. These include the claim that the conflict is the result of religious or political extremism among the elites; that it can be explained by economic exploitation superimposed on community divisions; that it is a product of archaic religious or political cultures; that the key to the conflict lies with the structural segregation of the two communities; and finally that individual discrimination underpins the antagonistic relations. Like Connor, McGarry and O'Leary stress the ethnonational nature of the conflict which they suggest will only reach a final resolution when the national aspirations of both sides have been adequated accommodated. The difficulty of doing this explains the tortuous nature of the negotiations that have marked the search for peace in the area.

10 Beyond Reason: The Nature of the Ethnonational Bond

Walker Connor

For the sake of clarity, we begin by noting that nationalism and patriotism refer to two quite distinct loyalties: the former to one's national group; the latter to one's state (country) and its institutions. For people, such as the Japanese, who possess their own ethnically homogeneous *nation-state*, and for *staatvolk* such as the French, who are culturally and politically preeminent in a state, even though other groups are present in significant numbers, the fact that nationalism and patriotism are two different phenomena is usually of little consequence. For such people, the two loyalties tend to blur into a seamless whole. But in a world containing thousands of ethnonational groups and less than two hundred states, it is evident that for most people the sense of loyalty to one's nation and to one's state do not coincide. And they often compete for the allegiance of the individual.

For example, a Basque or Catalan nationalism has often been in conflict with a Spanish patriotism, a Tibetan nationalism with a Chinese patriotism, a Flemish nationalism with a Belgian patriotism, a Corsican nationalism with a French patriotism, a Kashmiri nationalism with an Indian patriotism, a Quebec nationalism with a Canadian patriotism. The list could be lengthened several times over. Nationalism and patriotism are vitally different phenomena and should not be confused through the careless use of language.

We know from the comparative study of nationalism that when the two loyalties are perceived as being in irreconcilable conflict – that is to say, when people feel they must choose between them – nationalism customarily proves the more potent. A most vivid recent illustration of the relative strength of these two loyalties took place in the Soviet Union, wherein a beleaguered Soviet President Gorbachev only belatedly discovered that a sense of loyalty to the Union of Soviet Socialist Republics (what, for seventy years had been termed Soviet patriotism) was no match for the sense of nationalism demonstrated by nearly all of the peoples of the Soviet Union, including even the Russian nation. And obviously, events within what, until recently, was known as the Federal Republic of Yugoslavia certify that Albanian, Bosnian, Croatian, Macedonian, and Slovene nationalism has each proven itself far more potent than a Yugoslav patriotism.

To understand why nationalism customarily proves to be a far more powerful force than patriotism, it is necessary to take a closer look at national consciousness and national sentiment. What, for example, is the nature of the bond that both unites all Poles and differentiates them from the remainder of humanity? Until quite recently it was the vogue among prominent writers on nationalism to stress the tangible characteristics of a nation. The nation was defined as a community of people characterized by a common language, territory, religion, and the like.

Probing the nation would be a far easier task if it could be explained in terms of such tangible criteria. How much simpler it would be if adopting the Polish language, living within Poland, and adhering to Catholicism were sufficient to define membership in the Polish nation – were sufficient to make one a Pole. But there are Germans, Lithuanians, and Ukrainians who meet these criteria but who do not consider themselves Polish and are not considered Polish by their Polish fellow citizens.

Objective criteria, in and by themselves, are therefore insufficient to determine whether or not a group constitutes a nation. The essence of the nation is a psychological bond that joins a people and differentiates it, in the subconscious conviction of its members, from all non-members in a most vital way.

With but very few exceptions, authorities have shied from describing the nation as a kinship group and have usually explicitly denied any kinship basis to it. These denials are customarily supported by data showing that most nations do in fact contain several genetic strains. But this line of reasoning ignores the dictum that it is not *what is* but *what people perceive as is* which influences attitudes and behavior. And a subconscious belief in the group's separate origin and evolution is an important ingredient of national psychology.

In ignoring or denying the sense of kinship that infuses the nation, scholars have been blind to that which has been thoroughly apparent to nationalist leaders. In sharpest contrast with most academic analysts of nationalism, those who have successfully mobilized nations have understood that at the core of ethnopsychology is the sense of shared blood, and they have not hesitated to appeal to it. Consequently, nationalistic speeches and proclamations tend to be more fruitful areas for research into the emotional/psychological nature of nationalism than are scholarly works. Too often such speeches and proclamations have been precipitously dismissed as propaganda in which the leadership did not truly believe. But nationalism is a mass phenomenon, and the degree to which its inciters are true believers does not affect its reality. The question is not the sincerity of the propagandist, but the nature of the mass instinct to which he or she appeals.

Consider, then, Bismarck's famous exhortation to the Germans, spread at the time throughout more than thirty sovereign entities, urging them to unite in a single state: 'Germans, think with your blood!' Adolph Hitler's repeated appeals to the ethnic purity of the German nation (*Volk*) are notorious. To take but a single example: In a 1938 speech in Konigsburg (now Kaliningrad, part of the Russian Republic), Hitler declared (1942, p. 1438):

> In Germany today we enjoy the consciousness of belonging to a community, a consciousness which is far stronger than that created by political or economic interests. That community is conditioned by the fact of a blood-relationship. Man to-day refuses any longer to be separated from the life of his national group; to that he clings with a resolute affection. He will bear extreme distress and misery, but he desires to remain with his national group. [It is this noble passion which alone can raise man above thoughts of gain and profit.] Blood binds more firmly than business.

Although it may be tempting to pass off such allusions to the blood-bond as the exaggerations of a demagogue and zealot, what should not be forgotten is that it was precisely through such allusions that Hitler was able to gain the intense, unquestioning devotion of the best educated, the most literate nation in Europe. As earlier noted, it is not the leader but the mass instinct to which he or she appeals that interests us. And, by appealing to common blood, Hitler was able to wrap himself in the mantle of German nationalism – to become the personification of the nation in German eyes.

It is ironic that Benito Mussolini, to whom Hitler was indebted for the inspiration behind numerous nationalistic motifs, should have come to power in a state characterized by significant ethnic heterogeneity. His task was therefore far more difficult: if he were to mobilize all segments of the population through nationalistic appeals, he must first convince the Lombards, Venetians, Florentines, Neapolitans, Calabrians, Sardinians, Sicilians et al. of their consanguinity. To this end, the local vernaculars were outlawed, and state propaganda seldom passed up the opportunity to exphasize a common Italian ancestry. As but one example, the following is an extract from a manifesto promulgated throughout all of Italy in 1938 (as cited in Delzell 1970, pp. 193–4):

> The root of differences among peoples and nations is to be found in differences of race. If Italians differ from Frenchmen, Germans, Turks, Greeks, etc., this is not just because they possess a different language and different history, but because their racial development is different.... A pure 'Italian race' is already in existence. This pronouncement [rests] on the very pure blood tie that unites present-day Italians.... This ancient purity of blood is the Italian nation's greatest title of nobility.

Nationalistic appeals to ethnic purity were fully consonant, of course, with fascist dogma. More surprising is that Marxist–Leninist leaders, despite the philosophical incompatibility between communism and nationalism, should feel compelled to resort to nationalistic appeals to gain the support of the masses. But both Marx and Lenin, while insisting that nationalism was a bourgeois ideology that must be anathema to all communists, nonetheless appreciated its influence over the masses. They not only condoned but recommended appealing to it as a means of taking power. Even with this background, however, it appears strange to encounter Mao Tse-tung, when appealing for support from the Chinese masses, referring to the Chinese Communist Party *not* as 'the vanguard of the proletariat,' but as 'the vanguard of the Chinese nation and the Chinese people' (Brandt et al. 1952, p. 260). The Chinese communists in Mao's propaganda became 'part of the Great Chinese nation, flesh of its flesh and blood of its blood' (Mao Tse-tung 1975, p. 209).

In another proclamation (Brandt et al. 1952, p. 245), Mao appealed directly to the family ties deriving from a single common ancestor:

> Beloved Compatriots! The Central Committee of the Chinese Communist Party respectfully and most sincerely issues the following manifesto to all fathers, brothers, aunts, and sisters throughout the country: [W]e know that in order to transform this glorious future into a new China, independent, free, and happy, all our fellow countrymen, every single zealous descendent of Huang-ti[1] must determinedly and relentlessly participate in the concerted struggle.

Ho Chi Minh, the father of the Vietnamese communist movement, also appealed to common ancestors and made use of terms connoting familial relationships, when courting the support of the masses. For example (Ho Chi Minh 1967, p. 158), in 1946 he stated:

> Compatriots in the South and the Southern part of Central Viet-Nam! The North, Center, and South are part and parcel of Viet-Nam! ... We have the same ancestors, we are of the same family, we are all brothers and sisters.... No one can divide the children of the same family. Likewise, no one can divide Viet-Nam.

Democratic leaders have also appealed to a sense of shared blood in order to gain mass support for a course of action. Somewhat paradoxically, the early history of the American people – that human collectivity destined to form the polygenetic immigrant society *par excellence* – offers two noteworthy examples, one involving the decision to separate from Britain and the other the decision to form a federal union. The explanation for the seeming paradox again lies in what we earlier termed *staatvolk* psychology. The political elite of the period did not believe that they were leading an ethnically heterogeneous people. Despite the presence of settlers of Dutch, French, German, Irish, Scottish, and Welsh ancestry – as well as, of course, the presence of native Americans and peoples from Africa (the latter accounted for one of every five persons at the time) – the prevalent elite-held and mass-held self-perception of the American people was that of an ethnically homogeneous people of English descent. As perceived by would-be revolutionary leaders of the time, if popular support for separation from Britain was to be propagated, a major problem to be overcome was the colonists' sense of belonging to a larger English family. Therefore, the framers of the Declaration of Independence apparently concluded that the feeling of transatlantic kinship should be directly confronted and countered in order to ensure popular support for the separation. After itemizing the grievances against the king, the Declaration turned to the transgressions of the branch of the family still in Britain:

> Nor have we been wanting in attention to our British brethren.... We have appealed to their native justice and magnanimity, *and we have conjured them by the ties of our common kindred to disavow these usurpations*, which, would inevitably interrupt our connections and correspondence. *They too have been deaf to the voice of justice and of consanguinity.* We must, therefore...hold them, as we hold the rest of mankind, Enemies in War, in Peace Friends.

In sum, from the American viewpoint, the apostates were 'they,' not 'we.' It was 'they' who had destroyed the family through faithlessness to the sacred bond between kindred, through having been 'deaf to the voice of consanguinity.'

Eleven years later, political reformers were trying to entice the population, now spread throughout thirteen essentially independent countries, to adopt a federal constitution. The situation was therefore not unlike that which, as we earlier noted, would face Bismarck nearly a century later: How to appeal to people, strewn throughout a number of states, to join together. And, just as Bismarck, one of the authors of the *Federalist Papers* (which were designed to elicit popular support for union) appealed to the popularly held self-perception of the society as an ancestrally related nation. In the second of the eighty-five papers, John Jay wrote (Hamilton, Jay, Madison 1937, p. 9):

> With equal pleasure I have as often taken notice, that Providence has been pleased to give this one connected country to one united people – *a people descended from the same ancestors, speaking the same language, professing the same religion*, attached to the same principles of government, very similar in their manners and customs . . .
>
> This country and this people seem to have been made for each other, *and it appears as if it was the design of Providence, that an inheritance so proper and convenient for a band of brethren, united to each other by the strongest ties*, should never be split into a number of unsocial jealous, and alien sovereignties.

Jay was saying in effect, we are members of one family and the family should be reunited.

And so, in the case of the United States, charges of betrayal of an ancestral bond were first used to gain popular support for politically dividing the family, and this was followed years later by appeals to the ancestral bond to bring about the political union of the American section of the family.

Americans of Anglo-Saxon ancestry (the so-called WASPS) continued for decades to manifest the *staatvolk* perception that all Americans – or rather 'all true Americans' – were blood relatives of the English. For example, in a mid-nineteenth century poem, entitled '*TO ENGLISHMEN*,' American John Greenleaf Whittier wrote:

> O Englishmen! – in hope and creed,
> In blood and tongue our brothers!
> We too are heirs of Runnymede;
> And Shakespeare's fame and Cromwell's deed
> Are not alone our mother's.
>
> . . .
>
> 'Thicker than water,' in one rill
> Through centuries of story
> Our Saxon blood has flowed, and still
> We share with you its good and ill,
> The shadow and the glory.

Paeans to the greatness of the Anglo-Saxon strain said to be inherited by the true Americans were plentiful well into the twentieth century. Fear of diluting or polluting that strain with immigrants of inferior ethnic background undergirded the country's immigration policy until after World War II.

Numerous other cases of democratic leaders who have appealed to a blood link could be cited. Mustafa Kemal (Attaturk), whose vision for Turkey was a secular and democratic society, often did so. In a 1927 address to the youth of Turkey, he charged them as follows (Attaturk 1929, pp. 723–4):

> This holy treasure I lay in the hands of the Youth of Turkey. Turkish Youth! Your primary duty is to preserve and defend the National independence, the Turkish Republic . . . The strength that you will need for this is mighty in the noble blood which flows in your veins.

For a more recent illustration, we can turn to Yitzhak Rabin who, in, his 1992 inaugural address to the Knesset as the new Israeli Prime Minister Designate, said of the Jewish diaspora (FBIS, p. 26):

> In recent years, the gates have been opened to Jewish immigration. Hundreds of thousands have come here from all ends of the earth... We are their home and family. We have no closer kin than they.

Transborder appeals of common ancestry are particularly evident throughout the Middle-East. Gamal Abdel Nasser – the ruler of Egypt between 1954 and 1970 and the most idolized pan-Arabist – was unswerving in his evocation of a single Arab nation populating the area between the northwest coast of Africa and the Persian Gulf. For example, in a 1961 speech before the Parliament of Lebanon, Nasser said (Nasser, 1961, p. 72):

> We are united by ties of blood, spirit, and language, and these cannot be easily dissolved by the forces of aggression. There may be crises, but these shall pass like clouds in the sky and matters return to their natural state. *Our common origin shall remain, it bears feelings of love, amity, and brotherhood.*

Later – at a time of great personal disappointment following a decision by the Syrian government to annul a short-lived union with Egypt, Nasser took pains to insist that this setback did not reflect on the viability of a sense of common Arabness (Nasser 1961, p. 141).

> Our feeling of brotherhood and unity with them (the Syrians) is constantly getting stronger. The unity linking us is the unity of blood. It was never the unity of politicians. It is rather the unity of peoples and of blood which associates us with the Arab nation at large.

In yet another speech, Nasser exclaimed (Nasser 1961, p. 159):

> There is an Arab proverb that says my brother and I go into alliance together against the stranger. We might dispute each other, but we will never allow imperialism or a foreigner to shed the blood of an Arab, any Arab.... Regardless of where this blood is shed, it is Arab blood.

We have thus far confined our illustrations mainly to in-state situations. But because political and ethnic borders seldom coincide, appeals in the name of the nation have often jumped state borders. A shared sense of ancestral ties can become intermeshed in foreign policy and raise the issue of divided loyalties if important segments of the group are separated by political borders. Hitler's appeals in the name of the *Volksdeutsche* to all Germans living within Austria, the Sudetenland, and Poland are well known. More recently, Albania has claimed the right to act as the protector of Albanians within Yugoslavia on the ground that 'the same mother that gave birth to us gave birth to the Albanians in Kosovo, Montenegro, and Macedonia' (King 1973, p. 144); China has proclaimed its right to Taiwan on the ground that 'the people of Taiwan are our kith and kin' (*New*

York Times 1975); the former leader of North Korea, Kim Il Sung, declared the need to unify Korea in order to bring about the 'integration of our race' (*Atlas* 1976, p. 19). And in 1990, those who advised Germans in the Federal Republic of Germany and in the German Democratic Republic to approach most cautiously the question of reuniting the family in one state were no match for the kinship-evoking strategy of Chancellor Helmut Kohl, who appealed successfully for support of immediate unification by employing the disarmingly simple slogan: *Wir sind ein Volk!* We are one nation!

Unlike most writers on nationalism, then, political leaders of the most diverse ideological strains have been mindful of the common blood component of ethnonational psychology and have not hesitated to appeal to it when seeking popular support. Both the frequency and the record of success of such appeals attest to the fact that nations are indeed characterized by a sense – a feeling – of consanguinity.

Our answer, then, to that often asked question, 'What is a nation?' is that it is a group of people who feel that they are ancestrally related. It is the largest group that can command a person's loyalty because of felt kinship ties; it is, from this perspective, the fully extended family.

The sense of unique descent, of course, need not, and *in nearly all* cases *will not*, accord with factual history. Nearly all nations are the variegated offsprings of numerous ethnic strains. It is not chronological or factual history that is the key to the nation, but sentient or felt history. All that is irreducibly required for the existence of a nation is that the members share an intuitive conviction of the group's separate origin and evolution. To aver that one is a member of the Japanese, German, or Thai nation is not merely to identify oneself with the Japanese, German, or Thai people of today, but with that people throughout time. Or rather – given the intuitive conviction that one's nation is unique in its origin – perhaps we should say not *throughout time* but *beyond time*. Logically, such a sense of one's nation's origin must rest upon a presumption that somewhere in a hazy, prerecorded era there existed a Japanese, German, or Thai Adam and Eve. But logic operates in the realm of the conscious and the rational; convictions concerning the singular origin and evolution of one's nation belong to the realm of the sub-conscious and the non-rational (note: not *ir*-rational but non-rational).

This distinction between reason and the emotional essence of the nation was expressed in a tract written a few years back by a person in solitary confinement within the Soviet Union (Moroz 1974, p. 54). He had just been found guilty of anti-state activities in the name of Ukrainian nationalism. He wrote:

> A nation can exist only where there are people who are prepared to die for it;
> ...Only when its sons believe that their nation is chosen by God and
> regard their people as his highest creation.
> I know that all people are equal.
> My reason tells me that.
> But at the same time I know that my nation is unique...
> My heart tells me so.
> It is not wise to bring the voices of reason and of emotion to a common denominator.

The dichotomy between the realm of national identity and that of reason has proven vexing to students of nationalism. With the exception of psychologists, people trained in the social sciences tend to be uncomfortable in confronting the non-rational. They are inclined to seek rational explanations for the nation in economic and other 'real' forces. But national consciousness resists explication in such terms. Indeed, in a strong testament to the difficulty of explicating national consciousness in any terms, Sigmund Freud, who spent so many years exploring and describing what he termed 'the unconscious,' acknowledged that the emotional well-springs of national identity defied articulation. After noting that he was Jewish, Freud made clear that his own sense of Jewishness had nothing to do with either religion or national pride. He went on to note that he was 'irresistibly' bonded to Jews and Jewishness by 'many obscure and emotional forces, *which were the more powerful the less they could be expressed in words*, as well as by a clear consciousness of inner identity, a deep realization of sharing the same psychic structure.'[2]

Having noted that national identity defied articulation in rational terms, Freud made no attempt to further describe the national bond and the feelings to which it gives rise, but there is no mistaking that the sentiments he was trying to express are the same as those more concisely and enigmatically summed up in the German maxim, 'Blut will zu Blut!', a loose translation of which might be 'People of the same blood attract!' A nineteenth-century author, Adolph Stocker, expanded on this sentiment (Hayes 1941, p. 258):

> German blood flows in every German body, and the soul is in the blood. When one meets a German brother and not merely a brother from common humanity, there is a certain reaction that does not take place if the brother is not German.

'German' in this passage could, of course, be replaced by English, Russian, Lithuanian, etc. without affecting the passage's validity. Indeed, the thrust of the passage is remarkably similar to the sentiment expressed by a young Chinese nationalist revolutionary (Chen Tiannua) around 1900 (Dikötter 1990, p. 427):

> As the saying goes, a man is not close to people of another family. When two families fight each other, one surely assists one's own family, one definitely does not help the 'exterior' family. Common families all descend from one original family: the Han race is one big family. The Yellow Emperor is a great ancestor, all those who are not of the Han race are not the descendants of the Yellow Emperor, they are exterior families. One should definitely not assist them; if one assists them, one lacks a sense of ancestry.

No matter how described – Freud's interior identity and psychic structure, or blood-ties, or chemistry, or soul – it is worth repeating that the national bond is subconscious and emotional rather than conscious and rational in its inspiration. It can be analyzed but not explained rationally.

How can we analyze it? It can be at least obliquely analyzed by examining the type of catalysts to which it responds, that is to say, by examining the proven techniques for reaching and triggering national responses. And how has the non-rational core of the nation been reached and triggered? As we have seen in the case of numerous successful nationalist leaders, not *through* appeals to reason but *through* appeals to the emotions (appeals not to the mind but to the blood).

The non-rational core of the nation has been reached and triggered *through* national symbols, as historically varied as the rising sun, the swastika, Marianne, and Britannia. Such symbols can speak messages without words to members of the nation, because, as one author has noted, 'there is something about such symbols, especially visual ones, which reach the parts rational explanation cannot reach.'

The non-rational core of the nation has also been reached and triggered *through* nationalist poetry, because the poet is far more adept than the writer of learned tracts at expressing deeply felt emotion, as witness the following words written in 1848 by a Romanian poet to describe the Romanian nation (Tudor 1982, p. 61):

> It is in it that we were born, it is our mother;
> We are men because it reared us;
> We are free because we move in it;
> If we are angered, it soothes our pain with national songs.
> Through it we talk today to our parents who lived thousands of years back;
> Through it our descendants and posterity thousands of years later will know us.

The non-rational core of the nation has been reached and triggered *through* music popularly perceived as reflecting the nation's particular past or genius; the music may vary in sophistication, embracing the work of composers such as Richard Wagner, as well as folk music.

The core of the nation has been reached and triggered *through* the use of familial metaphors which can magically transform the mundanely tangible into emotion-laden phantasma; which can, for example, mystically convert what the outsider sees as merely the territory populated by a nation into a motherland or fatherland, the ancestral land, land of our fathers, this sacred soil, land where our fathers died, the native land, the cradle of the nation, and, most commonly, the *home* – the *home*land of our particular people – a 'Mother Russia,' an Armenia, a Deutschland, an England (Engla land: land of the Angles), or a Kurdistan (literally, land of the Kurds). Here is an Uzbek poet referring to Uzbekistan (Connor 1985):

> So that my generation would comprehend the Homeland's worth,
> Men were always transformed to dust, it seems.
> The Homeland is the remains of our forefathers
> Who turned into dust for this precious soil.

A spiritual bond between nation and territory is thus touched. As concisely stated in the nineteenth century German couplet, '*Blut und Boden*' blood and soil become mixed in national perceptions.

It is, then, the character of appeals made through and to the senses, not through and to reason, which permit us some knowledge of the subconscious convictions that people tend to harbor concerning their nation. The near universality with which certain images and phrases appear – blood, family, brothers, sisters, mother, forefathers, ancestors, home – and the proven success of such invocations in eliciting massive, popular responses tell us much about the nature of national identity. But, again, this line of research does not provide a rational explanation for it.

Rational would-be explanations have abounded: relative economic deprivation; elite ambitions; rational choice theory; intense transaction flows; the desire of the intelligentsia to convert a 'low,' subordinate culture into a 'high,' dominant one; cost–benefit considerations; internal colonialism; a ploy of the bourgeoisie to undermine the class consciousness of the proletariat by obscuring the conflicting class interests within each nation, and by encouraging rivalry among the proletariat of various nations; a somewhat spontaneous mass response to competition for scarce resources. All such theories can be criticized on empirical grounds. But they can be faulted principally for their failure to reflect the emotional depth of national identity: the passions at either extreme end of the hate–love continuum which the nation often inspires, and the countless fanatical sacrifices which have been made in its name. As Chateaubriand expressed it nearly 200 years ago (Sulzbach 1943, p. 62): 'Men don't allow themselves to be killed for their interests; they allow themselves to be killed for their passions.' To phrase it differently: large numbers of people do not voluntarily die for things that are rational.

The sense of kinship which lies at the heart of national consciousness helps to account for the ugly manifestations of inhumanity that often erupt in the relations among national groups. A chain of such eruptions in the late 1980s found Soviet authorities totally unprepared for the scale of the brutality that surfaced in the wake of *perestroika* and *glasnost*, as national groups across the entire southern USSR gave vent to their previously pent-up ethnic enmities.

Such behavior patterns are hardly unusual. The annual reports of organizations such as Amnesty International offer a dismal recitation of officially condoned oppression of national minorities: Tibetans by Han Chinese; West Bank Arabs by Jews; Kurds by Iraqi Arabs, by Persians, and by Turks; Dinkas and other Nilotic peoples by Sudanese Arabs; Quechuans by Peruvian mestizos; Ndebele by Shonas; Turks by Bulgars; Mayan peoples by Guatemalan mestizos; Kachins, Karens, Mons, and Shans by Burmese. The list could be lengthened. Moreover, as suggested by earlier described events in the Soviet Union, genocidal tendencies towards members of another nation have often surfaced without governmental approval. Recent non-Soviet illustrations of sets of nations who have manifested such tendencies are Xhosa and Zulu, Serb and Croat, Serb and Albanian, Irishman and 'Orangeman,' Greek and Turk, Kashmiri and Hindi, Punjabi and Sindhi, Sindhi and Pushtun, Hutu and Tutsi, Ovambo and Herero, Corsican and Frenchman, Vietnamese and Han, Khmer and Vietnamese, Assamese and Bengali, Malay and Han. Again, the list could be lengthened.

Not all relations among nations are so hate-filled. Popular attitudes held by one nation toward another are often quite positive. But while attitudes toward various other nations may vary across a broad spectrum, the national bond, because it is based upon belief in common descent, ultimately bifurcates humanity into 'us' and 'them.' And this propensity toward bifurcating the human race has a long history. Notice the simple cause-and-effect relationship between ethnic purity and hatred of all outsiders that Plato has Menexos ascribe to that most cultured and sophisticated of ancient peoples, the Athenians:

The mind of this city is so noble and free and so powerful and healthy *and by nature hating the barbarians because we are pure Hellenes* and not commingled with barbarians. No Pelops or Cadmus or Aegyptus or Danaus or others who are barbarians by nature and Hellenes only by law dwell with us, but we live here as pure Hellenes who are not mixed with barbarians. *Therefore, the city has acquired a real hate of alien nature.*

Because the sense of common kinship does not extend beyond the nation, that sense of compassion to which kinship usually – not always – but usually gives rise is lacking in the relations among national groups. The fault lines that separate nations are deeper and broader than those separating non-kindred groups, and the tremors that follow those fault lines more potentially cataclysmic. What underlies the now commonplace phrase, 'man's inhumanity to man' is all too often 'nation's inhumanity to nation.'

Failure on the part of scholars to appreciate the psychological wellsprings of the nation most certainly contributes to the tendency to undervalue the potency of nationalism. As earlier noted, when nationalism and patriotism are perceived as in conflict, it is nationalism that customarily proves the more powerful allegiance.

This is not to deny that patriotism can be a very powerful sentiment. The state has many effective means for inculcating love of country and love of political institutions – what social scientists collectively term 'political socialization.' Not the least effective of these is control of public education and particularly control over the content of history courses.

Moreover, even governments of complex multiethnic states are free to – and often do – adopt the idiom of nationalism when attempting to inculcate loyalty to the state. From my own primary school education, I recall how we students – many, probably most, of whom were first, second, or third generation Americans from highly diverse national backgrounds – were told we shared a common ancestry. We were programmed to consider Washington, Jefferson, et al. as our common, 'founding fathers.' We memorized Lincoln's reminder in the Gettysburg Address that four score and seven years earlier, it was 'our fathers [who had] brought forth upon this continent a new nation.' We repetitively sang that very short song – 'America' – one of whose seven lines reads 'land where my fathers died.'

But despite the many advantages that the state has for politically socializing its citizens in patriotic values, patriotism – as evident from the multitude of separatist movements pockmarking the globe – cannot muster the level of emotional commitment that nationalism can. Loyalty to state and loyalty to nation are not always in conflict. But when they are perceived as being in irreconcilable conflict, nationalism customarily proves the more potent.

Again, perhaps the most instructive case is that of the Soviet Union – wherein a most comprehensive, intensive, and multigenerational program to exorcise nationalism and exalt Soviet patriotism proved remarkably ineffective. Similar programs throughout Eastern Europe also clearly failed – most glaringly in Yugoslavia. As noted in a piece written decades ago (Connor 1967, p. 52): 'Political developments since World War II clearly establish that national consciousness is not on the wane as a political force, but is quite definitely in the ascendency.'

Notes

1   Huang-ti was the legendary first emperor of China.
2   The quotation interutilizes translated extracts of Leon Poliakov, *The Aryan Myth* (London: Sussex University Press, 1974, p. 287), and the more clumsy translation in The Standard Edition of the Complete Psychological Works of Sigmund Freud, Vol. XX (1925–6) (London: The Hogarth Press, 1959, pp. 273–4.

References

Atlas 1976 (February).
Attaturk 1929 *A Speech Delivered by Ghazi Mustapha Kemal, President of the Turkish Republic October 1927*, Leipzig: K. F. Kohler.
Brandt, Conrad et al. 1952 *A Documentary History of Chinese Communism*, London: Allen & Unwin.
Connor, Walker 1967 'Self-Determination: The New Phase', *World Politics*, vol. 20 (October 1967).
—— 1985 'The Impact of Homelands upon Diasporas', in Gabriel Sheffer (ed.), *Modern Diasporas in International Politics*, London: Croom Helm, pp. 16–46.
—— 1987 'Ethnonationalism', in Samuel Huntington and Myron Weiner (eds.), *Understanding Political Development*, Boston: Little Brown & Company.
Delzell, Charles 1970 *Mediterranean Fascism*, New York: Harper & Row.
Dikötter, Frank 1990 'Group Definition and the Idea of "Race" in Modern China (1793–1949)', *Ethnic and Racial Studies*, vol. 13 (July 1990).
FBIS-NES-92-135 (14 July 1992).
Freud, Sigmund 1959 *The Standard Edition of the Complete Psychological Works of Sigmund Freud, Vol. XX (1925–260)*, London: The Hogarth Press.
Hamilton, Alexander, John Jay, James Madison 1937 *The Federalist: A Commentary on the Constitution of the United States* 1937 New York: The Modern Library.
Hayes, Carlton 1941 *A Generation of Materialism, 1871–1900*, New York: Harper & Row.
Hitler, Adolph 1940 *Mein Kampf*, New York: Reynal & Hitchcock.
—— 1942 *The Speeches of Adolph Hitler, April 1922–August 1939*, vol. 2, London: Oxford University Press.
Ho Chi Minh 1967 *On Revolution: Selected Writings 1920–1966* [edited by Bernard Fall], New York: New American Library.
King, Robert 1973 *Minorities Under Communism*, Cambridge, MA: Harvard University Press.
Mao Tse-tung 1975 *Selected Works of Mao Tse-tung, Vol. 2*, Peking: Foreign Languages Press.
Moroz, Valentine 1974 *Report from the Beria Reserve*, Chicago: Cataract Press.
Nasser 1961 *President Gamal Abdel Nasser's Speeches and Press Interviews*. Cairo, n.p.
New York Times 1975 1 September.
Poliakov, Leon 1974 *The Aryan Myth*, London: Sussex University Press.
Sulzbach, Walter 1943 *National Consciousness*, Washington, DC: American Council on Public Affairs.
Tudor, Corneliu Vadim 1982 'Humanism, Fraternity of National Minority Policy Stressed', *JPRS* 81624 (25 August).

11 Nationalism and Modernity

Anthony D. Smith

In his 1986 lectures entitled *Polyethnicity and National Unity in World History*, the great world historian William H. McNeill argued that nations and nationalism are phenomena peculiar to a particular period of history, the age of Western modernity, and that just as in pre-modern ages nations and nationalism were unknown, so in the future we shall witness the demise of the nation and the withering away of nationalism. It was only in a short, but vividly documented period of modern European history, from about 1789 to 1945, that the ideal of national unity held sway, and the nation-state became accepted as the political norm. Before and after, the norm was not national unity, but polyethnic hierarchy.

Polyethnicity, Past and Future

For McNeill, only barbarism is monoethnic. The moment we reach the stage of civilisation, polyethnicity becomes the norm. The reasons are relatively straightforward. Civilisation is largely metropolitan, so centres of wealth and power require many kinds of skilled labour, and attract envious outsiders. Military, demographic and economic reasons support the polyethnic character of urban civilisation. After the 'cavalry revolution' of the early first millennium B C, we find a common pattern of conquest of civilised societies by nomadic tribesmen. Frequent epidemics among concentrated urban populations also encouraged urban polyethnicity, since depleted centres continually need to be replenished by rural populations to meet labour needs. Finally, long-distance trade gave rise to far-flung, alien merchant communities, often with their own portable religions. The overall result was that pre-modern civilisations with labour specialisation were necessarily culturally pluralist and soon bred ethnic hierarchies of skill; only those populations and polities far removed from the centres of civilisation like Japan, and perhaps England, Denmark and Sweden, could retain their ethnic homogeneity (McNeill 1986: ch. 1).

It was only after about 1700 that the ideal of independence for ethnically homogeneous populations, or nations, emerged. This was the result of a confluence of four factors. The first, and least important, was the influence of classical humanism, and hence the models of civic solidarity found in classical city-states like Athens, Sparta and republican Rome, which captured the imaginations of humanist intellectuals. More important was the growth of reading publics, versed in standardised forms of vernacular languages, which formed the elite basis of future nations. To this we must add the rapid growth of population in Western Europe, which allowed depleted cities to be replenished by ethnically homogeneous migrants from the countryside, and in the process fuelled revolutionary discontent among superfluous labour. Finally, and perhaps most important, was the new emphasis on modern infantry drill, which from this period became increasingly allied to state power, and by encouraging military participation on a large scale, also induced a new sense of civic solidarity and fraternity. McNeill argues that all these factors 'came together in western Europe at the close of the eighteenth century to give birth to modern nationalism', first in France and then throughout Europe. Although ethnic pluralism remained the social norm even in Western Europe, no state could henceforth afford to be without a 'national identity', for the unitary nation state and 'the myth of national brotherhood and ethnic unity' justified self-sacrifice in national wars, sustained public peace domestically and strengthened the state and the hand of government in everyday life (ibid.: 51, 56).

All this came apart after 1945. Two world wars revealed the immense costs of nation-states and nationalism. Revulsion against Nazi barbarism and the huge military sacrifices, was followed by a realisation that no nation-state could prosecute such a total war alone. They had to coordinate their efforts, and in the process draft in thousands of ethnically heterogenous soldiers and labourers, free or enslaved. This set the precedent for the flow of *Gastarbeiter* from alien cultures and lands; with higher birth rates and access to mass communications, these ethnic enclaves were able to perpetuate themselves on Western soil. In addition, the emergence of vast transnational companies and the internationalisation of military command structures have severely curtailed the autarchy of even the richest and most powerful nation-states. All this has undermined the power and the unity of 'nation-states', and presages the pluralisation of nations. For McNeill, once again, 'Polyethnic hierarchy is on the rise, everywhere'. Nations and nationalism are transitory phenomena, reversions to a barbarian ideal of ethnic purity which is crumbling before our eyes because of the urgent need for adequate supplies of alien skilled labour. Only a moment in the much-read histories of the classical city-states made it appear otherwise (ibid.: 82).

In fact, for McNeill as for many others, this short aberrant period of national unity is really only a matter of ideology; the social reality was always that of polyethnic hierarchy, even in the nation-states of Western Europe. One is left wondering how the nationalist mirage was created, and why so few people saw through it.

But the point I want to concentrate on here is McNeill's prognosis of a return to polyethnic hierarchy at the cost of national unity, that is, through the breakdown of the nation-state and nationalism. McNeill appears to assume that the nation-state and its nationalism is the antithesis of polyethnic hierarchy, although in practice, as he himself demonstrates, they are coextensive, if not symbiotic. But this is to forget the 'onion character' of ethnicity, its capacity for forging 'concentric circles' of identity and loyalty, the wider circle encompassing the narrower. This is not the same as the much-spoken-of 'multiple identities'. The latter often create competition and rivalry for people's loyalties; class, region, religion, gender, ethnicity all create identities and loyalties that may cut across each other. Whereas ethnicity can operate at several levels, the wider identity and community encompassing the narrower, so that a person may be equally and harmoniously a

member of a clan, an ethnic group, a national state, even a pan-national federation: a member of a tartan clan, a Scot, a Briton and a European.

If this was the case in the 'age of nationalism', according to McNeill, might it
not continue to operate, even within the more continental and global contexts of
the next century? This is just as plausible a scenario as the imminent breakdown
of the nation-state into its constituent ethnic parts. In other words, it is too easy to
assume a zero-sum relationship between ethnicity and nationalism, the *ethnie* and
the nation. Such a relationship needs to be tested empirically in each case, and the
conditions for the relationship specified.

The Post-national Agenda

McNeill's tripartite periodisation of history – pre-modern polyethnic hierarchy,
modern national unity and postmodern polyethnicity provides the historical setting
for the main themes of discussion and research on nations and nationalism in the
last decade. These themes include:

1 the impact of current population movements on the prospects of the national
   state, and especially the fragmentation of national identity and the rise of
   multiculturalism;
2 the impact of feminist analysis and issues of gender on the nature of national
   projects, identities and communities, and the role of gendered symbolism and
   women's collective self-assertion;
3 the predominantly normative and political debate on the consequence for citizenship and liberty of civic and ethnic types of nationalism, and their relations
   with liberal democracy;
4 and the impact of globalisation trends, and of 'postmodern' supranational projects, on national sovereignty and national identity.

With the exception of gender issues, each of these themes is prefigured and encom-
passed by McNeill's world-historical framework. Even the changed role of women
and the impact of gender divisions can be viewed, on this reading, as the final
extension of a 'post-national' citizenship to the largest and most underprivileged,
because hitherto invisible, 'minority', as a result of the pressing needs for skilled
labour in civilised polyethnic societies. Immigration and hybridisation; processes
of globalisation and supra-nationalism; and the transition to a looser, civic form of
liberal nationalism; all these issues and debates can be seen to form elements in
that trend to re-establish polyethnic hierarchies portrayed by McNeill.

Here I can only touch on the most salient of these issues, and try to show that,
while they ostensibly turn their backs, not only on modernism, but on all large-
scale narratives and higher-level theorising, these discussions and debates, and the
research they have spawned, constitute in reality one part (the last epoch) of that
larger framework which McNeill's analysis exemplifies. Theirs is an analysis which
attempts to go beyond the modernist paradigm of nations and nationalism, and
reveal its necessary supersession alongside the decomposition of its objects of
reference, that is, the nation and nationalism. Yet in going beyond modernism they

do not mean to challenge its assumption of the modernity of nations and national-ism. The 'postmodernist turn' does not seek to overturn the modernist paradigm, as does perennialism; nor does it seek to revise the modernist analysis 'from within', by revealing the debts of the modern nation to pre-modern ethnic ties, in the manner of the ethno-symbolists. Rather, it seeks to extend the range of mod-ernism to what it sees as a 'postmodern' phase of social development. But in doing so it subtly undermines and problematises some of the basic assumptions of mod-ernism, notably its belief in the sociological reality of nations, and the power of nationalist ideologies.

The underlying leitmotif of the most recent phase of theorising in the field of ethnicity and nationalism, which we may very loosely call 'postmodern', is that of cultural and political fragmentation coupled, in varying degrees, with eco-nomic globalisation. Let me try to sketch this leitmotif in each of the themes listed above.

Fragmentation and Hybrid Identities

Of course, Anderson's analysis of the literary tropes and devices which sustain the narratives of 'nation-ness' foreshadowed the uses of deconstructionist techniques in the analysis of ethnic and national phenomena. For many his example has served as the inspiration, and point of departure, for their own more radical application of these techniques. For Homi Bhabha, for example, the very idea of a 'national identity' has become problematic. That idea had first emerged in the totalising project of the Enlightenment which sought to incorporate all being, including the Other. Hence the nationalist narratives of the national self (which was, in fact, always constructed and defined by the Other, the significant outsider) always claimed to incorporate the Other and purported to create total cultural homogeneity. But such a claim is fictitious. Cultural difference is irreducible, and it reveals the hybrid quality and ambivalence of national identity in every state (Bhabha 1990).

For Bhabha, national identities are composed of narratives of 'the people', and they operate under a 'doubled' and 'split' signifier – split between past and present, the self and the other, and above all between pedagogical and performative narra-tives. This superimposed dualism fragments the nation. The received versions of national identity inculcated by the nationalists are always challenged and decom-posed into their component cultural parts by the alternative narratives based on the actions and performances of members of the designated community. In the manner of Simmel, Homi Bhabha directs our attention to the impact of the stranger and the outsider in defining the national identity of the host group. Only here the host is an imperialist national community, acting as magnet to the ex-colonised. The great influx of ex-colonials, immigrants, *Gastarbeiter* and asylum-seekers has eroded the bases of traditional narratives and images of a homo-geneous national identity, revealing their fragmented and hybrid character. Today, every collective cultural identity has become plural. Housed in 'anxious states', national identities have become precarious and hybridised, as they face in different directions. Composed of cultural elements from the ex-colonial periphery, which are neither able nor willing to be incorporated and assimilated, national identities have fragmented and lost their erstwhile hold on people (ibid.: ch. 16).

A similar emphasis on the importance of the cultural fragment, and the irreducibility of its experience and testimony, can be found in the work of Partha Chatterjee. In general, he is concerned with the relationship between the hegemonic nationalist discourses of the West which for Benedict Anderson provide 'modular' forms for pirating by nationalist elites in Asia and Africa, and the indigenous nationalisms created by those non-Western elites. In his earlier work Chatterjee had demonstrated how, typically, the nationalist discourses of Asia and Africa both derived from Western models and at the same time opposed a 'material' outer world dominated by the West and the colonial state, to an inner, 'spiritual' domain which was the preserve of the national culture being created by indigenous elites since the mid-nineteenth century (Chatterjee 1986). In *The Nation and Its Fragments* (1993) Chatterjee shows, through a richly detailed analysis of nationalism in Bengal, how in such institutions as language, drama and the novel, art, religion, schooling and the family, a new, creative 'inner domain of national culture' was fashioned by nationalist Indian elites which is simultaneously modern and non-Western, using both Western and indigenous (Sanskrit) models. At the same time, this dominant Indian nationalist discourse is influenced by those of the many marginalised groups outside the mainstream of politics, the 'fragments of the nation' which in this case include Bengalis, women, peasants and outcastes, even when their alternative images of the nation were bypassed or suppressed, and their aspirations 'normalised' by an incorporating Indian nationalism. The interesting point here is that such nationalist culture creation precedes the political challenge to the West, and the ensuing nationalist conflict, a point also made by John Peel in his analysis of the 'cultural work' of Yoruba ethnogenesis in the same period. The encounter with the Other is certainly crucial, but the forms and contents of the Indian, Middle Eastern or African nationalism which that encounter triggers are also derived from other, non-Western sources within the traditional cultures of the community (albeit greatly modified) (Chatterjee 1993: chs 1, 5; Peel 1989).

Such readings still leave intact the cultural differences which fragment the nation. But here too some radical postmodernist theorising has decentred and decomposed ethnicity. For Stuart Hall, Etienne Balibar and others, ethnicity must be viewed as a plastic and malleable social construction, deriving its meanings from the particular situations of those who invoke it and the relations of power between individuals and groups. Not only is it one among many competing identities, it derives its meanings from its articulation with other kinds of identity, notably class and gender. Shifting, permeable and 'situational', ethnicity has no essence or centre, no underlying features or common denominator. For Etienne Balibar, there is only a discourse of 'fictive ethnicity'. Thus:

> No nation possesses an ethnic base naturally, but as social formations are nationalised, the populations included within them, divided up among them or dominated by them are ethnicised – that is, represented in the past or in the future *as if* they formed a natural community, possessing of itself an identity of origins, culture and interests which transcend individuals and social conditions. (Balibar and Wallerstein 1991: 96, original emphasis)

Ethnicity itself is produced through two routes, those of the language community and the race, both of which create the idea of predestined, autonomous communities.

In similar vein, Stuart Hall views a sense of ethnicity as the expression of a hegemonic national identity, as in the concept of 'Englishness'. But Hall also sees the new 'identity politics' of representation in the West as constructing a new 'positive conception of the ethnicity of the margins, of the periphery'. This kind of voluntary ethnicity involves a

> new cultural politics which engages rather than suppresses *difference* and which depends, in part, on the cultural construction of new ethnic identities. (S. Hall 1992: 257)

Once again, the hegemony of a dominant discourse of national (and racial) identity is challenged by alternative discourses of peripheral ethnicity, newly constructed out of popular experiences, and predicated on the celebration of diversity. This is the premise, and justification, of the politics of multiculturalism, to which I shall return.

In sensitising us to the more complex and multifaceted nature of contemporary national identities in the West, and in revealing the differences between the older received traditions of the nation and the much more varied, and contested, understandings of national community among and within the many cultural groups that comprise most modern national states, this kind of postmodern analysis has done much to illuminate the latest phase of national formation, especially in the West. There is little doubt that modern Western nations have become 'frayed at the edges', and that their members have had to rethink former assumptions about national community and identity in the light of much larger movements of population. It is also true that different groups in both Western and non-Western societies such as India have had quite different visions and interpretations of the 'nation'. At the same time, we should not underestimate the continuing hold of a sense of national identity among the majority of the population in Western states, nor the desire of many members of immigrant communities to become part of a reshaped nation, while retaining their ethnic and religious cultures, perhaps increasingly in the form of a 'symbolic ethnicity'. Nor should we overestimate the degree to which most Western nations either were or felt themselves to be homogeneous in earlier periods. To do so is to set up a false 'before-and-after' dichotomy. National unity was never so assured in the past, even when it was sought by nationalists, nor today are fragmentation and voluntary ethnicity so marked. For most people, even in the West, there remain clear boundaries in determining their ethnic identities and national allegiances, even when they may dissent from them or their power-holders. They can change their national allegiances, though often with difficulty, and perhaps modify their ethnic identities, usually through their children, for example in mixed marriages. But this enhanced individual latitude in the West does not allow people to 'pick and mix' or consume at will among ethnic identities; their choices remain restricted by ethnic history and political geography. As Michael Billing put it:

One can eat Chinese tomorrow and Turkish the day after; one can even dress in Chinese and Turkish styles. But *being* Chinese or Turkish are not commercially available options. (Billig 1995: 139, original emphasis)

For most people, 'voluntary ethnicity' is not an option, even in democratic societies, if only because other ethnic communities are unlikely to accept such a radical boundary change; an example is the failure of Mauritian Muslims in the 1970s and 1980s to become accepted as of Arab rather than Indian descent (Gans 1979; Eriksen 1993: 72; Billig 1995: ch. 6).

Gender and Nation

The second major theme which overlaps with that of fragmentation is the mutual impact of gender and nation. Early feminist analyses did not seek to address the issues of ethnicity and nationalism, but from the mid-1980s there has been a growing literature in this area. Gender theorists complain, rightly in my view, of the failure of theories of nationalism to address either the role of women in national projects or the impact of gender cleavages on our understanding of nations and nationalism.

Of course, modernists might claim that their theories are universal and there is no need for a separate account of the role of women and gender in nationalism. But, if the very nature of nations and nationalism (or national projects) is gendered, then a separate, or at least, a different kind of theory is required, one which takes this key attribute of the *explanandum* into account – particularly from those who regard nationalism as linked to ethnicity and ethnicity to kinship, or from ethno-symbolists for whom ethno-history and 'myth-symbol' complexes are central to the development of nations.

To date, the question of the relations between issues of gender and nationalism has been pursued at a number of levels, and with very different assumptions and methodologies. These are lucidly set out in a masterly survey of the main works in the field to date by Sylvia Walby.

The role of women in nationalism

The first such level is empirical: the varying role of women in nations and nationalist projects, and the differential impact of such projects on women and their prospects. Here, Walby cites Kumari Jayawardena's seminal study which demonstrated that women's movements were active in many non-Western nationalisms, and were an integral part of national resistance movements; they were, according to Jayawardena,

acted out against a backdrop of nationalist struggles aiming at achieving political independence, asserting a national identity, and modernising society. (Jayawardena 1986: 3)

Jayawardena nevertheless emphasised the separate demands and roles of feminist movements alongside, or within, the nationalist movements; they might even be at variance with its goals or interpretations, as Haleh Afshar stresses in her analysis of women's struggles in Iran (Afshar 1989).

Conversely, nationalist movements view the question of women's emancipation in quite a different light. Walby points out how in the older nations of the West, the formation of nations was long drawn out and women's emancipation came very late in their 'rounds of restructuring'; whereas in the new states of Africa and Asia, women were accorded full citizenship rights with independence.

> Indeed the granting of full citizenship to all was one of the ways in which previously dominated colonies could make a claim to a nationhood. (Walby 1992: 91)

But, as Deniz Kandiyoti points out in a scholarly study of the Turkish emancipation movement, it was only on their own terms that nationalists accorded women full rights. In the Turkish case, their emancipation as equals flowed, in the eyes of the influential Turkish social theorist Ziya Gökalp, from ancient Turkish egalitarian mores. Kandiyoti perceptively concludes:

> Thus, there appears to be one persistent concern which finally unites nationalist and Islamist discourses on women in Turkey: the necessity to establish that the behaviour and position of women, however defined, are congruent with the 'true' identity of the collectivity and constitute no threat to it. (Kandiyoti 1989: 143; cf. Kandiyoti 1991)

Female symbolism of the nation

Deniz Kandiyoti here touches on a second level of analysis, the ideological and symbolic uses of women. Symbolism and ideology are two of the main dimensions along which Floya Anthias and Nira Yuval-Davis, in their pioneering volume, locate women within ethnic and national processes. They regard women as central to the creation and reproduction of ethnic and national projects, and list five major dimensions of their activity and presence. Women, they argue, should be seen:

(a)   as biological reproducers of members of ethnic collectivities;
(b)   as reproducers of the boundaries of ethnic/national groups;
(c)   as participating centrally in the ideological reproduction of the collectivity and as transmitters of its culture;
(d)   as signifiers of ethnic/national differences – as a focus and symbol in ideological discourses used in the construction, reproduction and transformation of ethnic/national categories;
(e)   as participants in national, economic, political and military struggles. (Yuval-Davis and Anthias 1989: 7)

In a later thought-provoking and systematic survey of the field, Nira Yuval-Davis goes on to apply a deconstructionist analysis to the relationships between gender and nation, and includes the ideological and symbolic modes of locating women (c and d above) as vital components of cultural reproduction. Culture or 'cultural stuff', she argues, rather than being fixed and homogeneous, should be seen as

> a rich resource, usually full of internal contradictions, which is used selectively by different social agents in various social projects within specific power relations and political discourse in and outside the collectivity. (Yuval-Davis 1997: 43)

As a result, hegemonic symbols and cultures are generally strongest in the centre of the polity and always evoke resistance, particularly at the periphery. Hegemonic nationalist symbols and narratives proclaim the need for men to defend both the 'Motherland' and the nation's women who symbolise and express its 'purity'. They call on men to sacrifice themselves for their women and children, so that they may be eulogised by their women in the manner of Plutarch's Spartan women, whom Rousseau so admired.

Yuval-Davis points out that women 'are often constructed as the symbolic bearers of the collectivity's identity and honour':

> A figure of a woman, often a mother, symbolises in many cultures the spirit of the collectivity, whether it is Mother Russia, Mother Ireland or Mother India. In the French Revolution its symbol was 'La Patrie', a figure of a woman giving birth to a baby; and in Cyprus, a crying woman refugee on roadside posters was the embodiment of the pain and anger of the Greek Cypriot collectivity after the Turkish invasion. (Yuval-Davis 1997: 45)

This is in line with the central nationalist construction of the 'home'. In the home gender relations become constitutive of the 'essence' of cultures, which in turn are to be seen as intergenerational ways of life that include such facets as family relations, ways of cooking and eating, domestic labour, play and bedtime stories (ibid.: 43).

Nationalism as a male phenomenon

Yet another level of analysis of gender–nation relationships concerns the nature of nations and nationalisms as largely masculine organisations and projects. For Cynthia Enloe, indeed,

> nationalism has typically sprung from masculinised memory, masculinised humiliation and masculinised hope. (Enloe 1989: 44)

And this is also the burden of Jean Bethke Elshtain's analysis of masculine patriotic self-sacrifice. Such considerations lead Sylvia Walby to argue that men and women are differentially involved in the nation and nationalism. Perhaps, she reasons, this is why many women, for example those in the Green and anti-nuclear movements, often display more international commitments and less militarism; alternatively, their greater pacifism and internationalism may make women less involved with the nation and nationalism than men (Elshtain 1993; Walby 1992: 92–3).

Against this view, we have seen plenty of evidence of women's political and even military involvement in national liberation struggles, even if the reasons are as much instrumental as expressive. This suggests that there are times, at least, when the national struggle supersedes or subsumes all other struggles, including those of class and gender. This does not mean that 'nationalism' as a discourse is not oriented primarily to the needs of men and for this reason possesses a 'masculine' symbolic content. In an age of revolutionary nationalism, after all, such neo-classic images as David's painting of the *Oath of the Horatii* (1784), West's *The Death of Wolfe* (1770) and Fuseli's *Oath of the Rütli* (1779) focus explicitly on the traditional masculine attributes of energy, force and duty.

How do we explain the basic male character of this nationalism? George Mosse draws on his earlier path-breaking analyses of the choreography of mass nationalism to reveal how its rise and development, particularly in Central Europe, was conditioned by the Western bourgeois family morality with its concern for 're-spectability', moral character and physical (Greek) beauty. This produced a sharp differentiation, not only in gender roles but also in gendered attributes and stereotypes, already evident in the anti-revolutionary German-speaking regions, which identified the French forces as 'loose-living', in opposition to the respectable, masculine German morality, which nationalists like Ernst Moritz Arndt embraced. As the nineteenth century progressed, the integral nationalist search for a specific masculine morality, 'Aryan' male beauty and a respectable and distinctive 'national character' merged with racist fascism's cult of male activism and aggressive virility (Mosse 1985, 1995; cf. Leoussi 1997).

More recently, Glenda Sluga, in a penetrating historical investigation, traced the gendered nature of both nations and nationalist ideologies further back to their origins in the French Revolution, where by 1793 'the legislators of the new French Republic had defined popular national sovereignty in terms of its masculine citizenry'. In the name of social order, women were returned to the private sphere as patriot wives and mothers of citizens, as Rousseau had recommended. Drawing on the work of Joan Landes, Sluga shows how the division between public and private spheres, stemming from the scrutiny of boundaries initiated by the Enlightenment, not only excluded women from the Revolution's invocation of universal rights, but ensured the entirely masculine character of the nation-state. Like Rousseau, Fichte, Michelet and Mazzini all emphasised the different roles of the sexes in national education, the supportive, nurturing function of women and the heroic, military role of men:

> Mazzini, like Michelet and Fichte, drew on the image of the patriarchal family (with the father at its head) as a natural unit to shore up the legitimacy of the fraternal nation-state and determine its preference for the male citizen as the active and military patriot. (Sluga 1998: 9, 24; see also Landes 1988)

Feminism and identity politics

Finally, there is the normative level of analysis: the ways in which feminists should address 'identity politics' and the politics of multiculturalism. For Nira Yuval-Davis the problem with 'identity politics' is that it tends to harden ethnic and gender boundaries, and homogenise and naturalise categories and group differences (Yuval-Davis 1997: 119). Similarly with multiculturalism. Here too the dangers of reifying and essentialising cultures ignore power differences between and within minorities, overemphasise the differences between cultures and privilege as 'authentic' the voices of the most unwesternised 'community representatives'. This can have particularly detrimental effects for women in terms of encouraging minority male control over their behaviour. Even allowing for the 'counter-narratives' which emerge from the nation's margins and 'hybrids', there is always the danger that homogeneity and essentialism

> are attributed to the homogeneous collectivities from which the 'hybrids' have emerged, thus replacing the mythical image of society as a 'melting pot' with the mythical image of society as a 'mixed salad'. (Yuval-Davis 1997: 59; cf. Kymlicka 1995)

Given the differential positioning of minorities and of women among and within them, there can be no simple approach to a 'feminist agenda'. For Yuval-Davis, feminists can only construct identities across difference by a 'transversal politics' which starts from different cultural roots and aims to 'shift' and move towards those from other cultures whose values and goals are compatible with one's own (ibid.: 130).

From this all too brief summary of some of its major themes, it is clear that the 'gender-nation' field is rich in potential for analysing the character and effects of nations and nationalism. How far it is useful to deconstruct its concepts and issues in terms of various 'narratives' and 'discourses', and whether we need to describe them as hegemonic (or otherwise) 'constructs', is open to question. Certainly, employing this kind of postmodernist approach sensitises us to the great complexity of women's positions in ethnic and national projects, and vice-versa, but it does so at a cost: a clear shift away from the task of causal explanation. It is noteworthy that, for all their analytical insights, only a few of the works discussed above (specifically, those that opt for a historical modernist approach) are concerned with the origins and formation of nations and the role of gender relations therein, or with why nations and nationalism have become so ubiquitous, or indeed, except in passing, with the issue of why nations and nationalisms evoke such passions among so many people (including so many women) across the globe. This suggests that 'nation–gender' theories have considerable work to do if they are to provide a more comprehensive causal analysis of the ways in which the complex interrelations of gender and nation contribute to the formation of nations and the spread and intensity of nationalism.

Liberalism and Civic or Ethnic Nationalism

Yuval-Davis' espousal of 'transversal politics' makes sense only in a more liberal democracy where the form of nationalism is inclusive, participant and relatively open in character. This is the type of nationalism which the 'nation-building' theorists had in mind, and it is this 'civic' version of nationalism that has been taken up by some liberals and social democrats, in opposition to its antithesis, 'ethnic' nationalism.

There is a burgeoning literature on the relationship between liberalism and/or social democracy and this form of nationalism, but most of it is philosophical and normative, and so lies outside the scope of my enquiry. I should only like to mention the debate provoked by David Miller's lucid defence of a civic version of the doctrine of nationality (his preferred term to 'nationalism'). Miller starts by discussing the idea of national identity or the nation, and lists five distinguishing marks of a nation as a community:

> it is (1) constituted by shared belief and mutual commitment; (2) extended in history; (3) active in character; (4) connected to a particular territory; (5) marked off from other communities by its distinct public culture. (O'Leary 1996a: 414; see Miller 1993: 6–8, and Miller 1995: ch. 1)

For Miller, nations can be defended on three grounds. First, they are valid sources of personal identity. Second, they are ethical communities, and as members we owe special obligations to our compatriots. Finally, nations have a valid claim to be self-determining, so as to allow their members to decide matters for themselves. Despite our commitment to ethical universalism, Miller argues, in practise we are ethical particularists, and the nation affords a larger and better basis for performing duties and achieving social justice. Moreover, the nation offers a better arena for achieving liberal and social democratic goals than radical multiculturalism, which cannot restrain the rich and strong and only encourages fragmentation. Nationality is also superior to citizenship and a purely abstract 'constitutional patriotism' of the type favoured by Jürgen Habermas, since it connects political principles and practice to a sense of shared history and culture, and a sense of place and time (Miller 1995: chs 2–3; O'Leary 1996a: 419–20).

One of the difficulties in Miller's approach, as Brendan O'Leary points out, is that he qualifies the claim to national self-determination in ways that tend to favour the powers-that-be, and is especially critical of the claims of ethnic communities in polyethnic nations. In effect, Miller comes down, as do so many others, in favour of a civic form of nationalism which is ultimately dependant on the state and its liberal practices. Yet Miller is also careful to distinguish nations from states. What then of all those ethnic groups that aspire to the status of nationality and desire to determine their own destinies? How shall we judge the claims of separatists and irredentists? (O'Leary 1996b: 445–7; cf. Beitz 1979).

Recognition of the political power of ethnicity has inspired a number of cognate debates, mainly in political science, notably about the ways of managing or eliminating ethnic differences and conflict. As McGarry and O'Leary demonstrate, these methods range from the extremes of partition, population transfer and genocide to assimilation, consociationalism and federation, and they reveal much about the consequences of nationalism in a world of mainly polyethnic states. Three topics have provoked particular controversy. The first is the merits (and features) of the 'consociational democracy' model associated with the work of Arend Lijphart, and its relationship to both class conflict and liberalism. The second is the meanings and political uses of concepts of 'ethnic democracy' and/or 'herrenvolk democracy' to characterise exclusive dominant-*ethnie* democracy in polyethnic states, and the differences of such regimes from liberal democracies. The third theme, the vicissitudes of ethnic minority rights and their relations with states and the inter-state system, has only recently been linked to questions about the nation and nationalism. However, in most of the literature these issues have a strong normative (and legal) content and have only been tangentially related to issues of national identity and nationalism. On the whole, therefore, they lie outside the scope of this survey (Lijphart 1977; McGarry and O'Leary 1993).

The debate about the civic or ethnic character of nationalism, on the other hand, is directly related to our concerns. It has, as one might expect, received much attention from analysts of immigrant societies like Canada and Australia. Raymond Breton's analysis of the evolution of English-speaking Canada, for example, emphasises a long-term shift from 'ethnic' to 'civic' nationalism. Even in Quebec, he can trace a similar, albeit slower development: as a result of immigration, both the French language and Catholicism have become increasingly detached from their Québécois ethno-cultural base, and

> membership cannot be defined in terms of ethnic attributes, but in terms of citizenship. As in English Canada, the collective identity has to be redefined in such a way as to incorporate the people of non-French origins who are legally members of the polity. (Breton 1988: 99–102)

In reality, few modern national states possess only one form of nationalism. Nevertheless, we *can* usefully distinguish between 'ethnic', 'civic' and 'plural' types of nation and nationalism; and these analytical distinctions may help to explain, for example, different traditions of state immigration policies. Thus Rogers Brubaker has shown how the territorial conception of belonging which formed the French tradition gave rise to a civic policy that naturalised immigrants on the basis of prolonged residence in France (*ius soli*); whereas the German conception of ethnic belonging entailed a genealogical policy (*ius sanguinis*) that till recently denied German citizenship to migrants and *Gastarbeiter*, however long their residence on German soil, while at the same time according immediate rights of citizenship to dispossessed ethnic Germans from the East. Similarly, Daniele Conversi has contrasted the pattern of cultural values among Basques and Catalans, revealing how Sabino Arana's influence has incorporated the Basque concern with purity of blood and exclusive rights, whereas the Catalan tradition of linguistic and cultural nationalism has encouraged a more open, assimilationist and inclusive Catalan nationalism, one that is far more respectful to immigrants (Brubaker 1992; Conversi 1997).

Yet in practice, these types frequently overlap, and a given national state will often display ethnic as well as civic components in its form of nationalism, sometimes in a historical layering, or its nationalism may move some way from one type to another and back. Moreover, each type, as I have argued, has its peculiar problems. If the ethnic-genealogical type tends towards exclusivity (though not necessarily), the civic-territorial type stemming from the French Revolution is often impatient of ethnic difference; it tends towards radical assimilation, some might call it 'ethnocide', of cultural differences and minorities. As for the 'plural' type of nationalism found mainly in immigrant societies like Canada and Australia, its celebration of cultural diversity risks a loss of political cohesion and tends towards a national instability which could in turn provoke reactive nationalisms (and in extreme cases like Quebec, secession movements) (A. D. Smith 1995: ch. 4).

For these reasons, those scholars who, in the tradition of Hans Kohn and John Plamenatz, oppose a 'good' civic to a 'bad' ethnic nationalism, overlook the problems associated with each type and in particular rewrite the civic version to accomodate the new politics of multiculturalism. Not only does this conflate, unhistorically, the civic and the plural types of nationalism; it fails to see how closely intertwined all three conceptions of the nation tend in practice to be, and how easy it is to move from one version to another as circumstances dictate. Nationalism will not be easily tamed and categorised to fit the prescriptions of moral and political philosophers (Kohn 1967: ch. 7; Plamenatz 1976; Ignatieff 1993; Kristeva 1993).

Nor can we easily accept the prescriptions of those who, like Habermas, would replace nationalism by a form of 'constitutional patriotism' that would make the political institutions and the constitution the focus of collective loyalties. Perhaps the most plausible of these prescriptions is that provided by Maurizio Viroli, who argues for a break with nationalism and a return to a modernised form of democratic republicanism. After a rich survey of the republican and nationalist traditions (nationalism here being exclusively of the German 'ethno-cultural' variety), Viroli argues that a territorially and historically grounded republicanism would replace nationalist exclusivity with a truly democratic and civic loyalty appropriate to the modern era. But, we may ask, is such a proposition feasible in large-scale industrial societies? If it were, why is it that nationalism rather than republicanism has swept the globe and drawn so many peoples and areas into its orbit? Besides, as we saw, there is no proof that republicanism might not turn out to be just as exclusive as (ethnic) nationalism; was not Athens after the citizenship law of 451 BC, were not Sparta and republican Rome, or many of the medieval Italian city-states, just as exclusive and rigorous? (Viroli 1995).

It is a welcome sign that there has been a renewed interest in the ethics of nationalism, after so many decades when nationalism was equated with fascism and was felt to be morally untouchable. But as long as ethnic nationalism – still the most popular and frequent of the versions adopted by elites and peoples around the world – continues to occupy a pariah status, and like the head of Medusa, turns the philosophic mind to stone, a large part of the subject, and that the most vexed and explosive, will remain unaddressed and unanalysed. . . .

Beyond Modernism?

Does all this suggest that we have moved beyond the nationalist epoch, in tandem with the shift away from modernism? Is a 'postmodern' epoch *ipso facto* a 'post-national' one, and are both reflected in 'postmodernist' styles of analysis?

The suspicion that 'objective' referents and empirical trends are, in some sense, a reflection of a particular style of analysis suggests a measure of caution in accepting the last part of McNeill's tripartite periodisation. Perhaps the reality we see here is the reflection of the kind of mirror 'held up to nature'; the evidence of 'fragmentation' may be as much a product of the deconstructive modes of analysis employed as of any empirical trends. Just as a perennialist paradigm looks for and finds continuity and rootedness, so the various postmodernist modes of analysis seek out and discover contestation, flux and fragmentation. And, of course, one can find plenty of evidence for both.

Looked at strictly from the standpoint of a theory of, or at least a fruitful perspective on, nations and nationalism, neither approach appears very helpful. Both have important things to tell us about aspects of the field of ethnic and national phenomena; and surely even from the brief survey I have conducted, it is clear that the themes of fragmentation and globalisation of the loosely labelled 'postmodern/post-national' approaches are rich in suggestion and insight into *contemporary* problems of ethnicity and nationalism. But here lies the rub. Except for some of the feminist accounts, there is a lack of historical depth to so many of the analyses under this broad heading, in a field that above all demands such depth, and for phenomena that are so historically embedded. It is as if the analysts had entered the drama in the third act (in terms of William McNeill's periodisation), taking for granted some version of modernism's script for the two previous acts. But which version, and why modernism? After all, both McNeill and the cultural fragmentation school of postmodernists stress the hard bedrock of 'cultural difference'. That suggests a joining of hands with perennialism over the heads of the modernists. Yes, the nation, the nation-state and all its works may be modern, contested, multi-stranded and fluid; but, in surpassing it and them, contemporary societies have rediscovered the power of fundamental cultural differences. Is this not, as Nira Yuval-Davis pointed out, just another form of 'essentialism', perhaps even of primordialism? (Yuval-Davis 1997: 59).

It is not only in their lack of historical depth that most of the recent analyses appear partial and 'fragmentary'. Again, with the exception of some feminist analyses, they propose no general explanation of nations and nationalism, and make no attempt to uncover the mechanisms by which they were formed, developed and spread. This is, in many cases, a consequence of postmodernism's anti-foundationalism and decentred analysis. But it is also evident in discussions of globalisation and Europeanisation, and of the civic or ethnic types of nationalism, which adhere to the usual canons of subject-centred and causal analysis. They too tend to take the phenomena of ethnicity and nationalism, and their cultural and political significance, as historical givens, even when they recast them as discursive narratives and deconstruct their meanings. But they offer no general explanation for their presence, variations and significance, no understanding of which nations emerged and where, why there are nations and nationalisms at all, and why they evoke so much passion.

This lack of theorising may have something to do with the deep ambivalence or, in the case of nationalism, downright hostility to these phenomena on the part of most of the analysts. This is not without its interest in that unpoliticised ethnicity, by itself, often evokes some sympathy, as 'cultural difference'; and, on the other side, a purely civic form of nationalism is commended by some analysts. It is the fatal combination of ethnicity and nationalism, as 'ethno-nationalism', that, in the tradition of Elie Kedourie, provokes the greatest fear and condemnation. But, as many of these analysts realise, it is precisely this combination that, whether it is tacit and 'unflagged', as in parts of the West, or explicit and explosive, as in Eastern Europe and parts of Africa and Asia, most requires to be addressed and explained. The fact that it is so deeply ingrained and routinised ('enhabited', in Michael Billig's term) in the West, also requires explanation. To see it as a de-ethnicised, civic form of nationalism is, I would suggest, not only a historical and analytical, but also a policy error, and to that extent, misleading and unhelpful (see Billig 1995: 42–3).

Common to most of these analyses, with the exception of McNeill's brief account and a few of the historical gender analyses, is a turning away from any 'grand narrative' like modernism or perennialism at the very moment when ethno-nationalism is resurgent and when the national state and national identity have once again become central to arguments about the direction of politics and society. Without an explicit theory of the character, formation and diffusion of nations and nationalism, such arguments will lack depth and validity. In the absence of a new encompassing grand narrative, all the partial 'little narratives' will have to lean on, and tacitly take their meaning from one or other version of the existing grand narratives. That can be good neither for systematic social understanding nor for political and social policy. Of course, research can be conducted on only a small part of the overall canvas; but equally its meaning and significance can only be clarified in terms of that wider framework or canvas. If that framework is tacitly assumed in the research without it being subjected to scrutiny, then the results of that research will be called into question along with its research programme. In these circumstances it is more helpful to relate the research directly to one or other version of the major paradigms, or fashion a new one that can justify the particular research programme.

References

Afshar, Haleh (1989) 'Women and reproduction in Iran', in N. Yuval-Davis, and F. Anthias (eds) *Woman–Nation–State*, London: Sage, 110–25.

Balibar, Etienne and Wallerstein, Immanuel (1991) *Race, Nation, Class*, London: Verso.

Beitz, Charles (1979) *Political Theory and International Relations*, Princeton NJ: Princeton University Press.

Bhabha, Homi (ed.) (1990) *Nation and Narration*, London and New York: Routledge.

Billig, M. (1995) *Banal Nationalism*, London: Sage.

Breton, Raymond (1988) 'From ethnic to civic nationalism: English Canada and Quebec', *Ethnic and Racial Studies*, 11, 1, 85–102.

Brubaker, Rogers (1992) *Citizenship and Nationhood in France and Germany*, Cambridge MA: Harvard University Press.

Chatterjee, Partha (1986) *Nationalist Thought and the Colonial World: A Derivative Discourse*, London: Zed Books.

——(1993) *The Nation and Its Fragments*, Cambridge: Cambridge University Press.

Coleman, James (1958) *Nigeria: Background to Nationalism*, Berkeley CA and Los Angeles CA: University of California Press.

Conversi, Daniele (1997) *The Basques, the Catalans and Spain: Alternative Routes to Nationalist Mobilisation*, London: C. Hurst & Co.

Elshtain, Jean Bethke (1993) 'Sovereignty, identity, sacrifice', in Marjorie Ringrose and Adam Lerner (eds) *Reimagining the Nation*, Buckingham: Open University Press, 159–75.

Enloe, Cynthia (1989) *Bananas, Beaches, Bases: Making Feminist Sense of International Politics*, London: Pandora.

Eriksen, Thomas H. (1993) *Ethnicity and Nationalism*, London and Boulder CO: Pluto Press.

Gans, Herbert (1979) 'Symbolic ethnicity', *Ethnic and Racial Studies*, 2, 1, 1–20.

Hall, Stuart (1992) 'The new ethnicities', in J. Donald and A. Rattansi (eds) *Race, Culture and Difference*, London: Sage.

Ignatieff, Michael (1993) *Blood and Belonging: Journeys into the New Nationalism*, London: Chatto and Windus.

Jayawardena, Kumari (1986) *Feminism and Nationalism in the Third World*, London and Atlantic Highlands NJ: Zed Books.

Kandiyoti, Deniz (1989) 'Women and the Turkish state', in Nira Yuval-Davis and Floya Anthias (eds) *Woman–Nation–State*, London: Sage, 126–49.

——(1991) 'Identity and its discontents: women and the nation', *Millennium, Journal of International Studies*, 20, 3, 429–44.

Kohn, Hans (1967) [1944] *The Idea of Nationalism*, 2nd edn, New York: Collier-Macmillan.

Kristeva, Julia (1993) *Nations without Nationalism*, New York: Columbia University Press.

Kuper, Leo (1981) *Genocide*, Harmondsworth: Penguin.

Kymlicka, William (1995) *Multicultural Citizenship: A Liberal Theory of Minority Rights*, Oxford: Clarendon Press.

Landes, Joan (1988) *Women in the Public Sphere in the Age of the French Revolution*, Ithaca NY: Cornell University Press.

Leoussi, Athena (1997) 'Nationalism and racial Hellenism in nineteenth-century England and France', *Ethnic and Racial Studies*, 20, 1, 42–68.

Lijphart, Arend (1977) *Democracy in Plural Societies: A Comparative Exploration*, New Haven CT and London: Yale University Press.

McGarry, John and O'Leary, Brendan (eds) (1993) *The Politics of Ethnic Conflict Regulation: Case Studies of Protracted Ethnic Conflicts*, London and New York: Routledge.

McNeill, William (1986) *Polyethnicity and National Unity in World History*, Toronto: University of Toronto Press.

Miller, David (1993) 'In defence of nationality', *Journal of Applied Philosophy*, 10, 1, 3–16.

——(1995) *On Nationality*, Oxford: Oxford University Press.

Mosse, George (1985) *Nationalism and Sexuality: Middle Class Norms and Sexual Morality in Modern Europe*, Madison WI: University of Wisconsin Press.

Newland, Kathleen (1993) 'Ethnic conflict and refugees', *Survival*, 35, 1, 81–101.

O'Leary, Brendan (ed.) (1996a) 'Symposium on David Miller's *On Nationality*', *Nations and Nationalism*, 2, 3, 409–51.

——(1996b) 'Insufficiently liberal and insufficiently nationalist', in Brendan O'Leary (ed.) 'Symposium on David Miller's *On Nationality*, *Nations and Nationalism*, 2, 3, 444–51.

Peel, John (1989) 'The cultural work of Yoruba ethno-genesis', in Elisabeth Tonkin, Maryon McDonald and Malcolm Chapman (eds) *History and Ethnicity*, London and New York: Routledge, 198–215.

Plamenatz, John (1976) 'Two types of nationalism', in Eugene Kamenka (ed.) *Nationalism: The Nature and Evolution of an Idea*, London: Edward Arnold, 22–36.

Sluga, Glenda (1998) 'Identity, gender and the history of European nations and nationalism', *Nations and Nationalism*, 4, 1, 87–111.

Smith, Anthony D. (1995) *Nations and Nationalism in a Global Era*, Cambridge: Polity Press.

Viroli, Maurizio (1995) *For Love of Country: An Essay on Nationalism and Patriotism*, Oxford: Clarendon Press.

Walby, Sylvia (1992) 'Woman and nation', in A. D. Smith (ed.) *Ethnicity and Nationalism: International Studies in Sociology and Social Anthropology*, volume LX, Leiden: Brill, 81–100; reprinted in Gopal Balakrishnan (ed.) (1996) *Mapping the Nation*, London and New York: Verso, 235–54.

Yuval-Davis, Nira (1997) *Gender and Nation*, London: Sage.

Yuval-Davis, Nira and Anthias, Floya (eds) (1989) *Woman–Nation–State*, London: Sage.

12 Northern Ireland and the Liabilities of Liberalism

John McGarry and Brendan O'Leary

Liberal explanations of ethnic and ethno-national conflicts and liberal prescriptions for their resolution enjoy wide currency in the academic world. In the classical liberal perspective properly-ordered states are composed of individuals who are self-interestedly rational; for instance, they establish states to provide for their security, and they join groups or political parties to advance their own interests. Society itself is conceived of as an arrangement to satisfy pre-existing individual interests, a 'co-operative venture for mutual advantage' (Rawls 1971, p. 4). In liberal ideology it is only in benighted and backward societies that individuals put an unchosen group identity – such as membership of an ethnic group or nation – ahead of their interests as individuals. Such societies are irrational, pre-modern, 'tribal' or 'primordial', outside the pale of the civilized liberal world (Ignatieff 1993). Ethnic and ethno-national identifications lead to 'mindless' conflict – characteristic of Bosnia, Rwanda, the Middle East and, of course, Northern Ireland. Communities sunk in illusory primordial identifications are seen as over-isolated from the Enlightenment; their hostilities explained by isolation and ignorance which cause negative stereotyping and the spread of disapproving myths about those outside the ethnic *laager*. Ghettoization, segregation, sectarianism and pillarization obscure the fundamental interests which humans have in common, especially those economic interests which cross-cut ethnic cleavages.

There are variations in the liberal world-view. Ethnic attachments and conflict are not always explained by underdevelopment, ignorance, isolation and unreasoning communalism. They may, on occasion, be attributed to opportunistically rational individuals pursuing their political or economic self-interest. Thus instrumental machinations of self-interested élites, eager to exacerbate (or even to create) ethno-national divisions for their own narrow ends, are often 'exposed' by liberal authors. For example, the conflict in the former Yugoslavia is held to stem from the ambitions of Tudjman and Milosevic, among other 'warlords', who saw in the collapse of Communism the opportunity to gain power by stirring up national antagonisms (p. 6). Similarly, conflict in South Africa in the run-up to the transitional constitutional deal was attributed to the scheming of Buthelezi, who, it was said, had chosen to promote Zulu nationalism as a means to power rather than accept the more progressive liberal agenda of Mandela and de Klerk. Exposing rational and amoral opportunism is not limited to individuals when liberal muck-rakers are in full flow. Entire ethnic collectivities may be seen as aggregates of individuals who have organized to ensure a greater share of scarce material resources. In this respect they are treated as no different from other 'rent-seeking' associations, like trade unions or interest groups. The closely related argument often follows that ethno-national conflict is caused by disputes over material resources; or it is said to be determined by inequality, deprivation, or the desire to profit. Conflict, in a more broad-minded liberal view, may be rooted in injustice, the result of opportunistic ethnic élites capturing state power and using it in a discriminatory fashion. Injustice often causes material inequality, and thereby causes resentment, but can extend beyond material concerns, touching on more abstract notions of fair play. Thus discrimination along ethnic, religious or racial lines promotes what is otherwise an artificial solidarity: winners defend the status quo; losers organize to dismantle it.

Liberal prescriptions for ethno-national conflict flow from these premises. If conflict is caused by backwardness, salvation lies in the bracing free air of modernity. If the problem is segregation, liberals seek to break down the barriers, including trade barriers, which exist between groups, and to expose them to each other. They espouse measures which 'reduce differences' between groups, and believe in what Steve Bruce has termed a 'mix and fix' philosophy (1994, p. 135). If the problem is scheming élites, the solution is opening the polity to alternative liberal voices. Thus, liberals advocate the formation of liberal political parties to counter ethnic entrepreneurialism. They launch liberal newspapers to combat ethnic propaganda. A recent article in the *Economist*, entitled 'Try words, they come cheaper', put matters thus: the 'warlike tribal myth[s]' of ethnically partisan media must be countered with stories of 'inter-tribal respect, co-operation and solidarity'. This prescription is intended to help ethnic divisions in places like Rwanda and the former Yugoslavia (*Economist*, 3 September 1994). Liberals also advocate electoral systems which facilitate 'vote-pooling' to make it more difficult for ethnic entrepreneurs to win with exclusivist appeals, and to help make 'moderation pay' (e.g. Horowitz 1989; 1991).

Alternatively, populist liberals advocate the bypassing of opportunistic political élites by appealing to the fundamentally individualist (and more moderate) sentiments of the people, and therefore support referenda or other instruments of direct democracy. If ethnic conflict is caused by material deprivations or inequalities, liberals seek to remove these causes and to create material incentives for peace. They call for economic aid for conflict-zones, or, alternatively, for economic sanctions to bring warring factions to their senses. If conflict is caused by ethnic élites' discriminatory use of state power, the liberal solution is civic integration: the creation of a neutral state in which discrimination is banned. With equal citizenship guaranteed, irrespective of people's ethno-national origins, it becomes irrational for political élites to make ethnic appeals, and so ethnic bonds wither away. The key instrument in the construction of such a liberal state is an individualist Bill of Rights which bans discrimination. Some liberals go beyond neutrality and require the liberal state to redress the consequences of historic discrimination through affirmative action policies. Such 'temporary' policies will create 'a level playing field' in which the difference-blind rules of egalitarian liberalism can apply. Whatever the method employed, the goal of liberals is straightforward: the erosion of ethnic solidarities, at least in the public realm, and the promotion of a more rational state and society based on equal individual rights.

Liberal Perspectives on Northern Ireland

Liberal views have shaped analysis of and prescription for Northern Ireland in a rich variety of ways. Here we summarize five liberal theses about Northern Ireland. We label each of them fallacious, for reasons which we shall subsequently defend.

Fallacy One: The conflict is the responsibility of extremist élites

There is a popular journalistic view that the conflict can be traced to the machinations of political or religious élites rather than to differences among the people. Such thinking is prevalent in Northern Ireland's 'independent' magazine, *Fortnight*,[1] which regularly launches editorials on the need to unleash 'people power' to circumvent the politicians – as if the conflict is analogous to that which led to the downfall of the Marcos regime in the Philippines, or the communist regimes of Eastern Europe. Supporters of this view cite opinion polls which consistently appear to show overwhelming popular support for compromise and peace. The view that the political class is to be blamed for the conflict informed the establishment of the Opsahl Commission in 1992 whose self-appointed task was to bypass the stonewalling of local élites by appealing to the people directly, and by allowing them to express their views before the Commission. The report of this self-appointed liberal élitist Commission was called, with no hint of irony, 'A Citizens' Inquiry' (Pollak 1993). It argued that politicians in Northern Ireland had much more latitude for compromise than they imagined (or pretended), and that they would benefit from educational courses on democratic conduct, available from the American, Scandinavian and German governments. . . .

When local élites are not being blamed directly for the conflict, they are held responsible for the social segregation which allegedly causes it. The segregated school system is sometimes seen as the direct by-product of church élites with interests in sustaining religious and ethnic differences. Characteristically, opinion polls are invoked to show substantial parental support for integrated education (Irwin 1991). High rates of endogamy are also sometimes attributed to the Roman Catholic Church because of its traditional position that the children of 'mixed' marriages should be brought up as Catholics. One study concludes that the Church's role in fostering segregated education and endogamy 'is the most significant aspect of the role of religion in the divisions and conflicts in Ireland and goes to the heart of the matter' (Fulton 1991, p. 131; see also Jenkins 1986, pp. 6–7).

Fallacy Two: The conflict has fundamental economic and material foundations

Liberal economists and other liberals share with Marxists the temptation to suggest that ethno-national conflicts are fundamentally rooted in economic and material interests. Some claim that it is the existence of economic deprivation in Northern Ireland, particularly in working-class ghettos, which has caused conflict.

The evidence seems strong: in numerous socio-economic indicators Northern Ireland is by far the most deprived region of the United Kingdom (Smith and Chambers 1991, pp. 51–2); a considerable amount of violence originates from people who live in deprived Catholic and Protestant 'ghettos'; and the most militant political parties – Sinn Féin [SF] and the Democratic Unionist Part [DUP] – draw disproportionate support from the less well-off. The reasoning is also straightforward. Those with little stake in society have little interest in stability and are more likely to be lured into militant ethnic organizations.

These views are popular within the British labour movement and within Conservative Party circles. Northern Ireland Office minister Richard Needham claimed in 1989: 'If work can be found for 10,000 unemployed boys in West Belfast,... that in itself will do more to impact on the political and security areas than anything else' (*Fortnight*, no. 276, 1989). The supposedly liberal prime minister of Northern Ireland put the logic a little more memorably in 1969: 'If you give Roman Catholics a good job and a good house, they will live like Protestants, because they will see neighbours with cars and television sets' (*Belfast Telegraph*, 5 May 1969). Sometimes it has been argued that the conflict is not only caused by deprivation but that the goal of those engaged in conflict is to end deprivation. In hearings held by the Opsahl Commission in the Shankill area in early 1993, some speakers attributed republican violence to the calculation that it would lead the government to transfer (financial) resources to Catholic areas. They attributed the more recent escalation in loyalist violence to the fact that Protestants had learned this lesson (*Fortnight*, no. 316, 1993, pp. 29–30). If the cause of the conflict is deprivation, then, so it seems, its resolution requires prosperity or economic growth – executed through greater governmental intervention on the left-wing view, or by the development of an 'enterprise culture' on the right-wing view.

The more cynical liberal economic perspective detects economic opportunism at the root of the conflict. Political élites, it is said, refuse to compromise because they derive material perks from continuing antagonism.... The prescription, implicit or explicit, is for tougher anti-racketeering measures and a clamp-down by the security forces.

Fallacy Three: The conflict flows from archaic cultures

The region's cultural backwardness and lack of exposure to the forces of modernization are dominant liberal orthodoxies. Many liberals confidently assert, for example, that the conflict is pristinely religious – a rerun of struggles which more modern regions fought and resolved in previous centuries. This claim is buttressed by evidence of high levels of religiosity in the region, by the fact that the rival political parties and paramilitary organizations draw their support almost entirely from different religious groups (Catholics and Protestants), and by the high profile of certain clergymen in politics, such as the Reverend Ian Paisley.

The view that the conflict has a fundamental religious dimension is endorsed by humanist organizations, ecumenical groups, journalists, historians, psychologists, political scientists and sociologists. Four distinct variants exist. First, liberal humanists blame the peculiar, anachronistic and uncompromising devoutness of both

Catholics and Protestants. This view, endorsed by some local atheists, is especially popular with outsiders. Here is a leading moralizing English journalist: 'The passions which are shared by Mass-going Gael and Calvinist planter, which sustain them indeed in the fashion of two drunks tilted out of the horizontal into a triumphal arch, are nothing to us' (Pearce 1991). Secondly, ecumenists, inside and outside the region, blame the conflict on the churches because they stress their differences and act as sectarian apologists for the political communities in their midst (Mawhinney and Wells 1975; Gallagher and Worrall 1982). Thirdly, there is the thesis of sociologists of religion (and of liberal Irish nationalists) that it is the exclusivist and peculiar nature of the Protestantism in Northern Ireland which underlies the conflict. In this perspective unionism is Protestantism, pre-national and religiously contractarian, whereas Irish nationalism is a secular ideology in which Irish Catholics can separate their faith and politics (Rose 1971, pp. 216–17; FitzGerald 1972; O'Brien 1974; Heskin 1980, p. 47; Buckland 1981, p. 100; O'Malley 1983, p. 178; Bruce 1986). Finally, evangelical Protestants and liberal unionists blame the conflict on the authoritarian Roman Catholic Church which they claim underpins an exclusivist and culturally coercive Irish nationalism (Aughey 1989, ch. 7; Wilson 1989, pp. 213–14).

Prescriptions follow. Humanists see secularization as the best chance for peace. Ecumenists seek the promotion of common Christian values. Those who regard unionism and Protestantism as identical divide in their proposals. If they are sympathetic, they defend the status quo; if they are unsympathetic, they argue either that unionists need not be taken seriously in a modern secular world, or that unionists would have no national objections to a united Ireland provided that their religion was protected (e.g. FitzGerald 1972). Those who blame the conflict on the Roman Catholic Church (and who fear its influence within a united Ireland) seek the reconstruction of the 1688 Protestant theocracy if they are evangelicals, and a secular integrated United Kingdom if they are liberal unionists.

However, the conflict is also attributed to a general cultural backwardness, rather than to religion *per se*. There is a long-established view in Great Britain that the Irish are 'culturally' primitive and disposed towards violence. In international folklore, from the bar-rooms of Chicago to the bar-rooms of Melbourne, the Irish male can be found displaying the alleged traits of his people: aggressive and unreasoning violence, facilitated by excessive alcohol consumption. What could be more natural therefore that in the homeland of the 'fighting Irish' there should be endless violence and intransigence. In this view, the Northern Ireland conflict is a protracted 'donnybrook'. . . .

The claim that the Northern Irish are unhealthily preoccupied with the past is, understandably, closely associated with professional historians. Oliver MacDonagh turns Oscar Wilde's witty dictum that 'Irish history is something which Irishmen should never remember, and Englishmen should never forget' into a sober cultural observation: the Irish never forget and the English never remember (MacDonagh 1983). Other historians, much less sympathetic to Irish nationalism, add that Irish republicans interpret their past through the distorting lens of Gaelic romanticism and Catholic mysticism (Dudley-Edwards 1977; Foster 1988; Elliott 1989). The thinly veiled implication is that the Provisional IRA is the current bearer of an irrational, romantic, religiously enthused communal hatred, which takes its 'cultural' polish from the Gaelic and Catholic revivals of the nineteenth century. Religious and romantic spiritualism are identified as key traits of Irish political culture, and impliedly culpable for its lack of modernization. Nationalist violence stems from this romanticism. Young people join paramilitary organizations after being schooled in histories of oppression and sacrifice or after imbibing republican songs on similar themes. In one account, even the hunger strikes of 1980–1, in which ten men died, are attributed to Gaelic and Brehon cultures, the sacrificial themes in Christian thought, and the tradition of republican protests and hunger striking stretching back to the Fenian movement founded in the 1850s (O'Malley 1990). The homily for Irish nationalists is clear: abandon the culture which caused these suicides and which still fuels mayhem and antagonism.

A leading historian of Ulster unionism, places special emphasis on the historically rooted siege mentality of the Protestant settlers and their descendants, and maintains that '... it is precisely because the most cruel and treacherous warfare has broken out over and over again, and usually after a period of relative security, as in 1641 or 1798 or 1920 or 1969, that the besieged suffer such chronic insecurity'. They fear insurrection by the natives/Catholics; betrayal from within their own ranks – the archetypal figure here being Governor Robert Lundy, the traitorous governor at the siege of Derry in 1690; and betrayal by Britain. 'The factor which distinguishes the siege of Derry from all other historic sieges in the British Isles is that it is still going on' (Stewart 1986, pp. 56–7).

Fallacy Four: The conflict is caused by segregation

Another liberal interpretation of Northern Ireland, often influenced by the history of black–white and Christian–Jewish relations in North America and Europe, is that conflict is caused (or at least exacerbated) by the isolation of the two communities from each other, an isolation more important than their alleged isolation from modernity. Numerous commentators highlight the denominational education system, in which 99 percent of pupils are segregated by their religion of origin. These voluntarily (and state-subsidized) segregated schools are seen as indoctrination camps for the rival ethno-national communities. Teaching different histories causes hostile feelings towards the other community; segregation facilitates negative stereotypes and myths of the Other, and prevents the establishment of cross-communal friendships; learning culturally specific sports inhibits mixing even after graduation; and segregated education reinforces residential segregation. The high rates of endogamy are also reinforced – research suggests that mixed marriages formed 6 percent of the total in Northern Ireland during the four decades 1943–82 (Fulton 1991, p. 199).

The liberal cure for segregation is to expose the rival groups to each other. Steve Bruce describes this 'mix and fix' mentality:

> Liberals get on well with each other. In such middle-class suburbs as the Malone Road area of Belfast, in such organizations as the [moderate] Alliance Party, and in such associations as Protestant and Catholic Encounter, Protestant and Catholic liberals mix and find they have much in common. They are thus readily drawn to the idea that the

conflict is caused by misunderstanding and ignorance. If working-class people also mixed, they would learn that their stereotypes are mistaken – "they" do not have horns – and that they are just like us. End of conflict (Bruce, 1994, p. 134).

. . .

Fallacy Five: Individual discrimination is the primary motor of antagonism

Perhaps the most important liberal explanation of the conflict is that it is caused by discrimination – it is the one with which we have most intuitive sympathy. In the 1960s the Northern Ireland Civil Rights Association [NICRA] sought equal citizenship for Catholics to end their second-class status and their exclusion from the institutions of the devolved government at Stormont. A government inquiry into the violence which flowed from the civil rights demonstrations attributed it to the absence of civil rights for Catholics (Cameron 1969). According to one distinguished political scientist had there been a Bill of Rights and judicial enforcement of its provisions against discriminations, as in the USA, there might have been no sustained political violence (Rose 1976). American civil rights leaders were able to pursue a successful strategy of non-violence because they could secure redress of black grievances through the courts. The Northern Ireland civil rights movement, denied similar opportunities, had no alternative strategy to offer militants, and the region became embroiled in violent conflict.

The British government has periodically expressed sympathy for this perspective and has introduced a range of measures to prevent discrimination against the Catholic minority. After a Fair Employment (Northern Ireland) Act (1976) failed miserably to achieve its objectives the British government, under pressure, eventually introduced a tougher law in 1989. It not only bans discrimination in hiring but requires employers to monitor the religious composition of their workforce and to take affirmative action if necessary. Liberal critics argue for a vigorous pursuit of this logic: they call both for explicit employment targets and a timetable for these to be achieved.

The most comprehensively researched statement that discrimination is at the centre of the conflict has been made by researchers from the Policy Studies Institute working for the Standing Commission on Human Rights (Smith and Chambers 1991). The work of Smith and Chambers is not, like that of many commentators, ahistorical. They observe that the seventeenth-century plantation of Ulster gave the best land to Protestants and relegated the Catholics to less fertile hilly land or to the status of landless labourers. Colonial disparities were reinforced by penal legislation which prevented Catholics from owning land and thereby acquiring the wealth in the period preceding industrialization (pp. 1–3, 368). Discrimination in employment and the allocation of public housing after 1921, the result of informal social practices and overt exhortations by successive unionist leaders, reinforced the legacies of colonialism. The result has been persistent and significant divergences between Catholics and Protestants in unemployment rates, quality of employment and overall living standards. For instance, Catholic men are about two and a half times more likely to be unemployed than Protestant men (pp. 161–2, 212). . . .

Having identified inequality as a central cause of conflict, Smith and Chambers rejected the unionist contention that this is a result of unequal abilities, or that it is a hangover from a bygone age which will gradually dissipate without corrective measures. Instead, they argued it can be accounted for significantly by continuing direct and indirect discrimination in the private and public sectors. Their prescription is for more effective policies for equal opportunity.

The Liabilities in Liberal Readings of Ethno-national Conflicts

All the foregoing liberal explanations have flaws. They either ignore or gloss over one or more of three essential facts: first, that the conflict is fundamentally rooted in ethno-national antagonism; secondly, that there is nothing pre-modern about conflicts which flow from such antagonism; and thirdly, that these antagonisms are intense because of their political and institutional setting. Liberals often make the mistake of reducing ethno-national conflicts to religious cultural or material differences between the ethno-national groups (Connor 1994). Such conflicts are better understood as socio-psychological, rooted in historically established collective identities and motivated by the desire to be governed by one's co-nationals, both for security and for collective freedom. These motivations have not been absent from liberal bastions like the United States, Great Britain or France. What distinguishes these territories from those presently embroiled in conflict are that their national questions have (largely) been settled. There is also nothing pre-modern about ethno-national conflicts. Western Europe has been embroiled in them for the best part of this century, and Canada's unity is currently threatened by nationalist separatism. Northern Ireland's ethno-national antagonisms have been intense, more like Bosnia's than Belgium's or Canada's and that must largely be explained by its political setting rather than its cultural environment. These considerations, simply asserted here, render the preceding liberal explanations and prescriptions problematic (see O'Leary and McGarry 1993; McGarry and O'Leary 1995).

Are political or religious élites to blame?

Élites play an important role in mobilizing nationalist movements. However, these movements usually have some pre-existing collective bases – the Achilles' heel in most instrumentalist readings of ethno-nationalist conflicts. What is more important is that once mobilized, and especially after protracted violence, ethno-national divisions become rooted, and are not easily dismantled without mutual collective security. In a deeply divided territory, with a long history of conflict, élites are more likely to reflect the divisions than to be responsible for them. Moreover, they respond to the incentives which they face. Leaders who underestimate the extent of those divisions and assume moderate positions often find themselves jobless or worse. Moderates in Northern Ireland have found no significant electoral niche. If moderate to begin with, they cannot compete with more chauvinistic leaders – as is evident in the electoral performances of the moderate Northern Ireland Labour Party [NILP] in the late 1960s and the Alliance Party [APNI] since the 1970s. If politicians experience Pauline conversions to moderation, as with unionists like Brian Faulkner in 1974 and William Craig in 1975, or nationalists like Gerry Fitt in 1980, they may be abandoned by their grass roots. Contrary to the Opsahl commissioners, little in the recent history of Northern Ireland suggests that political élites can easily compromise on the national question while retaining support. If in conditions of peace it becomes evident that public opinion has changed, then political élites will be capable of greater flexibility – but this change will not suggest that conflict was sustained by unrepresentative élites.

The popular moderation that is often displayed in opinion polls must also be treated with scepticism. Polls are imperfect, especially so in deeply divided territories where respondents may be unwilling to tell the pollster what they really think. They may judge their views to be outside conventional norms, or that their real views, given to a stranger, may put them at considerable risk. The evidence from Northern Ireland is that opinion polls tend to over-emphasize moderation and downplay extremism. Consider the following facts:

- opinion-poll support for the moderate Alliance party is roughly twice what it receives in elections (Whyte 1986, p. 232);
- cross-community power-sharing has received high cross-community support in opinion polls while unionist politicians advocating it have so far floundered at elections;
- support for Sinn Féin and the DUP in elections has always exceeded their support in opinion polls;
- huge numbers of unionists vote for Ian Paisley while hesitating to admit it in public.

It therefore cannot be confidently asserted that a referendum on a constitutional settlement will produce the same moderation we sometimes see in surveys.[2] To put matters in another way, selling any negotiated settlement successfully in a referendum will have to offer security to both ethno-national communities and not just to their moderates. . . .

The view that segregated education and endogamy can be blamed in any significant fashion on self-interested communal élites must also be treated with caution. Despite the existence of polls showing support for integrated education, there has been no significant public response to various government initiatives to facilitate integrated education. The high rate of endogamy, at least in urban areas, is probably caused as much by residential segregation and the lack of social interaction as it is by church policy (Whyte 1986; Whyte 1990, pp. 33–9). If Catholics do not meet Protestants, they are unlikely to want to marry them. Where there is an emphasis on ethnic solidarity and maintaining demographic numbers, and a distrust of the 'other side', endogamous practices prevail even among those who do not practise their religion. One sociologist of religion while attaching primary blame to the Catholic Church policy for endogamy, acknowledges that Catholics may have non-religious reasons for not marrying Protestants: they may consider them 'bigots, or oppressors or ethnic aliens' (Fulton 1991, p. 226). Endogamy, after all, helps to ensure that the offspring will not only be of the same religion, but also of the same national and political persuasion. Marriage across religious lines carries more than dangers of religious censure: it can mean ostracism, accusations of treachery and, in the more extreme cases, assassination (Whyte 1990, p. 41).

Has conflict been economically rooted?

Few commentators have reduced the conflict to deprivation. This is just as well, because there are many areas of the world much more deprived than Northern Ireland yet they are free of intense national conflict. Deprivation without the mobilizing glue provided by insecure ethno-national identity is mostly associated with apathy and criminal violence rather than with the organized and goal-oriented political violence characteristic of Northern Ireland. Moreover, unionists and nationalists draw support from right across the social spectrum, and not just from the deprived. Lastly, if deprivation was an important cause of conflict, we would expect the conflict to be worse in bad economic times than in good. Conflict should have been at its most intense during the Great Famine, rather than in 1798 or 1916–21 or after 1969. The current conflict broke out during a period of rising prosperity, suggesting a political trigger rather than an economic one. Similarly, its fluctuations in intensity have been more closely related to political events, such as internment without trial or the deliberations of the Constitutional Convention for example, than to changes in the economic cycle (see McGarry and O'Leary 1995, ch. 7). These arguments suggest that giving a republican a house and a TV set is unlikely to turn that republican into a unionist, certainly not in the short to medium term (see also Rose and McAllister 1983).

Opportunistic explanations are also suspect. The view that Catholics engage in conflict because it 'pays', overlooks the destruction which violence has wrought in Catholic areas and the economic plight of the Catholic community. The claim that the pursuit of personal profit is an important motive for paramilitaries downplays their ethno-national motivations: the paramilitary groups are ethnically exclusive, and direct practically all of their violence against other ethnic groups or state officials. Unlike mobsters, they have political goals and react to political stimuli. They also receive more support from their respective communities than those significantly engaged in criminal activities, and they have been resistant to prison management that criminals normally accept without rancour. By suggesting that the paramilitaries are opportunistic criminals, analysts overlook the contributions of repression and the behaviour of the security forces to the popularity of paramilitarism. . . .

Within the UK Northern Ireland has the lowest levels of criminal violence per capita but the highest levels of political or ethnic violence. The conflict over the last twenty-five years has also not produced the 'societal disintegration' associated with the triumph of anarchic and anomic criminality in some of the world's cities – which further underlines the national and political nature of the conflict (O'Leary and McGarry 1993, ch. 1).

Are backward cultures the problem?

Religion in Northern Ireland (or in Bosnia) is best seen as an ethnonational marker rather than as an important independent motivator of violent conflict. Religious labels distinguish the ethno-national groups, the descendants of settlers and natives, from each other. While the ethno-national groups are composed largely of 'Catholics' and 'Protestants', in many cases individuals do not practise their religion or do not allow their religion to determine their politics. It is this which occasions the well-known oxymoron of the 'Catholic (or Protestant) atheist'. Religious beliefs clearly play some role in shaping people's politics, and they may even be predominant for some, but there is significant evidence that they are less important than national identity in motivating behaviour and political dynamics.

First, the conflict started, escalated and has continued during the start of significant secularization[3] which has done little to undermine ethno-national conflict, and so it is questionable whether more secularization will make a significant difference. Secondly, there is no noticeable correlation between those areas most affected by violent conflict and areas of intense religious devoutness. In West Belfast, an epicentre of conflict, there have been significant declines in church-attendance in both communities (Wilson 1989, p. 204; Whyte 1990, p. 27). The spatial and per capita distribution of violence is highly concentrated in urban sites, which are, as elsewhere in the world, less religious than rural zones. Thirdly, relations between the Churches were improving when conflict erupted in the late 1960s. The second Vatican Council had formally abandoned the Roman Catholic claim that 'outside the Church there is no salvation', and there has been considerable ecumenical activity and inter-church cooperation during the current conflict, very different from what occurred in earlier crises. Fourthly, political activists avoid religious labels and make non-religious claims. The organizations of the minority embrace secular political values in their titles: 'nationalism' or 'republicanism', 'social democracy' and 'socialism' provide their vocabularies. No minority party or paramilitary group describes itself religiously. Politically they describe themselves as 'the northern nationalist community', and have shown willingness on many occasions to support individuals who enjoyed a closer relationship with Trotsky than with the Pope....

The absence of denominational titles in political and paramilitary organizations is more remarkable given their existence in other countries which are not racked by conflict, religious or otherwise. The high profile of Protestant clerics notwithstanding, the overwhelming majority of unionist politicians are lay people. They address secular issues, calling for a strengthening of the Union and for stronger security policies. The clerics who are politicians are best known for being hard-liners on the Union and security policy. Of course, national preferences might be dictated partly by religious motivations – a united Ireland, after all, would be 80 per cent Catholic, while the UK is over 80 percent Protestant or secular – but if most nationalist and unionist politicians are primarily interested in these religious agendas, they have done a good job of concealing it, from their followers, as well as from others. Loyalist paramilitaries generally shun overtly religious targets.

Catholic churches have remained relatively inviolate and priests have not been targets. It must be perplexing for those who believe that the paramilitaries are involved in a jihad that 'Protestant' gunmen assiduously have avoided clearly marked, accessible and unarmed priests and nuns when searching for targets. Individuals engaged in authentic religious wars – during the Inquisition, the Reformation and the Counter-Reformation – had no difficulty in dispatching heretics to hell.

The view that the Irish are culturally more disposed to be violent than other peoples is a colonial stereotype. The English, in the classic imperialist tradition, maintained that the Irish were murderous savages while murdering and savaging many of the natives. Such arguments justified conquest and expropriation in Ireland as they did in the Americas and elsewhere (Williams 1990). As for their alleged prowess with the beer glass, paramilitaries are more likely to be recruited for their disciplined, ascetic and puritanical characters. English stereotypists are best directed to the mirror of world-history, in which they will find that they (and their American cousins) have a much more widespread reputation for being an aggressive, warlike, piratical and imperial people. They are also well advised to ask themselves which nation's soccer fans are most welcome outside the islands of the North Atlantic? ...

Liberals who see the Northern Irish as unusually preoccupied with the battles of their ancestors usually live in states which are reasonably homogeneous or which have reached institutional accommodations between previously antagonisitc groups. Liberal Irish élites from the fabled 'Dublin 4', who now find their northern cousins embarrassing, come from an area which settled its national quarrel over seventy years ago. Rather than insulting the Northern Irish, they and others like them would be better advised to reflect on their good fortune.

Is segregation the problem and mixing the answer?

The idea of social mixing as a useful prescription faces major problems. To begin with it is impractical on a very significant scale. Residential segregation, particularly in working-class areas, is both extensive and voluntary. The desire to live among 'one's own' has been reinforced by twenty-five years of violence. Those who suffered most at the outbreak of the conflict in the late 1960s were those housed outside their respective ghettos. They experienced the Irish version of 'ethnic cleansing'. Without significant residential integration, however, there is unlikely to be support for integrated education. This would require bussing into threatening territory or at least out of the ghetto, and few parents will buy this idea. The same holds for workplace integration. There is also unlikely to be significant exogamy, because people from both communities are unlikely to meet and interact in the required fashion.

Even if social integration could be increased, it is questionable whether the consequences would necessarily be beneficial. In deeply divided territories, increased exposure to the 'other' may make group members more aware of what their group has in common and what separates them from the others. Exposure may cement group solidarity rather than diffuse it. There may, sadly, be something in the North American folk wisdom that white liberals are those whites who do not live near blacks. Analogously, Richard Rose warns that in Northern Ireland

> A Catholic in a mixed school may learn that when Protestants say 'Not an Inch' they mean it, just as a Protestant may learn that his Catholic schoolmates refuse to regard the Union Jack as the flag to which they give allegiance. (Rose 1971, p. 337)

As Connor writes, 'the idea of being friends presupposes knowledge of each other, [but] so does the idea of being rivals (1994, p. 48)....

The alternative to regarding 'mixing and fixing' as a panacea is to encourage it where it is feasible and wanted, but also to recognize durable divisions and ensure that both groups are treated in an equal manner and that both can be sure of their collective and cultural security. Just as many blacks in the USA now realize, ironically, that an authentic version of the separate but equal doctrine in *Plessey v. Ferguson* may be more attractive than the separate means unequal doctrine of *Brown v. Bd. of Education*, so many northern nationalists insist that they want equality and autonomy rather than equality and integration. Full funding for denominational and state schools, and a fair allocation of resources for job creation and public housing, are more important for them than integration. Lest we are misinterpreted, perhaps we should spell out that we believe that sufficient provision must be made for all those who wish to be schooled, live or work with members of the other community.

Is individual discrimination the problem?

The existence of significant economic inequality between Catholics and Protestants is undeniable. It has been convincingly argued that this gap exists because of discrimination, direct or indirect, that discrimination needs to be ended to reduce minority alienation, and that British efforts have not been far-reaching enough (e.g. Smith and Chambers 1991).

However, we take issue with the implicit liberal individualist supposition that the conflict centres on individual inequality and discrimination, and the implication that treatment of these matters will lead to a settlement. The liberal assumption is that people exist primarily as individuals with a fundamental (and moral) desire to be treated equally by others, and that states act justly and enjoy stability to the extent that they satisfy this yearning. This prescription is appropriate in societies where there is a consensus on national identity – in ethnically homogeneous states or in multi-ethnic immigrant societies with a shared civic identity, that is, where citizens see their relationship with the state through individualist lenses. However, in binational or multinational states, where there is no agreement on a common national political identity, matters are rather different. When the national nature of the state is at stake, many see themselves not just as bearers of individual rights but also as members of distinct communities.

Unable to recognize the importance of national identity or argue for the equal validity of rival versions of it, conventional liberalism not only fails to grasp what is at stake but ends up accepting the nationalism of the dominant community by default (Kymlicka 1991; 1995; Taylor 1992; 1993). In Northern Ireland, liberals characteristically prescribe that members of the nationalist minority should enjoy equality as individual citizens within the United Kingdom. However, by failing to recognize what most Catholics consider integral to their conception of the good life, i.e. the appreciation, recognition and institutional equality of their Irish national identity, this prescription falls short of authentic collective equality, including equality of individual self-esteem. Authentic collective equality requires that both groups' (national) identities be accepted as equally valid and legitimate – an argument refused by individualist liberalism. . . .

Just as 'unionist' civic integrationism downplays the national identity of the minority community, Irish nationalist civic integrationism, such as that represented by Dr Garret FitzGerald in the 1970s, downplays the British national identity of unionists. Unionists do not want to be treated as equal citizens within a united Ireland any more than Irish nationalists want to be treated equally within the United Kingdom. They want the preservation of their nation through the preservation of the UK.

Conclusion

There have been two conflicts going on in and over Northern Ireland: the conflict between the parties and paramilitaries of the ethno-nationalist communities and their respective patron-states, and the conflict about what the conflict has been about. It is this latter conflict, the meta-conflict, waged primarily by intellectuals, with which this article has been concerned. The two conflicts are intimately connected because misinterpreting the conflict has consequences for public policy. The premise of this article is that five liberal fallacies have persistently blocked a surer understanding of Northern Ireland. The conflict is primarily ethno-national and it is this dimension which must be addressed, and addressed fairly if the conflict is to be ended, and durably satisfy the nationalism of the current minority while protecting the nationalism of the current majority. The construction of such a settlement will be difficult, of course, though not impossible.

Liberalism should not be tossed away with its bath water. There is clearly independent merit in the arguments that deprivation should be targeted by public and employment policy, that discrimination should be firmly tackled and affirmative action vigorously pursued, and that obstacles to voluntary interaction between the two communities should be dismantled. There is, however, no merit, in the smug 'cosmopolitan' view that the conflict has been caused by unrepresentative and extremist élites, or by religiously or culturally retarded peoples incapable of the reasonable compromises allegedly characteristic of moderns. Analysts should always analyse themselves as a check on their interpretations of ethno-national conflicts.

Notes

This article abbreviates some of the principal arguments in McGarry and O'Leary (1995), to which interested readers are referred for defence in depth.

1   The independence of the magazine has become questionable since it now receives a subsidy from the British government.
2   When Canadians have been consulted in referenda they have always shown themselves to be more divided than their élites. Two referenda on prohibition and conscription split the country along linguistic lines. In a third referendum the political élites (the prime minister, ten provincial premiers, two territorial leaders, and four native leaders) submitted a package which they had unanimously negotiated. The package was rejected outside Quebec because it gave too much to that province, and within Quebec because it did not give enough.
3   Weekly church attendance among Catholics and Protestants has fallen since the 1960s. The divorce rate, while absolutely lower, has been increasing at about the same rate as in Great Britain. The rate of births outside marriage has also increased.

References

Aughey, Arthur 1989 *Under Siege: Ulster Unionism and the Anglo-Irish Agreement*, London: Hurst.
Bruce, Steve 1986 *God Save Ulster! The Religion and Politics of Paisleyism*, Oxford: Oxford University Press.
——1994 *The Edge of the Union: the Ulster Loyalist Political Vision*, Oxford: Oxford University Press.
Buckland, Patrick 1981 *A History of Northern Ireland*, Dublin: Gill and Macmillan
Cameron, Lord 1969 *Disturbances in Northern Ireland*, Report of the Commission appointed by the Governor of Northern Ireland, Belfast: HMSO.
Connor, Walker 1994 *Ethnonationalism: The Quest for Understanding*, Princeton, NJ: Princeton University Press.
Dudley-Edwards, Ruth 1977 *Patrick Pearse: The Triumph of Failure*, London: Gollanez.
Elliott, Marianne 1989 *Wolfe Tone: Prophet of Irish Independence*, New Haven CT: Yale University Press.
FitzGerald, Garret 1972 *Towards a New Ireland*, London: Charles Knight.
Foster, Roy 1988 *Modern Ireland: 1600–1972*, London: Allen Lane.
Fulton, John 1991 *The Tragedy of Belief: Division, Politics and Religion in Ireland*, Oxford: Oxford University Press.
Gallagher, Eric and Worrall, S. 1982 *Christians in Ulster, 1968–1980*, Oxford: Oxford University Press.
Heskin, Ken 1980 *Northern Ireland: A Psychological Analysis*, Dublin: Gill and Macmillan.
Horowitz, Donald 1989 'Making moderation pay: the comparative politics of ethnic conflict management', in J. P. Montville (ed.), *Conflict and Peacemaking in Multiethnic Societies*, Lexington, MA: Heath.
——1991 *A Democratic South Africa? Constitutional Engineering in a Divided Society*, Berkeley, CA: University of California Press.
Ignatieff, Michael 1993 *Blood and Belonging: Journeys into the New Nationalism*, Toronto: Viking.
Irwin, C. 1991 *Education and the Development of Social Integration in Divided Societies*, Belfast: Queen's University of Belfast.
Jenkins, Richard 1986 'Northern Ireland: In what sense "religions" in conflict?' in R. Jenkins, H. Donnan and G. McFarlane (eds), *The Sectarian Divide in Northern Ireland Today*, London: Royal Anthropological Institute of Great Britain and Ireland.
Kymlicka, Will 1991 *Liberalism, Community and Culture*, Oxford: Oxford University Press.

—— 1995 *Multicultural Citizenship: A Liberal Theory of Minority Rights*, Oxford: Oxford University Press.

Macdonagh, Oliver 1983 *States of Mind: Two Centuries of Anglo-Irish Conflict, 1780–1980*, London: Pimlico.

Mawhinney, B. and Wells, R. 1975 *Conflict and Christianity in Northern Ireland*, Grand Rapids: Erdman.

McGarry, John, and O'Leary, Brendan 1995 *Explaining Northern Ireland: Broken Images*, Oxford, England, and Cambridge, MA: Basil Blackwell.

O'Brien, Conor Cruise 1974 *States of Ireland*, London: Panther Press.

O'Leary, Brendan and McGarry, John 1993 *The Politics of Antagonism: Understanding Northern Ireland*, London and Atlantic Heights, NJ: Athlone.

O'Malley, Padraig 1983 *The Uncivil Wars*, Belfast: Blackstaff Press.

—— 1990 *Biting at the Grave: The Irish Hunger Strikes and the Politics of Despair*, Belfast: Blackstaff Press.

Pearce, Edward 1991 'One long piece of perplexity', *Fortnight*, no. 296, p. 15.

Pollak, Andy (ed.) 1993 *A Citizen's Inquiry: the Opsahl Report on Northern Ireland*, Dublin: Lilliput Press.

Rawls, John 1971 *A Theory of Justice*, Oxford: Oxford University Press.

Rose, Richard 1971 *Governing Without Consensus: An Irish Perspective*, London: Faber and Faber.

—— 1976 'On the priorities of citizenship in the Deep South and Northern Ireland', *Journal of Politics*, vol. 38, no. 2, pp. 247–91.

Rose, Richard and McAllister, Ian 1983 'Can political conflict be resolved by social change?' *Journal of Conflict Resolution*, vol. 27, no. 3, pp. 533–57.

Smith, David and Chambers, Gerald 1991 *Inequality in Northern Ireland*, Oxford: Oxford University Press.

Stewart, A.T.Q. 1986 *The Narrow Ground: Patterns of Ulster History*, Belfast: Pretani Press.

Taylor, Charles 1992 'The politics of recognition', in C. Taylor and A. Gutman (eds), *Multiculturalism and 'The Politics of Recognition'*, Princeton, NJ: Princeton University Press.

—— 1993 *Reconciling the Solitudes: Essays in Canadian Federalism and Nationalism*, Montreal: McGill-Queen's University Press.

Whyte, John 1986 'How is the boundary maintained between the two communities in Northern Ireland?' *Ethnic and Racial Studies*, vol. 9, no. 2, pp. 219–34.

—— 1990 *Interpreting Northern Ireland*, Oxford: Clarendon Press.

Williams, R. 1990 *The American Indian in Western Legal Thought: The Discourses of Conquest*, New York: Oxford University Press.

Wilson, Tom 1989 *Ulster; Conflict and Consent*, Oxford: Basil Blackwell.

Part V

Violence, Genocide, and War

INTRODUCTION TO PART V

One of the unfortunate consequences of the failure to resolve ethnic and racial conflicts is the extent to which this can lead to violent confrontation and even outright warfare. It may well be true that a seemingly stable system of racial hierarchy can be based on the implicit threat of violence of one group against another, and it is generally when there is a change in the structure of power that these latent antagonisms begin to come to the surface. Beth Roy examines the consequences of two violent incidents that took place in the 1950s in very different circumstances but which illustrate some surprising similarities. The first involved a riot over grazing rights between Muslim and Hindu villagers in what was later to become Bangladesh; the second, the integration of a public school in Little Rock, Arkansas at the the start of the post-war Civil Rights movement in America. In each situation, Roy examines the interpretations of different members of the groups involved in the conflicts and their later assessments several decades after these pivotal events. In the first case, changing rule over the land, from British colonial jurisdiction to Pakistani and later Bangladeshi control, placed the two key groups in a variety of different circumstances. What had been a region almost entirely free from the communal massacres that had marked the partition of India in 1947, was slowly transformed, after the riot, into a situation of considerable mistrust, at least on the part of the now less powerful Hindu community.

The changes in Little Rock also symbolized a major transformation in Southern society and the break up of traditional patterns of black–white segregation. Roy documents the manner in which attitudes lag behind legal changes and how the discourse of the various parties involved was shaped by the changing power relations. The political strategy of silence, of "inside talk" and the various ways in which groups communicate among themselves but not to outsiders, helps to explain the glaring difference in perceptions that has been shown to divide America, and other racially diverse societies, along group fault lines.

When societies are riven by extreme violence, leading to the widespread massacre of one group by members of another, there is an understandable tendency to attribute such genocides to primordial or historical hatreds. How else can we explain the levels of brutality that accompany these genocidal outbursts? However, on closer inspection such analyses often demonstrate the triumph of contemporary propaganda over historical reality. This conclusion is particularly troubling since it suggests that hideous cruelty may be a much more common potential of many more societies than we have previously thought. The situation of Burundi, the central African state and close neighbour of Rwanda, is explored by René Lemarchand who attempts to dispel many of the common misconceptions about the nature of ethnic conflict in that small central African state. Lemarchand reveals the true complexity of social relations in Burundi, the forms of identification and systems of reciprocal obligations and intermarriage that make the antagonism between Hutu and Tutsi a special product of the last thirty years. Far from representing the inevitable outcome of "primordial" differences, the fate of Burundi must be seen as the interplay between instrumental factors and a range of possible group affiliations. One such important influence has been the genocidal massacres taking place in Rwanda, and the wider geo-political context, affecting the internal developments in post-colonial Burundi.

It is precisely these geo-political forces that are emphasized by Dusko Sekulic in his attempt to explain the dissolution of Yugoslavia. Based on Collins's elaboration of Max Weber's model of political legitimacy, Sekulic exposes the limitations of any diagnosis tied to claims about primordial hatreds between diverse ethno-national groups in the Balkans. Rather, both the foundation of Yugoslavia, after the collapse of the Ottoman and Austro-Hungarian empires at the end of the First World War, its survival under Tito during the communist period, and its final collapse in the wake of the disintegration of the Soviet empire, should be explained in relation to the shifting external political forces and the calculations of the various ethnic elites. Yugoslavia, as a federation of South Slav communities made sense to Croats, Slovenes and other non-Serbs in the early part of the twentieth century, given the threat of Italian or Hungarian expansionism. Ties to Serbia, even a politically dominant Serbia, were better than the alternatives. After the Second World War, Yugoslavia was caught between East and West in a position that did little to encourage ethnic autonomy – Tito was clearly preferable to Stalin and all versions of communism were suspicious of nationalist sentiments. The collapse of the Communist bloc removed that particular geo-political threat to Yugoslavia's independence but the socialist and Serbian nationalist goals of the Milosevic regime, rapidly lead to warfare, secession and the break up of the state.

13 Rioting Across Continental Divides

Beth Roy

Introduction

In 1954 in a small East Pakistani village called Panipur, a cow ate a lentil plant in somebody else's field and a fight ensued. The cow was owned by a Muslim family, the plant by Hindus. Before too many days, a riot grew to enormous proportions and was put down by official force. Four people died, and relations between Hindus and Muslims in Panipur were never quite the same again.

In 1957 in a medium-sized city called Little Rock in the state of Arkansas in the USA, nine black students tried to enroll in a public high school that had always educated only white teenagers. The Nine were turned away by official force, while a crowd of angry white people raged outside. No one died but many were injured in one way or another, and relations between black and white people in Little Rock were never quite the same again.

Despite near-universal assumptions that conflict among people of unlike identities is a natural thing, old as history, destined to exist as long as humanity lives, just below the surface of the obvious swim many questions about these two events. In both places, the communities had lived side by side in apparent amity until the time when crisis hit. People in both places prided themselves on their record of peaceable relations. When a black man was lynched in Little Rock in the 1920s, white upper class women organized an effective anti-lynching movement that accounted for the absence of any lethal violence ever after. Indeed, it was because it was reputed to have good race relations that Little Rock was chosen as a site to start desegregating public schools following a Supreme Court order to that effect three years earlier – the same year the cow ate the plant in Panipur. Similarly, Panipur lay in a region in which Muslims had come forward in the years before the riot during the worst period of communal slaughter to protect Hindus and insist that their fellow religionists abstain from violence. It had been a model of intentional harmony in an era of uncontrolled communal frenzy elsewhere in Bengal.

Why then at those particular moments in time had both places exploded into hostilities? To assume the inevitability of identity-based conflict is to rule out all the most interesting questions. Drawing on research I've conducted over the past decade, I propose in this paper to compare two seemingly dissimilar occurrences in order to harvest insights into how group identities are constructed through acts of history-making, and in turn how the making of history shapes group identities.

1 Unlikely Comparisons

In a sense, it was a matter of irrationality as curious as the events I researched that led me to study two such disparate sites as Panipur and Little Rock. What most obviously bound together these two places was my own biography. I grew up in the southern part of the United States, in a place struggling with the same racial issues that exploded in Little Rock. Years later, I lived in West Bengal and, also somewhat by chance, worked across the border in the Panipur region, in what by then had become Bangladesh. On both continents, I puzzled long and hard over animosities among people I both liked and respected. Disbelieving deeply that irrationality exists, I searched for reasons that explained hostilities so resistant to reasoned intervention. As a psychotherapist I have learned that context is everything in making sense of mysteries on a psychological level. Viewed from the perspective of an outsider, feelings and ideas may be incomprehensible, but from the perspective of the individual involved, every emotion and belief makes sense. As a sociologist I apply this theory to social issues, studying oral histories of those involved to make sense of puzzling social conflicts.

It was also a matter of biography that gave me access to the stories of Panipur villagers and white graduates of Central High School in Little Rock. Harboring great bitterness for the ways they felt they'd been misrepresented in previous representations of the Little Rock story, the graduates made a considered decision to talk with me. Because I, too, had graduated from a segregated southern high school in the same time frame, they believed I could tell their story with sympathy. So, too, the villagers in Bangladesh talked with me because I was introduced by development workers they respected, who in turn knew me through a project for which I'd volunteered the year before.

In the end, what both villagers and graduates told me spoke volumes about ambitions and problems in their own lives expressed in the language of social action, formulated in terms of identities. My study of each case delineated meanings in terms specific to that group and that time; to analyze both in the same breath is a tricky proposition, but nonetheless productive. Let us look at some dissimilarities and congruencies as focal points for a meaningful comparison.

Some contrasts are obvious:

- In Panipur, the Hindus and Muslims who fought were social equals in many respects. The Hindus involved were members of a lowly tribe called Namasudra; both communities consisted of poor farmers with many similar complaints of oppression at the hands of caste-Hindu landlords, most of whom had left for India after partition. Indeed, the Namasudras consciously opted to remain in Pakistan because they viewed their class alliance with the Muslim tillers as more advantageous to them than any gains they might reap from migration. Said Sunil, a Namasudra farmer, "Many of us believed then, 'Let the caste Hindus go, but those of us who are peasants, whether Hindus or Muslims, can live together as brothers.'" In Little Rock, however, there were vast social, economic, and political distinctions between the white and black people who came to blows. The whites who protested desegregation at Central High School were greatly privileged in contrast to the black students seeking entry, although many of them were disadvantaged *vis-à-vis* other whites.

- While Namasudras and Muslims distinguished themselves by all sorts of cultural practices, ranging from modes of religious worship to dress to details of diet, they nonetheless shared an ethnic and racial commonality. Historically, each group probably derived from subaltern Bengali peoples (there is some question about the origins of Bengali Muslims, some scholars contending they were poor peasants who converted, others arguing that they were descendants of immigrants from Islamic lands.) In Little Rock, both whites and blacks at some point in their histories had arrived from other places, but by significantly different routes. White Arkansans descended from yeoman settlers making their way across the American continent in the 18th and 19th centuries and choosing for a variety of reasons to stop in that particular territory. Black Arkansans were the offspring of slaves, unwilling migrants to the new world who had won freedom but not liberty less than a hundred years before. Racially distinct (although frequent rape of black women by white slave owners accounted for a fair degree of genetic intertwining) and culturally different, the two groups interacted prototypically as servant to employer, not as economic actors with articulated class interests in common.

- Both occurrences I studied happened in a time of important change on a national level. But the specific contention involved was initiated and took place very differently. In Panipur, the immediate dispute was ordinary; cows ate neighbors' plants all the time. The conflagration appeared to be impulsive and spontaneous, although my study of it revealed that a good deal more consideration had gone into it than first met the eye. In Little Rock, the confrontation grew from many years of thoughtful action, both legal and political. African-American activists viewed school desegregation as only one step among many intended to advanced racial equity. They carefully prepared the ground for change, building a body of legal decisions on which the Supreme Court's order to desegregate schools was based. The selection of Little Rock as a site for desegregation and the publicity surrounding its achievement happened with intention, through political negotiation, according to plan. Similarly, the resistance to desegregation was engineered and encouraged through acts of rhetoric, community-level organizing, and political and economic coercion. There was little impulsive or spontaneous about events in Little Rock.

Despite these differences, Panipur and Little Rock have similarities that make their comparison fruitful:

- In both places, ordinary people, folks who did not normally see themselves as capable of influencing history, acted in ways that had historical impact.
- In both places, the state played an active role in complex interaction with the citizenry.
- In both places, the act of acting changed not only relationships between the identity groups involved, but the identities themselves. Moreover, those changes revealed interconnections among different identities, linking race, class, gender, and community in ways that made understandable the power and tenacity of each.

- Perhaps most striking, in both places ordinary people first described themselves as swept passively along by powerful forces not of their own making. But as their stories unfolded in detail, it became apparent that in fact they had made choices to act as they did, and those decisions made sense in the context in which they lived at the time.

2 Action and Intentionality

It is this last observation that opens up the theoretical territory I wish to explore. Why people made the choices they did became clear to me as I talked at length with them about the particular moments of crisis in the broader context of their life-stories. The unraveling of those puzzles is the subject of my two studies, *Some Trouble with Cows* and *Bitters in the Honey*. In brief, particular public behaviors expressed distinct problems of class and aspects of gender. Rather than elaborate these meanings further here, what I will address in this paper is *how* people made their choices. While every individual to whom I spoke told a story of his or her thinking and feeling at the time, I was very conscious of how interactions among individuals, and particularly how the modes of talk through which they communicated with each other, gave social significance to their individual decisions.

That the Bangladeshi Muslims made decisions as a community was clear in everybody's narrative. They met together and decided to stop tolerating minor village frictions which had been an irritating but acceptable part of life until that moment. As a community, they asserted a new set of rights and possibilities by declining traditional routes to peacemaking, taking stands which only a few years before would have been unthinkable. Golam, the Muslim man whose cow ate the plant, described how conscious that process was:

> That evening, we Mussalmans held a meeting. We thought we could not go on living like this. They often threatened us, they threatened to beat us.

So, too, in Little Rock, the fracas was occasioned by thoughtful strategies of the black community to change accepted norms of their rights and possibilities. In both these cases, a particular group acted assertively to challenge a perceived injustice.

The other group, however, resisted that change. The Namasudras in Panipur acted in self-defense, believing themselves to be in jeopardy at the hands of the Muslims. Said Sunil, the Namasudra farmer:

> Some people came and said, "They have damaged our crop. Moreover, they are saying provocative things. They're preparing themselves to beat us. What are we to do now?" The guardian sort of people among us said, "Don't do anything in advance. But be prepared to protect yourselves."

"The Mussalmans hit them and tore them up and burned their houses. How could they sit and tolerate it?" commented a Muslim villager sympathetically.

In Little Rock, white people often insisted they did *not* feel threatened by school desegregation. But neither did they welcome it. Said Jane, a white woman studying at Central High:

> At best [they wanted to] ignore [it]. I can't remember anyone saying, "I can't wait to be nice to black kids coming to school." That was never discussed. ...I remember words like law and order. They would use those phrases: "Are you going to be a law and order kind of person?"

While some white people took to the streets outside the school and violently threatened the black students, for many others, the majority of white students inside the school, for instance, resistance took the form of inaction, of technical obedience to a disagreeable law. Passivity was an effective political act for two reasons: first, the mobs outside and a significant minority of students inside who harassed and tormented the Nine formed a coercive context which cast neutrality in a hostile light, and, second, the historic context of racial inequity was so profoundly normalized that doing nothing intrinsically supported the *status quo ante*. Another white student, a man named Wesley, told me:

> Young people today, in my own family, my nephews, have asked me, "Well, what did you think about segregation?" And the answer is, I didn't think about it. It was just the way it always was, and it was like, we don't think about it being Sunday morning when it's Sunday morning.

When one group of people *asserts* its rights or campaigns for improvements in its lot, other groups can respond in a limited number of ways. They can *resist*, and resistance can take active forms, often couched in terms of self-defense as in Panipur, or passive ones as in Little Rock. They can *accommodate* change, shifting slightly to allow it to happen on the smallest scale possible. Finally, a group which has not initiated change can nonetheless *cooperate* with it, embracing one group's progress as a shared opportunity for furthering common objectives or joining disparate goals in alliance. Why and how one group opts for a particular response and another a different one is a crucial question for social theorists and activists.

All these relationships to change involve discourse with others. What is said and not said, who is and is not included in the conversation, how communication is constructed, all shape the social meaning of what happens. By comparing the stories of Panipur and Little Rock, I seek deeper understandings of how these interactions, some ordinary, some dramatic, shaped collective action and with it the meaning of social identity.

3 History and Change: Talking Law and Order

Mofizuddin, a lively Muslim gray-beard with wisdom, humor, and passion twinkling behind Coke-bottle eyeglasses, reflected on the Panipur riot thirty years after the event:

These cows and plants are symbols. After Partition, the minority community didn't take it well. There was Hindu–Muslim tension.... There's a song, "*Azad* Pakistan," it says there is anger in us, even if we don't express it. That's internal talk, not something you speak about openly.... In our *rastriya* [state], now it's Bangladesh, we all have to stay like Bangladeshis. In the British time, we had to obey the British laws. In the Pakistani time, we had to abide by those laws. There was no point in being angry. We felt it, but we didn't express our anger. Why couldn't they now accept our rules?

In describing the stance "we" took in response to alien rule, Mofizuddin echoed the philosophy of the white students of Central High who talked about "law and order." But he added an important emotional point: while their behavior was obedient, their feelings were angry. Not to express that anger was a strategic decision born of Mofizuddin's recognition of futility. There was "no point" in expressing it – *then*.

But *now* it was different. When Mofizuddin concluded by questioning why *they* couldn't *now* accept *our* rules, the *now* to which he referred was actually three decades past. "They" could equally have been caste Hindus or West Pakistanis. Often enough in the past, Namasudras and Muslims had formed alliances to contest particular issues, and the definitions of *them* and *us* had been based on class or politics, not communal identities. Indeed, when speaking of the state, of any one of three different states – British, Pakistani, Bangladeshi – Mofizzudin did include both Hindus and Muslims in his *we*. Yet suddenly at the end of his thoughtful statement, he distinguished a Namasudra *them* from a Muslim *us*. Why?

In the context of the changes of state he listed, all of them occurring within his lifetime, it makes sense that Mofizuddin's construction of his identity as a Muslim might be strengthened by the creation of Bangladesh. In the British time, all "Indians" were oppressed by rule of the "other." So, too, during the Pakistani era, when West dominated East, Bengalis were victimized as a group. In each of these cases, Mofizzudin's reference point in delineating *us* and *them* was more likely to have been political than religious, or even cultural. He referred to who had to obey whose rules. Now, with the advent of home rule, what Mofizzudin was therefore articulating was a sense of his own newfound identity with the state, based on his Muslim-ness as distinguished from his Hindu neighbors' absence of such a claim.

But the *now* to which Mofizzudin referred was symbolically, not temporally, now. He spoke of a moment which in actuality occurred when it was Pakistan, not Bangladesh. That was the moment when the riot took place, and in the context of Mofizzudin's eloquent statement to me, what he expressed was a moment back then when he and his fellows chose one identity over others. The definition of *us* became not peasant (as Sunil had defined it), not Bengali (as national political leadership defined it a few years later), but Muslim. That he made that particular choice was, I suspected, very purposeful, for Mofizzudin was a purposeful sort of fellow. Indeed, in the *now* we shared at that moment, I listened closely for his purpose in making the statement he had just made.

4   Passive Resistance in Little Rock

What that purpose might be is clarified by a contrast between Mofizzudin's evocation of law and order and that of the white Little Rock students. As the year of crisis began at Central High School, the editor of the student paper, Jane, wrote an editorial urging her peers to "act right" over the months to come. Her essay was given widespread national media coverage and was considered extraordinarily courageous by adult on-lookers all over the country:

> You are being watched! Today the world is watching you, the students of Central High. They want to know what your reactions, behavior, and impulses will be concerning a matter now before us. After all, as we see it, it settles now to a matter of interpretation of law and order.
>
> Will you be stubborn, obstinate, or refuse to listen to both sides of the question? Will your knowledge of science help you determine your action or will you let customs, superstition, or tradition determine the decision for you?

Jane posited obedience to the law as a moral virtue. Characteristic of the times, she joined that notion to the superiority of science over tradition. That she needed to invoke some alternative to custom was necessitated by the fact that the law to which she urged obedience was one challenging the traditional order of things. When the Supreme Court declared that segregated schools violated the national mandate to provide education of equal quality to all students of whatever race, they challenged an order of racial separation that was deeply structured into hierarchic relations in the South. Joined in ways not altogether evident to the racial hierarchy was also a mystified order of class stratification, and more subtly an arrangement of gender relations as well. To have welcomed the nine black students into Central High would have been to accept something far more profound than a simple co-existence of youngsters of different races in common classrooms.

Many of Jane's classmates did believe they could accept the latter without consenting to more fundamental change. "There was plenty of room for all of us there," declared Helen. "Now, I'm not trying to be Goody Two-Shoes, think about it. The school was big enough to accommodate everybody, so who cares?" The generous sentiment that the school was big enough for everyone was problematized just a bit by Helen's declaration, "Who cares?" Outside the school raged mobs of people who cared very much. Helen's way of dealing with that protest was to go round-about: "I didn't see if there was commotion going on up here, I didn't see it," she said. "Cause I came in the side door, went to my locker, did my thing." Nonetheless, inside the school, daily acts of harassment of the black teenagers by other white students constituted effective resistance to the change taking place. The Nine were tripped in the halls, surreptitiously attacked in their classrooms, tormented in the locker rooms, teased and humiliated in the lunchroom. "Going in the side door" in that context was a political act; to look the other way was to collude with the resistance.

But Helen didn't see it that way. She typified her fellow graduates when she told me she agreed to be interviewed in order to set the record straight. She had done exactly what Jane urged, had abided by the law and kept personal order, and yet she felt herself to have been misrepresented by history, vilified and demonized by false association with those "others" of her own race who acted badly. She had been watched by the world and, despite her own decorum, she had been judged wanting because of the bad behavior of others of her racial identity group. Her statements to me, like Mofizuddin's, served to justify her behavior and declare her innocence in the court of history.

Helen's attitude contained a particular view of history and relationship to the state which contrasted with Mofizuddin's perspective. Helen believed herself to be accommodating history, tolerating social change and thereby containing its consequences. I asked Helen what her parents would have thought had she brought a black friend home with her, and she replied with energy, "Well, I wouldn't have even thought about it. I would not have invited them into my home." Other women of Helen's group told me they, too, accepted the presence of the Nine in "their" school, but problems arose when one of the Nine, a feisty girl named Minnijean, walked the corridors proudly, as if she belonged there. Desegregation was all right, but true integration? Never! Helen and her peers therefore sought to obey the new law but defend the old order.

Mofizzudin, on the other hand, had tolerated an old order by abiding by the laws of the British. But when people took power some of whom shared with him religious identity, he recognized a new opportunity. By an old and familiar act, obedience to the law, he declared a new order. In the past both he and his Nama-sudra neighbors shared oppression, but now the ways parted, and he acted to secure privileges for himself and his group at the expense of the Hindus. Indeed, what he called for was Hindu acquiescence to *his* order. Where Helen sought to bend to winds of change but not break, Mofizzudin tried to ride the winds of change to his own ascendancy. Helen was part of a dominant group protecting that position from challengers. Mofizuddin was redefining his position in society by nuances of behavior in order to assert his superior rights *vis-à-vis* the Hindus.

Law is the embodiment of state power. How was it that in the same act, pledging allegiance to the law, Helen and Mofizuddin could accomplish opposite aims? Indeed, what law was it they were obeying? The laws of the new Pakistani state did not condone rioting, and in fact when the state did intervene, they squashed the melee and imposed equal punishment on Hindus and Muslims. On a literal level, then, Mofizuddin was rebelling, not obeying the state whose laws he exhorted Hindus to obey. His statement was, thus, more metaphoric than factual. But the spirit of the statement was true. He was imposing a new order, if not a new law, on the village polity.

So, too, in Helen's case, her evocation of law and order chose a particular segment of the state to which to ally herself. Desegregation embodied many kinds of conflict between different levels of state authority. The federal government, in the form of the Supreme Court, mandated that schools be integrated. The federal executive, however, in the person of the president, Dwight Eisenhower, did not personally support racial integration and quietly balked at implementing the court's order. The head of the state of Arkansas, Governor Orval Faubus, on the other hand, was a man who claimed to have no problem with integration. But for political reasons, he allied himself with people who did, using the armed force available to him, the non-professional National Guard, ostensibly to protect public safety, but actually to bar the black students from the school. Only when matters reached crisis point did the president send federal troops to Little Rock, breaking a stalemate so that the nine black youths could attend classes but doing nothing to promote change at the level of the human heart.

Helen could, therefore, opt for behavioral order within the letter of the law without wholeheartedly participating in a new social order. She could remain a faithful citizen and resist change. In some measure, she could do that because the immediate authority, the Governor of the state, was a person with whom she identified. He, too, was a native of Arkansas; he, too, considered himself to be open minded yet fundamentally pragmatic; and he, too, chose behaviors that furthered his own interests without regard to a larger good.

Both Helen and Mofizuddin thus based their responses to historic change on their identity – racial and political in Helen's case, communal in Mofizuddin's. In both cases, that act was based on their understanding of where power lay, for they took issue with a group whose access to power was even more compromised than their own. In neither case did they challenge those whose privilege in society might truly interfere with their well-being. The enemy they identified was, stripped of religious or racial characteristics, a person much like themselves, an ordinary soul eking out an existence, seeking at most a little betterment but not dominance. How did a given community define itself such that its gaze was deflected from upper levels of the social pyramid to that social level closest to its own?

5 Constructing Power: Inside Talk

"There's a song, 'Azad Pakistan'," Mofizuddin said, "it says there is anger in us, even if we don't express it. That's internal talk, not something you speak about openly." The second part of Mofizuddin's statement to me described the political use of silence.

Perhaps the most dramatic behavioral change by the Panipur Muslims was speaking openly through the act of rioting. Internal talk – careful choices about what is said to whom – both define community and indicate choices of political action. To talk internally is to select listeners; the criteria for selection speak eloquently of where people locate themselves in society. Internal talk defines inner and outer worlds, allies and enemies, peers and oppressors. To take that talk public is an act intended to make change in the world. The anthropologist James C. Scott writes of "hidden transcripts," those stories people exchange among themselves but not in public. Differences between private and public talk map power relations; secrecy and subterfuge are acts of resistance or rebellion done by people lacking more overt resources for pursuing their political objectives. Both the peasants of Panipur and the citizens of Little Rock told vivid stories of strategic choices about when to talk privately or publicly, and therefore about their definitions of those realms.

On a public level, the Muslim chairman of Panipur Union, Altaf-uddin, and informal village authorities called *matabbars* were making moves to reconcile the fight before it got out of hand. Golam was instructed by Altaf to convene a meeting: "I was asked to invite . . . people to a meeting to be held at Panipur High School. They were to sit in that meeting at the high school the next afternoon and settle the dispute." The *matabbars* appeared and talked in conciliatory ways. But privately:

> our *matabbars* decided that there would be no *nishputi* [compromise]. They often made compromises, but then again there would be a fight. So there was no need to compromise. They spoke this way after the meeting, not in Altaf's presence.

Terrified he'd be held responsible for the whole thing, Golam went back to Altaf to warn him of the *matabbars'* intentions:

> I went back . . . alone, to hear what he would say. I was very young, and I thought about it a lot, and worried about what would happen to me in the future. He told me there was no need for me to worry. It was necessary to teach them a lesson. Otherwise they would not stop. They would reap the paddy that grew on a *char* [sand-bar] and use it to feed their cows.

The chairman's double-dealing was confirmed by others. "Altaf was the leader here," said a Hindu who participated in the riot. "He led the first group of fighters to the field."

"Altaf told me," I replied, "that he tried to make peace."

"The chairman?" said my interviewee, surprised. "No, no. . . . I witnessed the whole thing. I saw Altaf carrying a gun."

Subterfuge and duplicity are both everyday acts of power management and crucial elements of rebellion. The Muslims were deciding to do something that broke with tradition. "I was very surprised," said Sunil, the Namasudra farmer who'd stayed in Pakistan because he saw his best advantage to lie in alliance with other peasants of whichever community. "How can it be? I thought. They damaged our crops, and when we protest there is this reaction. It was totally counter to the social rules." Publicly they said that which conformed to the social rules, while privately they determined to establish a new set of rules. It makes sense they would resort to duplicity to do so, assuming as they did that physical force was required to establish an order in which they could with impunity protest those grievances that had so long been the stuff of "inside talk."

There is a second reason why the Muslims of Panipur did not sit down to negotiate change verbally and cooperatively, and that is that they had not in the moment of action articulated their objectives. When speaking with me, they suggested the talk within the community back then was all about ceasing to tolerate that with which they had put up for so long. Only later, I suspected, did Mofizuddin formulate his reflections in terms of rules of state they had obeyed in the past and cows and plants as symbols. At the time, they were focused on another level of protest: against face-to-face wrongs done them by their Hindu peers. Imbedded in their assumption that the moment had come to protest openly and to refuse to compromise was another assumption: that the state was now "theirs," which is to say that a state in which Muslims, people "like" themselves, were in power would support, or at least condone, their changing the social rules at the village level. In other words, they did that which seemed possible in a context in which power had shifted, a different sort of power, not that wielded between neighbors, but the rules writ large to which Mofizuddin referred. In between these two levels of power there had been a third, caste Hindu landlords, and it, too, had also dramatically altered when the Hindus migrated to India. The landlords had been the visible personification of state power, not because they were themselves in control of the state (for they, too, were neither British nor Pakistani but Bengali), but because the villagers understood quite well that the state protected and buttressed those economic relations they lived every day.

Thus, protest took the form of confrontation with those who were most accessible, because the conditions of life had changed enough to make that a promising thing to do. Only later did some Muslims like Mofizuddin formulate the connections. In general, however, the Muslim villagers flowed into the new relations their riot had constructed without awareness of what had changed. Again and again, Muslims told me everything was fine between the communities now. They felt no animosity, wished their neighbors no ill, respected their rights, participated in their rituals, were content to coexist in the village.

But the Namasudras' story was quite different. Having lost power, they gave voice quite explicitly to the change that had resulted from the riot. After the riot, Sunil told me, the government officers "tried to make a reconciliation, tried to make us join hands."

"Was it a true reconciliation?" I asked.

"We were forced to reconcile," Sunil replied, putting his finger directly on the contradiction. "But in our hearts we have never reconciled. We still have the apprehension that it could happen again in future."

As I listened to this statement, I knew I was once again hearing "inside talk." Muslims who heard statements like Sunil's were universally surprised. They experienced relations between the communities as entirely harmonious. Their superior power was not visible to them, especially since many Namasudras like Sunil himself had prospered economically in the years since the riot. In their hearts, the Panipur Muslims felt no ill-will; how could it be, then, that their Hindu neighbors lived in fear?

6   Inside Talk in Little Rock

This phenomenon of power in its most subtle forms influencing perceptions of safety and therefore constructing power relations on the transactional level of talk is very familiar. People who experience themselves as vulnerable pay close attention to nuances in which their opportunities for advancement, chances for expression, ability to prevail in a conflict are reflected. A vivid representation of this phenomenon was given me by an elderly African-American minister in Little Rock. I visited him in his tidy home where he sat comfortably ensconced in a well-worn arm chair, surrounded by books and piles of magazines, spinning out story after story of his life and times. After awhile, I commented on the many forms of quiet protest I heard imbedded in his tales of segregation. While on the surface black people complied with the apartheid rules, in many, many little ways they subverted them. Rev. Young replied, "Oh, yeah. They do what you call complain down at the big gate."

"Down at the big gate?" I questioned.

"Now that's an expression that came out of a story," he went on.

One Negro said [to another], "I cussed that old boy [the white boss] out."

Says [the second man], "You did?"

"Yeah, cussed him out."

"What did he do?"

"He didn't do nothin', I cussed him out."

So [the second man] decided he's going to cuss him out, too. [But] that boy [the boss] beat him up. Went back, told his friend, "I thought you said that old boy didn't do anything. When I cussed him out, he beat me up."

"Where did you cuss him?"

"I cussed him to his face."

"I did better than that. I cussed him down at the big gate."

So always been protests down at the big gate, where they couldn't hear what you said. Down at the big gate, that kind of cussing going on, where you're grinnin' when you ain't tickled and scratchin' where you don't itch.

Rev. Young's description from the black point of view brilliantly reflects the sort of calculation of power and risk socially vulnerable people do all the time. If you know the "old boy" is going to beat you for speaking your mind, you don't stay silent; you speak up where you can't be heard. Rev. Young understood equally well the consequences of that choice:

[When the Supreme Court ordered desegregation] then all these white politicians, they'd get up and make statements, "We're getting along all right. If these outside agitators didn't come in here, well, everything all right." They thought the Negro wasn't protesting out loud, because they were protesting down at the big gate. They thought they were satisfied, happy with the way it was. They ain't never been satisfied or happy with the way they were treated.

But you ought to go and listen to them down at the big gate. When they get up there in front of you, they smile and scratch whether or not they itching. Grin when they not tickled. That what you call Uncle Tomming, that's a method of survival. Surviving in the situation. So they mistook that for their being satisfied, but they weren't satisfied.

Tolerating intolerable conditions is made easier by "inside talk" or complaining in safe quarters. At the same time, "inside talk" creates a sense of solidarity among fellow sufferers, defines groups capable of taking concerted action when at last conditions are right, and keeps alive a spirit of dignified resistance to oppression.

On the other hand, the sense of surprise of those in relative ascendancy when change hits is genuine, not only because they have failed to notice oppression from which they benefit, but also because they have been insulated from expressions of distress by the oppressed. Thought of from this perspective, it makes more sense that many of the white students at Central High would first seek to accommodate the presence of black students. Not perceiving how profound the victimization had been, they also failed to understand how deep school desegregation would cut. That insight was, paradoxically, first made apparent not by black activists but by white resisters rioting outside the schoolhouse. When people of their own racial identity rose up in an effort to prevent the change the students were willing to tolerate, the latter first disassociated themselves from the mob, making distinctions of identity based primarily on class. Describing the mob Dale, a white alumnus, said, "There was a bunch of rednecks out in front of the school." He then went on to define what he meant by the expression:

> A redneck was the farmer who, you know, followed behind the mule, watching the rows. And that's how it came about, because you got sunburned back there. I think it's kind of a connotation of, you mentioned the caste system yesterday? I think it's a connotation of probably experiences in life and people who were closer to rural America and didn't have the broadness of experience. . . . They were the guys that chewed tobacco and cut wood for a living out there, probably somewhere out on my grandfather's farm. That was my impression of the people out there, as being significantly from the vast unwashed and I wasn't.

When the name of a girl who'd been a segregationist leader inside the school came up in conversation with Helen and her friend Betsy, the latter said, "Now I didn't know her, [but] I remember she was *so* pretty and so cute. But they were what we considered white trash, really." Betsy and Dale spoke coded designations for lower class white people, and in the very process of naming them as they did disassociated themselves.

Whiteness in America is a contradictory phenomenon. So hegemonic is white dominance that whiteness does not seem a category at all, no less an identity. To be white is to be "normal"; to be anything else is to be "other." Yet allegiances based on a defense of white privilege abound, expressed by all but a very small minority of ideologically racist people in highly disguised forms – so disguised that they appear to the people talking not to be talk at all.

"If you don't talk about some things you're better off," Maddie told me. An old woman whose daughter had attended Central High in the year of crisis, Maddie was outrageous and outspoken.

"Why are you better off?" I pressed, naively.

She laughed uproariously. "You need to learn something, see."

"Teach me," I prompted.

"You need to learn something," she repeated, her lesson to me couched in her refusal to elaborate. "No, some things are just better not discussed."

Many people insisted they had not discussed the desegregation of Central High, a claim I had trouble taking at face value. As a standard part of my interviews with white Central High graduates from Little Rock, I asked what kinds of conversations were going on at home, with friends, and elsewhere. Many people replied there were none. I began to understand that statement was a misperception – and an interesting one – when Jane, the editorial writer who was sympathetic to desegregation, gave me a more elaborate answer:

> Well, I don't remember any white kid ever defending blacks in that sense, like, "They really should be here," or, "They have a right for education." Never, okay.
>
> What you did hear was – and I would say this was a majority of the middle class white kids – a feeling like, "Well, the most important thing we want to do is finish our high school, and this is something that eventually the South has got to deal with. And we really wish it were slower." There was a lot of that feeling like, "We're not ready yet." "Why should we be the first high school?" Discussion like that. Like, "What can we do to make sure we can continue having football games?" because that was so important, or dances on Friday nights.

What they were talking about, according to Jane, was defending normalcy rather than supporting or resisting social change, and therefore they did not believe they were talking about social change at all. But among the white Central High students who accommodated desegregation without truly accepting it, there were ways and means to enforce the very restricted boundaries of acceptance. While they talked around the issue of desegregation, the co-eds of Central High were indirectly exchanging opinions, values, and directions about how to behave, sometimes without speaking a word. "One of the things that happened at Central had to do with a *very* close friend of mine," Joyce told me. She was a year younger than Helen and Jane and the daughter of folks from Kansas, a state north of Arkansas. Joyce went on to tell me the story of her friend:

> She and I were just like sisters. We spent the night at each other's house. We walked to school together. We studied together. We went to church together. I would go home with them for chicken dinner after church on Sunday. She'd come home with me. I mean we were very, very, very close.
>
> I remember one time – have you had a chance to go by Central? Of course people have seen it in pictures and everything. Well, if you recall, the front of the school that faces on Park Street has stairs that go down, and there used to be a fishpond down there that was full of water and had goldfish in it, and so forth. And I remember one day, my friend (her name was Lydia) and another friend of ours, a mutual friend Joanna, the three of us were walking down those stairs and I was between Joanna and Lydia.

> And I don't even remember what brought the conversation to a start or anything, but I made the comment that I just, using the language of the day, I said, "Well, I don't see what's wrong with going to school with colored kids." And Lydia and Joanna both, and Lydia predominantly, got behind me and physically shoved me all the way down the stairs and right to the edge of the fishpond and I honest-to-god thought at that moment they were going to shove me into that fishpond. And they stopped right there.

Where friends agreed, little was said. When Joyce spoke a minority viewpoint, however mildly, her friends quashed the heresy without a word. Their message was contained in the spirit or emotional feeling of the transaction, conveying the intensity with which they disagreed with Joyce, a disagreement so profound it, too, went without saying.

"I don't remember whether the lesson came to me immediately," Joyce reflected as she told me the story:

> I think some kernel of it did, but it has grown over the years to the point that I realize that if you take a stand, if you believe in something that is not popularly accepted, if something like that is in your mind, then you either do one of two things: you either keep your mouth shut, or you be prepared to stand your ground. Because something's gonna happen. And that was a real shocking lesson to me, that even people you consider friends would take something like that so personally and focus so much anger on someone very close to them. That's the lesson I got from that.

What did you do?

> I think I kept my mouth shut for the rest of the school year with my friends.

Joyce did not keep her mouth shut forever; she became an activist and an outspoken social critic. But at the time she was effectively silenced, her unpopular beliefs becoming "internal talk," and in the process strengthening her resolve to speak out when she had attained more security for doing so.

Coercion to keep silent melds into colluding not to speak. Both serve to impede social change. Both convey messages that control the behaviors of those who would protest the social order. Both place individuals in social groups and craft collective behaviors that support or resist particular laws and orders.

"Inside talk" thus has a purpose. It teaches realities of power, who can expect what protection, who enjoys which rights. It also defines the local world in contrast to the outside.

Conclusion: Identifying Power, Negotiating Well-being

"These cows and plants are symbols," said Mofizuddin, and indeed they symbolized many things: normalcy and its redefinition in the context of changing social orders; community and its realignment with changing state power; identity and its uses in constructing effective collective action. Contained within the story of the cows and plants was a narrative about change. Bengali Muslims asserted their reformulated identity in recognition of a presumed alliance with other Muslims now holding state power. African-American activists seized upon post-war conditions to win a Supreme Court ruling against school segregation that nurtured a movement to dismantle Jim Crow laws and customs in the South, and de facto segregation in the North. In both cases, other groups of citizens took positions, for different reasons, that resisted the sought-after changes. In East Pakistan, the Namasudras handled their surprise at the loss of what they had perceived to be an alliance with fellow *krishaks* by organizing to defend themselves against physical predations. In Little Rock, the white students in the school either joined an organized campaign of harassment against the black students, or through acts of social coldness passively allied themselves with the active resistance.

In each drama, the state was a presence both symbolically, through evocations of law and order, and protestations of obedience, and materially, by the exercise of armed force to keep the nine black students out of the schoolhouse and by quelling the riot in Panipur by a rain of bullets. How the state intervened, however, was different in the two cases. In Panipur, it pretended to a neutrality it did not in fact have, because its identity with the Muslims, as perceived by both communities, turned literal neutrality, or a failure to punish Muslims more than Namasudras, into partisanship. In Little Rock, different levels of state authority battled each other, allying now with one civil force, now with another. But as in Panipur, groups of citizens read nuanced lessons about their identity and power in particular acts of officialdom.

In both Panipur and Little Rock, too, the dramas of change involved significant transformations of "inside talk" into public declarations. African-American activists used the courts to confront the "old boy" squarely inside the big gate. In doing so, they relied on more protection from the rule of law than, in the event, occurred. But once launched, they went on to "cuss the old boy out" vocally and effectively in very public forms. Where talk retreated to the big gate, however, was among the white students. In resistance to the changes afoot, they resorted to rules of propriety and studiedly did *not* talk about certain things, thereby seeking to reinforce a social order built on things not said. "Inside" talk for them thereby became a strategy for reconfirming a southern social order in which white people dominated.

For the Panipuri Namasudras, however, talk retreated decisively to outside the big gate, so much so that their Muslim neighbors had no idea thirty-five years later that all was not well between the two groups. For Sunil and his fellow Namasudras, their identity as Namasudras, an identity which in 1947 had become subordinate to their interests as *krishaks*, now became primary. Through acts of inside talk, that identity was called upon for mutual protection.

While those cows and plants symbolized all these dynamics and more, what they did not symbolize was collaborative social action. None of the citizens involved in Panipur or Little Rock were people of great means; all of them had need to struggle if they were to attain economic well-being. All of them had genuine conflicts of interest with people of higher class status. In the compelling dynamics of conflict with each other, however, all sense of that commonality, of a set of shared interests, was lost and remained lost in part because of the tacit agreement within each community to suppress open talk. The Muslims in Panipur established slight advantages for their group; the white people of Helen's class in Little Rock preserved racial privileges for theirs. But neither group secured true well-being. That project required a unity among communities that was retarded, not advanced, by the fight over cows and plants, by the passive resistance of white youths to embracing students of a different race.

14 Burundi: Ethnic Conflict and Genocide

René Lemarchand

A country of almost Lilliputian dimensions (27,834 square kilometers) and facing colossal difficulties at almost every level, Burundi is also a striking anomaly on a continent of artificially fashioned state systems. Because of its long pedigree as an archaic kingdom, few other polities on the continent seemed better equipped to cope with the crises of legitimacy that have beset African states. Its existence as a national entity preceded by centuries that of some European states. Although it is now a republic, its boundaries have remained virtually unchanged since the spurt of territorial expansion in the nineteenth century. Nor were its political institutions imported from abroad. As far back as can be remembered, the kingship served as the prime focus of popular loyalties. The legitimacy of the kingship as an institution was never seriously questioned. And yet, though spared the most crippling institutional disabilities faced by other African states, Burundi proved more vulnerable than most to the searing trauma of ethnic strife.

Here, then, is the central paradox of the Burundi situation. By what extraordinary combination of circumstances could centuries of relatively peaceful commingling between Hutu and Tutsi, cemented by their shared loyalty to a common set of institutions, suddenly dissolve into fratricide? References to "atavistic hatreds" and "ancestral enmities" are, of course, the stock-in-trade of journalists and scholars trying to make sense of an otherwise inexplicable state of affairs. For Irvin Staub, a distinguished academic (whose doctorate in psychology does not exonerate him from historical naïveté), in Burundi as in Biafra, both typifying the "genocides and mass killings that follow decolonization," "deep-seated historical conflicts can come to the fore in the context of profound social-political change." In both instances, he adds, "a history of conflict and antagonisms fuels a power struggle that ends in genocide" (Staub 1989, 86). From this perspective, there is little about the ethnic conflict in Burundi that makes it qualitatively different from what can be observed in other strife-torn areas of the continent. Tribalism, in short, is the age-old monster that suddenly rears its head from the mists of time to spread violence and bloodshed.

Scarcely more convincing is the notion of caste or class, occasionally offered as a corrective to "tribe." Although the reference groups are different, they too have a timeless quality embedded in the distant past. In a collective statement written by a distinguished roster of Africanists in the wake of the 1988 massacre, Burundi is described as historically "stratified into castes of different rank and privilege, the primarily pastoral Tutsi minority closely linked to the ruling group, and the agricultural majority Hutu under their domination" (*ASA Newsletter*, October–December 1988, 8). A reasonably accurate portrayal of precolonial

Rwanda, this statement is totally at odds with what we know of precolonial Burundi.

The same applies to class-based explanations. Attention here is drawn to the presence in precolonial Burundi of "unequal economic relations," with the Hutu cast in the role of an oppressed, landless peasantry from which "surplus labor" is exacted by the dominant, landowning class (Botte 1974). Although he puts a more nuanced construction on class phenomena, Roger Botte finds in Burundi's landless peasant stratum (*bashumba*) a striking example of social class formation in a precapitalist society. It is but a small step to the conclusion that the key to an understanding of contemporary strife lies in the projection of age-old class antagonisms in the context of a modernizing society.

That these explanations are little more than caricatures of a more complex reality emerges with reasonable clarity from a close examination of the historical record. The important point to note, however, is that they are treated as irrefutable verities by a fair number of Hutu intellectuals. How a mythical rendering of the past becomes incorporated into an ethnic ideology, the better to fortify the claims of the majority, is what we shall explore in the next chapter. Here, our main concern is to take a closer look at traditional patterns of stratification and, in so doing, take a more realistic measure of the distance that separates past from present.

Tribalism Reconsidered

When Hutu elites insist on being recognized as a political majority, they are usually branded as "tribalists" by their Tutsi opponents; for many Hutu, however, the label is exclusively reserved for the Tutsi because of their "Hamitic" origins and unswerving commitment to the supremacy of their kin. Adding to the confusion, some Western observers gravely conclude that both sides are victims of "tribal" enmities.

This is not the place for a lengthy refutation of the tribalist argument. That it is singularly unhelpful for a comprehension of African conflict situations has been demonstrated repeatedly. Suffice it to note that its explanatory merits are nowhere more questionable than in the case of Burundi. For one thing, the tribalist argument connotes a degree of cultural and physical distance among groups not found between Hutu and Tutsi. Besides perpetuating the myth of ancestral incompatibilities, the concept of tribe is patently inappropriate to describe communities that speak the same language (Kirundi), that share much the same type of social organization, and whose members lived peacefully side by side for centuries. Moreover, in its most common usage, the concept suggests cultural entities that are horizontally structured or merely juxtaposed to each other. Burundi, by contrast, can best be described as a vertical system of stratification, in which social aggregates stand in ranked relationship to each other. What the term *tribe* fails to capture are the complex hierarchies of power, status, and privilege that cut across ethnic identities and that once formed the axis around which revolved much of the country's social and political life. Finally, and most obviously, by reducing collective identities to the common denominator of an age-old, immutable commitment to the "idols of the tribe" (Isaacs 1975), the argument omits the most critical aspect of ethnicity – its contextual dimensions.

Students of ethnicity have long alerted us to the considerable analytic mileage to be gained from looking at collective identities as a "contextually shifting phenomenon" (Young 1976, 46). What the current debate on ethnicity fails to clarify is where, exactly, Burundi fits in the classic dichotomy between "primordialist" and "instrumentalist" interpretations. The first focuses on the essentialist character of cultural identities, on the symbols and enduring dispositions – what Pierre Bourdieu would call "habitus" (Bourdieu 1976) – that give such identities their distinctive texture; the second tends to emphasize the central role played by processes of political mobilization in shaping collective identities. From this vantage point, ethnicity emerges as a political resource deliberately manipulated by ethnic entrepreneurs for the specific purpose of facilitating their entry into the political arena.

Although the history of Burundi since independence shows ample evidence of "instrumentalism," this is not to argue that the primordialist dimension is nowhere to be found. Nor is there any reason to assume that one of these dimensions should exclude the other. This is the crux of the argument advanced by A. L. Epstein in his plea "to avoid...regarding 'affect' and 'circumstance' as variables to be handled separately, but to be treated in their complex interaction" (Epstein 1978, 112). It is at the level of the cultural construction of social identities that the interaction between "affect" and "circumstance" emerges in full force among Hutu ideologues. The cultural underpinnings of Hutudom are little more than the essentialist component of a strategy designed to maximize their ideological appeal.

What is involved here is an attempt to inflate, objectify, and ultimately distort the cultural "givens" of social identity. The aim, in short, is to reduce the inherent complexity of Burundi society to a set of greatly simplified and presumably irrefutable propositions about the roots and nature of social identities. What follows is an attempt to bring out the gray areas in the social landscape and, in so doing, draw attention to the selective sifting of the evidence that has presided over the birth of Hutu and Tutsi as "imagined communities" (Anderson 1991).

Hutu and Tutsi: Primordial Illusions

In terms of their respective numbers, physical characteristics, and occupational ties, Hutu and Tutsi are as different from each other as from any other group on the continent; this, in a nutshell, is the primordialist argument. In one form or another, this is the leitmotiv that runs through many of the official pronouncements of Hutu intellectuals, for whom these differences are treated as self-evident. But if we are to escape the confinement of the apparently obvious, we need to take a more critical look at the evidence and see how much of the primordialist view is grounded in reality.

That Hutu and Tutsi differ from each other in terms of numbers is hardly in doubt. In the absence of reliable census figures, however, observers inevitably tend to use population estimates dating back to the 1930s: today 85 percent of an estimated population of perhaps 6 million is said to be Hutu, 14 percent Tutsi, and 1 percent Twa. Though often treated as dogma, such statistics involve serious distortions. They not only leave out of the picture an undetermined number of people of princely origins, or *ganwa* (whose identity is distinct from that of both Hutu and Tutsi), as well as the Swahili-speaking and other immigrant communities, but also fail to take into account a substantial number of individuals of mixed origins. Nor is any attempt made to factor in the massive losses suffered by the Hutu as a result of the terrible bloodlettings of 1965, 1972, 1988, and 1991, followed by the exodus of tens of thousands of refugees into neighboring states. That perhaps as much as 20 percent of Burundi's population is Tutsi is not an unreasonable guess. But then who, exactly, are the Tutsi?

The more important point to note for the time being is that for many Hutu, the logic of numbers offers a devastating commentary on the methods used by the Tutsi minority to place the majority of the population into bondage. Only through deceit and ruse could the Tutsi assert their political hegemony over a vastly more numerous population. The Tutsi stratagems, as we shall see, are said to include offerings of cattle and gifts of "beautiful women," both designed to hoodwink the unsuspecting Hutu agriculturalists. The Tutsi's occupational status as pastoralists and the proverbial beauty of their women (tall and thin) were supposedly key ingredients in the historical process of feudal domination of Tutsi over Hutu. Only by taking into account the objective characteristics of physical traits and occupational ties can one comprehend the social dimension of Tutsi hegemony.

On both counts, proponents of the primordialist argument are on shaky ground, however, and particularly so when trying to discriminate between Hutu and Tutsi on the basis of physical traits. To note, as does Jean-Pierre Chrétien, that the average size of the Tutsi is 1.75 meters and that of the Hutu 1.66 meters is not particularly illuminating (Chrétien 1967, 13). Physical characteristics, after all, are notoriously unreliable to distinguish Hutu from Tutsi. Given the extraordinary amount of nonsense that has been written about the "short and stocky Hutu" and the "tall, lash-thin and graceful" Tutsi (Perlez 1988, 92), the point deserves the strongest emphasis. That physical characteristics may sometimes send the wrong ethnic message is nowhere more aptly illustrated than in the story told by the late President Michel Micombero (a Tutsi-Hima) to a group of foreign journalists, shortly after the 1972 bloodbath. Micombero stated: "When I returned from Belgium in 1964 I was the first Murundi to claim the rank of officer in the army. Some thought that I was a Hutu because of my physique, and thus tried to get me involved in a plot against the Tutsi. After I refused, saying that I did not want to kill innocent people, someone went to have a look at my father and saw that he had a Tutsi nose. From then on no one asked me any question" (*Livre blanc* 1972, 59). That Micombero may have made up the story to discredit the Hutu is immaterial; the important point is that the element of ethnic ambiguity conveyed by his story is entirely plausible.

The issue of "false" ethnic identity surfaced early in the months preceding independence, when the time came for the trusteeship authorities to Africanize civil service positions on the basis of ethnic parity. Thus in a statement released on September 16, 1960, the presidents of several newly founded, and mostly ephemeral, Hutu parties sharply criticized the newly appointed resident commissioner (*commissaire du pays*), Paul Baganzicaha, for officially identifying himself as a Hutu, "even though we know for sure that you are not Hutu but Tutsi."

Precisely because physical appearance is not an infallible guide to identity, ethnicity offers social actors opportunities for manipulation; as Micombero's story makes plain, the assumption that somatic traits are a reliable index of identity is likely to engender serious misperceptions, some of which may carry considerable political significance. Although we will probably never know how many Tutsi were "mistakenly" eliminated by other Tutsi, and Hutu by Hutu, in the 1972 crisis, the fact that survival – or death – may ultimately depend on one's "body map" is one of the more bizarre lessons to be drawn from Burundi's recent history.

Nor are ethnic identities immutable. Passage from one group to another (that is, from the status of Hutu to that of Tutsi, the opposite being virtually unheard of) was not uncommon. The phenomenon – known as *kihutura* in Kirundi – allowed for some degree of upward mobility in an environment in which social status and ethnic identity were closely aligned but by no means rigidly coterminous. Downward mobility, on the other hand, threatened all *ganwa* at one time or another. They lost their princely status and became Tutsi whenever a king bearing their dynastic name ascended to the throne – a phenomenon know as *gutahira*, loosely translated as "social demotion."

More subtle were the distinctions in mixed marriages. How much status a Hutu could claim for himself from marrying a Tutsi woman depended in part on his wife's lineage (*imiryango*). It is interesting to note that three of the most influential Hutu leaders of the 1960s (Paul Mirerekano, Pascal Bubiriza, and Joseph Bamina) were married to Tutsi women. Though far less frequent today than in the past, the number of Barundi claiming a Hutu father and a Tutsi mother is quite striking. And although in theory the child is expected to assume the identity of its father, the offspring of such mixed unions can reposition themselves with relative ease.

It is one thing to stress the fluctuating character of social identities, but it is quite another to argue, as some Tutsi do, that ethnic differences simply do not exist, except in the form of imported "tribal ideologies." Until recently, even when confronted with the most dramatic evidence of ethnic conflict, Burundi authorities consistently shoved the existence of separate ethnic identities under the rug. Thus, in August 1988, when asked by a journalist what proportion of Hutu and Tutsi had been killed, President Buyoya laconically brushed aside the question. "We are all Barundi," he replied. The assumption, presumably, is that by eliminating all public references to ethnic identities, ethnic discrimination will no longer matter as a policy issue or a source of intergroup conflict. Proceeding from the axiom that ethnic labels and stereotypes belong to the dustbin of colonial historiography, the official view has been that ethnic references are, at best, a figment of the colonial imagination and, at worst, part of a neoimperialist plot aimed at pitting one group of citizens against another.

Where the primordialist argument does take on a measure of cogency, however, is with regard to occupational differences between Hutu and Tutsi, between pastoralists and agriculturalists. Yet even here the dichotomy is not quite as rigid as some might think. After all, the Tutsi did not have a monopoly on cattle herding. Even though most cows were indeed the property of Tutsi elements, it was by entrusting their cattle to the Hutu that the Tutsi were able to establish clientage ties with Hutu elements, thus bringing Hutu and Tutsi together into a complex web of reciprocal rights and obligations. Far from driving a wedge between Hutu and Tutsi, their different occupational statuses provided the basis for a closer union.

But if the assumption of objective cultural differences between Hutu and Tutsi is largely illusory, how far did social inequality enter into the definition of ethnic "selves"?

Social Rank and Ethnicity

That someone might assume a double identity and be identified as both Hutu and Tutsi is one of the more puzzling aspects of traditional Burundi society. The key to the puzzle lies in the different semantic fields associated with the term *Hutu*. In Kirundi, the term has two separate meanings: one refers to its cultural or ethnic underpinnings, the other to its social connotations. In the latter sense, Hutu refers to a "social subordinate" in relation to somebody higher up in the pecking order. The definition given by Father F. Rodegem – *fils social*, or "social son" – is perhaps even more accurate, since it denotes not just social inferiority but a measure of affectivity (Rodegem, personal communication, 1991). Thus a Tutsi cast in the role of client *vis-à-vis* a wealthier patron would be referred to as "Hutu," even though his cultural identity remained Tutsi. Similarly, a prince was a Hutu in relation to the king, and a high-ranking Tutsi was a Hutu in relation to a prince.

Status, not ethnic identity, was the principal determinant of rank and privilege. Not only were there significant discrepancies between social ranking and ethnic identity, but many variations could also be detected within the broad range of dependency relations subsumed under the term *Hutu*. If we are to believe the testimony of a leading Hutu intellectual, the social dimension of the term never disappeared from the rural landscape. "Even during the Bagaza regime [1976–87], when references to Hutu and Tutsi were strictly forbidden, people in the country-side continued to use them on a daily basis to refer to social contracts among individuals" (Sindayigaya 1991, 94).

If so, our earlier characterization of Burundi society as a vertically ordered social system needs to be clarified. The basic distinction here is between vertical systems of stratification, where ethnic differences tend to coincide with the status differences, and horizontal systems, where the juxtaposition of discrete ethnic entities produces "unconnected coexistences," to use Max Weber's terminology, and where "each ethnic community is allowed to consider its own honor as the highest one" (quoted in Gerth and Mills 1958, 189). That traditional Burundi showed a close resemblance to the first of these categories is beyond dispute. Nonetheless, ethnic identities did not always coincide with status differences. There was, to be sure, a large measure of coincidence at the top and bottom of the social pyramid. Thus the ruling princely oligarchy (*ganwa*), forming a separate ethnic entity different from both Hutu and Tutsi, stood at the very top of the sociopolitical hierarchy; they were the supreme holders of power and privilege. Conversely, the Pygmoid Twa were clearly at the bottom of the heap. Among Hutu and Tutsi, the pecking order was immensely more complicated. The logic of numbers meant that there was, on the whole, greater socioeconomic inequality between Hutu and Tutsi than within either community. It is equally true, however, that depending on luck and individual ability, some Hutu elements could end up with considerably more influence, wealth, and social recognition than the average Tutsi. To view all Hutu as hewers of wood and drawers of water is clearly untenable.

The foregoing argues for extreme caution in the definition of Hutu and Tutsi, yet the picture is made more complex still by the different social rankings within each group. A classic and much misunderstood example is the distinction between the Tutsi-Banyaruguru and Tutsi-Hima elements (hereafter referred to as Banyaruguru and Hima) within the Tutsi community. Contrary to widespread opinion, the two groups are not distinguished by geographical distribution. Status is the critical differentiating factor here. Compared with the Hima, whose traditional social image evoked disdain if not outright contempt, the Banyaruguru (literally "the people from above") enjoyed considerably higher social status, a fact traceable to their historical connections to the monarchy. That the most violently antimonarchical elements among the Tutsi in the early 1960s happened to be of Hima origins is perhaps not entirely coincidental.

Important status differences also characterize the various clans or patrilineages (*imiryango*) within both Hutu and Tutsi. The usual distinctions made by the Barundi are between the very good families (*imiryango myiza*), and those that are rather good (*imiryango myiza cane*), those neither good nor bad (*imiryango mibi*). Kinship affiliations thus entailed a spectrum of social rankings that had little or nothing to do with one's membership in a particular ethnic group. For example, as a member of the prestigious Muhanza clan, the late Paul Mirerekano, a Hutu, could claim far more "honor" for himself than many Tutsi of more humble social background. And Pierre Mpozenzi, another leading Hutu figure, was a member of the Bajiji clan, among whom court dignitaries were normally recruited; thus it was entirely consonant with traditional norms for Mpozenzi to be appointed master of ceremonies at the royal court in 1963.

Patron–client ties, once the linchpin of Burundi society, added yet another element of flexibility to the social pyramid. In the repertoire of traditional social roles, few assumed greater significance than those of patron (*shebuja*) and client (*mugererwa*); none have been more consistently misunderstood. Formalized through the institution of *bugabire*, the patron–client relationship stands as a metaphor for the ambiguities inherent in the traditional social order. A multiplicity of meanings enters into the patron–client nexus: differentiation and cohesion, protection and oppression, deference and resentment. Whether a particular connotation takes precedence over another is an empirical question. To argue, with some Hutu intellectuals, that the patron–client relationship served the Tutsi as a social mechanism for placing the Hutu masses into bondage is arrant nonsense; yet it would be just as naive and uncritical to assume that patron–client interactions were invariably marked by undiluted social harmony.

As in other forms of clientage, at the heart of the institution was a relationship of exchange between individuals of unequal status, between a client in need of protection and a patron with enough wealth (usually in the form of cows and land) and influence to provide such protection. Clients would reciprocate through services and offerings in kind, but not the least of the benefits accruing to the patrons and clients alike was the sense of mutual loyalty and affection that normally accompanied the relationship. R. Bourgeois's intriguing rubric for his discussion of the *bugabire* – "devoirs moraux et courtisanerie contractuelle" – captures the normative and contractual dimensions of the relationship (Bourgeois 1954, 284). In a fundamental sense, clientage relations served as the normative frame of reference for the institutionalization of political ties; that ethnic identities did not necessarily correlate with the status of client and patron added immeasurably to the legitimacy of the institution.

The stability of the relationship owed much to the maintenance of a fair pattern of exchange between patrons and clients. "It was in the interest of the patron not to be too demanding or else he might risk losing his clients, who are always free to leave him" (ibid., 230). Of course, fairness of exchange did not always resist the strains of resource scarcities, warfare, or individual exploitation. And the social cohesion that once inhered in patron–client ties could hardly persist in a context of growing ethnic conflict. Once recast in the social fields of ethnically homogeneous nets, as happened after independence, patron–client ties served only to accelerate the process of ethnic polarization.

The language of clientelism gives us important clues to an understanding of the cultural frame of the patron–client nexus and by the same token brings into focus the normative aspects of power relationships. The semantic root of *ubugabire* is the verb *kugaba*, meaning both "to rule" and "to give." The all-important term *ubugabo* – meaning, depending on the semantic field, man, husband, umpire, authority, virility, or force – is likewise derived from the root term *kugaba*. In the popular consciousness of most Barundi, the exercise of power is virtually synonymous with gift giving. This is true not only of the patron, of the chief, of the king, but also of God, sometimes referred to as *Rugaba*, "He Who Gives," the supreme benefactor on whom depends the well-being of the nation. Just as power holders are expected to display generosity, the status of dependents is conceptually linked to the verb *ukusaba*, variously translated as "to solicit," "to implore," or "to submit oneself." There is no implication here of dependence being forced on the weak by the strong, but there is a sense of the former actively seeking the latter's protection.

The dynamics of the relationship are inscribed in terms like *ingabire* (the flow of resources from patron to client), *ingorore* (the goods and services offered by the client), *ukunyaga* (the withdrawal of a gift by a superior), and *ukukura ubwatsi* (the expression of gratitude for receiving gifts from a superior). All of these suggest opportunities for bargaining, for give-and-take, and sometimes for simply taking back. Inequality, in short, was the precondition of social exchange and the prime motive for seeking the protection of a superior, yet the basis of the relationship between patron and client, ruler and subject, was both utilitarian and sentimental, jural and moral. Countless proverbs bring out the positive affects (and effects) built into dependency relations: *Amasabo arakize* ("Dependence makes one wealthy"); *Udasavye ntakira* ("He who does not have a protector will never get rich"); *Amasaka aba ku masabo* ("Sorghum grows in the shade of subjection").

This is not to suggest that the use of force never entered the patron–client nexus. As has been pointed out, coercion was by no means infrequent at the highest echelons of the social pyramid. "At the level of the political authorities," writes Albert Trouwborst, "the system of exchange takes on special characteristics. ... One of the partners, the senior one, can specify the terms of exchange. ... Here one cannot freely choose one's partner; at this level constraints are real, and sometimes even physical" (Trouwborst 1961, 13). Very different, however, was the situation prevailing at the societal level, where the terms of exchange between patron and client were infinitely more flexible and always negotiable.

The picture that emerges, then, is that of a highly complex society, in which ethnic affiliations were by no means the most reliable indicator of social ranking. Kinship and clan ties played a critical role in shaping the contours of the pecking order, and the opportunities for improving one's chances in life (and changing one's ethnic identity) through clientage ties added yet another crucial variable to an already complicated social pyramid.

The Restructuring of Identities

Writing in 1931, from the perspective of seventeen years of intimate contacts with Burundi society, missionary Bernard Zuure of the White Fathers reached the conclusion that it would be pointless to try to look for basic differences of attitude and behavior between Hutu and Tutsi. These, he said, "have become so minimal that one can speak of a common culture" (Zuure 1931, 14).

Sixty years later, Zuure's statement strikes us as strangely anachronistic. The discovery of separate ethnic identities, under the twin stimuli of rapid social change and growing political competition, has altered the social landscape of the country in ways that Zuure could not possibly have imagined. What Zuure could not have anticipated was the rise of an ethnic consciousness nurtured and stimulated by new ideological commitments. The phenomenon is excellently described by Alphonse Rugambarara: "The use of the terms Hutu and Tutsi reflects a deliberate effort to create and maintain a Tutsi ideology and a Hutu ideology.... These two ideologies, born in the womb of the political class shortly before independence, have created and maintained this so-called ethnic consciousness, which may not have come into being had the experience of politics been lived and defined differently.... Behind the problem of definition (of ethnic categories) lies a problem of perception" (Rugambarara 1990, 37).

From a society characterized by complex sociopolitical hierarchies, Burundi has now become greatly simplified, consisting of separate and mutually antagonistic ethnic aggregates. In a time of crisis, Hutu and Tutsi emerge as the only relevant defining characteristics of group identities, reducing all other social roles to phenomena of marginal social significance. A whole range of social identities – associated with clan and family ties, patron–client nets, princely affiliations, and court connections – seems suddenly to recede from the social horizon, leaving only Hutu and Tutsi in sight. Admittedly, clan and lineage affiliations tend to surface periodically in the interstices of the ethnic struggle; the pulsations of ethnic consciousness impose a certain rhythm on the salience of subsidiary solidarities. Collective identities thus tend to shift back and forth from one level to another, from clan and lineage affiliations to ethnic identities. Once all is said and done, however, there can be little question that ethnic self-awareness has now asserted itself as the central element in the social landscape.

In the crucible of the Hutu-Tutsi conflict, other ethnic categories have simply disappeared. Always marginal, in terms of both numbers and status, the Pygmoid Twa are by now excluded from the realm of public discourse, perhaps not too surprisingly. More intriguing is the case of the princely elites, or *ganwa*, who not only were the real power holders in the traditional society but also were generally perceived as a distinct ethnic category, not identified with either Hutu or Tutsi. By 1972 they had become virtually assimilated into the Tutsi frame of reference.

The hardening of the Hutu-Tutsi dichotomy presumably rules out alternative forms of social identity, including those born of the reciprocities that once formed the core of clientage relations and ran through the entire social pyramid, holding it together in a seamless web of mutual rights and obligations. It rules out the presence of local notables (*bashingantahe*), mostly of Hutu origins, whose wisdom and sense of equity were recognized by Hutu and Tutsi alike. It rules out the hierarchy of chiefly roles, some of which, below the princely establishment, were occupied by both Hutu and Tutsi. And it rules out the appointment of Hutu dignitaries at the court – those in charge of administering the royal domains, of milking the king's cows, and of presiding over the annual harvest celebrations (*umuganuro*). In short, numerous social and political roles that once gave meaning and cohesion to membership in a "national" community have vanished.

Perhaps the best way to conceptualize the nature of this all-encompassing metamorphosis is to return for a moment to our earlier definition of the term *Hutu*, referring to both ethnic and social identities. Unlike in the traditional society, where one type of identity did not necessarily coincide with the other, in today's society the two meanings of the term have become almost interchangeable. With few exceptions, in the urban sectors most Hutu are in a position of social and economic inferiority *vis-à-vis* Tutsi elements. Furthermore, the Tutsi – more specifically the Hima – are the preeminent power holders. And because of their privileged access to the social and economic benefits of power, their collective self-awareness as Tutsi is inextricably bound up with their politically, socially, and economically dominant position. This is not to say that all Tutsi are rich and powerful, but compared with those Hutu elements who can legitimately claim such attributes, the Tutsi are clearly the overwhelming majority in absolute and relative terms.

Inequality has always been pervasive in Burundi society. That there is no equivalent in Kirundi for *equality* – or for *liberty* – speaks volumes for the nature of traditional Burundi underpinnings. And yet, strange as it may seem, a convincing argument can be made for the view that inequality among individuals was a major source of social cohesion. Protection of the poor and the weak by the rich and the powerful was part of the normative frame of clientage ties. Social inequalities tended to generate their own mechanisms of social cohesion. Today, however, inequality has taken on a radically different connotation, not only because the Hutu masses see it as morally objectionable but also because social actors view it primarily through an ethnic lens. Social inequality is thus increasingly correlated to ethnic identity. This is an unprecedented phenomenon in the history of the country.

Ironically, by projecting the present into the past, Hutu politicians end up with a vision of history totally at odds with every shred of evidence available; and by doing precisely the opposite and refusing to acknowledge a Hutu-Tutsi problem, Tutsi politicians have consistently turned a blind eye to the radical transformations that followed in the wake of their own discriminatory policies. As we now realize, the Burundi society that came into existence in the middle of the nineteenth century in the heart of Central Africa – inegalitarian yet cohesive, hierarchical yet not so rigidly stratified as to rule out social mobility, deeply divided at the top yet unified behind the symbols of kingship – was totally unlike that which emerged from the ashes of the colonial state. Nothing is more revealing of the gap that separates one from the other than the manner in which history is now "deconstructed" and incorporated into rival ethnic ideologies.

References

Anderson, Benedict. 1991. *Imagined Communities*. Rev. ed. London: Verso.

Botte, Roger. 1974. "Processus de formation d'une classe sociale dans une société africaine précapitaliste." *Cahiers d'Etudes Africaines* 14, no. 4: 605–26.

Bourdieu, Pierre. 1976. *Outline of a Theory of Practice*. Cambridge: Cambridge University Press.

Bourgeois, R. 1954. *Banyarwanda et Barundi: La coutume*, vol. 2. Brussels: Institut Royal Colonial Belge.

Chrétien, Jean-Pierre. 1967. "Le Burundi." *Notes et Etudes Documentaires* (17 Février). Paris: La Documentation Française.

Epstein, A. L. 1978. *Ethos and Identity*. London: Tavistock.

Gerth, H. H., and Mills, C. Wright, trans. and eds. 1958. *From Max Weber: Essays in Sociology*. New York: Oxford University Press.

Isaacs, Harold. 1975. *The Idols of the Tribe*. Cambridge, Mass.: Harvard University Press.

Kiraranganiya, Boniface. 1985. *La vérité sur le Burundi*. Sherbrooke, Canada: Editions Naaman.

Lemarchand, René. 1970. *Rwanda and Burundi*. London: Pall Mall.

Livre blanc sur les évènements survenus aux mois d'avril et mai 1972. 1972. Bujumbura: Ministère de l'Information.

Perlez, Jane. 1988. "The Bloody Hills of Burundi." *New York Times Magazine*, November 6.

Rugambarara, Alphonse. 1990. "Conscience ethnique." *Le Réveil*, July–August, 35–40.

Sindayigaya, J. M. 1991. *Sortir de la violence*. Bujumbura: Presses Lavigerie.

Staub, Irvin. 1989. *The Roots of Evil: The Origins of Genocide and Other Group Violence*. Cambridge: Cambridge University Press.

Trouwborst, Albert. 1961. "L'organisation politique en tant que système d'échange au Burundi." *Anthropologica* 3, no. 1: 1–17.

Young, Crawford. 1976. *The Politics of Cultural Pluralism*. Madison: University of Wisconsin Press.

Zuure, Bernard. 1931. *L'ame du Murundi*. Paris: Beauchesne.

15 The Creation and Dissolution of the Multinational State: The Case of Yugoslavia

Dusko Sekulic

Geostrategy and Legitimacy

Why was Yugoslavia created and why did it disappear from the map of the world? Under the impact of its forceful and bloody dissolution many are inclined to assert that it was an artificial creation from the beginning. But what does an artificial creation mean? Clearly the concept of artificiality required qualification, unless we accept the proposition that every multinational state is an artificial creation.

If we try to operationalise the concept then its meaning would stem from the fact that Yugoslavia was created at Versailles by the victorious powers, against the will of the people, most internal political actors and the historical viability of the region. We would be able to claim this only if the forces in favour of the creation of a Yugoslav state did not exist. But they did exist, so we cannot argue that Yugoslavia was imposed against the will of all the people, unless we propose (as, for example, many nationalists or Marxist philosophers claim) that we know some iron law of history and that the formation of a Yugoslav state was violating some such basic law (e.g., the impossibility of the long-term survival of multinational states, or the reversal of the trends of history in the direction of socialism etc.).

Denying the artificiality does not mean that I am advocating some *a priori* historical viability of this state, or an historical necessity of south Slav people to form such a state. In my opinion this approach is fruitless and instead of engaging in such discussions I think that a much better procedure is to analyse the social forces, strategies and goals of different actors, as well as the geopolitical factors leading to the creation, and later dissolution, of Yugoslavia. Historical options are always open and only an analysis of these complex forces can give us an answer to any particular outcome.

The concrete social reality of a particular event, in this case the creation and dissolution of a state, is a complex phenomenon, which is very difficult to explain with a single theory. It is a reality where a multitude of social processes, actors and events are going on in parallel. Usually theoretical approaches have a tendency to grasp one of these processes, but not the totality of them. We can say that these approaches are possible explanations of different levels of reality, which are not mutually exclusive but interactive. Geostrategical explanations are important, but different from cultural explanations, although geostrategical and cultural processes are often linked. Where one or the other approach has the tendency to diminish the significance of the processes on the other level, this is not dealt with from the perspective of a single approach.

We will start to explore the creation and dissolution of Yugoslavia from the geostrategical perspective. The framework used will be Collins' elaboration of Weber's theory of politics (Collins 1986). The main theme is that the internal legitimacy of the regime is the result of the geostrategical success of the state. Of course, geostrategy is not only important as an independent variable producing legitimacy but is also an explanatory scheme for interpreting the strategies used by different actors involved in geostrategical games. In the following analysis I will try to explore this theme using the example of Yugoslavia.

The Creation of Yugoslavia

Legitimacy

The central thesis in Collins' (1986) interpretation of Weberian political sociology is legitimacy. What is new is the emphasis on the importance of the external success of the state for its internal legitimacy.

> The thrust of Weber's thought is...that politics works from the outside in, and that external, military relations of states are crucial, determinants of their internal politics ...How is legitimacy gained and lost, and who will get it under what conditions? Weber is suggesting that it is tied to the power position of the state in the international arena. (p. 145)

The legitimacy of the Yugoslav state, and the differing prestige of the leading elites of various South Slav national groups, can be explained exactly in these terms. South Slavs were ruled by the two empires which went into decay at different periods in time. The fact that the Ottoman empire entered the period of its decline first, contributed to the earlier emancipation of the Slavs under its control. The Serbs, being the strongest group, regained in this way the role of the 'Piedmont' of the South Slavs (MacKenzie 1994). Croat and Slovenian political leaders could only envy the expansionism and gradual success of the struggle for independence of the newly created Serbian political elite. Starting with the revolt of 1804 the process of gaining autonomy within the Ottoman empire began, and from 1830s on it evolved into gradual expansion of the Serbian state. From that time on, with many set-backs, the Serbian political leadership gradually created and then expanded its autonomous state, first under the formal Turkish protectorate and later as an independent political entity. The Croat and Slovenian political leaderships, being part of the still strong Austrian (and later Austro-Hungarian) empire were not in a position to realistically aspire for independence.

During its successful expansion, Serbia gained control over Macedonia, Kosovo and Sandzak as a result of the uprisings against the Turks and the two subsequent Balkan wars. Serbia was also on the victorious side at the end of the First World War. At this time, the programme of the Serbian interior minister, Ilija Garasanin, called 'Nacertanije', which designed expansionist long-term goals for Serbian policy as outlined in the Memorandum of 1844, could finally be realised (Mac-Kenzie 1985).

From the standpoint of legitimacy the most important element in this whole development was that the status of Serbia among other South Slav elites was tremendously enhanced. For a moment we can return to Collins:

> the prime example of modern 'national autonomy' movements are those that disman-tled the Austro-Hungarian and Ottoman empires in the Balkans. Yet these were pre-cisely the states that were crumbling under the external geopolitical pressures; 'ethnic' nationalism is merely the form in which the fragmentary states surviving the breakup were organised. The ethnic purity of many of these states has been a myth; Yugoslavia, for example, incorporated several ethnic groups, as a kind of miniature Austria–Hun-garian empire in itself. And at the same time that Austria–Hungary was breaking up, the Russian empire was incorporating even more disparate ethnic groups in central Asia and the Caucasus, having overridden the ethnic division of the Ukraine, White Russia, and the Baltic. In this case, 'ethnic nationalism' was cast in a different form, one appropriate for a consolidating empire – pan-Slavism and its extensions, which at-tempted to claim a greater ethnic unity appropriate to an expanding state. (Collins 1986: 153)

The essence of Collins' argument is a denial of the perception that states are simply created along ethnic lines. Depending on the geostrategical advancement, at the same time that some multinational empires were disintegrating, others (for example, the Russian empire), were expanding. The creation of Yugoslavia follows a very similar logic to the creation of the Russian empire. On the one hand, it was the result of the disintegration of the greater multinational Austro-Hungarian empire, but, on the other hand, it was a culmination of the expansion of the smaller, Serbian empire. Yugoslavia was *de facto* created as the result of a Serbian mini-expansion as a stage in the process which began in the nineteenth century. As Russia was expanding, regardless of its ethnic boundaries, even some potentially new ethnic groups were merging (Ukrainians and White Russians, for example). The same logic was guiding Serbian expansionism. Although in comparison with Russia, it should be noted that by 1900 perhaps only half of the ethnically Serbian population lived within the boundaries of a Serbian state. The other half lived within the Ottoman and Habsburg monarchies. Because of that fact the expansion of the Serbian state was justified by the incorporation of the ethnic Serbs into it. But parallel with this incorporation process a peculiar expansionism was going on. The essence of this expansionism was the denial of ethnic separateness to some groups clearly developing separate identities. The cases in point are Macedonians, Bosnian Muslims and even Montenegrins. The non-existence of clear ethnic boundaries among many Slavic and even non-Slavic groups in the Ottoman and Habsburg empires was used as a pretext for territorial expansion. If everywhere around the Serbian state Serbs are living under foreign rule, then it is a 'natural' right of the Serbian state to incorporate these territories. The roots of this type of expansion can be found in the famous Vuk Karadzic pamphlet (1849) claiming that all stokavian speaking people are *de facto* Serbs. This type of analysis was used later to justify the expansionist policy of the Serbian state. We can conclude that the expansion of the Serbian state was on the one hand based on the incorporation of the ethnic Serbs into the Serbian state. When that basis for expansion was shaky the ethnic groups inhabiting the targeted territories were simply proclaimed to be Serbs unaware of their true identity.

In that process the role of the ideology of Yugoslavism was a very complex one. The fact that Yugoslavism was advocated even more by the non-Serbian political elites indicates the importance of the geostrategical explanation. On the one hand, the idea was stronger in the 'Slavic periphery' (Slovenia, Istria, Dalmatia) constantly under pressure of Germanisation, Hungarisation and Talianisation. Support of the Slavic hinterland, unification of fragmented Slavic cultural and political 'space' was the only hope for resisting the pressures of expanding 'western' empires. On the other hand, the Serbian political elites, especially after 1830s, were much weaker supporters of the Yugoslav idea seeing it as 'calculated to stop the expansion of the Serbian national consciousness to its rightful limits' (Banac 1984: 79). The legitimacy that Serbia had achieved as the result of its long-term geostrategical success helped to enhance Serbian prestige. Stronger ties between Serbs and Croats in 1848 were significant signal of this. Under Prince Mihajlo Obrenovic, Serbia become a magnet for Serbs, Bulgars and even some Croats. One of the originators of the Yugoslav idea, Bishop Josip Juraj Strossmajer of Croatia was attracted by the Mihajlo's policies and successes of Serbia (MacKenzie 1994: 162). Yugoslavism was the form in which these political elites were able to participate in the successes of the Serbian elites (Korunic 1989). In the same way, the merging of ethnonational identities was also going on with attempts to replace the particular identities with the Yugoslav one (Marijanovic 1913).

We can conclude that the legitimisation of the creation of Yugoslavia was the result of the Serbian geostrategical advances starting at the beginning of the nineteenth century. We can also regard Yugoslavism as Pan-Slavism in miniature. As Pan-Slavism was a reflection of the Russian geostrategical advances, so the strengthening of the Yugoslav idea can also be seen as a reflection of Serbian geostrategical successes. The geostrategical weakening of Austria–Hungary undermined the political forces loyal to it and gave strength to 'pro-Yugoslav' sentiments. On the other side, the earlier weakening of the Ottoman empire allowed for the earlier Serbian autonomy and then expansion without the need of the backing of the Yugoslav idea.

Geopolitical context

The creation and dissolution of Yugoslavia came about as a consequence of major geopolitical changes. The creation of the first Yugoslav state was the result of the First World War, the dissolution of the Austro-Hungarian empire and the 'New World Order' established at that time. I am not denying the obvious fact that the creation of the Yugoslav state was a consequence of the peace process after the First World War, and that the major power players of that time had their own interests in creating and shaping the Yugoslav state.

One important goal was the creation of viable states preventing the German *Drang nach Osten*. (Although here it must be noted that many were claiming that the preservation of the Austro-Hungarian empire in some democratised form would serve the purpose much better.) For this reason Yugoslavia appeared to be a much more viable solution than the eventual small patchwork of states created out of the wreckage of the Austro-Hungarian empire. A special role was the impression created in France and Great Britain by the heroic actions of the Serbian army. The creation of Yugoslavia was at that moment regarded as a simple extension of the base of this Serbian army for its eventual role in some future conflict. An echo of these views can be heard even today by some Western leaders' statements about the 'Serbs as traditional allies', a statement of very dubious validity taking into account developments during and after the Second World War.

But the role of these strategic interests are in my opinion of secondary importance. The role of the political forces inside Yugoslavia, favouring the creation of such a state, were of much greater significance.

Italian and Austrian aspirations for Yugoslav territory were another important factor influencing the developments towards Yugoslav unity (Tepsic 1970). Yugoslavia, or rather the political elites of the different national groups, were in different positions regarding the neighbours' territorial aspirations. Croatian and Slovenian elites, with no armies, being part of the defeated empires and under the pressure of internal revolutionary turmoil, were in no position to resist Italy and even Austria, without Serbian military backing. On the other hand, Serbia was in a much better position to solve satisfactorily its disputes and problems with Bulgaria, Romania and Albania.

The defeated states in the First World War waited for their 'revenge' until the Second World War, and their revanchist appetites put them on the side of the Axis powers. Yugoslavia was then dismembered to satisfy these aspirations. That came more than twenty years later. At the moment of the creation of the Yugoslav state the outside threat of Italy and Austria was a crucial one. The fact that this threat was mainly oriented towards Slovenia and Croatia, the parts of the former Austro-Hungarian empire in internal disarray, with no army and a very unstable international position, significantly influenced the internal bargaining relations of the Croatian and Slovenian political elites (Jankovic 1983).

Internal strategies

The internal strategies could be divided according to the main calculations about the future of this part of the world. There was almost a consensus among the political elites in the Slavic parts of the Austro-Hungarian empire, encompassing Slovenian and Croatian lands, that the goal should be increased autonomy and self-determination. The difference was in the estimation of how this should be achieved and what would be the main course of events and international changes creating a framework for action in the direction of self-determination.

The crucial division was based on the projection of the future of the Austro-Hungarian empire. If the empire survived, it should be changed from within according to federal principles, so that the dreams of Southern Slav unification held by the South Slavs within the empire would be realised. The opposite viewpoint started from the proposition that the empire would not survive (that it would be destroyed) so that the future realisation of hopes for self-determination lay in the creation of the new state of South Slavs – which meant unification with Serbia. The first line was more popular among the politicians active within the Austro-Hungarian empire, whereas the second approach was advocated more by those who left the Austrian empire and formed the London committee (Krizman 1977, 1989).

As it became obvious that the empire could not survive, the second line of thinking prevailed and unification became predominant. But, as described earlier, the main division emerged between those who advocated unification as a more or less disguised Serbian expansion and those who saw in this unification the creation of a new entity where the three national groups (Serbs, Slovenes and Croats) would have the same rights and equal status. Politically this division was operationalised as the centralism–federalism dilemma. Centralism was advocated mostly by the Serbian political elite, which was in the strongest political position, and federalism proposed mostly by the Croat political leaders.

This controversy ended with the clear victory of the Serbian political elites and the new state, the Kingdom of Serbs, Croats and Slovenes, was established as a centralised monarchy. The reason for this was the fact that the political and military positions of the advocates of centralism, Serbian politicians, on the one hand, and advocates of federalism, mostly Croatian political leaders, on the other, were very different. Serbia was on the victorious side with the army as the basis of its political power. On the other hand, the political leaders of Croatia (and Slovenia) were an appendage of a multinational state which was defeated in the war and was in the process of disintegration. The revolutionary ferment from inside, the international threats (the Treaty of London of 26 April 1915 promised Italy large portions of Slovenia, the whole of Istria, northern Dalmatia and most of the islands in exchange for a declaration of war on Austria–Hungary), and the lack of a reliable army, weakened the bargaining position of the non-Serbian political elites. They rushed into the creation of a common state clearly under Serbian domination.

It is often claimed that the unification and creation of the Yugoslav state was the result of the 'will of the people', which is a highly dubious statement. The willingness of the political elites of the Slav parts of the Austro-Hungarian empire to unite under Serbian leadership could be ascribed mainly to its politically weak position and hopes for democratic equality in the new state. It is very difficult to judge the prevailing attitudes of the ordinary people. If the results of the parliamentary elections of 1920 are interpreted as some kind of plebiscite for or against unification then support for unification in Croatia was relatively weak. In Croatia–Slavonia, the only region where it competed, the HPSS (Croat People's Peasant Party) won a clear majority of 52.55 per cent of votes. If we add the votes of autonomists and Frankists who were also clearly against unification (5.23 per cent and 2.48 per cent respectively), it would show over 60 per cent of voters were against unification in that region. In Dalmatia the support for unification was much stronger with votes in favour of the 'Yugoslav Club' parties of almost 28 per cent, compared to less than 3 per cent in Croatia–Slavonia (Burks 1961; Banac 1984: 387–92).

These results, combined with the history of uprisings and dissatisfaction, especially among peasants in Croatia, are a clear indicator that the rushed unification was more the result of the actions of political elites than of any kind of political movement based on popular support.

With the centralisation of Yugoslavia and the dissatisfaction of Croatian, but also other non-Serbian, anti-centralist political elites, the stage was set for the constant conflicts and instability which characterised the Yugoslav political scene between the two world wars. Because of these deep divisions Yugoslavia was unable to maintain parliamentary democracy and in 1929 (after the leader of the Croat Peasant Party, Stjepan Radic, was assasinated in parliament) King Alexander introduced a dictatorship in the hope that with it the warring national divisions could be overcome. That proved to be a false hope and in 1934 the king was assassinated by Croat and Macedonian extremists during his visit to Marseilles.

On the eve of the Second World War, in 1939, the regent Pavle negotiated the autonomy of Croatia, although this autonomy was never accepted by a majority of the political elite in Serbia. Banovina Croatia, created as a possible first step toward the federalisation of Yugoslavia, was short lived because Yugoslavia was occupied and divided by Germany, Italy, Hungary and Bulgaria.

Some major conclusions from this brief analysis of the political and historical forces operating in the period of the creation of Yugoslavia are the following.

First, the international environment, hostile and with territorial aspirations towards the South Slav part of the dissolving Austro-Hungarian empire, pushed the Croat and Slovenian political elites into Yugoslavia as a second-best solution. These elites rushed into Yugoslavia, even under centralist conditions unacceptable to them, because they perceived it as a lesser evil than the loss of territory and division between Italy, Serbia and eventually Hungary and Austria. This rush into Yugoslavia was also stimulated by the pre-revolutionary ferment and civil disorder, which threatened to slip control out of the hands of the new government.

Second, popular support for unification was never tested, and according to the results of the elections in 1920, together with unrest, specially among Croat peasantry, it did not enjoy widespread popularity.

Third, the concepts and ideological bases of unification differed significantly between the Serbian and the non-Serbian (Croat-led) political elites. Serbian elites viewed centralisation and the destruction of the cultural and political traditions of the autonomous regions as a prerequisite for building a strong and unified state. In practice that meant Serbian domination in the newly formed state, and for all practical purposes the expansion of the Serbian political institutions to the rest of the state. In contrast, the political leaders of the Austro-Hungarian South Slav regions were advocating the creation of a federal state, and not the simple expansion of the pre-existing Serbian state.

These ideologies of the Serbian and non-Serbian political elites were the basis of the permanent conflict in the Yugoslav state. One view was based on expansion (liberation from the Ottoman empire, the Balkan wars and now victory in the First World War), which was linked to the territorial enlargement of the Serbian state, and viewed the creation of the new state as a simple extension of the process which started with the anti-Ottoman uprisings and the creation of a free Serbian state in the second half of the nineteenth century. The other elite view hoped to create a completely new political structure as the culmination of long-existing hopes for South Slav unification but on a democratic and egalitarian basis.

This division underpinned all the conflicts of the 'old' Yugoslavia. At first it was limited only to the upper strata of the respective societies. Although anti-monarchist (anti-Austrian, -Hungarian and -Italian) feelings were strongly present among the wider Croat, Slovenian and Bosnian population, the Yugoslav idea did not have much popular support. Unification, except of course among Serbs living in Austria-Hungary, was not deeply rooted either. Animosity against Serbs was not based on traditional hostility and Croat peasants lived peacefully together or alongside Serbian settlers in Croatia. There is no history of their mutual conflicts, but, on the contrary, there is a history of mutual cooperation. It was only when the Yugoslav state was created that anti-Serbian feeling started and spread to the non-elite strata of society over persecution and resentment concerning the denial of some basic rights (e.g. discrimination against practising the Catholic faith). The lack of interest in Yugoslavism among the wider population of non-Serbs evolved on the basis of negative experience. It moved in the direction of anti-Serbianism and anti-Yugoslavism, because the Yugoslav idea, although historically mostly advocated by Croatian elites, became equated with Serbian domination.

The Dissolution of Yugoslavia

Legitimacy

In accordance with the Weber–Collins approach to legitimacy based on geostrategical success, we will try to interpret the decline of the legitimacy of Yugoslavia. Many have attributed the dissolution of Yugoslavia to the death of the great leader, but the disintegration started six to seven years after Tito's death and culminated only ten years later. The main reasons for this slow dissolution lay in the fact that basic legitimacy was preserved because the fundamental geopolitical position stayed unchanged. This static geostrategical situation is the true explanation of Yugoslavia's survival. It did not disintegrate because of Tito's death, although there was an undeniable weakening of central power after that event. However, its demise occurred because of change in the wider political environment and the total decline of internal legitimacy which resulted from it.

The legitimacy of the Yugoslav regime was not based on support for communism, which was an ideology accepted by only a small minority of the population. It was based much more on memories of the liberation war against Nazi occupation where the resistance was led by the communists. Nationalism, Weber insists, is a specially political sentiment. It is 'linked to memories of a common political destiny' (Weber 1922/68: 923). 'It was the history of having fought together, as part of a common state, against common enemies, for common political ideals, that constitutes the bond of political solidarity' (Collins 1986: 152). In that sense, a particular nationalism, different from 'ethnic nationalism', was created in Yugoslavia. The fact that Yugoslavia was defended against a common enemy, that through this struggle it became a part of the victorious coalition (as Serbia was in the First World War) helped to create a special sense of belonging to the state. This was also enforced by the new political elite emphasising the dangers of an internal enemy, those political forces defeated in the civil war which was going on in parallel with the liberation struggle:

> The ruling class need not base its claims to domination entirely on some ideology proclaiming the justice of its rule; a challenge from some other class can be even more effective in stirring up the emotions buttressing or establishing its legitimacy. It then becomes the defender of order against the party of disorder, where 'disorder' means explicitly violence in the streets, threats to persons and property. (Collins 1986: 160–1)

This 'internal enemy', in the form of political exiles, was constantly elevated in political importance regardless of its actual fragmentation and political insignificance, and depicted as a part of the fascist world (which was partially true). The fear of civil disorder was constantly evoked by reminding the people of the atrocities of the civil war and by creating the perception that the existing regime was the only guarantor of peace and stability. The source of this power to maintain peace and stability was based on the fact that the communist regime was part of the victorious coalition and that the nationalist forces were allied with the fascist powers. The post Second World War order was based on anti-fascism which gave an important element of legitimacy to the communist regime.

The most important single source of legitimacy was the threat from the 'East'. The Yugoslavs lived in a relatively open and liberal society compared to other Eastern bloc countries. The fact that in spite of being a communist country, they enjoyed greater freedoms and a higher standard of living than their communist neighbours created a specific 'negative legitimacy' and pride in being a liberal communist society. This negative comparison was more important than the positive comparison with the Western European countries. On several occasions, particularly in 1948 and 1968, the Yugoslavs expected an invasion from the East and according to many the important element in Tito's decision to crush the Croatian Spring was the threat from Brezhnev. (Of course it is an open question whether he used this threat as an excuse to create a consensus within the elite circles or whether it was a real threat.) With the geostrategical retreat of the Soviet Union from Eastern Europe the reasons for this negative legitimacy disappeared, attention was focused on positive legitimacy towards the West, and ethnic nationalist mobilisation prevailed.

Geopolitical context

The geopolitical context also played a crucial role in the dissolution of Yugoslavia. But this time the forces operating on the political leaders, especially on the leaders of the 'western' part of Yugoslavia, were pushing them in the opposite direction from that which had prevailed at the time of the creation of Yugoslavia.

In the case of the creation of Yugoslavia, the West, particularly Italy, was the 'danger' pushing the leaders into the arms of Serbia. But in the eighties the West was not perceived as a danger any more. It was the other way around; the process of European integration, economic prosperity and the disappearance of any revanchist aspirations made Europe attractive for the reform-minded, communist leaders of Slovenia and Croatia. Their main preoccupation became how to join Europe and not how to escape it. The last congress of the Communist Party of Slovenia, still in communist-ruled Yugoslavia, was held under the slogan *Evropa zdaj* (Europe now). This evolution toward liberal communism, first in Slovenia and later in Croatia, was accompanied by the opposite process in Serbia. There the evolution went in the reverse direction culminating in the replacement of the moderate leadership of Ivan Stambolic with the radical Slobodan Milosevic. Milosevic's leadership was much more reluctant regarding the opening towards Europe as reflected in a stronger alliance with the Soviet Union, particularly when Gorbachev slowed down the reform process. This pro-European strategy, characterising the western part of the still communist Yugoslavia, and the pro-Eastern stance, characterising Milosevic's leadership in Serbia, were important elements in the division of Yugoslavia. The split became final when, after the first free elections, the western part (Slovenia, Croatia, Bosnia and Herzegovina, but also Macedonia) elected anti-communist and nationalistic governments, while Serbia and Montenegro kept their communist regimes (in Serbia under a new socialist label, while in Montenegro the name was not even changed).

The survival of such an unlikely alliance of communist and anti-communist parts of the country was possible only in two ways. First, by creating an even looser federation-confederation, in order to allow the western part to go its own way toward further integration into the Western world and the east to stay on as the bulwark of communism. Second, by the use of force to crush one or the other option. Taking into account the imbalance of military power, and the inclinations of the Yugoslav army, the chances of the western part using force against the eastern part were minimal, but the chances of the east achieving military victory over the west were substantial.

The western republics (Slovenia and Croatia) offered a new confederal treaty (Cohen 1993: 178–81). The idea of an asymmetric federation was for a long time in use, especially in Slovenia (59–65). Milosevic, encouraged by European pressure to keep Yugoslavia intact, flatly rejected the proposals directed toward further confederalisation and instead offered the solution of centralisation. When that was unacceptable to the western part of the country, he started the war to restructure Yugoslavia.

Another element should also be taken into account, and that is the dissolution of world communism and the lack of pressure from the USSR. From the moment when communist Yugoslavia become an independent actor on the international scene, and that means after the Tito–Stalin split in 1948, its autonomy was dependent to a very extensive degree on the balance of power between two antagonistic world blocs. Yugoslavia was probably saved from a Soviet invasion mainly because of the fear of Western counter-intervention in 1948 (Bilandzic 1985: 158–63). The position of Yugoslavia from that time on can be described as a free floating entity kept alive by contradictory pressures from the West and East. With the disappearance of the one supportive pressure, the Warsaw Pact–USSR, the balance was lost and Yugoslavia fell.

This balance was important not only from a geostrategic standpoint but also because it enabled Yugoslavia to enjoy significant economic help from the West, as the show case communist state breaking its ties with the USSR, and at same time not being forced to fully join, in the sense of internal changes, the Western camp. That also increased the internal legitimacy of Tito's communist regime creating the image of liberating Yugoslavia from Soviet domination, in spite of the fact that it had brought it under the Soviet sphere of influence in the first place.

The interest and involvement of the West in Yugoslav affairs faded with the disappearance of Yugoslavia as an example of a communist dissident, while the capability and willingness of the USSR to intervene also diminished. Yugoslavia, without outside pressures to hold it together, no charismatic leadership, and with no possibility of creating and sustaining internal legitimacy, because of the crisis of communism and the deteriorating economic situation, simply exploded. The internal forces keeping it together were too weak or too clumsy, but the forces acting in the direction of dissolution were not capable of managing the transition in a peaceful way. A bipolar world held Yugoslavia together as the result of pressures from both sides; the disappearance of bipolarity meant the collapse of the outside forces keeping Yugoslavia intact.

Conclusions

The geostrategical explanation is important in understanding the dynamics of the creation and dissolution of Yugoslavia. Geostrategy operates on three different levels. First, on the level of international actors and their perception of the importance of the creation or the dissolution of an entity like Yugoslavia; Second, on the level of the interaction of geostrategical considerations and internal elite strategies; Third, on the production of legitimacy as the result of geostrategical success or failure.

The important element in the short-term explanation of the creation of Yugoslavia was the willingness of the non-Serbian elite to accept the Yugoslav state as a better solution than its disintegration and domination by the hostile surrounding powers. In that perspective Serbian domination looked to be a lesser evil than domination by Italy or Hungary. This consideration was also strengthened by the high esteem the Serbian elite was held in, resulting from its successes in creating and maintaining independence over the longer run.

These different perceptions, determined by different, long-term, historical positions, planted the seeds for the conflict which would constantly undermine the stability of Yugoslavia between the wars. This was a conflict between centralisation, rooted in the perceptions of the Serbian elite that Yugoslavia was just an extension of the long-term expansion of Serbia, and federalism, where Yugoslavia was perceived by the non-Serbian elites as the framework for an equal development of all national entities included in the new state. It was only from this period that we have, for example, the widespread Serbo-Croatian conflict at the popular level. Before the creation of Yugoslavia, the popular nationalisms of the two nations were not directed against each other. At the elite level, we have anti-Croatianism and anti-Serbianism, which is the logical consequence of nation formation and consolidation in the nineteenth century. At the popular level, before the peasant masses in Croatia began to feel that Serbian domination in Yugoslavia was directed against their interests, there was no popular anti-Serbianism. This internal divisiveness contributed to the fast dissolution of Yugoslavia as a consequence of Nazi aggression.

In explaining the events of post Second World War communist Yugoslavia, geostrategical factors were again of immense importance. Yugoslavia was between two existing blocs, balancing between the two. Internal stability was maintained exactly on the basis of this balance. The pro-Western forces were kept at a distance because of the 'reality' of Soviet influence. Any move directly outside the 'socialist camp', could bring the danger of internal dissolution and 'brotherly help' from the Eastern neighbour. On the other side more dogmatic, communist forces were kept at bay because the whole internal legitimacy of the system was built on the fact of successful struggle against Nazi occupation and Soviet pressure. This perception of the successful maintenance of independence created some deep inroads into the popular legitimacy of the communist regime. We can say, paradoxically, that the regime was popular not because it was communist, but because it successfully resisted the Soviet communist pressure and created stability where nobody expected that it could be achieved.

With the dissolution of world communism the situation dramatically changed. The fact that the west, particularly Italy, Austria and Germany, was not perceived by elites and the population at large to be any kind of danger, but, on the contrary, pillars of the European integrative processes, removed the motivation so important in the creation of the first Yugoslavia. The goal of the political leaders in Slovenia and Croatia was not to escape but to join Europe. They were prevented in their moves by the Serbian integrationalist strategy of unifying Yugoslavia on a more pro-Russian and anti-European basis. The disappearance of the Soviet threat removed the sources of internal legitimacy of the regime and allowed the explosion of pro-Western sentiments. Consequently the shifts in external pressures, the attractiveness of the West and the disappearance of the threat from the East, totally destroyed the internal consensus and Yugoslavia exploded under cross-pressures and the attractions provided by the changes in the geopolitical environment.

References

Banac, Ivan. 1984. *The National Question in Yugoslavia*. Ithaca: Cornell University Press.

Bilandzic, Dusan. 1985. *Historija Socijalisticke Federative Republike Jugoslavije*. Skolska Knjiga: Zagreb.

Burks, R. B. 1961. *The Dynamics of Communism in Eastern Europe*. Princeton: Princeton University Press.

Cohen, Leonard, J. 1993. *Broken Bonds. The Dissintegration of Yugoslavia*. Boulder, CO: Westview Press.

Collins, Randal. 1986. *Weberian Sociological Theory*. Cambridge: Cambridge University Press.

Jankovic, Dragoslav. 1983. 'Oko unitarnog ili federativnog uredjenja prve zajednicke Jugoslavenske drzave', in Nikola Popovic (ed.), *Stvaranje Jugoslavenske drzave 1918*. Belgrade: Institut za savremenu Istoriju.

Karadzic, Vuk. 1849. 'Srbi Svi i Svuda. Kovcezic za istoriju, jezik i obicaje Srba sva tri zakona. Bec, Jermenski manastir', quoted in M. Grmek, M. Gjidara and N. Simac, *Etnicko Ciscenje. Povijesni dokumanti of jednoj srpskoj ideologiji*. Zagreb: Globus, 1993. pp. 29–35.

Korunic, Petar. 1989. *Jugoslavizam i Federalizam u Hrvatskom nacionalnom preporodu. 1835–1875.* Zagreb: Globus.

Krizman, Bogdan. 1989. *Hrvatska u prvom svjetskom ratu.* Zagreb: Globus.

Krizman, Bogdan. 1977. *Raspad Austro-Ugarske i stvaranje jugoslavenske drzave.* Zagreb: Skolska knjiga.

MacKenzie, David. 1985. *Ilija Garasanin: Balkan Bismarck.* Boulder, CO: East European Monographs.

MacKenzie, David. 1994. 'Serbia as Piedmont and the Yugoslav Idea 1804–1914', *East European Quarterly* 28, 2: 153–82.

Marjanovic, Milan. 1913. *Narod konji nastaje. Zasto nastaje i kako se formira jedinstveni srpskohrvatski narod.* Rijeka: Knjizara G. Trbojevic.

Tepsic, Dragan. 1970. *Italija, Saveznici i jugoslavensko pitanje.* Zagreb: Skolska knjiga.

Weber, Max. 1968. *Economy and Society.* New York: Bedminster (original work published in 1922).

Part VI

Migration in a Transnational World

INTRODUCTION TO PART VI

One important feature of the trend towards globalization has been the ease with which capital can cross state boundaries at the speed of the Internet. Another aspect of the same development, and one with an even more critical impact on ethnic and racial conflict, has been the greater ability of people to move to those parts of the world offering them better prospects for economic success. Labour migration is never as rapid and volatile as capital transactions but its long-term consequences are likely to be far more profound. In the next section, we consider some of the implications of increasing population movements for race and ethnic relations in the modern world.

Since its birth, the United States has celebrated its foundation as a "nation of immigrants." While this may be a somewhat distorted interpretation of American history, downplaying the role of conquest and slavery in the last three centuries, it does provide a different founding myth from the territorial states of Europe, Asia and Africa. However, despite a more pluralistic ideology in the United States, the emphasis on assimilation has still been an important part of the experience that successive waves of migrants have had to contend with. Rubén Rumbaut considers some of the complexities of immigrant assimilation in America over the past thirty years and demonstrates that many of the outcomes of these processes may in fact be a mixed blessing. Far from automatically benefiting newcomers, some aspects of becoming more like mainstream Americans can be harmful to health and educational achievement. In many ways this analysis supports the general argument found in Seymour Martin Lipset's *American Exceptionalism*, that the advantages of life in the United States – individualism, opportunity, and freedom – have to be balanced against a set of corresponding disadvantages – inequality, crime, and family instability. American exceptionalism is indeed a two-edged sword. Rumbaut warns against an uncritical acceptance of the United States as a promised land and provides some evidence that America may be faced as much with a "native problem" as with an "immigrant problem."

Whatever the "discontents" of the assimilation process in contemporary America, no one can dismiss the power of the American economy to attract new migrants. In the period 1970–2000 almost as many immigrants have come to America as during the years of the transatlantic mass migrations from 1880–1920. What is, perhaps, somewhat different during this recent phase has been the extent to which changes in transportation and communications have enabled new migrants to maintain links with their countries of origin. Peggy Levitt examines one transnational community in detail, a group of Dominicans living in Boston. After exploring the diverse economic, social and political consequences of migration, and return migration, for several members of this community, she then considers other variations on a transnational theme. Unlike the Boston Dominicans, who are examples of what Levitt terms "transnational villagers," the recent Brazilian migrants to that city can be better characterized as transnational townspeople. Still further variants are illustrated by Gujaratis, whose members are drawn from a broad catchment area in India, and are best seen as transnational regional communities, in much the same way as the indigenous Mexican groups widely scattered across northern Mexico and southern California. By analysing the variety of factors influencing the types of communities and showing the dialectical impacts of the sending and receiving communities, Levitt demonstrates the complexity of migration and assimilation in contemporary America.

The third extract, shifts the focus to migrant groups who are as much influenced by political as economic pressures in their decisions to move from one state to another. Ellen Oxfeld looks at a small entrepreneurial community of Chinese tanners in Calcutta whose niche economy was threatened by the border war between India and China in 1962. Oxfeld follows the fortunes of an extended family, some of whose members remained in India, while others migrated to Canada. This fascinating case study raises many of the issues associated with "middlemen minorities" – a concept developed from the earlier analyses of Park on marginality and Du Bois and Weber on "pariah groups" – and is likely to have further relevance as diaspora communities become an increasingly common characteristic of the globalized world economy.

16 Assimilation and its Discontents

Rubén G. Rumbaut

Introduction

Few concepts in the history of American sociology have been as all-encompassing and consequential as "assimilation," or as fraught with irony and paradox. Few have so tapped and touched the pulse of the American experience. That master concept long ago penetrated the public discourse and seeped into the national narrative, offering an elemental explanation for a phenomenal accomplishment – the remarkable capacity of a self-professed nation of immigrants to absorb, like a giant global sponge, tens of millions of newcomers of all classes, cultures and countries from all over the world. And yet, few concepts have been so misused and misunderstood, or erected on such deep layers of ethnocentric pretensions. Few have so thoroughly conflated the real with the rhetorical, the idea with the ideal and the ideological, mixing descriptions of what is observable with prescriptions of what is desirable. And few have so tellingly entailed and entangled an attempt to support national illusions with arguments.

There is a certain fateful passivity and one-way-ness implied in "assimilation." As it is most commonly used, which is to say, unthinkingly, the term connotes a more or less fixed, given, and recognizable target state to which the foreign element is to "Americanize," dissolving into "it," becoming, in that elusive and expansive word, "American." That exosmotic usage recalls the no-nonsense coerciveness of Theodore Roosevelt's plain formulation of a century ago: "There can be no fifty–fifty Americanism in this country...there is room here only for 100 percent Americanism, only for those who are American and nothing else." But it also recalls Ralph Linton's devastating spoof of the "100 Percent American," as well as Henry James' contemporary critique of Roosevelt: "impaired...by the puerility of his simplifications," James wrote bitingly in 1898, "Mr. Roosevelt makes very free with the 'American' name, but it is after all not a symbol revealed once for all in some book of Mormon dug up under a tree. Just as it is not criticism that makes critics, but critics who make criticism, so the national type is the result not of what we take from it, but of what we give to it, not of our impoverishment, but of our enrichment of it."

That critical interactive view was not, to be sure, in vogue in sociological treatments of the subject around mid-century. In *The Social Systems of American Ethnic Groups* (1945), for example, Warner and Srole described the straight-line "progressive advance" of eight immigrant groups in the major status hierarchies of Yankee City (Newburyport, Massachusetts), explicitly linking upward social mobility to assimilation, which they saw as determined largely by the degree of ethnocultural (religion and language) and above all racial difference from the dominant group. While "racial groups" were subordinated through caste restrictions on residential, occupational, associational and marital choice, the clash of "ethnic groups" with the dominant institutions of the "host society" was not much of a contest, particularly among the young. The polity, the industrial economy, the public school, the American family system all undercut and absorbed ethnicity in various ways, so that even when "the ethnic parent tries to orient the child to an ethnic past...the child often insists on being more American than Americans" (p. 284). And for the upwardly mobile, with socioeconomic success came intermarriage and the further dilution of ethnicity.

That view of assimilation as linear progress, with sociocultural similarity and socioeconomic success marching in lock step, was not so much challenged as refined by Milton Gordon in *Assimilation in American Life* (1964), published ironically on the eve of the beginning of the latest era of mass immigration to the United States – and of the denouement of the concept itself in the wake of the 1960s. He broke down the assimilation sequence into seven stages, of which "identificational assimilation" – i.e., a self-image as an unhyphenated American – was the end point of a process that began with cultural assimilation, proceeded through structural assimilation and intermarriage, and was accompanied by an absence of prejudice and discrimination in the "core society." Once structural assimilation had occurred (i.e., extensive primary-level interaction with members of the "core group"), either in tandem with or subsequent to acculturation, "the remaining types of assimilation have all taken place like a row of tenpins bowled over in rapid succession by a well placed strike" (p. 81). For the children of white European immigrants, in fact, the acculturation process was so "overwhelmingly triumphant" that "the greater risk consisted in alienation from family ties and in role reversals of the generations that could subvert normal parent–child relationships" (p. 107). Still, what it was that one was assimilating to remained largely taken for granted.

Gordon was aware of the ways in which the ideal and the ideological get wrapped up in the idea of assimilation, and saw "Anglo-conformity" as the most prevalent ideology of assimilation in American history. But he was about to be ambushed by the unexpected: he could not have guessed at the time, not even in a wild flight of fancy, what was in store both for American society and his assimilation paradigm. What had seemed like a bland and straightforward enough description – an observable outcome of adaptation to new environments, a familiar process of "learning the ropes" and "fitting in" through which "they" become like "we," a convergence hypothesis, a sort of regression to the mean – could become an explosive and contested prescription, value-laden with arrogant presumptions of ethnic superiority and inferiority and fraught with the bitter baggage of the past and the fractious politics of the present. By 1993, after years of academic neglect and disrepute, no longer privileged in intellectual circles as either proverbial or canonical, Nathan Glazer could ask, matter of factly, "Is Assimilation Dead?"

Yet no sooner was that funereal question posed that, in what may be yet another of the pendulum swings that have characterized scholarship on American immigration, incorporation, and ethnicity in this century – as well as an effort to rescue the baby from the bath water – several major essays appeared that provide thorough-going reappraisals of the sociology and historiography of assimilation, casting a critical look not only at the concept, theory, and latest evidence, but also at the historical contexts that have shaped the ideas and ideals embodied in the notion of assimilation (see especially Alba and Nee 1997; Barkan 1995; Kazal 1995; Morawska 1994). Thus Kazal (1995) sees the apogee of the concept in the 1950s and early 1960s as reflecting the need generated by World War II for national unity and the postwar tendency to see American history as a narrative of consensus rather than conflict; and the political and social upheavals of the 1960s as shattering the "consensus school" and the rationale for studying assimilation, bringing back instead a focus on the ethnic group and ethnic resilience, and more inclusive conceptions of American society. "To know how immigrants came to fit in, one had to understand what it was they were fitting into... When the notion of an Anglo-American core collapsed amid the turmoil of the 1960s, assimilation lost its allure" (1995: 437). The point is well taken, an invitation to a self-reflexive sociology of knowledge that is keenly conscious of the fact that all our theories of reality are socially and historically grounded (cf. the essays in Kivisto and Blanck 1990).

Still, in the ideological contest, partly through policies and programs of "Americanization" and other intentional efforts, coercive or not, to make a process described by social observers into a practice prescribed by the guardians of the social order; partly by the patronizing ethnocentrism built into assumptions about immigrant adjustment that equated "foreign" with "inferior" and the ways of the "host" or "core" society and culture with "superior"; partly as a product of the linear logic of a positivist narrative within which the tale, and the *telos*, of assimilation is told; indeed, partly as a corollary to the central myth of progress at the heart of the core culture – in these and other ways it became difficult to disentangle the rhetorical from the historical, and the use of the term itself was tarred with the suspicion that an Anglo-conformist demand hid within it, like an ideological Trojan Horse. As a result, as Alba and Nee (1997) argue, "assimilation as a scientific concept has fallen into undeserved disrepute."

It is in these conceptual interstices between theory, rhetoric, and reality that irony and paradox emerge (or at least what may appear paradoxical from the vantage of the prevailing worldview). By focusing on ironies and paradoxes – on evidence that contradicts orthodox expectations and points instead to assimilation's discontents – my aim in this paper is to test empirically the conception of assimilation as a linear process leading to improvements in immigrant outcomes over time and generation in the US, to unmask underlying pre-theoretical ethnocentric pretensions, and to attempt to identify areas in need of conceptual, analytical, and theoretical refinement. For it is precisely through the examination of ironic and paradoxical cases – in effect, deviant case analyses of "outcomes of events that mock the fitness of things" – that fruitful reformulations can be stimulated, considered and advanced.

Assimilation and its Discontents

A few years ago, I heard a Vietnamese physician present data he had collected each year since 1975 on blood cholesterol levels of Vietnamese children in Connecticut.

As the only co-ethnic physician in the area, he provided primary health care services for the bulk of Vietnamese families who had been resettled there – including routine annual physical exams and blood tests. The results of those blood tests among the children showed that their cholesterol levels increased without exception for each year of residence in the United States. On reflection, that by-product of assimilation to the American diet should surprise no one, but that is not, needless to say, the sort of assimilative upward mobility Warner and Srole had in mind.

Nor does it fit with the view that assimilation is a more or less linear process of progressive improvement in the immigrant's adjustment to American life. That view is premised on an implicit deficit model: to get ahead immigrants need to learn how to "become American," to overcome their deficits with respect to the new language and culture, the new health care and educational systems, the new economy and society. As they shed the old and acquire the new over time, they surmount those obstacles and make their way more successfully – a process more or less completed by the second or third generation. Since today's immigration is overwhelmingly composed of newcomers from developing nations in Asia and Latin America, concerns have been raised about the speed and degree to which they can become assimilated – and hence about the social "costs" of the new immigrants – before they begin to produce net "benefits" to the new society. Recent research findings, however, especially in the areas of immigrant health, risk behavior, educational achievement, and ethnic self-identity, raise significant questions about such assumptions. Indeed, the findings often run precisely in the *opposite* direction of what might be expected from traditional perspectives on assimilation. Some of those findings on the relationship of assimilation, broadly conceived, to various types of outcomes, are highlighted below.

Epidemiological paradoxes: Is assimilation hazardous to infant health?

It seems only appropriate to begin at the beginning: with babies. Over the last decade a remarkably consistent and compelling body of evidence about the pregnancy outcomes of immigrant and native-born women has been emerging that turns the usual hypotheses about assimilation and socioeconomic status on their head. In particular, the research literature has pointed to an infant health "epidemiological paradox" among new immigrants (cf. Markides and Coreil 1986). It turns out that high-risk groups, particularly low-income immigrants from Mexico and Southeast Asia, show unexpectedly favorable perinatal outcomes. When these findings first came to light, particularly with reference to those classified as Hispanics, there was a tendency to dismiss them as being a result of migration selectivity or incomplete data. After all, lower socioeconomic status immigrants, such as refugees from Vietnam, Cambodia and Laos, and undocumented migrants from Mexico, El Salvador and Guatemala, generally combine high fertility rates with high poverty rates, and face formidable barriers in accessing health care and prenatal care services (Rumbaut et al. 1988). Conventional wisdom would expect these least "Americanized" groups of disadvantaged newcomers to exhibit worse than average health outcomes; but the opposite is true. Indeed, it soon enough became clear that these results could not be explained away by special circumstances or bad data.

In one of the first such reports, Williams and his colleagues (1986) analyzed data from California's matched birth–death cohort file for four groups: non-Hispanic whites, blacks, US-born Hispanics (mostly of Mexican descent), and Mexican immigrants. In terms of maternal risk factors, the Mexican-born women had less education, more children, shorter birth spacing, and a later start to pre-natal care than any of the other three groups. Yet, in terms of perinatal outcomes, the Mexican-born women had the lowest percentage of low birthweight babies, the lowest postneonatal infant mortality rates, and neonatal and total infant mor-tality rates that just matched the lower-risk white mothers. African Americans had the highest rates in these categories, followed by US-born Hispanics, and whites. The authors could not explain why the Mexican immigrants, despite their adverse socioeconomic circumstances and higher risk factors, produced such positive out-comes, but they speculated that it could be "the result of better nutrition, lower rates of smoking and alcohol consumption, or a higher regard for parental roles ... [or that] migration has selected out healthier individuals among newly arrived Latinos" (1986: 390). An earlier study had found similarly that Chinese-Americans had lower fetal, neonatal and postneonatal mortality rates than whites and other major ethnic/racial groups, and the superior health profile of Chinese infants was observed at every level of maternal education and for all maternal ages (Yu, 1982). Again, the available vital statistics lacked data with which to measure possible explanatory factors.

We reported similar evidence in a study of linked live birth and infant death records in San Diego County for the period 1978–85, covering some 270,000 live births (Rumbaut and Weeks 1989). The data showed that the infant mortality rate was lowest for Southeast Asians (6.6 per 1,000), followed by other Asians (7.0), Hispanics (7.3), non-Hispanic whites (8.0), and African Americans (16.3). In fact, among the Southeast Asians, the lowest infant death rates in the County were found for the Vietnamese (5.5) and the Cambodians (5.8). These highly positive outcomes were all the more remarkable because the Indochinese refugee groups (including the Vietnamese) had significantly higher rates of poverty, unemploy-ment, welfare dependency, fertility, prior infant mortality (before arrival in the US), and late use of prenatal care services than any other racial-ethnic groups in the San Diego metropolitan area, and because a high proportion of refugee mothers came from rural backgrounds with little or no prior education or literacy, proficiency in English, or readily transferable occupational skills. We also found that those results were not unique to San Diego, but were reflected statewide. In 1985 the State of California began publishing data on live births and infant deaths for more detailed ethnic groupings, including Vietnamese and Cambodians, using mother's place of birth as the principal criterion for ethnic identification. We compiled these statewide data and confirmed that during the late 1980s the Cam-bodians and Vietnamese had infant mortality rates of 5.2 and 7.5, compared to 7.7 for Mexican-born women, and 8.5 for non-Hispanic whites (Weeks and Rum-baut 1991). These differences were statistically significant. But just what was it that explained these differences could not be determined on the basis of the avail-able vital statistics. The Indochinese and Hispanics had lower infant mortality rates regardless of whether the mother was a teenager or not, and regardless of whether the mother was married or not; the findings also held after controlling for birth weight and onset of prenatal care.

Other regional studies with widely different ethnic populations in different parts of the country have reported similarly unexpected outcomes. In Illinois, Collins and Shay (1994) discovered that foreign-born Mexican and Central American mothers residing in very-low-income census tracts had much better pregnancy outcomes than either Puerto Rican or other US-born Hispanics. In Massachusetts, a study of low-income black women served by Boston City Hospital found significant differences in health behaviors and birth outcomes between natives and immigrants – the latter mostly from Haiti, Jamaica, and other Caribbean and African countries (Cabral et al. 1990). Compared to the US-born, the foreign-born women had better pre-pregnancy nutrition; they were far less likely to use cigarettes, marijuana, alcohol, cocaine or opiates during pregnancy; and they gave birth to babies that were larger in head circumference and significantly less likely to be of low birth weight or premature – health advantages that remained even after controlling for many of the factors suspected to influence fetal growth.

Research with national-level data sets confirms these findings across the board – while their significance grows: by 1995, foreign-born mothers accounted for nearly a fifth of all US births (18%), but over four-fifths (82%) of all Asian-origin babies and nearly two-thirds (62%) of all Hispanic-origin babies in the US were born to immigrant women (see Landale et al., 1999). A recent review of the literature (Eberstein 1991) cites research indicating that among blacks and Hispanics nationally, pregnancy outcomes (birth weight, infant mortality) are better for babies born to immigrant than to native mothers. Among Hispanics, an analysis of the 1983 and 1984 national data sets showed that infant mortality and low birthweight rates were lower for babies born to foreign-born vs. US-born Mexican and Cuban mothers, and for island-born vs. mainland-born Puerto Rican mothers, again despite a lack of correspondence between the socioeconomic profiles of these Hispanic groups and their health outcomes (Becerra et al. 1991).

More conclusive evidence comes from a new study using the 1989, 1990 and 1991 Linked Birth/Infant Death national data sets (Landale et al., 1999). The study examined the birth outcomes of immigrant vs. native-born mothers among ten ethno-racial groups – Chinese, Filipino, Japanese, Other Asian, Mexican, Puerto Rican (island-born vs. mainland-born), Cuban, Central/South American, non-Hispanic blacks and non-Hispanic whites. The babies of immigrant mothers had lower rates of prematurity, low birth weight, and infant mortality than those of US-born mothers. For each of the main groups, native-born mothers were also more likely than foreign-born mothers to be young (less than 20) and single, and to have smoked cigarettes during their pregnancies. In multivariate models the gap in birth outcomes by nativity and ethnicity was attenuated, but the offspring of immigrant mothers retained a health advantage over those of native-born mothers.

We attempted to unravel the reasons for this infant health paradox by examining an in-depth data set drawn from a Comprehensive Perinatal Program (CPP) in San Diego County providing prenatal care services to low-income pregnant women (see Rumbaut and Weeks 1996, 1998). The CPP data set consisted of nearly 500 independent variables per case (including most of those listed in the research literature as likely biomedical and sociocultural determinants of pregnancy outcomes), for a large sample of both foreign-born (mostly immigrants from Mexico and various Asian countries) and US-born women, matched to infant health outcome measures collected from hospital records for every baby delivered by CPP mothers during 1989–91. The analysis focused on the identification of maternal risk factors that best explained observed ethnic and/or nativity differences in pregnancy outcomes, such as birth weight, diagnoses at birth, complications, and length of hospitalization of the baby. Our findings caution from jumping too quickly to conclusions based solely on racial classifications, nativity status, education, or length of time in the US. For instance, it turns out that the best infant health outcomes were observed for certain "Asian" immigrant groups (the Indochinese, who were also the least educated of all), but the worst outcomes for a "white" immigrant group (Arab Muslims from countries in the Middle East, who were also the most educated of all). And while immigrants indeed do better than natives overall, the most assimilated immigrants (white Europeans and Canadians) do worse than US-born Asians, Hispanics, and blacks.

Still, given these caveats, the following general picture emerges from our data: Asians and Hispanics (mostly foreign-born) clearly had superior outcomes relative to non-Hispanic whites and blacks (mostly US-born); and within racial-ethnic groups, outcomes were better for immigrants than for natives. Specifically, native-born women (who in this sample were mainly non-Hispanic whites) were significantly more likely than immigrant women (who in this sample were mainly Mexicans and Indochinese) to: (1) have higher levels of education, employment, and per capita income; (2) be taller, heavier, and gain more weight during their pregnancies; (3) have had fewer live births and more abortions; (4) have diets lower in fruits and cereals and higher in fats and milk products; (5) report more medical conditions, especially venereal disease and genitourinary problems; (6) smoke, abuse drugs and alcohol, and be at risk for AIDS; (7) have a personal history of significant psychosocial problems, including having been a victim of child abuse and now of spousal abuse, and having currently stressful relationships both with the father of the baby and with their own family and parents; (8) be depressed, considered at risk psychosocially, and referred to a social worker; and (9) have generally poorer pregnancy outcomes – which is why infant health outcomes seem to worsen as the levels of education, English literacy, and general assimilation of the mother increase. In this context, then, part of the assimilation puzzle begins to clear up: that is, relative to the foreign-born in this sample of low-income women, the comparative socioeconomic advantages of the US-born appear to be overwhelmed by biomedical, nutritional, and psychosocial disadvantages.

The 1982–4 Hispanic Health and Nutrition Examination Survey (HHANES), with a very large regional sample of Mexicans, Puerto Ricans and Cubans, has also provided a wealth of evidence that contradicts orthodox theoretical expectations. For example, low-birth weight (LBW) rates were significantly higher for (more acculturated) second-generation US-born women of Mexican descent compared with (less acculturated) first-generation Mexico-born women, despite the fact that the latter had lower socioeconomic status, a higher percentage of mothers over 35 years of age, and less adequate prenatal care (Guendelman et al. 1990). The risk of LBW was about four times higher for second than first generation primiparous women, and double for second than first generation multiparous women. Other studies based on the Hispanic HANES have also observed this association between greater acculturation and low birth weight (Scribner and Dwyer 1989). In addition, first-generation Mexican women, despite their socioeconomic disadvantages, had a lower risk of eating a poor diet than second-generation Mexican-American women, whose nutrient intake resembled that of non-Hispanic white native women (Guendelman and Abrams 1995). For the immigrants, food choices actually deteriorated as income increased – and as the degree of assimilation increased (as indicated in this study by generational status).

Findings from the HHANES have shown a link between increasing acculturation and health risk behaviors (Marks et al. 1990), cigarette smoking (Haynes et al. 1990), and drug use (Amaro et al. 1990; see also Vega and Amaro, 1994). Adverse effects of acculturation have also been reported among Mexican Americans with respect to alcohol consumption patterns (Gilbert 1989) and psychological distress (Kaplan and Marks 1990). Indeed, intriguing questions have been raised by recent research on the mental health of ethnic minorities in the US, including immigrants and refugees. A review of prevalence rates reported in the most important research studies conducted over the past two decades suggests that rapid acculturation does not necessarily lead to conventionally anticipated outcomes (Vega and Rumbaut 1991). Thus, teenage children of middle-class Filipino immigrants, the most "Americanized" of contemporary Asian-origin newcomer groups and among the most socioeconomically advantaged, exhibit higher rates of suicidal ideation and attempts than most other immigrant groups (cf. Wolf 1997; Kann 1995; Rumbaut 1994, 1999).

Adolescent health and risk behavior: Patterns of intra- and intergenerational assimilation

Perhaps at no stage of the life course are assimilative processes more intensely experienced, or assimilative outcomes more sharply exhibited, than during the formative years of adolescence. A new source of data – the National Longitudinal Study of Adolescent Health (Add Health) – provides a unique opportunity to examine intragenerational and intergenerational processes and outcomes of assimilation among a large, nationally representative sample of adolescents. The data come from the first wave of the study, which in 1995 surveyed over 20,000 adolescents (and their parents) enrolled in grades 7 to 12 in 80 high schools drawn from a stratified probability sample of high schools nationwide, and included an oversample of high-income black youth and several ethnic samples. The sample includes sizable numbers of immigrant children and children of immigrants, and for the former data were collected on age at arrival and length of residence in the US. An analysis focusing on physical health characteristics and risk behaviors of three generational groups – first (immigrant children), second (native-born children of immigrant parents), and third or higher (native-born of native-born parents) generations – broken down by major national-origin groups, provides a tell-tale test of the linear progress hypothesis (Harris 1999).

First, looking at intergenerational results, for virtually every empirical indicator, second-generation youth have poorer physical health outcomes and are more prone to engage in risk behavior than the foreign-born-youth. In particular, Harris found that second-generation youth were more likely than the first generation to report poor or fair health, to have missed school due to a health or emotional problem in the previous month, to have learning disabilities, to be obese, to have asthma, to ever have had sex and at a younger age, and to have engaged in deviant behaviors (delinquency, violence, and substance abuse). Outcomes for the third+ generation vary significantly across race and ethnic groups, but in general native minorities report the poorest health and the highest levels of risk behaviors. The findings, which remain after adjusting for age differences, suggest a strongly linear assimilative pattern – but in the direction of deteriorating rather than improving outcomes.

Secondly, looking at intragenerational results for the foreign-born youth (that is, by length of residence in the US), the pattern of assimilation outcomes reinforces the above conclusion: the longer the time in and exposure to the US, the poorer are the physical health outcomes, and the greater the propensity to engage in each of the risk behaviors measured. Furthermore, a breakdown by national or regional origin for the most sizable subsamples – Mexico, Cuba, Puerto Rico (island-born vs. mainland-born youth and parents), Central/South America, China, the Philippines, Vietnam, Other Asia, Africa and the Afro-Caribbean, Europe and Canada – generally confirm the intergenerational patterns, with outcomes worsening the further removed from the immigrant generation, most strongly seen among Mexicans and Filipinos. A main exception – where first-generation youth are more likely to engage in some risk behaviors than the second generation (earlier sexual initiation and more substance abuse) – involves, interestingly enough, youths who were in some respects more Americanized prior to immigration: those from the English-speaking Caribbean and from Europe and Canada.

Despite these positive results among immigrant youth, their families actually had the highest poverty rates in the sample (38%), while the third-generation+ natives had the lowest (20%). By contrast, third-generation youth were the least likely to live in intact families, and the most likely to live with a single parent, whereas second-generation youth were most likely to live with both natural parents. Controlling in multivariate analyses for socioeconomic status, family structure, degree of parental supervision, and neighborhood contexts actually increased the protective aspects of the immigrant first generation on both physical health and risk behavior outcomes. In fact, on both of these outcome indices, the results showed that every first-generation nationality (with the sole exception of island-born Puerto Ricans, who are not immigrants but US citizens) had significantly fewer health problems and engaged in fewer risk behaviors than the referent group of native non-Hispanic whites. These findings vividly parallel those discussed above with respect to infant health and mortality, and, while still consistent with a linear hypothesis of assimilation to native norms, run directly contrary to the expectation of progressive improvement over time.

The assimilation of criminal propensities? A look at young adult men

Equally striking and unexpected are the results of a systematic analysis of patterns of incarceration among immigrants and natives in the United States over the past two decades, which suggests that "immigrants may assimilate to the (higher) criminal propensities of natives" (Butcher and Piehl 1997). The study, carried out by two economists, was aimed as a contribution to the economic research literature and the public policy debate on the consequences of immigration, focusing on an outcome that had received virtually no scholarly attention despite its clear societal significance: the social costs of crime and punishment. Indeed, during the 1980s, a decade which saw the largest (legal and illegal) flows of immigrants to the US since the turn of the century, the number of people incarcerated in state or federal prisons skyrocketed, doubling from 138 per 100,000 population in 1980 to 271 per 100,000 in 1989. In addition, since conventional theories of crime and incarceration predict higher rates for young adult males from racial-ethnic minority groups with lower educational attainment – characteristics which describe a much greater proportion of the composition of the immigrant population than of that of the native-born – it followed that immigrants would be expected to have higher incarceration rates than natives. But the results turned these expectations on their head.

The study used data from the 5% Public Use Microdata Samples of the 1980 and 1990 censuses to measure the institutionalization rates of immigrants and natives at both time periods. Since only the 1980 census identifies the type of institutional setting (correctional facilities, mental hospitals, homes for the aged, drug treatment centers and other institutions), the analysis focused on men aged 18–40, among whom the vast majority of the institutionalized are in correctional facilities (for them, with disability status controlled, the data confirm that institutionalization is a good proxy for incarceration). Among men 18 to 40, immigrants in both 1980 and 1990 had significantly lower educational attainment than natives, with the gap widening over the decade; Mexicans accounted for fully 30 percent of all male immigrants in the US in that age group. The institutionalization rate for men 18 to 40 increased sharply from 1980 to 1990, with the most dramatic increases registered among native-born blacks and Hispanics. But immigrant men had much *lower* institutionalization rates than the native-born in both 1980 and 1990, and the advantage for immigrants held when broken down by race-ethnicity and education; e.g., the rates for US-born blacks, whites, Asians and Hispanics were consistently higher than for foreign-born blacks, whites, Asians and Hispanics.

Butcher and Piehl examined the rates for national-origin groups and for refugees vs. immigrants, finding that Mexicans and refugees had *lower* institutionalization rates than other immigrants and *much lower* rates than natives in both years; and that Cuban, Colombian, and Afro-Caribbean groups all had lower rates than natives in 1980 but somewhat higher rates in 1990 – with the Cubans who came in the controversial 1980 Mariel boatlift having the highest rate of any group in 1990 (indeed, many of them were placed directly into institutional facilities in the US upon arrival, and were still held in 1990). Still, in models controlling for country of origin and likely determinants of institutionalization, the only immigrant "group" that always had higher rates than native-born men was "country not specified." Further, the authors showed that "if natives had the same institutionalization probabilities as immigrants, our jails and prisons would have one-third fewer inmates;" conversely, "in 1990, if immigrants had the same 'returns' to their characteristics as natives, they would have almost double the institutionalization rates of natives" (Butcher and Piehl 1997: 34, 11).

Finally, to examine what happens as immigrants spend more time in the United States, the study focused on the experience and characteristics of different cohorts who had arrived at 5-year intervals. Most of these cohorts of immigrants were found to be less likely to be institutionalized than the native-born, and the difference in institutionalization probabilities between natives and these cohorts only became wider as race, ethnicity, and education controls were added. More to the point, in both the 1980 and 1990 samples, the longer immigrants had resided in the US, the higher were their institutionalization rates (the sole exception involved those who arrived in the early 1980s, a cohort skewed by the composition of the Mariel entrants); that is, immigrants assimilate to the rates of the native born – but again in this instance, the assimilative pattern is in the direction of worsening outcomes. For reasons that remained unclear, the more recent immigrants were not only less likely to be institutionalized (relative to natives) than earlier arrivals were after a similar length of residence in the United States, but also appeared to assimilate to native norms less quickly than earlier immigrants.

Educational paradoxes: Is assimilation detrimental to academic achievement?

What is the relationship of immigrant assimilation to academic achievement? Given the enormous variability in the socioeconomic status of immigrant families in the US today, their language handicaps, and the relative recency of arrival of so many, how does the school performance of their children stack up with that of natives? Relatively few studies, including a handful of ethnographies, have explored these questions systematically, but still their results are also remarkably consistent and relevant to our concerns in this paper.

Part of the difficulty in obtaining useful data to address these issues is that school systems do not collect information on the nativity or immigration status of their students or their parents. A rough proxy for immigrant family status may be obtained from the home-language census that is mandated by law in public school systems such as those in California to ascertain the English proficiency of students whose primary home language is not English. Those students are then assessed and classified as LEP (Limited English Proficient) or FEP (Fluent English Proficient). One large-scale study in the San Diego Unified School District (the country's eighth largest, with a sizable and diverse immigrant population) obtained data on educational achievement for the entire high school student cohorts (all sophomores, juniors and seniors, including all active and inactive students) for two periods: the 1986–7 and 1989–90 school years, a combined total of nearly 80,000 students (see Rumbaut 1995; Portes and Rumbaut 1996). Among Asian and Hispanic students, about a quarter spoke English only, while three-fourths spoke a language other than English at home (with a larger proportion of FEPs than LEPs overall among them, although varying greatly by national-origin: the overwhelming proportion of Filipinos were FEP, while an equally large proportion of Cambodians and Laotians were LEP). Cumulative academic GPAs earned by the students since the ninth grade were compared for all the ethnic groups by language status.

The overall GPA for white non-Hispanic students was 2.24, above the overall district norm of 2.11; but (except for Hispanics) all of the non-English immigrant minorities outperformed their English-only co-ethnics as well as majority white students. This applied in most cases to FEP and LEP students alike, though clearly FEP students did significantly better. The highest GPAs were found for immigrant Chinese, Korean, Japanese, Vietnamese, and Filipino students. More remarkable still, even the Hmong, whose parents were preliterate peasants from the Laotian highlands (and who were at the time referred derisively by US Senator Alan Simpson as "the most indigestible group in society"), and the more recently arrived Cambodians, who were mostly rural-origin survivors of the Khmer Rouge "killing fields" of the late 1970s, were outperforming all native-born English-only American students; and again this pattern applied for both FEP and LEP students among these refugee groups. This finding held for GPAs in both ESL (English as a Second Language) and mainstream courses; that is, the refugees' GPAs were not an artifact of the curriculum (Rumbaut and Ima 1988; cf. also Caplan et al., 1991).

A more systematic analysis of the educational progress of children of immigrants in San Diego City Schools was recently provided by our Children of Immigrants Longitudinal Study (CILS). Survey data (supplemented by academic records from the school system) were collected in 1992 (T1) and again over three years later in 1995–6 (T2). The T1 sample totaled 2,420 Mexican, Filipino, Indochinese (Vietnamese, Cambodian, Lao, and Hmong), and other Asian and Latin American students who were enrolled in the eighth and ninth grades in San Diego city schools (a grade level at which dropout rates are still relatively rare, to avoid the potential bias of differential dropout rates between ethnic groups at the senior high school level). Most of the respondents were 14 or 15 years old at T1, and the sample was evenly split by gender, grade, and generation: 45% were US-born children of immigrant parents (the "second generation"), and 55% were foreign-born youths who immigrated to the US before age 12 (the "1.5" generation). Only 1.4% of the sample in San Diego checked "white" to a structured question on racial self-identification. The respondents were tracked over time, including students who dropped out or transferred from the school district, and over 85% (2,063) were successfully reinterviewed by T2. By that time most were about 18 years old and entering young adulthood.

Academic grade point averages for all schools district-wide in San Diego were compared against the GPAs earned in grades 9–12 in those schools by the entire original T1 sample of 2,420 children of immigrants during 1992–5. The result showed that at every grade level the children of immigrants outperformed the district norms, although the gap narrows over time and grade level. For example, only 29% of all ninth graders in the district had GPAs above 3.0, compared to a much higher 44% of the ninth graders from immigrant families; and while 36% of ninth graders district-wide had low GPAs under 2.0, only half as many (18%) of the children of immigrants performed as poorly. Those differentials decline over time by grade level, so that the advantage by the twelfth grade is reduced to a few percentage points in favor of the children of immigrants. Part of that narrowing of the GPA seemed to be due to the fact that a greater proportion of students district-wide dropped out of school than did the youth from immigrant families. The multi-year dropout rate for grades 9–12 in the San Diego schools was 16.2%, nearly triple the rate of 5.7% for the entire original sample of children of immigrants. That dropout rate was significantly lower than the dropout rates for preponderantly native non-Hispanic white (10.5%) and black (17.8%) high school students. Among the students from immigrant families, the highest dropout rate (8.8%) was that for Mexican-origin students, but even that rate was noticeably lower than the district norm, and slightly lower than the rate for non-Hispanic whites.

These results are remarkable enough in view of the relatively low socioeconomic status of a substantial proportion of the immigrant families. They become all the more remarkable in the context of other school data. At T1, over a quarter (29%) of the sample were classified as LEP, ranging from virtually none of the native-born Filipinos to around two-thirds of the foreign-born Mexican, Cambodian and Hmong students. That classification is supported by nationally standardized ASAT (Abbreviated Stanford Achievement Test) scores measuring English reading skills: the sample as a whole scored just below the 40th percentile nationally, and the foreign-born groups with the highest proportion of LEP students scored in the bottom quartile nationally. On the other hand, all groups do better in math computation than English reading tests. At T1, their ASAT math achievement test scores placed the sample as a whole at the 50th percentile nationally, with some students achieving extraordinarily high scores (notably the "first-wave" Vietnamese and Chinese, Japanese, Indian, and Korean students, placing most of them in the top quartile nationally).

One key reason for these students' above-average academic GPAs, despite significant socioeconomic and linguistic handicaps, is elementary: they work for it. At both T1 and T2, these students reported spending an average of over 2 hours per day on homework, with the foreign-born students compensating for language and other handicaps by significantly outworking their US-born peers (by comparison, national data suggest that American high school students average less than an hour daily on homework). From the end of junior high at T1, to the end of senior high at T2, the level of effort put into school work increased across all nationalities. The sole exception in this regard were the Hmong, who at T1 posted the highest average number of daily homework hours (2.9), but decreased to 2.6 hours at T2 (still above the sample average and well above the national average); not surprisingly, that drop in effort was matched by the drop in their GPAs from 2.92 (at T1) to 2.63 (at T2), the main drop in GPA among all the groups in the sample. Overall, the children of immigrants generally maintained their level of GPA attainment from T1 (2.80) to T2 (2.77).

In multivariate analyses at T1, examining a wide range of likely predictors, the number of daily homework hours emerged as the strongest single predictor of higher GPAs, while the number of hours spent watching television daily was significantly associated with lower GPAs (see Rumbaut, 1995, 1997). By T2, the data show that students who had dedicated more hours to school work in junior high did significantly better in terms of educational achievement three years later. More significant for our purposes here is the *negative* association of length of residence in the US and second-generation status with both GPA and educational aspirations. What is more, students whose parents were both immigrants outperformed their counterparts whose mother or father was US-born. Those results do not support a conventional linear assimilation hypothesis.

Similar findings on educational achievement, aspirations and attitudes have been reported by Kao and Tienda (1995) with national-level data from the National Educational Longitudinal Study (NELS) with a 1988 sample of over 25,000 eighth graders, and by a secondary analysis of the earlier High School & Beyond (HSB) data set, with a sample of over 21,000 10th and 12th graders followed since 1980 over a six-year period (Vernez and Abrahamse 1996), both finding a deterioration in outcomes over generations in the U.S. Essentially the same general intergenerational pattern has also been reported in ethnographic case studies in California of Mexican-origin and Punjabi Sikh students (see Matute-Bianchi 1991; Gibson 1989), and by a comparative cross-generational and cross-national study using projective tests (such as the TAT) of Mexican, Mexican immigrant, Mexican-American and non-Hispanic white students (Suárez-Orozco and Suárez-Orozco, 1995). And remarkably consistent results about the erosion of an ethos of achievement and hard work from the immigrant generation to the third generation have also been recently reported from a three-generational study of a sample of 1,100 secondary school students in California (Fuligni 1997), and from a survey of more than 20,000 teenagers from nine high schools in Wisconsin and California (for an overall summary, see Steinberg 1996).

The Arrow and the Boomerang: Linguistic assimilation and ethnic self-identity

Similarly provocative findings come from our panel study (CILS) of the adaptation of children of immigrants in San Diego, described above, focusing for our purposes here on changes in their patterns of English preference and proficiency, and in their ethnic self-identities. Indeed, language and identity are presumed to be intimately linked. A "straight-line" hypothesis would predict additional movement over time and generation in the direction of both increasing linguistic assimilation (anglicization) and increasing identificational assimilation (Milton Gordon's term) – i.e., of a primary self-identity as an unhyphenated "American." We can check that with the newly available evidence.

Our findings on language preference, a key index of cultural assimilation, are unequivocal. Over 90% of these children of immigrants report speaking a language other than English at home, mostly with their parents. But as seen in table 16.1, at T1 two-thirds of the total sample (66%) already preferred to speak English instead of their parents' native tongue, including 56% of the foreign-born youth and 78% of the US-born. Three years later, the proportion had grown significantly to over four fifths (82%), including 76% of the foreign-born and over 90% of the US-born. The most linguistically assimilated in this respect were the Filipinos, among whom 92% of those born in the Philippines (where English is an official language) and 98% of those born in the US preferred English by T2. But even among the most mother-tongue-retentive group – the Mexican-origin youth living in a Spanish-named city on the Mexican border with a large Spanish-speaking immigrant population and a wide range of Spanish radio and TV stations – the force of linguistic assimilation was incontrovertible: while at T1 only a third (32%) of the Mexico-born children preferred English, by T2 that preference had doubled to 61%; and while just over half (53%) of the US-born preferred English at T1, that proportion had jumped to four-fifths (79%) three years later.

A main reason for this rapid language shift in use and preference has to do with their increasing fluency in English (both spoken and written) relative to their level of fluency in the mother tongue. Respondents were asked to evaluate their ability to speak, understand, read and write in both English and the non-English mother tongue; the response format (identical to the item used in the US census) ranged from "not at all" and "not well" to "well" and "very well." Over two-thirds of the total sample reported speaking English "very well"(67% at T1, 71% at T2), compared to only about a third who reported an equivalent level of spoken fluency in the non-English language. Naturally, these differentials are much more pronounced among US-born youth, most of whom (87%) spoke English "very well," while only a fourth of them could speak the parental language "very well." But even among the foreign-born, those who spoke English very well surpassed by 59% to 44% those who spoke the foreign language just as well.

And the differences in reading fluency (not shown) are much sharper still: those who can read English "very well" triple the proportion of those who can read a non-English language very well (68% to 23%). Only the Mexico-born youth maintained by T2 an edge in their reported knowledge of Spanish over English, and even they nonetheless indicated a preference for English. The ability to maintain a sound level of literacy in a language – particularly in languages with entirely different alphabets and rules of syntax and grammar, such as many of the Asian languages brought by immigrants to California – is nearly impossible to maintain in the absence of schools that teach it, and a community that values it and in which it can be regularly practiced. As a consequence, the bilingualism of these children of immigrants becomes increasingly uneven and unstable. The data vividly underscore the rapidity with which English triumphs and foreign languages atrophy in the United States – even in a border city like San Diego – as the second generation not only comes to speak, read and write it fluently, but to prefer it overwhelmingly over their parents' native tongue. This linear trajectory of rapid linguistic assimilation is constant across nationalities and socioeconomic levels and suggests that, over time and generation, the use of and fluency in foreign languages will inevitably decline – and at an even faster clip than has been the age-old pattern in American history.

In both surveys, an identical open-ended question was asked to ascertain the respondent's ethnic self-identity. The results (and the wording of the question) are presented in the middle panel of table 16.1. Four main types of ethnic identities became apparent: (1) a plain "American" identity; (2) a hyphenated-American identity; (3) a national-origin identity (e.g., Mexican, Filipino, Vietnamese); and (4) a pan-ethnic minority identity (e.g., Hispanic, Latino, Chicano, Asian, black). The way that adolescents see themselves is significant. Self-identities and ethnic loyalties can often influence patterns of behavior and outlook independently of the status of the families or the types of schools that children attend. But unlike language, which changes in straight-line fashion, like an *arrow*, ethnic self-identities vary significantly over time – yet not in linear fashion but in a reactive, dialectical fashion, like a *boomerang*. The data in table 16.1 illustrate that pattern compellingly.

Table 16.1 The Arrow and the Boomerang: Language shifts, ethnic self-identity, and perceptions of discrimination among children of immigrants in San Diego, California, by nativity of the children (FB = foreign-born, US = US-born) and national origin of their parents, in 1992 (T1) and 1995 (T2)

Characteristics by National Origin and Nativity	Time	Mexico FB	Mexico US	Philippines FB	Philippines US	Vietnam FB	Vietnam US	Cambodia FB	Laos Lao Hmong FB	Laos Lao Hmong US	All Others FB	All Others US	Total FB	Total US	Total
Language:															
% Prefers English	T1	32.1	52.8	81.4	95.8	43.9	91.5	67.0	51.7	66.0	55.7	92.9	56.1	78.4	66.0
	T2	62.5	78.2	92.6	98.0	69.0	91.5	85.2	74.1	58.0	72.7	99.0	75.8	89.8	82.0
% Speaks "very well:"															
English Language	T1	38.5	74.1	75.2	94.3	45.9	95.7	48.9	44.1	22.0	59.8	93.9	52.2	86.2	67.3
	T2	48.2	77.7	83.3	93.6	47.8	89.4	50.0	49.0	30.0	70.5	93.9	58.5	87.0	71.2
Non-English Language	T1	74.0	44.8	23.2	2.0	41.3	10.6	33.3	42.0	50.0	49.4	11.2	43.4	20.3	33.1
	T2	78.1	49.9	23.0	3.6	38.7	4.3	33.3	40.6	44.0	50.6	18.2	43.7	25.7	36.3
Ethnic Self-Identity:[a]															
% "American"	T1	0.0	2.8	0.3	5.2	2.4	8.5	2.3	0.7	4.0	3.4	18.4	1.3	5.8	3.3
	T2	0.0	2.0	1.0	2.0	0.0	2.1	0.0	0.7	0.0	3.4	9.2	0.6	2.7	1.6
% Hyphenated-American	T1	14.7	40.4	50.8	66.2	43.9	70.2	46.6	28.7	26.0	18.2	38.8	35.8	53.0	43.4
	T2	12.1	39.3	21.9	48.4	28.2	51.1	30.7	19.6	12.0	9.1	25.5	20.2	42.4	30.1
% National origin	T1	33.5	8.2	41.8	21.5	45.9	19.1	40.9	61.5	62.0	44.3	11.2	44.3	15.7	31.6
	T2	67.9	26.3	72.7	42.5	56.1	36.2	48.9	67.1	48.0	18.2	11.2	60.7	32.3	48.1
% Racial/panethnic	T1	51.3	44.9	3.5	1.2	0.4	0.0	1.1	2.1	2.0	22.7	17.3	13.2	19.8	16.1
	T2	18.8	27.7	0.6	2.0	14.5	8.5	20.5	11.2	38.0	58.0	40.8	15.8	16.8	16.2
% Mixed ethnicity, other	T1	0.4	3.7	3.5	5.9	7.5	2.1	9.1	7.0	6.0	11.4	14.3	5.4	5.7	5.5
	T2	1.3	4.8	3.9	5.2	1.2	2.1	0.0	1.4	2.0	11.4	13.3	2.7	5.7	4.0
Discrimination:[b]															
% Has experienced being discriminated against	T1	62.5	63.8	60.8	66.2	65.5	70.2	61.4	71.3	56.0	64.8	58.2	63.7	64.5	64.0
	T2	68.8	64.4	69.1	68.9	71.8	70.2	65.9	74.8	82.0	60.2	63.3	69.9	66.8	68.5
% Expects discrimination regardless of merit	T1	33.5	35.6	35.0	41.0	33.3	40.4	38.6	46.2	40.0	29.5	32.7	35.8	37.9	36.7
	T2	39.3	38.4	43.7	44.2	36.9	40.4	39.8	43.4	50.0	42.0	31.6	40.9	40.7	40.8

[a] Responses to the open-ended survey question: "How do you identify, that is, what do you call yourself?" "Hispanic," "Chicano," "Latino," "Black," and "Asian" are classified as racial/panethnic identities; a Hmong ethnic identity is included under "national origin;" "Cuban-Mexican" or "Chinese-Thai" under "mixed" identities.

[b] Responses to (1) an open-ended question on experiences of discrimination, and (2) an item asking to agree or disagree with the statement: "No matter how much education I get, people will still discriminate against me." Data above show percent who agreed.

In 1992, almost a third (32%) of the sample identified by national origin; the largest proportion (43%) chose a hyphenated-American identification; a small fraction (3.3%) identified as plain "American"; and 16% selected pan-ethnic minority identities. Whether the youth was born in the US or not made a great deal of difference in the type of identity selected at T1: the foreign-born were three times more likely to identify by national origins (44%) than were the US-born (16%); conversely, the US-born were much more likely to identify as "American" or hyphenated-American than were the foreign-born, and somewhat more likely to identify in pan-ethnic terms. Those findings at T1 seemed suggestive of an assimilative trend from one generation to another. But by the T2 survey – conducted in the months after the passage, with 59% of the vote, of Proposition 187 in California in November 1994 – the results were quite the opposite from what would have been predicted by a straight-line identificational assimilation perspective.

In 1995, the biggest gainer by far in terms of the self-image of these youths was the foreign nationality identity, increasing from 32% of the sample at T1 to nearly half (48%) now. This boomerang effect took place among both the foreign-born and the US-born, most notably among the youth of Mexican and Filipino descent – the two largest immigrant groups in the US – an apparent backlash during a period (1992–6) of growing anti-immigrant sentiment and at times overt immigrant bashing in the country, above all in California. Overall, pan-ethnic identities remained at 16% at T2, but that figure conceals a notable decline among Mexican-origin youth in "Hispanic" and "Chicano" self-identities, and an extremely sharp upswing in the proportion of youths now identifying pan-ethnically as "Asian" or "Asian American," especially among the smallest groups such as the "Other Asians" (Chinese, Korean, Japanese, Thai) and the Hmong. The simultaneous rapid decline of both the plain "American" (cut in half to a miniscule 1.6%) and hyphenated-American (dropping from 43% to 30%) self-identities points to the rapid growth of a reactive ethnic consciousness (cf. Portes 1984; Rumbaut 1994). Furthermore, the measure of the salience or importance that the youths gave to their chosen identities showed that the strongest salience scores were reported for national-origin identities, and the weakest for plain "American" ones, with hyphenates scoring in-between in salience.

Change over time in this context, thus, has been not toward assimilative mainstream identities (with or without a hyphen), but rather toward a more proudly militant or nationalistic reaffirmation of the immigrant identity for the largest groups, and toward pan-ethnic identities among the smallest groups, as these youths become increasingly aware of the ethnic and racial categories in which they are persistently classified by mainstream society. While the results are based on a limited measure taken at two points in time spanning the period from mid to late adolescence, still they go against the grain of a linear assimilation perspective. In any case, "becoming American" for these children of immigrants may well turn out to be a lifelong occupation, itself a suggestion in turn of the importance of applying a contextualized life-course perspective to the analysis of social change and individual identity.

This process of growing ethnic awareness is in turn intertwined with their experiences and expectations of racial and ethnic discrimination. These are detailed in the bottom panel of table 16.1. Reported experiences of discrimination increased somewhat from 64% to 69% of the sample in the last survey. Virtually every group reported more such experiences of rejection or unfair treatment against themselves as they grew older, with the Hmong registering the sharpest increase (to 82%), but about two-thirds of every other nationality in San Diego uniformly reported such experiences. Among those suffering discrimination, their own race or nationality is overwhelmingly perceived to account for what triggers unfair treatment from others. Such experiences tend to be associated over time with the development of a more pessimistic stance about their chances to reduce discriminatory treatment on meritocratic grounds through higher educational achievement. As table 16.1 shows, in both surveys the students were asked to agree or disagree with the statement, "No matter how much education I get, people will still discriminate against me." In 1992, 37% of the total sample agreed with that gloomy assessment; by 1995–6, the proportion agreeing had edged up to 41%. Such expectations of external discrimination on ascribed rather than achieved grounds – and thus of perceived danger and threatening circumstances beyond one's control – have also been found, in multivariate analyses of both the T1 and T2 survey data, to be significant predictors of depressive symptoms (see Rumbaut 1994 and Rumbaut and Weeks 1998).

Still, it is important to underscore the fact that despite their awareness of the realities of American racism and intolerance, most continued to affirm a sanguine belief in the promise of equal opportunity through educational achievement – including nearly 60% in the latest survey who disagreed with the statement that people will discriminate against them regardless of educational merit. Even more tellingly, 63% of these youths agreed in the original survey that "there is no better country to live in than the United States," and that endorsement increased to 71% three years later. Significantly, those most apt to endorse that view were the children of Vietnamese exiles whose families had found a favorable context of reception in the US through a historic refugee resettlement program organized by the federal government. The groups least likely to agree with that statement were those who had most felt the sting and the stigma of racial-ethnic discrimination. Milton Gordon's assimilation sequence, it is well to recall here, ultimately required routine social acceptance and an absence of prejudice and discrimination in the "core society." It takes two to tango, after all – and to assimilate.

Assimilation From What? To What? For What?

As has by now been amply documented, the diversity and dynamics of the "new immigration" to the United States over the past few decades differ in kind, in many respects, from that of the last period of mass immigration in the first few decades of the century. The immigrants themselves differ greatly in their social class and national origins, and so do the American society, economy, and polity that receive them – raising perennial questions about their modes of incorporation, and challenging conventional accounts of assimilation processes that were framed during previous epochs of mass migration. In this respect, the differences in the *historical contexts* of immigration and incorporation themselves need to be taken far more seriously and systematically into account if we are to deepen our understanding of these processes; too often sociological analyses present "structural" and "cultural" explanations in a decontextualized historical vacuum, to their impoverishment. It may be useful to glance briefly backward at the original canonical statement, too often misread and trivialized – the seminal work by Park and Burgess – and see what may still be gleaned from it.

Accommodation and assimilation: A generational divide?

In their *Introduction to the Science of Sociology* ([1921] 1924), arguably the most influential single text in the history of American sociology, Park and Burgess gave the concept of assimilation its classic formulation: "a process of interpenetration and fusion in which persons and groups acquire the memories, sentiments, and attitudes of other persons and groups, and, by sharing their experience and history, are incorporated with them in a common cultural life" (p. 735). They distinguished systematically between "four great types of interaction" – competition, conflict, accommodation, and assimilation – which they related respectively to economic, political, social, and cultural institutions. The distinction they elaborate between accommodation and assimilation is instructive. An *accommodation* (of a conflict, or to a new situation) may take place quickly, and the person or group is typically a highly conscious protagonist of the process of accommodating those circumstances. In *assimilation*, by contrast, the changes are more subtle and gradual, and the process is typically unconscious, so that the person is incorporated into the common life of the group largely unaware of how it happened. Assimilation thus takes place most rapidly and completely in primary – intimate and intense – social contacts; whereas accommodation may be facilitated through secondary contacts, but they are too distant and remote to promote assimilation. Since the nature (especially the interpersonal intimacy, "the great moral solvent") of the social contacts is what is decisive, it follows that "a common language is indispensable for the most intimate associations of the members of the group," and its absence is "an insurmountable barrier to assimilation," since it is through communication that gradual and unconscious changes of the attitudes and sentiments of the members of the group are produced.

The psychosocial mechanisms through which assimilation occurs, a key issue but one addressed by Park and Burgess only in passing, are those of "imitation and suggestion." The end result is not "like-mindedness," but rather "a unity of experience and orientation, out of which may develop a community of purpose and action." Race and place become critical structural determinants of the degree of assimilation precisely insofar as they delimit possible forms of primary social contact; for Park and Burgess, social relations are inevitably embedded and bounded in space, which is why social distance is typically indexed by physical distance and patterns of residential segregation. In sum, an exegesis of their argument compels the conclusion that *accommodation* is the modal adaptation of first-generation adult immigrants, while *assimilation* can become a modal outcome ultimately only for the malleable young and for the second generation, who are like palimpsests, and then only if and when permitted by structural conditions of inclusion at the primary group level.

This formulation underscores the centrality of both the 1.5 and the second generations of children of immigrants as strategic research sites (cf. Merton 1987) for the study of assimilation processes and outcomes. Or perhaps it may be more precise to say that the *family*, albeit an underprivileged social structure in most of our professions, may be *the* strategic research site for understanding the dynamics of immigration and of immigrant adaptation processes, as well as for their long-term consequences. Indeed, immigration to the United States is largely a family affair, and kinship is the basis for longstanding selection criteria built into US immigration law. Haves and have-nots alike, from manual laborers to professionals to entrepreneurs to once well-heeled exiles, immigrant families come in all shapes, and confront dramatically different contexts of adaptation. To make sense of their diversity – and of the complexity of assimilation processes and outcomes that then ensue, particularly among the 1.5 and second generation – we need to recognize from the outset that it makes no sense to speak of a singular immigrant or immigrant family experience.

Often the most insightful statements of what goes on within such families are found in both fictional and non-fictional autobiographical (yet not filiopietistic) tracts written with a perspicaciously nuanced mastery of the new language by children of immigrants (for a selected list see Rumbaut 1997). Why and how? Perhaps because of the emancipatory and innovative energies that marginality, for all and possibly because of all its emotional costs, can release in individuals who come of age between colliding cultural worlds, between centripetal and centrifugal force fields, outside of the routinized social comfort zones that ossify reflection, less bound to worship the idols of any tribe, and who manage to achieve a creative synthesis of insiderness and outsiderness, proximity and distance, aloofness and involvement; perhaps when such marginal and malleable individuals in their formative years, in whose minds those dissonant worlds and memories conflict and fuse (cf. Park 1928), become critically self-conscious of the relativity of intergroup boundaries and "imagined communities" and assimilation processes and can make them an object of sustained inquiry, becoming not so much "citizens of the world" or of "America" as of their own imaginations. We can learn much from that literature – often much more than from academic texts. . . .

References

Alba, Richard D., and Victor Nee. 1997. "Rethinking Assimilation Theory for a New Era of Immigration." *International Migration Review*, 31, 4: 826–74.

Amaro, Hortensia, R. Whitaker, J. Coffman, and T. Heeren. 1990. "Acculturation and Marijuana and Cocaine Use: Findings from HHANES 1982–84." *American Journal of Public Health*, 80 (supplement): 54–60.

Barkan, Elliott R. 1995. "Race, Religion, and Nationality in American Society: A Model of Ethnicity – From Contact to Assimilation." *Journal of American Ethnic History*, 14, 2: 38–75.

Becerra, J. E., C. Hogue, H. K. Atrash, and N. Pérez. 1991. "Infant Mortality among Hispanics: A Portrait of Heterogeneity." *Journal of the American Medical Association*, 265, 2: 217–21.

Butcher, Kristin F., and Anne Morrison Piehl. 1997. "Recent Immigrants: Unexpected Implications for Crime and Incarceration." NBER Working Paper 6067. Cambridge, MA:
National Bureau of Economic Research.

Cabral, H., L. E. Fried, S. Levenson, H. Amaro, and B. Zuckerman. 1990. "Foreign-Born and
US-Born Black Women: Differences in Health Behaviors and Birth Outcomes." *American
Journal of Public Health*, 80, 1: 70–2.

Caplan, Nathan, Marcella H. Choy, and John K. Whitmore. 1991. *Children of the Boat
People: A Study of Educational Success*. Ann Arbor: University of Michigan Press.

Collins, J. W., Jr., and D. K. Shay. 1994. "Prevalence of Low Birth Weight among Hispanic
Infants with United States-Born and Foreign-Born Mothers: The Effect of Urban Poverty."
American Journal of Epidemiology, 139, 2: 184–92.

Eberstein, Isaac W. 1991. "Race/Ethnicity and Infant Mortality." Paper presented at the
annual meeting of the American Sociological Association, Cincinnati, August.

Fuligni, Andrew J. 1997. "The Academic Achievement of Adolescents from Immigrant
Families: The Roles of Family Background, Attitudes, and Behavior." *Child Development*,
68: 261–73.

Gibson, Margaret A. 1989. *Accommodation Without Assimilation: Sikh Immigrants in an
American High School*. Ithaca, NY: Cornell University Press.

Gilbert, M. 1989. "Alcohol Consumption Patterns in Immigrant and Later Generation Mexican American Women." *Hispanic Journal of Behavioral Sciences*, 9: 299–313.

Guendelman, Sylvia, and B. Abrams. 1995. "Dietary Intake among Mexican American
Women: Generational Differences and a Comparison with White Non-Hispanic Women."
American Journal of Public Health, 85, 1: 20–5.

——, J. Gould, M. Hudes, and B. Eskanazi. 1990. "Generational Differences in Perinatal
Health among the Mexican American Population: Findings from HHANES 1982–84."
American Journal of Public Health, 80 (supplement): 61–5.

Harris, Kathleen Mullan. 1999. "The Health Status and Risk Behavior of Adolescents in
Immigrant Families." In *Children of Immigrants: Health, Adjustment, and Public Assistance*,
edited by Donald J. Hernández. Washington, DC: National Academy of Sciences Press.

Haynes, S. G., C. Harvey, H. Montes, H. Nicken, and B. H. Cohen. 1990. "Patterns of
Cigarette Smoking Among Hispanics in the United States: Results from the HHANES
1982–84." *American Journal of Public Health*, 80 (supplement): 47–53.

Kann, L., et al. 1995. "Youth Risk Behavior Surveillance—United States, 1993." *Morbidity
and Mortality Weekly Report*, 44 (SS-1): 1–56.

Kaplan, M., and G. Marks. 1990. "Adverse Effects of Acculturation: Psychological Distress
among Mexican American Young Adults." *Social Science and Medicine*, 31, 12: 1313–19.

Kazal, Russell A. 1995. "Revisiting Assimilation: The Rise, Fall, and Reappraisal of a Concept
in American Ethnic History." *American Historical Review*, 100, 2: 437–71.

Kivisto, Peter, and Dag Blanck, eds. 1990. *American Immigrants and Their Generations:
Studies and Commentaries on the Hansen Thesis After Fifty Years*. Urbana: University of
Illinois Press.

Landale, Nancy S., R. S. Oropesa, and Bridget K. Gorman. 1999. "Immigration and Infant
Health: Birth Outcomes of Immigrant and Native Women." In *Children of Immigrants:
Health, Adjustment, and Public Assistance*, edited by Donald J. Hernández. Washington,
DC: National Academy of Sciences Press.

Markides, K. S., and J. Coreil. 1986. "The Health of Hispanics in the Southwestern United
States: An Epidemiological Paradox." *Public Health Reports*, 101: 253–65.

Marks, G., M. García, and J. Solis. 1990. "Health Risk Behaviors in Hispanics in the United
States: Findings from HHANES 1982–84." *American Journal of Public Health*, 80 (supplement): 20–6.

Matute-Bianchi, María Eugenia. 1991. "Situational Ethnicity and Patterns of School Perform-ance Among Immigrant an Non-Immigrant Mexican-Descent Students." Pp. 205–47 in *Minority Status and Schooling: A Comparative Study of Immigrant and Involuntary Minorities*, edited by Margaret Gibson and John U. Ogbu. New York: Garland.

Merton, Robert K. 1987. "Three Fragments from a Sociologist's Notebook: Establishing the Phenomena, Specified Ignorance, and Strategic Research Materials." *Annual Review of Sociology* 13: 1–28.

Morawska, Ewa. 1994. "In Defense of the Assimilation Model." *Journal of American Ethnic History* 13, 2: 76–87.

Park, Robert E. 1928. "Human Migration and the Marginal Man." *American Journal of Sociology* 33, 6: 881–893.

——, and Ernest W. Burgess. [1921] 1924. *Introduction to the Science of Sociology*. Chicago: University of Chicago Press.

Portes, Alejandro. 1984. "The Rise of Ethnicity: Determinants of Ethnic Perceptions Among Cuban Exiles in Miami." *American Sociological Review*, 49: 383–97.

——, and Rubén G. Rumbaut. 1996. Second edition. *Immigrant America: A Portrait*. Berkeley and Los Angeles: University of California Press.

Rubén G. Rumbaut. 1994. "The Crucible Within: Ethnic Identity, Self-Esteem, and Segmented Assimilation Among Children of Immigrants." *International Migration Review*, 28, 4: 748–94.

——. 1995. "The New Californians: Comparative Research Findings on the Educational Progress of Immigrant Children." Pp. 17–70 in *California's Immigrant Children: Theory, Research, and Implications for Educational Policy*, edited by Rubén G. Rumbaut and Wayne A. Cornelius. La Jolla: Center for U.S.–Mexican Studies, University of California, San Diego.

——. 1997. "Ties That Bind: Immigration and Immigrant Families in the United States." Pp. 3–46 in *Immigration and the Family: Research and Policy on U.S. Immigrants*, edited by Alan Booth, Ann C. Crouter, and Nancy S. Landale. Mahwah, NJ: Lawrence Erlbaum Associates.

——. 1999. "Passages to Adulthood: The Adaptation of Children of Immigrants in Southern California." In *Children of Immigrants: Health Adjustment, and Public Assistance*, edited by Donald J. Hernández. Washington, DC: National Academy of Sciences Press.

——, Leo Chávez, Robert Moser, Sheila Pickwell, and Samuel Wishik. 1988. "The Politics of Migrant Health Care: A Comparative Study of Mexican Immigrants and Indochinese Refugees." *Research in the Sociology of Health Care*, 7: 148–202.

——, and Kenji Ima. 1988. *The Adaptation of Southeast Asian Refugee Youth: A Comparative Study*. Washington, DC: Office of Refugee Resettlement.

——, and John R. Weeks. 1989. "Infant Health Among Indochinese Refugees: Patterns of Infant Mortality, Birthweight and Prenatal Care in Comparative Perspective." *Research in the Sociology of Health Care*, 8: 137–96.

——, 1996. "Unraveling a Public Health Enigma: Why Do Immigrants Experience Superior Perinatal Health Outcomes?" *Research in the Sociology of Health Care*, 13: 335–88.

——, 1998. "Children of Immigrants: Is 'Americanization' Hazardous to Infant Health?" In *Children of Color: Research, Health, and Public Policy Issues*, edited by Hiram E. Fitzgerald, Barry M. Lester, and Barry Zukerman. New York: Garland.

Scribner, R., and J. Dwyer. 1989. "Acculturation and Low Birthweight among Latinos in the Hispanic HANES." *American Journal of Public Health* 79: 1263–7.

Steinberg, Laurence, 1996. *Beyond the Classroom*. New York: Simon & Schuster.

Suárez-Orozco, Marcelo, and Carola Suárez-Orozco. 1995. "The Cultural Patterning of Achievement Motivation: A Comparison of Mexican, Mexican Immigrant, Mexican American, and Non-Latino White American Students." Pp. 161–90 in *California's Immi-*

grant *Children: Theory, Research, and Implications for Educational Policy,* edited by Rubén G. Rumbaut and Wayne A. Cornelius. La Jolla: Center for U.S.–Mexican Studies, University of California, San Diego.

Vega, William A., and Hortensia Amaro. 1994. "Latino Outlook: Good Health, Uncertain Prognosis." *Annual Review of Public Health,* 15: 39–67.

———, and Rubén G. Rumbaut. 1991. "Ethnic Minorities and Mental Health." *Annual Review of Sociology,* 17: 351–83.

Vernez, Georges, and Allan Abrahamse. 1996. *How Immigrants Fare in U.S. Education.* Santa Monica, CA: RAND.

Warner, W. Lloyd and Leo Srole. 1945. *The Social Systems of American Ethnic Groups.* New Haven, CT: Yale University Press.

Weeks, John R. and Rubén G. Rumbaut. 1991. "Infant Mortality Among Ethnic Immigrant Groups." *Social Science and Medicine,* 33, 3: 327–34.

Williams, R. L., N. J. Binkin, and E. J. Clingman. 1986. "Pregnancy Outcomes among Spanish-Surname Women in California." *American Journal of Public Health,* 76: 387–91.

Wolf, Diane L. 1997 "Family Secrets: Transnational Struggles Among Children of Filipino Immigrants." *Sociological Perspectives,* 40, 3: 455–82.

Yu, Elena. 1982. "The Low Mortality Rates of Chinese Infants: Some Plausible Explanations." *Social Science and Medicine,* 16: 253–65.

17 Transnational Villagers

Peggy Levitt

Not very much about Cecilia Jiménez's life changed when she returned to Miraflores after fifteen years in Boston. She had the refrigerator and television she had always wanted. She had enough money to live comfortably because her children sent her something every month from the United States. In general, though, things were pretty much as they had always been. The tin roof on her house still leaked. The family still used an outhouse instead of an indoor bathroom. And she complained that there were still too many noisy children running around her yard in the afternoon when she was trying to rest.

This was not the case for Pablo Liriano. He returned to a new home with air-conditioning and marble-tile floors. He had all the latest appliances in his kitchen. His children played with imported toys and always wore clean, neatly pressed clothing. Community members elected him leader of the MDC's sports committee. But although he had dreamed for years about his return to Miraflores, it was not as easy as he had thought to readjust to village life. He had trouble figuring out how to form new relationships with his neighbors and old friends. They either kept him deferentially at bay or treated him as if his pockets were lined with gold. And though he spent months searching for some business idea to invest in, he was still living off his savings more than a year after his return.

Both Cecilia's and Pablo's experiences speak to the paradoxical relationship between transnational migration and development. Most Mirafloreños have more income and enjoy a more comfortable lifestyle since migration began. They have a better school, health clinic, and water supply. They feel a stronger sense of civic responsibility and a desire to challenge the political status quo. But they have achieved these gains only through the graces of those in Boston. They cannot sustain this higher standard of living on their own. They have lost faith in Dominican values and in their country's ability to solve its own problems. They have become so dependent on the money, ideas, and values imported from Boston that migration has become an integral part of their everyday lives.

Immigrant life also yields ambiguous rewards. Most Mirafloreños work at jobs that pay more than they have ever dreamed of. The new furniture and electronics that fill their homes please them. They are proud of their English-speaking children when they do well in school. On the weekends, they go to the mall, where they can choose from a range of products so vast it is almost unimaginable. But work consumes them. They leave at five o'clock in the morning, return at two, eat, bathe, and then work again until ten at night. Their jobs give them little besides a paycheck. Many live near the bottom of the socioeconomic ladder. Since they often work alone, they generally learn little English and few new skills, meaning they have few opportunities to get ahead. They watch the Anglo world from its margins, not knowing how to negotiate their way in. They feel more capable when they compare themselves to those who remain in Miraflores and diminished when it comes to their dealings in the larger world. Those who regret their choices find it difficult to turn back because so many family members and friends depend on their support.

Transnational migration opens up opportunities for some and constitutes a deal with the devil for others. One factor shaping this relationship is class. Those who start out with more generally finish with more. Mirafloreños who arrived with more education, money, and contacts were more likely to get ahead. Those with more human and social capital could raise families, start businesses, and express political demands across borders more easily. Pablo had completed primary school when he arrived in Boston. He already spoke some English. He had an uncle already living in the city who helped him get a job at a factory where he eventually became a supervisor. He worked hard and learned how to handle himself among Anglos. When he moved back to Miraflores, he did so with more than $50,000 in his bank account.

Cecilia, on the other hand, left Miraflores with much less on her side. She could barely read and write and spoke little English. She did not know anyone who could help get her a "good" job where she had a chance to get ahead. While migration catapulted Pablo into the elite ranks of Miraflores, Cecilia's minimal social and cultural capital meant that for her, migration was like treading water. With some slight improvements, her life upon return was very similar to the one she led before she left.

The experiences of the five Paniagua family siblings further highlight the equivocal relationship between transnational migration and development. They also underscore how status and power differences within households are renegotiated such that norms of bounded solidarity and enforceable trust still hold sway across borders. Teresa Paniagua ascended into the American middle class. She married a small business owner who is a widely respected leader of the Latino community in Boston. Together they run a successful children's clothing store and own several residential and commercial properties in Jamaica Plain. Her children are doing well in school. Teresa sends back money regularly to her mother in Miraflores and generally visits at least once a year. Success has been more elusive for her brother Ricardo. After working two part-time jobs for nearly ten years, he also tried his hand at small business ownership but went bankrupt within a year. He is now trying to put together another strategy for escaping out of permanent part-time employment. Things are looking up. He recently moved to Providence, Rhode Island, where he and his wife both found work easily. He also purchased a home with help from a program for first-time home buyers.

For Anthony, migration has been a disaster. During his first stint in Boston, he and his wife, Ana, lived separately for three years until she got a visa and was able to join him. Together they saved enough money to return to Miraflores, where they opened a small *colmado* and bar. When this failed, after only six months, Anthony returned to Boston, but this time, by the time Ana and their children could follow him, he was living with another woman; he and Ana subsequently divorced. Anthony later got arrested on a drug-related charge and spent three years in prison before being deported back to the Dominican Republic. He now works as an itinerant barber, traveling to Santo Domingo several times a week to cut hair, which is exactly what he did before migrating more than twenty years ago. He also sells hotdogs in front of one of Miraflores's main squares – a newly acquired taste among visitors and nonmigrants alike.

Teresa and Ricardo support their mother, Doña Silvia and, by default, their older sister Concepción, who lives next door. Doña Silvia is satisfied, though there are times when she waits anxiously for her money because she owes so much on credit at the corner grocery store. She and Concepción never complain. They are grateful for their family's support and know that receiving without ever directly asking for anything is their part of the bargain. Last year Teresa and Ricardo finally had enough money to renovate the family's home. They expanded the kitchen and added an extra bedroom, where they stay when they visit. And their youngest sister, Iris, who had been *loca por irse* (crazy to go) ever since she was a teen, finally made it to the United States on her second try at crossing the border. Her fate remains to be seen.

The Impact of Dual Memberships

Though many scholars have abandoned the notion of fixed identities for one that acknowledges their malleability, much research still assumes that individuals have a "master," overarching identity that is fundamentally rooted in a single place. In contrast, transnational community members develop several fluid, sometimes con-flicting identities. Rouse (1991) called the Mexican Americans he studied "bifocal" because their multiple roles enabled them to view the world through different types of lenses simultaneously. Mahler (1998) described the migrant who left El Salvador as an impoverished peasant but eventually earned enough money to buy a house and land back in his village. While he worked in the United States, he hired a man to care for his property, paying him barely a subsistence wage. By asking if he is exploiter, exploited, or both, she brings to light the contradictory roles migrants play and how each repositions the individual with respect to the locus of power in the sending- and receiving-country context.

In the case of Miraflores, and other transnational communities like it, identity construction is even more complex. Mirafloreños simultaneously managed several sometimes-contradictory roles and identities that divided their attachments be-tween their home and host countries. The same individual is not just peasant or owner, leader or follower, exploiter or exploited, but a political, religious, and social actor who might earn her livelihood in the United States, dedicate most of her time toward achieving political goals on the island, but feel equally comfort-able as a member of a transnational Dominican – US church. She is able to maintain these multiple, partial memberships without conflict. One can see such individuals as hedging their bets. A more accurate description is that they belong to and are making a future in two places. They are assimilating and remaining transnational at the same time. Increasing numbers of migrants and nonmigrants now understand their roles of parent, moral compass, breadwinner, and political claims maker as ones they will carry out across borders over time.

The individual and household-level connections that form across borders reinforce and are reinforced by the transnationalization of organizational life. How individuals distribute their loyalty and energy between sending- and receiving-countries depends upon how political, religious, and social life is organized across space. The organizations I described here each manifested their transnational character along different dimensions. All three groups were structured transnationally, though in distinct ways. In the case of the church, autonomous chapters of the same global institution were connected to one another through informal, interpersonal ties between religious and lay individuals. The PRD created a franchise in the United States that was supervised directly by its organization on the island. The Miraflores Development Committee, also an entirely Dominican group, consisted of linked chapters in Boston and the Dominican Republic that were, at least initially, equal partners.

These organizations were also transnational to the extent that they carried out their activities across borders. They each raised funds, recruited members, and carried out strategies and goals in two settings. The Miraflores experience demonstrates, though, that articulating a transnational agenda and acting transnationally to accomplish it does not automatically produce transnational results. While the Catholic Church acted and achieved transnationally, cross-border politics and community development had a much greater impact in the Dominican Republic. The proliferation of political, religious, and community organizational transnational membership challenges the meaning and content of citizenship and participation. More and more residents of contemporary nation-states are non-nationals or hold multiple citizenships. Many aliens enjoy political and social rights previously reserved only for citizens. However, a high proportion of ethnic minority members, regardless of their citizenship status, are excluded, discriminated against, and treated as second-class citizens. Furthermore, naturalization does not necessarily signal a shift in allegiance from one national culture and identity to another. Instead, a number of sometimes-conflicting motivations underlie citizenship choices. These trends take place in a world in which rights can be claimed, demands articulated, and interests organized at multiple levels. It is not just the nation-state that endows individual rights but also international and supranational organizations that guarantee certain basic protections.

A number of researchers convincingly argue that earlier migrants and nonmigrants also sustained strong ties to one another. As far back as 1927, Thomas and Znaniecki observed that nonmigrants held fast to their hopes that migrants would return and take up their original place in their communities of origin. Earlier migrants managed business and real estate transactions transnationally and supervised the emotional affairs of their nonmigrant kin through their letters, telegrams, and visits just as migrants do today. Their loyalty and worth were also measured against the yardstick of how much money they remitted. And migrants' home-country political focus, and the efforts of sending states to perpetuate it, persisted over time, in some cases up through World War II (Morawska 2001a; Foner 2000; Glick-Schiller 1999).

But clearly these relationships have also changed. The strength of migrants' attachments ebbed and flowed depending upon sending- and receiving-country opportunities and constraints. The motivations underlying them also shifted, ranging from mere interest in keeping up with home-country news to actively mobilizing against home-country rule. Morawska (2001b) argues that the New Deal and immigrant-friendly labor organizations encouraged the foreign-born to become more active in US politics. Their transnational attachments did not wane, however, but were "reconfigured through the ethnicization process into new compositions" as their experiences in America gained preeminence in shaping their reference frames (Morawska 2001b, 15–16). They could do so, she argues, because they enjoyed a great deal of flexibility with which to create the meaning and content of their ethnic and immigrant identities, as well as their home-country attachments. The present-day US context endows migrants with even more room with which to invent who they are and gives them access to an even broader range of elements, including transnational ones, to use in identity construction.

Several additional factors reinforce contemporary transnational attachments. Ease of transport and cheap travel increase the intensity and immediacy of these relationships. Unlike the 1920s, when restrictive laws dramatically reduced the numbers entering the United States, migration that began in the 1950s is likely to continue at a steady rate. Because sending states need migrants' remittances, they are allowing expatriates to assert their continued membership from their host-country base. More and more states are putting into place formal mechanisms, such as dual citizenship, the expatriate vote, and various investment incentive schemes, that enable migrants to maintain official, long-term dual loyalties. Finally, conditions in the United States make it more difficult for some low-skilled individuals to assimilate to the same degree as migrants in the past. Institutions like political wards and unions that fostered political integration among earlier groups are on the decline. Economic restructuring during the past two decades narrows opportunities for social and economic mobility. Contemporary migrants, who are more likely to be nonwhites, often encounter discrimination. Transnational practices allow some individuals to compensate for these limits to their economic advancement. They choose to remain transnational to overcome the blocked opportunities they face in the United States.

Increasing numbers of migrants, then, have the ability and the incentive to sustain some combination of long-term formal or informal political, religious, and civic attachments to their countries of origin even as they assimilate into the United States. The rest of this section highlights what Mirafloreños' experiences reveal about the consequences of different membership choices. It also examines the relationship between transnational political, religious, and civil-society memberships. Tens of millions of people are said to live in one state as citizens but be subject to another state where they are also citizens. The 1997 European Convention on Nationality reflected a heightened recognition among governments that dual nationality is not a short-term aberration that should be eliminated, but a growing reality that must be accommodated (Aleinikoff and Klusmeyer 1998). Thus far, dual citizenship has not posed a major threat to the security and stability of the nation-state regime, nor do I expect it will do so in the future. Isolated examples, such as that of the US – Israeli dual citizen Samuel Scheinbein, whom the Israeli government refused to extradite to the United States, where he was accused of murder, highlight some of the practical problems that need to be addressed (Katzenell 1999).

States need to iron out which government is ultimately responsible for these individuals and where dual citizens will vote, pay taxes, be punished for the crimes they commit, or serve in the military. They need to decide where dual citizens will fulfill the duties and responsibilities of citizenship. They need to sort out how best to protect transnational actors' interests without neglecting the needs of those who stay behind. Though some states may do so by disallowing dual membership, it makes more sense to acknowledge that increasing numbers of individuals already live their lives across borders and to create mechanisms to allow them to contribute fully and equally to both polities. The issue is not whether migrants should or should not belong, in some way, to two polities but that, given that increasing numbers live transnational lives, how their rights and representation can be best guaranteed.

If migrants do not have the option to hold dual citizenship, or they decide not to exercise it, they can configure their membership in a number of ways. They can become US citizens but still continue to participate in home-country affairs, or they may opt for long-term resident alien status, participate in civic and religious groups, and exercise their political citizenship rights in their countries of origin.

To date, most Mirafloreños have chosen long-term partial membership in the United States as legal resident aliens in combination with continued full, though often unexercised, membership in the Dominican Republic. As noncitizens, many participated in nonelectoral forums. Membership in church, school, or civic groups allowed them to address their everyday concerns fairly effectively. These kinds of groups successfully pressure government officials to keep the local health clinic open, provide after-school care, or install more streetlights in their neighborhood. Belonging to the Catholic Church also integrated Mirafloreños into a strong, well-endowed institutional network that afforded them some basic protections and representation.

Even the largest, most well-organized groups, however, will not sway politicians if their members do not vote or make campaign contributions. Participation and representation through local-level civic groups still leaves migrants out of the loop with respect to electoral politics. While citizenship cannot predict social and economic status or guarantee that those who hold it will exercise their rights or receive equal representation and protection, long-term partial membership leaves individuals without an electoral voice.[4] It also excludes them from the political agenda-setting process. They have little say over what issues are put on the table and who is invited to discuss them.

Until 1996, permanent resident aliens enjoyed almost the same set of rights and privileges as citizens. Green-card holders could not vote, serve on juries, run for certain elected offices, or hold government positions considered politically sensitive (Schuck 1998). Apart from this, though, they received the same basic protections and benefits as citizens. Legislative reforms subsequently scaled back welfare benefits and food stamps for many legal immigrants. Though some states reinstituted benefits, and Congress restored some benefits at the national level, the tenuousness of social rights without full political membership in the United States is clear.[5]

In some areas, long-term permanent residents have won the right to participate in local politics. Noncitizens can vote in New York City School Board elections and in elections for Chicago school advisory boards.[6] Takoma Park, Maryland, granted noncitizens the right to vote in municipal elections in 1992. For the second time since 1993, non-citizen voting is being considered by the Cambridge, Massachusetts, City Council (McNaught 1999). The New York State Assembly's Task Force on New Americans recommended a similar proposal in 1992 (Sontag 1992). Some level of local political rights has also been granted to noncitizens in a half-dozen European countries since the 1970s (Miller 1989). While these arrangements mediate against complete disenfranchisement, limited, localized citizenship still means migrants have minimal say over state and national issues. They enhance migrants' ability to sustain multiple memberships but allow them to do so only from a position of second-class membership. Furthermore, noncitizen voting rights are still reversible. In fact, the eighteen states that granted some form of noncitizen suffrage between 1789 and 1924 repealed these rights in the face of heightened anti-immigrant sentiments (Jones-Correa 1998).

Given their limited rights as noncitizens in the United States, migrants may turn to their sending states for protection and representation if the need arises. But to what extent can this compensate for partial host-country membership? There are an increasing number of cases in which sending states have intervened on migrants' behalf. In 1998, for example, the Paraguayan government, acting through the World Court, tried unsuccessfully to stay the execution of a Paraguayan national sentenced to death in Virginia (Jacobs 1998). Clearly, some countries are in a much stronger position to advocate for their citizens than others. The Mexican government, for example, is more likely to be successful at protecting its emigrants than smaller, less influential states because Mexico sends such large numbers and plays such a significant role in US economic and political affairs. Countries that send fewer migrants and that are less important economically and politically have much less bargaining power.

And what of migrants' continued political participation in their home countries? The rise in multiple, differentiated memberships is important not only for receiving-country politics but also for the politics of the homeland. Not only do increasing numbers of sending-country politicians campaign and raise money regularly among their migrant constituents in the United States, but migrants' participation in the civil societies of the countries that receive them, and their exposure to the political life around them, also has the potential to transform their political culture and behavior. The social remittances they send back can contribute to local-level reform just as the political skills and resources they bring with them can heighten participation and introduce new ways of doing politics in receiving states.

How migrants' long-term participation without residence will affect Dominican formal politics is difficult to predict. By allowing dual citizenship, and by mandating that all those born to Dominican parents outside the country are eligible for Dominican citizenship, the Dominican government institutionalized the long-term incorporation of its expanding diaspora. It also granted formal recognition to an emerging transnational elite who could challenge traditional power holders (Guarnizo 1998). Before expatriate voting was approved, Dominicans often returned to the island to cast their ballots (Sontag 1997; Rohter 1996a). Thus, presidential candidate José Francisco Peña Gómez acknowledged that "the part they [migrants] play is absolutely decisive, especially in terms of campaign finances." Migrants' influence will increase considerably if and when the Dominican government agrees on an implementation plan for the expatriate ballot.

Though it is too soon to assess the effect of expatriate voting in the Dominican Republic, voter turnout among expatriate Brazilians and Colombians has been low. These numbers may increase as registration and vote casting become easier. The Brazilian consulate in Boston, for example, planned to open three polling stations during the 1998 election to allow migrants to vote closer to their homes and workplaces. If participation remains low, despite efforts to encourage it, this may indicate that migrants are satisfied with their ability to influence politics through their financial contributions or through reciprocal exchanges, such as lobbying host-country legislators in exchange for home-country legislation favorable to migrant interests. It may also indicate that transnational actors are being left out or are opting out of the political process on both sides of the border and that they will remain marginal to politics for the long-term in both settings.

It is important to remember, however, that transnational political outcomes are context-specific. The Dominican community in New York has been much more successful than the community in Boston at acting and achieving transnationally. Dominicans play an increasingly important role in New York City politics while they continue to influence political outcomes on the island. Several factors, unique to the New York experience, encouraged this, including the Dominican community's growing numbers, long history, and ability to form alliances with other racial and ethnic minorities who have served as their guides.

Migrants from larger, more distant countries that have less history of political and economic dependence on the United States are unlikely to play such a significant role in national-level, home-country politics as those from the Dominican Republic. There are a number of reasons for this that a comparison with Mexico brings to light.

First, the high residential concentration among Dominicans in the United States is unmatched by most other groups. Though there are large communities of Mexicans in Texas, California, and Illinois, it is much more difficult to organize them around a united agenda than it is to mobilize Dominicans, nearly two-thirds of whom live in the Northeast.

Second, when 10 percent of the Dominican Republic's 7.5 million residents migrate from several parts of this small country, it affects the nation as a whole. When 10 percent of 90 million Mexicans enter the United States from specific regions, its impact on Mexico is concentrated in just those regions. When many people have particular cities or states in large countries, regionalized political effects, similar to those occurring nationally in the Dominican Republic, are more likely to result.

A number of cases come to mind. Significant numbers have migrated from the Brazilian city of Governador Valadares and the Mexican state of Zacatecas, to name two; both send significant numbers who tend to residentially cluster near one another in the United States. These migrants send high levels of remittances that the sending-country regional economy is increasingly dependent on. The strength of Mexican and Brazilian migrants' influence over home-country regional electoral politics depends upon the distribution of power between federal and state governments. It also hinges on the likelihood that migrants will be granted the right to vote in state or provincial elections. Whether they are allowed to vote or not, however, migrants may still shape nonmigrant voter preferences, encourage reforms, and influence campaigns in their home country region in much the same way that migrants from smaller countries do nationally.

The Miraflores experience also sheds light on how transnational religious affiliations interact with political memberships and shape the relationship between transnational religion and politics. Transnational religious membership involved few costs. Mirafloreños belong to the Catholic Church wherever they reside. Their home-and host-country religious practices often had much in common. Unlike the PRD, which had to forge relationships with a host-country organizational partner to achieve transnational results, migration merely extended and deepened the scope of this already transnational religious institution. Organizational and ritualistic similarities allowed Mirafloreños to circulate fairly effortlessly between religious arenas in Boston and on the island.

Mirafloreños left a church that often substituted for or pressured the state to solve their problems for them. They also brought with them a strong tradition of lay leadership. Migrants' interactions with the church in Massachusetts taught them new skills but also allowed them to introduce their own traditions into the receiving-country arena. They modeled these experiences for fellow church members and by so doing opened up space for greater participation and voice in the receiving church. Because of the ease of entry and exit afforded by these transnational connections, iterative skill transfers and democratization between sending-and receiving-countries are likely to continue. Verba et al. (1995) have demonstrated the role that church-going plays in encouraging civic engagement, but the Miraflores case makes clear that skill development and institution building are processes that occur increasingly across boundaries.

Religious participation also encourages mobilization and voice indirectly because it can result in panethnic participation and cooperation that other groups are unable to achieve. Efforts to create panethnic economic and political coalitions in Boston have met with limited success. The Latino Democratic Committee in Massachusetts, for example, has undergone several waves of active mobilization to near collapse. In contrast, at church, different country-of-origin groups consistently come together around worship and parish governance. Under the right circumstances, these alliances could be mobilized more explicitly to achieve political goals.

Finally, transnational religious membership incorporates migrants into potentially powerful, politically influential institutional networks where individuals can also express their interests and make claims. They are transnational religious members, regardless of their political citizenship. Though migrants' direct ties to states may weaken because of their divided political membership, they are reconnected to the state by virtue of the church–state relationship.

Variations in this church–state relation shape the extent to which transnational religious memberships compensate for or complement partial political membership. Religion has been a catalyst for opening up totalitarian and authoritarian regimes, raising new democratic demands in established democracies, and in building stronger institutions (Casanova 1994; C. Smith 1996). It has also clearly thwarted political change. In countries like the Dominican Republic, where there is a close marriage between the government and the church, religious institutions are unlikely to be effective platforms from which to challenge the state. In countries like Brazil, where the church has a strong history of advocating for the poor, religious participation integrates migrants into an influential, well-endowed organization that can represent them and help them access resources.

How the relationship between religion and politics changes when it is negotiated across borders has to do with the match between sending-and receiving-country churches. At the local level, the direction and impact of these activities depend upon each clergyman's particular vision, how much autonomy he grants his followers, and how much autonomy he is granted by his superiors. In the Miraflores case, some priests have played an active role in community-development efforts. It was parish priests, for example, who convinced the first commercial bank to locate in Jamaica Plain and who fought to convert what had been a French Canadian and Italian national parish in Lawrence, Massachusetts, into a church dedicated to the growing Latino community.

But there are also many cases where the church has done little to raise concerns about social justice despite the growing impoverishment of its members. In their current incarnations, the Boston and Dominican churches are fairly conservative. In contrast, similar transnational ties linking Brazilian Catholics and their sending church bring new members from a much more liberal religious environment into the fold. Depending upon how much freedom the archdiocese grants its new Brazilian parishioners, these differences could act as catalysts for liberalization in Massachusetts. In Brazil, these cross-border ties could make the church more conservative as leaders back away from their social reform agenda and focus on individual spiritual growth.

Community organizational participation is a third way that Mirafloreños exercise dual membership. To date, participation in the MDC has done little to encourage incorporation into US society or to compensate for migrants' political marginalization. In fact, it strongly reinforces their ties to their sending communities and privileges migrant members over those who stay behind. In addition, these activities have not taken into account that transnational villages need transnational development strategies. Community development is not a zero-sum game, in which migrants must rob Peter to pay Paul, but one in which outcomes on both sides are inextricably linked.

Proponents of postnational or transnational citizenship would argue that rights guarantees by the sending or receiving states are increasingly irrelevant because individuals are ensured a set of universally accepted rights regardless of their membership in particular states. There are, indeed, a growing number of examples where extra-state entities bestow rights. In exchange for greater access to Indian and other markets by US financial services corporations, the United States agreed to grant 65,000 visas for professionals entering as temporary workers as well as the continued admission of intracompany transferees. Although mirroring provisions already in domestic law, these guarantees were made in the context of negotiations over the General Agreement on Trade in Services (GATS) and, having treaty status, can be made more restrictive only with the consent of other signatories. The Working Group on Migration and Consular Affairs of the US–Mexican Binational Commission on Migration, which began meeting as an independent entity in 1992, has also become a useful mechanism for bilateral dialogue and for coordinated efforts between Mexican and US officials (Mexican Ministry of Foreign Affairs and U.S. Commission on Immigration Reform 1998).

While I believe we are moving toward a world in which some rights are universally accepted and guaranteed by extra-state entities, there is still a long way to go. States still matter. The institutional mechanisms that guarantee universal rights are weak at best. States regularly disregard international treaties they have signed when it is in their perceived best interest. The United States, for example, ignored the World Court's recommendation to stay the Paraguayan's execution, saying that the court did not have the jurisdiction to order it to do so. Though the UN Declaration of Human Rights was signed more than fifty years ago, a 1999 US State Department report on the state of human rights in the world documents a significant increase in abuses (U.S. State Department 1999). In the interim, more and more migrants sign on to dual, partial memberships that postnational citizenship does not, at present, adequately compensate for.

Variations in Transnational Community Forms

Miraflores exemplifies one type of transnational community, which I call a transnational village, that emerges when large numbers of people from a small, bounded sending community enact their lives across borders. But migrants and nonmigrants create other kinds of transnational social groups through their enduring ties.

Relations between Boston and the sending city of Governador Valadares in Brazil produce a second kind of community. Governador Valadares is a city of approximately 270,000 located in Minas Gerais, one of Brazil's largest states. North Americans came to Valadares during World War II to get minerals for their war efforts. Migration to Boston is said to have begun when mining-company executives brought back young Valadarense women to work for them as domestic servants when they returned to the United States.

An estimated 20,000 Valadarenses have settled in eastern Massachusetts (Sales 1999; Braga Martes 1999). Though significant numbers reside in other, smaller cities in the area, such as Allston and Somerville, one center of the Valadarense community is Framingham, where an estimated 5,000 Brazilians are living. Most work in restaurants, hotels, or cleaning homes, though a good number have started their own small stores and home- or car-cleaning businesses. The Valadares economy depends strongly on *Valadólares* (Valadollars), or migrant remittances, so much so that when the Brazilian government devalued its currency in 1999, Valadares was said to be the only place in the country where the devaluation had a positive effect.

The urban to urban transnational social group linking Boston and Valadares differs from the Mirafloreño transnational village. The strong connection between Valadares and Boston is widely recognized throughout Brazil. That "there is not one house in Valadares that doesn't have family in the United States" is a constant refrain. When one walks through both poorer and upper-class neighborhoods in the city, it is easy to identify the many houses that have been built or renovated with US money. There are strong formal and informal ties between Protestant and Catholic churches in Valadares and those in Massachusetts. Yet not all potential members have joined elites' efforts to create a transnational community. Leaders have laid down a foundation for such a group but, so far, it does not figure large in the everyday lives of ordinary people.

The mayor of Valadares, for example, visited Framingham and several other East Coast cities with large concentrations of Valadarenses in 1997. Just as he visits his constituents in the neighborhoods of Valadares, he said, so should he visit those living in the United States. The publisher of the daily newspaper, *O Diario Rio Doce*, added a two-page section with news and advertising from community members in Massachusetts. The Banco do Brasil, in conjunction with the Mayor's Office, created a Valadares-focused investment fund that pays higher interest rates to those who deposit their remittances. The Federacao das Industrias do Estado de Minas Gerais (FIEMG, or the Federation of Industries in Minas Gerais) mounted a technical-assistance program to help returning migrants set up businesses in Brazil. FIEMG also organized a trade fair at the Massachusetts Institute of Technology to attract recent graduates to return to work in Brazil. There is, however, no specific Valadares–Framingham association equivalent to the hometown associations created by so many immigrant groups. The Brazilian Workers' Party is the only Brazilian political organization that has been at all active in the area.

Unlike Mirafloreños, then, who continue to place a higher priority on staying involved in Dominican affairs, those Valadarenses who participate in politics and community organizations are directing more of their energy toward US concerns. They seem to be travelling a more traditional route toward social and political incorporation, though religious arenas facilitate dual memberships for those who choose them. Thus far, this urban transnational community is constituted primarily by a single class. Though many Valadarenses perceive themselves as being one of many who keep their feet in two worlds, they have largely rejected elites' invitations to express this collectively.

Migration between Gujarat, India, and Massachusetts forms a third type of normative transnational community, one that initially arises from shared geographic ties but gradually matures into a social group based on migrants' common identities and values. In 1990 there were more than 815,500 Indian immigrants living in the United States. An estimated 30,000 Indian immigrants currently reside in Massachusetts, more than half of whom arrived in the 1980s. Many of those living around the city of Lowell are Patidars or Patels, who belong to a subcaste from the Baroda and Anand Districts. Like Indians throughout the United States, they are likely to be college educated (49%), well represented in professional (49%) and technical (47%) occupations, and home owners (63%) (U.S. Census 1992). But there is also a growing number, originally from rural towns and villages, who find blue-collar jobs when they arrive in the States.

At first glance, Patidars might be expected to be weakly united with one another and to be only weakly connected to Gujarat. Though there is a critical mass of Gujaratis in Massachusetts, there are also large communities in New Jersey, California, and Texas. The Indian government and Indian political groups have played a minimal role in reinforcing these ties. But geographic dispersion and limited transnational institutional development are counteracted by the multiple overlapping identities community members share with one another. Larger, more inclusive identities, such as being from Gujarat or belonging to the same caste, are reinforced by membership in smaller endogamous marriage groups of residents from particular towns or religious organizations. The requirements of membership in many of these groups, the values that guide them, and the substantive content of their activities, isolate members from the host society and constantly remind them of their attachments to their home state. In the case of Gujaratis, then, the nature of their transnational normative community may mean strong, continuous ties to Gujarat combined with abbreviated participation in US political and civic institutions.

Indigenous Mexicans in northern Mexico and southern California form a similar normative transnational group. The goal of the Frente Indígena Oaxaqueño Binacional, a coalition of Mixtec-Zapotec groups, is to promote and defend the human rights of indigenous migrants and improve living and working conditions for indigenous migrants on both sides of the border. These groups are said to do better at organizing transnationally than their Mixtec counterparts because their shared ethnicity enables them to mobilize unique cultural and social resources, traditional forms of self-government, and a strong political identity. Their common ethnic ties supersede attachments to particular localities. Since the transnational goals of these indigenous groups are not rooted in tightly circumscribed geographies, people, regardless of their location, are the object of these efforts (Rivera-Salgado 1999).

What other types of cross-border communities does transnational migration give rise to, and how do we explain variations within and among them? What is the relationship between these transnational social groups and broader, diasporic ones? How do migration-generated, place-based, or normative communities compare to the epistemic, professional, or issue-oriented transnational social groups and movements that are becoming increasingly common? What does this tell us about how ordinary people live their lives in this increasingly globalized world? There is much research to be done.

References

Aleinikoff, Alexander, and Douglas Klusmeyer. 1998. Plural Nationality: Facing the Future in a Migratory World. Paper presented at the Conference on Demography and Security, 11–12 December, MIT Center for International Studies, Cambridge, Massachusetts.

Braga Martes, Ana Cristina. 1999. *Brasileiros Nos Estados Unidos*. São Paulo, Brazil: Editora Paz e Terra, SA.

Casanova, José. 1994. *Public Religions in the Modern World*. Chicago: University of Chicago Press.

Foner, Nancy. 2000. *From Ellis Island to JFK: New York's Two Great Waves of Immigration*. New Haven: Yale University Press.

Glick Schiller, Nina. 1999. Transmigrants and Nation-States: Something Old and Something New in the U.S. Immigrant Experience. In *The Handbook of International Migration*, edited by Charles Hirschman, Philip Kasinitz, and Josh DeWind. New York: The Russell Sage Foundation.

Guarnizo, Luis. 1998. The Rise of Transnational Social Formations: Mexican and Dominican State Responses to Transnational Migration. *Political Power and Social Theory* 12: 45–94.

Jacobs, Margaret. 1998. Legal Beat: World Court Orders U.S. to Stay Virginia Execution of Paraguayan. *Wall Street Journal*. 10 April.

Jones-Correa, Michael. 1998. *Between Two Nations: The Political Predicament of Latinos in New York City*. Ithaca and London: Cornell University Press.

Katzenell, Jack. 1999. Israel's Supreme Court Blocks Sheinbein's Extradition. Associated Press, 25 February.

Mahler, Sarah. 1998. Theoretical and Empirical Contributions Toward a Research Agenda for Transnationalism. In *Transnationalism from Below: Comparative Urban and Community Research, Vol. 6*, edited by M. P. Smith and Luis Guarnizo. New Brunswick, New Jersey, and London: Transaction Publishers.

McNaught, Sarah. 1999. Alien Ballot: A Novel Idea in Cambridge: Give Non-citizen Immigrants the Vote. *Boston Phoenix*, 18–25 February.

Mexican Ministry of Foreign Affairs and U. S. Commission on Immigration Reform. 1998. *Migration Between Mexico and the United States: A Binational Study*. Austin, Texas: U.S. Government Printing Office.

Miller, Mark. 1989. Political Participation and Representation of Noncitizens. In *Immigration and the Politics of Citizenship in Europe and North America*, edited by W. Rogers Brubaker. Lanham, Maryland, and New York: University Press of America and the German Marshall Fund.

Morawska, Ewa. 2001a. The New-Old Transmigrants, Their Transnational Lives, and Ethnicization: A Comparison of 19th/20th- and 20th/21st-Century Situations. In *Immigrants, Civic Culture, and Modes of Political Incorporation*, edited by Gary Gerstle and John Mollenkopf. New York: Russell Sage Foundation.

———. 2001b. Becoming Ethnic, Becoming American: Different Patterns and Configurations of the Assimilation of American Jews, 1890–1940. In *Divergent Centers: Shaping Jewish Cultures in Israel and America*, edited by Deborah Dash Moore and Ilan Troen. New Haven: Yale University Press.

Rivera-Salgado, Gaspar. 1999. Political Organizing Across the U.S.–Mexican Border: The Experience of Mexican Indigenous Migrant Workers. Paper presented to the University of California Comparative Immigration and Integration Program Research Workshop, February, San Diego.

Rohter, Larry. 1996. New York's Dominicans Taking Big Role in Island Elections. *New York Times*, 26 June.

Rouse, Roger. 1991. Mexican Migration and the Social Space of Postmodernism. *Diaspora* 1: 8–24.

Sales, Teresa. 1999. *Brasileiros Longe de Casa*. São Paulo, Brazil: Editora Cortês.

Schuck, Peter H. 1998. *Citizens, Strangers, and In-Betweens*. Boulder, Colorado: Westview Press.

Smith, Christian. 1996. *Disruptive Religion: The Force of Faith in Social Movement Activism*. New York: Routledge.

Sontag, Deborah. 1992. New York Dominicans to Vote in Homeland Elections. *New York Times*, 15 November.

———. 1997. Advocates for Immigrants Exploring Voting Rights for Non-citizens. *New York Times*, 31 July.

U.S. Department of State. 1999. 1998 *Human Rights Report*, released by the Bureau of Democracy, Human Rights, and Labor, 26 February.

Verba, Sidney, Kay Lehman Scholzman, and Henry Brady. 1995. *Voice and Equality*. Cambridge, Massachusetts: Harvard University Press.

18 Blood, Sweat, and Mahjong

Ellen Oxfeld

It is a warm August morning in Scarborough, an eastern suburb of Toronto. As I walk along the quiet empty streets lined with rows of two-story brick houses, my thoughts shift from the setting before me to the energetic and densely inhabited streets of Calcutta, where I lived between 1980 and 1982.

Calcutta is a pulsating city, a mosaic of different ethnic, caste, and religious groups. The worldwide fame of Mother Teresa, and other individuals who work with Calcutta's poor, has created a popular image of Calcutta as a sea of poverty and destitution. But while the poor are indeed present in Calcutta, the city is also the commercial, industrial, and intellectual center of northeast India. It is a city of many faces. As the journalist William Stevens wrote: "For a city long pictured as the ultimate urban disaster area, a place of putrefying decay and absolute human misery, Calcutta rises awfully early, works awfully hard and radiates an astonishing amount of energy" (1983).

Chinese Tanners of Calcutta – Remembering the Setting

During the years 1980–2, and again in the summers of 1985 and 1989, I conducted fieldwork in a community of Hakka Chinese who had found a profitable niche in Calcutta's leather industry. The Hakka are a distinctive speech group who live in certain regions of the southeastern Chinese provinces of Guangdong, Fujian and Jiangxi. It is thought, however, that they migrated to south China several centuries ago from the north. Indeed, the word *hakka* means "guest people" in Cantonese, and the Hakka therefore received their name from speakers of the Cantonese language, who consider themselves to be the natives of Guangdong Province (Cohen 1968:247).

A small number of Hakka Chinese immigrants to Calcutta entered into the manufacture of leather during the World War I era. This occupation, considered to be polluting by high-caste Hindus and normally left to untouchables or Muslims, proved to be a lucrative source of income. Although the entire Chinese population of Calcutta consists of no more than eight thousand individuals, the Hakka Chinese now own and operate the vast majority of tanneries there, and their contribution to the Indian leather industry is far from negligible on a national scale. Calcutta is one of three major centers of the tanning industry in India, surpassed only by the cities of Madras in the south and Kanpur in the north.

The Hakka do not comprise Calcutta's entire Chinese population. Cantonese-speaking immigrants from Guangdong Province and immigrants from the central

Chinese province of Hubei have also settled in Calcutta. The Cantonese are known primarily as carpenters, whereas the major business of the small Hubeinese community is the operation of dental clinics. In addition, the Hakka Chinese themselves are involved in other industries besides tanning. They own and operate shoe shops, hairdressing salons, and restaurants. But the tanning industry still engages the largest number of Calcutta's Hakka population, and the Hakka community itself is by far the largest of the three Chinese subgroups.

The Chinese tanning area is situated on the eastern periphery of Calcutta in an area known as Dhapa. Approximately three hundred tanning businesses, the majority employing between five and fifty workers each, are found there. Housed in large concrete buildings of two and three stories, or small one-story structures with tile roofs, these factories are connected by a maze of unpaved, frequently muddy paths as well as open sewers through which the by-products of the tanning process flow. Yet the tanneries in this rust-colored industrial environment serve as both residences and factories for the Hakka Chinese who live and work there.

At the entrance to each factory stand large impressive wooden doors, above which the name of the enterprise is painted in Chinese characters. As you pass through these doors into the main manufacturing areas, you may notice decorative sheets of red paper with gold lettering pasted on the walls. These are popular Chinese proverbs, and most of them – such as *yi ben wan li*, which means that for each unit of currency invested, one should profit ten thousand times, and *huo ru lun zhuan*, the hope that one's goods will rotate like a wheel, in other words, be in high demand – express the desire for business success. Frequently, there is an altar at one end of the factory floor, on which sit such popular deities as Guanyin, the Buddhist goddess of mercy, and Guangong, a god of war, but perhaps more significant, a god of wealth and stores. Images of the spirits of happiness, wealth, and longevity, Fu, Lu, and Su, are also commonly displayed.

Once inside the tanneries, you may notice that in many of them kitchens and dining spaces are placed directly on the factory floors. Chinese women cook in areas adjacent to those where their Indian employees shave pieces of leather or throw rawhides into tanning solutions. Drying vegetables hang beside drying hides. Small children run about the factories, and elderly and middle-aged women often sit outside the large factory doors and gossip. In the early morning, you can see these women, dressed in Chinese pajamas, shopping for food in a market near the center of the district. Meanwhile, Indian laborers deliver rawhides to the tanneries, and the tannery employees themselves, mostly Chamars, an untouchable caste associated with leather work, arrive at the factories to begin their workday. Later in the day, these workers can be seen nailing semifinished pieces of leather to dry on boards under the hot sun.

The tanning area presents a mixed impression. The strong odor emitted by the tanning process, workers sweating under the hot sun, pushcarts, trucks, and machinery all suggest an industrial locale. The children running about while playing and buying snacks from vendors, and the groups of Chinese women, standing or sitting while gossiping in front of the big factory doors, suggest a residential area. The industrial waste, mud, and smell hardly make the outdoor areas a garden spot. Yet the residential quarters within the tanneries are often quite large and amply furnished.

In the living rooms, finely crafted woodwork is highlighted by Chinese wall hangings, usually delicately stitched embroidery pictures of birds, trees, and flowers. The latest rages in high-tech consumer gadgets may also be present (while I was there in 1982, videocassette recorders were just beginning to catch on). The one constant reminder of the community's occupational calling is that leather seems to be everywhere. Not only is leather used for covering chairs, but large pieces also cover the broad wooden beds, creating cool, comfortable platforms for sleeping – and for gossiping, taking tea, and for children's play.

Five Years Later – A Calcutta Chinese Family in Toronto

All the aforementioned images, and even my memories of the stench of tanning, pass through my mind on this particular August morning in Toronto in 1986. Perhaps it is because the Toronto street on which I walk, almost antiseptic in appearance, and without a soul passing by, is at such variance with the tanning area. And yet, the association in my mind is natural, for I am going to interview a man whom I knew from the Calcutta Chinese community.

With a prosperous tanning business back in Calcutta, and two married sons who attend to its daily operation, Mr. Kong now has both the economic where-withal and the time to make fairly frequent trips abroad. This is especially the case during the monsoon season in India, when the tanning business is rather slow (since most tanners rely on steady sunshine rather than expensive automation to dry their semi-finished leather). Every few years, Mr. Kong, his wife, or sometimes both of them, visit their four other children, two married sons and two married daughters, who now live in Toronto.

Mr. Kong is known in the Calcutta community as an expansive talker. He likes to boast that he runs one of the most successful tanning enterprises in the community and to extol the merits of his youngest son, who has taken on a good portion of the responsibility for their business. He complains with equal animation about his eldest son, who he feels lacks talent, is lazy, and does nothing to further the fortunes of the enterprise.

During my initial fieldwork, verbose Mr. Kong naturally became one of the first residents of the Calcutta Chinese community with whom I was able to talk at some length about their lives in India, particularly the histories of their families and businesses. I learned from Mr. Kong how his father and father's brother journeyed to India in the early 1920s, how they became involved in tanning, and how the business, which they started in a bamboo shed, grew and divided among their descendants into several separate factories.

Now, during the summer of 1986, I am conducting further research in Toronto, because a considerable number of Calcutta Chinese have immigrated there. Earlier in the week I telephoned Mr. Kong's son Stephen, whom I had never before met, and I was rather relieved to find out that his parents were visiting, thus saving me the problem of approaching him as a total stranger. I arranged for an interview with Stephen, at which time I also met with his brother and sisters in Toronto; after the interview, we all went out to a famous *dim sum* restaurant. But soon after this excursion, I realized I still had some questions for Mr. Kong himself; hence, the reason for my visit this August morning.

As I enter Stephen's house, I find in progress a small celebration in honor of his son's second birthday. Two lighted candles top a cake. Stephen's parents, wife, and two small children are present, as well as his wife's father and sister, his own sister, and her young son. After enjoying our cake and exchanging pleasantries, Mr. Kong looks at me. Not wishing to forget the purpose of my visit, he says, "Ou Xiaojie [literally, Miss Ou – Ou being my Chinese surname], why don't you ask your questions now?"

I sit down at the table and begin to ask questions, most of which pertain to family and kinship in the Calcutta Chinese community. As had been the case in Calcutta, Mr. Kong seems to enjoy holding court, speaking in Mandarin and sprinkling his remarks with four-character phrases, or aphorisms, which he writes down for my benefit. I have gotten onto the subject of marriage and marriage negotiations in Calcutta, and want to know why the services of a matchmaker are deemed so essential among Calcutta Chinese when people all know one another so well; as in many small communities, there are few strangers. Mr. Kong proceeds to discuss the difficulties and embarrassments that are avoided by not conducting face-to-face negotiations with the family of a potential bride or groom. Then he turns around toward his daughter Sheila, who is standing in the corner of the room, and exclaims emphatically, "She didn't have a matchmaker when she got married, and now look, they can't agree on anything!"

I try unsuccessfully to move the discussion away from his daughter's situation and back to more general considerations, but somehow Mr. Kong continues pointedly returning to his daughter and her marriage. For instance, after more discussion about the merits of having a third party to mediate in disputes, Mr. Kong remarks that in the Calcutta community, matchmakers sometimes intervene in clashes between spouses, helping them to come to amicable settlements. He notes that divorce is practically nonexistent there. "It's not like here," he states acidly, "people get in an argument and the next thing you know they're stirring up a divorce.... They start to talk, and before they talk reason [daoli], they talk law [falu]!"

At times, Sheila also interjects a comment. When I ask about Canada and whether matchmakers are used there, she remarks, "No, we don't use [them] here, it's like in Western countries." In fact, I later discover that this is not always the case, and that some members of the community in Toronto still use matchmakers. But Sheila's defensiveness this morning can easily be understood, for I soon learn that not only is she in the middle of a divorce, but she is also the first emigrant from her community to face such a prospect, and it is the cause of many of her father's pointed remarks this morning.

Much on this trip to Canada annoys Mr. Kong. His grandchildren misbehave wildly in front of him, whereas the presence of a grandfather in the Calcutta Chinese community is usually enough to put a damper on most children's rowdy horseplay. The same grandchildren pay no heed to their elders during mealtimes, simply digging into the food without waiting for a signal to begin from the most senior individual at the table. And now, Mr. Kong's youngest daughter is getting divorced!

Mr. Kong uses a phrase to describe divorce (*hen duibuqi de shiqing*), which roughly means that divorce is "a very rude affair" but really conveys much more. The word *duibuqi* can indicate not only that you have been unfair to someone, but more than that, that you have caused that person to lose face. If you *duibuqi* a person, you've acted in very bad form, stepped on his or her toes. In a sense, Mr. Kong indicates that by getting a divorce, the couple offend not only each other, but their family and community as well.

Indeed, the birthday party this morning symbolizes to me the changes that have occurred after immigration both in his family and among other community members. In Calcutta, birthdays are celebrated every ten years, beginning only when one turns sixty-one. These are large gatherings attended by hundreds of guests and are public testimonials to the standing or the status an individual and his family have achieved over long years in the community. This Canadian birthday party could not be at greater variance with those in Calcutta; it is held in honor of a two year old, and it is small, private, and modest.

Yet although he is dissatisfied because he believes his family in Toronto has abandoned some important principles of proper Chinese living, it is still important to Mr. Kong that at least some of his children settle in Canada. His family, like many others in the Calcutta community, is dispersed around the globe, just as his father and his brother, who left China to come to India, were part of an earlier process of dispersion and resettlement.

Families across Time and Space: Agency, Constraint, and Contradiction

What has prompted the emigration of Mr. Kong's children and other members of their community? To answer this question, we need to understand three conceptually separable, but in fact interrelated, processes: the internal dynamics within their families, their entrepreneurial ideology and practice, and their role as a pariah ethnic group in their host society of India. I focus on the relationship between these three factors – family, entrepreneurship, and ethnic role – in an attempt to understand the dynamics of Chinese families in an overseas and entrepreneurial setting. Such an analysis must of necessity view the trajectories and strategies of families and family members across both time and space, and as such, while I concentrate my analysis on the Calcutta community, I also consider the lives of their predecessors who emigrated from China, and the dispersion of community members to North America, particularly to Toronto.

Studies of immigrant entrepreneurs, including the overseas Chinese, have paid insufficient attention to the connections between the internal dynamics of their families and the exigencies of their host societies. These internal family dynamics and external social structures work together in ways that both constrain and enable ethnic minority entrepreneurs in their particular economic roles. While the social, class, and ethnic composition of these host societies often structure the types of economic activities that such immigrant groups may pursue, members of these groups may also actively manipulate their kinship systems to gain economic advantages in those spheres of activity open to them. Moreover, kinship obligations may limit as well as open up economic possibilities, and family arrangements may themselves change in response to the exigencies of life in a particular host society.

Further, as I show in this study of the Calcutta Chinese and their relatives in Toronto, the underlying ideologies and motivations of such immigrant entrepreneurs are neither straightforward nor simple. First, family relationships often create ambivalence in regard to economic action. Does one work single-mindedly toward a profit or give a break to a relative? Moreover, the entrepreneurial ethic itself is often riddled with contradictory imperatives and evaluations, such as the notion that one can control one's fate through wise investment and decision, and the idea that economic outcomes are ultimately a matter of mere luck.

Indeed, the title of my book refers to just such a contradictory imperative. The reference to "blood and sweat" comes from a phrase that community members frequently quote about hard work. Mahjong, on the other hand, is a Chinese gambling game played frequently in Dhapa. While the Dhapa Chinese condemn all gambling as wasteful when done to excess, they also acknowledge that gambling ironically reenacts some of the central contradictions of the entrepreneurial ethic itself, such as the injunction to rely on one's skills and hard work versus the undeniable factor of luck in one's ultimate success or failure.

On a more general level, I hope through my analysis of Hakka Chinese families in India, their predecessors in China, and their family members in Toronto, to add a new emphasis to the understanding of families in terms of both their spatial and their temporal dimensions. Of course, in any account of human agency or action, time is of paramount importance. As Jean-Paul Sartre observed, cultural behavior is "temporal." It is not simply "past determinations ruling men in the way a cause rules its effects." For "everything changes if one considers that society is presented to each man as a perspective of the future and that this future penetrates to the heart of each one as a real motivation for his behavior" (1963:96). Thus, "our roles are always future, they appear to each one as tasks to be performed, ambushes to be avoided, powers to be exercised, etc." (1963:107). In other words, people create agendas. That these agendas may themselves be the product of a distinctive cultural and social environment should not blind us to the fact that while people are indeed acted upon by outside forces, they respond to these forces with an array of individual, familial, and extra-familial strategies, and these strategies are worked out over time.

The French sociologist Pierre Bourdieu, in a classic work based primarily on his fieldwork in Algeria, has called attention to the importance of time, strategy, and cultural aims in the study of kinship. Bourdieu emphasized the idea that kinship structures and rules, or kinship relations, are used strategically to fulfill "vital material and symbolic interests" (1977:38). Like Sartre, Bourdieu emphasizes the importance of time in the study of social forms; for strategy is nothing less than the playing out of aims and goals over time. Yet his conception of strategy does not ignore the very real fact that all strategies are pursued within existent social frameworks, and that the motivations themselves, the aims and goals which people strategically pursue, are culturally constructed.

This last point is critical. To say that people use their kinship systems in a strategic way does not necessarily imply that all people have the same strategy, or even the same goals. Some writers, Sylvia Yanagisako, for example, have criticized

Bourdieu's approach for ignoring culture, reducing kinship to "rational utilitarian calculation" (Yanagisako 1985:13). Yet people can utilize their kinship systems in pursuit of a variety of goals. And Bourdieu clearly states that kinship fulfills not only "material" but also "symbolic" interests (1977:38).

Most analysts recognize time as an important aspect of social action; space, however, is often given less attention. In David Harvey's words, "Social theories...typically privilege time over space in their formulations. They broadly assume either the existence of some pre-existing spatial order within which temporal processes operate, or that spatial barriers have been so reduced as to render space a contingent rather than fundamental aspect to human action" (1989:205). But, in fact, space both shapes and is shaped by human action.

In the case of Hakka Chinese families like Mr. Kong's, the dispersal of family members over space is part of a strategy through which economic and political risks are contained. But, in addition, as their family histories have unfolded, the nature of space has itself been transformed. While populations have migrated to various parts of the globe throughout history, people have been able to communicate and move with relatively greater speed in recent years. This ability is one aspect of the phenomenon that David Harvey calls "time–space compression" (1989), a phenomenon that involves the breaking down of spatial impediments to more rapid movements of humans and capital.

The increased rapidity and ease with which populations can move around the globe, however, has led to some ironic results. Diverse peoples come into more frequent contact through both physical proximity and satellite communications. But at the same time, they are also able to maintain links more easily with their "home" territories. Thus, it cannot be assumed that movement and contact will lead to a blending of cultures or the loss of a sense of cultural distinctiveness by different groups of migrants. Rather, "time–space compression" may also help engender a sense of cultural distinctiveness. Indeed, the maintenance of distinct cultural identities may be a response to flux and movement itself. Thus, while the Hakka Chinese families who are the subject of this book have *used* space in their strategies, the changing nature of space itself has had implications in their continuing social relations.

In attempting to understand the organization and development of family and firm among Hakka Chinese tanners, therefore, we must think in terms of both temporal and spatial strategies, and in terms of both human agency and social and cultural constraints. Further, these strategies have evolved in the pursuit of goals that are often ambiguous and contradictory as well as clear-cut. I now turn to a brief summary of theories about pariah capitalism and middleman minorities.

Pariah Capitalists and Middleman Minorities

When Stephen Kong decided to migrate from Calcutta to Toronto, one of his first considerations was political security. The Chinese of India have faced political insecurity ever since the Sino-Indian Conflict of 1962, which engendered very bitter feelings in India and therefore had severe repercussions for the small Chinese community. Although the Chinese were not physically attacked by members of the general populace, their Chinese ancestry was used as a basis for governmental restrictions and deprivations of rights. Many lost citizenship; others were interned or deported; still others lost their freedom of unmonitored movement. The experience created a feeling of insecurity among Indian Chinese, and many fear that it might reoccur, or that they might suffer even more dangerous retribution if the political situation between China and India becomes tense again. As Stephen stated, "We look at what happened to the Sikhs [referring to the period when Indira Gandhi was assassinated in 1984, and there were physical attacks and killings of Sikhs by angry and revengeful crowds], and we think we are just as noticeable. If China goes to war with India again, it could happen to us."

In their relative degree of commercial success, and their lack of political power, the Calcutta Chinese resemble a type of social group often referred to as "pariah capitalists" (Hamilton 1978) or "middleman minorities" (Bonacich and Modell 1980). The key characteristics of all such groups are a fair to high degree of economic success coupled with lack of political power and social status. The Chinese of Southeast Asia, the Jews of pre-World War II western Europe, and the Indians of East Africa have all been used by theorists as examples of pariah entrepreneurs. I turned first to literature about these groups in trying to understand the intricacies of the Calcutta Chinese social situation.

The term *pariah capitalist* was coined by Max Weber in the early 1920s, when he wanted to distinguish between a system of *rational capitalism*, which he described as having originated in the West, and the economic activities of alien groups, which he termed *pariah capitalism* (1983:131). For Weber, rational capitalism entailed several specific requirements including systematic accounting of profit and loss, a free market for both goods and labor, and a uniform code of law, uniformly applied (1983:110). Thus, capitalism, as opposed to the one-time pursuit of "booty," entails the operation of "continuing rational capitalistic enterprise: that is, for the constant *renewal* of profit, or *profitability*" (1978:333).

Pariahs, said Weber, are a "hereditary social group lacking autonomous political organization and characterized by internal prohibitions against commensality and intermarriage....Two additional traits of pariah people are political and social disprivilege and a far-reaching distinctiveness in economic functioning" (1978:493). Because pariah groups were kept apart from the rest of civil society, said Weber, they could utilize different standards when dealing with outsiders and insiders (1983:131). Accordingly, Weber held that they were not responsible for the development of rational capitalist practice as he defined it, since it entailed uniformity and universality.

But many subsequent social theorists pointed out that it was precisely among alien populations that trade and entrepreneurship developed first. The economist Karl Polanyi, for instance, suggested that market activity as opposed to reciprocity was unlikely to occur in small solidary communities. Bargaining activity could more easily transpire between groups, rather than within them, because of the nature of the social relationships it entailed. As Polanyi pointed out, "Exchange at fluctuating prices aims at a gain that can be attained only by an attitude involving a destructive antagonistic relationship between the partners" (1957:255).

In many early civilizations, merchants and traders were outsiders, although they worked in the interests of native rulers, helping them to extract taxes from the populace. Most of the traders mentioned by Homer, for instance, were non-Greeks, just as the majority of those written about in the Bible were non-Jews (Jiang 1968:151). Indeed, rulers and merchants often had a relationship fraught with contradictions. Rulers were unwilling to do the "dirty work" entailed in the day-to-day contact with the masses in which merchants engaged. But at the same time, because of their wealth, merchants were a potential threat to ruling powers. When the merchant class was composed of aliens, however, they were easier to control. They lacked a native power base from which they could challenge rulers, and should their actions become menacing, they could be threatened by the rulers with deportation, or deprivations of political rights.

By utilizing a group of aliens as merchants, governments could also maintain greater control over the common folk among the native populace. In nineteenth-century Thailand, for instance, all male Thai freemen were bound by the requirements of corvée labor (Skinner 1957:96). But Chinese were exempt from corvée labor requirements, and unlike Thai agricultural freemen, who were bound to a patron, they could travel freely. This arrangement was most beneficial to the Thai kings. As G. William Skinner points out, Chinese could serve as procurers, traders, and shippers of commercial agricultural products in Thailand, and in lieu of serving as corvée laborers, they were charged a tax high enough to add revenue but not so high as to discourage them from continuing to immigrate to Thailand (1957:97).

The Jews in Poland filled a niche similar to that of the Thai Chinese. When the Jews began to settle in Poland in the twelfth century, no native commercial class existed. In addition, the Polish aristocracy needed tax collectors. In order for Poles to perform these functions, it would have been necessary to liberate the serfs (Eitzen 1968:225). Thus, the Jews were at first welcomed by the Polish aristocracy, although as with most pariah minorities, their welcome did not last forever.

Gary Hamilton cogently defined the nature of pariah capitalism when he said, "The essence of pariah capitalism...is a structure of power asymmetry which enables an elite group to control and prey upon the wealth generated by a pariah group" (1978:4). The most extreme instance of this power asymmetry was that of the Jews in Christian Spain. The Jews were legally the property of the king, who was the sole grantor of Jewish rights and privileges (Hamilton 1978:4).

Of course, pariah capitalism was not the only form of relationship that existed between trading diasporas and host communities. Philip Curtin points out that trading communities, such as those established by the Europeans in Asia from the sixteenth through the eighteenth centuries, actually brought their "trade enclaves under their own military control." And ultimately, "toward the end of the eighteenth century, they had used force so effectively that at least the British East India Company in India and the Dutch East India Company on Java had stopped being militarized trade diasporas and became true territorial empires" (Curtin 1984:5).

Nevertheless, the development of colonialism and international marketing did not put an end to pariah capitalism as one form of relationship between traders and host society. Rather, the nature of connections between pariahs and ruling elites changed from personalized forms, such as that between the Jews and the king in medieval Spain, to contractual relationships between members of pariah groups, who acted as middlemen, and members of the elite. Indeed, as colonialism emerged, the elite who were served by these middlemen were frequently the colonial occupiers. In Indonesia, for instance, Chinese ventured into the interior and bought produce, which they would then sell to Dutch export firms (see Furnivall 1944; Purcell 1965).

Needless to say, such activities did not always endear the pariahs to the native populace, and they have frequently been the targets of mass hostility and resentment. Indeed, one of the difficulties often faced by such groups is that they, rather than the ruling groups which may profit from their activities, are viewed by the poor members of the native populace as their true agents of oppression.

Edna Bonacich has developed this concept further in her analysis of "middleman minorities" (Bonacich and Modell 1980; Bonacich 1973). For Bonacich, middleman minorities are groups that exhibit a number of common characteristics. First, they fill a "status gap" between elites and masses – a fitting example is that of the Chinese of Mississippi, described in a work by James Loewen (1971). The Mississippi Chinese owned and operated small retail stores in rural areas. They thereby engaged in daily and constant contact with blacks, something which white Mississippians were reluctant to do in a highly segregated society. At the same time, the white power structure had an interest in keeping the blacks themselves from entering business. Since the blacks were much more numerous than the Chinese, and had resided in Mississippi for so many generations, they could presumably utilize increased economic resources to threaten the whites politically – something which the small community of immigrant Chinese could not do.

Bonacich points out that middleman minorities often engage in activities that the host society considers to be impure, unholy, or degrading (1973:584). Christians, for instance, were not allowed to lend money, whereas the Jews were bound by no such restrictions. In Thailand, pigs were slaughtered and butchered by Chinese, since the Buddhist Thais regarded such activity as a violation of the Buddhist precept of nonviolence (Skinner 1957:217).

Middleman groups, says Bonacich, often have a "sojourner mentality" (1973:584); that is, they think they will not settle where they are living. They come to the host society to make money, and often "since they plan to return [to their country of origin]...have little reason to develop lasting relationships with members of the surrounding host society" (1973:286). This mentality results in a savings rather than a spending orientation and enables them to accumulate more capital which can be invested in other enterprises (1973:584). Of course, sojourner orientations are often the result of discrimination or persecution by the host society. As playwright and essayist Frank Chin has so powerfully argued:

> We [Chinese in the United States] did not make life bearable here with idealized notions of Chinese culture and a dream of going home rich until an honorable life in America was made impossible. We were fishermen, farmers, shoemakers, cigarmakers, laundrymen, miners all over the West wherever we could go, until we saw that America...was determined to wipe us out. The California laws against entry of Chinese women had been struck down in court, because the Constitution didn't allow states to mess with immigration; that was for Congress to do, and in 1924, Congress did. (1972:62)

Bonacich does not deny that host hostility contributes to the sojourning orientation of middleman groups; what is important for her is that both host hostility and sojourning orientations help to establish another common characteristic of middle-man minorities – a high degree of internal solidarity. Although middleman groups may be "riddled with division and conflict, based on regional, linguistic, political or religious differences found in the homeland," asserts Bonacich, these differences are put aside in the face of the host society (1973:586). In a work coauthored with John Modell, she goes on to state that while such solidarity may enable middlemen to cooperate efficiently economically, it also opens them up to even greater attack from host populations, who see them as clannish, disloyal, and as draining the host society of money (Bonacich and Modell 1980:20).

Bonacich's final points about middleman minorities concern the nature of their enterprises. It is the family firm, she says, that typifies the economic activity of middleman minorities. Furthermore, she insists that industrial entrepreneurship is rare among middlemen groups, since it requires a long-term investment in nonmo-vable assets, preventing such entrepreneurs from leaving their host society if cir-cumstances demand it (1973:585).

Because of their involvement with industrial entrepreneurship, an activity which requires them to invest in a great deal of nonliquid wealth, the Calcutta Chinese deviate from the patterns delineated by Bonacich and others. Yet they retain many other characteristics of the groups described in this chapter. Like pariah capitalists, they lack political security and work in occupations denigrated by the host society; in this case, jobs associated with the lowest rungs of the Hindu caste system. And, like middleman minorities, they run family businesses and display ambivalence, even antagonism, toward their host society. Furthermore, although industrial entre-preneurship might be a barrier to geographical mobility in some cases, this has not been the situation with the Calcutta Chinese. As illustrated by Mr. Kong's family, this group has been able to achieve a high degree of movement and mobility through the use of ties to and assistance rendered by family and kin.

It is in this area, the analysis of kinship and family, that theories about pariah capitalism and middleman minorities tell us little. Bonacich, for example, empha-sizes the fact that middleman businesses tend to be family businesses. But she gives no details about how differing kinship systems might influence either the organiza-tion of these businesses or the strategies used by group members in the host society. A kinship system in which only one heir inherits, for instance, would certainly have different implications for the organization of family firms than one in which all sons inherit equally. And yet, discussion of the effects of particular kinship structures on middleman minority firms has not been prevalent in the literature.[3]

Therefore, though I found middleman minority theory useful in explaining the status and position of a certain type of minority group, I had to look elsewhere for an analysis of how the microdynamics within families articulate with and affect the ethnic roles that middleman minorities play. One work that does address some of these problems is James L. Watson's study of a Chinese lineage village in Hong Kong and its emigrants in England (1975). Watson not only analyzes the effects of Chinese lineage organization on patterns of emigration to Britain but also examines the use of lineage ties in the villagers' new economic niche in England – the restaurant business. Watson's book, however, is concerned primarily with the effects of emigration on the home community. For at the time of his research, the majority of emigrants studied by Watson still intended to return to Hong Kong. The Chinese of Calcutta, on the other hand, dispensed with plans to return permanently to their home communities in China after the revolution of 1949. For whatever their political allegiances might be, most seem to agree that their standard of living is higher as overseas Chinese entrepreneurs than it is likely to be in China for the foreseeable future. Accordingly, I focus not on the communities of origin in an indigenous Chinese setting, but on the community in Calcutta, where the Chinese are an ethnic minority. . . .

Understanding the dynamics within Calcutta Chinese families is absolutely critical to understanding both the development of their businesses and the strategies adopted by individuals and families in their host society. In Stephen Kong's case, for instance, familial factors have been as important as political ones in his decision to emigrate. In a family structure in which all brothers inherit equally, there is always a chance that even a prosperous enterprise will be less lucrative when the business is split up among five or more brothers. Some brothers may have to leave if the enterprise is to provide any kind of a living for those who remain behind. Although Stephen's family is prosperous, his emigration still lessens the economic risks of keeping all sons together in one business. And it does so while also providing an overseas connection, a connection which other family members can utilize if they later need to emigrate because of changes in India's political climate.

References

Bonacich, Edna. 1973. A Theory of Middleman Minorities. *American Sociological Review* 38 (October):583–94.

Bonacich, Edna, and John Modell. 1980. *The Economic Basis of Ethnic Solidarity.* Berkeley: University of California Press.

Bourdieu, Pierre. 1977. *Outline of a Theory of Practice.* Cambridge: Cambridge University Press.

Chin, Frank. 1972. Confessions of the Chinatown Cowboy. *Bulletin of Concerned Asian Scholars* 4 (Fall):58–70.

Cohen, Myron. 1968. The Hakka or 'Guest People': Dialect as a Sociocultural Variable in Southeastern China. *Ethnohistory* 15(3):237–92.

Curtin, Philip. 1984. *Cross-Cultural Trade in World History.* Cambridge: Cambridge University Press.

Eitzen, D. Stanley. 1968. Two Minorities: The Jews of Poland and the Chinese of the Philippines. *Jewish Journal of Sociology* 10:221–40.

Furnivall, J. S. 1944. *Netherlands India: A Study of Plural Economy.* New York: Macmillan.

Hamilton, Gary. 1978. Pariah Capitalism: A Paradox of Power and Dependence. *Ethnic Groups* 2:1–15.

Harvey, David. 1989. *The Condition of Postmodernity: An Enquiry into the Origins of Cultural Change.* New York: Basil Blackwell.

Jiang, Joseph P. L. 1968. Toward a Theory of Pariah Entrepreneurship. In *Leadership and Authority: A Symposium,* ed. Gehan Wijeyewarndene, 147–162. Singapore: University of Malaya Press.

Loewen, James W. 1971. *Mississippi Chinese: Between Black and White.* Cambridge, Mass.: Harvard University Press.

Polanyi, Karl. 1957. The Economy as Instituted Process. In *Trade and Market in the Early Empires*, ed. Karl Polanyi, Conrad Arensberg, and Harry Pearson, 243–70. Chicago: Henry Regnery.

Purcell, Victor. 1965. *The Chinese in Southeast Asia*. London: Oxford University Press.

Sartre, Jean-Paul. 1963. *Search for a Method*. New York: Vintage.

Skinner, G. William. 1957. *Chinese Society in Thailand: An Analytical History*. Ithaca: Cornell University Press.

Stevens, William K. 1983. Calcutta, Symbol of Urban Misery, Won't Give Up. *The New York Times*, 5 June, sec. 1, p. 10.

Watson, James L. 1975. *Emigration and the Chinese Lineage*. Berkeley: University of California Press.

Weber, Max. 1978. *Max Weber: Selections in Translation*. Ed. W. G. Runciman. Trans. E. Matthews. Cambridge: Cambridge University Press.

——. 1983 [1920–21]. *Max Weber on Capitalism, Bureaucracy, and Religion*. Ed. Stanislav Andreski. London: Allen and Unwin.

Yanagisako, Sylvia Junko. 1985. *Transforming the Past: Tradition and Kinship among Japanese Americans*. Stanford: Stanford University Press.

Part VII

Boundaries, Citizenship, and Identity

INTRODUCTION TO PART VII

The final decades of the twentieth century witnessed important political developments that profoundly altered established relationships between ethnic groups and states. Three examples of these changes can be seen in the changing political boundaries in Europe, the Americas, and the former republics of the Soviet Union. The unification of the European Community, the fragmentation of the Soviet empire, and the continuous migration into the United States, all raise fundamental questions concerning the meaning of citizenship and the types of identity that are becoming salient in these three regions.

Yasemin Soysal considers how the arrival of guestworkers, refugees, and ex-colonial migrants has transformed the debate about citizenship in Europe. This has occurred at the same time as the structure of the typical European state was being transformed by moves towards continental economic and political unification. Rights that had previously been bestowed on citizens by virtue of their membership in a specific state have been slowly expanded to apply to individuals on a more universal basis. This, Soysal argues, requires us to construct a new postnational model of membership to capture the fluidity and flexibility of contemporary European society. In such a situation, dual citizenship is increasingly common and political participation and access to welfare rights is guaranteed for all people living within a country's borders. While the growth of supranational institutions and transnational laws can be seen in the post-war European experience, this is by no means an inevitable trend. In many other parts of the world, particularly in states undergoing the process of nation building, the insistence on exclusive citizenship rights may be working in the opposite direction.

A further set of issues are raised by the developments in the city of Miami, particularly since the Cuban Revolution in 1959. As Portes and Stepick explain, Miami represents a very different experience from those other cities, like Chicago and New York, that played such an important part in the development of earlier patterns of American race and ethnic relations. The theories developed by Du Bois, Park, and Weber were set against a background of economically-driven migrants competing in the industrial and transportational hubs of the North-East and Mid-West. In contrast the city of Miami, created almost accidentally as a tourist resort and gateway to the Caribbean, was crucially shaped by the Cold War politics of the 1960s. The arrival of Cuban émigrées fleeing the Marxist regime of Fidel Castro was to transform the politics and economy of Miami and dominate the other major communities of Anglos and Blacks. Furthermore, the rise of an ethnic enclave economy and the strident anti-Castro politics of an exiled community – seen in the Elian Gonzalez case during the millennium year – raise important questions about the long-term impact of this politically inspired migration. What will happen when Castro finally goes and will the younger generation of Cuban Americans turn out to be more American than Cuban?

A third major development, resulting from the momentous political changes of the latter part of the twentieth century, concerns the future of the "Russian diaspora." Igor Zevelev sets out to explain why this potentially explosive situation did not degenerate into ethnic cleansing and bloody reprisals. While there are many examples of tough rhetoric from the Russian leadership little action was taken to support this stance. The problems of economic decline and military disorganization in the post-Soviet era have diverted priorities away from the plight of the diaspora communities. Secondly, Russia's need to prevent ethnic secessionist movements within the Russian federation acted as a major restraint on openly encouraging irredentist activities among the Russians abroad. Furthermore, the great diversity of circumstances faced by the many diaspora communities from societies as different as Tadjikistan and Latvia; the lack of organization and solidarity among groups who previously enjoyed a dominant social and political position; and the overwhelming capacity of the Russian state to retaliate should their co-ethnics face genuine persecution, acted as a major brake on the escalation of intergroup violence. The extent to which these circumstances will persist and the long-term stability of the complex ethnic mix in the former states of the Soviet Union, as well as within the Russian Federation, are questions of the utmost importance. Experience in the Balkans, and in the protracted and bloody wars in Chechnya, suggests just how dangerous the current situation remains.

19 Toward a Postnational Model of Membership

Yasemin Nuhoğlu Soysal

Guestworkers and Citizenship: Old Concepts, New Formations

The postwar era is characterized by a reconfiguration of citizenship from a more particularistic one based on nationhood to a more universalistic one based on personhood. Historically, citizenship and its rights and privileges have expanded in waves, with changes in how the national public is defined in relation to class, gender, and age (Marshall 1964; Ramirez 1989; Turner 1986a, 1986b). Each wave has represented the entry of a new segment of population into the national polity; workers, women, and children were eventually included in the definition of citizenship. This universalizing movement has made exclusions based on any criteria of ascribed status incompatible with the institution of citizenship (Turner 1986a:92–100). The expansion, however, was limited from within: the rights of men, women, and children, as individuals, were defined with respect to their membership in a particular nation-state. In that sense, the expansion of rights protracted and reinforced particularities ordained by national attributes. In contrast, in the postwar era, an intensified discourse of personhood and human rights has rent the bounded universality of national citizenship, generating contiguities beyond the limits of national citizenry. Accordingly, contemporary membership formations have superseded the dichotomy that opposes the national citizen and the alien, by including populations that were previously defined as outside the national polity. Rights that used to belong solely to nationals are now extended to foreign populations, thereby undermining the very basis of national citizenship. This transformation requires a new understanding of citizenship and its foundation.

Recent studies recognize the disparity between the national citizenship model and the membership of postwar migrants in European host countries. Tomas Hammar (1986, 1990a), for instance, argues that foreigners who are long-term residents of European states, and who possess substantial rights and privileges, should be given a new classification, and suggests the term *denizen*. In the same vein, Brubaker (1989a, 1989b) maintains that the membership forms generated by postwar immigration deviate from the norms of classical nation-state membership, which he views as "egalitarian, sacred, national democratic, unique, and socially consequential." In acknowledging these deviations, he offers a model of "dual membership" organized as concentric circles: an inner circle of citizenship, based on nationality, and an outer circle of denizenship, based on residency. Both Hammer and Brubaker contend that, in regard to rights of immigrants, the crucial determinant is residence, not citizenship.

Heisler and Heisler (1990) attribute the emergence of the denizenship status to the existence of a "mature" welfare state. They suggest that the elaborate redistribution machinery and the "ethos of equality" of the welfare state have led to the widening of the scope of citizenship in European societies. However, there is nothing inherent about the logic of the welfare state that would dictate the incorporation of foreigners into its system of privileges. Welfare states are also conceived as "compelled by their logic to be closed systems that seek to insulate themselves from external pressures and that restrict rights and benefits to members" (Freeman 1986: 51; see also Leibfried 1990). Not that this logic of closure is empirically realized in the world of welfare states. Many of the most advanced welfare states, especially those that are small in size and trade-dependent, have open economies that operate as part of an increasingly integrated global economy (Katzenstein 1985; Cameron 1978). Nevertheless, welfare states are expected to operate with the assumption of closure: the effective distribution of welfare among citizens and maintenance of high standards of benefits and services require the exclusion of noncitizens (see Schuck and Smith 1985; Walzer 1983). As such, the welfare state is universal only within national boundaries.

The denizenship model depicts changes in citizenship as an expansion of scope on a *territorial* basis: the principle of domicile augments the principle of nationality. Denizens acquire certain membership rights by virtue of living and working in host countries. Within this framework, denizenship becomes an irregularity for the nation-state and its citizenry, that should be corrected in the long-run (see Heisler and Heisler 1990, and the articles in Brubaker, ed., 1989 and Layton-Henry 1990).

In construing changes in citizenship as territorial, these studies remain within the confines of the nation-state model. They do not recognize the changing basis and legitimacy of membership or the recent, fundamental changes in the relationship between the individual, the nation-state, and the world order. As I see it, the incorporation of guestworkers is no mere expansion of the scope of national citizenship, nor is it an irregularity. Rather, it reveals a profound transformation in the institution of citizenship, both in its institutional logic and in the way it is legitimated. To locate the changes, we need to go beyond the nation-state.

A Model for Postnational Membership

Time period

The modern history of citizenship begins with the French Revolution. Although the idea of national citizenship emerged at the time of the Revolution, the realization of this particular form of membership occurred much later. Only quite recently has national citizenship become a powerful construct. The classical instruments for creating a national citizenry, the first compulsory education laws and universal (male) suffrage acts, were not enacted before the mid-nineteenth century (Ramirez and Soysal 1989; Soysal and Strang 1989). Moreover, construction of the dichotomy between national citizens and aliens, through the first immigration and alien acts, and made visible in the introduction of passports, identity cards, and visas, did not take place until as late as the First World War.

Table 19.1   Comparison of national and postnational models of membership

Dimension	Model I: National Citizenship	Model II: Postnational Membership
Time period	19th to mid-20th centuries	Postwar
Territorial	Nation-state bounded	Fluid boundaries
Congruence between membership and territory	Identical	Distinct
Rights/privileges	Single status	Multiple status
Basis of membership	Shared nationhood (national rights)	Universal personhood (human rights)
Source of legitimacy	Nation-state	Transnational community
Organization of membership	Nation-state	Nation-state

The reconfiguration of citizenship is mainly a postwar phenomenon. Even as the nation-state and its membership became authorized and taken-for-granted, its classificatory premises were beginning to be contested. By the 1960s, the classical model of nation-state membership was loosening its grip on the Western world, while consolidation of national polity and citizenship was an impassioned item on the agenda of many countries in Africa and Asia. The increasing flow of goods and persons and the large magnitude of labor migrations after World War II have facilitated this process.

Territorial dimension

The classical model is nation-state bounded. Citizenship entails a territorial relationship between the individual and the state (Bendix 1977; Weber 1978). It postulates well-defined, exclusionary boundaries and state jurisdiction over the national population within those boundaries. The model thus implies a congruence between membership and territory: only French nationals are entitled to the rights and privileges the French state affords – nobody else.

In the postnational model, the boundaries of membership are fluid; a Turkish guestworker can become a member of the French polity without French citizenship. By holding citizenship in one state while living and enjoying rights and privileges in a different state, guestworkers violate the presumed congruence between membership and territory. The growing number of dual nationality acquisitions further formalizes the fluidity of membership.

The fluid boundaries of membership do not necessarily mean that the boundaries of the nation-state are fluid. Neither does it imply that the nation-state is less predominant than before. Indeed, the nation-states, still acting upon the national model – since their existence is predicated on this model – constantly try to keep out foreigners by issuing new aliens laws and adopting restrictive immigration policies. However, these continued attempts testify that European states have not succeeded in controlling the influx of foreigners. In particular, such measures have failed to prevent migratory flows justified on humanitarian grounds – political asylum and family unification, two major sources of persisting immigration to European countries.

Rights and privileges

The classic order of nation-states expresses formal equality in the sense of uniform citizenship rights. Citizenship assumes a single status; all citizens are entitled to the same rights and privileges. The postnational model, on the other hand, implies multiplicity of membership – a principal organizational form for empires and city states. As we have seen in the case of guestworkers, the distribution of rights among various groups and citizens is not even. In the emerging European system, certain groups of migrants are more privileged than others: legal permanent residents, political refugees, dual citizens, and nationals of common market countries.

In earlier polities, multiplicity of membership was also a given, but inequality was considered a "natural" characteristic of social order. Differential membership status, such as that of slaves, was thus constructed as part of the formal definition of the polity. Modern polities, however, claim a uniform and universal status for individuals. As Turner (1986a:133) comments, in the modern polity "the particularistic criteria which define the person become increasingly irrelevant in the public sphere." What makes the case of the guestworker controversial is that it violates this claim for unitary status. Rendering differential status unjustifiable within the framework of universalistic personhood, the modern polity encourages a climate for diverse claims to and further expansion of rights.

Basis and legitimation of membership

In the classical model, shared nationality is the main source of equal treatment among members. Citizenship invests individuals with equal rights and obligations on the grounds of shared nationhood. In that sense, the basis of legitimacy for individual rights is located within the nation-state.

However, guestworker experience shows that membership and the rights it entails are not necessarily based on the criterion of nationality. In the postnational model, universal personhood replaces nationhood; and universal human rights replace national rights. The justification for the state's obligations to foreign populations goes beyond the nation-state itself. The rights and claims of individuals are legitimated by ideologies grounded in a transnational community, through international codes, conventions, and laws on human rights, independent of their citizenship in a nation-state. Hence, the individual transcends the citizen. This is the most elemental way that the postnational model differs from the national model.

Universal personhood as the basis of membership comes across most clearly in the case of political refugees, whose status in host polities rests exclusively on an appeal to human rights. Refugees are in essence stateless (some carry a United Nations passport) but are nonetheless still protected and granted rights as individuals. Similarly, the most universalized aspects of citizenship are those immediately related to the person – civil and social rights – which are often the subject of international conventions and discourse. These rights are more commonly secured in international codes and laws, and they permeate national boundaries more easily than universal political rights that still imply a referential proximity to national citizenship.

Organization of membership

While the basis and legitimation of membership rights have shifted to a transnational level, membership itself is not really organized in a new scheme. In both models, the responsibility of providing and implementing individual rights lies with national states. In other words, one still has to go through, for instance, the German, British, or French welfare system. The state is the immediate guarantor and provider, though now for "every person" living within its borders, noncitizen as well as citizen. Actually, the very transnational normative system that legitimizes universal personhood as the basis of membership also designates the nation-state as the primary unit for dispensing rights and privileges (Meyer 1980).

This is critical to explaining why residency in a state is consequential in securing various rights. The world is still largely organized on the basis of spatially configured political units; and topographic matrixes still inform the models and praxis of national and international actors. Hence the nation-state remains the central structure regulating access to social distribution. The material realization of individual rights and privileges is primarily organized by the nation-state, although the legitimacy for these rights now lies in a transnational order.

Transnational Sources of Membership

How can we account for the manifest changes in national citizenship, that celebrated and stubborn construction of the modern era? As it stands, postnational membership derives its force and legitimacy from changes in the transnational order that defines the rules and organization of the nation-state system. I regard two interrelated lines of development as crucial in explaining the reconfiguration of citizenship.

The first one concerns a transformation in the organization of the international state system: an increasing interdependence and connectedness, intensified world-level interaction and organizing, and the emergence of transnational political structures, which altogether confound and complicate nation-state sovereignty and jurisdiction (Abu-Lughod 1989a, 1989b; Boli 1993; Meyer 1980; Robertson 1992). I refer not only to growth in the volume of transactions and interactions, which, in relative terms, has not changed significantly over the last century (Thomson and Krasner 1989). More important are qualitative changes in the intensity of these interactions, and their perception by the parties involved.

In the postwar era, many aspects of the public domain that used to be the exclusive preserve of the nation-state have become legitimate concerns of international discourse and action. The case of guestworkers clearly demonstrates this shift. The host states no longer have sole control over migrant populations. The governments of the sending countries and extranational organizations of various kinds also hold claims *vis-à-vis* these populations, in regard to their lives, education, welfare, family relations, and political activities. A dense set of interactions facilitated by inter- and transnational market and security arrangements (NATO, the EC, and the UN system) constrain the host states from dispensing with their migrant populations at will. In fact, this system not only delegitimizes host state actions that attempt to dispense with foreigners; it obliges the state to protect them.

This is a different picture than that of nineteenth-century conceptions of the international system, which assume a world of discrete nation-states with exclusive sovereignty over territory and population. In the postwar period, the nation-state as a formal organizational structure is increasingly decoupled from the locus of legitimacy, which has shifted to the global level, transcending territorialized identities and structures. In this new order of sovereignty, the larger system assumes the role of defining rules and principles, charging nation-states with the responsibility to uphold them (Meyer 1980, 1994). Nation-states remain the primary agents of public functions, but the nature and parameters of these functions are increasingly determined at the global level.

The intensification and connectedness of the global system do not necessarily signal that nation-states are organizationally weaker or that their formal sovereignty is questioned. Rather, it refers to the explicitness of global rules and structures, and the increasing invocation of these rules. In that sense, nation-states, as authorized actors, function concurrently with inter-and transnational normative structures, ordering and organizing individuals' lives.

The second major development is the emergence of universalistic rules and conceptions regarding the rights of the individual, which are formalized and legitimated by a multitude of international codes and laws. International conventions and charters ascribe universal rights to persons regardless of their membership status in a nation-state. They oblige nation-states *not* to make distinctions on the grounds of nationality in granting civil, social, and political rights. The Universal Declaration of Human Rights (1948) unequivocally asserts that "all beings are born free and equal in dignity and rights, independent of their race, color, national or ethnic origin." The International Covenant on Civil and Political Rights (1966) further imposes a responsibility on the state to respect and ensure the rights of "all individuals within its territory and subject to its jurisdiction" (Goodwin-Gill, Jenny, and Perruchoud 1985:558). The European Convention on Human Rights (1950) expounds almost identical provisions, with further protection against the collective expulsion of aliens. Both the Universal Declaration of Human Rights and the European Convention have been incorporated into the constitutions and laws of many countries.

In addition to these principal codes of human rights, many aspects of international migration, including the status of migrant workers and their particular rights, have been elaborated and regularized through a complex of international treaties, conventions, charters, and recommendations. Some of these instruments originated in the early 1950s, at the onset of largescale labor migration. Over time, their span has expanded to include entry and residence, the rights to choice and security of employment, working conditions, vocational training and guidance, trade-union and collective bargaining rights, social security, family reunification, education of migrant children, and associative and participatory rights, as well as individual and collective freedoms. These conventions differ in scope. Some have universal application; others are country-specific. Nonetheless, they all aim to set standards for the "equitable" treatment of migrants and the elimination of disparities between nationals and migrants of different categories.

The conventions concluded under the aegis of the International Labor Office (ILO) and the Council of Europe are especially noteworthy. According to the ILO Convention of 1949, the contracting states agree to treat migrant workers "without discrimination in respect of nationality, race, religion, or sex" regarding employment, conditions of work, trade union membership, collective bargaining, and accommodation (ILO n.d.:2). The 1975 convention goes further, promoting the social and cultural rights of migrant workers and their families, in addition to provisions strictly concerned with labor. It explicitly states that the participating countries will take all steps to assist migrant workers and their families "to maintain their own culture" and to provide for their children "to learn their own mother tongue" (ILO 1986:7).

In a similar vein, the 1955 Convention of the European Council on Establishment requires the contracting parties "to treat the nationals of the other contracting states on a basis of equality and to secure for them the enjoyment of civil rights...[and] the same economic rights as are possessed by nationals of the state in which the alien is established" (Plender 1985:3). Later conventions of the Council (1961, 1977) introduce provisions regarding freedom of association and information, residence and work permits, social security, social and medical assistance, and family reunification. More recently, the Council has given priority to extending the lists of individuals' rights, specifically to include further rights in the cultural and political spheres. The Council organizes meetings and conferences to promote cultural rights and make national and local authorities aware of "specifities" of minorities, both native and foreign.

More generally, the United Nations has produced a series of instruments with implications for international migration and migrants. The UNESCO Declaration on Race and Racial Prejudice (1978) extends provisions for the cultural rights of migrants – the right to be different, to have one's cultural values respected, and to receive instruction in one's mother tongue. The United Nations convention on the Protection of the Rights of All Migrant Workers and Their Families, adopted in 1990, aims to establish universal standards that transcend national definitions of foreigners' status. The convention guarantees minimum rights to every migrant, including women and undocumented aliens and their families (see *International Migration Review* 1991). In doing so, it constructs the category of "migrant worker," including such subcategories as "seasonal worker," and "frontier worker," as a universal status with legitimate rights. The ILO and the European Council also have provisions dealing specifically with illegal aliens and their protection (Niessen 1989).

Lastly, political refugees are protected by a set of international legal instruments designed to ensure their rights. According to the Geneva Convention on the Legal Status of Refugees (1951), persons shall not be forced to return to their country of origin if they have a "well-founded fear of persecution" for reasons of race, religion, nationality, membership of a particular social group or political opinion. The Convention further guarantees treatment in the country of asylum equal with that of nationals in regard to religious freedom, acquisition of property, rights of association, and access to courts and public education (Plender 1985).

The multitude and scope of these instruments are impressive. The rights defined and codified assure not just the economic, civil, and social rights of individual migrants – membership rights, in Marshall's terms – but also the cultural rights of migrant groups as collectivities. Within this context, the collective rights of foreigners – the right to an ethnic identity, culture, and use of one's native tongue – emerge as a locus of international legal action.

The most comprehensive legal enactment of a transnational status for migrants is encoded in European Communities law. Citizenship in one EC member state confers rights in all of the others, thereby breaking the link between the status attached to citizenship and national territory. The provisions specify a migrant regime under which European Community citizens are entitled to equal status and treatment with the nationals of the host country. The basic tenets of this regime are as follows:

- Citizens of member states have the right to free movement, gainful employment, and residence within the boundaries of the Community.
- Community law prohibits discrimination based on nationality among workers of the member states with regard to employment, social security, trade union rights, living and working conditions, and education and vocational training.
- Community law obliges host states to facilitate teaching of the language and culture of the countries of origin within the framework of normal education and in collaboration with those countries.
- The Commission of the European Community recommends full political rights in the long run for Community citizens living in other member states. Under current arrangements, they have the right to vote and stand as candidates in local and European elections.

These rights are protected by a growing body of directives, regulations, and laws that locates them within a human rights context (Commission of the European Communities 1989b). Moreover, the 1991 Maastricht treaty has created the status of citizen of the Community, to "strengthen the protection of the rights and interests of the nationals of its member states." The treaty foresees a multilevel citizenship structure that guarantees rights independently of membership in a particular state. Thus, the Community as a supranational organization establishes a direct relationship with individuals in the member nation-states. As such, "European citizenship" clearly embodies postnational membership in its most elaborate legal form. It is a citizenship whose legal and normative bases are located in the wider community, and whose actual implementation is assigned to the member states.

At the present, the new Community citizenship and the free-movement provision do not apply to nationals of non-EC countries, who constitute the majority of the migrant populations in Europe. For non-EC migrants, the Community has issued guidelines toward the equalization of their status with that of nationals of EC countries. In 1989, for example, the Community adopted the Charter of the Funda-mental Rights of Workers, which requires the member states to guarantee workers and their families from non-member countries living and working conditions com-parable to those of EC nationals. More directly, with its authority to engage in international treaties, the Community has made agreements with several non-EC sending countries. These bilateral agreements incorporate the rights of non-EC for-eign workers into the legal framework of the Community with provisions in regard to social security, working conditions, and wages, under which workers and their families from signing countries can claim benefits on equal terms with community citizens (Callovi 1992).

My intention in citing all of these instruments and regimes is to draw attention to the proliferation of transnational arrangements, grounded in human rights dis-course, that address the rights and interests of migrants and refugees. These instru-ments and regimes provide guidelines as to the management of migrant affairs for national legislation, by standardizing and rationalizing the category and status of the international migrant. Like other transnational instruments, the charters and conventions regarding guestworkers do not for the most part entail formal obliga-tions or enforceable rules. This does not mean that they do not effect binding dispositions. By setting norms, framing discourses, and engineering legal categories and legitimate models, they enjoin obligations on nation-states to take action. They define goals and levels of competence, and compel nation-states to achieve specific standards. They form a basis for the claims of migrants shaping the plat-forms of migrant organizations as well as other public interests. They generate transnational activity and stir up publicity regarding migrant issues.

One of the ways international instruments affect nation-state action on migrants is through the construction of migrants as a legal category. Statutes on aliens, migrant workers, and refugees, which entitle migrants to claim legal protection on the basis of human rights, are now established branches of international law (Per-ruchoud 1986). In the case of the European Community and the European Coun-cil, extragovernmental bodies have been established, to interpret and give meaning to international codes and laws, thereby both constraining and enabling nation-state jurisdiction in many ways. One such examples is the European Court of Human Rights. According to the European Convention of Human Rights, individ-ual citizens of the European Council countries, as well as nongovernmental organ-izations or groups, can appeal directly to the European Court, whose decisions are binding on member states. In the last two decades, the caseload of the European Court has increased drastically, with some 5,500 complaints filed each year (Lester 1993). The Court has given a significant number of rulings on individual rights in recent years, including decisions on immigration and family unification.

Corresponding to this growth in the activity of the European Court, national courts increasingly invoke the European Human Rights Convention. The resulting panoply of human rights arrangements generates interesting cases. For example, in 1992, a Sudanese political refugee in Germany fled to Britain for asylum, fearing racial persecution in Germany. The British government decided to send him back to Germany, his first port of entry; however, a British high-court judge ordered the government to halt the deportation in accord with the European Convention on Human Rights, acknowledging that in Germany he might be in danger of attack by neo-Nazis (*The Economist*, 15 February 1992). In an earlier case, some East-African Asians, by appealing to the European Convention of Human Rights, were able to contest their exclusion from the United Kingdom under the 1968 Commonwealth Immigrants Act, which subjected the populations from the New Commonwealth to immigration controls (Plender 1986). Thereby, an international human rights instrument superseded the decision of the British Parliament.

The Court of Justice of the European Community, another supranational legal arrangement, oversees individual or state-level complaints that fall within Community Law. The Court has the task of harmonizing national laws with those of the Community. Fourteen percent of the cases brought before the European Court of Justice between 1953 and 1986 were related to the free movement of workers and their dependents, the right of abode and work, and other social issues (Commission of the European Communities 1987). The European Convention on Human Rights has been cited frequently by the Court of Justice in elaborating the general principles of Community Law and making decisions (Brown and McBride 1981).

In addition to their effect in the realm of legal rights, transnational laws, rules, conventions, and recommendations also directly influence nation-state policy and action. Let me cite some examples to illustrate this point. The inspiration for foreigners' assemblies and advisory councils came from a directive of the fifth session of the European Conference on Local Powers in 1964 (Sica 1977). Acting upon this directive, European host governments established several such assemblies and councils between 1968 and 1978 (Miller 1981). In creating specialized social service centers for migrants, the EC Commission's recommendation of 1962 constituted the basis upon which many national governments acted (Dumon 1977). In the early 1970s, the participation rights for foreigners in the work place were mainly introduced by the expansion of the European Community law and practice. Similarly, the European Community General Directive on Education of Migrant Workers (1977) afforded a backdrop for national provisions for teaching migrant children their own language and culture. In collaboration with sending countries, many European host states have established arrangements for such instruction.

Existing national policies are also sometimes revised in response to transnational instruments. In Sweden, limitations on the political activity of aliens were rescinded in 1954 as an effect of the European Convention on Human Rights and Fundamental Freedoms (Hammar 1985). Similarly, in 1985 the Austrian Supreme Court ruled the Foreigners Police Law unconstitutional, "since it did not accord with Article 8 of the European Convention on Human Rights, . . . interfering with private and family life" of migrants (Bauböck and Wimmer 1988:664). This decision resulted in an amendment of the law, requiring the foreigners police to take into account an individual's family situation and length of residence before making a decision about deportation.

All of these examples substantiate the impact of transnational instruments in the rationalization of the status of international migrant. Migrants' rights increasingly expand within the domain of human rights, supported by a growing number of transnational networks and institutions. The crucial point is that this intensified transnational modus operandi very much determines the discourse of membership and rights on the national level. The universalistic conceptions of rights and personhood become formally institutionalized norms through the agency of an array of collectivities – international governmental and nongovernmental organizations, legal institutions, networks of experts, and scientific communities. These collectivities, by advising national governments, enforcing legal categories, crafting models and standards, and producing reports and recommendations, promote and diffuse ideas and norms about universal human rights that in turn engenders a commanding discourse on membership. The same discourse is adopted by states, organizations, and individuals in granting and claiming rights and privileges, thereby reenacting the transnational discourse.

Human rights discourse is widely evoked in national policy language and government rhetoric pertaining to the rights of international migrants. As Catherine de Wenden remarks, since 1981, French immigration policies have been transformed from "a mere body of laws dealing with labor" to legislation and governmental guidelines that prescribe "equal treatment of foreigners and nationals, and human rights." Over the years, the basic rights of migrants, including "the fundamental right to a family life" and the "expression and representation of migrants in a multicultural France," have become part of policy discourse (de Wenden 1987). After the electoral victory of conservative and centrist parties in 1993, the French parliament passed a series of restrictive laws concerning the nationality code, family unification, and illegal immigration. The restrictions were criticized not only by civil rights groups and opposition parties, but also by prominent cabinet members, expressing concerns about human rights (New York Times, 23 June 1993). The French Constitutional Council ruled against the legislation concerning family unification on the grounds that it would violate the rights of migrants as individuals. The Council reasoned that "foreigners are not French, but they are human beings" (Le Monde, 16 August 1993).

Germany's policy language and official rhetoric have also changed over time. In 1981, Richard von Weizsäecker, then the mayor of West Berlin, insisted that foreigners must decide between repatriation and becoming Germans (Castles 1985). In the 1990s, however, Berlin offers its foreign residents a "multi-cultural society" and "no forced integration," as was noted in the official address of the secretary of the Berlin City State at a conference at the Free University in June 1990. The term multi-cultural society is invoked in public debates and has gained currency among experts on foreigners' issues and government officials responsible for implementing policies of integration.

As attacks on migrants and asylum seekers have risen, the debate about easing Germany's restrictive nationality law and allowing dual citizenship has intensified. The argument of the Social Democratic Party for extending dual citizenship was that "it would send a signal to our foreign residents that we fully recognize them as human beings" (Reuter News Agency, 4 June 1993). The major rally organized by the government to protest the killings of three Turkish migrants by neo-Nazis convened under a banner proclaiming that "Human Dignity is Inviolable" (Boston Globe, 8 November 1992). In addressing another such protest, Richard von Weizsäecker, the president of Germany, reasserted the theme of human dignity: "The first article of our constitution does not say 'the dignity of Germans is inviolable' but 'the dignity of man is inviolable'" (United Press International, 3 June 1993).

In much official debate, arguments for furthering the rights of migrants are typically presented in terms of the inalienable right of personhood. For example, the Belgian delegation to the 1981 Conference of European Ministers, in making a case for multicultural policies, reasoned that "any attempt to deprive a people of its history, culture, and language produces human beings who are incomplete and incapable both of forming plans for the future and of participating in community life and politics. It is to prevent alienation of this kind that any initiative permitting multilingual and multicultural education and a well-developed community life must be encouraged" (Council of Europe 1981:205). Claims for the political rights of migrants are framed within the same discourse: "The migrant's integration – apart from economic, social, and cultural aspects – involves the question of political participation, since the migrant has a political dimension, as does any other human being; his status in the receiving country cannot be divorced from this fundamental dimension" (*International Migration* 1977:78, citing the conclusions of the seminar on Adaptation and Integration of Permanent Immigrants of the Intergovernmental Committee for Migration [ICM]). Such an understanding of political rights clearly contradicts the construction of the individual's political existence as a national citizen.

Migrants themselves repeatedly urge the universalistic concept of personhood as the grounding principle for membership rights. Claims for membership become publicly coded as human rights, as is clearly discernible from the platforms and action programs of foreigners. In its sixth congress in Stockholm, the European Trade Union Confederation called for a more "humanitarian European unity," referring to the rights of migrant workers, especially those from the non-EC countries (*Ikibin'e Doğru*, 29 January 1989). Debates about local voting rights invariably center on the universal/humanistic versus national/particularistic controversy. The most notable argument put forth is that "the right to take part in the political process of one's country of residence is an essential aspect of human life" (Rath 1990:140). In their manifesto for local voting rights, the foreigners' organizations in Switzerland explicitly referred to humans' "natural right" of self-determination. The motto of the 1990 voting rights campaign of migrants in Austria was "Voting Rights Are Human Rights" (*Milliyet*, 10 October 1990). All these claims portray suffrage not only as a participatory right, but as an essential aspect of human personhood.

Human rights discourse dominates calls for cultural rights, as well. Multiculturalism, the right to be different and to foster one's own culture, is elementally asserted as the natural and inalienable right of all individuals. What is ironic is that the preservation of particularistic group characteristics – such as language, a customary marker of national identity – is justified by appealing to universalistic ideas of personhood. The Turkish Parents Association in Berlin demands mother-tongue instruction in schools on the grounds that "as a human being, one has certain natural rights. To learn and enrich one's own language and culture are the most crucial ones" (from the 1990 pamphlet of the association). In the same vein, the Initiative of Turkish Parents and Teachers in Stuttgart publicized its cause with the slogan "Mother Tongue is Human Right" (*Milliyet*, 4 October 1990).

Urging Islamic instruction in public schools, migrant associations also assert the natural right of individuals to their own cultures. During the 1987 national elections, Islamic associations in Britain justified their demands for the observance of Islamic rules in public schools and the recognition of Muslim family law by invoking the Declaration of Human Rights and the Declaration on the Elimination of All Forms of Intolerance based on Religion or Belief (Centre for the Study of Islam and Christian-Muslim Relations 1987). In May 1990, when the local authorities refused to permit the opening of another Islamic primary school, the Islamic Foundation in London decided to take the issue to the European Court of Human Rights. As part of the debate over the *foulard* affair in France, the head of the Great Mosque of Paris declared the rules preventing the wearing of scarves in school to be discriminatory. He emphasized personal rights, rather than religious duties: "If a girl asks to have her hair covered, I believe it is her most basic right" (*Washington Post*, 23 October 1989). Accordingly, the closing statement of the fourth European Muslims Conference made an appeal for the rights of Muslims as "human beings" and "equal members" of European societies (*Kirpi*, July 1990, p. 15).

In all of these examples, the prevalence of transnational discourse is evident. Membership rights are recast as human rights; governments, organizations, and individuals recurrently appeal to this "higher-order" principle. The changes I have delineated indicate, not only the empirical extension of rights, but the existence of legitimate grounds upon which new and more extensive demands can be made. The dominance of human rights discourse, and the definition of individuals and their rights as abstract universal categories, license even foreign populations to push for further elaboration of their rights. The fact that rights, and claims to rights, are no longer confined to national parameters, supports the premise of a postnational model of membership.

References

Abu-Lughod, Janet L. 1989a. *Before European Hegemony: The World System, A.D. 1250–1350*. London: Oxford University Press.
——. 1989b. Restructuring the Premodern World System. Paper presented at the annual meeting of the American Sociological Association, San Francisco.
Bauböck, Rainer, and Hannes Wimmer. 1988. Social Partnership and 'Foreigners Policy': On Special Features of Austria's Guest-worker System. *European Journal of Political Research* 16:659–82.
Bendix, Reinhard. 1977. *Nation-Building and Citizenship: Studies of Our Changing Social Order*. Berkeley and Los Angeles: University of California Press.
——. 1993. Sovereignty from a World Polity Perspective. Paper presented at the annual meeting of the American Sociological Association, Miami.
Brown, L. Neville, and Jeremy McBride. 1981. Observation on the Proposed Accession by the European Community to the European Convention on Human Rights. *The American Journal of Comparative Law* 29:691–705.
Brubaker, William Rogers. 1989a. Introduction. In *Immigration and Politics of Citizenship in Europe and North America*, ed. W. R. Brubaker. Lanham, Md.: University Press of America.
——. 1989b. Membership without Citizenship: The Economic and Social Rights of Noncitizens. In *Immigration and Politics of Citizenship in Europe and North America*, ed. W. R. Brubaker. Lanham, Md.: University Press of America.
Brubaker, William Rogers, ed. 1989. *Immigration and Politics of Citizenship in Europe and North America*. Lanham, Md.: University Press of America.

Callovi, Giuseppe. 1992. Regulation of Immigration in 1993: Pieces of the European Community Jig-Saw Puzzle. *International Migration Review* 26:353–72.

Cameron, David R. 1978. The Expansion of the Public Economy: A Comparative Analysis. *American Political Science Review* 72:1243–61.

Castles, Stephen. 1985. The Guests Who Stayed – The Debate on 'Foreigners Policy' in the German Federal Republic. *International Migration Review* 19:517–34.

Centre for the Study of Islam and Christian–Muslim Relations. 1987. Muslim Demands of the British Political Parties. *News of Muslims in Europe*, no. 40, pp. 6–7. Birmingham.

Commission of the European Communities. 1987. New Rights for the Citizens of Europe. *European File*, no. 11/87. Luxembourg: Office for Official Publications of the European Communities.

Commission of the European Communities. 1989b. The European Community and Human Rights. *European File*, no. 5/89. Luxembourg: Office for Official Publications of the European Communities.

Council of Europe. 1977. *European Convention on the Legal Status of Migrant Workers*. Strasbourg.

Council of Europe. 1981. *European Migration in the 1980s: Trends and Policies*. Conference of European Ministers Responsible for Migration Affairs, Strasbourg, 6–8 May 1980, Records. Strasbourg.

Dumon, W. A. 1977. The Activity of Voluntary Agencies and National Associations in Helping Immigrants to Overcome Initial Problems. *International Migration* 15:113–26.

——. 1986. Migration and the Political Economy of the Welfare State. *Annals of the American Academy of Political and Social Science* 485:51–63.

Fullinwider, Robert K. 1988. Citizenship and Welfare. In *Democracy and the Welfare State*, ed. A. Gutmann. Princeton: Princeton University Press.

Goodwin-Gill, Guy S., R. K. Jenny, and Richard Perruchoud. 1985. Basic Humanitarian Principles Applicable to Non-Nationals. *International Migration Review* 19:556–69.

Hammar, Tomas, ed. 1985. On Immigrant Status and Civic Rights in Sweden. Paper presented to the research group, European Consortium for Political Research, Paris.

——. 1986. Citizenship: Membership of a Nation and of a State. *International Migration* 24:735–47.

——. 1990a. *International Migration, Citizenship, and Democracy*. Aldershot: Gower.

Heisler, Martin O., and Barbara Schmitter Heisler. 1990. Citizenship—Old, New, and Changing: Inclusion, Exclusion, and Limbo for Ethnic Groups and Migrants in the Modern Democratic State. In *Dominant National Cultures and Ethnic Identities*, ed. J. Fijalkowski, H. Merkens, and F. Schmidt. Berlin: Free University.

ILO (International Labor Office). 1986. *The Rights of Migrant Workers: A Guide to ILO Standards for the Use of Migrant Workers and Their Organizations*. Geneva: ILO Publications.

——. N.d. *Provisions of the ILO Conventions and Recommendations Concerning Migrant Workers*. Geneva: ILO Publications.

Informatie Amsterdam. 1985. *Adviesraden-Danişma Kurullari*. City of *International Migration*. 1977. Third Seminar on Adaptation and Integration of Permanent Immigrants: Conclusions and Recommendations, vol. 15:17–83.

International Migration Review. 1991. U.N. International Convention on the Protection of the Rights of All Migrant Workers and Members of Their Families. Special Issue 25(4).

Katzenstein, Peter J. 1985. *Small States in World Markets: Industrial Policy in Europe*. Ithaca: Cornell University Press.

Leibfried, Stephan. 1990. Sozialstaat Europa? Integrationsperspektiven europäischer Armutsregimes. *Nachrichtendienst des Deutschen Vereins für öffentliche und private Fürsorge (NDV)* 70:296–305.

Lester, Anthony. 1993. Britain Wrong on Human Rights. *Financial Times*, 26 May.

Marshall, T. H. 1964. *Class, Citizenship and Social Development*. Garden City, N.Y.: Doubleday.

Meyer, John W. 1980. The World Polity and the Authority of the Nation-State. In *Studies of the Modern World System*, ed. A. Bergesen. New York: Academic Press.

——. 1994. Rationalized Environments. In *Institutional Environments and Organizations*, ed. W. R. Scott and J. W. Meyer. Newbury Park, Calif.: Sage.

Miller, Mark J. 1981. *Foreign Workers in Western Europe: An Emerging Political Force*. New York: Praeger.

Niessen, Jan. 1989. Migration and (Self-) Employment, Residence, and Work Permit Arrangements in Seventeen European Countries. Maastricht: European Center for Work and Labor. Manuscript.

Perruchoud, R. 1986. The Law of Migrants. *International Migration* 24:699–716.

Plender, Richard. 1985. Migrant Workers in Western Europe. *Contemporary Affairs Briefing*, vol. 2, no. 14.

——. 1986. Rights of Passage. In *Towards a Just Immigration Policy*, ed. A. Dummett. London: Cobden Trust.

Ramirez, Francisco O. 1989. Reconstituting Children: Extension of Personhood and Citizenship. In *Age Structuring in Comparative Perspective*, ed. D. Kertzer and K. W. Schaie. Hillsdale, N.J.: Lawrence Erlbaum Associates.

Ramirez, Francisco O., and Yasemin Nuhoğlu Soysal. 1989. Women's Acquisition of the Franchise: An Event History Analysis. Paper presented at the annual meeting of the American Sociological Association, San Francisco.

Rath, Jan. 1990. Voting Rights. In *The Political Rights of Migrant Workers in Western Europe*, ed. Z. Layton-Henry. London: Sage.

Schuck, Peter H., and Rogers M. Smith. 1985. *Citizenship Without Consent: Illegal Aliens in the American Polity*. New Haven: Yale University Press.

Sica, Mario. 1977. Involvement of the Migrant Worker in Local Political Life in the Host Country. *International Migration* 15:143–52.

Soysal, Yasemin Nuhoğlu, and David Strang. 1989. Construction of the First Mass Education Systems in Nineteenth-Century Europe. *Sociology of Education* 62:277–88.

Thomson, Janice E., and Stephen D. Krasner. 1989. Global Transactions and the Consolidation of Sovereignty. In *Global Changes and Theoretical Challenges: Approaches to World Politics for the 1990s*, ed. E. O. Czempiel and J. N. Rosenau. Lexington, Mass.: Lexington Books.

Turner, Bryan S. 1986a. *Citizenship and Capitalism: The Debate over Reformism*. London: Allen and Unwin.

——. 1986b. Personhood and Citizenship. *Theory, Culture, and Society* 3:1–16.

Walzer, Michael. 1983. *Spheres of Justice: A Defense of Pluralism and Equality*. New York: Basic Books.

Weber, Max. 1978. *Economy and Society: An Outline of Interpretive Sociology*, vol. 1, ed. G. Roth and C. Wittich. Berkeley and Los Angeles: University of California Press.

de Wenden, Catherine Wihtol. 1987. France's Policy on Migration from May 1981 till March 1986: Its Symbolic Dimension, Its Restrictive Aspects and Its Unintended Effects. *International Migration* 25:211–20.

20 The Transformation of Miami

Alejandro Portes and Alex Stepick

Since their origins in the nineteenth century, theories about the growth of cities have emphasized economic causes. Cities arise out of the imperatives of economic life and develop according to their importance in the larger economy. Their location can be analyzed by means of the same logic: urban concentrations emerge as marketplaces for settled hinterlands, as places where sources of energy converge with sources of labor, and as "breaks" in transportation routes requiring the physical transfer of commodities.[1]

This economic emphasis is sufficiently broad to encompass both mainstream and Marxist theories of the city. The Marxist school follows the theme of economic determinism and endows it with greater intentionality than do more conventional theories in sociology and economics. For Marxists, it is not accidents of geography and prior population settlement, but the deliberate hand of capital seeking to organize the various factors of production, that accounts for urban growth. Thus, while the German sociologist Max Weber referred to the city as a "marketplace" and the American economist Adna Weber portrayed it as a transportation hub, Marxists have consistently defined it as the site where industrial labor power is sold and commodities are produced for profit. As François Lamarche states:

> If the city is considered to start with as a market where labour power, capital, and products are exchanged, it must equally be accepted that the geographical configuration of the market is not the result of chance.... The main hypothesis underlying our argument can be summarized as follows: the urban question is first and foremost the product of the capitalist mode of production which requires a spatial organization which facilitates the circulation of capital, commodities, and information.[2]

Given the vast body of theoretical literature coming from both sides of the ideological spectrum, the story of Miami is remarkable indeed. It is not a story that fits "central place" theory very well, because Miami at its beginnings was not the center of anything; it did not serve as a "marketplace" for a settled hinterland, of which there was very little, and it did not sit at the "break" between alternative transportation routes, because these did not exist at the time. Certainly, the city was a product of nineteenth-century capitalism, but in a way that deviated significantly from classic orthodox and Marxist theories on the origins of cities. Miami did not attract industrial capital or industrial labor, and it did not produce anything of significance. Nor did it serve as a commercial hub for agricultural products, or for any other good – except one. Its sole assets were sun and beach, sold by the square foot. Since the Florida peninsula boasts hundreds of miles of similarly endowed shoreline, the location of the city was accidental. The metropolis that grew by Biscayne Bay could equally well have been located in Palm Beach, by the mouth of the New River in today's Ft. Lauderdale, or even in the Florida Keys.

The origins of the city were hence *economically underdetermined*, more the result of chance and individual wills than of any geographic or commercial imperative. This accidental birth, added to the peculiar asset that was the lifeblood of the city, accounted for Miami's sense of suspension above real life and the feebleness of its civic organizations. The exotic theme parks dreamed up for the place by northern entrepreneurs – pseudo-Arab minarets, mock-Andalusian towers, "Venetian" palaces – did nothing to reduce the feeling of separation from the surrounding landscape or diminish the city's political fragmentation. Compared to Chicago, Cincinnati, Cleveland, or Pittsburgh – "real" cities growing at the break points of railroad and water routes and attracting industrial capital – Miami's social organization and civic leadership seemed at best a poor imitation. People came here to retire, enjoy the weather, and play. Apart from the real estate business, few serious economic and civic pursuits could attract their attention.

The poor fit with economic theories about the origins of cities, however, is only the first half of Miami's exceptionality. The flows of men and materials that crisscrossed the Florida peninsula at the turn of the century left their mark on the city, but in different manners and at different times. The Flagler-led feverish building of railroad and hotels gave Miami a distinct profile that, during the first half-century of its existence, separated it from cities up north. The equally busy ferrying of arms to the rebellious Spanish colony of Cuba prefigured its character during the second half. Geography is destiny, but in Miami's case it was not so much economic as political geography that played the determining role.

America in the Caribbean: The Origins of Contemporary Immigration

If the nineteenth-century creation of Miami was due to chance and individual initiative rather than economic imperatives, its late-twentieth-century transformation under the impact of successive waves of migration was without question politically overdetermined. Miami was a choice target for two reasons: first, its geographic proximity and connections to the Caribbean by air and sea routes made the city a logical entry point into the United States; and second, its close ties to Cuba gave it a major role as backstage in Cuban politics.

A more refined understanding of why Caribbean migration arose in the first place and why it came to the United States, however, requires a brief excursus into another body of theory. Explanations of international migration are commonly based on a "push–pull" mechanism that depicts migrants as people encouraged to leave by unfavorable circumstances in their own countries and attracted by conditions in the receiving ones. Although plausible on the surface, these theories do not explain why migrant flows emerge from some countries and not from others at similar levels of disadvantage, or why these flows are directed toward certain receiving countries but not others. In short, the theory fails to recognize that decisions to migrate are not made in a social vacuum. Individuals do not simply sit at home and ponder the costs and benefits of going to country X versus country Y. Instead they are guided by precedent, by the experience of friends and relatives, and by the alternative courses of action held to be acceptable and realistic in their own societies.

The social environment of migration is molded, in turn, by the history of prior relationships between the country of origin and those of potential destination. People seldom move to completely unfamiliar places; rather, they seek out those made accessible by past contacts. This is why a great deal of migration from former Third World colonies is directed today to the original *métropoles* – Algerians and Tunisians go to France; Indians, Pakistanis, and West Indians move to Britain; South Americans frequently migrate to Spain; and Koreans go to Japan.

No other region of the world has experienced greater American economic and political penetration than the Caribbean. Although the United States did not become a colonial power in the mold of older European nations, the heavy hand of North American intervention has made itself particularly felt in the smaller countries of its southern fringe. During the last century, US military occupations have been a fact of life throughout the region: Mexico, Puerto Rico, Cuba, the Dominican Republic, Haiti, Nicaragua, Panama, and Grenada have all been, at one time or another, under direct US military rule. In addition, the United States has exercised overwhelming economic dominance in the region and has saturated it with its values, diffused through the media. Consequences of this historical relationship have been the mass adoption of American consumption patterns and the creation of economic elites that are profoundly "Americanized" in their outlook. Of these, none was more typical than the prerevolutionary Cuban bourgeoisie, molded by the hegemony of North American interests in the island.

A series of grave economic and political crises during the second half of the twentieth century led to enhanced out-migration from a number of Caribbean countries. Migration took place not on the basis of detached calculations of costs and benefits, but along the lines of least resistance opened by the prior history of the region. Hence, when confronted with overwhelming threats to their well-being, Cuban and Nicaraguan elites did not think of going to Japan, Germany, or Canada, but rather to the country whose influence had shaped their own position and mental outlook. Less well-to-do groups followed suit.

The recent waves of Caribbean migration demonstrate how past penetration and molding of weak peripheral societies by a dominant power can turn upon itself. To a large extent, Cubans and Nicaraguans, Haitians and Dominicans, came directly to the United States because they had been socialized in that direction. The same explanation covers the particular destinations of each migrant flow: Caribbean refugees did not distribute themselves evenly across the United States, but concentrated in a few spots. These were the places most salient in the newcomers' mental map as centers of North American influence and power and as logical entry points into the country. For Caribbean immigrants, "America" did not mean Arkansas or North Dakota, but, almost exclusively, New York and Miami.

The 1959 Cuban Revolution was, of course, the decisive event that initiated Miami's politically led transformation. As entire layers of the formerly privileged were forced to leave Cuba, they went to the only country and the only city where, given their history, it made sense to go. And once the defeated Cuban bourgeoisie reestablished itself in Miami, the city became the almost inevitable destination of all major refugee streams fleeing political instability. Nicaraguans crossing the Mexican border caught the bus not to nearby Houston or New Orleans, but to Miami; leaving their desperately poor and repressive country behind, Haitians pointed their boats in the same direction; and less numerous flows from Panama, Colombia, and Honduras followed the same course.

Political migrations then produced a novel economic phenomenon as the rise of the Cuban enclave and the availability of large pools of bilingual labor turned Miami into a major trade entrepôt. The city shed its role as a seasonal resort town to become, as David Rieff put it, a "real" place.[3] Real in the sense that its new economic diversification occurred not by accident, but on the basis of resources that only that city had. While Orlando and other northern locales chipped away at Miami's traditional tourist trade, no other city could outcompete it in the role of "Capital of the Caribbean."

Table 20.1 illustrates this economic change by showing the decline in the proportion of Dade County's economically active population employed in hotels and restaurants, mainstays of the tourist industry, and the rise in the proportion employed in banking and FIRE (finance, insurance, and real estate) sectors, elements of the city's new economic profile. Also shown is the parallel surge of small businesses, many started by recent immigrants. "Very small" establishments, defined as those employing fewer than ten people, grew more rapidly during the 1970s and 1980s than did business establishments overall, reversing the trend observed in the preceding two decades.

Table 20.1   Employment and business establishments in the Miami metropolitan area, 1950–87

	1950	1960	1970	1980	1987
Economically active population (EAP)	157,321	282,774	467,992	788,249	712,568
Percent EAP in services	21.3	25.9	24.8	27.0	30.9
Percent EAP in hotels and restaurants	17.4	13.6	11.0	—	9.1
Percent EAP in banking	1.4	2.4	2.3	2.9	3.6
Percent EAP in finance, insurance, and real estate	6.2	7.6	8.7	7.5	9.4
Total business establishments	14,894	23,051	27,140	42,817	58,036
Percent growth during preceding decade	—	54.8	17.7	57.8	35.5
Business establishments with fewer than 10 employees	11,566	17,178	18,840	32,368	45,617
Percent growth during preceding decade	—	48.5	7.6	75.2	40.9
Banks and finance agencies	141	309	398	671	981
Percent growth during preceding decade	—	119.1	28.8	68.6	46.2

Sources: U.S. Bureau of the Census, *Country Business Patterns.* (Washington, D.C.: U.S. Department of Commerce, indicated years); *County and City Data Book* (Washington D.C.: U.S. Department of Commerce, indicated years).

Traversing the Miami River in the direction of Biscayne Bay is a way of gaining firsthand evidence about Miami's Caribbean nexus. Freighters from Honduras, Haiti, Colombia, and the Dominican Republic crowd this working river, loading diverse cargoes for their countries. At the river's mouth, one suddenly leaves Third World trade behind to admire the gleaming silhouettes of the Royal Caribbean pleasure boats anchored in Biscayne Bay. Formerly a tourist destination itself, Miami is now the world's main port of embarkation for vacation cruises, most of them to the Caribbean. Hence, an interesting dynamic sets in as well-heeled tourists depart Miami for enchanted and romantic Caribbean islands, which the native people are often desperately trying to leave...for Miami. The freighters in the river also do their part as they haul from Miami the luxuries and conveniences to which tourists are accustomed and which they will consume in their "exotic" Caribbean destinations.

What makes Miami a unique experiment is its peculiar reversal of established patterns of urban growth. Here, politics determines economics rather than vice versa. Almost alone among major American cities, Miami did not originally grow out of economic locational advantages, but acquired them only afterward as an outgrowth of its unplanned political role. The latter did not involve domestic forces, but rather the international dynamics unleashed by the United States' domination of its immediate periphery.

This singularity does not, however, mean that Miami's experiences are not replicable. In this sense, its "uniqueness" may hold important lessons for other cities. The international forces that transformed Miami are still at play, and have, if anything, grown stronger: people worldwide are increasingly bound together by expanding trade and information networks; consumption expectations diffused from the developed world translate into immigrant flows seeking to satisfy those expectations; the dialectics whereby past colonialism begets refugee movements to the old dominant powers is still very much alive.

For its size, Miami is easily the most "internationalized" of American cities, but others may follows suit as they respond to global social and political dynamics. Today, Boston plays host to a rapidly accelerating Irish immigration, while Los Angeles, San Diego, and San Francisco do the same for the vast Mexican inflow, augmented by refugees from the Central American conflicts. Miami's experience may not reveal to other cities the image of their own future, but the forces that led to its transformation will surely manifest themselves elsewhere, leading to significant social and political outcomes.

Ethnic Discourses

What are some of these outcomes? The arrival of sizable foreign groups necessarily produces a resurgence of ethnicity and, along with it, a transformation in the fabric of local society. Depending on the strength of preexisting elites and the character of the migrant community, newcomers may take their place in the ethnic queue, awaiting their turn to move slowly upward; they may remain entirely outside the playing field as marginal workers; or they may actually transform the rules of the game. In Miami, the politically led transformation of the social structure gave rise to the emergence of alternative discourses about the city and to a rapid shift in local power.

Table 20.2 presents the evolution of Miami's metropolitan population, providing the background against which the transformation of its political structure must be understood. The table illustrates the dramatic changes in the ethnic composition of the population that led to the shift in elected leadership. Whereas Hispanic (that is, Cuban) political representation was nonexistent in 1950 and 1960, in 1990 it accounted for four mayoral posts in Dade County (including those of the two largest municipalities, Miami and Hialeah), the majority of the councils of these two cities and several smaller ones, the Miami City and Dade County managers, seven state delegates and two state senators (one-third of the entire county's delegation), and a US congressional representative. Cuban representation among elected officials will only grow further in the coming years. Redistricting required by the 1990 Voting Right Acts will increase the number of "Hispanic" seats in the state House to as many as eleven out of eighteen total; four of the six state senators are likely to be Cuban-American, as well as two out of four members of Dade's congressional delegation. "Politically, we'll hardly recognize the place," writes the *Miami Herald*'s political editor.[4]

Table 20.2   Ethnic composition of metropolitan Miami, 1950–90

	1950	1960	1970	1980	1990
Population total	495,000	935,000	1,268,000	1,626,000	1,937,000
U.S. rank[a]	—	19	17	12	11
Percent increase in preceding decade	—	88.9	35.6	28.2	19.1
White, non-Hispanic	410,000	748,000	779,000	776,000	586,000
Percentage of total	82.8	80.0	61.4	47.7	30.3
Percentage increase/decrease in preceding decade	—	82.4	4.1	−0.4	−24.5
Hispanic[b]	20,000	50,000	299,000	581,000	953,000
Percentage of total	4.0	5.3	23.6	35.7	49.2
Percentage increase in preceding decade	—	150.0	498.0	94.3	64.0
Black[c]	65,000	137,000	190,000	280,000	369,000
Percentage of total	13.1	14.7	15.0	17.2	19.5
Percentage increase in preceding decade	—	110.8	38.7	47.4	31.8

Sources: Metro-Dade Planning Department, Research Division, *Dade County Facts* (Miami: Metropolitan Dade County Government, 1990); *Persons of Hispanic Origin by Race, City, and Census Tract* (Miami: Metropolitan Dade County Government, 1990).
[a] Among standard metropolitan statistical areas.
[b] Hispanics can be of any race.
[c] There is some overlap between the Hispanic and Black categories owing to the presence of black Hispanics. In 1980, the Metro-Dade Research Division reported 11,000 blacks of Hispanic origin; in 1990, there were 28,372 such persons. The table includes them as "Black" for the sake of congruence with earlier figures where this separation was not made.

This transformation of the political order is taking place in a context where the rupture of the old hegemonic discourse has not yet given rise to a new one. Indeed, the distinct ethnic frames of reference continue to hold sway, each having its own cogent reading of the principal features of the city and its main problems. This situation has two noteworthy aspects. First, the various frames seldom incorporate points salient to the others but rather slide, as it were, on different planes. The result is that several mutually unintelligible perceptual "maps" coexist in the same physical space. Second, the existence of these separate "maps" plays back on everyday reality, leading to more stereotyped behavior by members of the different communities. Anglos, Blacks, and Latins lead their lives in separate worlds, but when meeting each other in public places they tend to adopt a ritualized stance, influenced by their own particular discourse.

"This microphone has an accent," says the Cuban businessman addressing a meeting of the Miami Chamber of Commerce. But this concession to the cultural sensibilites of his Anglo hosts is followed by a vigorous telling of the familiar "success story."[5] In interethnic public gatherings, Miami Cubans are likely to behave as "up and coming, in-charge Cubans," Anglos as "on the defensive, holding-the-fort Anglos," and Blacks as "entitled and doubly aggrieved citizens of color." This ritualized ballet is guided less by the specific situation of the individual than by his or her perception of the general context, guided by the respective frame of reference.

Every large city possesses a coterie of civic figures who attempt to rise above current problems in order to present the place in the best possible light. The result may be called a "normalizing" narrative that links the city with familiar and valued features of the national culture. Despite its fragmentation, Miami also has a version of this narrative; though its authorship still falls to the editors of the *Miami Herald* and a small group of Anglo business leaders, the content of the message has changed significantly over the last decade. In the 1960s and 1970s, Miami was portrayed as an all-American city, the playground of the nation affected by the "problem" of immigration but ultimately very much in the mainstream. This picture coincided with the then-hegemonic Anglo discourse.

During the eighties, however, the native white population plummeted to just one-third of Dade County's total population. In the city of Miami proper, Anglos shrank in number from an absolute majority in the 1960s to just 10 percent in 1990; in the latter year, meanwhile, Hialeah was over 88 percent Latin.[6] Accompanying this demographic revolution were major changes in local culture. Cuban and to a lesser extent other Latin festivities, music, and cuisine became integral to the city's lore. It was now increasingly common for Anglos and Blacks to learn Spanish, just as Latins were trying to learn English. In response, Miami's "normalizing" narrative shifted to encompass a very different message. See the remarks of the new CEO of the same company, James K. Batten, on the occasion of the October 1991 visit of President George Bush to the city:

> Those of us who live and work and raise our children in Miami have big aspirations for this vibrant young city. We are only 95 years old, but those 95 years have been jammed with endless change, especially over the last tumultuous three decades.... At the beginning of 1959, only a few thousand people of Hispanic descent lived in Dade

County. Today the number of Hispanics here has jumped to close to one million or roughly half the population of this community. Their presence here has transformed Miami, and enriched life here in profound and countless ways.[7]

And consider this prediction by presidential son Jeb Bush, cited by Batten: "By the turn of the century, Miami will have completed its evolution into a major world city – a center of international trade, culture, education, health care, and recreation, providing a desirable quality of life for our residents and visitors."[8]

The content of the Anglo elite's portrait of their city thus evolved from one embodying mainstream American customs and traditions to one in which Miami was nothing short of a harbinger of the national future. Immigrants and their foreign languages were transformed from a "problem" into an "enrichment." In a remarkable article entitled "Get on the Ball ... Learn a Language," *Miami Herald* publisher David Lawrence, Jr., set multicultural Miami as an example to the entire nation and at the "cutting edge" of the America to come. He then urged his fellow Miamians to "get on" and enroll in a foreign language class.[9]

The newer Cuban-American political leadership chimed in with its own tentative attempt at a "normalizing" narrative. Mayor Xavier Suárez regularly raised the "City of the Future" theme, though he tempered it with jabs at the county and state governments for not helping Miami fulfill its destiny. At the City Commission inauguration ceremony in 1989, for example, Suárez declared:

> Our own government has been drastically streamlined by our reform-minded city manager. Our own police department has been decentralized under a forward-thinking chief. When are we going to see the same efficiencies in the County which now pays its attorney 50 percent more than we pay ours? And when are we going to see State legislation to provide substantial help to poverty-stricken areas so that commercial growth is fostered and police presence less needed? How long can we remain a high-taxed city in a low-taxed state?[10]

Pursuing the same theme of normalization, a Cuban-American *Herald* columnist went so far as to chide his compatriots for their excessively "Cuban" child-rearing methods. In his view, although the original exiles might remain contentedly within their enclave, their American-born offspring could not afford to do so: "No matter how Latinized Miami continues to become, it is still and always will be in the United States. Thus our children are first generation Americans. That is an important distinction to make if we are to avoid burdening them with identity problems in the future."[11]

Ethnicity in Miami is still paramount, and the fragmentation brought about by the breakup of the old hegemonic discourse remains the city's dominant reality. Anglos, Blacks, and Jews, Nicaraguans, Haitians, and Cubans, tend to stay within their ethnic circles and to greet calls for intermingling with skepticism, if not hostility. Yet at the edges and in the better-educated sectors, there are visible signs of convergence. This trend fits a thus far neglected but fundamental lesson in the history of past immigration and ethnic adaptation in American cities. The story is worth reviewing, for no matter how distinct Miami is at present, it is likely in time to follow a path similar to that taken before by other communities.

Who Rules?

In *Who Governs?* (1961), his classic book on American urban politics, political scientist Robert A. Dahl traced the transformation of New Haven, Connecticut, from a city ruled by its old white Protestant elite to one in which immigrants – in this case Irish, Jews, and Italians – gradually gained the upper hand. He forcefully argued that power had indeed come to be shared between old and new elites rather than being retained by old WASPs behind a façade of ethnic politicians. Not surprisingly, the book became the standard reference for the pluralist perspective on urban community power.

The pluralist-elitist controversy over who "really" rules obscured an important aspect of the book, however, namely its analysis of how the immigrants became integrated into American culture through their participation in politics and management of local institutions. No matter that the first impulse of newly elected Irish mayors was to distribute patronage among their own, the important long-term consequence of institutional participation was to integrate each group firmly into local society:

> Hence the politics of New Haven became a kind of ethnic politics; it was a politics of assimilation rather than a politics of reform, a politics that simultaneously emphasized the divisive rather than the unifying characteristics of voters and yet played upon their yearnings of assimilation and acceptance. The very success of politicians who use the ethnic approach leads to the obsolescence of their strategy.[12]

The point of Dahl's analysis, in short, is that ethnic politics provides an effective vehicle for convergence because the achievement of political power socializes immigrants into the functioning of mainstream institutions and gives them the necessary "voice" to feel that they are part of those institutions. Immigrants do not first learn to be "Americans," and only then are freely admitted into the mainstream. Rather, they become Americans by elbowing their way into centers of local power through the political mobilization of ethnic solidarity. The very success of that strategy in turn leads to its gradual dissolution.

The common view of the process of assimilation, unfortunately, tends to reverse this sequence, with acculturation coming before social acceptance. From that perspective, ethnic politics is seen as a looming threat, a fear on which nativist emotions thrive. In a book titled *The Immigration Time Bomb*, former Colorado governor Richard D. Lamm expressed the theme with notable clarity:

> The political power of more than fifteen million Hispanics is being used not to support assimilation but to advance "ethnic pride" in belonging to a different culture. The multiplication of outsiders is not a model for a viable society.... If immigrants do not feel that they are fully part of this society, as American as everyone else, then we are failing.[13]

First-generation immigrants have seldom felt "as American as anyone else" because natives have repeatedly reminded them of their cultural and linguistic differences. The error in Lamm's formulation is to believe that cultural diversity and ethnic pride must disappear before immigrants can take part in the institutions of society. As Dahl's study suggests, the opposite has often been the case. The process is exemplified not only in New Haven, but in large cities that have been major recipients of immigration. The Irish of Boston, the Italians and Jews of New York, the Poles of Chicago first mobilized around the symbols of a common ethnicity precisely because that was how they had been defined and often ostracized in their places of settlement.

Hence "ethnic pride" arising out of reactive formation is the first and natural rallying point for immigrant groups entering the political system. Through the defense of particularistic goals, they are socialized into national political values. Before politicians of Irish, Greek, and Italian origin learned how to interpret mainstream sentiment and to represent broad constituencies, their predecessors had spent considerable time in ward politics fighting for the narrow interests of their group.

We examined the reactive formation process of Cuban refugees in the aftermath of Mariel, a process that gave rise both to a novel discourse and to strong participation in local politics. The above quotes from the Cuban-American mayor of Miami and the Cuban-American columnist of the *Herald* resemble hundreds that could be used to illustrate how far the process of integration has advanced in a decade. Concerns about a more equitable tax distribution for the city and how to avoid the ghettoization of the next generation are hardly the worries of a refractory minority. Gradual convergence toward the cultural mainstream, however, is attributable more to the entry of former exiles into local political institutions than to the assimilationist sermons of the past.

The extraordinary division of Miami along ethnic lines continues to define its reality, but there are at present a number of Anglo and Cuban leaders who prefer to advance the "Capital of the Caribbean" and "City of the Future" themes over segmented ethnic perspectives. Left out of this endeavor, however, are Miami's black minorities. The double-subordination discourse forged by Black leaders during the last decade represents both an original form of reactive ethnicity and an attempt to gain entry into the city's power structure. So far the attempt has been unsuccessful.

The continuing exclusion of Blacks from true political participation virtually guarantees new episodes of ethnic strife in Miami's future. From the perspective of Dahl's analysis, their position is the precise opposite of the Cubans'. Blacks are thoroughly acculturated, "as American as everyone else" – yet this achievement has yielded nothing near political or economic parity. Indeed, the situation has become so bad in recent years that many Black leaders recall almost wistfully the days of segregation. A principal Black community leader, interviewed in 1987, had this to say about Black Miami five years later:

> The changes have been for the worse, not for the better; violence is rampant and uncontrollable.... What oppression does is that it makes the oppressed group also aspire to be like the oppressor. And if I am able to be like the oppressor, then the things that I was forced to develop by virtue of my oppression are no longer valued.... It's a question of emulation having to do with assimilation. Without a doubt, Blacks are the most American people in America....

> When things were colored, *when things were colored*, then the same kind of business enclave that exists in the Cuban community, in the Jewish community, also existed in the Black community, because the consumer base was contained.[14]

Lacking an ethnic economy and sufficient political power for effective representation, Black Miami remains marginal to the process of integration-through-participation described by Dahl. Daunted but not beaten, Haitians nevertheless continue striving to build their enclave, and Black leaders still seek a voice in local power circles. If their efforts are not successful, the "Capital of the Caribbean" is in for some tough times no matter how much it has moved toward convergence between its other major groups.

Politics During the Deathwatch

In February 1990, Governor Bob Martinez appointed a twelve-member commission to study the potential effects that a change in government in Cuba would have on the state of Florida. The idea for the commission came from the Cuban-American National Foundation, whose president, Jorge Mas Canosa, was subsequently appointed chair of the panel. Meeting for the first time on the twenty-ninth floor on the Miami-Metro building, the commission discussed such things as preventing widespread absenteeism among Cuban-American workers celebrating the fall of Fidel, controlling the festivities in South Florida, and coping with the influx of Cubans from elsewhere in the United States who would use Miami as a "staging area" to reach Cuba.[15]

The gap between the important-sounding commission and the shallow topics it discussed reflects the fact that neither the participants nor anyone else had the slightest idea of what would happen were Castro's regime to fall. The creation of the panel was, in other words, largely symbolic; it signaled the clout that right-wing exiles had with the Republican governor and their sense that the long-awaited downfall was imminent. That sense permeated the Cuban enclave, being reflected both in the public utterances of its leaders and in street culture. The Cuban-American Foundation, for example, announced with much fanfare a plan for "the future governance of Cuba."[16] So did almost every other exile political group. Salsa singer Willy Chirino's hit song of 1990 proclaimed, "Ya viene llegando" (It's just around the corner); another popular rap singer, perhaps with a keener instinct about the future, announced that "soon in Cuba, English will be spoken."

In 1990, Cuban Miami embarked on the deathwatch for its enemy. Events in Europe had converted Cuba into the single Western country still governed by orthodox communism. The fall of East European regimes and the end of the Soviet Union left the island nation bereft of allies and protectors, and the defeat of the Sandinista regime in Nicaragua and the end of the Salvadoran insurgency entirely isolated Cuba in the Western Hemisphere. Widespread domestic scarcities and rising popular discontent made it clear to many that the end was near. After three decades, the revolutionary episode that had transformed Miami appeared to be near an end, and not only Cubans, but the entire city, watched with both anticipation and foreboding. What new surprises did the convulsed island hold in store? Would the "City of the Future" be suddenly abandoned by half its population, as militant exile leaders promised? Or would it, on the contrary, be inundated by a still larger inflow of post-Castro refugees?

Both scenarios are probably overdrawn. A massive return to Cuba is unlikely because of the roots established during three decades of settlement and the growing process of social convergence. Few well-established former exiles are likely to pack up and leave all they have accomplished behind. A recent survey on the topic by researchers at Florida International University shows that only a third of adult Cuban residents (38 percent) in Dade County would consider returning to the island to live in the event of Castro's downfall. Such a move is even less probable among U.S.-born Cuban-Americans. Only the most recent refugees, those with the least social roots and smallest economic assets, are likely to find the return option attractive.

And although a new refugee influx is more likely because of widespread material scarcities in Cuba, it would probably be checked by the end of the island's special status as America's main adversary in the Western Hemisphere. With the conversion of Cuba into just another Caribbean country, new arrivals would necessarily be labeled conventional immigrants rather than political refugees.

If the downfall of Castroism would not lead to a major demographic movement, it could have a subtler but still far-reaching effect, namely, the end of the monolithic ideological outlook that undergirds the Cuban ethnic economy. For more than three decades, ideological fervor and tight social controls have been maintained on the strength of a single theme: irreconcilable opposition to Castro and communism. This has been the message hammered out daily by the Cuban exile media, and it has furnished the frame according to which all other domestic and world events are interpreted. Castro's end would remove the raison d'être of this fierce preaching and put the bellicose radio commentators and militant activists on the spot: either they move back to Cuba as announced for so long, or they accept their role as regular immigrants and, hence, the inevitable reality of assimilation.

The same is true, in fact, for the entire community. Among those former exiles who choose to remain in Miami – easily the majority – the claim of a unique status based on principled opposition to a dictatorial regime would dissolve. The social mechanisms that underlie business success in the enclave may remain, on the strength of habit and past practice, but would weaken over time because of the loss of social controls rooted in exile ideology. In these circumstances, the most likely prognosis is the gradual end of the ethnic economy and the acceleration of the process of cultural convergence, already under way.

Yet Miami will never return to what it was before its transformation. The former exiles will still be there, and new Caribbean and South American inflows will replace them in number, if not in ideological fervor. Even today, in the midst of the deathwatch, the process of acculturation-in-reverse continues. Every year, new parts of Miami become more like Havana, or at least like the nostalgic image that Cubans have of their capital city. In an article entitled "Miami's Crossroads of the Vanities," *Herald* columnist Howard Kleinberg lamented that the streets in the "Latin quarter" were being named for "Latin American militarists and romantics who never had been to Miami and whose names barely made it into any encyclopedia."[17] He proposed instead that the City Commission name a street for John Reilly, the city's first mayor, and another for Francisco Villareal, the Spanish friar who in 1567 established the first Catholic mission on the site of today's Hyatt Regency.

Despite his otherwise keen observations, Kleinberg failed to understand the driving force behind all this name changing. The intention was not to memorialize Miami as it had been until 1959, but rather to celebrate pre-Castro Havana. In their symbolic reenactment of a lost past, Cubans and their elected leaders could not be counted on to know much about the Merricks, the Reillys, and the Deerings, though these were prominent men in the city's modest history. Instead a much older past was imported, so that the friars, scholars, and soldiers whose names now adorned the streets of Miami were also those who gave their names to streets and schools in Cuba.

With or without Castro's downfall, a long-term trend toward integration and cultural convergence appears inevitable. In the short to medium term, however, Miami will continue to be characterized by ethnic fragmentation, strife, lack of a hegemonic discourse, and the nostalgic reproduction of a foreign past. For Karl Marx, great historical dramas are often enacted twice, the second time as farce. There are indeed tragicomic aspects to the exiles' single-minded attempt to reenact past lives in South Florida. There is nothing farcical, however, in the depths of the transformation that they have wrought and in the unique urban experiment that their presence, along with that of natives and newer immigrants, have forged in their adopted city.

Notes

1   Adna F. Weber, *The Growth of Cities in the Nineteenth Century: A Study in Statistics* (Ithaca, N.Y.: Cornell University Press, 1967), 172. See also the classic essay on the origins of European urbanization by Henri Pirenne, *Medieval Cities: Their Origins and the Revival of Trade* (Princeton: Princeton University Press [1925] 1970); and Max Weber, *The City* (New York: Free Press [1921] 1966), chap. 1.

2   François Lamarche, "Property Development and the Economic Foundations of the Urban Question," in *Urban Sociology: Critical Essays*, ed. C. G. Pickvance (New York: St. Martin's Press, 1976), 86.

3   Rieff, *Going to Miami*.

4   Tom Fielder, "Politically, We'll Hardly Recognize the Place," *Miami Herald*, October 6, 1991, 5C.

5   Field observations by the authors, Miami, 1989. The speaker went on to become a prominent member of the Miami Chamber of Commerce.

6   Richard Wallace, "South Florida Grows to a Latin Beat," *Miami Herald*, March 6, 1991, 1–2Z; Carl Goldfarb, "Alienation Keeps Miami's Anglos away from Polls," *Miami Herald*, November 19, 1989, 1–2B.

7   James K. Batten, "Miami's Can-Do Spirit Remains Strong Even in Tough Times," *Miami Herald*, October 10, 1991.

8   Ibid.

9   David Lawrence, Jr., "Get on the Ball...Learn a Language," *Miami Herald*, March 24, 1991, 2C.

10 Xavier L. Suárez, "Miami Is Poised to Fulfill 'City of the Future' Role," *Miami Herald*, December 6, 1989.
11 Lopez-Miró, "Where the 'Cuban' Ends."
12 Dahl, *Who Governs?*, 33–4.
13 Richard D. Lamm and Gary Imhoff, *The Immigration Time-Bomb: The Fragmenting of America* (New York: E. P. Dutton, 1985), 123–4.
14 Field interview, January 7 and 8, 1992.
15 Sandra Dibble, "Think Tank Seeks Wide-Ranging Plan for Life After Castro," *Miami Herald*, February 23, 1990, 1–3B.
16 Pablo Alfonso, "Panel Offers a Plan for Governing New Cuba," *Miami Herald*, March 3, 1990.
17 Howard Kleinberg, "Greater Miami's Crossroads of the Vanities; City Renames History Streets at the Whim of Politicians," *Miami Herald*, July 31, 1990.

21 Russia and the Russian Diasporas

Igor Zevelev

The collapse of the Soviet Union occurred remarkably swiftly and relatively smoothly, especially when compared to the debacle of another multinational communist federation: Yugoslavia. All armed conflicts have occurred on the periphery of the former Soviet empire, while its core, though not very stable, thus far has avoided major violence. Such a situation stands in sharp contrast to the fact that the core nation, the Russians, appear to have been the greatest losers in the aftermath of the Soviet Union.

Since late 1990, there have been many predictions that the real trouble in Eurasia would start when the interests of Russians are challenged by other ethnic groups (Carrere d'Encausse, 1990, p. 389; Shlapentokh and Sendich, 1994, pp. xx, xxiii). With the disintegration of the USSR, Russia (apparently) lost its imperial role, while more than twenty-five million Russians suddenly found themselves outside of Russia, creating an instant diaspora and their instant transformation from a dominant group to an ethnic minority within the new states. Many of these Russians have never reconciled themselves to this change in status and to the open or hidden discrimination they may face. Millions of them have voted with their feet and migrated to Russia.

Nevertheless, the issue of Russians in the "Near Abroad" seems now to be less intense then had earlier been predicted. Why? Why has there been no open violence between Russians and other groups, with the partial and isolated exception of *Pridnyestrooye*, where ethnicity is only one of several factors in the conflict? Why has not the specter of the former Yugoslavia come to the former Soviet Union?

In this article, we shall argue that a key to answering this question may lie in the restrained or muted policies of the Russian Federation. Contrary to the belief that Russian policy in the "Near Abroad" has been imperialistic and aggressive over issues concerning the new Russian diasporas, we find that Russian policy has instead been reasonably moderate in some of its features and tremendously ineffective in others. Indeed, in those undertakings that could destabilize the whole region, Russian policy has been particularly ineffective. As a result of both moderation and ineffectiveness, there is a great discrepancy between the boastful, assertive rhetoric of Russia's leaders and the actual policy of Russia in its relations with the Russian diasporas.

We will test this hypothesis by analyzing three Russian policies toward Russian diasporas in the "Near Abroad": (1) Russia's lost battle for dual citizenship; (2) the adoption of a very moderate governmental program (Osnovnyye, 1994) and its actual conversion into the cornerstone of the official perspective of the Russian

state; and (3) the strengthening of multilateralism as a restraining factor in relations among the successor states. All three of these are recent manifestations that
surfaced fully only in 1995. They belie generalizations about contemporary Russian policy that are based on the rhetoric and aspirations of 1993–4.

Dual Citizenship

Many people who found themselves in other successor states after the disintegration of the Soviet Union looked upon Russia as a destination of possible migration
or as a power that might help to ensure their rights and interests. However, their
bonds with Russia were not always clear. For some, these were ties of ethnicity.
For others, Russia was a place of birth and/or long-time residence. And for many
Russified intellectuals of non-Russian origin, it represented the center of "Soviet
civilization," as a prominent dissident (Sinyavsky, 1990) called the cultural context
of the Soviet Union. These people viewed Russia as the successor of a culturally
diverse Soviet Union that was very different from the more ethnically-oriented
newly independent states. In most cases, this viewpoint had nothing to do with a
nostalgia for the USSR or communism.

Recent demographic trends illustrate the pull of Russia for so many citizens of
successor states. More people migrate to Russia than out of Russia. More people
in the "Near Abroad" want to establish some sort of cultural, business or political
relations with Russia than do residents of Russia with other former Soviet republics. Moscow and other large Russian cities are full of cosmopolitan businesses,
criminal organizations, and cultural elites, political dissidents and opposition activists from every former republic of the Soviet Union. But most of those who
immigrate into Russia are ethnic Russians, and most of those who seek to establish
some sort of secure ties with Russia, while residing permanently in another state,
are also ethnic Russians.

The Russian government has felt the tension between the concept of a Russian
state within the arbitrarily-drawn borders of the RSFSR, on the one hand, and the
actual domain of Russian culture, language and national consciousness, on the
other. The idea of dual citizenship was originally perceived as something of a
panacea for all the problems associated with this discrepancy between the boundaries of the newly emerging state and those of the newly emerging nation. Seizing
upon this idea, the Russian government decided to grant Russian citizenship to all
Russians, as well as to people of other nationalities who had some sort of historic
tie with the territory of Russia. This was to be a supplement to the local citizenships granted by the other independent states.

To officials in the Russian government, the advantages of such dual citizenship
for Russians in the "Near Abroad" seemed to be threefold. First, such a policy
looked much more "civilized" (a favorite term of the Russian political elite) than
would the establishment of some sort of "special relationship" with coethnics
abroad. It stressed the civic, not ethnic, nature of the Russian polity and policy,
and thus held promise of protecting the Russian nation without exacerbating ethnic conflict. Indeed, Andrey Kozyrev wrote in precisely such terms in
his memoirs (Kozyrev, 1995, p. 98): "We cannot put an ethnic factor in the

foundation of our policy. It would lead to conflicts among nationalities like those in Yugoslavia."

A second perceived advantage of the dual citizenship policy was that it could help curb an uncontrolled flow of migrants to Russia by providing them some sort of security and peace of mind in their host state. At the same time, it could also help to prevent irredentism. Russia, being in deep economic crisis, could not accommodate millions of newcomers or fight wars for new territories. Abdulakh Mikitayev, chief of the Citizenship Directorate of the President's Administration, and chairman of the Presidential Commission on Citizenship, expressed the sentiment candidly in an interview in an official Russian publication: "One of the major tasks of state policy, in my view, is the prevention of a mass exodus of people from the states of the former Union" (*Rossiyskaya Federatsiya*, 22–4, November–December, 1994, p. 55).

The third advantage of dual citizenship was more self-aggrandizing than geared toward conflict-avoidance. The policy could serve as a convenient source of leverage and influence on the neighboring states and as an instrument for implementing a Russian policy of domination and hegemonism. The protection by a powerful state of its citizens abroad has become a normal practice in modern international relations. This policy has been used often by the United States in Latin America and by France in Africa. If Russia could have millions of its citizens in neighboring states, no one would be able to challenge its absolute and unrestrained domination in Eurasia.

The idea of dual citizenship actually replaced an earlier policy that was less attentive to the interests of Russians in the "Near Abroad." In 1992, Russia instead adopted a strategy of "denationalized state-building," defined as the creation and stabilization of new state institutions within the borders of RSFSR, establishment of the inviolability of borders between the former Soviet republics, and development of relations with neighboring states as equal, fully-independent entities. This official policy lasted only about a year. Indeed, it stood in tension with the supplementary political rhetoric of top officials, who boasted of their willingness to defend "compatriots abroad." In April 1992, only four months after the Byelovezhskaya Pushcha agreements, Boris Yeltsin, in a speech at the Sixth Congress of People's Deputies, declared: "Twenty-five million of our compatriots in these countries must not and will not be forgotten by Russia" (*Nezavisimaya gazeta*, January 1, 1994). In another speech at the same congress a few days later, he admitted: "we still defend our compatriots poorly" (*Nezavisimaya gazeta*, January 1, 1994). But in 1992, these sentiments remained at the level of rhetoric.

In 1993, the idea of dual citizenship, as a concrete tool for the defense of compatriots, started to take shape. President Yeltsin took the lead. The concept then found supporters in the Supreme Soviet, and was promoted by the Foreign Ministry and personally by Andrey Kozyrev, by the Presidential Commission on Citizenship and, importantly, by the Ministry of Defense. The new Russian military doctrine, adopted in 1993, identified as an "external danger" abuse of "the rights, freedoms and legal interests of citizens of the Russian Federation in foreign countries" (*Voyennaya mysl'*, [special issue], November 1993, p. 5). The creation of such a category of citizens abroad was a precondition for subsequently justifying intervention by the Russian military in their defense. Thus, with his usual grace, General Pavel Grachyov entered the arena of discourse and inadvertently undermined the undertaking by showing Russia's neighbors all the possible consequences of the new strategy.

The parliamentary elections of December 1993 strengthened the assertive, nationalistic trends in official policy. In January 1994, Foreign Minister Kozyrev organized a conference of Russian ambassadors to the countries of the Commonwealth of Independent States and the Baltics. Also participating were the Russian Minister of Interior, Deputy Minister of Defense and other high officials. In his speech to the conference, Kozyrev declared that protection of the rights of "compatriots" in the near abroad was "the main strategic task of Russia's foreign policy," and that dual citizenship was the major instrument for fulfilling that task. This was the first time that the issue of dual citizenship was elevated to such a high place on Russia's foreign policy agenda.

In 1994, important support for the idea came from the Federal Migration Service (FMS), an agency of the Russian government. According to the Federal Migration Program, adopted by presidential decree in August 1994, "it is necessary to strive for recognition of dual citizenship by these states" (Federal'naya, 1994, Art. 2.2, p. 37). The reason for support of the idea from this quarter was clear. According to the FMS's minimal forecast, the number of forced migrants from the "Near Abroad" to Russia in 1994–6 was projected to be more than 800,000. Their intermediate variant projected 2–3 million; the maximal projection, 4–6 million. Yet the Federal Migration Program is financed to accommodate only 400,000 people, or half the minimal forecast. Accordingly, the position of the Federal Migration Service is easy to explain: it hoped that dual citizenship would keep many potential migrants to Russia at home.

By 1994 there had formed a strong coalition for dual citizenship. It included the major branches of the Russian government, significant constituencies within Russia who did not want to acknowledge that Russians outside Russia suddenly found themselves turned into foreigners, and Russian communities in the "Near Abroad." This coalition was opposed by the governments of all other successor states, which feared that their nation-building tasks would be undermined by dual citizenship. The non-Russian population of the Eurasian republics was also suspicious of the idea. It was unclear by what criteria Russia intended to confer Russian citizenship on persons who, in most cases other than Latvia and Estonia, already were citizens of other countries. The selection process might contradict the principle of equal rights regardless of ethnicity, religion, or language.

In spite of vigorous promotion of the idea of dual citizenship by Boris Yel'tsin, Andrey Kozyrev, Abdulakh Mikitayev and others, all bilateral talks with their counterparts from the Eurasian republics have achieved virtually nothing. The only significant result of the attempts to use this "major instrument" in fulfilling "the main strategic task of Russia's foreign policy" has been an agreement with Turkmenistan signed in December 1993. At that time, Boris Yel'tsin was solemnly granted a Turkmen passport in Ashgabat. It is noteworthy that the Russian diaspora in Turkmenistan is one of the smallest in the former USSR.

Four developments in 1995 were indicative of the complete and, apparently, final failure of Russian policy in this area. First, Ukrainian President Leonid Kuchma took a firm stand against dual citizenship, despite his presidential campaign pledges of 1994. In February 1995, after talks with President Yeltsin in Moscow, Mr. Kuchma said that he would not sign any agreements with Russia if they so much as mentioned dual citizenship (*Kommersant-daily*, February 2, 1995). Disagreement on dual citizenship was one of the reasons that a comprehensive treaty between Russia and Ukraine was not signed in 1995. The main reason for postponement, however, lay elsewhere – in disputes over the Black Sea fleet – and the treaty still had not been signed at the time of the June 1996 Russian presidential elections.

Second, the analogous comprehensive treaty with Belarus (Dogovor, 1995b) was signed in February 1995, but contained no provisions on dual citizenship. Third, after long, persistent and desperate Russian pressure on Kazakhstan regarding dual citizenship, Yeltsin's government retreated and signed two documents that contained no provisions for dual citizenship (Dogovor, 1995a; Soglasheniye, 1995). Instead of dual citizenship, these documents offered easier acquisition of the new citizenship with simultaneous loss of the previous one.

It is worth bearing in mind that 75 percent of the new Russian diasporas reside in the three countries just discussed: Ukraine, Belarus and Kazakhstan. The failure to achieve progress on dual citizenship with all three countries signified the practical collapse of Russia's strategy.

The fourth indicator of failure was a policy document (Strategicheskiy kurs, 1995) signed into law by President Yeltsin in September 1995. This document did not contain a single word about dual citizenship. Instead, it outlined different, and in most cases much less effective, measures for establishing relations with the Russian diaspora. It called for smooth adaptation by Russians to their host societies, preservation of their culture, and the use of trade sanctions by Moscow in case of serious violations of their rights.

The State Duma Committee on CIS Affairs and Relations with Compatriots, headed by Konstantin Zatulin, was one of a few state agencies that stood firm on issues of dual citizenship in 1995. It stated that it would oppose ratification of any treaty with the newly independent states if there was no provision for dual citizenship (*Nezavisimaya gazeta*, February 23, 1995). Yet even this threat was muted when it clashed with realities. Thus, during the second half of 1995, which was marked by a heated preelection campaign, the Committee's level of activity was low. Its last achievement was to establish a "Council of Compatriots," an analytical-consultative body of the State Duma charged with representing the interests of *rossiyanye* residing abroad – that is, of Russian citizens and their descendants who acknowledge cultural "belonging" to Russia. It is noteworthy that there was no mention of dual citizenship in the Declaration of the Constituent Congress of this Council. Instead, it called for reintegration of the former Soviet republics and Moscow's benevolence toward compatriots living in the Near Abroad (Deklaratsiya, 1995).

The current law on citizenship (Zakon, 1993) is a very good indicator of the nature and evolution of Russia's policy toward Russians living abroad. In accordance with international norms, Russia acknowledged that dual citizenship could exist only in the context of a treaty relationship with a particular state. The law on citizenship is very friendly to those former Soviet citizens who reside in other successor states and wish to *move to Russia* and become Russian citizens. Indeed, all changes and amendments to the law, since its initial adoption in November 1991, have made it progressively easier to obtain Russian citizenship by broadening the categories of individuals who can obtain such citizenship automatically, by registration and not through an application process, once they have moved to Russia. In 1995, the period for obtaining Russian citizenship by registration after migration to Russia was extended until the year 2000. But, facing strong opposition from virtually all its neighboring states, and especially vigorous protests in Estonia and Ukraine, Russia did not dare to extend the same rights to those who preferred to stay in their host state. This opportunity had been granted to residents of former Soviet republics for only one year, from June 17, 1993 to June 17, 1994. The subsequent retreat meant that Russia, aside from the failure with dual citizenship, never introduced a permanent mechanism for creating "pure" Russian citizens in the "Near Abroad."

Though obtaining Russian citizenship, either by registration or application, was rather easy, very few people from the "Near Abroad" dared to obtain it at the price of losing their citizenship of the state in which they were residing. There are no reliable statistics on this, but the number of registered voters for elections to the State Duma in December 1995 may suffice as an indirect indicator. Only 200,000 were registered (OMRI, 1995), or less than 1 percent of Russians residing in the "Near Abroad." This figure is very low, even if some "illegal" dual citizens, who obtained Russian passports without revoking their previous ones, did not want to expose themselves by registering as voters.

Thus, dual citizenship, once elevated to a strategic task of Russian foreign policy, started disappearing from the political agenda in 1995. A very important instrument of the Russian policy of hegemony and dominance, one with great destabilizing potential, has not been created, despite energetic efforts by the Russian government. When Moscow encountered determined resistance from other governments on this issue, it simply backed off.

The Concept of "Compatriots Living Abroad"

In 1994, the Russian government decided to supplement the idea of dual citizenship with a broader strategy of building special relations with Russians living abroad. It officially endorsed the concept of "compatriots" (fellow countrymen). Abdulakh Mikitayev claimed that it was he who persuaded Mr. Yeltsin to adopt a special government program to this effect (*Rossiyskaya Federatsiya*, 22–4, November–December 1994, p. 56). Andrey Kozyrev reported in his memoirs (Kozyrev, 1995, p. 105) that he was proud of the fact that his Ministry for Foreign Affairs initiated the program.

According to Mr. Mikitayev, there are three categories of residents of the neighboring states who qualify as "compatriots": (1) Russian citizens residing in the "Near Abroad"; (2) former Soviet citizens who have not obtained new citizenships (apatriates, or stateless persons, most of whom live in Latvia and Estonia); and (3) those who obtained citizenship of the host country but wish to maintain their own culture and ties with Russia (Mikitayev, in *Diplomaticheskiy vestnik MID RF* (Diplomatic herald of the Ministry of Foreign Affairs of the Russian Federation),

2, 1995, p. 52). From this perspective, "compatriots" form a broader circle, with Russian citizens residing abroad as its core. Russia's ties with this broader entity were seen as a bit looser than those with Russian citizens.

On August 11, 1994, President Yeltsin signed a decree (Ukaz Prezidenta, 1994) that called for the government to formulate the major components of this policy. On August 31, 1994, the government adopted such a program (Osnovnyye napravleniya, 1994). This document defined the "strategic line of Russia's policy towards the compatriots" as promotion of their voluntary integration into the host states in a way that both adapted to local culture and preserved their own distinctive culture. The program read like a manifesto of multiculturalism. It avoided any indications that it had been designed for ethnic Russians alone. It spoke for all nationalities whose roots lay in the territory of Russia.

According to this program, the Russian government's primary means for defending the rights and interests of compatriots must be diplomatic and economic. It suggested the use of international human rights instruments and, in extreme cases, economic pressure. It called for strengthening cultural ties with the compatriots by broadcasting Russian-language television in the neighboring states, supporting other Russian-language mass media, assisting cultural centers, and the like. It also called for the promotion of economic ties between Russia and those enterprises in the "Near Abroad" in which most employees were "compatriots."

Generally, the structure, language and style of the program were reminiscent of documents designed by the Central Committee of the CPSU under the old regime: much abstract terminology, lack of clarity about implementation, and poor guidelines for coordination among governmental bodies. It did not read as if decision-makers in the government truly believed that the program would ever be fully implemented. Many provisions required financial resources the government evidently lacked in the face of severe budget constraints. The real significance of the program seemed to be in its spirit: it reflected the strategy of state-building within the borders of present-day Russia, supplemented by moderate support for compatriots in the "Near Abroad." The primary aim of this support was defined in the program as preventing the mass immigration of those "compatriots" into Russia.

Once the attempt to introduce dual citizenship began to fail, this program became the primary framework for Russian policy toward Russians in the "Near Abroad." Designed originally as a supplement to the strategy of dual citizenship, it came to be the heart of the policy. Dual citizenship had the potential to be converted into a very strong instrument of domination within the Eurasian region. The program of aid to compatriots, by contrast, lacks that kind of potential.

Multilateralism

A third component of Russian policy in this realm has been efforts undertaken within the multilateral framework of the Commonwealth of Independent States (CIS). Andrey Kozyrev, a dedicated neo-liberal in his views on world politics, assumed in his memoirs that the problems of the Russian-speaking population could not be addressed as a bilateral issue in relations between Russia and other Soviet successor states. Instead, he wrote, "Russian diplomacy seeks to make the defense of human rights and the rights of ethnic minorities one of the major policy directions of the Commonwealth." He also admitted: "I will tell you straight: the human rights dialogue is not proceeding easily. There are still misgivings that Russia will use it to interfere in the domestic affairs of its neighbors" (Kozyrev, 1995, p. 99).

As a result of such "misgivings," no document adopted within the framework of CIS thus far has directly addressed the issue of the Russian or any other diasporas. Nevertheless, in 1994–5 several important declarations and agreements were signed that have borne on the issue. The "Declaration on Sovereignty, Territorial Integrity, and Inviolability of Borders" (Deklaratsiya, 1994) and the "Memorandum on Peace and Stability in the CIS" (Memorandum, 1995) were among the first multilateral CIS documents that strongly and unconditionally condemned separatism and any support of separatism. Russia, by supporting these principles, actually sent a message against irredentism to the Russian diasporas in Kazakhstan, Ukraine, Moldova and other newly independent states.

In May 1995, adoption of the CIS "Convention on Human Rights and Fundamental Freedoms" (Konventsiya, 1995) was still another indicator of the moderation of Russian policy. Notably, the Convention addressed all problems of human rights as individual rights, not as collective or group rights. True, Article 21 declared that persons belonging to ethnic minorities shall not be denied the right to express, maintain and develop their distinctive ethnic, linguistic or religious culture. However, this simply echoed article 27 of the 1966 United Nations' International Covenant on Civil and Political Rights. This right, in the particular wording of the UN Covenant, is an individual right. It is attributed to "persons belonging to...minorities," not to communities (United Nations, 1985, p. 31). This means that no affirmative action on the part of the state is required. The only obligation of the state is not to prevent individuals from enjoying their distinctive culture. Article 27 of the CIS Convention confirmed this principle by stating that each participating state must "respect the right of parents to provide their children with education and teaching that corresponds to their own beliefs and national traditions." The CIS Convention, following the 1966 UN Covenant, is much more conservative and limited than the OSCE approach, which includes acknowledgment of the group rights of ethnic minorities.

The CIS Convention provides almost no basis for governments to support ethnic minorities living abroad. Instead, it creates a legal framework for the multilateral support of individual human rights. This is not exactly what Russia is seeking, if she is concerned to bolster her instruments of domination in the region. Nevertheless, Russia was a driving force for adoption of the Convention. Immediately after the signing of the document, Russia started lobbying for the establishment of a CIS Commission on Human Rights to monitor compliance by parties to the Convention.

In 1993–4, some politicians and officials within Russia were hoping to promote the idea of a convention on the rights of ethnic minorities within the CIS. Thus far, however, all attempts to elaborate this idea, and to persuade other countries to back it, have failed. The result has been an ambiguous situation wherein multilateral instruments of the CIS are oriented toward individual rights, while unilateral Russian policy is oriented toward supporting the rights of collectivities ("compatriots").

The multilateral regimes and agreements, in turn, serve as an important obstacle to any attempt to use the issue of diasporas as an instrument of Russia's hegemony or dominance in Eurasia.

Nationalist Rhetoric and Imperatives of State-building

The evidence adduced thus far suggests that, with respect to three areas of policy toward Russian diasporas, the most assertive strategy (introduction of dual citizenship) has been a failure, while the others (strengthening ties with compatriots and creation of multilateral instruments within the CIS) have been very modest and moderate in content. Let us now turn, however, to the opposition to these outcomes within Russia.

Opponents of moderation during 1992–5 urged the adoption of three highly assertive policies: (1) trade sanctions against Latvia and Estonia as punishment for their citizenship policies toward Russian-speakers; (2) pressure for the elevation of Russian language to the status of the second official language in states with a significant Russian-speaking population (Ukraine, Kazakhstan, Belarus, Moldova, Latvia and Estonia); and (3) pressure for the self-governance of Russian communities within the "Near Abroad" (*Sovremyennaya*, 1995, pp. 87–93).

In the chaotic years that followed the disintegration of the USSR, some high-ranking members of the Russian government actually sided with the opposition on the issue of relations with the Russian diasporas. This was especially the case during the period December 1991–December 1993, up through the forcible dissolution of the Supreme Soviet and the adoption of a new constitution. For example, former vice-president Aleksandr Rutskoy and Yel'tsin's advisor, Sergey Stankevich, were much tougher then the rest of the government and suggested that Russia recognize Crimea and Pridnyeprovye as sovereign entities because the large majority of their populations were Russian (Kolstoe, 1995, p. 271)

Although none of these hardline measures were adopted by the Russian government, there has been plenty of tough rhetoric on the issue. The gap between rhetoric and action has been a large one throughout the period of Russian independence. Thus, in 1992, Boris Yeltsin, looking and sounding tough, made an explicit linkage between the treatment of Russian minorities on issues of citizenship in Latvia and Estonia and the withdrawal of Russian army troops from those countries. But this in no way affected the schedule of troop withdrawals. And since 1992, Andrey Kozyrev, following Yeltsin, had been threatening to implement "forceful methods" to protect Russians in the "Near Abroad." The gap between Kozyrev's rhetoric and actual policies remained large until his resignation in 1996.

What, then, explains this gap? First, defense of the rights and interests of Russian minorities is seen by the current regime as an instrument, not a goal, of domination throughout the territory of the former Soviet Union. That instrument has consistently been compromised for the sake of other policies that are considered to be of higher priority. However, the regime has found it convenient to keep the issue alive. But the gap cannot be explained by reference to a *general* lack of will or capacity to dominate. In some other areas Russia has been more successful in establishing its regional hegemony: (1) the dependency of new states on Russia's energy resources; (2) success in wringing concessions from certain neighbors on the retention of Russian military bases on their soil; and (3) joint patrolling of borders.

Second, and these successes notwithstanding, there remains a large gap between Russia's ambitions of domination in the whole Eurasian region and its current limited ability to carry out this burden. Being in deep economic crisis, facing tremendous social problems, having a significantly weakened and disorganized army, and being politically unstable, Russia hardly matches the portrait of a regional hegemon. It is only Russia's potential, combined with the extremely frail condition of most neighboring states, that gives some basis for its stated aspirations. But that potential cannot be realized until Russia has gone through several years of stabilization.

A third reason for the gap between rhetoric and policy relates to the contradictions between the principles being espoused by Russian officials and the realities of Russia's *internal* federative structure. For example, had Russia officially supported Crimean demands to join Russia, or even to elevate significantly its level of autonomy from Ukraine, there could have been serious repercussions for the nature and legitimacy of regional demands within Russia. While working hard to "strengthen" the "integrity" of Russia and the Russian state, Yeltsin's regime could not afford to prevent other newly independent states from consolidating their own statehood.

Stephen Sestanovich (1995, p. 78) recently suggested a thoughtful parallel between France of the 1960s and Russia of the 1990s, relying on a three-decade-old analysis by Henry Kissinger of President Charles De Gaulle's leadership. De Gaulle, according to Kissinger, attempted to revive the glory of France with the help of tough, nationalistic, often anti-American rhetoric that resonated in a humiliated country that was experiencing a crisis of identity. Contemporary Russia has even fewer resources than did De Gaulle's France to back up its rhetoric. But what is common to the two cases is the therapeutic effect of words. They help to heal wounds and, when they are not backed by aggressive policies, they need not destabilize international relations. The real danger in this situation is in the overreaction of other actors in the international arena to the threatening noises. Thus, Russian rhetoric on protection of compatriots might help to offset psychologically the shock of the actual division of the Russian nation once the Soviet Union broke up. Such rhetoric can help to ease the tensions engendered by a policy of statebuilding within the current, artificial borders of Russia, which reflect neither historical experience nor the perceptions of Russians regarding the spatial distribution and formal subordination of their nation. Thus far at least, verbal imperialism (rhetoric) may have helped to prevent a real policy of imperialism.

In 1992, Russian policy toward the Russian diasporas was entirely rhetorical. During 1993–4, there took place an attempt to back up the rhetoric with some assertive measures, including the advocacy of dual citizenship. By 1995–6, after the failure of this undertaking, there remained only a combination of moderate policy and tough rhetoric.

Contemporary Russia is neither a nation-state nor an empire. It is, rather, in the process of becoming a hegemonic regional power. The thrust of its policy is to combine state-building within its current borders with the creation of a zone of formally sovereign, but effectively dependent countries around Russia. Our analysis of one of the key components of this policy – building special relations with the new Russian diasporas – has demonstrated that this is no easy task. It has also shown that, whatever their ideal aspirations, Russian policymakers have adjusted their policies to real-world constraints, while compensating for the adjustment with boastful rhetoric.

Future Prospects

Will the issue of Russian diasporas remain in its current dormant form? There are many reasons to believe that the situation will not change as a result of assertiveness on the part of the diasporians themselves. First, there are no noticeable, horizontal ties between the Russian communities (Teague, 1994, p. 82), and few prospects that they will be constructed. As a result, without involvement by the government of Russia, problems arising within the diasporas are likely to remain local issues. Differences in the characteristics of these communities, moreover, bode ill for their developing horizontal ties. They are very different in size, lifestyle, and level of integration into their host societies. They do not have a common enemy or a single vision. The percentage of Russians knowing, as a second language, the titular language of the republic in which they lived in 1989 (the year of the last Soviet population census) varied from more than 30 percent in Ukraine, Lithuania, and Armenia to 1 percent in Kazakhstan and Kyrgyzstan. Russians constituted more than 70 percent of those employed in the sciences in Kazakhstan and Kyrgyzstan, while the same indicator for Armenia was only 6 percent (Harris, 1993, pp. 22, 24). After the breakup of the Soviet Union these differences were dramatically increased by the variety of internal conditions among the newly independent states. Thus, it is very difficult to find a common denominator for Russians fleeing the horrors of the civil war in Muslim Tadjikistan versus the relatively affluent Russian community in "European" Latvia, where the major problem is acquiring citizenship. Perhaps only two factors unite all Russian communities: a common culture and an "external historic homeland": Russia.

Second, Russian communities are very poorly organized. Political or any other mobilization, solidarity and cooperation along ethnic lines are entirely new concepts for the formerly dominant people.

Third, there is a widespread belief in Eurasia that only the existence of Russia can prevent the Russian communities from repeating the historic experience of some other diasporas: Jewish, Greek, Armenian. This belief gains support from comparative perspectives on the fates of diasporas. As the late Ernest Gellner (1983, p. 105) wrote: "The disastrous and tragic consequences, in modern conditions, of the conjunction of economic superiority and cultural identifiability with political and military weakness, are too well known to require repetition." All the former Soviet republics have adopted ethno-political myths (Connor, 1986) identifying the state as a homeland of a specific, indigenous people. This is reflected in the names of the new states, their flags, anthems, emblems, official histories and holidays. Walker Connor's generalization (1986, p. 18) about the impact of such developments upon diasporas more generally is quite applicable to the current environment in most Soviet successor states:

> Diasporas are viewed at best as outsiders, strangers within the gates. They may be tolerated, even treated most equitably, and individual members of the diaspora may achieve highest office. Their state may be multigenerational, but they remain outsiders in the eyes of the indigenes, who reserve the inalienable right to assert their primary and exclusive proprietary claim to the homeland, should they so desire. Moreover, in a number of cases what superficially might pass for the peaceful acceptance of a diaspora has been due to the lack of means to purge the homeland of an alien presence.

In most cases, Russian diasporas themselves, without the assistance of Russia, are unable to prevent unfavorable developments in the "Near Abroad."

In sum, the diasporians themselves are unlikely to force a change in their status. The governments of the successor states, by endorsing or initiating persecution of the Russian diasporas, could well trigger a backlash by the Russian government. Short of that, what are the chances that the Russian government will more actively use its preponderance of power *vis-à-vis* the "Near Abroad" to protect the interests of Russian diasporas, or manipulate the issue in order to create leverage against the governments of those states? Our analysis of Russian policy to date showed that Moscow has been restrained and moderate thus far, especially when facing resistance. However, the issue of the diasporas, and the alleged responsibility of Russia to them, have been injected into the theoretical discussions of state-building and nation-building that have helped to shape Russia's political agenda.

One of the currently influential, though not politically well organized, perspectives on state-building and nation-building in Russia is ethno-nationalism (Zevelev, 1995, pp. 28–9, 35). This viewpoint begins with the observation that the Russian people do not occupy the same juridical territory, now that the Soviet Union has collapsed. The essence of the ethnonationalist program is to restore a geographical congruence between state and nation: to build the Russian state within the area of settlement of the Russian people and other Eastern Slavs. Politically, this means the reunification of Russia, Ukraine, Belarus, and Northern Kazakhstan, called "Southern Siberia and Southern (Trans) Urals" by Aleksandr Solzhenitsyn, the founder of ethnonationalism in modern Russia (Solzhenitsyn, 1990, p.7).

Two consequences of the collapse of the USSR bear on the prospects that this ethnonationalist tendency might emerge ascendant in Russian politics. First, and on the one hand, Russian ethnic identity, no longer hidden under the imperial veil, has become more salient to Russians in both the Russian Federation and other successor states. Ethnonationalists, therefore, now have less grounds for complaining that the imperial role deprives Russians of their ethnicity. Second, and on the other hand, the emergence of fifteen independent states inevitably leads to the weakening of political connectedness among Russians. This ruptures the centuries-old tradition of Russians grouping themselves around the state. Sooner or later, these two trends may start seriously to contradict each other. As has happened many times in the history of Europe, a well-articulated common culture may come to be defined as the ideal political boundary, leading to strong claims that all Russians be reunited under one political roof. Current Russian policy, after the failure to secure dual citizenship agreements, resists such a trend by concentrating on state-building within the Russian Federation and by limiting itself mainly to the promotion of Russian culture in its relations with the diasporas. But we should not assume that current policy will necessarily prevail over ethnonationalist sentiments indefinitely.

How can such ideological currents make their way onto the political agenda? Thus far, the issue of diasporas has been kept mainly behind the lines of Russian politics, but under specifiable conditions it can be dragged to the front lines. Studies of nationalist movements in other parts of the world, for example, led James Mayall (1994, p. 272) to the conclusion that irredentist claims "are available to governments as a mobilization instrument, a means of securing popular support at times when, for whatever reason, such support seems particularly desirable." In Russia, the issue of the diasporas in any form, including, irredentism, can be used to generate popular support by defining it credibly as a major concern of national interest and security.

But when are circumstances most propitious for credibly floating such an idea? George Breslauer (1995, p. 19), in a recent analysis of political leadership in post-Soviet Russia as it relates to the decision to invade Chechnya, identified one circumstance that catalyzes unexpected military adventures from the Russian government:

> In contrast to leaders in more strongly institutionalized (or constitutionalized) regimes who may seek only "minimal winning coalitions" on policy, both Soviet and post-Soviet leaders have felt the need to *over*insure themselves. This may explain why they all embraced programs that promised a great deal to almost everybody, and that therefore proved impossible to fulfill. In the presence of dashed promises, the insecurity of tenure becomes ever-more-salient and the leader becomes ever-more-sensitive to a growingly hostile or skeptical climate of opinion within the political establishment. When threats to fundamental state interests, at home or abroad, coincide with this stage of an administration, the conditions sufficient for brinkmanship or military intervention have crystallized.

Then too, the Leninist legacy provides justification for subordinating current problems to urgent political tasks. This could facilitate the efforts of a Russian leader who decides, for reasons of state or personal authority, to declare as unacceptable the continued division of the Russian people.

In sum, there are many conditions within Russia and the Russian polity that could undermine the current policy of restraint. Much will depend on the direction taken by ongoing redefinitions of the Russian nation; much will also depend on the kinds of political institutions that develop, and their implications for political authority maintenance. At present, "integrationalism," or expanded economic reintegration of the former Soviet republics, leading to some sort of a voluntary political union, may be the only viable alternative to both "denationalized state-building," which is unrealistic, and ethnonationalist or imperialistic programs, which are destabilizing and threatening to peace in Eurasia. Indeed, some sort of integration of the former Soviet republics would have the additional virtue of decreasing the political salience of the issue of Russian diasporas, and reducing the chances that these diasporas would become pawns in a political game.

References

Breslauer, George, "Yeltsin's Political Leadership: Why Invade Chechnya?," in *Russia: Political and Economic Development*. Claremont, CA: The Keck Center for International and Strategic Studies, 1995.

Carrere d'Encausse, Helene, *La gloire des nations, ou La fin de l'Empire sovietique*. Paris: Fayard, 1990.

Connor, Walker, "The Impact of Homelands Upon Diasporas," in Gabriel Sheffer, ed., *Modern Diasporas in International Politics*. New York, NY: St. Martin's, 1986.

"Deklaratsiya o soblyudenii suvereniteta, territorial'noy tselostnosti i neprikosnovennosti granits gosudarstv – uchastnikov Sodruzhestva Nezavisimykh Gosudarstv (Declaration on observing the sovereignty, territorial integrity and inviolability of the borders of states that are parties to the Comonwealth of Independent States)," *Diplomaticheskiy vestnik MID RF* (Diplomatic herald of the Ministry of Foreign Affairs of the Russian Federation), 9–10, 1994.

"Deklaratsiya Uchreditel'nogo S" yezda upolnomochennykh predstaviteley zarubezhnykh rossiyskikh obshchin, organizatsiy i ob"yedineniy (Declaration of the Constituent Assembly of the empowered representatives of Russian communities, organizations and associations living abroad)," *Delovoy mir*, July 11, 1995.

"Dogovor mezhdu Respublikoy Kazakhstan i Rossiyskoy Federatsiey o pravovom statuse grazhdan Respubliki Kazakhstan, postoyanno prozhivayushchikh na territorii Rossiyskoy Federatsii, i grazhdan Rossiyskoy Federatsii, postoyanno prozhivayushchikh na territorii Respubliki Kazakhstan (Treaty between the Republic of Kazakhstan and the Russian Federation on the legal status of citizens of the Republic of Kazakhstan who are permanently residing on the territory of the Russian Federation, and citizens of the Russian Federation who are permanently residing on the territory of the Republic of Kazakhstan)," *Rossiyskaya gazeta* (departmental supplement), February 25, 1995a.

"Dogovor o druzhbe, dobrososedstve mezhdu Rossiyskoy Federatsiey i Respublikoy Belarus (Treaty on friendship, good-neighborliness and cooperation between the Russian Federation and the Republic of Belarus)," *Rossiyskaya gazta* (departmental supplement), May 5, 1995b.

"Fedcral'naya migratsionnaya programma," in *Pereselentsy: Federal'naya migratsionnaya programma* (Migrants: The federal migration program). Moscow: Izdatel'stvo "Rossiyskaya Gazeta," 1994.

Gellner, Ernest, *Nations and Nationalism*. Ithaca, NY: Cornell University Press, 1983.

Harris, Chauncy, "The New Russian Minorities: A Statistical Overview," *Post-Soviet Geography*, 34, 1: 1–28, January 1993.

Kolstoe, Paul, *Russians in the Former Soviet Republic*. Bloomington and Indianapolis, IN: Indiana University Press, 1995.

"Konventsiya Sodruzhestva Nezavisimykh Gosudarstv o pravakh i osnovnykh svobodakh cheloveka (Convention of the Commonwealth of Independent States on human rights and fundamental freedoms)," *Rossiyskaya gazeta* (departmental supplement), June 23, 1995.

Kozyrev, Andrey, *Preobrazheniye*. Moskva: Mezhdunarodnyye otnosheniya, 1995.

Mayall, James, "Irredentist and Secession Challenges," in John Hutchinson and Anthony Smith, eds., *Nationalism*. Oxford, UK and New York, NY: Oxford University Press, 1994.

"Memorandum o podderzhanii mira i stabil'nosti v Sodruzhestve Nezavisimykh Gosudarstv (Memorandum on the maintenance of peace and stability in the Commonwealth of Independent States)," *Diplomaticheskiy vestnik MID RF* (Diplomatic herald of the Ministry of Foreign Affairs of the Russian Federation), 3, 1995.

"OMRI Special Report: Russian Election Survey," *Open Media Research Institute Daily Digest*. Prague: OMRI, December 22, 1995.

"Osnovnyye napravleniya gosudarstvennoy politiki Rossiyskoy Federatsii v otnoshenii sootechestvennikov, prozhivayushchikh za rubyezhom (Basic directions of the Russian Federation's state policy toward compatriots living abroad)," *Rossiyskaya gazeta*, September 22, 1994.

Sestanovich, S., "Vozdat' Rossii dolzhnoye (Give Russia her due)," *Polis*, 1, 1995.

Shlapentokh, Vladimir and Munir Sendich, "Preface," in Vladimir Shlapentokh, Munir Sendich, and Emil Payin, eds., *The New Russian Diaspora, Russian Minorities in the Former Soviet Republics*. Armonk, NY and London: M. E. Sharpe, 1994.

Sinyavsky, Andrei, *Soviet Civilization: A Cultural History*. New York: Arcade Publishing, 1990.

"Soglasheniye mezhdu Respublikoy Kazakhstan i Rossiyskoy Federatsiey ob uproshchonnom poryadke priobreteniya grazhdanstva grazhdanami Respubliki Kazakhstan, pribyvayushchimi dlya postoyannogo prozhivaniya v Rossiyskuyu Federatsiyu, i grazhdanami Rossiyskoy Federatsii, pribyvayushchimi dlya postoyannogo prozhivaniya v Respubliku Kazakhstan (Agreement between the Republic of Kazakhstan and the Russian Federation on simplified acquisition of citizenship by citizens of Kazakhstan coming to Russia for permanent residency and by citizens of Russia coming to Kazakhstan for permanent residency)," *Rossiyskaya gazeta* (departmental supplement), February 25, 1995.

Solzhenitsyn, Aleksandr, *Kak nam obustroit Rossiyu* (How we should redesign Russia). Leningrad: Sovetskiy pisatyel', 1990.

Sovremennaya russkaya ideya i gosudarslvo. Moscow: RAU-Korporatsiya, 1995.

"Strategicheskiy kurs Rossii s gosudarstvami – uchastnikami Sodruzhestva Nezavisimykh Gosudarstv (The strategic course of Russia in its relations with the states that are parties to the Commonwealth of Independent States," *Rossiyskaya gazeta*, September 23, 1995.

Teague, Elisabeth, "Russians Outside Russia and Russian Security Policy," in Leon Aron and Kenneth Jensen, eds., *The Emergence of Russian Foreign Policy*. Washington, DC: United States Institute of Peace Press, 1994.

"Ukaz Prezidenta Rossiyskoy Federatsii 'Ob Osnovnykh napravleniyakh gosudarstvennoy politiki Rossiyskoy Federatsii v otnoshenii sootechestvennikov prozhivayushchikh za rubyezhom' (Decree of the President of the Russian Federation 'On the basic directions of the Russian Federation's state policy toward compatriots living abroad')," *Rossiyskaya gazeta*, August 18, 1994.

United Nations International Convention on Civil and Political Rights 1966, United Nations, New York/Geneva, 1985.

"Zakon o grazhdanstve Rossiyskoy Federatsii (The law on citizenship of the Russian Federation)," *Vedemosti S"yezda narodnykh deputatov Rossiyskoy Federatsii i Verkhovnogo Soveta Rossiyskoy Federatsii* (The Record of the Congress of People's Deputies and Supreme Soviet of the Russian Federation), item 1112, 29, 1993.

Zevelev, Igor, "Building the State and Building the Nation in Contemporary Russia," in *Russia: Political and Economic Development*. Claremont, CA: The Keck Center for International and Strategic Studies, 1995.

Part VIII

The Policy Debate: Levelling the Playing Field

One of the most controversial policy issues raised by racial and ethnic inequality centers on the need for action to redress disparities in economic rewards, social status, and political power between groups. While the debate over affirmative action in the United States has been given considerable prominence in the social science literature – the "mend it, don't end it" formula of the Clinton adminis-tration being a compromise similar to the "don't ask, don't tell" strategy for gays in the military – it is by no means a North American issue. Preferential policies designed to help disadvantaged groups have been in operation for more than a century in India, for three decades in Malaysia, and since the transition to non-racial democracy in South Africa in the mid-1990s. Of course, preference policies for privileged minorities and majorities are as old as history, and it is this associ-ation that has caused some advocates of greater ethnic and racial justice to have severe reservations about any policies that appear to discriminate on the basis of race, ethnicity or any other group criteria. The issues are complex as the next three articles reveal.

A major criticism raised by opponents of affirmative action is that it differen-tially aids the minority middle class, those least in need of special assistance. It is on this question that Bowen and Bok's analysis of minority students in elite Ameri-can universities provides a much more positive assessment. Following in the trad-ition of W. E. B. Du Bois who argued that a "talented tenth" of black intellectuals would be an essential element in leading African Americans to full equality, Bowen and Bok document the successful career paths of the affirmative action cohort in the most prestigious American universities. Despite often being admitted with lower test scores and other "objective" measures of academic achievement, these black students have demonstrated that they have the potential and motivation to excel in their studies and to go on to have very successful careers. Bowen and Bok raise important questions about the meaning of "merit" and the complexities in-volved in the selection practices used by admissions officers in their attempts to identify the true potential of individual applicants. They argue that colleges and universities seek to serve a variety of goals which include the recognition of long-term societal needs. What is more, their study shows how most of the non-minority students generally express their appreciation of an education in a diverse environment that more nearly reflects the multicultural reality of contemporary America.

Daniel Monti takes a middle position in the American debate on the subject, thereby exposing the limitations of both the supporters and the critics of current policies. He points to a central weakness in the outcomes of such approaches: that affirmative action may be a very successful strategy for improving minority repre-sentation among the elite professions and other lucrative occupations, but of little use, if not harmful, to the least advantaged members of the group. One answer to this critical objection to preference policies is to recast them in a communal rather than an individualistic direction by expanding opportunities in the ethnic economy. By linking the benefits derived from affirmative action to the minority community, rather than to specific minority individuals, the destructive consequences of a flight of the upwardly mobile out of the ghetto is reduced. Preventing the loss of the best and the brightest, which places those left behind in an environment of increasing deprivation, is the basis of a policy that aims to mine the "cultural capital" of the community and invest it in ways that uplift the group as a whole. The practical implementation of this refined version of affirmative action is a major challenge.

In Europe, affirmative action policies have not been pursued in a manner similar to the United States. Most Europeans, as Christian Joppke explains, have failed to see the plight of their racial and ethnic minorities as paralleling the historical and ethical claims of African Americans or Native Americans. Many of the minority groups are linked to more recent patterns of immigration and, as a result, the claim that these groups deserve some form of reparations or "compensatory justice" – as argued for America by Randall Robinson in his book *The Debt: What America Owes to Blacks* (New York: Dutton, 2000) – has met with limited support. The nearest approach to this argument has been voiced by former colonial migrants ("We are over here, because you were over there") and has rarely received much of a response from the dominant societies. In Germany, because of its restrictive citizenship laws and the historical legacy of the Nazi era, a very complex situation has arisen in relation to anti-discrimination policies. Unification after the fall of the Berlin Wall in 1989, and the changing political configuration of both Western and Eastern Europe, have put pressure on Germany to move from an ethnic to a more civic model of citizenship. While in general German law has avoided the use of ethnic or racial categorization, two interesting exceptions are the cases of the ethnic Germans from Eastern Europe and the former Soviet Union, and Russian Jews. Both groups have received special treatment as compensation for the hardships suffered as a direct or indirect consequence of the Nazi period and both have been given relatively easy access to citizenship status. By the end of the century, Germany was moving gradually towards a territorial definition of citizenship that should start to incorporate its long-settled Turkish and other immigrant communities, and bring it into line with the dominant trends of the rest of the European Union. While this situation established the basis for a more tolerant multicultural citizenship, there is little support in Europe for the redistributive policies associated with American-style affirmative action.

22 The Shape of the River

William G. Bowen and Derek Bok

Here was a piece of river which was all down in my book, but I could make neither head nor tail of it; you understand, it was turned around. I had seen it when coming upstream, but I had never faced about to see how it looked when it was behind me. My heart broke again, for it was plain that I had got to learn this troublesome river *both* ways.

Mark Twain, *Life on the Mississippi*

The "river" that is the subject of this book can never be "learned" once and for all. The larger society changes, graduates of colleges and universities move from one stage of life to another, and educational institutions themselves evolve. Similarly, there is much yet to be learned about the future lives of those who have attended selective colleges and professional schools over the last thirty years. This study, then, does not purport to provide final answers to questions about race-sensitive admissions in higher education. No piece of this river can ever be considered to be "all down" in anyone's book. But we are persuaded of the value of examining each piece "*both*" ways" – when "coming upstream," as students enroll in college, and "when it was behind me," as graduates go on to pursue their careers and live their lives.

So much of the current debate relies on anecdotes, assumptions about "facts," and conjectures that it is easy for those who have worked hard to increase minority enrollments to become defensive or disillusioned. It is easy, too, for black and Hispanic graduates, as well as current minority students, to be offended by what they could well regard as unjustified assaults on their competence and even their character. Some of the critics of affirmative action may also feel aggrieved, sensing that they are unjustly dismissed as Neanderthals or regarded as heartless. In short, the nature of the debate has imposed real costs on both individuals and institutions just as it has raised profound questions of educational and social policy that deserve the most careful consideration. In the face of what seems like a veritable torrent of claims and counterclaims, there is much to be said for stepping back and thinking carefully about the implications of the record to date before coming to settled conclusions.

On inspection, many of the arguments against considering race in admissions – such as allegations of unintended harm to the intended beneficiaries and enhanced racial tensions on campus – seem to us to lack substance. More generally, our data show that the overall record of accomplishment by black students after graduation has been impressive. But what more does this detailed examination of one sizable stretch of the river suggest about its future course? What wide-angle view emerges?

The Meaning of "Merit"

One conclusion we have reached is that the meaning of "merit" in the admissions process must be articulated more clearly. "Merit," like "preference" and "discrimination," is a word that has taken on so much baggage we may have to re-invent it or find a substitute.

Still, it is an important and potentially valuable concept because it reminds us that we certainly do not want institutions to admit candidates who *lack* merit, however the term is defined. Most people would agree that rank favoritism (admitting a personal friend of the admissions officer, say) is inconsistent with admission "on the merits," that no one should be admitted who cannot take advantage of the educational opportunities being offered, and that using a lottery or some similar random numbers scheme to choose among applicants who are over the academic threshold is too crude an approach.

One reason why we care so much about who gets admitted "on the merits" is because, as this study confirms, admission to the kinds of selective schools included in the College and Beyond universe pays off handsomely for individuals of all races, from all backgrounds.[1] But it is not individuals alone who gain. Substantial additional benefits accrue to society at large through the leadership and civic participation of the graduates and through the broad contributions that the schools themselves make to the goals of a democratic society. These societal benefits are a major justification for the favored tax treatment that colleges and universities enjoy and for the subsidies provided by public and private donors. The presence of these benefits also explains why these institutions do not allocate scarce places in their entering classes by the simple expedient of auctioning them off to the highest bidders. The limited number of places is an exceedingly valuable resource – valuable both to the students admitted and to the society at large – which is why admissions need to be based "on the merits."

Unfortunately, however, to say that considerations of merit should drive the admissions process is to pose questions, not answer them. There are no magical ways of automatically identifying those who merit admission on the basis of intrinsic qualities that distinguish them from all others. Test scores and grades are useful measures of the ability to do good work, but they are no more than that. They are far from infallible indicators of other qualities some might regard as intrinsic, such as a deep love of learning or a capacity for high academic achievement. Taken together, grades and scores predict only 15–20 percent of the variance among all students in academic performance and a smaller percentage among black students. Moreover, such quantitative measures are even less useful in answering other questions relevant to the admissions process, such as predicting which applicants will contribute most in later life to their professions and their communities.[2]

Some critics believe, nevertheless, that applicants with higher grades and test scores are more deserving of admission because they presumably worked harder than those with less auspicious academic records. According to this argument, it is only "fair" to admit the students who have displayed the greatest effort. We disagree on several grounds.

To begin with, it is not clear that students who receive higher grades and test scores have necessarily worked harder in school. Grades and test scores are a reflection not only of effort but of intelligence, which in turn derives from a number of factors, such as inherited ability, family circumstances, and early upbringing, that have nothing to do with how many hours students have labored over their homework. Test scores may also be affected by the quality of teaching that applicants have received or even by knowing the best strategies for taking standardized tests, as coaching schools regularly remind students and their parents. For these reasons, it is quite likely that many applicants with good but not outstanding scores and B+ averages in high school will have worked more diligently than many other applicants with superior academic records.

More generally, selecting a class has much broader purposes than simply rewarding students who are thought to have worked especially hard. The job of the admissions staff is not, in any case, to decide who has earned a "right" to a place in the class, since we do not think that admission to a selective university is a right possessed by anyone. What admissions officers must decide is which set of applicants, *considered individually and collectively*, will take fullest advantage of what the college has to offer, contribute most to the educational process in college, and be most successful in using what they have learned for the benefit of the larger society. Admissions processes should, of course, be "fair," but "fairness" has to be understood to mean only that each individual is to be judged according to a consistent set of criteria that reflect the objectives of the college or university. Fairness should not be misinterpreted to mean that a particular criterion has to apply – that, for example, grades and test scores must always be considered more important than other qualities and characteristics so that no student with a B average can be accepted as long as some students with As are being turned down.

Nor does fairness imply that each candidate should be judged in isolation from all others. It may be perfectly "fair" to reject an applicant because the college has already enrolled many other students very much like him or her. There are numerous analogies. When making a stew, adding an extra carrot rather than one more potato may make excellent sense – and be eminently "fair" – if there are already lots of potatoes in the pot. Similarly, good basketball teams include both excellent shooters and sturdy defenders, both point guards and centers. Diversified investment portfolios usually include some mix of stocks and bonds, and so on.

To admit "on the merits," then, is to admit by following complex rules derived from the institution's own mission and based on its own experiences educating students with different talents and backgrounds. These "rules" should not be thought of as abstract propositions to be deduced through contemplation in a Platonic cave. Nor are they rigid formulas that can be applied in a mechanical fashion. Rather, they should have the status of rough guidelines established in large part through empirical examination of the actual results achieved as a result of long experience. How many students with characteristic "x" have done well in college, contributed to the education of their fellow students, and gone on to make major contributions to society? Since different institutions operate at very different places along our metaphorical river (some placing more emphasis on research, some with deeper pools of applicants than others), the specifics of these rules should be expected to differ from one institution to another. They should also be expected to change over time as circumstances change and as institutions learn from their mistakes.

Above all, merit must be defined in light of what educational institutions are trying to accomplish. In our view, race is relevant in determining which candidates "merit" admission because taking account of race helps institutions achieve three objectives central to their mission – identifying individuals of high potential, permitting students to benefit educationally from diversity on campus, and addressing long-term societal needs.

Identifying individuals of high potential

An individual's race may reveal something about how that person arrived at where he or she is today – what barriers were overcome, and what the individual's prospects are for further growth. Not every member of a minority group will have had to surmount substantial obstacles. Moreover, other circumstances besides race can cause "disadvantage." Thus colleges and universities should and do give special consideration to the hard-working son of a family in Appalachia or the daughter of a recent immigrant from Russia who, while obviously bright, is still struggling with the English language. But race is an important factor in its own right, given this nation's history and the evidence presented in many studies of the continuing effects of discrimination and prejudice. Wishing it were otherwise does not make it otherwise. It would seem to us to be ironic indeed – and wrong – if admissions officers were permitted to consider all other factors that help them identify individuals of high potential who have had to overcome obstacles, but were proscribed from looking at an applicant's race.

Benefiting educationally from diversity on the campus

Race almost always affects an individual's life experiences and perspectives, and thus the person's capacity to contribute to the kinds of learning through diversity that occur on campuses. This form of learning will be even more important going forward than it has been in the past. Both the growing diversity of American society and the increasing interaction with other cultures worldwide make it evident that going to school only with "the likes of oneself" will be increasingly anachronistic. The advantages of being able to understand how others think and function, to cope across racial divides, and to lead groups composed of diverse individuals are certain to increase.

To be sure, not all members of a minority group may succeed in expanding the racial understanding of other students, any more than all those who grew up on a farm or came from a remote region of the United States can be expected to convey a special rural perspective. What does seem clear, however, is that a student body containing many different backgrounds, talents, and experiences will be a richer environment in which to develop. In this respect, minority students of all kinds can have something to offer their classmates. The black student with high grades from Andover may challenge the stereotypes of many classmates just as much as the black student from the South Bronx.

Until now, there has been little hard evidence to confirm the belief of educators in the value of diversity. Our survey data throw new light on the extent of inter-action occurring on campuses today and of how positively the great majority of students regard opportunities to learn from those with different points of view, backgrounds, and experiences. Admission "on the merits" would be short-sighted if admissions officers were precluded from crediting this potential contribution to the education of all students.

Imposition of a race-neutral standard would produce very troubling results from this perspective: such a policy would reduce dramatically the proportion of black students on campus – probably shrinking their number to less than 2 percent of all matriculants at the most selective colleges and professional schools. Moreover, our examination of the application and admissions files indicates that such substantial reductions in the number of black matriculants, with attendant losses in educa-tional opportunity for all students, would occur without leading to any appre-ciable improvement in the academic credentials of the remaining black students and would lead to only a modest change in the overall academic profile of the institutions.

Addressing long-term societal needs

Virtually all colleges and universities seek to educate students who seem likely to become leaders and contributing members of society. Identifying such students is another essential aspect of admitting "on the merits," and here again race is clearly relevant. There is widespread agreement that our country continues to need the help of its colleges and universities in building a society in which access to pos-itions of leadership and responsibility is less limited by an individual's race than it is today.

The success of C&B colleges and universities in meeting this objective has been documented extensively [in this study]. In this [final] chapter, it is helpful to "look back up the river" from a slightly different vantage point. Some of the conse-quences of mandating a race-neutral standard of admission can be better under-stood by constructing a rough profile of the approximately 700 black matriculants in the '76 entering cohort at the C&B schools whom we estimate would have been rejected had such a standard been in effect. Our analysis suggests that:

- Over 225 members of this group of retrospectively rejected black matriculants went on to attain professional degrees or doctorates.
- About 70 are now doctors, and roughly 60 are lawyers.
- Nearly 125 are business executives.
- Well over 300 are leaders of civic activities.
- The average earnings of the individuals in the group exceeds $71,000.

- Almost two-thirds of the group (65 percent) were *very* satisfied with their undergraduate experience.

Many of these students would have done well no matter where they went to school, and we cannot know in any precise way how their careers would have been affected as a result. But we do know that there is a statistically significant association, on an "other things equal" basis, between attendance at the most selective schools within the C&B universe and a variety of accomplishments during college and in later life. Generally speaking, the more selective the school, the more the student achieved subsequently. Also, we saw that C&B students as a group earned appreciably more money than did the subgroup of students in our national control with mostly As, which suggests that going to a C&B school conferred a considerable premium on all C&B students, and probably an especially high premium on black students. Black C&B students were also more likely than black college graduates in general to become leaders of community and social service organizations. These findings suggest that reducing the number of black matriculants at the C&B schools would almost certainly have had a decidedly negative effect on the subsequent careers of many of these students and on their contributions to civic life as well.

Even more severe effects would result from insisting on race-neutral admissions policies in professional schools. In law and medicine, all schools are selective. As a consequence, the effect of barring any consideration of race would be the exclusion of more than half of the existing minority student population from these professions. Race-neutral admissions policies would reduce the number of black students in the most selective schools of law and medicine to less than 1 percent of all students. Since major law firms and medical centers often limit their recruitment to the most selective schools, this outcome would deal a heavy blow to efforts to prepare future black leaders for the professions.

But what about the other students (most of them presumably white) who would have taken the places of these retrospectively rejected black students in selective colleges and professional schools? There is every reason to believe that they, too, would have done well, in school and afterwards, though probably not as well as the regularly admitted white students (who were, after all, preferred to them in the admissions process). Still, on the basis of the evidence in this study, the excluded white male students might have done at least as well as their retrospectively rejected black classmates, and probably even better in terms of average earnings. On the other hand, fewer of the "retrospectively accepted" white women would have been employed, and those who were employed would have earned about the same amount of money as the retrospectively rejected black women. Fewer of the additional white students, women and men, would have been involved in volunteer activities, especially in leadership positions.

Would society have been better off if additional numbers of whites and Asian Americans had been substituted for minority students in this fashion? That is the central question, and it cannot be answered by data alone.

Fundamental judgments have to be made about societal needs, values, and objectives. When a distinguished black educator visited the Mellon Foundation, he noted, with understandable pride, that his son had done brilliantly in college and was being considered for a prestigious graduate award in neuroscience. "My son," the professor said, "needs no special consideration; he is so talented that he will make it on his own." His conclusion was that we should be indifferent to whether his son or any of the white competitors got the particular fellowship in question. We agreed that, in all likelihood, all of these candidates would benefit from going to the graduate school in question and, in time, become excellent scientists or doctors. Still, one can argue with the conclusion reached by the parent. "Your son will do fine," another person present at the meeting said, "but that isn't the issue. *He may not need us, but we need him*! Why? Because there is only one of him."

That mild exaggeration notwithstanding, the relative scarcity of talented black professionals is all too real. It seemed clear to a number of us that day, and it probably seems clear to many others, that American society needs the high-achieving black graduates who will provide leadership in every walk of life. This is the position of many top officials concerned with filling key positions in government, of CEOs who affirm that they would continue their minority recruitment programs whether or not there were a legal requirement to do so, and of bar associations, medical associations, and other professional organizations that have repeatedly stressed the importance of attracting more minority members into their fields. In view of these needs, we are not indifferent to which student gets the graduate fellowship.

Neither of the authors of this study has any sympathy with quotas or any belief in mandating the proportional representation of groups of people, defined by race or any other criterion, in positions of authority. Nor do we include ourselves among those who support race-sensitive admissions as compensation for a legacy of racial discrimination. We agree emphatically with the sentiment expressed by Mamphela Ramphele, vice chancellor of the University of Cape Town in South Africa, when she said: "Everyone deserves opportunity; no one deserves success."[3] But we remain persuaded that present racial disparities in outcomes are dismayingly disproportionate. At the minimum, this country needs to maintain the progress now being made in educating larger numbers of black professionals and black leaders.

Selective colleges and universities have made impressive contributions at both undergraduate and graduate levels. To take but a single illustration: since starting to admit larger numbers of black students in the late 1960s, the Harvard Law School has numbered among its black graduates more than one hundred partners in law firms, more than ninety black alumni/ae with the title of Chief Executive Officer, Vice President, or General Counsel of a corporation, more than seventy professors, at least thirty judges, two members of Congress, the mayor of a major American city, the head of the Office of Management and Budget, and an Assistant U.S. Attorney General. In this study, we have documented more systematically the accomplishments of the nearly 1,900 black '76 matriculants at the twenty-eight C&B schools, and the evidence of high achievement is overwhelming – there is no other word for it. These individuals are still in their late thirties, having entered college just over twenty years ago. We shall be very surprised if their record of achievement is not magnified many times as they gain seniority and move up various institutional ladders. If, at the end of the day, the question is whether the most selective colleges and universities have succeeded in educating sizable numbers of minority students who have already achieved considerable success and seem likely in time to occupy positions of leadership throughout society, we have no problem in answering the question. Absolutely.

We commented earlier on the need to make clear choices. Here is perhaps the clearest choice. Let us suppose that rejecting, on race-neutral grounds, more than half of the black students who otherwise would attend these institutions would raise the probability of acceptance for another white student from 25 percent to, say, 27 percent at the most selective colleges and universities. Would we, as a society, be better off? Considering both the educational benefits of diversity and the need to include far larger numbers of black graduates in the top ranks of the business, professional, governmental, and not-for-profit institutions that shape our society, we do not think so.

How one responds to such questions depends very much, of course, on how important one thinks it is that progress continues to be made in narrowing black–white gaps in earnings and in representation in top-level positions. As the United States grows steadily more diverse, we believe that Nicholas Katzenbach and Burke Marshall are surely right in insisting that the country must continue to make determined efforts to "include blacks in the institutional framework that constitutes America's economic, political, educational and social life."[4] This goal of greater inclusiveness is important for reasons, both moral and practical, that offer all Americans the prospect of living in a society marked by more equality and racial harmony than one might otherwise anticipate.

We recognize that many opponents of race-sensitive admissions will also agree with Katzenbach and Marshall, but will argue that there are better ways of promoting inclusiveness. There is everything to be said, in our view, for addressing the underlying problems in families, neighborhoods, and primary and secondary schools that many have identified so clearly. But this is desperately difficult work, which will, at best, produce results only over a very long period of time. Meanwhile, it is important, in our view, to do what can be done to make a difference at each educational level, including colleges and graduate and professional schools.

The alternative seems to us both stark and unworthy of our country's ideals. Turning aside from efforts to help larger numbers of well-qualified blacks gain the educational advantages they will need to move steadily and confidently into the mainstream of American life could have extremely serious consequences. Here in the United States, as elsewhere in the world, visible efforts by leading educational institutions to make things better will encourage others to press on with the hard work needed to overcome the continuing effects of a legacy of unfair treatment. Leon Higginbotham spoke from the heart when, commenting on the aftermath of the *Hopwood* decision, he said, "I sometimes feel as if I am watching justice die."[5] To engender such feelings, and a consequent loss of hope on the part of many who have not attained Judge Higginbotham's status, seems a high price to pay for a tiny increase in the probability of admission for white applicants to academically selective colleges and universities.

Notes

1 "The College and Beyond Database" (C&B) was produced by a Mellon Foundation study conducted from 1994–7. It included 80,000 undergraduates who matriculated at 28 academically selective colleges and universities in the fall of 1951, the fall of 1976, and the fall of 1989. (Editors' note.)
2 Martin Luther King, Jr., now regarded as one of the great orators of this century, scored in the bottom half of all test-takers on the verbal GRE (Cross and Slater 1997, p. 12).
3 Ramphele 1996.
4 Katzenbach and Marshall 1998, p. 45.

References

Cross, Theodore, and Robert Bruce Slater. 1997. "Why the End of Affirmative Action Would Exclude All but a Very Few Blacks from America's Leading Universities and Graduate Schools." *Journal of Blacks in Higher Education* 17 (Autumn): 8–17.

Higginbotham, A. Leon, Jr. 1998. "Breaking Thurgood Marshall's Promise." *New York Times*, January 18, sec. 6.

Katzenbach, Nicholas de B., and Burke Marshall. 1998. "Not Color Blind: Just Blind." *New York Times*, February 22, sec. 6.

Ramphele, Mamphela. 1996. "Equity and Excellence – Strange Bedfellows? A Case Study of South African Higher Education." Paper presented at The Princeton Conference on Higher Education, March 21–23.

23 Ethnic Economies and Affirmative Action

Daniel J. Monti

Nine thousand persons marched across San Francisco's Golden Gate Bridge on August 28, 1997, to protest the implementation of a 1996 California law, based on the hotly debated Proposition 209, that effectively bans affirmative action in public employment, education, and in the awarding of state contracts. An anticipated challenge to California's law before the US Supreme Court promises to keep much attention focused on this sensitive matter, especially since President Clinton openly declared his support for federal affirmative action laws and programs during the summer of 1995. Many organizations and politicians no doubt will issue principled and impassioned statements for or against affirmative action and "quotas" as they have in the past, thus, continuing to throw more heat than light onto a subject that seems all but immune to reasoned debate or a satisfying resolution.

Any resolution to our arguments over affirmative action will require us to strike a better balance between our over-heated rhetoric and inability to imagine alternatives to current state and federal programs that many persons find either insufficient or offensive. In the spirit of trying to search for just such a balance, the National Italian American Foundation brought together a few lawyers, activists, and professorial types, like myself, to discuss what might happen if affirmative action were ended. The goodness or badness of affirmative action was not supposed to be at issue, although it seemed to several of the more bookish among us that the Senate chamber in which we conferred did not bring out the best in our legal and activist brethren. Our formal charge was to imagine how the world might look after affirmative action and to speculate about what might replace it.

This was an interesting challenge, particularly for a sociologist who had written extensively about school desegregation but not on affirmative action as such. There were parallels, to be sure, between desegregating schools and bringing more minorities and women into the workplace or treating them better once they arrived. Notable among these parallels was a peculiar tension between rhetoric that spoke of improving the condition of "groups" and reforms that had affected only small numbers and select representatives of certain types of citizens.

It is true that our rhetoric in matters of civil rights always has been more ambitious than our actions. This difference has made it easier for us to accept the piecemeal changes we imposed on ourselves as a bigger deal than they actually were.[1] Affirmative action controversies, however, carry at least three additional risks that are not as obvious in school desegregation cases. The size of the affected "classes" in affirmative action plans, for instance, is much greater than it is for school-aged children; and adults can vote. Moreover, unlike school desegregation orders, the impact of affirmative action programs extends beyond the public arena and carries over into private businesses. Indeed, the whole economy could be affected by a truly ambitious affirmative action program. By extension, questions about economic inequality and social class differences are harder to avoid in the debate over affirmative action. They are more easily masked in school desegregation disputes.[2]

The challenge in writing about alternatives to affirmative action, then, is that the stakes – both real and imagined – are much greater than they are for other civil-rights issues. The challenge of doing something about economic inequality is that one must discover ways for persons to improve their economic standing in a market which, unlike the public schools, is not so easily protected from the vagaries of competition. Fortunately, sociologists have studied and written extensively about a system that provides both a measure of success and security for persons enmeshed in a local economy. It is called an "ethnic economy," and it holds some intriguing possibilities for framing a kind of home-grown affirmative action program in our nation's cities.

Making Affirmative Action Effective

It does not help a community when some of its residents become more successful and then move away or fail to invest their money, knowledge, and good will in the place where they live. Yet, affirmative action as it has been practiced up to now puts no larger social obligation on those who benefit from it other than perhaps to serve as models for "racial progress." A more effective way of doing something like affirmative action would enhance the strength of communities whose members gained some advantage from it.

Supporters of affirmative action cannot claim this as a goal except in a most abstract way, and probably not even then. No less a liberal thinker than Philip Selznick has argued, for instance, that "programs of the welfare state are mainly designed to serve individual needs . . . (not) the integrity and well-being of groups and institutions." Indeed, as "government moves in . . . the fabric of community is weakened. Kinship, religion, locality, employment, friendship, social networks, voluntary associations: all diminish in relative importance as centers of moral obligation."[3] If Selznick is right, whatever benefit individuals may take from affirmative action must be weighed against the damage it does to communities and traditional centers of moral obligation.

There is another way to think about affirmative action and to do something like affirmative action, however, that is not burdened by such problems. This alternative is found in so-called "ethnic economies" that originate – not surprisingly – in ethnic enclaves. These economies operate in ways that make it easier and more attractive for local residents and businesses already committed to the community to stay and increase their ties to each other. Furthermore, inasmuch as ethnic economies tend to tap into new markets they also have the unintended effect of helping an ethnic population reach out to groups with which they have had little contact in the past.

Models for an affirmative action policy that would mimic the effects of ethnic economies have sprung up in many United States cities since the mid-nineteenth century. Based in equal measure on personal mobility and the promotion of a community's well-being, the key to effective affirmative action would become the successful mining of a people's "cultural capital."[4]

An affirmative action policy that complements the work of ethnic economies and develops a people's cultural capital would have several advantages over current approaches to reducing economic inequality. First, *the primary burden for defining and implementing affirmative action programs would shift to local communities.* There was a time not too long ago when such a proposal might have struck one as unimaginable. In light of the federal initiative to support the development of new welfare programs at the state level, however, this proposal appears much less radical today. The history of different ethnic peoples in the United States shows how their members developed collective strategies – social, political, and economic – to help them meet the challenges of a new and often unsettled world. These strategies enabled them to make a more secure place for themselves in the local economy *and* a better community. Ethnic economies do not discourage their fellow ethnics from finding employment in the larger economy. In fact, such strategies make it easier for their fellow ethnics to move into the general economy by expanding business contacts with persons not like themselves. The collaboration of ethnic leaders with local businessmen and officials actually helps able-bodied and talented, but otherwise disadvantaged, persons to move into growing areas of the local economy. Local leaders are in a good position to judge where and how to improve the fortunes of area residents who had been unable to make as full a contribution to the local economy as they might like. The federal government is not.

Second, *promoting a community's economic well-being and turning the immediate beneficiaries of assistance into a communal resource would become the primary goals of affirmative action.* The foremost objective would not be to improve the life chances of individuals with no connection to the community. It would be to help persons committed to the place where they live. A community benefiting from affirmative action policies should be able to capitalize upon the talents and good fortune of the individuals in whom it invested much time and to whom it provided support. Persons who take some advantage from an affirmative action program supported by the community ought to give something back to the community that promoted their well-being. Such an approach would spread the costs and the benefits of affirmative action far beyond their typical resting place.

Third, *the success of affirmative action would be measured against the distribution of all jobs held by community members and relevant comparison populations, not simply by the number of specific jobs acquired or lost by a minority person.* There are practical problems associated with making affirmative action workable and credible that have nothing to do with politics or principle. These problems deal instead with the thorny matters of measuring how successful an affirmative action program has been and in knowing when enough progress has been made so that the program no longer is needed. An emphasis on making affirmative action work for an entire community and across the whole spectrum of job opportunities requires us to examine changes in jobs held by all members of the community. It also would help to reduce disparities among the members of a given population as well as inequities between themselves and other populations.

Looking at the effects of affirmative action in this way is intuitively appealing and has obvious benefits. We would for the first time actually treat affirmative action as something that has an impact on an entire population and not just some of its individual representatives. The members of a community would compare their progress to that enjoyed by persons like themselves as well as to persons different from themselves. This, too, is an idea that builds on principles put into practice in ethnic economies.

Shifting the Burden for Affirmative Action

Our economy is supposed to work something like this: individuals compete in an open market, rent their services to an employer, and are compensated for their labor. Unfortunately, certain types of individuals have not been able to participate fully in that marketplace. The market is rigged, many persons believe, or at least it works in a manner that makes it easier for some types of persons to succeed more often and better than do others.

The ostensible purpose of affirmative action policies is to fix the way our economy works for persons who are members of certain disadvantaged "classes," the ones who consistently enjoy less success in a rigged market. Proponents of affirmative action suggest that the commonweal is served when such persons acquire jobs they have not held in the past, or when these individuals begin to earn salaries commensurate with those of workers who are not from disadvantaged classes. Affirmative action, then, is a device to promote the economic fortunes and social mobility of individuals who are representatives of these disadvantaged classes.

The problem, as we all know, is that there is disagreement about how severely the marketplace is rigged, how much can be done to make it less rigged, and who really should benefit from adjustments that are made. Furthermore, when we look at the entire membership of the "disadvantaged class" within the confines of its own community, it is clear that not every member is equally disadvantaged. Many are doing well.

There is a range of success stories in these communities. However, the way we typically think about affirmative action and measure its effectiveness does not take these success stories into account. Given the way affirmative action usually works, the cumulative effect of changes in the lives of individuals aided by affirmative action programs do not redound to the larger minority community except in an abstract way.

It is not hard to imagine why this is the case. The "existence of profound racial disparities, higher poverty and unemployment rates, greater welfare dependency, inner-city problems, and the like," Glenn Loury has argued, "provides a primary justification" for affirmative action policies. Nevertheless, "the evidence suggests that preferences have played a marginal role in alleviating these problems." The reason for this, he argues, is that "hiring preferences are a poorly targeted method of intervention for the task of reducing racial inequality, since... their benefits are (acquired) most readily by those... who are least disadvantaged."[5]

Affirmative action, as it has been practiced, does not work often or well for less skilled workers. Nor is it viewed as community property. If it were, we would worry about the impact such policies have on the overall rate of inequality *within* the minority community as well as rate of inequality *between* it and other relevant comparison populations.

Ethnic economies operate in a manner that allow for this fuller view of inequality and efforts to reduce it. These economies spread the benefits of work and business investment across several social classes inside a minority community. Less well-to-do persons often are hired by fellow ethnic group members, a relative who owns a business, or other businessmen who operate in the general area and customarily hire them. The relevant comparison for persons working in and around such an economy is as much their own group as it is groups composed of persons not like themselves. In this case, the question of how one is doing "relative" to others takes on a new and fuller meaning – one that spreads the burden and advantages of affirmative action beyond where they typically are placed.

Minority Persons and Ethnic Peoples

Central to understanding why this has not happened and how to make affirmative action laws and policies more corrigible is the distinction between minority persons and an ethnic group or people. A minority person usually is someone who has physical or social traits that are – for whatever reason – not highly esteemed. It is possible, even likely, that a society will have substantial numbers of such persons. Their social significance comes by way of their inclusion in categories of persons that the rest of us talk about and sometimes try to influence. In principle, the only thing bigger than himself to which each minority person can claim membership is a statistical artifact that often is referred to as a "class" and sometimes mistakenly as a "group."

An ethnic group, or people, is much different. It is unlike the statistical class with which it sometimes is confused or the minority persons who are counted as a part of such a class. An ethnic group has a corporate history and a sense of itself as a distinctive people. It usually has a real or imagined place or homeland that its members claim as their own. It possesses organizations and institutions that work on behalf of some or all of these members. These persons share a set of beliefs or credo, if you like, that gives voice to who they are and renders what they do legitimate. An ethnic people always includes persons from different generations. In its modern form, ethnic groups also include persons of unequal wealth, power, and prestige.[6]

An ethnic people often is composed of individuals who have attributes that also qualify them to be called "minorities." Being a minority person, on the other hand, does not qualify one for membership in an ethnic people. One's status as a minority person can be traced to accidents of birth and an assignment to one or another demographic pothole. One's status as a member of an ethnic group is part of a larger corporate or communal accomplishment.

Proponents and critics of affirmative action conflate the two, arguing that affirmative action helps groups. One can think this a horrible idea or view it as a highly desirable outcome; but the truth is that affirmative action does not help any group. It certainly helps the individuals who get a better job or a higher wage; and in principle it could hurt persons who are not part of the disadvantaged class. The impact of affirmative action on the well-being of a larger community or people, if Philip Selznick is correct however, may not be good. It depends entirely on how well the individuals touched by it are tied to a larger community. The effect that even a fair-sized number of such persons has in a given place could be quite modest, particularly if they are not integrated well into their neighborhood. It can be harmful, if the persons who have been assisted leave or withdraw from the community.

The manner in which a community is put together, the kind of groups that work in it and for it, and how its residents relate to each other would make a great deal more difference to their sense of well-being and development as competent and more successful persons. Economist Glenn Loury has observed, and any sociologist would agree, that "societies are not simply amalgamations of individual(s)...nor are they simply coalitions of agents which form...to advance their individual interests." They are "networks of social affiliation" which "exert a profound influence upon...resources important to the development...of human beings."[7] Individuals who benefit from affirmative action programs are part of a much larger social and public mix, a community which may, or may not, be able to build on their private success.

Loury says this larger social and organizational milieu constitutes a form of "social capital." It is an asset that when combined with a complementary set of values accrues a form of interest on which it is hard to put a monetary value. Nevertheless, this interest can be invested or spent in a variety of ways that benefit a larger community as well as its individual members.[8]

Sociologist Peter Berger has used the term "mediating structures" to refer to the assemblage of groups, institutions, and networks of family, peer or neighborly support that give substance to a community and direction to its members.[9] I have gone a bit further here and said that under some conditions the persons enmeshed in such an array of social relations and institutions can grow into an ethnic people. This is accomplished when the members of this larger "group" have a sense of themselves as a distinct people, share a common set of values, and work together in behalf of a place that they call home. It is all part of their "cultural capital."

These larger social creations, no matter what name one puts to them, would have a big impact on the fate of an affirmative action program. The federal government, were it to start a new kind of affirmative action, would support community-based initiatives with it. One can imagine community leaders underwriting with some federal money the development of small retail establishments – owned and run by their fellow ethnics – that employ youths from the surrounding community. One might find local governments ceding control of certain properties to community development corporations that put local persons to work as builders, managers, and maintenance personnel. Large corporations seeking to expand their markets into certain areas dominated by a particular ethnic people might be convinced to provide franchises to area residents because they knew that the area was under constant surveillance by community members, only some of whom actually worked for the company. Finally, area banks could serve as loan guarantors and advisors to start-up companies in which both their customers and the federal government have a financial interest.

Profits from these different enterprises could be reinvested in the community either in the form of new and expanded businesses or as valuable services such as child care, tutoring, and assistance to the elderly. Community leaders could consult with established businesses and organizations belonging to other ethnic groups. An attempt could be made to match the strengths of these different peoples and to undertake joint ventures which simultaneously opened up new markets for both and provided for better social ties outside of the ethnic enclave. Area youngsters could be trained to set up and operate data banks that helped to match local groups with organizations from other ethnic communities that were willing to barter with them or to invest in local businesses.

The point of these and many other projects that could be imagined is that they would emerge because the community's organizational strength in concert with its residents' hard work was treated as a form of collateral. Credit in the form of grants, loans, and deferred or limited taxes from government agencies, loans from area banks, and the establishment of franchises by large corporations would be directed to areas covered under this type of affirmative action program. Local residents would be employed in a variety of capacities, and much of what they earned or spent would stay in the local area. Though more elaborate than traditional rotating credit associations or mutual trade associations found in ethnic economies, these enterprises are fashioned on the same principles and would have an impact on the whole community or big pieces of it.

The act of subordinating affirmative action programs to the workings of a larger ethnic economy may seem to diminish the symbolic importance of any federal effort. It certainly would make it harder to measure the precise impact of the program, inasmuch as it would supplement work undertaken by a variety of organizations. For that very reason, however, affirmative action implemented in this way would have more far-reaching consequences than it has in the past.

The comparatively modest accomplishments of established affirmative action programs for black Americans, for instance, are not surprising. Black Americans made much bigger advances when they moved into cities in order to take industrial jobs provided by war-time economies, events that took place well before the introduction of affirmative action programs. These changes introduced large numbers of black Americans to a wide range of occupations in an urban environment. Their most dramatic advances may have been in jobs requiring more education or technical training, precisely where affirmative action has enjoyed its greatest successes. It is too easy to lose sight of the fact, however, that advances in other occupational areas were every bit as important as those witnessed in the professions.

How are we to reconcile the modest accomplishments of these reforms with the overheated rhetoric of their proponents and detractors? I think re-casting affirmative action programs so that they build on the work of ethnic economies would accomplish such an end. We can begin to see how such reforms can complement the work of private companies and local groups that are in a good position to make life at least a little better for a variety of persons. We also can imagine a civil rights reform that empowers persons and communities and puts them more squarely in the midst of the conventional economy. It would not be the first time that minority communities had succeeded in this way. It only would be the most recent and ambitious attempt to build an ethnic economy within an unsettled urban world.[10]

Making Affirmative Action Count

One of the bigger impediments to initiating this kind of affirmative action program will likely be the persons responsible for making the laws and policies that we are supposed to follow. Lawyers and politicians are fond of creating elegant rules that often are ignored, so that they might protect abstract classes of citizens whose individual members may then dream about things that few have a chance of acquiring in real life. It is as if they imagined there were a single collection of persons "out there" who actually shared all of the burden and relief of oppression and reform. In practice we know that this is not so, and the dialogue over affirmative action points out clearly the limits of reform undertaken on behalf of disadvantaged "classes" of citizens.

Such "classes" or "groups" as rule makers deem necessary for the safe and effective conduct of their craft are little more than figments of their own, and our, imagination. Reified beyond the point of being a statistical artifact, they emerge full blown as corporate beings with a history and a name. They are, in reality, an intellectual contrivance with no life outside our animated discourse, or academic writing. That we appropriate them at all speaks more to a need on our part to talk about the stresses and strains built into our society than to any serious plan to make the world into a better place for the fictional groups in whose name we fabricate reforms. It is within the confines of the artfully scripted crises and reforms promoted as "social change" that we are to find the real significance of affirmative action policies and laws.

Our passionate arguments about how to describe and measure the impact of affirmative action until now have been exciting, if not especially convincing. Like two bickering archers locked in an unlit room, the advocates and detractors of affirmative action have taken turns shooting at each other's claims about the efficacy and necessity of government programs. Yet they have done this without any good view of where they were shooting or even without knowing at what target they should be aiming.

The goal of conventional affirmative action programs has been to help minorities and women to acquire specific jobs that they typically have not held. Not uncommonly, these jobs have been of a professional nature. Successful affirmative action led to more minorities or women being in the pool of potential candidates, being hired for such jobs, or acquiring salaries commensurate to those going to persons who typically hold them. As such, affirmative action did provide some individuals with an opportunity to improve their economic standing. Their private accomplishment was not tied to improvements in the life chances of minority persons or women in general, however, except in a most abstract way.

The true impact of an affirmative action plan cannot be measured convincingly by counting the number of persons who have managed to acquire a particular job. Nor is failure measured satisfactorily by counting the number of persons who had failed to secure employment in a given occupation. It may be nice to have three more doctors, five accountants, a lawyer, and a handful of investment bankers who come from the same background as I do. On the other hand, it is hard to know whether that is much of an accomplishment when so many other persons like me are finding it extremely difficult to achieve economic security, much less economic prosperity.

The problem with doing affirmative action in this way is that it presumes to deal with inequality in bite-sized pieces. Inequality is not a feature of individual lives and cannot be imagined or measured adequately in that way, anymore than my successful avoidance of lung cancer tells us anything about the prevalence of that affliction among middle-aged men in general. If inequality is better imagined as a social phenomenon, and subject at all to the influences of groups, then the appropriate focus of any affirmative action plan should be on how well or poorly an entire population is doing in a given locale. A better way to measure the success of efforts to ameliorate the effects of inequality, then, would be to look at how all the members of one population are doing in relation to the members of another population where they live. This would give them a much better feel for the changes that had occurred in their community over a period of time.

This approach is reasonable as far as it goes, but Glenn Loury correctly notes that it is haunted by a subtle logical problem. "A focus on group differences," as he refers to them, "in the presence of continuing overall inequality, amounts to a demand for equality *between groups* of the overall inequality *within groups*." "Why should inequality among individuals of the same group be acceptable," he wonders, "when inequality between groups is not?"[11] Why indeed?

Loury has put his finger on an important flaw in the logic informing affirmative action policies. In so doing, however, he also has inadvertently provided a rationale for amending affirmative action plans so that they build on the strengths of ethnic economies. The advantage of ethnic economies is not just that they can provide a modicum of success for some persons. It is rather that ethnic economies call attention to comparisons that are made by persons *within* their own group as well as the progress evidenced *between* themselves and persons from another population.

Someone is always going to be unequal in comparison to somebody else, and inequality among the members of a given population would remain even if it were all but eradicated between themselves and other peoples. "If we are to be concerned about group inequality," Loury asks, "how will we know which groups are the salient ones?"[12] The answer to his question is that ethnic economies call for such comparisons to be made both within the "disadvantaged" population and between it and other populations.

An affirmative action policy designed to mimic the workings of an ethnic economy would help to make the distribution of jobs and inequality within one population more like that of other relevant comparison populations in the community. Success would be measured locally and in terms of how similar the distribution of jobs and salaries among the members of a disadvantaged class is to the distribution of jobs and salaries for persons who are not in the disadvantaged class. Failure, by comparison, would be revealed in a distribution of minority jobs and salaries that was growing less like the distribution seen among persons who are not in that disadvantaged class or community.

Accounting for the success of affirmative action in this way is not arbitrary and it does not create an impossible standard to achieve. Furthermore, having achieved comparability in the distribution of jobs, salaries, and inequality one could make a convincing argument for ending affirmative action programs. Communities once considered underprivileged would have found ways to make their residents as well off as persons from other places around them, even though many of them individually were not at all well-to-do.

The central feature of ethnicity in modern societies is that persons of unequal wealth, status, or power find reasons to view themselves as part of the same people. This is an important accomplishment because it shows how significant differences in position and talent can be overcome by appeals to a common brotherhood. Affirmative action policies could help to foster that kind of brotherhood and build on the success fostered by the development of solid ethnic groups. It would do this by changing the way we look at inequality; making it easier for one's own group to look enough like other people so as to reduce the degree of tension between them *and* by making the members of these ethnic groups more responsible for each other's well-being.

The Problem with Group Solutions

Constitutional lawyers, politicians, and social scientists with an ideological or programmatic ax to grind could be expected to resist these proposals for any number of reasons. Conservatives who typically favor less intervention by federal rule-makers might well bridle at the idea of using "group-based" solutions to address pressing social problems. They probably would prefer to let individuals take care of themselves. More liberal persons might take issue with a proposal that takes the teeth out of existing federal programs and puts more of the responsibility for addressing such issues in the hands of the disadvantaged groups. The ideas laid out here could be perceived as coming perilously close to "blaming the victims" for not changing the sorry condition of their lives.

There surely is merit to these criticisms, if one accepts the logic that has informed the customary arguments of affirmative action's champions and detractors. In my estimation, however, their objections would drag us back to the same old tired and well-grooved "solutions" to inequality that have proven ineffective in the past. There would be great, and unfortunate, irony in looking backward at this important moment in our history. This irony, however, would be surpassed by the tragedy implied in discouraging communities from working harder to deal with a problem that no outsider has yet been able to show them how to address satisfactorily, but whose solution already is within their grasp.

Notes

1   Daniel J. Monti. (1985) *A Semblance of Justice* (Columbia, MO: University of Missouri Press).
2   Daniel J. Monti. (1995) "In the Black: School Desegregation and the Politics of Fiscal Redemption." *Urban Education*, 30(2): 150–74.
3   Philip Selznick. (1992) *The Moral Commonwealth* (Berkeley: University of California Press), p. 512.
4   Paul DiMaggio. (1982) "Cultural Capital and School Success." *American Sociological Review*, 47(2): 189–201.
5   Glenn C. Loury, "The Economics of Discrimination: Getting to the Core of the Problem." Public Lecture, Boston University, March 31, 1992, pp. 21–2.
6   Anthony D. Smith. (1993) *The Ethnic Origins of Nations* (London: Blackwell Publishers).
7   Loury, "The Economics of Discrimination," pp. 13–14.
8   Ibid., p. 15.
9   Peter Berger and Richard John Neuhaus. (1977) *To Empower People: The Role of Mediating Structures in Public Policy* (Washington, D.C.: American Enterprise Institute for Public Policy Research).
10 John Sibley Butler. (1990) *Entrepreneurship and Self-Help among Black Americans: A Reconsideration of Race and Economics* (Albany: State University of New York Press).
11 Loury, "The Economics of Discrimination," pp. 11–12.
12 Ibid., p. 12.

24 Multicultural Citizenship in Germany

Christian Joppke

Pierre Bourdieu and Loïc Wacquant (1998) have recently denounced as a 'trick of imperialist reason' the global spread of American concepts, such as 'multiculturalism' or 'underclass'. If detached from their historical context, the two French sociologists argue, these concepts must lead to a misreading of non-American realities. 'Affirmative action' is another case in point. This is a particularly American solution to a particularly American problem. 'American problem', that is, the legacy of black slavery, for which there is no equivalent in Europe; 'American solution', that is, to carry the American penchant for equality (which has amazed European observers since Tocqueville) so far that even its temporary violation was justified if it helped to bring about final, ultimate equality. Interestingly, in the finest theory of minority rights available today, which was written by a Canadian (Kymlicka 1995), there is no space for affirmative action. Kymlicka distinguishes between moderate 'polyethnic rights' for immigrants (which are to protect the culture and lifestyle of ethnic immigrants) and stronger 'self-determination rights' for national minorities. American blacks, who are neither immigrant nor national minority, and the affirmative action privileges accorded to them, fall entirely outside this scheme. While an 'omission' to some, the Canadian philosopher insisted that this was exactly the point: to develop a non-US centered theory of minority rights, and thus to escape the 'cultural imperialism' that seems to worry not only the French.

Turning from theory to reality, there is no 'affirmative action' in Europe, and it is nowhere seriously debated nor close to being established. Interestingly, in its practice of racial quotas the US has more in common with India or Malaysia (see Jalali 1993 and Lim 1985) than with Great Britain or the Netherlands. The latter two, due to their shared multiracial legacy of empire and postcolonial immigration, went further than most other European countries in creating approximations of affirmative action, such as anti-discrimination laws and multicultural integration policies. Britain is the most interesting case in this respect, because its race relations law is partially modelled on US civil rights law. But the 'positive action' that the Race Relations Act of 1977 allows is emphatically not affirmative action, because it sticks to the strict principle of non-discrimination and forbids reverse discrimination (see Teles 1998). Examples of positive action are special job training schemes by private employers for their underrepresented minority employees, or the placing of special job advertisements in the minority press. Such positive action is permissive rather than mandatory, and in the all-important field of employment some (reverse) discrimination may occur preceding to, but never, never at the point of selection or promotion. There is a simple reason for Britain's reticence: it has always viewed its racial minorities as voluntary immigrants toward whom no special obligations existed. As E. J. B. Rose's (1969:5) classic survey of New Commonwealth immigration formulated this view, due to their voluntary entry 'the descendents of Britain's slaves ... would not be on the conscience of the country in the way that the Negro had for generations been on the conscience of Americans.'

Against this backdrop, it is not surprising that Germany has never seriously considered introducing affirmative action for its immigrant minorities. But there is additional complexity to the German case, which merits further attention. The German case allows us to see, through their absence, some prerequisites of affirmative action (and of anti-discrimination laws and policies in general). The first prerequisite is citizenship. Because of its (until recently) restrictive citizenship laws, immigrants to Germany are mostly not citizens, even in the second and third generation. Citizenship, however, is a necessary condition for anti-discrimination measures, because – in international law – nationality is a legitimate marker of discrimination. Accordingly, the United Nations Convention Against Race Discrimination of 1966 prohibits discrimination on the basis of national or ethnic origins, but explicitly allows discrimination on the basis of nationality (in the sense of formal state membership). Not by accident, we find anti-discrimination laws mostly in countries with postcolonial immigration, where immigrants had arrived with (de facto) citizenship (which derived from their membership in the empire). A prime example is again Britain, whose race relations law was directed at immigrants who were from the start citizens. One may speculate that an anti-discrimination law, which Germany currently does not have, will become an issue when later-generation foreigners (especially Turks) acquire German citizenship in larger numbers. This situation has in principle arrived with the liberalization of citizenship law in 1999 (see Joppke 2000). Accordingly, the 1998 coalition treaty of SPD and Greens, which constitute the new federal government, promptly included a proposal for an anti-discrimination law as complementary to the envisaged liberalization of citizenship law.

A first movement for an anti-discrimination law had been launched already in the early 1990s, jointly by the Federal Commissioner for Foreigner Affairs, the Foreigner Commissioner of Berlin (see Senatsverwaltung fuer Soziales, 1992) and the Frankfurt Office for Multicultural Affairs (see Rittstieg and Rowe, 1992). It tackled the problem of the non-citizen status of immigrants by interpreting foreigner discrimination in terms of ethnic or racial discrimination, whereby UN Convention protection would apply (Mager 1992:121f), or by simply adding 'nationality' to the catalogue of prohibited discriminatory markers in a proposed statutory anti-discrimination law (Rittstieg and Rowe, 1992:92). The conservative government at the time resisted such a law, arguing that the existing legal provisions were sufficient. The most important is Article 3(3) of the Basic Law, which stipulates that 'nobody must be disadvantaged or preferred because of his sex, ethnic or national origins, race, language, and religious or political opinion'. Like the UN Convention, this constitutional article does not outlaw nationality-based discrimination, and would force a reinterpretation of nationality-based law in terms of ethnic or racial discrimination. And, interestingly, it prohibits positive discrimination, i.e., American-style ethnic or racial quotas. Furthermore, the article binds only the state, not private parties (who may invoke the liberty right of Article 2.1 to justify discriminatory contracts or other private transactions). However, courts have held that private actors, to the degree that they exert societal or economic power (for instance in education, housing, or public services) are indirectly constrained by the anti-discrimination provisions of Article 3. Additional already existing protection from race-based discrimination can be found in the articles 130 and 131 of penal law, which prohibit 'Volksverhetzung' and 'Incitement to Racial Hatred' (through offensive publications etc.), respectively. However, the advocates of an anti-discrimination law have stressed that the existing protections in the Basic Law and in penal law are not sufficient, first, because they leave the status of nationality-based discrimination unclear, and, secondly, because they erect high legal thresholds (for instance, in imposing on the discriminated party the difficult burden of proving intentional discrimination on the part of the offender). As a result, Germany today is a country in which even blatant, direct discrimination goes mostly unpunished in crucial private sector domains, such as housing, employment, and services.

A second prerequisite of affirmative action, which (unlike the partially remedied citizenship situation) *continues* to be absent in Germany, is a willingness of the state to assign public status to ethnic and racial groups. As is well-known, America's quest for racial equality started color-blind, in the Civil Rights Act's outlawing intentional discrimination, and ended color-consciousness, in the combating of non-intentional discrimination through achieving statistical parity between designated groups in the workforce, higher education, and political representation. In the original approach, color and group-status were to be eradicated; in the eventual approach, racial groups had to be carved out (and individuals attributed to them) as the targets of remedial measures, even though the main goal remained the same throughout: a society without racial discrimination. The turn from individual to group rights, and from anti-discrimination policy proper to affirmative action, was not the result of a conscious change of philosophy, but of slippage, in which administrative agencies acted under the political pressure of having to find fast and efficient solutions to the vexing problem of racial inequality (see Skrentny 1996). In Germany, such 'slippage' was factually impossible, because there was not even a modest anti-discrimination law that would target direct discrimination. But it was also ruled out in principle, because of a deep public aversion to categorize people in terms of ethnic or racial groups. The memory of the Nazi Regime, which had driven such categorization to the murderous extreme, is responsible for this. Accordingly, 'ethnicization' (Ethnisierung), which in the United States has the positive connotations of self-organization and group solidarity, figured in the German immigration debate as a negative word for the ghettoization and self-insulation of settled guestworkers (see Elwert 1982).

This aversion to ethnic categorization is ironic, because pre-unity Germany's exclusion of guestworker immigrants from the citizenry had to have exactly this effect, to 'ethnicize' its immigrants by keeping them in the separate legal and social status of – nationally divided – 'foreigners', in a kind of soft apartheid. Institutional ethnicization was furthered, for instance, through assigning the foreigner population to semi-public charity organizations according to their nationality and religion, and through incorporating foreigners into the symbolic 'foreigner parliaments' according to their nationality (see Joppke, 1999a:ch. 6). While Germany's institutional context furthered the ethnic or national group identifications of immigrants, claims and public policy making in these terms were still considered illegitimate. Interestingly, even the advocates of an anti-discrimination law have strongly rejected the idea of ethnic or racial quotas: 'Quotas in employment and housing have to be rejected, because they would encourage ethnic orientations and racist reactions' (Rittstieg and Rowe, 1992:92). This is almost identical with the language a conservative US Supreme Court has used to roll-back affirmative action and to reinstate the color-blindness that had guided the original civil rights law (see Rubenfeld, 1997:446).

Scattered (academic) voices for quotas were nonetheless raised in 1995, when second- and third-generation immigrant youth – the children and grandchildren of the guestworkers – ended up as losers in the increasingly competitive race for scarce slots in the German 'dual system' of combined schooling and employment training. Until the late 1980s, young foreigners (especially Turks) had made steady gains in schooling and employment. But this changed with the massive arrival of privileged ethnic Germans and the dramatic increase of mass unemployment in the early 1990s. However, the demand for quotas for foreign youth in the dual system never gained ground because of obvious inconsistencies – for instance, naturalized foreigners would fall out of this scheme, and it would disencourage their non-naturalized peers from acquiring German citizenship.

Even if the taboo of ethnic and racial labeling could be overcome, quotas would still clash with Article 3 (3) of the Basic Law, which prohibits negative *and* positive discrimination. The test ground for the constitutionality of quotas are the gender quotas practiced by most Laender (subfederal states) in civil service employment. The defenders of gender quotas refer to clause 2 of Article 3, which (in its amended version of 1994) mandates the state to 'further the actual equality of women and men and (to) remove existing disadvantages' (see the discussion in Degener, 1997). This was a concession to the more 'progressive' equality rights that women had enjoyed in the former GDR. As of today, the Constitutional Court has not decided on the constitutional legitimacy of affirmative action for women, and whatever decision it takes will throw the switches for or against similar claims by other groups.

In the context of immigration policy, there are two interesting exceptions to Germany's aversion to classify according to ethnicity or race: well known, the so-called ethnic Germans from Eastern Europe and the former Soviet Union; much less well known, Russian Jews, who in the 1990s were the only group to immigrate freely to Germany, without quota restrictions, and who upon arrival were entitled to generous social benefits and integration offers. If one looks for an equivalent in Germany to blacks in America, the original and primary beneficiary there of civil rights law and affirmative action, it would be ethnic Germans and Jews. Both groups, in diametrically opposed ways, are the victims of German history, and selected by the state for remedial treatment. Only, this remedial treatment did not entail affirmative action, in which the entitled minority, across generations, would have the edge over members of the majority society in key domains such as employment or higher education. Instead, remedial action followed the logic of welfare-state inclusion plus financial reparations for past damages or injustice, which were large enough to prevent the rise of disadvantaged ethnic German or Jewish "minorities" in the second generation.

To be sure, the case of ethnic Germans is paradoxical, because it meant carving out an ethnic group entitled to privileged treatment on the basis of a putative similarity (rather than difference) with the majority society. The motivation behind it is an obligation by the majority society to repay, as an act of national solidarity, the ethnic Germans for the disproportionate consequences of the war they had faced in terms of repression and persecution under Communism. Its most pertinent expression is the Lastenausgleichsgesetz (Equalization of Burdens Act), which compensated those who had lost their homes and properties in the eastern territories. Closer to the logic of welfare-state inclusion is the so-called Fremdrentengesetz (foreigner pension law), according to which ethnic Germans received old-age pensions equivalent to those of other Germans, even though they had not spent their working lives in the Federal Republic, and thus had not made the required contributions to the public pension fund. Indicating the logic of welfare state inclusion at work here, the pension-entitled ethnic Germans were treated 'as if' they had spent their entire working lives in the Federal Republic (see Preis and Steffan 1991).

It is interesting to note that the priority-immigration (and subsequent privileged treatment) of ethnic Germans has in principle been phased out, with the *Kriegsfolgenbereinigungsgesetz* of 1992. This law reflects that after the demise of Communism and the removal of exit restrictions in Eastern Europe and the former Soviet Union there could no longer be an automatic presumption of repression or 'expulsion pressure' (*Vertreibungsdruck*) for one's ethnic Germanness. The 1992 law, which is only the last in a series of laws since 1989 that chipped away the priority status of ethnic Germans, shifts the burden of proving 'expulsion pressure' from the government to the individual (with the important exceptions of ethnic Germans from the former Soviet Union), limits the right to claim the status of ethnic German to persons born before 1993, and imposes a quota of 225,000 ethnic Germans to be allowed in each year (see Levy 1999).

No such restrictions have been imposed on the priority-immigration of Russian Jews, which took off just when the priority-immigration of ethnic Germans became increasingly restricted. The 1991 Quota Refugee Law provides for the unrestricted migration and permanent settlement of Russian Jews to Germany – an opportunity that some 76,000 of them had seized before 1998, thus almost tripling the size of the Jewish community in Germany (Harris 1998). In fact, the rebuilding of the Jewish community in Germany has been the explicit purpose of this policy, which stands in complete contrast to the stern 'no-immigration' maxim of all German governments since 1973. To be sure, the Jewish exception has been forced upon a non-immigration minded government by a grassroots movement of Greens, SPD, and cities such as Frankfurt, which for a while accepted the Russian Jews – rather curiously – as non-acknowledged ethnic Germans. The interesting fact about this case is the complete incapacity of the federal government to impose any restrictions. Even when evidence abounded that the 'Jewish' migrants were not persecuted in their home countries, had few religious ties, or had used false documents to establish their Jewishness, there simply was no moral space for the government to formally examine the veracity of claims or to shift the burden of proof to the migrant. More than that, this policy went against the explicit request of Israel not to grant refugee-status to Russian Jews, because it needed them for its own nation-building purposes. Already in 1987, when the wave of Jewish migration from the Soviet Union had barely begun, Germany had refused such pressure by Israel: 'In view of her historical past, Germany does not want to close her borders just for Jews from the Soviet Union' (ibid., p. 117).

The asymmetric treatment of ethnic Germans and Russian Jews, successively restricting immigration of the former but allowing the continued immigration of the latter, suggests that an implicit ranking of victim groups is at work here. The claims of ethnic Germans, who had suffered retaliation for Nazism by communist regimes, were put below the claims of Jews, who had been persecuted and eliminated by the Germans themselves.

To sum up, citizenship and legitimate ethnic and racial categorizing are two minimal conditions for affirmative action, which – to varying degrees – have been absent in the German case. In fact, the German case is entirely outside the parameters of 'multicultural citizenship' (Kymlicka 1995), in which the debate about minority rights is usually placed. Regarding citizenship, the German case has inspired two very opposite lines of reasoning, one that sees citizenship devalued by the rise of 'postnational membership' based on 'universal rights of personhood' (Soysal 1994); and another one that sees citizenship as an ultra-stable institution determined by 'cultural idioms' of nationhood (Brubaker 1992). Both theories, as opposite as they seem, have caught a slice of truth. In pre-unity Germany, the integration of guestworkers was marked by the co-existence of traditional ethnic citizenship, closed to foreigners, and of postnational membership, in which the human rights provisions of the Basic Law endowed settled foreigners with most of the rights and privileges that Germans enjoyed (except political rights). Both were two sides of the same coin: postnational membership allowed the maintenance of ethnic citizenship, which survived after its delegitimization by Nazism only indirectly, as the homeland obligations of the Federal Republic to the ethnic German diaspora in communist Eastern Europe. West Germany was, like Israel, an incomplete ethnic state, which prioritized the immigration of co-ethnics. This was constitutionally enshrined in the reunification mandate of the Basic Law's preamble, and in Article 116 of the Basic Law that secured automatic citizenship to the ethnic Germans outside the Federal Republic. Allowing foreigners into the citizenry would have threatened the mandate of completing the nation-state. As a consequence, the status of 'foreigner' had to be upgraded into a safe membership status that approximated that of Germans – this is the concrete historical backdrop to 'postnational membership' in Germany. In a nutshell, pre-unity Germany's approach to guestworker integration was both maximally differentialist, designed to keep foreigners out of the citizenry, *and* maximally inclusionist, giving them most of the rights that Germans had. This is a constellation that forecloses the possibility of multicultural citizenship and minority rights, because the recognition of difference presupposes a common membership status, i.e., citizenship.

However, this constellation is now changing radically. National reunification and the end of Communism have put an end to the co-existence of ethnic citizenship and postnational membership, which had characterized the Bonn Republic. Two factors are responsible for this. First, there is no longer an ethnic diaspora to redeem, and with it the rationale for ethnic citizenship has disappeared. Germany is no longer like Israel. Secondly, the xenophobic violence in the early 1990s, directed indiscriminately against new asylum-seekers and long-settled Turkish immigrants, has thrown into sharp relief the problem of integrating second- and third-generation immigrants, who are forever locked out of the citizenry through the old *ius sanguinis* citizenship rules, which date back to 1913. In response to this double pressure, Germany has recently moved from an ethnic toward a civic-territorial citizenship regime, in which not descent, but residence and birth on territory matters. A first step in this direction was the introduction of as-of-right naturalization for second-generation immigrants in 1992, remarkably, just two years after reunification. Regarding this particular 'immigrant' group, it removed the two pillars of the old, restrictive naturalization rules: absolute state discretion and cultural assimilation as precondition for citizenship. 'Assimilation' is now simply deduced from the applicant's length of residence; it is no longer individually examined. This makes the German naturalization process in certain respects more liberal than the American one, which is still based on an individual assimilation test (however minimal). And, most importantly, membership in the German nation-state is no longer premised on being part of the ethnocultural nation. In this limited sense, German citizenship has already become 'multicultural citizenship'.

The second, and decisive, step toward civic-territorial citizenship occurred in the new citizenship law of 1999, which put an end to more than eighty years of exclusively *ius-sanguinis*-based citizenship. According to the so-called Option Model guiding the new law, the German-born children of long-settled, legal resident foreigners are German citizens at birth, but will have to decide between age 16 to 23 between their German or their foreign citizenship. The eased incorporation of Germany's immigrants is bound to foster new, and more urgent demands for policies of anti-discrimination and minority protection, and Germany's resistance to ethnic classifying may have to loosen a little. The existence of large pockets of disadvantaged ethnic minorities within the citizenry is likely to put pressure on the lawmaker to do something more for them, particularly in the two key areas of employment and education. Moreover, these groups are bound to transform from an object into a subject of politics. Interestingly, the fierce opposition by the conservative opposition parties (CDU/CSU) against the original plan of the SPD/Green coalition government to generally accept and tolerate dual citizenship was partially motivated by the fear that the massive increase of dual (especially Turkish-German) nationals could lead to the formation of a (homeland-oriented) 'Turkish Party', which on the basis of the minority protection already built into the Federal Election Law would be exempt from the five-percent threshold that normally excludes small splinter parties from seats in national parliament. This was doubly sloppy thinking, because, first, this minority protection is not contingent upon dual nationality status, and, secondly, it is still questionable in international and national law if a migrant group could be entitled to protections that are usually granted only to sedentary ('allochtone') national minorities. However, it was apt foreboding that with the granting of citizenship status especially, the sizeable Turkish-origin population would emancipate from a passive object of state policy into an active political player.

The German case has three implications for theorizing about immigration and citizenship. First, citizenship in liberal states is malleable. Contrary to Brubaker, states are not slaves of their 'cultural idioms' of nationhood, but may devise flexible citizenship policies in response to immigration pressures. Second, national citizenship remains indispensable for integrating immigrants. 'Postnational membership' à la Soysal may have a certain value to first-generation immigrants; it is a liability for later-generation immigrants, whose non-citizenship makes them vulnerable and stigmatizable minorities. Third, Germany's withdrawal from assimilation as a precondition for citizenship, which reflects a general European trend (see Hansen 1998), adds an important dimension to Kymlicka's theory of multicultural citizenship (to the degree that this is a theory with empirical, not exclusively normative claims). Kymlicka had looked only at the internal rights, not the external closure-dimension of citizenship. But even the closure-dimension has taken on some multicultural features, in decoupling citizenship acquisition from the tested assimilation of the applicant. This reflects the cultural neutrality of liberal states, which cannot commit their members to substantive life forms, but only to shared procedural rules. In this sense, liberal states (in Europe and elsewhere) are inherently 'multicultural', because they respect, sometimes even protect, the identities of their members. As Kymlicka outlined, this has occurred within various schemes of 'polyethnic rights', such as changes in the curriculum, bilingual education, and exemptions from laws and regulations that disadvantage minorities. If the United States has gone further in granting additional affirmative action privileges to minority groups, which are not just about recognition but redistribution, the question cannot be why Europe generally does not follow, but why the United States is so strangely different.

References

Bourdieu, Pierre and Loïc Wacquant. 1998. "Sur les ruses de la raison imperialiste," *Actes de la recherche en sciences sociales*, March issue.

Brubaker, Rogers. 1992. *Citizenship and Nationhood in Germany and France*. Cambridge, Mass.: Harvard University Press.

Degener, Theresia. 1997. "Der Streit um Gleichheit und Differenz in der Bundesrepublik Deutschland seit 1945," in: Ute Gerhard, ed., *Frauen in der Geschichte des Rechts*. Munich: Beck.

Elwert, Georg. 1982. "Probleme der Auslaenderintegration," *Koelner Zeitschrift fuer Soziologie und Sozialpsychologie* 34, pp. 696–716.

Harris, Paul. 1998. "Jewish Migration to the New Germany," in: Dietrich Traenhardt, ed. *Einwanderung und Einbuergerung in Deutschland*. Munich: Litt.

Hansen, Randall. 1998. "A European citizenship or a Europe of citizens? Third country nationals in the EU," *Journal of Ethnic and Migration Studies*, vol. 24, no. 4, pp. 751–68.

Jalali, Rita. 1993. "Preferential Policies and the Movement of the Disadvantaged: The Case of the Scheduled Castes in India," *Ethnic and Racial Studies*, vol. 16, no. 1, pp. 95–120.

Joppke, Christian. 1999a. *Immigration and the Nation-State: The United States, Germany, and Great Britain*. Oxford: Oxford University Press.

Joppke, Christian. 1999b. "How Immigration is Changing Citizenship," *Ethnic and Racial Studies*, vol. 22, no. 4, pp. 629–52.

Joppke, Christian. 2000. "Mobilization of Culture and the Reform of Citizenship Law," in: R. Koopmans and P. Statham, eds., *Challenging Immigration and Ethnic Relation Politics*. Oxford: Oxford University Press.

Joppke, Christian and Ewa Morawska (eds). 1999. *Integrating Immigrants in Liberal Nation-States*.

Kymlicka, Will. 1995. *Multicultural Citizenship*. Oxford: Clarendon Press.

Levy, Daniel. 1999. *Remembering the Nation*. Dissertation filed at Columbia University, New York.

Lim, Mah Hui. 1985. "Affirmative Action, Ethnicity and Integration: The Case of Malaysia," *Ethnic and Racial Studies*, vol. 8, no. 2, pp. 250–76.

Mager, Ute. 1992. "Schutz der Auslaender vor Diskriminierung durch Privatpersonen," in: Senatsverwaltung fuer Soziales (1992).

Preis, Ulrich and Ralf Steffan. 1991. "Harmonisierungsbedarf im (Fremd-)Rentenrecht," *Zeitschrift fuer Rechtspolitik*, no. 1, pp. 12–17.

Rittstieg, Helmut and Gerard C. Rowe. 1992. *Einwanderung als gesellschaftliche Herausforderung*. Baden-Baden: Nomos.

Rose, E. J. B. 1969. *Colour and Citizenship*. Oxford: Oxford University Press.

Rubenfeld, Jed. 1997. "Affirmative Action," *Yale Law Journal*, vol. 107, pp. 427–72.

Senatsverwaltung fuer Soziales. 1992. *Schutzgesetze gegen ethnische Diskriminierung*. Berlin: hectographed.

Skrentny, John. 1996. *The Ironies of Affirmative Action*. Chicago: University of Chicago Press.

Soysal, Yasemin. 1994. *Limits of Citizenship*. Chicago: University of Chicago Press.

Teles, Steven. 1998. "Why is There No Affirmative Action in Britain?", *American Behavioral Scientist*, vol. 41, no. 7, pp. 1004–26.

Part IX

Toward Ethnic and Racial Justice?

The final selections in the book are concerned with three major aspects of the quest for just and stable solutions to the problems generated by ethnic and racial conflict. Each extract focuses on certain fundamental questions: the conflicting demands of group protection and individual rights; the compromises that may be necessary to ensure the transition toward non-racial democracies, following violent ethnic and racial struggles; and the search for viable laws and institutions to provide a global framework for racial equality. These issues raise profoundly difficult political and ethical dilemmas to which there are no simple answers.

Charles Taylor sets the problems of multiculturalism within the long tradition of debates in political and social theory. The limited extent to which nineteenth-century liberalism responds to the recognition of diverse cultural identities can be seen against the complex political struggles in Canada over the past thirty years. Attempts to reconcile the diverse claims of Quebeckers, aboriginal peoples, immigrants and the English-speaking majority illustrate both the practical and theoretical issues in question. The failure of the Meech Lake Accord, in the early 1980s, to reach a sustainable compromise is explained by the inherent contradiction between a liberal model of individual rights and the collective goal of group survival that lies at the core of the Quebec nationalists' case. Taylor suggests that one type of liberalism is indeed "inhospitable" to difference, but another interpretation – what he calls the politics of equal respect – provides much greater latitude to those collective goals that seek the preservation of minority culture and the survival of community life. This discussion leads on to the contemporary debates about cultural diversity and whether the demand for equal recognition precludes any judgments about the relative merits of different cultures.

The practical consequences of making judgments about extreme types of human action is seen in the controversies concerning Truth Commissions set up to facilitate the transition from authoritarian to democratic regimes. In principle, the issues at stake are well known and stem from the Nuremberg and Tokyo trials at the end of the Second World War. To what extent is it possible to punish crimes against humanity, many of which involve the genocidal massacres of racial and ethnic groups, without creating an appearance of "victor's justice"? If the rape of Nanking or the atrocities committed by Japanese soldiers in Manchuria demand accountability, what about the atomic bombing of Hiroshima and Nagasaki? The same question may be raised against Nazi barbarities, but does this extend to the allied bombing of Dresden and other predominantly civilian targets? The problems become still more complicated in the democratic transitions of the end of the twentieth century, when oppressive regimes yield up their power on condition that there will be an amnesty for the perpetrators of gross human rights violations.

Adam and Moodley discuss these problems against the experience of the South African Truth and Reconciliation Commission. While some have seen this experiment as a magnanimous and creative method of bringing closure to the injustices and crimes of the apartheid era, thereby avoiding the perpetuation of bitter divisions and undermining the fragile new democracy, others have remained skeptical about its value.

The South African experience represents one of a series of attempts to establish some form of justice in a world plagued by racial and ethnic conflict. Michael Banton considers the case of global laws designed to reinforce fundamental human rights. These issues touch on basic problems of political theory as well as the overriding challenge of establishing an international rule of law. Abortive attempts to set up the League of Nations after the end of the First World War, and the terrible cost of its failure, have led on to the post-war treaties established under the auspicies of the United Nations. The great difficulties in getting member states to ratify conventions on human rights and genocide reflect the complex political and cultural questions involved. While pessimism about the glacial pace of progress is understandable, the fact that these issues are finally being debated in a global forum, and that tentative rules and institutions are being proposed and established, provides some measure of hope for the future.

25 The Politics of Recognition

Charles Taylor

The fact is that there are forms of the liberalism of equal rights that in the minds of their own proponents can give only a very restricted acknowledgment of distinct cultural identities. The notion that any of the standard schedules of rights might apply differently in one cultural context than they do in another, that their application might have to take account of different collective goals, is considered quite unacceptable. The issue, then, is whether this restrictive view of equal rights is the only possible interpretation. If it is, then it would seem that the accusation of homogenization is well founded. But perhaps it is not. I think it is not, and perhaps the best way to lay out the issue is to see it in the context of the Canadian case, where this question has played a role in the impending breakup of the country. In fact, two conceptions of rights-liberalism have confronted each other, albeit in confused fashion, throughout the long and inconclusive constitutional debates of recent years.

The issue came to the fore because of the adoption in 1982 of the Canadian Charter of Rights, which aligned our political system in this regard with the American one in having a schedule of rights offering a basis for judicial review of legislation at all levels of government. The question had to arise how to relate this schedule to the claims for distinctness put forward by French Canadians, and particularly Quebeckers, on the one hand, and aboriginal peoples on the other. Here what was at stake was the desire of these peoples for survival, and their consequent demand for certain forms of autonomy in their self-government, as well as the ability to adopt certain kinds of legislation deemed necessary for survival.

For instance, Quebec has passed a number of laws in the field of language. One regulates who can send their children to English-language schools (not francophones or immigrants); another requires that businesses with more than fifty employees be run in French; a third outlaws commercial signage in any language other than French. In other words, restrictions have been placed on Quebeckers by their government, in the name of their collective goal of survival, which in other Canadian communities might easily be disallowed by virtue of the Charter. The fundamental question was: Is this variation acceptable or not?

The issue was finally raised by a proposed constitutional amendment, named after the site of the conference where it was first drafted, Meech Lake. The Meech amendment proposed to recognize Quebec as a "distinct society," and wanted to make this recognition one of the bases for judicial interpretation of the rest of the constitution, including the Charter. This seemed to open up the possibility for variation in its interpretation in different parts of the country. For many, such variation was fundamentally unacceptable. Examining why brings us to the heart of the question of how rights-liberalism is related to diversity.

The Canadian Charter follows the trend of the last half of the twentieth century, and gives a basis for judicial review on two basic scores. First, it defines a set of individual rights that are very similar to those protected in other charters and bills of rights in Western democracies, for example, in the United States and Europe. Second, it guarantees equal treatment of citizens in a variety of respects, or, alternatively put, it protects against discriminatory treatment on a number of irrelevant grounds, such as race or sex. There is a lot more in our Charter, including provisions for linguistic rights and aboriginal rights, that could be understood as according powers to collect-ivities, but the two themes I singled out dominate in the public consciousness.

This is no accident. These two kinds of provisions are now quite common in entrenched schedules of rights that provide the basis for judicial review. In this sense, the Western world, perhaps the world as a whole, is following American precedent. The Americans were the first to write out and entrench a bill of rights, which they did during the ratification of their Constitution and as a condition of its successful outcome. One might argue that they weren't entirely clear on judicial review as a method of securing those rights, but this rapidly became the practice. The first amendments protected individuals, and sometimes state governments, against encroachment by the new federal government. It was after the Civil War, in the period of triumphant Reconstruction, and particularly with the Fourteenth Amendment, which called for "equal protection" for all citizens under the laws, that the theme of nondiscrimination became central to judicial review. But this theme is now on a par with the older norm of the defense of individual rights, and in public consciousness perhaps even ahead.

For a number of people in "English Canada," a political society's espousing cer-tain collective goals threatens to run against both of these basic provisions of our Charter, or indeed any acceptable bill of rights. First, the collective goals may require restrictions on the behavior of individuals that may violate their rights. For many nonfrancophone Canadians, both inside and outside Quebec, this feared outcome had already materialized with Quebec's language legislation. For instance, Quebec legislation prescribes, as already mentioned, the type of school to which parents can send their children; and in the most famous instance, it forbids certain kinds of commercial signage. This latter provision was actually struck down by the Supreme Court as contrary to the Quebec Bill of Rights, as well as the Charter, and only reenacted through the invocation of a clause in the Charter that permits legislatures in certain cases to override decisions of the courts relative to the Charter for a limited period of time (the so-called notwithstanding clause).

But second, even if overriding individual rights were not possible, espousing collective goals on behalf of a national group can be thought to be inherently discriminatory. In the modern world it will always be the case that not all those living as citizens under a certain jurisdiction will belong to the national group thus favored. This in itself could be thought to provoke discrimination. But beyond this, the pursuit of the collective end will probably involve treating insiders and outsiders differently. Thus the schooling provisions of Law 101 forbid (roughly speaking) francophones and immigrants to send their children to English-language schools, but allow Canadian anglophones to do so.

This sense that the Charter clashes with basic Quebec policy was one of the grounds of opposition in the rest of Canada to the Meech Lake accord. The cause for concern was the distinct society clause, and the common demand for amendment was that the Charter be "protected" against this clause, or take precedence over it. There was undoubtedly in this opposition a certain amount of old-style anti-Quebec prejudice, but there was also a serious philosophical point, which we need to articulate here.

Those who take the view that individual rights must always come first, and, along with nondiscrimination provisions, must take precedence over collective goals, are often speaking from a liberal perspective that has become more and more widespread in the Anglo-American world. Its source is, of course, the United States, and it has recently been elaborated and defended by some of the best philosophical and legal minds in that society, including John Rawls, Ronald Dworkin, Bruce Ackerman, and others.[1] There are various formulations of the main idea, but perhaps the one that encapsulates most clearly the point that is relevant to us is the one expressed by Dworkin in his short paper entitled "Liberalism."

Dworkin makes a distinction between two kinds of moral commitment. We all have views about the ends of life, about what constitutes a good life, which we and others ought to strive for. But we also acknowledge a commitment to deal fairly and equally with each other, regardless of how we conceive our ends. We might call this latter commitment "procedural," while commitments concerning the ends of life are "substantive." Dworkin claims that a liberal society is one that as a society adopts no particular substantive view about the ends of life. The society is, rather, united around a strong procedural commitment to treat people with equal respect. The reason that the polity as such can espouse no substantive view, cannot, for instance, allow that one of the goals of legislation should be to make people virtuous in one or another meaning of that term, is that this would involve a violation of its procedural norm. For, given the diversity of modern societies, it would unfailingly be the case that some people and not others would be commited to the favored conception of virtue. They might be in a majority; indeed, it is very likely that they would be, for otherwise a democratic society probably would not espouse their view. Nevertheless, this view would not be everyone's view, and in espousing this substantive outlook the society would not be treating the dissident minority with equal respect. It would be saying to them, in effect, "your view is not as valuable, in the eyes of this polity, as that of your more numerous compatriots."

There are very profound philosophical assumptions underlying this view of liberalism, which is rooted in the thought of Immanuel Kant. Among other features, this view understands human dignity to consist largely in autonomy, that is, in the ability of each person to determine for himself or herself a view of the good life. Dignity is associated less with any particular understanding of the good life, such that someone's departure from this would detract from his or her own dignity, than with the power to consider and espouse for oneself some view or other. We are not respecting this power equally in all subjects, it is claimed, if we raise the outcome of some people's deliberations officially over that of others. A liberal society must remain neutral on the good life, and restrict itself to ensuring that however they see things, citizens deal fairly with each other and the state deals equally with all.

The popularity of this view of the human agent as primarily a subject of self-determining or self-expressive choice helps to explain why this model of liberalism is so strong. But we must also consider that it has been urged with great force and intelligence by liberal thinkers in the United States, and precisely in the context of constitutional doctrines of judicial review. Thus it is not surprising that the idea has become widespread, well beyond those who might subscribe to a specific Kantian philosophy, that a liberal society cannot accommodate publicly espoused notions of the good. This is the conception, as Michael Sandel has noted, of the "procedural republic," which has a very strong hold on the political agenda in the United States, and which has helped to place increasing emphasis on judicial review on the basis of constitutional texts at the expense of the ordinary political process of building majorities with a view to legislative action.[2]

But a society with collective goals like Quebec's violates this model. It is axiomatic for Quebec governments that the survival and flourishing of French culture in Quebec is a good. Political society is not neutral between those who value remaining true to the culture of our ancestors and those who might want to cut loose in the name of some individual goal of self-development. It might be argued that one could after all capture a goal like *survivance* for a proceduralist liberal society. One could consider the French language, for instance, as a collective resource that individuals might want to make use of, and act for its preservation, just as one does for clean air or green spaces. But this can't capture the full thrust of policies designed for cultural survival. It is not just a matter of having the French language available for those who might choose it. This might be seen to be the goal of some of the measures of federal bilingualism over the last twenty years. But it also involves making sure that there is a community of people here in the future that will want to avail itself of the opportunity to use the French language. Policies aimed at survival actively seek to *create* members of the community, for instance, in their assuring that future generations continue to identify as French-speakers. There is no way that these policies could be seen as just providing a facility to already existing people.

Quebeckers, therefore, and those who give similar importance to this kind of collective goal, tend to opt for a rather different model of a liberal society. On their view, a society can be organized around a definition of the good life, without this being seen as a depreciation of those who do not personally share this definition. Where the nature of the good requires that it be sought in common, this is the reason for its being a matter of public policy. According to this conception, a liberal society singles itself out as such by the way in which it treats minorities, including those who do not share public definitions of the good, and above all by the rights it accords to all of its members. But now the rights in question are conceived to be the fundamental and crucial ones that have been recognized as such from the very beginning of the liberal tradition: rights to life, liberty, due process, free speech, free practice of religion, and so on. On this model, there is a dangerous overlooking of an essential boundary in speaking of fundamental rights to things like commercial signage in the language of one's choice. One has to distinguish the fundamental liberties, those that should never be infringed and therefore ought to be unassailably entrenched, on one hand, from privileges and immunities that are important, but that can be revoked or restricted for reasons of public policy – although one would need a strong reason to do this – on the other.

A society with strong collective goals can be liberal, on this view, provided it is also capable of respecting diversity, especially when dealing with those who do not share its common goals; and provided it can offer adequate safeguards for fundamental rights. There will undoubtedly be tensions and difficulties in pursuing these objectives together, but such a pursuit is not impossible, and the problems are not in principle greater than those encountered by any liberal society that has to combine, for example, liberty and equality, or prosperity and justice.

Here are two incompatible views of liberal society. One of the great sources of our present disharmony is that the two views have squared off against each other in the last decade. The resistance to the "distinct society" that called for precedence to be given to the Charter came in part from a spreading procedural outlook in English Canada. From this point of view, attributing the goal of promoting Quebec's distinct society to a government is to acknowledge a collective goal, and this move had to be neutralized by being subordinated to the existing Charter. From the standpoint of Quebec, this attempt to impose a procedural model of liberalism not only would deprive the distinct society clause of some of its force as a rule of interpretation, but bespoke a rejection of the model of liberalism on which this society was founded. Each society misperceived the other throughout the Meech Lake debate. But here both perceived each other accurately – and didn't like what they saw. The rest of Canada saw that the distinct society clause legitimated collective goals. And Quebec saw that the move to give the Charter precedence imposed a form of liberal society that was alien to it, and to which Quebec could never accommodate itself without surrendering its identity.

I have delved deeply into this case because it seems to me to illustrate the fundamental questions. There is a form of the politics of equal respect, as enshrined in a liberalism of rights, that is inhospitable to difference, because (a) it insists on uniform application of the rules defining these rights, without exception, and (b) it is suspicious of collective goals. Of course, this doesn't mean that this model seeks to abolish cultural differences. This would be an absurd accusation. But I call it inhospitable to difference because it can't accommodate what the members of distinct societies really aspire to, which is survival. This is (b) a collective goal, which (a) almost inevitably will call for some variations in the kinds of law we deem permissible from one cultural context to another, as the Quebec case clearly shows.

I think this form of liberalism is guilty as charged by the proponents of a politics of difference. Fortunately, however, there are other models of liberal society that take a different line on (a) and (b). These forms do call for the invariant defense of *certain* rights, of course. There would be no question of cultural differences determining the application of *habeas corpus*, for example. But they distinguish these fundamental rights from the broad range of immunities and presumptions of uniform treatment that have sprung up in modern cultures of judicial review. They are willing to weight the importance of certain forms of uniform treatment against the importance of cultural survival, and opt sometimes in favor of the latter. They are thus in the end not procedural models of liberalism, but are grounded very much on judgments about what makes a good life – judgments in which the integrity of cultures has an important place.

Although I cannot argue it here, obviously I would endorse this kind of model. Indisputably, though, more and more societies today are turning out to be multicultural, in the sense of including more than one cultural community that wants to survive. The rigidities of procedural liberalism may rapidly become impractical in tomorrow's world. . . .

The logic behind some of these demands [for multiculturalism] seems to depend upon a premise that we owe equal respect to all cultures. This emerges from the nature of the reproach made to the designers of traditional curricula. The claim is that the judgments of worth on which these latter were supposedly based were in fact corrupt, were marred by narrowness or insensitivity or, even worse, a desire to downgrade the excluded. The implication seems to be that absent these distorting factors, true judgements of value of different works would place all cultures more or less on the same footing. Of course, the attack could come from a more radical, neo-Nietzschean standpoint, which questions the very status of judgments of worth as such, but short of this extreme step (whose coherence I doubt), the presumption seems to be of equal worth.

I would like to maintain that there is something valid in this presumption, but that the presumption is by no means unproblematic, and involves something like an act of faith. As a presumption, the claim is that all human cultures that have animated whole socieities over some considerable stretch of time have something important to say to all human beings. I have worded it in this way to exclude partial cultural milieux within a society, as well as short phases of a major culture. There is no reason to believe that, for instance, the different art forms of a given culture should all be of equal, or even of considerable, value; and every culture can go through phases of decadence.

But when I call this claim a "presumption," I mean that it is a starting hypothesis with which we ought to approach the study of any other culture. The validity of the claim has to be demonstrated concretely in the actual study of the culture. Indeed, for a culture sufficiently different from our own, we may have only the foggiest idea *ex ante* of in what its valuable contribution might consist. Because, for a sufficiently different culture, the very understanding of what it is to be of worth will be strange and unfamiliar to us. To approach, say, a raga with the presumptions of value implicit in the well-tempered clavier would be forever to miss the point. What has to happen is what Gadamer has called a "fusion of horizons."[3] We learn to move in a broader horizon, within which what we have formerly taken for granted as the background to valuation can be situated as one possibility alongside the different background of the formerly unfamiliar culture. The "fusion of horizons" operates through our developing new vocabularies of comparison, by means of which we can articulate these contrasts. So that if and when we ultimately find substantive support for our initial presumption, it is on the basis of an understanding of what constitutes worth that we couldn't possibly have had at the beginning. We have reached the judgment partly through transforming our standards.

We might want to argue that we owe all cultures a presumption of this kind. I will explain later on what I think this claim might be based. From this point of view, withholding the presumption might be seen as the fruit merely of prejudice or of ill-will. It might even be tantamount to a denial of equal status. Something like this might lie behind the accusation leveled by supporters of multiculturalism against defenders of the traditional canon. Supposing that their reluctance to enlarge the canon comes from a mixture of prejudice and ill-will, the multiculturalists charge them with the arrogance of assuming their own superiority over formerly subject peoples.

This presumption would help explain why the demands of multiculturalism build on the already established principles of the politics of equal respect. If withholding the presumption is tantamount to a denial of equality, and if important consequences flow for people's identity from the absence of recognition, then a case can be made for insisting on the universalization of the presumption as a logical extension of the politics of dignity. Just as all must have equal civil rights, and equal voting rights, regardless of race or culture, so all should enjoy the presumption that their traditional culture has value. This extension, however logically it may seem to flow from the accepted norms of equal dignity, fits uneasily within them, because it challenges the "difference-blindness" that was central to them. Yet it does indeed seem to flow from them, albeit uneasily.

I am not sure about the validity of demanding this presumption as a right. But we can leave this issue aside, because the demand made seems to be much stronger. The claim seems to be that a proper respect for equality requires more than a presumption that further study will make us see things this way, but actual judgements of equal worth applied to the customs and creations of these different cultures. Such judgments seem to be implicit in the demand that certain works be included in the canon, and in the implication that these works have not been included earlier only because of prejudice or ill-will or the desire to dominate. (Of course, the demand for inclusion is *logically* separable from a claim of equal worth. The demand could be: Include these because they're ours, even though they may well be inferior. But this is not how the people making the demand talk.)

But there is something very wrong with the demand in this form. It makes sense to demand as a matter of right that we approach the study of certain cultures with a presumption of their value, as described above. But it can't make sense to demand as a matter of right that we come up with a final concluding judgment that their value is great, or equal to others'. That is, if the judgment of value is to register something independent of our own wills and desires, it cannot be dictated by a principle of ethics. On examination, either we will find something of great value in culture C, or we will not. But it makes no more sense to demand that we do so that it does to demand that we find the earth round or flat, the temperature of the air hot or cold.

I have stated this rather flatly, when as everyone knows there is a vigorous controversy over the "objectivity" of judgments in this field, and whether there is a "truth of the matter" here, as there seems to be in natural science, or indeed, whether even in natural science "objectivity" is a mirage. I do not have space to address this here. I don't have much sympathy for these forms of subjectivism, which I think are shot through with confusion. But there seems to be some special confusion in invoking them in this context. The moral and political thrust of the complaint concerns unjustified judgments of inferior status allegedly made of non-hegemonic cultures. But if those judgments are ultimately a question of the human will, then the issue of justification falls away. One doesn't, properly speaking, make judgments that can be right or wrong; one expresses liking or dislike, one endorses or rejects another culture. But then the complaint must shift to address the refusal to endorse, and the validity or invalidity of judgments here has nothing to do with it.

Then, however, the act of declaring another culture's creations to be of worth and the act of declaring oneself on their side, even if their creations aren't all that impressive, become indistinguishable. The difference is only in the packaging. Yet the first is normally understood as a genuine expression of respect, the second often as unsufferable patronizing. The supposed beneficiaries of the politics of recognition, the people who might actually benefit from acknowledgment, make a crucial distinction between the two acts. They know that they want respect, not condescension. Any theory that wipes out the distinction seems at least *prima facie* to be distorting crucial facets of the reality it purports to deal with.

In fact, subjectivist, half-baked neo-Nietzschean theories are quite often invoked in this debate. Deriving frequently from Foucault or Derrida, they claim that all judgments of worth are based on standards that are ultimately imposed by and further entrench structures of power. It should be clear why these theories proliferate here. A favorable judgment on demand is nonsense, unless some such theories are valid. Moreover, the giving of such a judgment on demand is an act of breathtaking condescension. No one can really mean it as a genuine act of respect. It is more in the nature of a pretend act of respect given on the insistence of its supposed beneficiary. Objectively, such an act involves contempt for the latter's intelligence. To be an object of such an act of respect demeans. The proponents of neo-Nietzschean theories hope to escape this whole nexus of hypocrisy by turning the entire issue into one of power and counterpower. Then the question is no more one of respect, but of taking sides, of solidarity. But this is hardly a satisfactory solution, because in taking sides they miss the driving force of this kind of politics, which is precisely the search for recognition and respect.

Moreover, even if one could demand it of them, the last thing one wants at this stage from Eurocentered intellectuals is positive judgments of the worth of cultures that they have not intensively studied. For real judgments of worth suppose a fused horizon of standards, as we have seen; they suppose that we have been transformed by the study of the other, so that we are not simply judging by our original familiar standards. A favorable judgment made prematurely would be not only condescending but ethnocentric. It would praise the other for being like us.

Here is another severe problem with much of the politics of multiculturalism. The peremptory demand for favorable judgments of worth is paradoxically – perhaps one should say tragically – homogenizing. For it implies that we already have the standards to make such judgments. The standards we have, however, are those of North Atlantic civilization. And so the judgments implicitly and unconsciously will cram the others into our categories. For instance, we will think of their "artists" as creating "works," which we then can include in our canon. By implicitly invoking our standards to judge all civilizations and cultures, the politics of difference can end up making everyone the same.

In this form, the demand for equal recognition is unacceptable. But the story doesn't simply end there. The enemies of multiculturalism in the American academy have perceived this weakness, and have used this as an excuse to turn their backs on the problem. But this won't do. A response like that attributed to Bellow, to the effect that we will be glad to read the Zulu Tolstoy when he comes along, shows the depths of ethnocentricity. First, there is the implicit assumption that excellence has to take forms familiar to us: the Zulus should produce a *Tolstoy*. Second, we are assuming that their contribution is yet to be made (*when* the Zulus produce a Tolstoy...). These two assumptions obviously go hand in hand. If they have to produce our kind of excellence, then obviously their only hope lies in the future. Roger Kimball puts it more crudely: "The multiculturalists notwithstanding, the choice facing us today is not between a 'repressive' Western culture and a multicultural paradise, but between culture and barbarism. Civilization is not a gift, it is an achievement – a fragile achievement that needs constantly to be shored up and defended from besiegers inside and out."[4]

There must be something midway between the inauthentic and homogenizing demand for recognition of equal worth, on the one hand, and the self-immurement within ethnocentric standards, on the other. There are other cultures, and we have to live together more and more, both on a world scale and commingled in each individual society.

What there is is the presumption of equal worth I described above: a stance we take in embarking on the study of the other. Perhaps we don't need to ask whether it's something that others can demand from us as a right. We might simply ask whether this is the way we ought to approach others.

Well, is it? How can this presumption be grounded? One ground that has been proposed is a religious one. Herder, for instance, had a view of divine providence, according to which all this variety of culture was not a mere accident but was meant to bring about a greater harmony. I can't rule out such a view. But merely on the human level, one could argue that it is reasonable to suppose that cultures that have provided the horizon of meaning for large numbers of human beings, of diverse characters and temperaments, over a long period of time – that have, in other words, articulated their sense of the good, the holy, the admirable – are almost certain to have something that deserves our admiration and respect, even if it is accompanied by much that we have to abhor and reject. Perhaps one could put it another way: it would take a supreme arrogance to discount this possibility *a priori*.

There is perhaps after all a moral issue here. We only need a sense of our own limited part in the whole human story to accept the presumption. It is only arrogance, or some analogous moral failing, that can deprive us of this. But what the presumption requires of us is not peremptory and inauthentic judgments of equal value, but a willingness to be open to comparative cultural study of the kind that must displace our horizons in the resulting fusions. What it requires above all is an admission that we are very far away from that ultimate horizon from which the relative worth of different cultures might be evident. This would mean breaking with an illusion that still holds many "multiculturalists" – as well as their most bitter opponents – in its grip.

Notes

1   Rawls, *A Theory of Justice* and "Justice as Fairness: Political Not Metaphysical," *Philosophy & Public Affairs* 14 (1985): 223–51; Dworkin, *Taking Rights Seriously* and "Liberalism," in *Public and Private Morality*, ed. Stuart Hampshire (Cambridge: Cambridge University Press, 1978); Bruce Ackerman, *Social Justice in the Liberal State* (New Haven: Yale University Press, 1980).
2   Michael Sandel, "The Procedural Republic and the Unencumbered Self," *Political Theory* 12 (1984): 81–96.
3   *Wahrheit und Methode* (Tübingen: Mohr, 1975), pp. 289–90.
4   "Tenured Radicals," *New Criterion*, January 1991, p. 13.

26 Reconciliation without Justice

Heribert Adam and Kogila Moodley

I

The South African Truth and Reconciliation Commission (TRC) represents a unique compromise between war tribunals and dealing with past atrocities by ignoring them. This amnesia would have shortchanged millions of victims of racial laws and weakened the moral foundations of the new order. Imposing justice or revenge by the new power holders, on the other hand, was ruled out by the need for reconciliation in an ethnically divided society. After all, the new order had been achieved through a negotiated revolution. Bilateral indemnity for past crimes formed a crucial precondition for the relatively peaceful changeover of political power. Amnesty upon full disclosure proved the mutually acceptable formula for future coexistence.

Revealing the truth is said to reconcile the nation if only in the next generation. However, the opposite effect could also happen: the more the gory truth is brought home, the greater the clamor for justice. Retaliation and punishment rather than forgiveness is the normal reaction to brutality. In short, the truth can undermine reconciliation – and herein lies the basic contradiction of the South African commission.

Moreover, genuine reconciliation presupposes a certain degree of forgetting. In the post-war German debate, Habermas has stressed that the "crass demand for reconciliation" necessitates "the promotion of forgetfulness".[1] Just as the old Nazis were exculpated as allies in the Cold War, so the apartheid advocates are now needed for growth and development. Cynics argue that the TRC merely uses the victims as legitimizing decoration for the ritual of exculpation in which the real beneficiaries are the past rulers who get away scot-free. Yet reconciliation or at least peaceful coexistence remains the prerogative of a society in which colonial settlers are as legitimately at home as their colonized subjects. Unlike the Nazis, they have not only been undefeated but also selectively implicated ideologically. Afrikanerdom produced many dissenters and even some martyrs to the anti-racist cause. Without a policy of pragmatic clemency, a reverse racial war could loom on the horizon to the detriment of all. That option did not exist in a defeated Germany and therefore the demonization of Nazi supporters occurred without political risk.

It has been pointed out that "reconciliation" amounts to the imposition of a Christian religious value on unwilling participants. Forgiveness cannot be engineered by bringing perpetrators and victims into contact. Some crimes remain literally "unforgiveable". Only victims can forgive. A strong minority opinion holds, as articulated by literary critic Benita Parry,[2] that "no government or leader has the moral authority to grant a people's pardon to their erstwhile oppressors, since here the consent and participation of neither party has been solicited and procured". While this position has been adopted and even legally pursued by prominent South African survivors, such as the Biko and Mxenge families, it can be argued that the people through their elected ANC representatives as well as their opposition negotiated precisely such consent. Initially, inclined to indemnify themselves, the contenders at least concurred with the ritual of public confessions before the pardon. Amnesty, however, does not require remorse that could expediently be feigned. Headed by two clergymen and a theologian as the chief research officer, the TRC thinking unfortunately slips frequently into the theological discourse of atonement and repentance. When Tutu feels "deeply distressed" by de Klerk's denial of "culpability" for gruesome acts committed by his security forces that "negate" his apology for apartheid, he applies religious assumptions of absolution requiring remorse. Absolution by an ambitious former archbishop is limited to the faithful, who value "healing" or the African philosophy of "ubuntu". It suggests that your own humanity can only be realized by recognizing the human qualities of your enemy. However, as Timothy Garton Ash has pointed out, "the reconciliation of all with all is a deeply illiberal idea".[3] Some values are irreconcilable. Liberalism teaches how to coexist tolerantly with irreconcilable conflicts rather than engineer totalitarian closure or normative homogeneity.

There are several features distinguishing the South African process from similar Latin American precedents, that served as a model for the South African legislation. As André du Toit has pointed out, unlike the Chilean Presidential Commission, "the TRC is essentially a public and democratic enterprise".[4] As a parliamentary commission it was forged through heated public debates, public hearings about the suitability of commissioners and regularly televised proceedings. Hence, the TRC reflected the new political power relations. Representatives of the old regime are underrepresented, unlike the parity of the eight person Chilean Commission. Although charged with quasi-judicial impartiality by the "Promotion of National Unity and Reconciliation Act" of 1995 and staffed by commissioners "who do not have a high political profile", most commissioners played highly active roles in the long anti-apartheid struggle. It would be hard to find any "fit and proper person" with a low political profile in a highly politicized society, apart from a few recently returned exiles. The perceived leanings of most of the sixteen commissioners and particularly their staff towards a broad ANC version of history affected the legitimacy of the TRC in the eyes of competing parties whose leaders feared being perpetually discredited.

This impression was reinforced by the wide publicity given to the harrowing accounts of victims, seeking acknowledgements and, hopefully, some later compensation. Unlike the dramatic impact of the Argentinian Nunca Mas report – which was released after long in camera investigations about the disappeared – Nunca Mas was spread over three years in South Africa. Moreover, the names of perpetrators were not kept secret but the faces of the torturers appeared each day in the South African media. One of the more popular SABC serials about a commander of an aberrant police unit was called "Prime Evil". Such a public discourse undoubtedly contributes to historical education or political immunization but whether it establishes a unifying truth is questionable.

Richard Goldstone asserts "Making public the truth is itself a form of justice." This may be true for the victims who have their suffering publicly recognized and dignity restored, but hardly applies to the perpetrators. Few of them seemed embarrassed or even shamed by the display of their atrocities. In their view, they merely fulfilled orders or fought a war against alleged foreign communists who are now fellow citizens. Yet seeing former regime representatives admit and apologize for their misdeeds is in itself a gain. Nobody can now deny past atrocities. As Michael Ignatieff has written: "Truth commissions ... can reduce the number of permissable lies in a society",[5] the Orwellian scepticism about an official truth notwithstanding.

While truth commissions laudably establish the fate of individual victims, redeem their suffering and compensate materially or symbolically, they also claim to heal a torn nation through a shared truth. However, the truth about the past is always contested. Historical meanings are constructed according to competing interests, and it is doubtful whether a "traumatized" nation can be cured by having her repressed memory restored. While the critical engagement with conflicting historical interpretations characterizes the developed political consciousness of the ideal individual citizen, nations do not possess collective psyches. The medical metaphors are misleading when applied to collectivities. Guilt can only be individual, not collective. The benefit of tribunals or truth commissions lies in disaggregating the misdeeds of individuals from the blame of all. Germans were freed by the persecutions of Nazis from being indiscriminately implicated as a society. The heated debate about Goldhagen's *Hitler's Willing Executioners* stems from the renewed claim of collective guilt. Therefore, advocates of communal reputations should have an interest in having guilty members brought to justice rather than having the name of the entire community smeared. From this perspective the South African TRC serves the opposite of "an exercise in Afrikaner bashing", as Constand Viljoen the former head of the military claimed.

II

Unlike the old security establishment had expected, no blanket and collective amnesty was granted. Instead amnesty was made contingent on (a) telling the truth by individuals and (b) demonstrating that their crimes were politically motivated and proportional to their assigned role in the conflict (Noorgard principles). Individual killings out of racial hate would not qualify as a political crime but acting within the perceived race politics of a political organisation, even if wrongly interpreted by a combatant, presumably will lead to acquittal. This trade-off between full confessions and amnesty has not been practiced anywhere else.

Whether the threat of future prosecutions of those who refuse to apply for amnesty will be realized, remains to be seen. Although more than 6000 applications have been received, most originated from common criminals in prison who invented political motives for their hoped for release. The success rate is mixed with regard to crucial senior political actors. Only two cabinet ministers of the previous regime applied before the cut off date of May 10, 1997; the top military brass had nothing to regret, as did most senior apartheid politicians and leaders of the Zulu-based IFP who boycotted the TRC as an instrument of their ANC enemies. Yet, the police chiefs related their stories to the commission, mostly out of spite for their civilian bosses of the NP they perceived as having given the orders but now refused to take responsibility. This breaking of the ranks of a once solid ethnonationalist supremacy clarified and confirmed the lines of command, although the originators of most atrocities were long known. With its powers of subpoena, the Commission can force unwilling suspects to testify, but has done so sparingly.

The TRC has highlighted *individual* gross human rights violations and *individual* fates of victims at the expense of institutional and corporate complicity. Although bodies such as political parties and professional associations (medical, judiciary, business, media) were invited to reflect on their contribution to sustaining or legitimizing apartheid, most denied such a role. From the ANC to the NP or military command they all took "collective responsibility" for the misdeeds of their underlings, which they "never condoned" or even knew about, although they should have known about it or in most cases, could have prevented it, had they shown the political will. Locked into political competition for votes or credibility, political parties can hardly be expected to discredit themselves if they were to admit honestly their involvement in breaking principles of natural justice. This applies no less to the ANC, as it obviously does to the National Party and the IFP.

With its current moral hegemony, the ANC confidently presented its struggle against an inhuman system as a heroic drama between black liberation and a repressive state on a different moral plane. This "just war" doctrine, however overlooks the fact that the defenders of an undoubtedly just cause must still adhere to the principles of "justice in war", for example, following the Geneva convention of not unnecessarily harming civilians or treating prisoners humanely. Such insistence does not imply "moral neutrality". It still recognizes the differential power of jailer and jailed but does not grant license to the jailed to free themselves "by all means necessary". Judging from the ANC's defence of just war against a "racist holocaust" and the reluctance of senior ANC leaders to appear before the TRC in the same ways as their tormentors, the liberators too have to take lessons in organisational responsibility. Both the ANC and the National Party publicly regretted deviations from well intentioned policies but failed to reflect on how their own internal mobilization and propaganda contributed to the brutalisation of their followers. Instead of admission of institutional guilt with concomitant remorse and offer of restitution as far as possible, all political actors scapegoat "bad apples" in their midst. As exceptions to the rule, the rule makers exonerate themselves by blaming lower-level executioners. Foot soldiers are targetted while those who gave orders or devised policies are left free on the whole.

III

An even more complex question than how to deal with torturers is posed by the many beneficiaries of the apartheid laws. Mahmoud Mamdani has pointed to

the difference between Rwanda where there are many perpetrators but few beneficiaries of genocide, and apartheid South Africa with few perpetrators and many
beneficiaries.[6] The focus of the Truth Commission on "gross human rights violations" obliterates the systemic discrimination and its beneficiaries. Individualising
the process ignores the many other victims of apartheid: the millions imprisoned
under the Pass Laws, the tens of thousands displaced from their homes by the
Group Areas Act and ultimately all disenfranchised whose life chances and dignity
were damaged. Should the beneficiaries of these practices pay compensation? Can
victims and beneficiaries be defined in racial terms – as there were also black
beneficiaries and white victims? Can there be reconciliation without economic
justice?

There is the possibility that a Truth Commission reinforces the fallacy that the
past has been put behind the nation, like the Germans called 1945 "Stunde Null"
(hour zero), as if a new counting has begun despite the continuing legacy of an
abominable past. Instead of actively engaging with the past, Adorno warned, the
past is always in danger of being committed to oblivion through the process of
accounting for it "once and for all". The final report of the Truth Commission "to
the nation" – according to the Act to establish "as complete a picture as possible
of the nature, causes and extent of gross violations of human rights" between
1960 and 1993 – therefore should not mark the end but the beginning of the
process of engagement. Ideally the TRC will stimulate the equivalent of the
German *Historikerstreit* (dispute about history) with many revisionist Goldhagens
to follow suit. The ultimate success of the TRC can be measured not in how
complete, let alone "accurate" a picture of the past it will paint, but in how much
future political education it will generate. Walter Benjamin suggests that the
proper mourning consists of recalling the past injustices in order to nourish the
current struggles for emancipation. Notions of justice are derived from the narratives of past iniquities, although a consciousness shaped solely by the vanquished
dead forgets the living now, as Nietzsche has reminded us.

Notes

1   Jürgen Habermas, *Die Einbeziehung des Anderen*, Frankfurt: Suhrkamp 1996.
2   Benita Parry, "Reconciliation and Remembrance", *Die Suid-Afrikaan*, No. 55, Dec. 95/
    Jan. 96, 10–12.
3   Timothy Garton Ash, "South Africa: True Confessions", *New York Review of Books*,
    XLIV, 12, July 17, 1997, 33–8.
4   André du Toit, "No Rest without the Wicked: Assessing the Truth Commission", *Indicator
    S.A.*, Summer 1997, 7–12.
5   Michael Ignatieff, "Truth, Justice and Reconciliation", *National*, November/December,
    1996, 30–7.
6   Mahmoud Mamdani, "Reconciliation without Justice", *Southern African Review of
    Books*, Nov./Dec. 1995, 3–5.

27 The International Defence of Racial Equality

Michael Banton

John Locke maintained that there was a natural law which regulated human society. From it human beings derived rights that those who governed them had to respect. Anyone, whether ruler or subject, who infringed the rights of either prince or people, and thereby threatened the constitution, was guilty of the greatest of crimes. Such a person was to be treated as the common enemy of mankind. In the nineteenth century this doctrine was assailed by utilitarians and positivists, most famously by Jeremy Bentham (1843, pp. 523, 501) when he declared: 'Right is the child of law; from real laws come real rights, but from imaginary law, from "laws of nature", come imaginary rights ... Natural rights is simple nonsense, natural and imprescriptible rights rhetorical nonsense, nonsense upon stilts.'

Hitler, Stalin and the architects of apartheid were neither utilitarians nor positivists but they took care to see that their legislatures passed law which authorized their actions. They aligned themselves with the positivists, in that they recognized only the laws placed upon their own statute books. There was no appeal to any higher law. International law, up to 1945, was powerless to challenge what such rules had done. The countries that fought Hitler were determined to change this. It has not been easy, but they have now secured agreement to a detailed code of international law defining the rights of individuals against the states that exercise power over them and the duties of states to the comity of nations. This code has been described by Sieghart in *The Lawful Rights of Mankind* (Sieghart 1986), which is admirably designed for the general reader. I shall draw upon it at several points.

Like other branches of international law, the code has two sources: custom and treaties. Among the latter are three global treaties: the Charter of the United Nations, the Covenant on Economic, Social and Cultural Rights, and the Covenant on Civil and Political Rights. There are four regional treaties for Europe, America and Africa. Mention should be made in addition of two declarations: the Universal Declaration of Human Rights, and the American Declaration of the Rights and Duties of Man. The former is becoming part of customary international law. There are also some twenty specialized treaties now in force concerned with genocide, apartheid, racial discrimination, refugees, forced labour, slavery and the rights of women.

The nature of customary law in this area can be illustrated by the acceptance, long ago, that when two states went to war with one another, each state was to allow the other's ambassador and staff to return with a safe conduct. This custom then became binding upon new states, even though there was no means of enforcing it. Nowadays the International Court of Justice at The Hague is able to declare that certain kinds of behaviour violate universally accepted norms of the international law of human rights but so far it has had few opportunities to do so, and then only incidentally to some other issue. Freedom from slavery, from genocide, from racial discrimination and from torture are rights protected, even if imperfectly, by customary international law as well as by treaties entered into by particular states. The rights and freedoms so protected are described as inherent, inalienable and equal. We all have our human rights in equal measure, which is why my title refers to the defence of racial equality.

The differences between the two Covenants have a bearing upon the legacy of John Locke. In 1946 a commission was appointed to submit to the United Nations General Assembly recommendations and reports regarding an 'International Bill of Rights'. English-speaking delegates proposed a treaty specifying rights that could be enforced by international institutions. First the Soviet Union and then the United States concluded that such actions would be premature. In 1948 the Universal Declaration of Human Rights was adopted but it took a further eighteen years before the Covenants were adopted and they did not enter into force until 1976. By September 1987 the Covenant on Economic, Social and Cultural Rights had been ratified by ninety states. The Covenant on Civil and Political Rights had been ratified by eighty-six states. The United States had not ratified either. Two Covenants were required because the socialist countries insisted on the pre-eminence of economic, social and cultural rights, while the West emphasized civil and political rights. Sieghart contrasts these as the view that human rights begin after breakfast and the view that human rights begin at the police station.

The Western philosophy has its sources in the influence of John Locke and in the English, French and American revolutions. It is concerned that individual rights be not violated by governments. Nineteenth-century socialists, by contrast, reacted against the inequalities they saw all around them and demanded that governments should intervene actively to redress social and economic injustices. Their successors see the state as the source of rights conferred upon individuals. Thus, one Soviet lawyer has stated: 'The individual has no rights as long as the State has not fulfilled its obligation to grant them. The State acts as a necessary channel of transformation of its obligations into individual rights'. The prominent Soviet lawyer Kartashkin has explained: 'The purpose of formalizing these rights and freedoms in international law is to help consolidate the guarantees for the observance of the fundamental rights and freedoms. However, that is not to say that human rights are now being directly regulated by international law or that they no longer fall within the internal competence of states'. According to this view international law is a body of norms established between states, and the individual is not a subject of international law. It cannot be expected that the socialist states will in the near future accept new or existing human-rights agencies in which the individual can take the initiative (Bloed and Van Hoof 1985, pp. 45–6).

The Convention

The proposal for a specialized convention on racial discrimination was triggered by incidents of swastika-painting, attacks on Jewish burial grounds and other manifestations of anti-Semitism in Western Europe during the winter of 1959–60. Memories of National Socialist ideology and of the Holocaust were important influences. To them were joined the concerns of newly independent African states about racial segregation and discrimination on their own continent and in North America. The General Assembly decided that two conventions would be required: one against racial discrimination and one against religious intolerance. So it was that in 1965 the General Assembly adopted the International Convention on the Elimination of Racial Discrimination. One who had worked for this result observed cautiously that 'it remains to be seen whether the enthusiasm expressed in these and other speeches will also be demonstrated by depositing instruments of ratification' (Schwelb 1966, p. 997). He misjudged the position because this Convention has now been ratified by 124 states, three-quarters of the number of states recognized by the United Nations. A representative of the United States signed the treaty in 1966. In 1978 President Carter sent it to Congress for ratification. This has yet to occur, although United States lawyers believe that ratification would be consistent with the country's domestic law (Nathanson and Schwelb 1975; Schroth and Mueller 1975).

When subsequently I refer to 'the Convention' I shall intend a reference to the International Convention on the Elimination of All Forms of Racial Discrimination. It was the first of the human rights conventions sponsored by the United Nations and has several distinctive features. Some of its provisions have worked well; others have been little used. Now that it has been in operation for eighteen years, it is possible to estimate its contribution to the defence of racial equality.

States that ratify the Convention bind themselves to work for the Convention's general objectives, to fulfil its particular requirements, and to report on their discharge of their obligations every two years to a committee of eighteen experts whom they themselves elect. The Committee (which is usually identified by its acronym, CERD) examines these reports and has itself to report the outcome to the General Assembly. It may make formal suggestions to particular states and may forward general recommendations to the General Assembly. The reporting process is the prime component of a tripartite system for international review. The second element is a set of provisions for considering state-to-state complaints; states parties have been reluctant to invoke it. The third establishes a right to individual petition when the state in question has made a declaration under Article 14. So far eleven states have done this and one petition has been submitted. The committee has a fourth principal function in respect of Trust and Non-Self-Governing Territories but this is rather different because in this matter it works with the competent bodies of the United Nations.

The Convention defines racial discrimination in a way that includes discrimination based on colour, descent, and national and ethnic origin. It specifies what states must do to eliminate it. Reflecting the circumstances that gave rise to its own establishment, it tends to treat 'ideas or theories of superiority of one race or group of persons of one colour or ethnic origin' as the main source or cause of racial discrimination. It therefore requires that the dissemination of ideas based on racial superiority be penalized, and this has caused some states parties to enter reservations designed to protect freedom of speech. In the very important Article 5 the Convention lists civil, political, economic, social and cultural rights in respect of which there must be no discrimination. Remedies must be available to those who are aggrieved and states must adopt educational measures to combat prejudices that lead to racial discrimination.

Achievements

In implementing the Convention, CERD's main achievements can be summarized under the headings of standard-setting, education and institution-building. The first of these is simple but vital. Most states, throughout the world, now have legislation against racial discrimination. That legislation is more comprehensive and better enforced than it would have been without CERD. In a few instances in the early years, states parties consulted the Committee in advance about contemplated changes in their legislation or in their administrative practice and indicated that they would take the Committee's advice into serious consideration before giving final form to those proposed changes (CERD/1, p. 203)....

An institutional structure for the elimination of racial discrimination has been built. There is now a routine whereby the world situation with respect to such discrimination is discussed annually at the United Nations, first in the Third (Social, Humanitarian and Cultural) Committee and then in the General Assembly on that Committee's resolution. It is discussed by all UN member states and not just those that are parties to the Convention. The UN's Economic and Social Council has organized a first, and now a second, decade for the Elimination of Racial Discrimination (ending in 1993). Every 21 March the UN and some of its member states observe the International Day for the Elimination of Racial Discrimination. Among the UN bodies concerned with racial discrimination there is a recognized division of labour to which the Human Rights Commission, the Sub-Commission on the Prevention of Discrimination and the Protection of Minorities, the International Labour Organization, UNESCO and CERD all contribute....

Operating Constraints

The chief constraint upon all bodies in the UN system is the sovereignty of member-states. In his introduction to the classical essays on social contract, Sir Ernest Barker wrote that 'the State, in the sense of a political community, and as an organized society, is based on a social contract – or rather upon myriads of such contracts – between each and every member of that community or society' (1947, p. xii). The more contracts there are between citizens, the more difficult it is for the community as a whole to agree on collective action. This sets an upper limit to the size of a society that can be conducted according to Athenian ideas of democracy and helps explain the Aristotelian belief that in a republic a small number of citizens must be supported by a large number of non-citizens. When the United States was founded comparable arguments about the need for communal homogeneity influenced the law of citizenship. The stupendous increase in the population of many states over the last two centuries and the doctrine of mass political participation have multiplied the number of contracts between individuals. It is difficult for states to get their citizens to agree upon what should be the priorities when negotiating with other states. Their freedom in inter-state negotiation is constrained by their domestic commitments.

For some states, certain issues have such an overriding priority that they will seize any opportunity to press their case. In inter-state relations, claims to territory are heavily prioritized and this can affect the implementation of a convention. Thus, in the 1985 debate on CERD's report in the Third Committee the representative of Algeria complained that CERD had considered a report

> one chapter of which was devoted to measures taken by the State party in a territory it occupied by force. That decision was a serious breach of the Committee's terms of reference and of article 15 of the Convention. By that act, the Committee had set a dangerous precedent by arrogating to itself the authority to decide on the territorial sovereignty of State parties. (A/C.3/40/SR.15 para 23)

This was a reference to the formerly colonial territory of Western Sahara, most of which has been incorporated within Morocco though fighting continues. At the end of the debate a group of states introduced a motion one paragraph of which proposed that 'The General Assembly ... considers that the Committee should not take into consideration information on Territories to which General Assembly resolution 1514(XV) applies unless such information is communicated by the competent United Nations bodies...' Morocco then secured a statement from the UN Office of Legal Affairs that the right to give authoritative interpretations of the Convention rested not with the General Assembly but, in the first instance, with CERD itself. Perhaps because it was confident that the resolution would therefore not change the prevailing situation, Morocco did not vote against this paragraph, which was adopted by ninety-eight votes to nine with thirty-six abstentions....

In the 1960s and 1970s many UN member-states prioritized action against racist regimes in southern Africa. When the Convention was being drafted the Third Committee decided not to include any reference to specific forms of racial discrimination. Nevertheless, there is a reference to apartheid in the ninth preambular paragraph and in Article 3. These references were cited in 1972 when CERD agreed a general recommendation expressing the view that measures taken on the national level to give effect to the provisions of the Convention were interrelated with measures taken on the international level, and that it therefore welcomed the inclusion in the reports of any state party which chose to do so, of information regarding the status of that state's diplomatic, economic and other relations with the racist regimes in southern Africa. The United Kingdom government objected that a state's international relations were not directly relevant to its obligations under Article 3, which concerned domestic relations, but the General Assembly commended the Committee's practice of welcoming such information. In 1975 CERD returned to this topic. It referred to various UN resolutions and to the phrase in the preamble to ICERD about the resolve of states parties 'to build an international community free from all forms of racial segregation and racial discrimination'....

The realist standpoint encourages people to assume that racial discrimination is something produced by particular social conditions and that this then takes on an existence of its own. It is said to be present in some countries and absent from others. The opposing view is that every individual is capable of discrimination; readiness to identify some people as members of an individual's own group is one of the things that makes society possible. Discrimination is therefore not a thing so much as a universal variable and the forms of racial discrimination are the outcomes of racially motivated behaviour in differing circumstances. This interpretation can derive support from the provision that enables a state to discriminate racially without breaking the Convention if it follows Article 2(2). This enjoins a state party to take 'special and concrete measures to ensure the adequate development and protection of certain racial groups or individuals belonging to them, for the purpose of guaranteeing them the full and equal enjoyment of human rights and fundamental freedoms'. One such measure might be the adoption of quota policies that are discriminatory but not necessarily unlawful. In the attempt to formulate or mobilize international opinion about such topics as apartheid or colonialism much of the debate is structured by differences in epistemological assumptions. The relative success of the realist view has encouraged members of CERD to believe that they should speak for international opinion and has motivated them to express themselves on matters that some states parties consider to be outside the scope of the Convention. . . .

A major constraint upon the Committee's work, and one of the reasons why it has concentrated upon the examination of legislation, is its lack of any independent fact-finding powers. It is difficult to form any estimate of the adequacy of measures taken by a reporting state if that state provides no demographic information about racial and ethnic minorities. Thus, its 1973 report observed that it was difficult to appraise the position of persons in Bulgaria of Greek, Turkish and Macedonian national or ethnic origin for lack of such information. The same issue was raised in 1986 when Bulgaria reported that there was no longer any Turkish or Macedonian minority in the country. The Yugoslav member of CERD testified that 'any visitor to Bulgaria could see and talk to Macedonians'. It would be possible on some definitions of 'minority' to conclude that there were Bulgarians of Macedonian origin but that they did not constitute a minority. This was not the position adopted by the representative to the reporting state. He recognized the existence of only three ethnic minorities; Jews, Armenians and Gypsies. Answering allegations that ethnic Turks had been forced to take Bulgarian names, he said that in changing all personal and place names of Turkish origin back to Bulgarian names, the Bulgarian people had given voice to its desire to sever the last remaining link to Turkish domination (CERD/C/SR, pp. 750–76, para 48). That most members of the Committee were dissatisfied with this reply and with their inability to obtain more information will be apparent from any reading of the records. In concluding this discussion of constraints it should also be noted that the Convention contains no provisions for bringing any sanctions to bear upon states parties that delay or fail to submit reports when due or that do not pay the sums assessed against them as contributions to the expenses of members of the Committee. . . .

An International Contract

It is easy to sympathize with the dismay that some have expressed over the failure of international organizations to act effectively against genocide and political massacre (e.g., Kuper 1985). Yet high standards in the field of human rights should be formulated, even if history suggests that practice will often fall short. The US Civil Rights Act of 1866 is rarely mentioned in histories of racial relations. It did not prevent the disfranchisement of black voters in the late 1890s or the rise of racial discrimination in northern cities as the new century opened, but it laid down a standard. In 1987 the US Supreme Court had to reach decisions about what groups Congress intended to protect by that act 121 years earlier because this was important to litigants in 1987. In the same way, courts in the year 2070 may have to decide which groups are protected by ICERD.

Hitherto the Convention has been used primarily to encourage action against racial discrimination, defining race in the sense it has acquired in west-European languages in the twentieth century and concentrating upon doctrines of racial superiority as a cause of discrimination. As yet the Convention's potentiality for action against discrimination based upon colour or descent, and for linking these with the more general principle of non-discrimination (on which see Partsch 1982), or for reducing the racial discrimination that has other causes, has scarcely been recognized. Much more work educating states parties will be necessary. We are at the beginning of a long-term task of delineating the natural law regulating the contracts between people who are physically or culturally distinguishable, and of specifying rights that must be respected by both individuals and governments. We are creating a new international contract. The parties to it are governments and it is they who have to prevent and punish breaches. When governments themselves are in default, their deficiencies are publicized before the General Assembly and one day there may be more effective means of securing compliance by governments. For the world as a whole the establishment since 1945 of this new branch of international law is as important as the Glorious Revolution of 1688 was for England.

Note

Since this lecture was delivered in 1988 there have been major advances. By the end of 2000 the USA had become one of the 156 states to have ratified ICERD and its initial report was due for examination in 2001. The Russian Federation had become one of the thirty states permitting individual petition under the Convention. The USA had also ratified the International Covenant on Civil and Political Rights, Article 26 of which requires the prohibition and prevention of discrimination. The protections against racial discrimination under the European Convention on Human Rights had been improved and the European Union had introduced a powerful new directive against racial discrimination in employment.*

*For further information relating to the UN see the website www.unhchr.ch and Michael Banton, *International Action Against Racial Discrimination* (Clarendon Press, 1996).

References

Bloed, Arie, and Hoof, Fried Van 1985, 'Some aspects of the socialist view of human rights' in Arie Bloed and Pietar Van Dijk (eds), *Essays on Human Rights in the Helsinki Process*, Dordrecht: Martinus Nijhoff, pp. 29–55.

Barker, Ernest 1947, Introduction to *Social Contract: Essays by Locke, Hume and Rousseau*, London: Oxford University Press.

Bentham, Jeremy 1843, *The Works of Jeremy Bentham, published under the superintendence of his executor, John Bowring*, Vol. 2, Edinburgh: Wm. Tait.

Buergenthal, Thomas 1977, 'Implementing the UN Racial Convention', *Texas International Law Journal*, vol. 12, pp. 187–221.

CERD/1. 1979, *Committee on the Elimination of Racial Discrimination and the progress made towards the achievement of the objectives of the International Convention on the Elimination of All forms of Racial Discrimination* (Initially issued as document A/CONF. 92/8), UN Publications Sales no E 79.XIV.4. New York: United Nations.

Kuper, Leo 1985, *International Action against Genocide*, New Haven, CT: Yale University Press.

Lerner, Nathan 1980, *The UN Convention on the Elimination of All Forms of Racial Discrimination*, 2nd ed., Alphen aan den Rijn: Sijthoff and Noordhoff.

Nathanson, Nathaniel L. and Schwelb, Egon 1975, *The United States and the United Nations Treaty on Racial Discrimination*, The American Society of International Law, Studies in Transnational Legal Policy no. 9, West Publishing Co.

Partsch, Karl-Joseph 1982, 'Fundamental principles of human rights: self-determination, equality and non-discrimination' in Karl Vasak and Philip Alston (eds), *The International Dimension of Human Rights*, New York: Greenwood and Paris: UNESCO, pp. 61–81.

Schroth, Peter W. and Mueller, Virginia S. 1975, 'Racial discrimination: the United States and the International Convention', *Human Rights*, vol. 4, pp. 171–203.

Schwelb, Egon 1966, 'The International Convention on the elimination of all forms of racial discrimination', *International Comparative Law Quarterly*, vol. 15, pp. 996–1068.

Sieghart, Paul 1986, *The Lawful Rights of Mankind: An Introduction to the International Legal Code of Human Rights*, Oxford: Oxford University Press.

Index

Hakka Chinese community in, 276–9
Treaty of London (1915), 224
tribalism, 209–10
Trouwborst, Albert, 216
Truth Commissions *see* South Africa, Truth and Reconciliation Commission
Turkey, genocide against Armenians by, 2
Turkish Parents Association (Berlin), 302
Tuskegee (Alabama), 43
Tutsi-Banyaruguru/Tutsi-Hima (Tutsi groups), 214, 217

Ukraine, 5, 324, 327, 328, 330, 331
UNESCO Declaration on Race and Racial Prejudice (1978), 297
United Nations, 3, 7, 88, 388–93
    United Nations Convention Against Race Discrimination (1966), 360
    United Nations Convention on Protection of the Rights of All Migrant Workers and their Families, 297
    United Nations High Commissioner for Refugees (UNHCR), 80
    United Nations Relief Works Agency for Palestinian Refugees (UNRWA), 80
United States, 28
    affirmative action in, 337–8, 346, 348, 366
    African Americans in, 15
    Army, segregation in, 3
    assimilation into, 238–57
    Civil Rights Act (1866), 393
    Civil Rights movement in, 4
    Civil War and Reconstruction, 2, 14, 45, 374
    Clinton administration and, 337
    construction of dual society in, 23
    Cuban refugees in, 6; *see also* Boston; Cuba; Mariel boatlift; Miami
    economy in, 351
    educational paradoxes in, 246–50
    epidemiological paradoxes in, 240–4
    ethnic relations in, 13–14
    formation of, 144
    foundation of, 390
    Great Depression in, 3
    immigrants in: 240–1, 256, 265–6; *accommodation* and *assimilation*, 255–6; birth statistics for, 242; family and, 256; Filipino, 244; first-generation, 314–15; historical

contexts of, 254–5; Indian, 271; institutionalization rates for, 246; Mexican, 246–7
    language and, 250–1
    as nation of immigrants, 5, 235
    Nicaraguans in, 110
    Northern cities, 29
    racial quotas in, 359
    racism in, 5, 45, 97, 99
    rights of resident aliens in, 265–6
    segregation in, 5
    Southern society, 29, 37–8, 43, 189, 205
    value of diversity in, 342–3
    white supremacy myth, 78
    whiteness in, 203–4
    World Court and, 270
Universal Declaration of Human Rights (UN), 270, 296, 387
universal personhood, 294–5, 364
universal rights, 269–70
USSR *see* Soviet Union
"utopian realism," 92

Verbindungsnetzschaft (network-based social system), 86
Versailles Peace Treaty, 3, 219
verzuiling puzzle (Dutch community model), 114, 116, 119, 120–3
    see also Netherlands
Viroli, Maurizio, 166
Voting Rights Act (1965), 4
Vuk Karadzic (Serb pamphlet), 221

Wacquant, Loïc, 359
Walby, Sylvia, 159–61
Wallman, S., 66
Warren, William Penn, 25
Watson, James L., 284, 285
Weber, Adna, 306
Weber, Max, 1, 6, 11, 12, 17, 69, 213, 289, 306
    and ethnicity, 30–9
    model of political legitimacy, 190, 220
    "pariah groups," 236, 281
    visit to United States, 28–9
welfare state, 292, 295
Wen Yiduo, 131
Wenden, Catherine de, 301
West, the, 158
West Germany, 364
    see also Germany

CPSIA information can be obtained at www.ICGtesting.com
Printed in the USA
LVOW11s0053040813

346097LV00005B/16/A